THE VISITOR

THE VISITOR

*André Palmeiro
and the Jesuits in Asia*

———

Liam Matthew Brockey

THE BELKNAP PRESS OF HARVARD UNIVERSITY PRESS

Cambridge, Massachusetts

London, England

2014

Library of Congress Cataloging-in-Publication Data

Brockey, Liam Matthew.

The visitor : André Palmeiro and the Jesuits in Asia / Liam Matthew Brockey.

pages cm

Includes bibliographical references and index.

ISBN 978-0-674-41668-0 (alk. paper)

1. Palmeiro, André, 1569–1635.   2. Jesuits—Asia—Biography.
3. Jesuits—Asia—History—17th century.   I. Title.

BX4705.P3655B76 2014

271'.5302—dc23

[B]

2014005698

For Mónica

Contents

Note on Orthography and Usage

The global span of this study necessarily involves the appearance of personal and place names and other citations in a host of foreign languages. Portuguese is the most frequently encountered, since André Palmeiro used it to write most of the documents analyzed here. European terms are given in standard modern spelling, while words from Asian tongues are romanized according to current practice. Personal names appear in hybrid form. Given names are presented according to their modern appearance in the person's mother tongue (for example, Joam is rendered as João; and Alexandro is rendered as Alessandro), whereas an attempt has been made to preserve the early modern spelling of family names. Latinized, castilianized, or gallicized versions common in an older historiography have been avoided. (Examples are André Palmeiro, not Andrea Palmieri, and Manuel Dias, rather than Emmanuel Diaz.) The main figures in this book come primarily from the Society of Jesus, so the reader should assume that all of the principal actors in the story are Jesuits unless otherwise indicated. An attempt has been made to include the dates for the live spans of all individuals who play roles in this story. Not all dates have been identified, however, and some individuals are only invoked tangentially. Place names are given according to their resonance for the modern reader of English. Modern place names will be given upon first mention, but the general rule will be to use commonly recognizable premodern place names in English or, when appropriate, in Portuguese (for example, the Moluccas and Malacca instead of Maluku and Melaka; Porto rather than Oporto). The Bible is cited in the Latin original of the Clementine Vulgate, with English translations drawn from the Rheims-Challoner edition. Except where otherwise noted, all translations are by the author, who accepts sole responsibility for their accuracy. Any errors in the text or notes likewise belong to the author.

THE VISITOR

Prelude

Nagasaki, 1635

Silence wrapped the apostate like a shroud. He had been broken under torture and kept under strict surveillance. Only his captors saw him regularly since October 18, 1633; they made him serve as an interpreter, but he was more prized as an informant. The authorities wanted to know the whereabouts of the remaining priests and their scattered flock, and the apostate was thought to have the answers. And so it had been a long while since any Christian had been with him. For the apostate's former friends and associates, rumors took the place of facts about what had happened. These rumors were a mixture of pious fabrications and malicious gossip: Some expressed an animus against the Society of Jesus; some lamented the grievous wound that had been inflicted on the Jesuits' honor. There were, nevertheless, certain parts of the apostate's story that were known to all. He had been bound and hung upside down from a scaffold over a pit, suspended in agony. This torture, invented with the aim of producing backsliders instead of martyrs, had not been very successful until that fateful day. Of the twenty-five men who had been tormented in this way since the new technique was first used in the late summer of 1633, only two Japanese laymen had been taken from the pits. No friar and no Jesuit had begged for mercy.[1] Rather, the torture of the pit had added a steady stream of pious heroes for the rolls of the beatified, as most of the missionaries and laymen expired without renouncing Christianity.

To those who caught sight of this episode from the Portuguese ships sailing out of Nagasaki harbor that October day, it appeared that a new group of martyrs was bound for glory. At the unfurling of the sails, the apostate seemed to be fighting the good fight alongside seven other missionaries. True, the departing observers had seen him taken down from the scaffold to receive medical attention, but this was a standard practice intended to prolong the suffering; it seemed certain that he would be hung over the pit again when he recovered. It was inconceivable to the Portuguese merchants, as it was to most of the underground Christians left in Nagasaki, that he could abandon the religion of his ancestors, the faith he had worked for decades to implant in Japanese soil. After all, this was no ordinary believer. He was a priest. He was, moreover, the nominal leader of a group of missionaries that had dwindled to single digits under the rigors of persecution. He had spent nineteen years living in the shadows, traveling under the cover of darkness and hiding in remote villages. How could he succumb in his final hour when so many others had resisted to the end? Yet it had happened: Cristóvão Ferreira, fifty-three years old, a native of Torres Vedras in Portugal, priest and professed member of the Society of Jesus, had abjured Christianity.

Between October 1633 and May 1635, few saw the apostate. Ferreira (ca. 1580–1650) was lodged in part of a house in Nagasaki that belonged to the widow of an executed Chinese merchant. He rarely came out of his quarters except to report to his captors. Those few who had seen him claimed that when he did come out, he was dressed as a Japanese and used a Japanese name. It was known that, after his fall, Ferreira had been summoned to Edo and afterward sent back to Nagasaki. One witness claimed to have seen him climb inside a closed sedan chair upon his departure for the court, and had shouted "May God go with you!" at Ferreira as the conveyance moved away. But only a mumble was heard from inside, as if a muzzle prevented the traveler from speaking. This lack of response had engendered hope among the European traders and the clandestine Christians that the former Jesuit had not in fact reneged. Other signs were interpreted to mean that although he might have fallen, he was prepared to beg for forgiveness. For example, a witness claimed to have seen Ferreira with beads in hand, praying aloud.[2] At best, these were no more than fleeting glimpses of a man whose thoughts remained a mystery, no more than pious speculations more revealing of others' hopes than of the apostate's actual condition. But there was one point upon which all who had seen him agreed: Ferreira was miserable. He was desperately poor and sorrowful, and given to crying loudly.

The silence lasted until the spring of 1635, when a group of Portuguese merchants traveled from Macau to Nagasaki with a sensitive mission. Their challenge was to quash the rumors by discovering the truth. Demanding to know if he had indeed abandoned the faith, Ferreira's superiors on the other side of the China Sea had written letters to be delivered in person to the apostate. But the merchants dared not attempt that, fearing swift and deadly reprisals from the Japanese authorities. The fleet's captain, Gonçalo da Silveira (d. 1639), had received specific orders from the Nagasaki officials not to contact hidden priests or Christians, or to forward money to them. The price for disobedience was prohibitively high: the Japanese authorities threatened to cut off all trade with Macau. To be sure, Silveira did not want to speak with those who remained in the faith; he wanted to hear from the one who had left it. Still, he deemed it too dangerous to attempt a rendezvous with the apostate, or even send him letters through a courier. After more than a year of silence, Ferreira also wanted to speak to his former countrymen but caution urged him against it, according to Silveira, who claimed that the apostate had twice appeared at his door in Nagasaki but had retreated without saying a word. Shame and fear prompted his flight on both occasions, as Ferreira had written in a short note that was smuggled to the captain.

While Silveira made no move to contact the apostate, other members of the 1635 trading expedition put less stock in the officials' prohibitions. These men, too, were anxious to know the truth about Ferreira. What would the apostate have to say for himself? The first one to break his silence was Manuel Mendes de Moura, about whom little is known. Mendes was a newcomer in East Asia and, although he was the nephew of an important senior member of the Society of Jesus, the Macau Jesuits had not thought to entrust him with their letters.[3] Mendes nevertheless found his way into the presence of the apostate to confront him, most likely at Ferreira's quarters; their location was no secret.

The conversation between the two men did not last long, choked as the apostate and his visitor were by tears at this emotional encounter of strangers. After over a year and a half of silence, Cristóvão Ferreira asked the first question: "How is André Palmeiro?" Mendes replied: "He is dead. And both the doctors and everyone else know that he died because of the fasting and mortifications he took upon himself after hearing about what had happened in Japan, especially the reports about you."[4]

Introduction

Company Man

André Palmeiro was a Jesuit priest entrusted with an enormous task. In an age when most people never journeyed farther than the immediate surroundings of their places of birth, he left his homeland in Portugal for an adventure that would take him to a grave on the far side of the earth. Palmeiro's challenge was to inspect the most extensive network of missions of the early modern age, his order's enterprises in Maritime Asia. He bore the title Father Visitor, and the aim of his visitation was to assess how the men of the Society of Jesus had acquitted themselves in their apostolic endeavors. The geographic space Palmeiro was sent to inspect was vast, stretching from the rivers of Mozambique in East Africa all the way to the northern reaches of the island of Honshu in Japan. Travel was difficult in the early modern era, and the Jesuit missions were often situated beyond areas under colonial control. For all that, Palmeiro did not shrink from his charge. His journeys took him by ship from Lisbon to Goa, by foot from Madurai to Cochin, and by riverboat from Macau to Beijing. And he conducted a lively correspondence with his fellow Jesuits, meaning that missionaries as far afield as Ethiopia, Tibet, Tonkin, and the Spice Islands received his orders.

Palmeiro embarked on his travels after attaining renown for his intellect. In contrast to the many Jesuits who left for Asia as unproven young men, the Visitor sailed for the East after reaching the summit of an academic career.

By the time he left on his one-way trip to India and beyond, he had taught rhetoric, philosophy, and theology in a formal academic setting. At the Jesuit college in Coimbra, Palmeiro held a chair of theology second only to that occupied by one of the most brilliant minds of his day, Francisco Suárez (1548–1617). In addition to his scholarly activities, Palmeiro was also a renowned preacher and a competent administrator, but he was not destined to live out his life in study, prayer, and pastoral work. Instead, at the age of forty-nine he was ordered to Asia. This was a dangerous voyage even for men in the prime of youth, but the superiors of the Society of Jesus deemed it essential that a mature figure be sent as inspector. Palmeiro's reputation for probity and his long experience in the highest ranks of his order made him an excellent candidate for the post. His task in Maritime Asia, one that called for a combination of intellectual rigor and administrative astuteness, was to evaluate the moral, spiritual, and temporal states of the Jesuits' affairs. Beyond seeking to conserve and advance the Society's missions, Palmeiro was to judge the various innovations in missionary policy that his subordinates had pioneered in India and China through their efforts at cultural accommodation.

Despite Palmeiro's important office and his decisive role in the shaping of early modern missions in Asia, he is virtually unknown outside scholarly circles. Even among the members of the Society of Jesus itself, he is far from a familiar figure. Since Palmeiro was not the founder of a mission, one of the celebrated martyrs of the period, or the cause of any scandal, he has not attracted attention from historians and has accordingly escaped being made the object of either praise or opprobrium. Moreover, because he traveled so much during the last two decades of his life, no specific Jesuit province could claim him, far less number him among its illustrious members. So it is that, with the exception of the chroniclers of his home Province of Portugal (as the Jesuits called their administrative unit corresponding to continental and insular Portugal, plus the missions to West Africa), few scholars past or present have devoted more than a few lines to Palmeiro's life and work.

Such a consignment to oblivion might be excusable in the case of figures who wrote little or disappeared off the map in distant missions, but a man like Palmeiro deserves better. He was a major figure in the early seventeenth century's Jesuit enterprises; he has claim to a larger place in the Society's history and, more generally, that of Christianity in Asia. Thankfully, European archives preserve a great number of Palmeiro's writings. Wherever he went in the world, he wrote letters to his fellow Jesuits, especially to the superior general in Rome who had sent him on his journey. Palmeiro also drew up rules for Jesuit life in the order's colonial colleges and in its missions. Rather than merely clarifying the contours of a shadowy historical figure, we can make his image not just visible but three-dimensional.

––––––––

The scenes of Palmeiro's life reenacted here take place at the foreground of unfamiliar stages. The first episodes occur at the Jesuit colleges in Portugal, situated at Europe's distant Atlantic edge; the next unfold in the heart of the Portuguese Empire in Maritime Asia, a colonial context where European and Asian influences converged; and the final events transpire in Asian lands during an age of upheaval, at the dawn of Tokugawa Japan and the twilight of Ming China. But even as the scenery changed over the course of Palmeiro's life, none of these backdrops receded completely from view. Indeed, it was essential that the memory of Jesuit life in Europe accompany him to the far side of the globe so that it might be recreated in the contexts of Portuguese Asia and even beyond the limits of colonial power.

The first of these three broad contexts for Palmeiro's life is the Society of Jesus itself. The order was a product of the great surge in religious energy that swept over Western Europe in the early sixteenth century. Its founder, Ignatius Loyola (1491–1556), left the life of a soldier to pursue a spiritual journey that took him from his native Spain to the Holy Land and eventually to the University of Paris. While in France, Loyola brought together a group of educated men who desired to form a new type of congregation. They styled themselves the Society of Jesus, which gained papal approval in 1540. Within a decade, the two defining marks of Jesuit activity in the early modern world became clear: education and mission. The order's men would dedicate themselves to the creation of schools for instructing young men in classical thought and Christian doctrine; and they would devote themselves to the work of preaching and indoctrination in rural Europe, across the confessional divides among Christians, and in the lands recently discovered by overseas explorations. The Society expanded dramatically before Loyola's death in 1556, and continued to attract thousands of recruits from across Europe during the second half of the sixteenth century.

From its headquarters in Rome, the fledgling Society sent men to establish branches of the order in the different nations of Catholic Europe. Among the first sovereigns to welcome its representatives was King João III of Portugal

(r. 1521–1557), who requested two priests and insisted that they commit themselves to working in continental Portugal and his overseas dominions. Simão Rodrigues (1510–1579) and Francis Xavier (1506–1552) arrived in Lisbon in 1541, with the former overseeing the opening of the order's first residence in the court city and the latter embarking for Goa, the capital of the Estado da Índia. Over the next dozen years royal favor ensured that the Jesuits could open schools in Lisbon and Coimbra, the seat of the only Portuguese university at the time. These institutions, and the ones opened by the Society elsewhere in Portugal in subsequent years, served to create a loyal following of former students as well as to attract scores of new recruits to the order. The *Companhia de Jesus* found fertile ground for its growth in Portuguese soil: the Province of Portugal was among the largest of all the early Jesuit provinces, and the order found no shortage of candidates eager to live in its spiritual and intellectual communities. One such individual was André Palmeiro, who attended lessons at the Jesuit college in Lisbon before joining the order at Coimbra in 1584.

While the Jesuits gradually established themselves amid the other religious orders in Portugal, a few of their number laid the foundations for an array of overseas missionary endeavors. Xavier sailed on the Cape Route in 1541 as the first member of the Society to work beyond Europe. Most of his decade of travels in Maritime Asia was spent visiting the colonial settlements in Mozambique, southern India, Malacca, and the Moluccas, where he sought to win converts and reform the moral and spiritual state of the European settlers. But Xavier's travels also included ventures beyond the bounds of the Portuguese Empire, including a stay of two years in Japan and an ill-starred visit to the China coast in 1552. By that time, the "Apostle of the Orient" had inaugurated a Jesuit presence across a vast space stretching from southern Africa to Japan. His successors built upon these initial efforts, expanding the order's recently founded enterprises and opening new missions in Ethiopia and China. In the cities of the Portuguese Estado da Índia, they would oversee the creation of schools offering the type of education, albeit on a smaller scale, that the Society provided in its European colleges. This was the missionary and educational network that Palmeiro would be sent to inspect in the early seventeenth century, as the Jesuit presence in Asia approached its centennial.

The Society's expansion in Asia would not have been nearly as rapid or as wide-ranging without the assistance and protection of the Portuguese colonial state. Having sailed to Asia aboard a fleet which traveled the *Carreira da Índia,* the Indies route from Lisbon to Goa, Xavier made his first

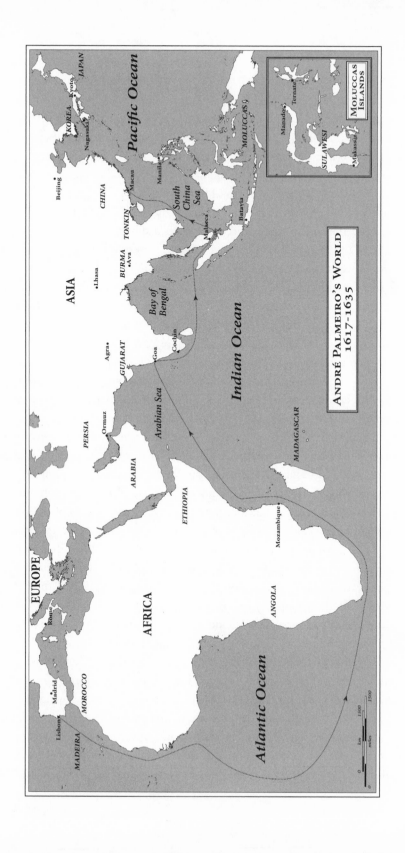

ANDRÉ PALMEIRO's WORLD
1617–1635

MOLUCCAS
ISLANDS

Inset (Moluccas Islands): Manado, Ternate, SULAWESI, Makassar

Main map labels:

EUROPE, Madrid, Lisbon, Rome, MADEIRA, MOROCCO

AFRICA, ANGOLA, ETHIOPIA, Mozambique, MADAGASCAR

Atlantic Ocean, Indian Ocean, Pacific Ocean

ASIA, PERSIA, ARABIA, Ormuz, Arabian Sea, GUJARAT, Agra, Goa, Cochin, Bay of Bengal, Lhasa, BURMA, Ava, TONKIN

CHINA, Beijing, Macau, KOREA, Kyoto, JAPAN, Nagasaki, Manila, South China Sea, Malacca, Batavia, MOLUCCAS

km 1500
miles 1500

home at the viceregal capital. He traveled to the far reaches of Maritime Asia aboard Portuguese ships and frequently found himself acting as ambassador for the viceroy or as pastor to the empire's soldiers and sailors. Capitalizing upon his reputation for sanctity, Xavier's successors extended the Jesuit reach throughout Portuguese Asia. It is not an exaggeration to affirm that by the end of the sixteenth century, the Jesuits were the most influential religious congregation in the Estado da Índia. In contrast to most of the other orders, the Society made its presence felt beyond Goa and the major colonial cities; Jesuits could be found in the empire's most distant outposts and well beyond them. Royal patronage for these endeavors was crucial, but so was the support of broad segments of the Portuguese, Luso-Asian, and indigenous Christian communities: A portion of the proceeds from the crown's customhouses was directed each year toward the support of the Society's missions; private individuals and lay congregations contributed substantial endowments for the creation of Jesuit colleges in cities across the empire. And the order's men were borne to their mission districts aboard merchant ships and the fleets outfitted by the Estado da Índia to link its distant entrepôts.

The benefits of this relationship between the Portuguese Empire and the Society of Jesus were mutual. In exchange for patronage, the Jesuits shared their varied forms of expertise with the empire's representatives and inhabitants. In the first instance (much like the other religious orders that worked in the Estado da Índia), they provided pastoral care to the colonial population: Jesuits celebrated memorial masses, heard confessions, organized devotional confraternities, and gave sermons at public celebrations. The Society's men also accompanied the military expeditions conducted by the colonial state, ministering to nobles and commoners alike in times of war. It was the Jesuits' academic training and readiness to travel that distinguished them from many of the members of other orders present in Portuguese Asia. Jesuits served as ambassadors and linguists in diplomatic negotiations with regional powers and helped Portuguese merchants open trading relations with their indigenous counterparts. The Society also put its members' engineering skills at the disposal of the crown officials who were charged with fortifying colonial outposts. In many of the empire's cities, Jesuits opened colleges where instruction in the rudiments of reading, writing, and Christian doctrine was made available gratis to young boys. At the larger Jesuit establishments, such as the colleges at Goa, Cochin, and Macau, a greater of number of courses, including instruction in rhetoric, philosophy, and theology, was offered at times.

The colleges and residences maintained by the Jesuits within the enclaves of the Portuguese Empire were also marshaling points for missions beyond colonial protection. Building upon the foundations laid by Xavier and his early companions, the Society's men created a network of inland missions during the second half of the sixteenth century. During that period, Jesuits pursued apostolic endeavors in the Zambezi River valley far from the coastal stronghold of Mozambique Island as well as in the highlands of Ethiopia. They sought political protection and patronage from indigenous rulers in both regions, and in the latter they eventually won royal backing for their ambitious project of reshaping Ethiopian Christianity in the Roman Catholic mold. In similar fashion, the Jesuits' colleges in the heart of the Estado da Índia were springboards for enterprises within the Mughal Empire and elsewhere in South Asia. In 1580 Emperor Akbar requested that priests from Goa be sent to his capital, a petition that resulted in the creation of a small but influential mission to the north. And the early work of Xavier had forged a bond between the Jesuits and the indigenous Christians of the Fishery Coast in the south, ensuring that pastors from the Society would minister there for decades. Further missions were launched in Madurai as well as in the inland areas of Sri Lanka. Some of the Jesuits there used forms of cultural adaptation that Palmeiro would have to assess.

Farther to the east the Jesuits conducted most of their activities in areas where Portuguese power meant little. Portugal's only significant colonial outpost in East Asia was Macau, a tiny trading port founded in 1556 by dint of diplomacy for the purpose of exchanging Chinese silk for Japanese silver. The flux of merchant activities carried the men of the Society from the China coast to Japan where, over the course of the second half of the sixteenth century, a symbiotic relationship between Portuguese merchants, Jesuit missionaries, and Japanese lords facilitated the creation of a mission church. By 1600 the Japan mission was the crowning glory of all of the Society's overseas endeavors: its hundreds of members ministered to hundreds of thousands of indigenous Christians. Seeking a complement to the rising tide of conversions in Japan, Jesuit superiors at Macau strategized about inaugurating a mission within the Ming Empire. A successful investment in acquiring the language of Chinese scholar-officials in the early 1580s at length earned a handful of the Society's men permission to stay in China beyond the close of the Canton trade fairs. Fashioning themselves as the exotic intellectual peers of the imperial bureaucrats, these Jesuits gained acceptance in influential circles in northern and southern China. Most famously, in 1610 the Wanli Emperor granted Matteo Ricci (1552–1610), the mission's founder, a plot of land for his tomb and state honors for his funeral. Local patronage in other Chinese cities permitted small groups of Jesuits to remain elsewhere in the Ming Empire, but their proselytizing activities yielded only a small fraction of the results garnered by their brethren in Japan during their mission's first decades.

———————

Upon arriving in Asia, André Palmeiro stood at the center of that Jesuit world. For nearly two decades he occupied the office of visitor, also known by its Latinate equivalent, visitator. His functions in that capacity constitute a model, a template for measuring Jesuit activities in the early modern period. But what was a visitor? The office was a temporary position created for the purpose of conducting inspections and most frequently used in ecclesiastical settings. In keeping with the reforming spirit of the mid-sixteenth century among sections of the Catholic hierarchy, especially after the Council of Trent (1545–1563), bishops were supposed to act as visitors in their own dioceses. That is, they were to inspect their parishes on a regular basis, ensuring that their clergy maintained discipline and that good pastoral and temporal administration extended to the lowest level. Among religious orders, the office of visitor was an ad hoc position that served a similar function. The post was not unique to the Jesuits; other orders, too, appointed inspectors. But no other made as much use of the position as the Society. Indeed, owing to the great distance between the order's Roman curia and its distant missions, visitors became a nearly permanent fixture of Jesuit administration in Asia. Elsewhere the order relied upon visitors less frequently, but periodic inspections by outsiders to a given province were not rare.

Two factors account for the Jesuits' frequent recourse to visitations. First, the Society of Jesus had a central administration, meaning that a wide range of decisions was taken in Rome rather than in the provinces. This style of governance was a departure from the traditions of monastic and mendicant religious life, where administration began at the local level in chapter meetings. By contrast, the Society's superior general in Rome was accorded executive power that reached to individual colleges, the basic unit of Jesuit organization. The general's duties included representing the order before popes and monarchs, overseeing personnel decisions within the provinces, and approving assignments to mission territories. He was given a life term to fulfill those responsibilities. By contrast, other Jesuit officials customarily served triennial terms, whether as residential superiors, rectors in colleges, or provincial officers. To be sure, the task of managing the whole order was too big for one man, and so the superior general worked in conjunction with a set of executive secretaries who represented the broad administrative units, which were made up of provinces, dubbed "assistancies." These executive secretaries, known as assistants, received reports from the superiors in the Society's provinces and responded with orders approved by the general. Individual assignments were made in Rome based on nominations made by men at the head of the provincial hierarchy, who provided candid assessments of all of their subordinates. While the ebb and flow of correspondence between Rome and the provinces was an effective way of transmitting orders up and down the hierarchy, it did not substitute completely for the personal presence of a higher authority. The post of visitor therefore emerged in the mid-sixteenth century as an occasional adjunct to the order's standard modes of governance. Briefly stated, the visitor acted in the superior general's stead while the general himself remained at the curia in Rome.

The second reason for the Society's reliance on inspectors was the order's rapid expansion in its first decades. After securing papal approval in 1540, the order grew rapidly. From ten members at its inception, it counted over a thousand at Loyola's death in 1556, over five thousand by 1580, and over ten thousand by the turn of the seventeenth century.[1] Just as impressive was the Society's geographic expansion across Europe and in the overseas colonial empires. Not long after 1540, in other words, the number of Jesuits had grown to the point where the spirit of its founders was something transmitted through texts and rules rather than through shared personal experience. The shift from the original matrix of Jesuit life—the way that Loyola and his companions lived and worked—to the forms that the Society would adopt as it grew, whether in colleges or missions, obliged oversight. In order to prevent the expanding order from losing its original identity, it was necessary to ensure that its "institute"—that is, the letter and spirit of its rules, codified in the *Constitutions* in the mid-1550s—was observed as closely as possible throughout the different provinces; for although the order's rules were lengthy and detailed, they explicitly allowed for local variations and relied on the good judgment of its superiors. Variances were permitted insofar as they were not at odds with the rules' oft-repeated phrase, *nuestro modo de proceder,* "our way of proceeding," a formulation that implies unity. Periodic inspections were therefore organized to verify that a recognizable style and general uniformity of practice was found in all Jesuit communities.

The Society's visitors were the plenipotentiary representatives of the superior general in the provinces. Although the first appointee to the office was Loyola's close associate and successor as superior general, Diego Laínez (1512–1565), responsibility for visitations during the early years of the Society belonged primarily to Jerónimo Nadal (1507–1580). One of the Society's first recruits after its foundation, Nadal not only played a crucial role in transforming Loyola's vision into its *Constitutions* but also served repeatedly as Loyola's emissary to the European provinces in the 1550s and early 1560s. Nadal's visitations were ambitious endeavors, planned as general inspections of all of the order's continental communities.[2] Yet toward the end of his life, it was clear that work on such a scale by one Jesuit was impractical, and that individual provinces needed their own inspections. And so it was during the generalate of Francis Borgia (r. 1565–1573) that the corps of inspectors grew to ensure visits to all provinces, including those overseas, and more specific rules for visitations were elaborated. During this period the ad hoc inspections of earlier times shifted to more formal exercises, a trajectory that continued during the generalate of Everard Mercurian (r. 1573–1580).[3]

What were visitors supposed to do during their inspections? Their principal task, a challenge originating in the first visitations, was to bring the spirit of the Society's founders from Rome to the provinces. That is, the inspections were intended as pastoral exercises, not inquisitorial ones. The visitor, as a representative of the superior general, was to act as a peacemaker between factions, or between the different ranks of the order, meaning between priests and brothers, as well as among the hierarchy of priests. Beyond this diplomatic task, inspectors were entrusted with verifying that the *Constitutions* were being observed. A visitor's powers therefore included the capacity to reprimand those who overstepped the boundaries of their station within the order. Over the middle decades of the sixteenth century, the inspector's charge was expanded to include oversight in temporal matters, such as approving the construction of new colleges, reviewing the negotiations between the Society and its patrons, inspecting the financial dealings of individual communities, and verifying the quality of studies at the order's schools.

In the 1570s the accumulation of powers in the hands of centrally appointed inspectors gave rise to conflicts between visitors and provincial officials, men to whom the *Constitutions* accorded similar responsibilities. In this
push and pull between Rome and the provinces over the locus of authority,
Rome would gradually triumph. The victory of curial authority came largely
as a result of factional struggles within the provinces, especially in Spain and
Portugal. In order to resolve the problem of dissent and disunion, the Society's generals granted further powers to their inspectors. Most importantly,
Superior General Mercurian charged his visitors with inquiring after religious observance, in addition to temporal and administrative matters. This
change meant that in the late 1570s the visitors were instructed to interview
all members of the order and ensure that ritual and theological norms were
respected. Visitations thus became a means for disciplining those who strayed
from the Society's rules and, above all, from Rome's understanding of the
order's corporate identity.[4]

This further expansion of the visitors' powers makes it unsurprising that the
tension within the order over the precise boundaries of the authority of visitors
versus that of provincials continued into the early years of the generalate of
Claudio Aquaviva (r. 1580–1615). The friction appears to have been greatly reduced by the early 1590s, with the passing of a generation and the successful extension of Rome's authority. In order to bring about this change subtly, however,
the visitors appointed during Aquaviva's generalate were often given only partial
assignments; that is, they were sent to inspect certain aspects of Jesuit life, such
as temporal management, religious observance, or academic standards. The result was a greater number of inspectors, whose more frequent visits to the provinces helped to strengthen Rome's position. Similar reinforcement ensued when
the curia made no move to clarify the boundaries between provincial administration and visitors. Aquaviva's delay in providing specific rules—and the acceptance of this state of affairs by the general congregations of provincial representatives that were summoned in the early seventeenth century—eventually
permitted the reintroduction of visitors with the full range of responsibilities. As
a result, when an official elaboration of the rules for visitations was published in
1607, it contained no more than general guiding principles. This ambiguity
about the precise role of the visitor would persist through the seventeenth century, including Palmeiro's time as inspector in the Asian provinces.[5]

In sum, by the early seventeenth century Jesuit visitors enjoyed considerable powers but were given ill-defined objectives. They were to be guided by

the spirit of the *Constitutions,* and their work was intended to make the order at once more harmonious and more faithful to its founding ideals. Despite the vagueness of this commission, the inspectors were also supposed to be thorough in their review of personnel matters, internal and external relations, temporal structures, and communal spiritual life. By leaving the specifics to the judgment of the individual visitors, the superiors general manifested their administrative shrewdness. Rome confided in the scruples of its representatives, selecting men who had long demonstrated loyalty to the order and entrusting them with great power. The lack of definition and the broad nature of their charge obliged visitors to maintain frequent communication with the curia. In the documents they sent to Rome, the visitors gave lengthy discussions of their findings and their decisions. Conscientious inspectors, such as Palmeiro, would provide detailed examinations of the state of affairs in their provinces, and would weigh the temporal and moral problems confronted by the Society. Therefore, their letters not only reveal how the Jesuits dealt with internal and external affairs but also how the decision-making process functioned at the highest levels of this centrally administered religious community.

For all of the authority wielded by the Society's visitors during the early modern period, they are little known even among Jesuits or outside scholars. Only one figure is commonly associated with the office. Indeed, a cursory inspection of the literature on the subject over the past generation would suggest that he was one of the few men, if not the only one, who served as visitor. This towering individual was Alessandro Valignano (1539–1606), an Italian priest who was sent to inspect the Asian missions in the 1570s. His visionary approach to his order's enterprises and his energetic direction of the Jesuits in Maritime Asia have rightly been judged of high importance for the history of the Society of Jesus and for the broader study of Catholicism in Asia.[6]

Valignano played a crucial role for the Society during his time as visitor, and the strategy of cultural accommodation that he elaborated had a decisive impact on its East Asian missions. In fact, in the mission context the very notion of adaptation has become synonymous with Valignano's name: It was he who insisted that the Jesuits in Japan should adopt as many cultural forms from their hosts as possible, so as to make Christianity a Japanese religion rather than one cloaked in an unshakeable mantle of foreignness. And it was Valignano who instructed his subordinates to study the Chinese language and adopt the dress and habits of the scholar-bureaucrats of the Ming

Empire in order to initiate a Jesuit mission in China. This visitor also played a strong role in the governance of the Indian missions, although his early work in that context has not been studied as thoroughly. By the time of his death in 1606 Valignano had earned a considerable share of the credit for establishing the Asian missions, even if his task as inspector meant that others would be responsible for putting his policies into effect.

A figure as important as he was inevitably casts a long shadow over his successors. Alessandro Valignano was André Palmeiro's most illustrious predecessor, and the two men had the same writ and sphere of activity. Like Valignano, Palmeiro would be commissioned with inspecting the Indian missions first, then the East Asian ones. But whereas Valignano elaborated and enacted a host of policies for advancing the missions, Palmeiro was charged with gauging the effectiveness of his predecessor's ideas and adjusting them as necessary. And so Palmeiro's activities and decisions were often in direct dialogue with the precedents set by Valignano, even if two or more decades had passed in the meantime. No previous knowledge of the overall development of the Society's Asian missions or of the specific policies elaborated by Alessandro Valignano is expected here, however. These aspects of Palmeiro's inheritance will be discussed at the moments when he confronts them.

––––––––––

Andrew the Apostle is quoted only once in the New Testament, but his few words are of considerable relevance to us. They help to understand some of the themes in this biography of his namesake. In the Gospel of John, when Jesus finds himself by the shore of the Sea of Galilee at twilight with a crowd of five thousand before him, He asks Philip where to find bread for the hungry multitude. This disciple responds that only a fortune would buy enough for everyone to have a small bite. But it is Andrew who, upon surveying the situation, asks the practical question of Jesus: "There is a boy here that hath five barley loaves, and two fishes; but what are these among so many?"[7]

The miracle of the feeding of the five thousand was the response, but the nature of Andrew's question is most important for this book. André Palmeiro was an eminently pragmatic man. Like the apostle, he looked at massive challenges that lay before him and tried to think of measured solutions. But unlike Andrew, André did not have access to miraculous means when worldly resources did not suffice. As inspector, he was confronted by a host of practical questions about how the Society should structure its resources to best meet its goals. He was also faced with a series of moral questions raised by the nature of the Jesuits' activities. Palmeiro's responses were marked by a degree of pragmatism that contrasted, at times starkly, with the charismatic idealism of his subordinates. In the midst of a crowd of men who hoped for divine succor and heavenly assistance, the Visitor stood out as one who urged caution, paused for reflection, and reined in the overly ambitious or the simply foolhardy.

The tension between missionary charisma and the Visitor's pragmatism will be revealed at several points in the following chapters. In southern India, in Southeast Asia, and in China, Palmeiro had occasion to review the novel approaches introduced by his men, whose inspirations and motivations often came from the heady cauldron of precedents set by the lives of the saints. Like their contemporary Don Quixote, whose mind was a clouded mirror of the paragons of chivalry, so some of the Jesuits in the Asian missions saw themselves as Catholic paladins confronting the "heathen" with only the Gospel and Christian ritual as their arms. To make this comparison is not to dismiss the insights of the ambitious early modern Jesuits in the pursuit of missionary experiments—especially those who pushed the boundaries of accommodation with their changes in dress, language, and style—but rather to recall that these men lived in a dangerous world where divine intervention could not be counted upon. None was more keenly aware of this than Palmeiro, who used his role to confront many of the pious fancies of his subordinates. It was the Visitor who would have to ask how the missions would be sustained after the charisma of their founders had disappeared and how the church would continue once the moment of conversion had passed. At times, such concerns were pedestrian. But they were of crucial importance not only to the Jesuits' Asian neophytes but also to the hierarchy of the Society of Jesus, among whom the expanding missions were viewed as the order's patrimony.

Insistence on this fundamental contrast should not be understood as unmitigated praise for the hard-headed, analytical approach of certain early modern Jesuits like Palmeiro but as a counterweight to those studies that place the original, the visionary, and the miraculous before practical considerations. Nowhere has the divergence between the two sides been so marked as in studies on cultural accommodation. Although signs of a change in the historical understanding of the Jesuits in East Asia are beginning to appear,

studies of the Society's enterprises still place great emphasis on certain visionary aspects of Jesuit strategy while ignoring other features. It is common coin
in the realm of Jesuit studies that Valignano in Japan, Roberto Nobili (1577–
1656) in Madurai, and Matteo Ricci in China were men possessed of a modern spirit, one of openness and tolerance. We are told that the precedent set
by these pioneers was a signal lesson for posterity, one that their successors
unfortunately did not learn. According to the standard line, the destruction
of the Asian missions before the end of the early modern period was the price
paid for the failure to replicate the spirit of this inspired trio. Alas, this vision
of the missionary strategy of the early Jesuits in Asia and its outcomes is
clouded by illusions. It forestalls consideration of the political, social, temporal, and theological constraints that bound the missionaries, and it seeks
communion with imagined historical precedents for the genius of the modern age. Because his Roman superior entrusted Palmeiro with examining the
practical and theological consequences of accommodation in South and East
Asia, there will be much discussion here of this strategy.

The questions of missionary policy addressed by the Visitor cannot be reduced to their proselytizing dimensions. Inherent in Palmeiro's assessment of
the attitudes and methods of his subordinates in Asia were inquiries into the
larger issues of translation and its limits. After all, what were the early modern Catholic missions if not ambitious exercises in translation? It should come
as no surprise that Palmeiro engaged with this broad issue. Intellectual concerns were proper for a man who had spent most of the first half-century of
his life in an academic milieu. In spite of his practical spirit, he was no stranger
to discussions of abstract notions or speculative matters. And he was not afraid
to apply his analytical skills to questions of missionary policy. His letters
therefore address many of the potential consequences of the Jesuits' attempts
at translating Christianity or the common forms of Catholic piety into alien
settings. This aspect of Palmeiro's biography is one of its most compelling elements because one finds here an example of a man who was at once an administrator and an intellectual.

On the question of translation as well as on the other abstract issues that
he would confront, Palmeiro consistently displayed a willingness to learn
from the experience of others. He was not quick to judge his subordinates but
conceived of his role as one obliging him to listen first. Although his position
gave him supreme authority, he used it judiciously, and while he enjoyed inquisitorial powers, he did not act the part of an inquisitor. Rather, during his

time as visitor Palmeiro revealed himself to have a great independence of mind. He did not arrive from Europe at the Asian mission fields with a strict vision of how Jesuits were to proselytize, or of how Catholic Christianity was to be practiced by non-Europeans. His thoughts on these matters were informed by reasoned observation, rigorous analysis, and continual reflection. As a result, Palmeiro frustrates attempts to pigeonhole him. Labels that might make him easy to understand do not apply; none of the stereotypical ideas associated with the Portuguese, with Thomistic theologians or, for that matter, with the Jesuits are useful here. The Visitor's writings will suffice to impress upon the reader that André Palmeiro cannot be reduced to caricature.

How the Society of Jesus functioned outside of Europe is the specific concern of this book, written in the midst of a sustained expansion of historical studies on the early modern Jesuits. In times past the history of the Society was written by its own members for its own members, just as other religious orders produced internal histories. Far from being uniformly celebratory, many of these studies were pieces of first-rate scholarship worthy of the order's centuries-long intellectual tradition. When the old generations of scholars passed in the second half of the twentieth century, lay scholars began to show interest in the Jesuits of the "Old Company"—that is, the men who belonged to the order prior to its suppression by papal command in 1773. The result of the kernel of interest planted in the 1970s is the current flourishing of Jesuit studies, a field sustained in large part by scholars outside the Society. But whereas the older Jesuit historians who wrote about the order for their peers implicitly shared their readers' understanding of how it functioned, many present-day scholars write about the Jesuits without the same awareness of the Society's history and traditions. Depicting an organization marked with an ironclad unity of formation, purpose, and outlook, recent studies have all too frequently turned the Jesuits into clichés. They are heroic; they are pious; they are scheming; they are intractable; they are learned; they are laxist; they are ambitious. What they are not are individuals. Too many works fail to consider the Jesuits as what, indeed, they were—a community representative of the rich variety of early modern Catholic piety and preoccupations.

Through a detailed analysis of Palmeiro's deeds and decisions, this book restores depth and texture to the men of the early modern Society of Jesus. The most important source for his story is the Visitor's correspondence with the order's superior general, Muzio Vitelleschi (1563–1645, r. 1615–1645). Letters have survived from nearly all of the years that Palmeiro spent in Asia, and their most valuable quality is that in them he addresses the superior general in the first person. In other words, his observations are candid and personal; they reveal much about the man who wielded the pen. Moreover, Palmeiro's tone differs from many other surviving documents written by early modern Jesuits, such as annual letters or compendia of rules. These were typically written in an impersonal voice, which served to underscore the Society's corporate unity. Although they are valuable for other inquiries, such documents are not useful for revealing the thoughts and concerns of specific individuals. As a result, scholars have tended to speak in general or abstract terms about the Jesuits and about the Society's initiatives. By contrast, this biography makes Palmeiro's voice heard across the centuries, just as it was heard across oceans and continents after he sealed his letters.

The close attention to the details of Palmeiro's life and thought is not an exercise in hagiography. At most it is an attempt at historical resurrection, but not of the religious kind. No apologetic or polemical intent lies behind this study: There is no need to celebrate the march of the faith among the non-Christian lands beyond Europe. Likewise, there is no aim here of valorizing the work of the Jesuits vis-à-vis the members of other religious orders, or of insisting on the visionary quality of Jesuit attitudes. This book is an attempt to describe the life of one man in a variety of different early modern contexts with the goal of enhancing understanding of that period.

One political context will receive considerable attention: the Portuguese Empire in Maritime Asia. To examine the place of religious orders within the Estado da Índia, a topic that has received relatively little scholarly attention, is an explicit goal of this study. High imperial history of the kind written in the late nineteenth and early twentieth centuries tended to focus on the highest ranks of the colonial nobility—its captains, admirals, and viceroys. Subsequent generations of historians turned their attention to the economic aspects of the Estado da Índia, linking political and mercantile concerns in an attempt to explain how a disjointed collection of colonial outposts could constitute a veritable empire. While the Portuguese ecclesiastical historians, whether laymen or from the clergy, have long been interested in the study of the colonial church, their analyses from the early twentieth century tended to discuss the ecclesiastical jurisdictions of the empire and the link between *igreja* and *estado*. As a result, the historiography of Portuguese Asia was most frequently concerned with the rights of patronage conceded by the papacy to the crown, known as the *Padroado,* and the various struggles to maintain these privileges in the face of encroachment by European rivals. And since the history of the missions within and beyond the empire was often written by members of the sponsoring religious orders, it focused in the main on the victories and virtues of the orders' members rather than on their links to the Portuguese colonial state.

The shift in scholarly concerns over the past two generations has changed historians' approaches to the Estado da Índia. The rise of social and cultural history has added new dimensions to the study of colonial life across Portuguese Asia, with special focus on the institutions that were common across the empire, such as city councils and the famous charitable brotherhood called the *Santa Casa da Misericórdia*. Similarly, there has been a thorough reevaluation of the intellectual pursuits among the elites of colonial Maritime Asia, in particular the production of ethnographic, medicinal, and cartographic knowledge. It should be noted that the lion's share of scholarly attention on premodernity has been accorded to the sixteenth century, when the Portuguese Empire was in its formative years, instead of later periods, such as the era discussed in this book. Examinations of religious life lagged behind this general curve of historiographical change, with the surge of interest commencing only in the past two decades. Taking their cue from the type of social and religious history pioneered in Europe using ecclesiastical archives, scholars have trained their attention on the Goan branch of the Holy Office of the Inquisition and some of the mission fields supported by the Portuguese Empire. More recently, there has been a flourishing of interest in the links between missions and empire as well as in the ecclesiastical fixtures of the Estado da Índia, such as its bishops and its inquisitors. Only in the past years has the subject of religious orders in Maritime Asia outside of the missionary context begun to attract scrutiny. The same may be said of the theme of relationships between the regular clergy, the secular church, and imperial administrators.

Palmeiro's story thus reveals the links and tensions between the Society of Jesus and the Portuguese Empire in the early seventeenth century. As visitor, he was also the chief representative of his order in Maritime Asia. He was responsible for dealing with his counterparts in other religious orders and for protecting and advancing the Society's interests before secular and ecclesiastical authorities. Archbishops, governors, inquisitors, and viceroys were therefore in Palmeiro's circle of acquaintances and often in his network of friends. But the Visitor knew that the interests of his order were not necessarily coterminous with those of the Portuguese Empire or the colonial church (especially when its hierarchy seemed keen to attack the Society in order to advance its own interests or those of other orders). There was constant competition between the men of the *Companhia* and their rivals for patronage as well as for missionary glory. In India and Japan, the Society engaged in bitter feuds with members of other religious orders. In Portugal and in the administrative centers of the Estado da Índia, the men of the Society were often in conflict with their fellow religious over the pecking order.

The two-part structure of this study of the life, thoughts, and deeds of André Palmeiro reflects the boundaries of the Portuguese Empire in the early modern period and the place of the Society of Jesus within it. The first section discusses Palmeiro's early years and his academic career in Portugal in addition to examining his two terms as visitor in South Asia, a combination that underscores the common structures of Jesuit life in these regions. The Jesuit colleges of India were close approximations of their counterparts in Europe, and the patterns of life among the Society's men in the heart of the Estado da Índia were similar to those maintained in Portugal. Although the Jesuits in India had significant missionary commitments beyond the boundaries of the Portuguese settlements, their bases of operation were colleges in the colonial cities, where pastoral and academic concerns took pride of place. Moreover, the types of concern that Palmeiro would face during his time as inspector of the Provinces of Goa and Malabar bore a greater resemblance to the challenges confronted by the Society in continental Portugal than to those found in lands farther to the east of India.

The second part of the book deals with the final nine years of Palmeiro's life, the time he spent as visitor of the East Asian missions. Although he remained at Macau, his charge was to administer the Jesuit enterprises in the vast area of mainland Southeast Asia, China, and Japan. European colonial power in the early seventeenth century did not extend far inland in any of these territories, and the growth of the Dutch presence on nearby seas checked Portuguese pretensions to greater dominion. In other words, Palmeiro's tasks during his last years required him to direct his attentions far beyond the bounds of the Estado da Índia and into the heart of Tokugawa Japan, Ming China, Nguyen Cochinchina, and Trinh Tonkin. While the situation in Southeast Asia and Japan was too unstable to permit him to visit those Jesuit enterprises in person, he would take the opportunity to inspect the

China mission. In fact, Palmeiro would be the first outside inspector to travel to the Jesuit residences in the Ming Empire, trekking all the way to Beijing, where he strategized with missionaries and mandarins about how to advance the Society's proselytizing endeavor. And his death would come as he anxiously awaited news about the dramatic events that transpired during the brutal anti-Christian persecutions in Japan, a land where neither he nor any Portuguese had the power to intervene.

André Palmeiro's biography is not the story of a hero, and this account of his life will not lead to his beatification. But this study does recount the career of a remarkable figure who left the comfort of academic life and communal spirituality at an advanced age to take on a daunting task. Moved by his vow of obedience, he risked his health on a journey that would take him from Europe to Asia, where he would end his days. But it is not the seven thousand miles that separate Lisbon and Macau, the sites of his birth and death, that make the Visitor special; other early modern men and women crossed equally great distances during their lives. And it is not the fact that he was a Jesuit living in a distant land that makes Palmeiro unique; other members of the Society made more ambitious treks than he did. Rather, it is the continual movement that he kept up *ad maiorem Dei gloriam* over the course of his twilight years, and the constant critical regard that he applied to his men and their endeavors that make the Visitor worthy of study. It is the vivid tone of the descriptions of his journeys, and the earnestness of his sustained reflections on the progress and setbacks of the Jesuit missions in Asia. Above all, it is the compelling story of adventures in distant lands, told in the first person by a man who was obliged to project his voice around the globe, that summons the attention of readers nearly four hundred years after his death. Let us listen to what André Palmeiro has to say.

PART ONE

Inside the Empire

1

Entering the Order

Plague swept across Portugal in the year of André Palmeiro's birth. The outbreak not only devastated the capital, it laid low cities and towns throughout the kingdom. Such was the ferocity of this epidemic that it became known to posterity as the *peste grande*. Rumors of disease began to spread about the capital city in June 1569, shortly after the first telltale growths were spotted on the dying.[1] The contagion spread rapidly in Lisbon, one of the largest cities in sixteenth-century Europe. Its roughly ninety thousand inhabitants lived in densely packed neighborhoods that sprawled over the hills on the northern bank of the Tagus River.[2] Contemporaries blamed the continual traffic of ships from around Europe and beyond for the outbreak but, whatever its cause, by midsummer there was no stopping its spread. According to one chronicler, between fifty and sixty people died every day in the capital in late June, and thousands fled in fear of a cataclysm predicted for the new moon of July 10. Before that fated night, "the city was emptied out in such a crazy rush, without order or direction, each one heading off without knowing where, going to the suburbs with women, children, and goods to huddle under the olive trees." Afterward, those who could proceeded beyond the city's outskirts while the poor, lacking alternatives, returned to weather the crisis.[3] Death was everywhere, but the infant André, who had been born to Salvadora Fernandes and António Palmeiro in Lisbon during the first days of 1569, was spared.[4]

Nothing else is known about the circumstances of Palmeiro's birth or infancy, and little information survives about his youth. No personal writings
describe his formative years, and the available sources are laconic. What data
are available were set down perfunctorily when he joined the Jesuits in 1584.
As was customary for those who entered religious life in the early modern
period, postulant Palmeiro made vows in which he identified himself. His
name, his parents' names, and his age were recorded, but that is all. The
Society of Jesus did not require any more in writing about his parents, their
professions, or their social status. The dates of their deaths are not recorded,
and Palmeiro does not mention them in his later correspondence. The only
reference to any aspect of his parents' presence in his life is a brief note that
Palmeiro's mother was still in Lisbon in 1617, the year he sailed to India.[5]

It is fitting that the man who would become such a loyal servant of the
Society of Jesus should only begin to appear in the historical record after entering its ranks. From the order's perspective, his life changed completely
when he took religion. For his brethren, Palmeiro's life in the secular world
was of little interest; it was as if his true date of birth was the moment in 1584
when he joined their number. But in an age when signs and omens enjoyed
widespread currency, they did record a story about the presage of piety that
young André showed while he was a student at the Jesuit Colégio de Santo
Antão in Lisbon.[6] Based on this reference—the only one identified for this
study—it is possible to reconstruct the general pattern of his primary education and give some idea of the context in which he spent his youth. There are
more frequent references to Palmeiro's training at the Jesuit college in Coimbra, as well as to his early career as a member of the Society in that city. Yet,
despite their greater number, those archival traces are rudimentary; they are
brief entries in personnel catalogues, the lists that served to record biographical information about all Jesuits in the order's provinces.

While Palmeiro gradually moves from obscurity to clarity in the historical record during the period from his birth until his ordination as a priest at
century's end, little can be said about his individual experience. It is therefore necessary to focus on the institutions and communities that gave him
an intimate knowledge of Jesuit patterns of life in late sixteenth-century
Portugal. This awareness of how the order functioned in Europe would be
the most valuable baggage that he would carry with him to Maritime Asia.
Palmeiro garnered this experience over the many years that he spent as a
student, novice, and instructor in the Society's colleges, and it was the yard-

stick that he would use to measure Jesuit life in the colleges and missions overseas.

The Colégio de Santo Antão was the Jesuits' main educational establishment in Lisbon in the early modern period. It stood just beyond the northern edge of the city's late medieval walls, just below the Castelo de São Jorge, in the newer districts that accommodated the capital's swelling population. The college opened in 1552, a decade after the first Jesuits arrived in Portugal, offering a curriculum of Latin grammar and rhetoric to boys and young men.[7] By the mid-1570s, when Palmeiro was a student, it provided nine levels of instruction in Latin and two in moral theology. Most of the Latin students were boys who ranged from seven to sixteen years of age. They were divided among classes in grammar and in the "humanities"—that is, Latin and Greek poetry and prose as well as rhetoric. The students of moral theology or, more specifically, casuistry were seminarians, parish priests, or members of other religious orders. According to reports from Palmeiro's time at Santo Antão, the students numbered from 1,300 to 1,500. These enrollments were so great that the Society purchased a nearby site for a more spacious college in the 1580s. As was customary in the Society's schools, education was provided tuition-free by the college's community of roughly sixty Jesuits, approximately fifteen of whom were priests and the rest brothers.[8]

Palmeiro would have followed the standard educational cursus at this Lisbon college in the late 1570s and early 1580s. Although the curriculum taught in the Society's schools evolved until 1599, when the final version of the *Ratio Studiorum* (Plan of Studies) imposed uniformity on Jesuit teaching, its general contours were established by the time he began his studies.[9] The youngest students at Santo Antão would first learn reading, writing, and religion in their native tongue. The transition to Latin was made gradually over the first three years. Afterward students were expected to compose texts and speeches in Latin, and to speak that language while at school. According to a mid-sixteenth-century Jesuit teaching guide, those who showed skill in composition were invited to perform public recitations. By the fourth or fifth years of the curriculum, students began to study the works of Roman authors, especially Cicero and Virgil. The final years of the program, when the students had reached adolescence, were devoted to rhetoric as well as to introductory Greek.[10] This last curricular stage consisted of repeated

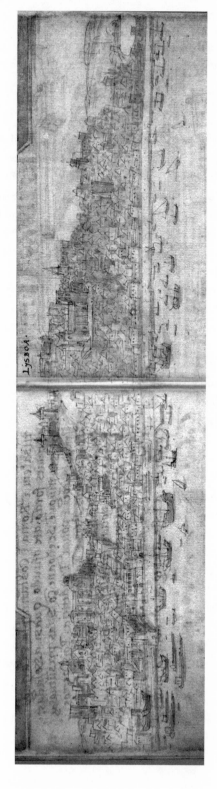

FIGURE 1.1. View of Lisbon, seen from the Tagus River, drawn in 1571 by Francisco de Holanda. The first Jesuit Colégio de Santo Antão was situated on the slope of the castle hill, behind the great Rossio Square at the center of the left side. The Society's Professed House of São Roque was located on the crest of the hill opposite the castle at the far left.

compositions, recitations, and examinations aimed at conferring eloquence in speech and writing.

Although the educational program at Santo Antão relied primarily on classical authors, Jesuit education was imbued with the spiritual charge of the Catholic Reformation. Students were obliged to attend doctrine classes and masses, and were assigned devotional topics for their compositions in poetry and prose. Membership in honorary clubs required students to participate in religious brotherhoods and assist at rituals such as the singing of the litanies. The student plays that were staged during the academic year typically had doctrinal or devotional content. For instance, in 1579, when Palmeiro would have been in the middle of his Latin studies, a "tragicomedy of the story of Jonah" was prepared by the college's oldest students.[11] The spiritual side of Jesuit education apparently appealed to him. While it is not known if Palmeiro participated in student devotions or theater, it is certain that he spent much time in the college chapel. Recalling fond memories from his youth as he lay dying on the far side of the world six decades later, he mentioned how he had eagerly helped the sacristan with duties such as placing the altar cloths.[12]

Palmeiro's time at Santo Antão was nevertheless not without incident. The late 1570s and early 1580s were a time of upheaval in Lisbon, and the college's community suffered with the general population. Famine came in 1578, appearing at almost the same moment that King Sebastian I (r. 1557–1578) decided to pursue his ill-advised Moroccan expedition. And the city once again suffered an epidemic: Palmeiro saw his studies interrupted in the late spring of 1579 when contagion forced the closing of Santo Antão. The annual report sent from the Portuguese Jesuits to their brethren in Rome painted a lamentable scene of that year's events. Sickness reigned over the kingdom for more than a year: First spread a catarrh, "which spared no one and could quickly ravage an entire college." Then came an outbreak of plague, which "raged furiously for the entire year, causing great damage throughout the city with the death of more than fifty thousand people." By the time the danger had passed and the schools could open once again, "the city was so devastated by the past troubles that very few students attended."[13]

Following upon famine, pestilence, and death, war came to Lisbon while Palmeiro was a student. The succession crisis that began in August 1578 at the Battle of Alcazarquivir would end in the summer of 1580 with the invasion of Portugal by Castilian armies. The dynastic transition culminated in the summer of the following year, when Don Felipe II of Castile arrived to be acclaimed as Dom Filipe I of Portugal (r. 1580–1598). Palmeiro thus lived most of his life as a subject of the Habsburg monarchs who reigned over Portugal and its empire from Madrid. What he felt about this is unclear: his voluminous later writings never mention his thoughts on royal affairs. In any case, it would seem that the greatest impact of all these political and social events on the eleven-year old boy was the sporadic interruption of his schooling. The repeated closures of Santo Antão due to disease and war meant that

Palmeiro did not finish his study of Latin and "humanities" before he headed to Coimbra to join the Society of Jesus at the customary age. He would therefore have to complete his early education at the same time as his novitiate.

Shortly after his fifteenth birthday, André Palmeiro entered the Society of Jesus. The motives for his decision are not clear. It is not surprising that a young man who had been a student at a Jesuit college would have considered joining the Society. By the time Palmeiro was a student, the Society's classrooms were the order's primary recruitment pools. It is likely that he was attracted by the Jesuits' spirituality, given his desire to frequent Santo Antão's chapel and in light of the ample proof of his piety from later on. Others may have joined the Society because they were attracted by its academic activities, or by the possibility of social promotion it offered to men of low birth, or even in order to attain stability in an uncertain age, but none of this appears to have driven Palmeiro's choice—at least to the extent that documents written at the time of his death can be trusted in their suggestion that he was a natural candidate for religious life. It is possible that his instructors encouraged him to join their order, but he may have made the request himself, as other young men did each year, not all of them successfully. For example, in 1578 the Jesuits at Santo Antão claimed that many of their students entered the religious life in other orders, while "the Society accepted three who were chosen from among the others who desired and requested entry."[14]

Such confidence about their selectivity should be expected in the annual reports that the Jesuits circulated among their Portuguese residences and then forwarded to the superior general in Rome. These reports were meant to be read aloud at mealtimes and therefore had the specific intent of both informing and edifying their readers (or listeners, as was more often the case). While one should not dismiss the Jesuits' boast that many sought to join them, it cannot be ignored that in the 1580s the Society was still a new presence in Portugal. Their "institute"—that is, the set of rules that constituted their manner of spiritual and communal life—was a recent addition to the spectrum of religious life. Not two generations had passed in the history of the order in Portugal, whereas three centuries had gone by since the arrival of the Dominicans and the Franciscans. The Augustinians, the Carmelites, and the Trinitarians enjoyed similar pedigrees, while the roots of the Benedictines and Cistercians stretched back to the Reconquista period. The Jesuits were by comparison upstarts in an age that resisted novelty and innovation, especially in matters of religion.

Despite its recent vintage, the Society enjoyed a rapid expansion in Portugal, as it did elsewhere in Europe. By early 1584, when Palmeiro joined the order, its members numbered 504 men distributed among ten residences. The Society's growth was due, above all, to royal favor. King João III helped the Jesuits acquire residences in Lisbon and Coimbra in the 1540s, and as their order began to focus pastoral energies on education, further endowments helped the Jesuits open colleges throughout the kingdom. The schools in Lisbon, Braga, Porto, and Funchal (on Madeira) offered a curriculum in Latin and Greek grammar and rhetoric in addition to courses in moral theology, while those in Coimbra and Évora presented those same classes as well as others in the higher sciences of philosophy and theology.[15] In the 1580s prospective Portuguese Jesuits were required to attend one of these last two colleges since they were the only ones that had novitiates. The Colégio de Jesus at Coimbra and the Colégio do Espírito Santo at Évora were thus the Society's largest communities in Portugal, accounting for over half of the order's priests and brothers. In Coimbra, Palmeiro joined the biggest of them all, where he was one of 178 Jesuits, 139 of them brothers like him.[16]

Jesuit sources indicate that Palmeiro made his first novice vows on January 14, 1584. Although the register he signed on that occasion seems not to have survived, a similar book for the novitiate at Évora has. In both colleges novices entered as brothers and pronounced initial vows binding them to observe the order's rules and their superiors' commands. In the early modern era great importance was placed on such vows because the entry into religious life meant that one left the jurisdiction of secular law and entered into that of canon law. For the parish clergy this meant being subject to the authority of their bishops, archbishops, and, in the last instance, the pope, while for members of religious orders there was yet another set of legal constraints. Jesuits, as well as other regulars—friars, monks, and nuns—were bound by the specific rules of their orders. So the Society's novices at Coimbra and Évora pledged themselves to the order by writing the following formula in Latin or Portuguese, depending on their level of schooling:

All Powerful and Eternal God, I [Name], despite being unworthy in every way of Your Divine Presence nevertheless trust in Your goodness and infi-

nite mercy; and, moved as I am by the desire to serve You, promise to the
most holy Virgin Mary and all of the celestial court of Your Divine Majesty, perpetual poverty, chastity and obedience in the Society of Jesus, and
promise to enter the same Society of Jesus in order to serve You perpetu-
ally, that is, according to the constitutions of the same Society, and I hum-
bly ask that by Your immense goodness and clemency, by the most precious blood of Jesus Christ Our Lord, You deign to receive this sacrifice
with the odor of sweetness, and in as much as You have given me the grace
to desire it and to offer it, grant me even more to fulfill it. [Place, Date, and
Signature][17]

Few documents testify to Palmeiro's early years in the Society. The Jesuits'
vertical hierarchy obliged its superiors to feed a constant flow of personnel
reports up the chain of command, so his name begins to appear in administrative sources after 1584. These reports range from lists of the residents of
each college, compiled on a yearly basis, to abbreviated biographies for every
Jesuit, drawn up every three years, in addition to the references to particular
individuals found in the correspondence between rectors, provincials, and
the order's curia in Rome. Personnel catalogues reveal that in January 1585
Brother André Palmeiro was a resident of the Colégio de Jesus and was en-
rolled as a student in the "first class" of the humanities sequence. In contrast
to the philosophy or theology courses, the "classes" of the lower schools were
ranked in descending order, putting him in the final year of the Latin grammar and rhetoric curriculum. Moreover, this brief notation confirms that
Palmeiro's superiors recognized his academic talents early on; he was allowed
to enter the novitiate as a scholastic, someone on track for higher academic
pursuits, rather than as a coadjutor, one who would remain in the Society's
lower ranks.[18]

The Colégio de Jesus would be Palmeiro's home for the next thirty years.
It was where he would embark on his distinguished academic career and gain
the reputation for intellectual ability that would contribute to his nomina-
tion as visitor in Asia. Coimbra was one of the few centers of cultural life in
sixteenth-century Portugal. Intellectual activities were typically the province
of court and church, so Lisbon naturally played an important role as the seat
of royal and ecclesiastical power. Outside of the capital, there were two significant concentrations of learned men: at Évora, whose university was administered by the Society of Jesus after its creation in 1559, and, even more

importantly, at Coimbra. It is therefore worthwhile to provide a sketch of intellectual life there and of the Jesuit presence in the city.

Crowning a hill on the banks of the Mondego River, the city was the seat of one of Europe's oldest universities. The Estudo Geral was first established in 1290 but moved back and forth to Lisbon before its definitive establishment in Coimbra in 1537. In the words of one early modern chronicler, King João III knew well that "the muses like solitude and, amid the traffic of customhouses and contracts, letters are smothered." So he moved the university far from the bustle of the court, to the site of a royal palace that had seen little use since the Middle Ages.[19]

With the permanent settlement of the university, Coimbra began to grow. Its population reached approximately ten thousand inhabitants by the end of the sixteenth century.[20] The city's privileged position as one of the poles of intellectual life meant that early modern *érudits* lavished praise upon it. They noted the city's temperate climate, its healthy air, the civility of its inhabitants, the purity of its waters, the bounty of its nearby farms, and, in the opinion of at least one commentator, the "benign influence of the stars."[21] Other authors celebrated Coimbra in terms they knew other Europeans would understand. Pedro de Mariz (ca. 1550–1615), a late sixteenth-century scholar, penned a dialogue in which an aged Italian wanderer came across a young student seated by the banks of the Mondego, asserting that Coimbra matched the highest standards: "If I did not know that this city was in Portugal and mine in Italy, I could have been easily fooled!"[22]

By the mid-1580s the university and the Society's college in Coimbra were in full expansion. The first Jesuits had arrived in the city only a few years after King João III ceded his palaces to be the seat of the university. In 1547 the Jesuits began construction on their Colégio de Jesus, following the pattern established by the religious orders that opened colleges in the city. But in 1555, after they had given proof of their ability to teach the trilingual curriculum that stood at the heart of a humanistic education—and after the Inquisition forced out its original professors—the king appointed the Jesuits to run the Colégio das Artes. This royal college had been founded to offer training in grammar and rhetoric as well as philosophy to future students of the university. The faculties of theology, law, and medicine made up the university's core, with the "arts" occupying a secondary status.[23] The two Jesuit-run colleges in Coimbra would remain in separate edifices until the Society built a massive new complex at the end of the sixteenth century.

There was considerable overlap between the university and the colleges of the religious orders in Coimbra. Although the university was an independent body of professors and students, bound by its own rules and traditions, it was permeated by members of the clergy who belonged to groups with different regulations and customs. The prestige of the university's faculties, especially in theology, meant that members of religious orders, including the Jesuits, sought positions there. But the orders also maintained their own faculties, which gave instruction to their members, often in the same subjects that were taught at the university. The Jesuits, for example, would convoke the same number of theology classes as the university, but neither the Society nor any other order could confer the degrees of bachelor, licentiate, master, or doctor. That remained the university's prerogative, a fact that led to confusion and conflict, especially with regard to the Colégio das Artes. By the terms of the university's royal charter, the university was obliged to pay for the college and its instructors, who, as Jesuits, were not subject to the university's rules.[24]

The rise of the Jesuits during their first decades in Coimbra astonished and annoyed contemporaries. Royal favor and, above all, funds ensured that the Society enjoyed a privileged spot just outside the university's doors. In contrast to other orders, most of whose colleges were located on the Rua da Sofia in the lower town, the Jesuits were granted a spacious plot at the city's highest point. They attempted to begin construction on a college there in 1547 but were met with resistance from the city council and the townspeople that lasted for over two decades.[25] Yet by the time Palmeiro arrived in 1584, construction of the Colégio de Jesus was well under way. Frequent work stoppages, however, kept it unfinished until long after he left for Asia. Indeed, the college church—today's New Cathedral—was only begun in 1598, and work on the new Colégio das Artes commenced more than a decade later.

Palmeiro spent most of his life in half-finished buildings, both in Europe and overseas, not in the massive building complexes that the Society would come to occupy later on. The spaces where he underwent his novitiate, the classrooms where he studied and later taught, and the chapels where he prayed in Coimbra were located for the most part in temporary quarters that would be dedicated to other uses when the college was completed. Nevertheless, in the late 1580s the Colégio de Jesus had room for more than 180 Jesuits and classroom space for almost 2,000 students. With four classes in theology, four in philosophy, eleven in Latin grammar and rhetoric, and one class each

FIGURE 1.2. View of Coimbra found in the fifth volume of *Civitates Orbis Terrarum* by Georg Braun, published in 1598. The Jesuits' Colégio de Jesus is situated adjacent to the university buildings in the upper right corner, while their Colégio das Artes is found on Rua da Sofia at the center left. The Convento de Santa Clara, site of the tomb of Queen Isabel, is situated on other side of the Mondego River at the lower right.

in Greek, Hebrew, and mathematics, this college was the center of Jesuit life in all of Portugal and its empire.[26]

The novitiate at Coimbra was intended to shock postulants out of their childish ways and to charge them with piety and obedience. Early modern Jesuit authors celebrated the rigors of their order's probation since it was a three-year process, a year longer than the common span for religious orders. To be sure, the Society of Jesus did not oblige its postulants to three continuous years of seclusion, privations, and menial chores. Rather, the novitiate lasted for two years when a candidate first joined and was completed several years later with a third year known as the tertianship. This third year was intended to remind Jesuits of the variety of Society's pastoral ministries, forcing them from the academic routines that consumed most of their time. Indeed, for men like Palmeiro who entered the order as scholastics, their early years combined the novitiate's probationary activities with continued study. Those who did not proceed through the academic track would endure the same trial phase but would be given a terminal rank as temporal coadjutors—that is, brothers. To be sure, the title "brother" was given to scholastics too. They remained brothers for a long time after the novitiate, their ordination only coming several years later after they completed part of their theology studies. For instance, Palmeiro remained "Brother André" through the 1580s and most of the 1590s.[27]

Most of the information that has survived about the Society's novitiates is prescriptive. It is known what postulants were supposed to do and what the order's founders considered the best type of experience for introducing them to religious life. What actually happened is harder to discern, given the variety of national settings in which the Society was found in early modern Europe. For the Province of Portugal, anecdotal information about the novitiates abounds in the work of António Franco (1662–1732). The *Imagem da Virtude* volumes which he wrote in the early eighteenth century describe the novitiate of Coimbra and offer accounts of the "lives and holy deaths of many men of great virtue who were trained in that holy house." While Franco's biographies are marked by pious nostalgia, they give insight into novitiate life in Palmeiro's time. Franco describes how the postulants were kept secluded from the rest of the college in a separate wing of the building, and how they lived under the strict rules of the master of novices.

The master was charged with ensuring that the brothers kept regular prayer routines, both communally and individually. He was also entrusted with their spiritual formation, restricting their readings to a handful of classics such as the *Contemptus mundi,* the *Stimuli divini amoris,* the letters of St. Catherine of Siena, a Hieronymite treatise called *El Desseoso,* and the *Institutions* of Johannes Tauler.[28] He appointed novices to take turns preaching to their fellow brothers and to hold daily examinations on the themes presented during mealtimes. In addition to acting as perpetual examiner, the master coordinated chores such as hanging laundry, sweeping the college, sifting flour, and kneading dough. Mortification was the watchword, and periodic fasts were imposed on the brothers to enhance their understanding of "holy poverty." One master invented the practice of reducing one meal each month to broth, fruit, and bread or, rather, slices from the burned loaves. Perhaps unsurprisingly, the brothers spent their rest hour talking about their meager meal—although Franco claims they saw the virtue in their frugal portions and ruminated on "how little our nature needs". Franco also remarks on how the first masters of novices at Coimbra had to clamp down on occasions for gluttony, "such as putting mustard on their cabbage," and to enforce decorum by combating the perpetual scourge of novices, laughter. "Since laughing ordinarily proceeds on these occasions from the body's being somewhat happy with eating," he continued, "when the Father Master saw that someone laughed, he would order his fruit or something else to be taken from the table."[29]

During Palmeiro's time, the master was Vasco Pires (1546–1590), who considered the novitiate to be a "workshop of the spirit" where one came to know the "shape of the perfect religious." Pires, who held this position for twelve years, was known for his extreme rigor. He dismissed immediately anyone who did not punctiliously conform to the Society's rules. According to Franco, Pires likened his charge to that of a gardener who "seeks to make good grafts and good stocks with all diligence, since in the future whoever eats the fruit will give thanks to him who produced it, but if it is bad, as soon as they touch it and discover its lack of taste, they will spit it out with disgust, cursing the one who wasted time grafting and growing such bad fruit."[30]

Pires's goal was to ensure that his subordinates kept the habits acquired as novices throughout their lives as Jesuits. He was particularly given to discipline and obedience, demanding that his novices detach themselves from all possessions and affectations; he insisted on conformity and sought to instill

control over individual passions, at times to the point of absurdity. On one
occasion Pires insisted on conquering two novices' aversion to cheese and eggs
by obliging them to finish their meals in the refectory with large portions of
each. The master only relented when their food allergies (and vomiting) refused
to subside, "seeing that it was not in his hands to defeat their repugnance of
these things." To further tame the postulants, Franco wrote, he "would not
suffer formalities or manners that smelled of hypocrisy or benevolent flattery,
desiring frankness and religious simplicity among them." Pires taught by
example, and he invited senior Jesuits and other venerable clergymen to examine the novices. Among them were Fernão Martins Mascarenhas (1548–1628),
the rector of the university and later inquisitor general, and Afonso de Castelobranco (1522–1615), the count-bishop of Coimbra and inveterate patron of
the Jesuits.[31]

It appears that Pires found an eager listener in Palmeiro, whose later actions mimic the virtues celebrated in the anecdotes about the novice master.
Pires was remembered above all for his obedience and his austerity. For instance, he was known to obey orders immediately without hesitation, as happened in one episode when he leapt from the barber's chair half shaven to
rush to the side of the (surprised) superior who had summoned him.[32] Palmeiro likewise was known for his unfailing obedience, not only in his willingness to depart on a dangerous journey but also in his scrupulous adherence to orders from the superior general. Pires displayed an almost apostolic
sense of personal rigor, choosing to proceed on foot rather than by horse or
mule whenever obliged to travel long distances. Palmeiro, too, would journey
far and wide on foot, eschewing the meager comforts of early modern con-
veyances in the name of mortification. And Pires's commitment to poverty
was such that he would not permit his novices to have their own devotional
objects or relics, calling them vanities and insisting that they be sent to India
for use in the missions instead.[33] Palmeiro observed a similar adherence to
poverty: When he was in Macau in his final years and one of his fellow Jesuits asked for a devotional object for his own use, the Visitor denied the request
and ordered the procurator to collect all of the plaques, images, and pendants
to send to the missions "because this was their purpose, and none other".[34]

As perhaps should be expected, the novitiate also produced lifelong friend-
ships. It is hard to underestimate the sense of solidarity and loyalty that this
experience engendered among the young Jesuits, especially those whose paths
took them to the far ends of the earth. The Colégio de Jesus was indeed a

"seminary of the world", in the words of a seventeenth-century chronicler, whence generations of young missionaries traveled to Asia, Africa, and the Americas, and bonds of the kind formed there were what held the Society of Jesus together.[35] Among Palmeiro's colleagues was Diogo Valente (1568–1633), a man whose career mirrors Palmeiro's. Valente, also from Lisbon, would teach in Coimbra and serve in the various colleges of southern Portugal before being named bishop of Japan in 1618. He would live out his final days with Palmeiro in Macau and be buried side by side with his longtime friend.[36] Also among Palmeiro's colleagues in the mid-1580s were Mateus de Couros (1568–1633), who left the novitiate for a long career as a missionary in Japan, and João Soeiro (1566–1607), who also departed for East Asia straight from the novitiate and became one of the first missionaries to work in China. In comparison to these Jesuit travelers, Palmeiro's future seemed less exotic: he would remain at Coimbra while they would head for the missions. Little did he know that their paths would one day cross again on the other side of the globe.

Palmeiro entered the novitiate as a scholastic, meaning that he would proceed along the Society's standard academic track. In 1584 he was in the final phase of the Latin program, which by that stage was devoted to rhetoric and literature. The central emphasis of this program was composition in classical languages as well as in Portuguese. Students not only wrote prose and poetry, they declaimed it to each other, and the best students were chosen to read their pieces aloud at the year-end student celebrations. While Palmeiro's voluminous writings from later in his life clearly attest to skills in Portuguese and Latin, the only piece of evidence of his early command of rhetoric is a short Latin poem about the Blessed Virgin titled *Magnae Matris carmen genethliacon*. This "birthday poem," most likely written on the occasion of the feast of the Nativity of the Virgin (September 8), is in dactylic hexameter and evokes the great changes in the history of humankind that were ushered in by Mary's birth. The images that the young Palmeiro includes are typical classical references, the stock photography of his day—especially appropriate topics for students in Jesuit colleges. They include evocations of the waters of the flood, the colors of the rainbow, the abyss of the underworld. The following is the first stanza of the poem, recorded in a miscellany of student poetry from the Colégio de Jesus in the 1580s:

Sistite largifluos, rorantia nubila, fontes
Sat pelago mortale genus commissa reprendit
Crimina. Iam roseis distincta coloribus Iris
Illucet terris, pacemque annuntiat orbi.
Hactenus undantes, resolutis nubibus, imbres
Alluvie tristi vastâqua voragine mundum
Immersum tenuere vadis. Proh! Quanta per undas
Millia Tartareo perierunt hausta profundo.

[Oh dripping clouds, cease your copiously flowing fountains,
humankind has blamed the sea enough of its crimes.
Already Iris, marked by rosy colors,
shines over the earth, and announces peace to the world.
The abundant rains from the breaking clouds have, by their waters,
until now kept the world immersed in a sad flood
and an enormous whirlpool. Alas! how many thousands
perished, swallowed by the waves into Tartarus's depths!][37]

There is little information about Palmeiro's first years at Coimbra beyond
the notations in the Society's personnel catalogues from the late 1580s that he
completed his rhetoric studies and the subsequent four-year course in philosophy. This lack of data is unsurprising because Palmeiro did not stray from
the standard course and so did not warrant any comments from his superiors.
Yet the lacuna means that his student years can only be examined through
descriptions of life at the Colégio de Jesus and the major events that would
have been witnessed, or at least talked about, by the men who lived there.

One such event occurred at the end of Palmeiro's first novice year, when
he was in the first humanities class. In December 1585 an "embassy" from
Japan arrived at Coimbra and was received with pomp by the local dignitaries before being escorted to the Jesuit college, where it spent three weeks.
This embassy was actually a publicity tour organized by the Society's superiors in Asia, who intended to supplement the frequent—and oftentimes
exaggerated—reports of missionary success in Japan with living proof. Four
teenagers from families of the arms-bearing gentry of Kyushu were escorted
by Jesuit handlers across Southern Europe, where they were presented to
noblemen, bishops, the king, and the pope as members of the highest ranks
of the Japanese aristocracy. Lasting from 1582 until 1590, the embassy's tour
took the youths across the Estado da Índia to Portugal, and from there to

Spain and Italy and back. The party reached Coimbra on their return journey, arriving in Portugal too early for the April fleets bound for India. In order to drum up missionary vocations, no less than to gather donations from Portuguese benefactors, the "ambassadors" were brought to Coimbra and presented to illustrious figures, including members of the Bragança family, the university's rector, and the count-bishop. As the bells of the city's churches rang out on the December day of their arrival, the party headed toward the Jesuit college amid a press of onlookers so great that "there was no space for them to dismount, until the justice officials who came with them and even the bishop with his authority cleared a space for them to enter the church."[38]

If he did not see the Japanese youths as they kissed the relics of the True Cross and the virgin martyrs during their welcome at the Colégio de Jesus, Palmeiro surely glimpsed them during a stage production that his class performed in their presence a few days later. The humanities students then enacted a dialogue between guardian angels about the heavenly protection of Europe and Japan. A contemporary account of the play based on the notes taken by the youths' escorts and embellished by the Society's superiors in Asia claims that the instructors adorned their classroom with tapestries and outfitted the student actors with luxurious clothes. The two angels celebrated the nascent East Asian church, recounting about Japan "many admirable victories and exploits redounding to the praise of the Christian religion." The figure of Faith appeared "together with a great company of the heavenly host" and confirmed these assertions, and all attributed the apostolic advance to the Holy Cross. Afterward the European guardian angel spoke about the embassy's success before handing over the emissaries to his Japanese companion to be guided safely back home. Palmeiro's instructor also played a role, interjecting to discourse on the similarity between the joyous entry of King Afonso Henriques into Coimbra after a rout of the Moors in the twelfth century and the success of the Christian mission in Japan. The latter feat took the better part, "for it was idolatry, which had long ruled throughout Japan, that had been vanquished."[39]

The farthest reaches of Asia thus bracket the story of Palmeiro's life in the Society of Jesus. Although he did not know it as a novice, he would end his days as a Jesuit just as he began them, in the pitch of fervor about the fate of Christianity in Japan. In the 1580s in Portugal, just as the missions in Japan entered their phase of maximum expansion, Palmeiro watched as great expectations filled the air—provoking several of his colleagues to petition for assignment to the Society's Asian enterprises. And he would follow the violent end of Christianity in Japan four decades later from a front row seat. In his waning years, he would address himself to other ambassadors, ones that the Society of Jesus had sent to Japan in the shadow of persecution and who faced cruel martyrdoms if they were caught. It was thus ironic that the theme chosen by the college faculty to enact for the ambassadors on the Feast of the Kings in 1586 was a tragic one, the decapitation of John the Baptist. But at that moment the star of the Japanese church was in the ascendant, and all present at the Coimbra festivities thought only of triumphal scenes.

After completing his rhetoric studies, Palmeiro began the *Curso das Artes,* which would occupy him until 1590. Not to be confused with the "classes" of the Latin track, the "arts course" was a three-year program in Aristotelian philosophy which included the examination of logic and metaphysics as well as substantial amounts of "natural philosophy"—that is, the study of the physical world and the heavens. By the late 1580s the Coimbra Jesuits had become known across Europe for their expertise in teaching philosophy and, at the request of the Society's superiors general, had begun to polish their lecture notes for publication. The glosses on Aristotle's core works compiled by a team led by Pedro da Fonseca (1528–1599), a series of texts known to posterity as the *Commentarii Collegii Conimbricensis Societatis Iesu,* became the standard resource for explaining the Philosopher's thought in Jesuit schools. The Coimbra Commentaries were not simply a straightforward analysis of Aristotelian thought. They were meant to supplement the synthesis between Greek thought and Christianity that Thomas Aquinas had begun in the thirteenth century. In other words, what Palmeiro heard presented in his philosophy classroom were the elemental texts of Aristotle supported by many layers of classical, patristic, medieval, and contemporary interpretation.[40]

The Coimbra course, and its equivalent at the Society's Roman College, aimed to demonstrate the practical relevance of Aristotelian thought to Christian theology. It was taught before theology in the standard academic sequence because the foundations of logical reasoning were deemed indispensable for the later study of speculative theology. Indeed, those young Jesuits who did not prove capable of handling the rigor of the first year logic lessons of the arts course were removed from the program. Their future studies, if they were permitted to pursue them, would only be in moral theology— that is, a path of priestly training that would enable them to hear confessions but not to preach. For those who successfully completed the logic syllabus and the rest of the *Curso das Artes,* however, the path of studies led through the whole theology course, both the moral and speculative components. So Palmeiro was in line to achieve his later rank by moving smoothly through his studies. He completed the arts course by 1590, meaning that by then he had studied logic, then natural philosophy (including astronomy and some mathematics), and finally ethics and metaphysics.[41]

Palmeiro did not begin the theology course immediately after finishing his philosophy studies. This was typical, and it implied no judgment on his capacities. By the 1580s it had become routine to assign junior Jesuits to teaching the first years of the grammar course in the hope that their youthful energy would match that of their pupils. The fact that the Colégio de Jesus was obliged by its founding charter to provide teachers for the courses at the Colégio das Artes meant that the Jesuits were always in need of grammar instructors. It appears that those freshest out of the arts course were the ones who were sent to the initial ranks of the Latin sequence, working their way up as the years progressed. Owing to a lack of personnel catalogues from the 1590s, it is not known which classes Palmeiro taught. Other sources, however, indicate that he spent six years teaching Latin.[42] Most likely he taught different classes within the grammar and rhetoric sequence since this seems to have been the case for other young Jesuits. The same lack of documentation means that little can be known of how Palmeiro's superiors or students evaluated his teaching, although the fact that he taught at Coimbra for twenty-five years suggests they were pleased.

Generally, Jesuit superiors held the College of Coimbra in high esteem. Except for a few complaints about a lack of austerity and of interest in public preaching and doctrine teaching, senior members of the Society communicated their approval to the order's Roman curia. The Colégio de Jesus, for good or for ill, was primarily an educational institution and so focused on academic activities instead of pastoral ones. Although there were "many priests and brothers of rare virtue," wrote Manuel Sequeira (1533–1595) after his 1593 inspection of the college, there were others "who see it as their only goal to become lettered men."[43] Such a focus smacked of vanity, Sequeira implied, but other superiors were not so ill at ease with the college's academic focus. One of the most important biblical exegetes of the later sixteenth century, Sebastião Barradas (1543–1616), reported that the college proceeded admirably. "There is nothing noteworthy to report to Your Paternity," he wrote to Superior General Claudio Aquaviva in 1595. "The rules and the institute are kept according to the limits of human frailty."[44] And Francisco de Gouvea (1540–1638), who conducted an inspection of the Province of Portugal in 1595, wrote of his satisfaction with the "diligence of the masters" who taught the various classes, among whom was Palmeiro. Gouvea only complained about the slow pace of construction that left the college intolerably overcrowded: "The classrooms are cramped, and since the number of students is so great, they are tightly squeezed and each master must remain the whole time in his chair, which is a hardship and affliction."[45]

After his first stint teaching, Palmeiro began his theology studies in the autumn of 1596. He would be ordained a priest by the end of the decade. Typically Jesuits who were on track to become professed members of the Society would take two years of moral theology and a further two years of speculative theology. While the first segment of the course was required for all priests, and many who were not Jesuits studied it at the Colégio de Jesus, the second part was reserved for those who had acquired the philosophical foundation needed for understanding the Thomistic texts that constituted most of the speculative program. This was no challenge for Palmeiro, who had completed the arts course and would become a philosophy instructor in the last years of the decade. According to personnel catalogues, Palmeiro studied theology for three years, from 1596 until 1599.[46] Why his program was more compact than the standard four-year sequence that would be employed in the Society in later decades is unclear, but he certainly mastered the material: it would not be long before he taught it himself.[47]

It is also unclear when Palmeiro completed his tertianship, the third year of novice training that was unique to the Society of Jesus. The order's personnel catalogues from the late sixteenth and early seventeenth century suggest this final step in Jesuit formation would have been taken upon completion of philosophy and theology studies, typically at about thirty years of age.[48] There is, however, no record of Palmeiro's tertianship, and his writings never mention it. It is also difficult to determine when exactly he took Holy Orders. The most likely date for this event is 1599 because from that point onward documents refer to him as Padre André Palmeiro.[49]

In contrast to the distant wanderings of his final eighteen years as a Jesuit, Palmeiro's initial decade and a half was spent largely within the Colégio de Jesus. Continuously occupied with either studying or teaching, his life was more monastic than one would expect of a member of the Society of Jesus. As a novice, he was obliged by his vows to live in seclusion, frequenting only the classrooms, the common meeting rooms, and the interior patios where songbirds gathered in the trees. As a brother, his sphere of movement grew only marginally larger to include the whole of the college complex. After ordination and once he commenced his teaching career, it again expanded, taking him about Coimbra from the Rua da Sofia and down along the banks of the Mondego. But the Colégio de Jesus, and especially its library, were his central reference point; there, surrounded by tomes in this "abundant Parnassus and Athenaeum" of philosophical and theological writings, he drew inspiration for his academic pursuits.[50] Palmeiro's mind, much like the college buildings he inhabited, was a work in progress. Yet in contrast to the Colégio de Jesus, whose massive church was only begun in 1598, his formation would be complete by the end of the sixteenth century.

The early period of Palmeiro's life was characterized by routines. His entry into the Society of Jesus brought him into a world marked by regular patterns of communal life, annual educational cycles, standard academic tracks, and normal progressions within Jesuit ranks. The routine nature of these activities served to inculcate norms and expectations, and were not supposed to occasion comment by those who experienced them. So it is unsurprising that Palmeiro was silent about his formative years, and that we have to rely on the testimony of his superiors, his peers, and later chroniclers. As Jesuits they knew that the process of creating members of the Society of Jesus was achieved as much in the classroom as it was in other common spaces. The yearly educational cycles and the common rhythms of devotional activities were the pulses of Jesuit life in early modern Europe. Long experience of them would be crucial to Palmeiro's future career as inspector. The inculcation of habits particular to Jesuits and the experience of life in the Society's colleges, especially in one as important as the Colégio de Jesus, endowed him with a set of standards that he would apply to all of the Jesuit communities he visited in Asia. But India was still a distant horizon for him at the turn of the seventeenth century, a place to which some of his friends and instructors had gone. He would have to begin to speak for himself before he would be chosen to join them.

2

The Visitor in Training

André Palmeiro spent the second half of his thirty-year stay at Coimbra as one of the senior Jesuits of the Province of Portugal. Although his formal education had ended with his successful completion of the course in speculative theology, his informal training as an administrator had only begun. By observing his colleagues at the Colégio de Jesus, he would learn how to serve as a professor of philosophy and theology, how to manage a community, and how to conduct inspections. Palmeiro's knowledge of how the Society of Jesus functioned would likewise increase as he climbed the hierarchical ladder from simple priest to professed Jesuit. Upon reaching that superior rank, he became a participant in the order's governance. Starting at the position of college consultor, an advisor to the Coimbra college's rector, Palmeiro would progress to the post of rector at the Jesuit college in Braga in northern Portugal. Only a few years after that he would receive his first commission as visitor in Asia.

It is only slightly easier to plot the course of Palmeiro's life during his final two decades in Portugal than it was for his first three. His name appears with greater frequency on documents from this period than from the earlier one; yet few significant traces remain. This is not surprising. The identity of early modern religious orders was explicitly corporate. Individual personalities were not supposed to be distinguishable from the mass of their brethren.

Moreover, the desire to demonstrate humility, one of the most prized qualities of pious brothers, priests, or nuns, encouraged many to self-effacement—indeed, to the point where they disappear from the historical record. For example, members of the Franciscan family changed their names upon entry into their orders as a sign of humility and subordination of individual identity to that of their order. Among Dominicans and Jesuits, to give but two examples, postulants retained their names, but a similar pressure nevertheless existed to downplay the individual in favor of the "spiritual family." As a result, someone like Palmeiro intentionally remained a face in a crowd even when he reached the Society's senior rank. He was known more by his position, whether in Coimbra or in Braga, than by his name. Moreover, the fact that Palmeiro sought to embody the virtue of humility by his rejection of worldly honors—that is, until he was obliged by obedience to take up the position of visitor and speak with his own voice—meant that he left few marks of his years as professor or even as rector.

The contrast between the ample testimony of Palmeiro's activities during his years in Asia and the scarcity of sources to describe his nearly fifty years in Portugal is striking. And so once again it is necessary to examine the environment within which he lived, rather than his own words and deeds. Much is known about the Jesuit communities of Coimbra and Braga in the first two decades of the seventeenth century, so to evoke life at those two colleges is not a difficult challenge. Still, the primary task of this stage in Palmeiro's biography is to understand what skills he would have acquired in Portugal that proved useful for the task of inspecting the Society's provinces in Asia. A secondary goal is to describe how he came by the gravitas that would be necessary in his later role as visitor.

———————

Two dramatic events occurred at the Colégio de Jesus in Coimbra while Palmeiro was finishing his theology studies. Both involved death and a rush of emotion, but in different ways: One was the passing of a renowned preacher, the other a case of murder. The two episodes illustrate some of the tensions latent in early modern religious life, albeit at moments of rare intensity. In the first case, the death of a man whose charisma made him one of the most famous preachers in sixteenth-century Portugal occasioned a great outpouring of grief. In the second, a web of jealousies ensnared a Jesuit brother and led to his violent death. These two events reveal aspects of the Society's internal and external relations, illuminating some of the dynamics of Jesuit life that Palmeiro would have to confront as visitor.

The first of these two events was the death of Inácio Martins. This charismatic Jesuit priest (b. 1531) was best known for his parades of doctrine-singing children, adolescents, and slaves in Lisbon as well as for his efforts to ban public comedies.[1] It is more than likely that Palmeiro knew Martins from his time at Santo Antão because the street preacher was one of the best-known Jesuits in the court city.[2] Martins had come to Coimbra in early 1598 to take part in the Society's triennial provincial congregation and had intended a brief stay. Unaware of a fatal illness, he ascended to the pulpits of the Colégio de Jesus and the university chapel to begin a cycle of Lenten sermons, which he would never complete. After collapsing twice, perhaps the victim of stroke, Martins was brought to the college infirmary. Although he had spent most of his career in Lisbon, the news of his illness caused commotion in Coimbra. Clergy and laity said prayers for his health, and the nuns of the Convent of Santa Clara sent a relic of the *Rainha Santa,* Blessed Queen Isabel of Portugal (1270–1336), to his quarters. At Martins's request, the Jesuit novices came to sing doctrine songs at his bedside, and holy water was brought to bless the spot where he would die. In his final hours on the night of February 28, Martins grasped tightly the cane with which he had shepherded young doctrine students for seventeen years and breathed his last.[3]

If Palmeiro was not present at the moment of the preacher's death, he could not have been absent from the flood of sentiment loosed by the priests and brothers at the college in the hours that followed as Martins's body was prepared for burial. According to a report sent to Rome, the corpse was "hard and blackened, since he had spent his whole life out in the sun, and it was covered with the signs of his penitential disciplines—with welts and calluses and, in some places, open wounds." These marks caused not pity but admiration. Knowing that many visitors would come to see the body, Provincial Cristóvão de Gouvea (1542–1622) ordered it to be laid in a chapel upon a high bier covered in carpets and surrounded by candles. News of Martins's death traveled along with the pealing of the college's bells, and the townspeople swiftly appeared at the Jesuits' doors. The local clergy and other worthies, including Count-Bishop Afonso de Castelobranco, appeared the following morning to offer their condolences. The rector of the university insisted on kissing the corpse's feet and hands, and some of the professors "cried like children" in its presence. After the chapel doors had been shut that night, the rector acceded to the pleas of a crowd of students and commoners who begged to venerate the corpse and acquire relics, and "there was no lack of those who came with scissors to cut pieces from his alb, and the tips of his nails." Swept up by similar emotions, the college's priests and brothers held their own viewing behind closed doors that night, "and set to obtaining relics of hair and nails with such devotion that the superiors had to visit them several times to calm their fervor."[4]

The crescendo of lamentation over Martins's death reached its height when the Jesuits attempted to bury him inside the college church. According to one report, the most loudly voiced emotions came from the university students from Lisbon who remembered the doctrine parades of their youth and felt that their city was being cheated of a holy treasure. During the vigils and ceremonies held at the college sanctuary, any mention of Martins set off "tears and trembling . . . cries and uncontrolled shouts like those heard when the Passion is preached." For the funeral mass, the Jesuits erected another bier in the center of the church, and welcomed a host of dignitaries and fellow religious, as well as the university faculty, students, and "innumerable" city dwellers. All sought to touch the body with their rosary beads, prayer books, or "whatever they had in their hands", while many even considered the candles distributed for the mass to be relics. After groups from different religious orders had sung their prayers while surrounding the body, the Jesuits attempted to bury it, but the crowd surged as soon as they lifted the corpse. In this scrum, some pushed forward "to touch, others to kiss, others to see, and so many were the scissors and knives around it that no threads were left" on either Martins's outer or inner garments. The slippers were taken from his feet and his socks thoroughly slashed, giving the university's most senior theology professor a last chance to kiss the exposed flesh. Even Martins's cap disappeared ("though it was later found"), before the body was removed to a smaller chapel, far from the violent grasp of popular piety. Only a day later could the corpse, dressed anew, be committed to the earth beneath the church's paving stones.[5]

The second dramatic event that occurred in 1598 at the Colégio de Jesus was not greeted with the same pious fervor. On the night of June 8, Brother António Antunes was murdered in the loft of the college's former pantry. His mangled body was found a day later. Such was the shock occasioned by this news that the Society's superior general sent orders from Rome for a special investigation. Martim de Mello (1548–1617), visitor of the Province of Portugal, traveled to Coimbra to conduct the inquest, interviewing both senior and junior Jesuits. According to his report, Brother Antunes was found cold, covered in blood, and bearing the marks of having been trampled. Mello's account is filled with gory details, stressing the "great hatred and strange cruelty" of the killing. It was clear that a club or staff had been used to beat Antunes, and the many penetrating wounds in his skull and chest were proof of the viciousness of the stabbing that followed. Indeed, his head was nearly severed.[6]

Who was responsible for this heinous crime? Although there was no one caught red-handed, there was no mystery about the identity of the culprit. The prime suspect was another coadjutor, João Álvares. It was widely known that he hated Antunes and had repeatedly cursed him. Moreover, Álvares, the brother in charge of the college's hired help, was described by witnesses in Mello's investigation as "choleric, wrathful, irascible, and with little truth or fear of God"—faults that contrasted starkly with the many virtues of his victim, who was described as cheerful, competent, and obedient. Álvares had an accomplice, a servant named Bastião who had recently been sacked. He, too, harbored a hatred for Antunes—not without reason, because Antunes was the one who had fired him. Álvares reportedly tricked Antunes into visiting the old building where the two men attacked him. Then, after stealing the money from Antunes's purse, the murderers fled on horseback, Bastião heading for his family home a short distance from Coimbra and Álvares riding south toward Santarém, where he sold his horse. Two Jesuit brothers spotted Álvares in Lisbon, but he claimed to be traveling on official business and headed across the Tagus River to parts unknown. Six months later his whereabouts were still unknown, and he continued "on the loose and in hiding." In Mello's summation, not only the Jesuits but the whole city were scandalized, "believing that the person or persons who committed such a crime were most worthy of the harshest punishment."[7]

The episodes involving Inácio Martins and António Antunes illustrate how external and internal forces exerted pressure upon the Society of Jesus. For Palmeiro, who lived at the Colégio de Jesus at the time, they were object lessons in the challenges faced by Jesuit superiors. During his time as inspector in Asia, he would be required to deal with such pressures, whether from individuals outside the order or among his subordinates. When dealing with external ones, he would have to guard the public image of the order. This was precisely the challenge that his superiors faced when Martins died.

After all, the Society was not a monastic order. Its men aspired to be "contemplatives in action," performing a variety of ministries to individuals across the social spectrum. One such figure was Martins, who preached in pulpits and on street corners, attracting public attention and solidifying the order's image of pious heroism. The success of this type of popular ministry was demonstrated by his large following as well as the deep strains of emotion intoned at his funeral. But individuals like Martins occupied a fringe of Jesuit life; they moved from their structured community out into the world, impelled by their charisma. By their public displays of fervor, such men stimulated the desires of laymen and women to partake in the Society's perceived sanctity.

Minding the divide between communal life and the demands of outsiders was a perennial problem for early modern religious orders. Although many entered religious life to "flee from the world," it remained close at hand. The question was therefore how close outsiders should come to the centers of communal piety and how much they should take from what religious communities created. To be sure, the Jesuits (and their peers) had to attract attention. The Society needed patrons, just as it required audiences for its preachers, penitents for its confessors, and members for its confraternities. The Jesuits' primary public ministry was, of course, its educational one, and they counted on their students to act as a spiritual clientele. Men like Martins expanded that pastoral audience to include larger segments of society. The order therefore had to respond to the devotional fruit produced by the charisma of its members. On some occasions, such as his funeral, the Jesuits were obliged to permit crowds of scissor-wielding relic-seekers to occupy their sanctuaries. Their interest in accommodating the desires of individuals from the higher ranks of society was scarcely less. The Jesuits provided confessors to kings, prelates, and noblemen and women; they made preachers available when requested by city councils or religious communities; and they discussed theology and morality with members of the learned elite. But the boundary between popular and elite devotions was not a hard and fast barrier, as the Coimbra Jesuits knew well. The priests and brothers who had obtained their own relics of Martins had to give up his clothes, beads, cilice, and flagellating whip "because the Dukes of Bragança and Aveiro, and other principal lords, had asked with much devotion for some particular piece belonging to Padre Inácio."[8] When he became an administrator himself, Palmeiro would be the Jesuits' principal representative before viceroys, *fidalgos,* merchants, commoners, and neophytes, and would have to respond to their desires and devotions in much the same way his own superiors at Coimbra did.

Internal tensions within religious orders were often no less difficult to manage than external ones. Preserving the internal harmony among the Jesuits themselves was of paramount concern to the order's superiors. In the case of Antunes, the jealousies between two temporal coadjutors came to a head in a brutal manner. The general tenor of violence in early modern Europe may account for the coarseness of social interaction and moments of explosive passion. Still, one does not expect to find reports of murder within religious communities. Independent of the question of justice (which would eventually ensnare Álvares, who died in prison four years after he committed his crime), the problem of group cohesion among the Jesuits was a concern that demanded the constant vigilance of rectors, provincials, and visitors.[9]

Their watchfulness was not limited to the lower ranks of the Society, as in the case of the two brothers at Coimbra and the college's hired help. It was also needed among the senior members of the order. Perhaps the Society's organization exacerbated jealousies and resentments because the decision-making process was more centralized and more vertical among the Jesuits than in other orders, where decisions were taken by vote in chapter. Favoritism at the top rungs of the administrative ladder was therefore just as dangerous as envy at the bottom end. For example, inspectors of the Colégio de Jesus in the early 1590s informed Rome that rector Nicolau Pimenta (1546–1613) gave better teaching assignments (that is, classes with older students) to "those for whom he has affection."[10] Such complaints, contemporaries knew, led to competition, conflict, and disunion. To prevent discord was accordingly one of the most important tasks of a Jesuit superior. It was the constant concern of one charged with the duty of inspecting residences and colleges, Palmeiro's future function.

Palmeiro began his career as a professor at Coimbra in the autumn of 1598. This is when his name, written in his own hand, first enters the archival record. The dispersion (or destruction) of Jesuit documents in the intervening centuries means that it is not in the Society's records that his first mark appears. Instead, the oldest record of his signature is found on the folio reserved for the names of the philosophy examiners in a register of academic degrees conferred by the University of Coimbra. This source records the names of students who received degrees in theology, medicine, civil and canon law, and philosophy, as well as the names of their examiners. Palmeiro's name appears as that of examiner for the first year of the philosophy course, which began on October 1, 1598. He is found in university documents by virtue of his assignment as philosophy professor in the Colégio das Artes, an institution that was linked to the university but was a wholly owned subsidiary of the Colégio de Jesus.[11]

Palmeiro's tenure as an instructor of the higher sciences got off to a rocky start. The academic year of 1598–1599 was an inauspicious one. In the spring of 1598 plague returned to Portugal, coming by sea from Galicia to Porto and Lisbon. By the end of the year the disease threatened Coimbra, and the city fathers began to plan for its arrival. The university requested permission from the crown to close, but this was denied until long after the initial outbreaks in late January 1599. By mid-February the city's inhabitants and students began to flee for the countryside, while the Inquisition began dispensing justice with singular alacrity in order to empty its prison. Only on May 4, after the disease had reached its most virulent stage, did word arrive at Coimbra that the crown had consented to the closing of the university, whose rector and two remaining professors abandoned the city that day.[12] Those too poor or too sick to flee faced scarcity and eventually famine, being reduced to eating "wild thistles boiled in water".[13]

The city's religious orders saw the moment of the plague as an opportunity to display their commitment to the care of the poor and the sick. "This occasion," wrote the chronicler of the Jesuits' novitiates, António Franco, "provided one of the great theaters for the charity of the *Companhia* in this kingdom".[14] The men of the Society, like the Franciscans, remained in Coimbra—largely within their walled compounds, of course—for the duration of the outbreak, sending only their afflicted members to *casas de saúde*, "houses of health," at their countryside farms. The Colégio de Jesus welcomed the poor at its gates, feeding a hundred people every day with meat broth and bread baked in the college ovens. Moved by the spectacle of misery, some priests, such as Manuel Rodrigues (ca. 1550–1612) and António de Proença (b. 1566), ventured out in the face of danger. Rodrigues made daily rounds between the Jesuits' farm and the plague victims' encampment in order to dress wounds and administer the sacraments, and Proença traversed the city pushing a cart filled with meat and bread for the hungry. One Sunday in the early summer Proença was joined by a number of friars who helped him carry twelve hundred loaves, four goats, and three sides of beef in a "beautiful procession" through the city streets. The nuns of the Convent of Santa Clara, whose convent was on the far side of the Mondego, sent three massive trays of sweets. According to Proença, Inquisitor Bartolomeu da Fonseca appeared at his window in the Convent of Santa Cruz to proclaim that this remarkable display would certainly drive the plague from the city.[15]

For those Jesuits like Palmeiro who remained inside the college walls, prayers were the best bulwark against disease. The intercession of the saints, especially St. Anthony's, vouchsafed their health, they believed. So convinced was Rector Jerónimo Dias (1545–1624) of the efficacy of this Portuguese saint's invocation that he dedicated a chapel to his honor as soon as the plague began to wane. Palmeiro was certainly part of the new devotional regime that Dias instituted with the intention of making the Jesuit community "a spiritual storehouse to placate heaven." In order to achieve this goal, groups for penitential discipline were organized to keep prayers being said "from ten at night until seven in the morning," after which the standard devotions took place.[16] These pious activities grew in intensity through the Lenten season in the spring of 1599, with rounds of prayers said at each altar in the college church and midnight flagellations led by the theology professors and their students.[17] When the "flag of health" was finally raised over the city in late September, the Jesuit community was largely intact: out of 196 men, only 1 priest and 2 brothers had succumbed.[18] The other residents of Coimbra were not so lucky—approximately 2,000 men and women died from plague and famine that year.[19]

The routines of academic life at the Colégio de Jesus and the university recommenced in October 1599. Palmeiro resumed his philosophy instruction for the same group, since it was customary to keep the same students during all four years of the arts course. University registers are extant for three of the four years of this period, indicating that he served as *regedor* (coordinator) and *examinador* (examiner) each year until the summer of 1602.[20] The Society's personnel catalogues confirm this information, supplementing it with the lists of his Jesuit students. There would have been additional pupils in his classes, but the eleven Jesuit scholastics who finished the course with Palmeiro are the only ones whose identities are known for certain.[21] At least two of these apparently found inspiration in his classes: António Simões (1581–1614) went on to make a public defense in philosophy in 1603, and Diogo Pereira (1580–1643) also became an instructor in the *Curso das Artes* and served as a philosophy examiner for the university.[22]

What did Palmeiro teach in the philosophy course? The standard program, one might assume, would have been the Aristotelian texts laid out in the *Curso Conimbricense.* This was not yet the case, however, since the final volume to be edited, which represented the first year of the course and dealt with logic, was printed in 1606.[23] So Palmeiro prepared his own lecture notes at least for the early stage of the course, in the same way as did the other instructors at the Colégio das Artes, and delivered them orally to his students, who took notes on them for future reference. (It is unlikely that the massive Coimbra Commentaries were intended to be purchased by students. Rather, they were used as reference tools by instructors and kept in the libraries of religious communities).

One text from Palmeiro's philosophy teaching has survived, a manuscript related to his discussion of dialectics from the first year of the arts course. This text examines themes in Porphyry's *Isagoge,* an introduction to Aristotle's *Categories.* Porphyry's text is an analysis of the fundamental terms of philosophy that preceded the study of the works on logic found in the Philosopher's *Organon.* Palmeiro's manuscript also discusses Aristotle's *Categories.* It bears the date February 5, 1601, suggesting that Palmeiro recopied his lecture notes after the end of this first section of the philosophy course. His presentation follows the lines established by Pedro da Fonseca in his published commentary on Porphyry (Coimbra: 1591), with minor variations in the choice of examples and citations from other authors. A detailed analysis of Palmeiro's text is beyond the scope of this study, but it suffices to say that his approach to Aristotle did not stray from the standard line. To be sure, innovation was not prized among the rank and file of the Jesuit teaching corps in early modern Europe.[24]

The subsequent semesters of the arts course that Palmeiro taught most likely followed the pattern described in contemporary sources. Classes met for five hours every day during the academic year, with a morning session from eight until ten-thirty, and an afternoon session from two until four-thirty. The first year of the course worked through the texts of the *Organon.* By the end of the first year, students were to have read through the *Prior Analytics,* and by Christmas of the second year were to have finished with Aristotle's logic. The second half of the second year was devoted to the *Physics* and

De Caelo (*On the Heavens*), with a selection of other works on natural philosophy chosen at the instructor's discretion. Despite the importance accorded by scholars to the teaching of "science" in Jesuit colleges, appropriately introduced at this phase of the philosophy course, it is doubtful that Palmeiro would have selected controversial texts to supplement his teaching. Indeed, much of the innovative work of contemporary "science" was classified as mathematics, which was taught as a separate discipline to Jesuit students at the Colégio de Jesus.[25] The third year of the course was dedicated to the *Metaphysics,* after which additional time was spent with texts on natural or moral philosophy, such as the *Parva Naturalia* and *Nicomachean Ethics.* In the final year, discussion centered on Aristotle's *De Anima* (*On the Soul*) and *De Generatione* (*On Generation*). These texts were considered to be an appropriate introduction to the theology program, but owing to their speculative nature (and their pagan cosmology) were reserved for those students who had passed the other phases of the course. The last semester of the arts course was used for reviewing the materials presented over the previous years and for holding public examinations.[26]

After the end of his term as philosophy instructor in the Colégio das Artes, Palmeiro appears in the Society's personnel catalogues with the degree of "Master of Arts."[27] To modern eyes, it seems strange that he should have attained what we would describe as a precondition for university teaching only after he had completed his assignment as instructor (he would not teach the arts course again). But this confusion can be explained, at least in part, by the ambiguous relationship between the Jesuits and the University of Coimbra. The Society was granted control of the Colégio das Artes by royal fiat, so it was not supervised by the university's rectors. As a result, some of the degrees granted by the Colégio das Artes were not included in the university's registers of graduates. Palmeiro's name is not to be found in that institution's archives as belonging to a bachelor, licentiate, master, or doctor.

The issue of academic jurisdictions was a continual cause of tension between the Jesuits and the university, who clashed over the matter in the late 1590s. The heart of that conflict was whether the Society's internal academic regime afforded its members qualifications to teach at the university. At issue was the decision made by Philip II in 1597 to oblige the university to award its most prestigious chair of theology to the Jesuit Francisco Suárez. Despite his long career in Spain and Italy as well as his reputation as one of the most brilliant minds of his day, Suárez had no doctorate and was therefore considered unqualified to hold the chair. So he traveled to Évora, where the Society's Colégio do Espírito Santo was also a university, and received a degree *honoris causa*. Upon returning to Coimbra in October 1597 he became *lente de prima,* that is, the reader of the canonical hour of prime, a position that Suárez would hold for two decades.[28]

It is also possible that the subordinate status of the Colégio das Artes vis-à-vis the higher faculties at the university accorded the Jesuits the right to attribute academic degrees without passing through the university's formal procedures. Surely Palmeiro deserved his degree since he could present a lengthy manuscript summary of Aristotle's works as proof of his competence in philosophy. But the degree of master of arts seems to have been given out to almost every Jesuit who taught the *Curso das Artes.* A glance at the biographical information found in the triennial catalogues for the Province of Portugal confirms this supposition and reveals that many Jesuits who did not teach the arts course also took the degree. Palmeiro seems to have attained his in the typical fashion: it was allotted to him when he finished teaching the four-year philosophy cycle. But others, such as Sebastião Barradas, who only taught the *Curso* for a year and a half, or Luis de la Cruz (1543–1604), who taught the humanities course for twenty-four years, were also *mestres em artes.*[29]

It appears that Jesuit instructors in philosophy and theology were granted the master's degree so as to be treated properly by the university faculty. When the Society of Jesus created its internal system for training its men, correlating academic progress to the attainment of the upper ranks within the order, it did so without contemplating the wider arena of early modern academic life. At Coimbra, much as at Alcalá or Salamanca, the Jesuits were one group of learned men among others. And since they endeavored to be regarded favorably by their intellectual peers, they required the trappings of academic achievement.

In the eyes of some Jesuits, however, to seek degrees for public display smacked of vanity. At the time when Palmeiro became *mestre em artes,* the question of degrees was mooted at the Society's triennial Provincial Congregation, held in Lisbon in April 1603. There it was voted that *mestrados* should only be granted "with much care and only to those most worthy in knowledge and ability," and among them only to those whose ministries included lecturing and examining (that is, the potential for public interaction with the university faculty). The decision was forwarded to Rome, where the Society's curia confirmed the rule: the superior general always assumed that those who "asked permission" for such degrees were qualified, and that the provincials would only permit the taking of a degree in cases where a degree was useful. From Rome's perspective, "degrees are not given within the Society simply for increasing authority but when and where they are necessary; nor do we grant them in those places where such sciences can be professed without them, regardless of how learned the petitioners may be."[30] Fortunately for *Mestre* Palmeiro and his brother instructors of philosophy and theology, the university town of Coimbra was precisely the kind of place where it was helpful to have an advanced degree.

The provincial consultors further agreed in 1603 that only those who had taught the philosophy course should be chosen to teach theology. Skill in logic and public disputation was indispensable for speculative theology, so this decision made sense.[31] Perhaps Palmeiro got his degree because the next step in his career was to be in the theology faculty of the Colégio de Jesus. Whatever the case may be, the eleven years he would spend teaching moral and speculative theology did not result in further academic degrees. In other words, Palmeiro would not receive a doctorate. But it was not the lack of qualifications that prevented him from attaining the same rank as his colleague Francisco Suárez, who held the titles of *mestre em artes e doutor em theologia.* Palmeiro had attained a sufficiently advanced academic level to earn recognition as a doctor, and many contemporaries were convinced that he actually held a doctorate. After all, he taught for years at an elite theology faculty and enjoyed prestige in Coimbra's scholarly circles. But, as his necrology reports, Palmeiro repeatedly refused to accept the doctoral degree offered him by the university. His gesture was made "out of humility," stemming from his desire to reject worldly honors rather than to embrace them.[32] This was an impressive display of virtue, since there were few doctors among the Coimbra Jesuits. In addition to Suárez, who was known to posterity by the honorific title *Doctor Eximius,* only Sebastião Barradas, the famous interpreter of sacred scripture, held a doctorate.[33] Yet what Palmeiro spurned was nevertheless attributed to him by others; one source from a non-Jesuit pen written in 1612 refers to him as a "doctor in sacred theology."[34]

In addition to being the year of his promotion to the highest ranks of the academic staff at the Colégio de Jesus, 1603 was also the year in which Palmeiro reached the senior level of the Society of Jesus. On July 27 he pronounced his fourth vow and became a "professed" member of the order. Scholars (and, of course, the Jesuits themselves) have long pointed to this fourth vow as the principal feature which set the Society apart from other orders. Beyond the three vows of poverty, chastity, and obedience that were common to all, professed Jesuits made a fourth vow of "mission." This vow put the Society's senior men at the disposition of the pope, who might send them wherever they would be most helpful to the church's pastoral goals.[35] "Mission" for the professing Jesuit did not necessarily imply work overseas (in fact, the Jesuits sent abroad to the missions left, almost without exception, years before they professed their fourth vow).[36] What this vow implied was a duty, a disposition for activity or service, be it preaching, teaching, writing, confessing, or even diplomacy. Since the pope rarely interfered in the administration of the Society—something the Jesuits would have seen as an affront to their independence regardless of their professed obedience—those who made the fourth vow placed themselves at the disposal of the superior general, whose authority enabled him to act, in this limited regard, in the pope's stead.[37] While "profession" was the rite that enabled Jesuits to play roles in the Society's governance, it rarely imposed the burden of obedience suggested by its formula. In Palmeiro's life in 1603, it was simply a pro forma event. But fourteen years later, when he was ordered to travel to the other side of the world, he would be obliged to obey the terms of the fourth vow in the strictest sense.

There is little information about Palmeiro's first years as a professed Jesuit. It appears that he was integrated smoothly into the theology teaching corps, starting out as an instructor of casuistry. In the personnel catalogues he is listed as a "master of cases" only for the academic year 1603–1604.[38] It is worth noting, however, that Palmeiro spent considerable time with moral theology, since much of his later work in Asia would revolve around "cases of conscience." Casuistry was the science of the confessional, where the boundaries of sinful behavior were drawn and the degrees of sinfulness detected. It was a requisite part of any Jesuit priest's theology training, the first step in an education that aimed to produce men skilled in the cure of souls. Many contemporaries—especially the Jesuits' detractors, such as Blaise Pascal—considered it the signature theological contribution of the Society of Jesus. Lectures in this discipline were typically drawn from numerous casuistry manuals that had flowed from printing presses in response to the rising desire for a better-trained clergy. What texts did Palmeiro use in his casuistry teaching? It is impossible to say for certain, but it is likely that he used the works of the influential Doctor Navarro,

Martin de Azpilcueta (1492–1586), who had also taught at Coimbra and there published his *Manual de Confessores & Penitentes* (1552).[39]

Palmeiro next appears in contemporary documents in 1605, when he is listed as the *lente de vespora* at the Colégio de Jesus.[40] This move was a shift from the teaching of moral theology to that of speculative theology. During Palmeiro's time there, the college had five theology professors whose subjects were indicated by the canonical hours at which they taught: *prima* (prime), *terça* (terce), and *vespora* (vespers). Of these, *prima* was the most important, with *vespora* second. A fourth class in sacred scripture was also taught, typically at the early afternoon hour of *noa* (none). Each of these courses covered different books of the scholastic canon, especially the works of Peter Lombard (1095–1160) and the summas of Thomas Aquinas (1225–1274). Theology instruction at the Colégio de Jesus was similar to that offered at the university, where the fifth Jesuit theologian (during the period examined here, Francisco Suárez) taught at the *prima* hour. This overlap also existed in the other religious houses in Coimbra, whose members also sought appointments to the university faculty. The difference between the university and the colleges was that the university had eight theology chairs (four major and four minor) reinforced by a faculty of canon law.[41] Since the Society's goal was to train its own preachers and confessors, and to supplement the pastoral training of the secular and regular clergy, it had no need to duplicate the university's offerings in law. And since Ignatius Loyola had prescribed the works of Aquinas for all Jesuits in the order's *Constitutions,* the Society was not obliged to offer instruction in other schools of thought, such as those of Duns Scotus (ca. 1265–1308) or Guillaume Durand (ca. 1230–1296).

Unlike his agitated younger years, Palmeiro's life in the first two decades of the seventeenth century seems to have been calm. In the Society's personnel catalogues he is listed as the *lente de vespora* until 1610, with the exception of one year, when he appears as *lente de terça*.[42] In his final years at Coimbra, Palmeiro would reach the summit of theology instruction in the Society of Jesus: he would be *lente de prima* from 1610 until 1614.[43] The curriculum that he taught during these years was a largely standardized series of discussions on the works of Aquinas. The vespers class was typically dedicated to the third part of Aquinas's *Summa Theologica,* which dealt with the Incarnation and nature of Christ, as well as with the sacraments.

Just as he had done with his philosophy lectures, Palmeiro produced polished copies of his lectures on theology. Once in 1611 and then again after he left Coimbra for the position of rector at the College of Braga, he dictated his exegeses to an amanuensis.[44] These manuscripts reveal that Palmeiro hewed to the standard lines of interpretation about the necessity of the sacraments and the indispensable role of the clergy. In these texts he neither produced original insights to familiar questions nor sought to combat Protestant polemics against the Catholic Church. In other words, his approach to Aquinas's thought did not seek to break new interpretive ground, as the work of his colleague Francisco Suárez had done. But this fact does not mean that Palmeiro was not creative in his approach to theological questions or resistant to original thought. Indeed, his training and his teaching occurred during the fullest flowering of the scholastic tradition and represented the most adaptive form of that theological mode. He was well equipped to examine the theological implications of rituals and terms, themes upon which he would be called to give judgment in both India and China. Baptism and marriage (the longest section of his lectures at Coimbra) were two other themes that he examined thoroughly. These were topics of particular relevance to missionary policy in Asia, where both rites had to be aligned with indigenous cultural practices.[45]

Just like his philosophy notes, Palmeiro's commentaries on Aquinas are peppered with citations from other theologians and biblical scholars. It is not surprising to find a mass of references to the works of others in his writing, and in such profusion that they almost occlude what might be identified as his own voice. He was clearly an assiduous reader, even if his later correspondence offers few demonstrations of this type of erudition. At Coimbra, he most likely made good use, as did other theology and philosophy instructors, of the well-stocked library of the Colégio de Jesus. There, before the portraits and devotional paintings which had been donated by the count-bishop of Coimbra in 1600, Palmeiro could immerse himself in the works of medieval and modern authors to produce his lectures.[46] Unlike the Coimbra Commentaries, there was no standard gloss for theology, although there was no shortage of useful texts at his disposal. The college library had an especially rich collection of Jesuit theological works, kept ready for "decapitating heresies."[47]

Palmeiro's ascension through Jesuit ranks came first through teaching and only later through administration. By the end of the first decade of the seventeenth century, it would have been logical for him to assume one of the order's positions of governance, whether at Coimbra or in one of the order's other residences. At the top of the hierarchy were the provincial-level appointments, and lower down were the rectorships, positions of master (of studies or of novices), designations as procurator, and other posts. But Palmeiro did not move through these administrative offices until the mid-1610s. It seems that he was given the opportunity, as a member of the theology staff, to demonstrate his academic skills without having other demands made upon him. The fact that he spent a decade as a theology instructor, with only the additional title of college "consultor" for some of those years, suggests that his superiors hoped he would follow in the footsteps of Suárez, composing treatises to enhance the Society's public image.[48] Unfortunately, the internal evaluations that were a standard part of the personnel catalogues later in the seventeenth century are lacking for this period. That type of information would have revealed more clearly the ministries for which Palmeiro's superiors considered him to be best qualified. Palmeiro was obviously well regarded by his peers and enjoyed the prestige that came from being a reader in theology, both inside and outside of the Society. His primary responsibility to the order beyond teaching, it would appear, was to maintain the order's reputation and to defend its honor.

These terms are admittedly vague, but they held specific meaning for the early modern Jesuits. They meant the external and internal demonstration of the order's central virtues of piety, obedience, and erudition. To be sure, the vows that Palmeiro made as a novice and those that he repeated every year obliged him to defend the Society's honor and maintain its reputation, but these demands took on a different meaning as one matured within the order. "Unto whomsoever much is given, of him much shall be required," Palmeiro and his brethren would have said in evocation of Luke's Gospel.[49] For the senior Jesuits, this maxim meant setting an example for their younger brethren, as Palmeiro did when he composed a lengthy Latin poem about Pentecost. Long after his years as a grammar and rhetoric teacher, he continued to produce verse for the purpose of edifying younger Jesuits. One of his poems can be found in a commonplace book kept by an unknown student, possibly a Jesuit, from the Colégio de Jesus. Here again, as with his earlier poetry, Palmeiro had recourse to references drawn from classical mythology. But here his references are a bit more recherché; they were intended to impress his listeners and to inspire them to similar flights of eloquence. His theme is the coming of the Holy Spirit, the powerful force that swept away the gloom of the pagan past. Here follows the first stanza of his multipage ode titled "De Sancte Spiritus adventu":

Castalei roris, musisque habitata canori
Flumina Parnassi, procul ite; quid undae
quid latices possint? Quid tristi lentus in antro
Phoebus? Olympiaca cum se diffundet ab arce
flamma tenebrosas humentis pectoris umbras
exsuperans lustratque animi splendore recessus.

[O dew from the Castalian spring, where the Muses lived, and
harmonious streams of Parnassus, be gone! What could the waters,
what could the springs do? What would slow Phoebus do in
his mournful cave? When the flame spreads itself from Olympus,
over the dark shadows of the wet breast
and shows its splendor to hidden places.][50]

More in keeping with his formal academic role, Palmeiro also served as an examiner in the public theological disputations held by the Society for its members. Here the reputation of the order was enhanced through the subsequent printing and distribution of the questions posted for debate and the answers given by the examinees. In one such pamphlet, Palmeiro is found sitting in judgment of a disquisition presented by João da Rocha (1587–1639) on a question pulled from the topics of the third part of Aquinas's *Summa Theologica:* Would the Incarnation have been necessary had Adam not sinned?[51]

Censorial duties were part of the broader charge to defend the honor of the Society of Jesus as well. In his role as one of the college consultors at Coimbra, Palmeiro worked closely with the rector on academic affairs and matters of governance. He was also one of the main interlocutors for a visitation conducted by João Álvares (1548–1623) between 1610 and 1613. Visitor Álvares, one of the most distinguished priests among the Portuguese Jesuits, had been rector of the College of Porto, provincial, assistant in Rome, and intermediary in the abjuration of Henry IV of France. Álvares's inspection tour of the Province of Portugal obliged him to visit all its colleges and residences (with the exception of the houses in Cape Verde and Angola). Álvares naturally spent a long span at the largest Jesuit community of them all, the College of Coimbra, and dealt at length with Palmeiro and the other consultors about its spiritual and temporal health.

The scope of Álvares's visitation was impressive: The compilation of rules and orders that Álvares produced after his travels fills almost two hundred pages and touches on general aspects of Jesuit life, the role of each position within the order, and practices specific to individual communities. For example, the color of the robes worn by novices is indicated, the need for lanterns when leaving the college at night is stipulated, and rules for expelling students from the Society's schools are laid out.[52] In Lisbon, care is to be taken with the pruning of the trees in the college yard; in Coimbra, those involved in studies are warned against taking long walks about the city after dinner, this practice being the cause of "so many sicknesses of the liver"; and

FIGURE 2.1. Frontispiece of the theological disputation presented by João da Rocha and judged by André Palmeiro on May 22, 1614.

in the far northern region of Minho at the Residence of San Fins, a pot of broth is to be prepared daily "in the months of May, June and July, when the poor suffer more need."[53] Since Palmeiro would later be called upon to make similar visitations and draw up similar orders, to remember the model employed by João Álvares would have been greatly to his advantage.

Beyond his active role within the Jesuit community at Coimbra, Palmeiro's position demanded that he lend his intellectual authority to public affairs. For example, he was summoned to help resolve a long running dispute between the Jesuits and the university over the Colégio das Artes. In 1610, in his capacity of consultor, he examined (and fortified) the requests that the Society had made for adequate classrooms for its grammar, rhetoric, and philosophy classes. In the Jesuits' understanding of the founding charter of the Colégio das Artes, it was part of the university, and the university was therefore obliged to pay for the construction of adequate (and appropriately situated) space for its classes. Convinced that the Society had received sufficient royal funds to pay for a large college on the grounds of the Colégio de Jesus, the university refused. So the Jesuits slowed the pace of construction at their new college from the 1570s until the late 1590s, when they moved to expand their living quarters but not their teaching facilities. According to one visitor to Coimbra who saw the place a decade later in 1609, "the College of the *Companhia* amounts to little more than foundations, and so there is little worthy of note beyond the refectory, which is a most capacious piece, as are the dormitories."[54] The Jesuits were willing to stall construction on the Colégio de Jesus, building only residential structures to house the more than two hundred men who lived there, while they waited for the university to pay for new classrooms.[55]

This forty-three year standoff between the Society and the university involved risks. After all, the Jesuits of the Colégio das Artes taught almost two thousand students in sixteen classes in buildings that were deemed temporary.[56] By 1610 the strain of overcrowding was clearly evident to all who visited the school. Francisco Suárez described the classroom edifice as "most uncomfortable and unworthy of this university," so old that it threatened to collapse. What was needed, he argued in a judicial opinion, was a new structure near the Jesuit college and the university but separate from the other faculties. It was important to keep the youths who attended the Colégio das Artes away from the older students since the mixing of the two groups would "present occasions for distraction, rumors, and disturbance." Moreover, the

Jesuits needed to have the school building near their college because, as religious, they could not be strolling about the city one by one but had to proceed "with their cloaks and companions" when going to their classrooms.[57] Finally, with the good will of the crown on their side, the Jesuits brought the university to the negotiating table to settle the affair. When the final documents were signed on June 17, 1610, the rector of the Colégio de Jesus, Nuno Mascarenhas (1552–1637), and the college consultor, André Palmeiro, were present to accept the university's payments on behalf of the Society of Jesus. In contrast to the lethargic pace of construction at the college from the early 1570s until the 1600s, this deal inaugurated a flurry of activity. By 1616 the first classes were held in the massive new Colégio das Artes, built only a few yards from the Colégio de Jesus.[58]

More appropriately for a theology professor, Palmeiro also served as a representative of the Society in public affairs of a religious character. While he does not appear to have played any role as a consultor for the Inquisition in Coimbra—which could draw on an ample supply of theologians and thus did not require Jesuits except for preaching occasionally at autos da fé—he did take part in one of the city's most important ecclesiastical events of the early seventeenth century, the canonization process of its most famous holy woman, Queen Isabel of Portugal. Under pressure from the Spanish crown, the papacy reinvigorated the process of saint-making, which had nearly ground to a halt in the early sixteenth century and resumed only fitfully in the late 1580s.[59] The *Rainha Santa,* a princess from Aragon who became the wife of King Dinis I (1261–1325), was the founder of the Convent of Santa Clara in Coimbra. She was renowned in her lifetime for her charity and piety, and in her, the Philippine Dynasty saw the opportunity to harness long-standing popular devotions to an ancestor of the Spanish Habsburg line. Moreover, she was a figure who underscored the historical unity of the Iberian Peninsula, linking Portugal, Castile, and Aragon. Isabel had been beatified by Leo X in 1516, but her canonization was not insistently sought until the early seventeenth century. The "Holy Queen" was nevertheless the object of popular and royal devotions from the mid-fourteenth century in Portugal, and especially in Coimbra.[60]

In order to meet the rigorous standards that the papal Congregation of Rites had imposed on new canonizations, an inspection of Queen Isabel's acts and relics had to be undertaken and testimony of popular devotion to her gathered. The first step in this process was to hold interviews to investigate miracles that had happened by her intervention. Under the auspices of Count-Bishop Afonso de Castelobranco, a schedule of twice-daily meetings was drawn up, the witnesses being summoned to appear in the high chapel of the church of São João de Almedina. This church was attached to the bishop's palace and situated across the Couraça dos Apostolos from the Colégio de Jesus. On February 9, 1612, the first individual to offer testimony was Palmeiro, "doctor in theology and *lente de prima* of this science at the college of the Jesuits in Coimbra, forty-five years of age." After confirming that he had recently taken the sacraments, was not under excommunication, and would not receive anything for this testimony, Palmeiro declared what he knew of the Portuguese queen. He stated that he had been aware "since the age of a child that it was public knowledge that this saint was dead and buried in the convent of Santa Clara in this city." While he lived in Coimbra, Palmeiro had the habit of going "to visit her tomb both to venerate the saint as well as to ask graces from her." Moreover, he claimed to have gone "many times to the church where she was entombed to say mass at the request of people from many places in order to attain remedy for their needs through her intercession." When he was asked why he would say masses there, Palmeiro replied that it was well known that she had performed miracles in the past and "worked them in the present."[61]

Taking Palmeiro's cue, his questioners asked him to explain these miracles. The first example he discussed was the intercessions that helped the women who visited the Rainha Santa's tomb when their milk dried up before it was time. More verifiable (for a priest) was the miraculous healing of Luís Pinheiro (1550–1620), one of Palmeiro's fellow Jesuits, upon whose forehead grew a tumor. After the usual remedies did not make it disappear, one of his confreres suggested saying a mass at the *beata*'s tomb and bringing some of the oil from the lamps found there to daub on his head. Palmeiro averred that this solution produced a miraculous cure because oil lacked the "natural forces" to produce such a rapid effect. Moving on to academic matters, the questioners asked him if he had any notion of the antiquity of the legends surrounding the queen's life and older miracles. Here tradition was called as a witness; Palmeiro affirmed that he had read the books by reputable authors which spoke of her.[62] In later questions, he asserted with his authority as a theologian what all of the subsequent 120 witnesses would confirm and, indeed, what everyone in Coimbra knew: *Beata* Isabel was truly *Santa* Isabel.[63]

More proof than just common consent was needed for the scales of judgment in Rome to tip against the devil's advocate at a canonization trial. So King Philip ordered her tomb to be opened to verify the state of her relics, in the hopes of finding the queen's body incorrupt. If it was, it would surely be a miracle because she had died in the heat of the summer in Estremoz, on the plains of southern Portugal, and it had taken seven days for her to be transported to Coimbra, 130 miles away.[64] On March 26, 1612, a crowd of about forty theologians, inquisitors, and physicians—Palmeiro and Suárez among them—proceeded across the Mondego River to the convent church where the body lay on a balcony inside a massive gothic stone tomb. The only interested parties not invited to this event were the nuns of Santa Clara, who

FIGURE 2.2. The first tomb of Queen Isabel of Portugal, the *Rainha Santa*. In Palmeiro's day, it was located in the church of the Convent of Santa Clara-a-Velha. Owing to the Mondego's repeated floods, however, the Poor Clares decamped to the convent of Santa Clara-a-Nova in the second half of the seventeenth century. They took the tomb to its current site in a minor chapel of that church, removing the wooden coffin with the saint's remains and displaying it in a silver and crystal case above that church's main altar.

remained in the choir of the lower church singing while they attempted to view the proceedings using a mirror.[65]

Under the direction of the Jesuit architect and mathematician João Delgado (1553–1612), the thick stone lid of the tomb was hoisted off, exposing a wooden coffin. The onlookers all noticed that the queen's pilgrim staff and purse lay undisturbed on top of the coffin, in the same spot where they had been placed almost three hundred years before. Once the planks were pried off and her clean, white shroud cut open, they beheld the body, "whole and without corruption, even very white and pleasant smelling, covered with flesh, in such a way that the head was full of blond hair." Under the direction of the physicians, Isabel's clothing was sliced open to reveal her chest, "with its nipples raised, and also very white and full, and when the chest was pressed by hand with great force, it remained firm without breaking or coming apart." When her right arm was inspected, it revealed the "veins and nerves" to be intact and the fingers and nails firmly attached. A retired theology professor reported that he had tugged on the saint's hair, and a physician claimed to have squeezed her shoulder and pulled on her arm, both men ensuring that their eyes did not fool them.[66] Modesty as well as the conviction that the rest of body was in as good a condition led the inspectors to halt the inspection at the saint's waist, and the body was wrapped and sealed once again in its wooden coffin.[67] Eyewitness accounts from the priests and the physicians present insisted that a "most suave scent" came from the body— literally the odor of sanctity they were seeking—and that the queen's body matched the well-known medieval reports about her: "Her body well formed and of tall stature, and seeing it confirmed that if she was beautiful during her life, even after death she appeared to be alive."[68]

The incorrupt corpse of Queen Isabel was clear proof to Palmeiro and the other witnesses that divine power continued to work in the world and that miracles could justly be expected from those who petitioned the *Rainha Santa*. No doubt inspired by this demonstration of veritable sanctity in Coimbra, the Jesuits decided to exhume the body of the saintly preacher Inácio Martins one month after the inspections at Santa Clara. With the construction on the new church at the Colégio de Jesus well under way, April 1612 was deemed the appropriate time for moving his remains to a new tomb. Full of expectation in the recent memory of his virtuous life and holy death, a team of priests and brothers pulled Martins's coffin from the earth and pried open its planks. But fourteen years in the grave had not been as good for Martins as 276 years had been for the Holy Queen. According to a contemporary report, "the priest's body was wasted away so that nothing was left of it but bones. The doctrine staff with which he was buried was also worn away so that only a small piece was left which looked more like a bit of bark than a staff." No odors of sanctity but only corruption came from the illustrious Jesuit, whose death was marked by such public outpourings of grief. Martins's remains were placed in a lead box which was reburied in a chapel dedicated to the Society's honored but not manifestly saintly dead.[69]

By the middle of the second decade of the seventeenth century, Palmeiro had enjoyed a long career in the most distinguished academic forum in Portugal. His intellect was sharp enough to win him the praise of individuals such as Francisco Suárez. For all that, he did not seem to be poised to launch a new phase of his academic work, that is, to publish books in the same manner as other illustrious Jesuit theologians. Had Palmeiro begun to compose during his time at Coimbra, he would most likely have remained in an academic setting for the rest of his life. But he did not. And so, even though he had held the coveted post of *lente de prima* for four years, his superiors thought his energies would be better applied to some other ministry or to an administrative post. After all, the Society had other talented theologians in waiting for Palmeiro's spot, and Jesuits did not typically hold such positions for life.

The moment of change finally came in 1614, when Palmeiro was forty-five years old. That year saw his renown as a theologian in Coimbra reach its height, and occasioned a decisive shift in his career. Even though he was a familiar figure within the Society in Portugal and had steadily climbed the order's academic ladder, he had not reached the forefront of attention of his superiors in Lisbon and Rome. But in 1614 they would be made aware of his talents. A report of a "very learned and very serious sermon" offered in the Cathedral of Coimbra to an audience of secular and ecclesiastical dignitaries during a time of crisis reached the Professed House in Lisbon, seat of the provincial leadership. Palmeiro's preaching had produced "great emotions and many tears, with universal satisfaction" for all who heard it.[70] Here was a man, the provincial superior was reminded, who was worthy of an administrative post that demanded being in the public eye.

The occasion for Palmeiro's sermon was a scandal in the city of Porto, sixty-five miles to the north of Coimbra. On May 11, a pyx containing more than sixty consecrated hosts was stolen from a chapel in the cloister of Porto's cathedral.[71] The news of the sacrilege spread rapidly about the kingdom, and anxiety grew from week to week, especially among the clergy and religious orders, as the crime remained unsolved. (In fact, the perpetrator was never identified.) The Society's men in Porto as well as their colleagues in Évora and Lisbon joined large numbers of Portuguese layfolk in prayers, penances, and processions aimed at atoning for the sins thought to have been the cause of the crime.[72] In Coimbra the Jesuits held continual vigils before the Blessed Sacrament for four days after hearing the news. According to one eyewitness, over fifty religious could always be found praying during that time, "many of them kneeling, and with their hands raised," and sometimes their number swelled to over two hundred. The strictest silence was observed at the college, and the "oldest and most important" Jesuits demonstrated their piety by fasting, flagellating themselves, singing the litanies daily, and taking their meager meals while sitting on the ground.[73]

On the orders of the count-bishop, the cathedral chapter arranged a citywide procession for the first Friday after the octave of Corpus Christi. On that day in early June the prelate carried a monstrance draped with a black silk veil from the cathedral through the streets of Coimbra, up to the university and down nearly to the riverbank. "More people than had ever been seen in the city" joined in the procession, forming a crowd so large that its front and back ends passed each other on the city's main thoroughfare. The procession ended when the count-bishop placed the monstrance on the cathedral's high altar, and Palmeiro ascended to the pulpit to preach on a verse from the Book of Lamentations: "The breath of our mouth, Christ the Lord, is taken in our sins; to whom we said: Under thy shadow we shall live among the Gentiles".[74] According to Afonso Mendes (1579–1659), a Jesuit professor of sacred scripture and future Latin Patriarch of Ethiopia, Palmeiro's sermon was divided into three parts: "The first about how serious an offense that bold sinner had committed by taking God Our Lord from us and locking Him up; the second about how we should fear that this had happened because of our sins and in order to punish them; and the third about how, in spite of our sins, we were right to hope that the Lord would gather us in His shadow and help us now, because He was the more offended party and because He could consider Himself satisfied with our tears and emotions." Palmeiro's words caused outbursts of crying, as did the singing of *Miserere mei Deus* by the count-bishop and the cathedral chapter as they retreated into the sacristy.[75]

Less than two months after this event, the superiors of the Province of Portugal gave Palmeiro his first assignment outside of a Coimbra classroom, and his wanderings about the globe began. By August 2, 1614, he had traveled 105 miles north through the coastal plain and across the Douro River to assume the position of rector at the Colégio de São Paulo at Braga in northern Portugal.[76] After his trip from Lisbon to the Colégio de Jesus in 1584, there is no evidence that he traveled far beyond the city limits of Coimbra during the three decades that he spent there. From this day forward, however, he would be in nearly constant motion. He would stay in his new home for just over two years, but that was enough time to gain firsthand experience at governance. Palmeiro's tasks in Braga included looking after the academic affairs of the college's Latin and theology classes; overseeing the management of the temporal needs of his community; and providing spiritual guidance to his subordinates as well as to outsiders, both religious and secular.

Beyond these common tasks for rectors, Palmeiro would also have to be a diplomat. A city of over ten thousand inhabitants, Braga was home to an array of religious houses as well as to an archbishop who held the lofty title of Primate of the Spains and whose see dated back over a millennium.[77] It was in the Society's best interest to keep up good relations with this prelate, who was among the most important political figures in Portugal. In fact, a previous *Arcebispo Primaz* had been responsible for bringing the Jesuits to Braga and endowing their Colégio de São Paulo. Frei Bartolomeu dos Mártires (1514–1590), a Dominican who had participated in the Council of Trent and was known for his charity and austerity, entrusted the Society with the grammar schools in Braga within a year of becoming archbishop in 1559.[78] By the time Palmeiro arrived in 1614, the see was held by Frei Aleixo de Menezes (1559–1617), an Augustinian from one of the most illustrious families in Portugal. Menezes had served for seventeen years as archbishop of Goa before returning to Europe in 1612 as archbishop of Braga. In both places he also shouldered secular responsibilities: he was viceroy of the Estado da Índia from 1607 to 1609, and viceroy of Portugal from 1614 to 1615. It is therefore unlikely that Palmeiro met Menezes in Braga since the archbishop resided in Lisbon at that time and later left for Madrid to serve on the Council of Portugal, but the Jesuit rector would necessarily have to deal with Menezes's influential deputies in the cathedral chapter.[79]

Palmeiro's primary task was to manage the College of Braga. This institution had grown over the course of the half-century between its founding and the time Palmeiro assumed the rectorship. Its school had eight masters responsible for five Latin classes, one philosophy class (the arts course), and two classes of moral theology. During the early seventeenth century, approximately six hundred students attended classes at the college.[80] The foundational charter for the Colégio de São Paulo required the Jesuits to teach three grammar classes and the two moral theology classes, but according to the Society's triennial accounting for 1614, the college offered two more classes "without obligation, only to spread out the multitude of students and to relieve the masters." Furthermore, the college hired a teacher to instruct its youngest students in reading and writing. Like other religious houses in the early modern period, the College of Braga was endowed with rental income from fields, mills, and church tithes to pay for its expenses. Having made vows of poverty, the Jesuits could not receive salaries themselves, but their colleges were allowed to have revenues (by contrast, professed houses, such as the São Roque residence in Lisbon, were not teaching institutions and therefore were required to be supported by alms). At Braga in 1614 the Jesuits had an income of 5,500 *cruzados*, enough to support up to forty men while paying down outstanding debts.[81]

Perhaps the most important training Palmeiro received at the Colégio de São Paulo in Braga was in the management of the Society's human resources. To be sure, his task involved far fewer men than that of the rector of the College of Coimbra. The personnel catalogue from January 1615, drawn up five months into his term as rector, indicates that there were thirty-four Jesuits in Braga. Of these, fifteen were priests, some of whom taught, others who preached and heard confessions, and still others who ministered to the college's students or served as procurators for the community's temporal needs. The teaching corps was made up of brothers who, like Palmeiro in the early 1590s, were sent to teach Latin before beginning their philosophy and theology studies. Four brothers were also in residence, studying the *Curso das Artes*, or moral theology. In addition to these scholastics, there were nine temporal coadjutors, that is, brothers who constituted the college staff. They served in jobs such as cook, sacristan, clothier, porter for carriages, and bellringer. There was also a "prefect of health," a Jesuit charged with assisting the elderly and the sick. During Palmeiro's first year in Braga, prefect of health was an important position because four of the temporal coadjutors were listed as old and infirm.[82]

Palmeiro's skill in managing his men was put to the test soon after his arrival in Braga in summer of 1614. One of the men studying philosophy at the college had an unusual background: João Cardim (1585–1615), the scion of an illustrious family of royal administrators, had studied canon law for ten years at Coimbra before joining the Jesuits. Cardim was a paragon of pious austerity and was later the subject of an unsuccessful beatification process. If the street preacher Inácio Martins represented the vigorous public piety of the earliest generation of Jesuits, João Cardim represented the interior intensity of a later era. Cardim was the product of an intellectual milieu; his extreme penitential practices and demanding prayer routines reflected the rigorous application to study that had earned him renown before he joined the order. Dealing with Cardim would give Palmeiro his first experience of trying to rein in the seemingly uncontrollable zeal of his men. Similar challenges would recur at several reprises in Palmeiro's career, at moments when his pragmatic outlook would move him to curb his subordinates' pious excesses.

The newly appointed rector learned of Cardim's piety as soon as he arrived in Braga. (It is possible that the two men knew each other in Coimbra, but there is no evidence to substantiate this claim). In the month of Palmeiro's arrival, Cardim requested permission to head off on a doctrine-teaching tour of the Minho region on foot. Despite Cardim's weak constitution, his superior acceded to the request owing to its manifest piety. But the accumulation of other extreme forms of devotion during the following months caused Palmeiro concern; for example, Cardim's insistence on distributing food and drink to the indigents who gathered at the college door and sharing their bowls and cups, and his frequent fasts during which he sat on the floor to eat scraps. Sensing excess in this piety, especially because of his extreme flagellation regimen, Palmeiro attempted to dissuade his subordinate from too much rigor. A contemporary account of Cardim's life claims that he ignored such calls for restraint, dismissing a remark from the rector that he was on the fatal path of Luigi Gonzaga (1568–1591), another fervent young Jesuit who met a tragic end while he tended to plague victims. But when the other priests called upon Palmeiro to intervene more forcefully in early 1615, "to stop the priest who seemed to want to kill himself with lashes," it was too late. Illness aggravated by overexertion put Cardim in his deathbed, where he expired on February 18. Stripping his clothes for burial, the college's brothers found his body to be "all one open wound from the stripes with which he continually bruised himself."[83]

Palmeiro viewed Cardim's premature death with mixed feelings. While the Society of Jesus had lost a talented young priest who might have gone on to do great things, the order had also added another demonstration of holiness to its growing register of venerable priests and brothers. Palmeiro was convinced of Cardim's sanctity and responded to the public demand to revere his corpse. As the Coimbra Jesuits had done for Inácio Martins, the rector welcomed the high-ranking churchmen and citizens who came to kiss Cardim's feet and touch his body with their rosaries, and permitted his fellow students to adorn his bier with flowers. Palmeiro also organized the funeral mass in the college church, at which a grasping horde of relic-seeking city dwellers had to be forced from the sanctuary's crossing by the closing of the altar rails. He likewise gathered the deceased's meager possessions, in particular his writings, to distribute as relics among the Jesuits and their patrons. Papers where Cardim had signed his name were deemed especially valuable reminders, but, as one hagiographer claimed, in the flurry of donations, "not even his cap was left to give away." In the days after the burial, Palmeiro organized a series of talks in order to bring together testimony about Cardim's virtues, drawing up accounts that were said to have circulated throughout the Province of Portugal and even to Brazil and Asia. In these accounts, Palmeiro averred that he had seen Cardim levitate "two or three palms high" during his prayerful ecstasies. Such an impact did this vision of piety make upon Palmeiro that, nearly fifteen years later, he clearly recalled the brief months he had spent with the would-be saint; from Macau, he sent testimony of Cardim's sanctity to Portugal as part of a beatification process.[84]

Palmeiro's proximity to the saintly Cardim and his important role in the distribution of relics certainly increased his visibility within the Province of Portugal. The rector's links to the other senior Jesuits were further enhanced by a series of meetings with provincial superiors. For in addition to dealing with his men and the local worthies at Braga, Palmeiro was also responsible ex officio for representing the college at provincial congregations. Typically these meetings, held either in Lisbon or Coimbra, were only summoned every three years, but Palmeiro attended two of them during his brief time as rector. The first was the regularly scheduled congregation, convened in October 1614 in Lisbon, only two months after he had become rector at Braga; he traveled the 225 miles from the Colégio de São Paulo to the Casa Professa de São Roque for the ten-day event. Among the topics discussed by the members at the congregation was whether the Portuguese province should prepare six to eight men each year for the overseas missions, and if the Society's men should be taught the history of the overseas missions as part of their formation.[85]

After the assembled provincial consultors intoned a final *Te Deum* on October 31, Palmeiro returned to Braga, only to receive another summons to Lisbon in May 1615. On this occasion the Portuguese Jesuits gathered to appoint representatives for the Society's Seventh General Congregation to be held in Rome in November of that year. So once again Palmeiro traveled to Lisbon, where he was one of the fifty members of the Society of Jesus who gathered at the Professed House to the strains of *Veni Sancte Spiritus*. The primary task of this gathering was to achieve a consensus about the desirable traits for a new superior general, since Claudio Aquaviva had died in January 1615 and a successor had to be chosen. When the meeting in Lisbon was adjourned on May 14, Palmeiro returned to Braga, having journeyed more than a thousand miles in eight months.[86]

Not much is known about Palmeiro's activities during the final year and a half of his stay in Braga. The sources available from that span of his rectorship are impersonal, saying little that is specific about the tenor of his governance. His necrology makes mention of his laudable combination of gentleness and rigor, noting that his zeal for observance of the Society's rules was noted by all who knew him. Perhaps the most illuminating vignette from that final phase as rector of the Colégio de São Paulo suggests that he was able to maintain the esteem that he had earned from local secular and ecclesiastical authorities during the period of João Cardim's death. In the words of Palmeiro's eulogist: "When it was known in the city of Braga, where he was rector at the time, that he was leaving for India, the city council ordered the gates closed, and the citizens pleaded with him insistently that he abandon his voyage, but to no avail."[87]

―――――――

Around the first of the year in 1617 Palmeiro received word from his superiors that he was to proceed to Lisbon and prepare for his passage to India. Apparently his appointment as visitor was decided in Rome and agreed to in Portugal before the formal orders and letters patent were issued by the new superior general, Muzio Vitelleschi. This was not unusual. News of ecclesiastical appointments often preceded the arrival of official notifications from Rome. High-ranking prelates tended to wait for their letters patent before taking office, so as to be able to mute any critics who might doubt their authority. But within the Society of Jesus there was no need for such a delay since the news of Palmeiro's appointment was not likely to be contested by his brethren.

Upon arriving in India, he would nevertheless elect to wait in Goa until he received his official commission from Rome, sealed on January 20, 1618, biding his time before sailing to his appointed district, the Society's Province of Malabar.[88]

Why was Palmeiro chosen for this important position? This question remains a mystery. No documents that would reveal the reasons for Vitelleschi's decision have been found for this study in Portuguese or Italian archives. Did Palmeiro voice a desire to travel to the overseas provinces while he was at the provincial congregation in Lisbon in 1615, a wish that was relayed to Rome? It could be that he harbored a desire for missionary work, since a few passing mentions of such an impulse can be found in his later writings. But the Roman Archives of the Society of Jesus contain no "Indies petition" of the type required for assignments to the missions. In the early modern period, Jesuits who sought to leave their home provinces in Europe in order to work in the overseas provinces typically wrote one or more letters to the superior general in which they described their missionary desires. If Palmeiro wrote such a letter, it was not placed alongside the thousands of other such missives preserved in Rome.

Perhaps his friend and former rector in Coimbra, Nuno Mascarenhas, suggested Palmeiro's name to the superior general after he arrived in Rome in 1615 to serve as the Portuguese Assistant. After all, there were important matters to settle in the Province of Malabar, and a talented outsider was needed to conduct a visitation. Mascarenhas knew that Palmeiro was an excellent candidate: He had considerable experience in an important college and had served, albeit for only a short term, as a rector. His talents were sure to be superior to those of the men in the Asian provinces, most of whom had been sent overseas as young men, long before their capacities were known, whereas Palmeiro had demonstrated his aptitude at the University of Coimbra. Moreover, he was a renowned preacher and academic with no obligations detaining him in Portugal. That is, he was not among the small circle of high-ranking Jesuits who had served as rectors of the major colleges and from whose number future provincial officers would be chosen. Palmeiro would have to spend a longer time governing different colleges before he could become a candidate for such a post. His long journey along the Society's academic track had left him far behind on its administrative path. Ironically, the position of visitor in the overseas provinces, although more important within the Jesuit hierarchy, was less prestigious than the rank of provincial in Europe. But barring an unlikely promotion to the rectorship of a major college, it was improbable that he would live long enough to ascend to a position like that of visitor in Portugal. The overseas provinces were thus the ideal place for a man such as Palmeiro.

The future visitor left Braga to make sure he reached the capital before the traditional departure date of the Indies fleets in late March or early April. According to the Annual Letter for the Province of Portugal for 1617, Palmeiro quit the Colégio de São Paulo amid an outpouring of tears, leaving behind sweet memories. He was forty-eight years old, long past the age when Jesuits usually left for the missions. This journey to India would be the crowning event of his illustrious career as a member of the Society, this narrative's author suggested.[89] Heading south, Palmeiro passed through Coimbra, where his former colleagues and the count-bishop had the chance to exchange parting words with him. Here he presented himself almost as a caricature of the virtues of apostolic poverty and obedience. When he returned to his alma mater, he wore the same worn and patched cloak that he had used for years, one that, according to his necrology, was "already proverbial at the University of Coimbra." Upon seeing him, Afonso de Castelobranco reportedly wept, and when Palmeiro inquired why, the count-bishop replied: "I am crying because of how poor Your Reverence's cloak is."[90] The same source also mentions that Palmeiro's rigor in observing his superiors' orders was such that he did not stop to see his mother during this final trip to Lisbon. But this anecdote seems a bit of pious exaggeration, meant to inspire his confreres by his example, since it is known that he visited his place of birth—and in all likelihood his mother—on two occasions in the months before he left for India.

Palmeiro clearly impressed his brothers in the Society of Jesus during his service in Portugal. There was no better proof of their respect than that which came from the pen of Francisco Suárez, who also traveled to Lisbon in 1617, summoned there by the crown to resolve an interdict crisis. Writing to a confrere in South Asia, the *Doctor Eximius* offered a tribute to his former Coimbra colleague who was poised to embark on the Cape Route: "Now Father André Palmeiro is leaving for India. He is in fine shape and a great man; there is none other in Portugal like him."[91]

3

Manager of Men

On April 21, 1617, the carrack *Nossa Senhora da Guia,* which carried André Palmeiro to India, left Lisbon harbor in the company of five other ships. This vessel was commanded by one of the most celebrated captains of the day, Nuno Álvares Botelho, the man who would be responsible for the heroic defense of Malacca in 1629. Three other Jesuits were on board along with Palmeiro; two of them were being sent to serve in the Society's Province of Goa and the third was destined for the Province of Malabar. For six and a half months they sailed toward India. First the fleet headed in the direction of the Madeira Archipelago, then the Cape Verde Islands, and afterward far out into the southwestern Atlantic, where the ships caught the west winds that propelled them past the Cape of Good Hope. By late summer, they reached the Indian Ocean. They sailed northward along the coast of Mozambique, passing the northern tip of Madagascar in time to catch the monsoon winds that drove them northeastward to India.[1]

Palmeiro's writings are silent about his journey on the *Carreira da Índia,* save for a passing mention in one letter to the effect that his voyage was nothing but smooth sailing; the seas were far rougher, he claimed, on a much shorter trip that he later took from Cochin to Colombo.[2] Indeed, a deathly monotony was characteristic of the half-year voyage to the East. There were no scheduled ports of call between Europe and Asia, the horizon dominated the view from all sides of the ship. Only misfortune waylaid fleets on their way to India. If they failed to reach Mozambique in time for the favorable southwest winds, they would be forced to winter on the coast of East Africa. The three carracks and three smaller ships that sailed in 1617, however, "all reached Goa on the ordinary monsoon," that is, in the final months of the year.[3] Palmeiro's vessel entered harbor there on November 9, three weeks after the fleet's earliest arrival dropped anchor near the mouth of the Mandovi River.[4]

The steady progress of the Indiamen that year did not mean that Palmeiro's voyage was without incident. All three of his confreres died or, or as that year's annual letter for the Province of Goa put it, "reached the heavenly port before they sighted the earthly one." This was not surprising since disease frequently haunted the ships of the Indies route but, just as he had escaped the plague in his first year of life, Palmeiro was again spared. Curiously, his survival and arrival went unremarked upon in that same annual letter. Rather, the Goa Jesuits recorded with surprise that three of their number died on the *Nossa Senhora da Guia,* which was assumed to be the better, safer ship, while all five members of the Society who sailed in the same fleet on the *Nossa Senhora do Cabo* arrived in good health. According to this report, the *Cabo* was so famous for its high numbers of shipboard deaths that it had earned the macabre nickname "the tomb."[5]

Palmeiro disembarked at Goa as a professed Jesuit with experience as an academic and an administrator. He was not yet visitor. It is therefore unlikely that his arrival was greeted with fanfare, although it was customary for the Jesuits in Goa to send a procession of singing children to the quayside to greet new arrivals from Europe. Senior priests were typically received by the provincial superior, who would escort them from the ships to the Professed House of the Bom Jesus.[6] It is not known if Palmeiro was given such special treatment, but a lack of pomp and circumstance no doubt would have suited him well. His elevation to visitor would occur a full year after his arrival in Goa, when he received his letters patent from Rome: Palmeiro's commission, signed by the superior general on January 20, 1618, first had to travel from Italy to Portugal and then halfway around the world on the Cape Route.[7]

With the exception of these first months at Goa, Palmeiro would spend the rest of his life holding the office of visitor. Each of the successive triennial assignments that he received from Rome granted him authority over a specific province or provinces. In other words, he would not be responsible for all of the Society's enterprises in Maritime Asia at once, he would inspect the provinces by turn: First he was visitor to the Province of Malabar, then to the Provinces of Goa and Malabar, and afterward to the Province of Japan. These "provinces" were geographical units created by the Society of Jesus to organize its overseas enterprises, and their headquarters were all situated in colonial cities of the Portuguese Estado da Índia. The Province of Malabar, centered on Cochin, encompassed the Jesuit enterprises along the coasts of southern India, in the inland region of Madurai, in western Sri Lanka, in Bengal, Burma, and Malacca, and in the Spice Islands. The Province of Goa, headquartered in Goa, subordinated the Society's colleges and missions in Mozambique, Ethiopia, Gujarat, western India, the Mughal court cities, and Tibet. And the Province of Japan, centered on Macau, included the missions to mainland Southeast Asia, China, and Japan. Palmeiro would have the chance to visit several of these regions during his eighteen years in Maritime Asia. At one point or another he would be responsible for managing all of them.

The Jesuit provinces were communities of men. Like the Province of Portugal, from where Palmeiro had come, the provinces of Malabar, Goa, and Japan were mixes of priests and brothers living in colleges or smaller residences. For the most part, these men had not chosen each other's company. The Asian provinces, like their counterparts in the Americas, were made up primarily of recruits from Europe. That is, with the exception of a minority who joined the Society from the Portuguese colonial population, most of the men in Asia had come there seeking missionary glory. Back in Europe, these recruits had successfully petitioned the superior general for an assignment to the "Indies" and had been sent to one of the overseas provinces. They came from a variety of different nations and brought varying notions of Catholic life to the Jesuit community in Asia. Many of them found outlets for their apostolic ambitions in the expansive mission districts, where opportunities for pious heroism or even martyrdom abounded. But the Asian provinces were not simply agglomerates of missionary outposts. Their colleges in colonial cities undertook the same type of ministries that the order offered at its European colleges. Teaching, preaching, and confessing were all parts of Jesuit life in Maritime Asia, much to the disappointment of many recruits who came seeking confrontation with non-Christian religions. So the Society's Asian provinces were also arenas for conflicts of expectations. They were places where the reality of life in highly structured religious communities clashed with baroque dreams of missionary travails and triumphs.

Palmeiro received his first commission as visitor of the Province of Malabar at a moment of crisis. The Jesuit community was rent by divisions, both
at its headquarters in Cochin and in the mission districts. The disputes among
its men had festered to such a point that they came to involve the highest
levels of church authority in India. As visitor, Palmeiro was entrusted by the
superior general in Rome with resolving these conflicts, and his mettle as a
manager of men was tested even before he set foot in his appointed district.
As soon as he received his patents as inspector from the mails carried to Goa,
Palmeiro had to use his analytical skills to evaluate a theological controversy
that had arisen over innovations in missionary method at one of the residences of the Province of Malabar. In an attempt to make conversions from
the social elite at Madurai, Roberto Nobili adopted the clothing and lifestyle
of an indigenous ascetic. While still at Goa, the Visitor took part in a confrontation between Nobili and the city's archbishop, who claimed jurisdiction over the Madurai mission and doubted the orthodoxy of the missionary's strategy. Palmeiro's role in this dispute was to defend the reputation of
the Society of Jesus, a task that included visiting Madurai to see if Nobili's
experiments produced the desired result: a thriving indigenous church. On
the way there, Palmeiro took the opportunity of assessing the state of affairs
at the College of Cochin, the principal Jesuit community in the Province of
Malabar. At Cochin, he found himself in the midst of another storm. The
city's college was the scene for vigorous sparring between different factions of
Jesuits, so Palmeiro faced the added challenge of bringing about harmony
among his men.

––––––––––

Palmeiro's first year in Goa, spent waiting for his commission as visitor to
arrive from Rome, was the only time when he figured as an honored guest of
the Goa Jesuits instead of the superior general's representative: when he returned to the viceregal capital of the Estado da Índia in the mid-1620s, he
would take up residence at the Professed House of the Bom Jesus as the
highest-ranking Jesuit in South Asia. Goa, in other words, was the Visitor's
base of operations for half of the time that he remained in India.

What kind of city was Goa? To put it succinctly, it was a mirror of its
metropolitan counterpart, Lisbon. Goa was a major urban center with a
population estimated at 75,000 at the beginning of the seventeenth century. European-born Portuguese were comparatively few; they were vastly

outnumbered in the city by indigenous peoples and imported slaves.[8] The commercial activities of its European, Eurasian, and Asian traders made Goa a major entrepôt, where resources were marshaled from afar for carrying out commercial and apostolic enterprises across the Indian Ocean. While being in a commercial center and transportation hub was important to Palmeiro for carrying out his tasks as Visitor, the city's role as a center of imperial administration was even more so, for Goa was also a court city, home to a concentration of secular and ecclesiastical power unlike any other in Portuguese Asia.[9] It was a stage upon which, in addition to his administrative tasks within his order, the Visitor would have to act as a diplomat. The role he played in seeking out the patronage of the great and the good in order to secure social, political, and economic advantages for the Society of Jesus should not be underestimated.

Despite the fact that he was a high-ranking member of an influential religious order, at Goa Palmeiro was a face in a crowd. At the summit of the local hierarchy sat the viceroy and the royal officials who were entrusted with the management and defense of the Estado da Índia in its legal, military, and economic affairs. *Fidalgos,* that is, noblemen, who were entrusted with the captaincies of the fortresses of Portuguese Asia or with command of the fleets that were the sinews of empire occupied positions of high eminence at this colonial court. The private traders (whether of noble status or not) who had become wealthy in the city's varied commercial enterprises also enjoyed considerable prestige. The *casados,* married men, formed the urban elite whose voice was heard through the workings of the *Câmara,* or city council, as well as through the important charitable brotherhood, the *Misericórdia.*[10]

The secular church in Goa was represented by men who held impressive titles. Its highest-ranking prelate was *Arcebispo Primaz da Índia Oriental,* not only an archbishop but primate of the East Indies. Just like his counterparts in Europe, the archbishop of Goa had his own ecclesiastical court of canons and suffragan bishops. When Palmeiro arrived, the reigning prelate was Frei Cristóvão de Sá e Lisboa (d. 1622), a Hieronymite friar who had served for five years as bishop of Malacca before being elevated to the archdiocese of Goa in 1612. Goa was also the seat of the only nonmetropolitan branch of the Holy Office of the Inquisition in the Portuguese Empire, staffed by a full complement of judges, deputies, and functionaries. And in addition to the Jesuits, the Dominicans, Franciscans, Carmelites, and Augustinians (who also had a sister branch of nuns in the city) could be found at Goa, each order with its own dignitaries.

For the year that he spent waiting for his credentials from Rome, Palmeiro held an ambiguous position among the Goa Jesuits. He was not formally a member of the Province of Goa, so he could not be assigned to tasks by the provincial superior. But he was too talented to be kept idle, and his skills were put to good use upon the death of Jerónimo Xavier (b. 1549). This famed missionary to the court of the Mughal emperors had assumed the post of rector of the Colégio de São Paulo-o-Novo in the summer of 1617, and his passing opened an administrative vacancy in Goa. Aware of his prior service at Braga, the provincial requested that Palmeiro fill in as head of this important Jesuit school until a suitable replacement could be found.[11]

Palmeiro's other main activity during his year in Goa was preaching. His fame in the pulpit had traveled from Coimbra to the East even before he disembarked, brought there by his former students and colleagues. Unfortunately, none of his sermons from this time has been preserved (indeed, exceptionally few sermons from early modern Portuguese Asia have come down to the present). Evidence of Palmeiro's status as a preacher can be found in the personnel catalogue for the Province of Goa for 1618.[12]

Palmeiro's preaching is also mentioned in the correspondence of the local branch of the Holy Office with the Supreme Council of the Inquisition in Lisbon. In their annual report to the inquisitor general, Goa's two inquisitors, Francisco Borges de Sousa (d. 1628) and João Fernandes de Almeida (d. 1624), gave an account of the auto-da-fé that was held on November 18, 1618. Sixty individuals, they noted with satisfaction, were sentenced in front of Viceroy João de Coutinho, the Count of Redondo (c. 1540–1619), and "a great crowd of noblemen, and countless plebeians." They lamented, however, that the archbishop had taken ill, was forced to miss the occasion, and could not give the erudite sermon that he had prepared. On the day before the event, the Holy Office therefore informed Palmeiro that he would have to preach. To help him prepare on such short notice, they gave him a list of the crimes that were to be condemned during the ceremony. Palmeiro's sermon was learned enough, the inquisitors thought, but it left them wanting something more. They complained that the renowned Jesuit preacher only denounced Judaizing, a crime whose perpetrators were "the least part of those condemned."[13] Surely Palmeiro could have risen to the occasion and denounced bigamy, homosexuality, blasphemy, turning Muslim, practicing Calvinism,

or defending Lutheran ideas—to cite only the list of crimes for which prisoners were held in the Inquisition's jail in the late 1610s—but he only seemed
able to recall the anti-Semitic refrains from the autos that he had witnessed
in Coimbra.[14] Needless to say, with so many other obliging priests, the Inquisition would not invite Palmeiro back to the pulpit for its next public sentenc-
ing in Goa, in 1623.

When he received his patents from Rome in the last weeks of 1618, Palmeiro rose in status both inside and outside the Society of Jesus. As far as
the Jesuits of the Province of Malabar were concerned, he now had many of
the powers of the superior general in Rome. The most important of these
was the ability to compel obedience. Yet unlike his famous predecessor Alessandro Valignano, Palmeiro did not engender respect by his imposing stature or commanding manner. Rather, his subordinates saw in him a scrupu-
losity possessed by few men of his rank. Outside the order, Palmeiro entered
the elite of the colonial clergy. As visitor (albeit for the Province of Malabar),
he was at least equal in status to the provincial superior of the Province of
Goa, who enjoyed as much prestige as his peers in the other orders. To be sure,
the Society of Jesus was one group among several, and the Franciscans and
Augustinians were also influential in Portuguese India. For example, the Augustinians saw several of their men raised to the status of bishops, and even
archbishops, where they outranked all other priests. Moreover, the judges of
the Holy Office enjoyed preeminence over the members of religious orders,
although they considered accomplished theologians like Palmeiro to be their
peers.

The Visitor would face his first major challenge regarding the Jesuit missions in Asia from bishops, inquisitors, and archbishops. The senior clergy at
Goa was starkly divided over a theological question borne of Jesuit missionary zeal. At issue were the missionary methods employed in the inland kingdom of Madurai, five hundred miles to the southeast. Since this mission district was part of the Province of Malabar, the controversy was Palmeiro's
concern. Such was the commotion created by the Jesuits involved in the affair that it drew the attentions of the archbishop of Goa and the judges of the
Inquisition. The involvement of these figures, who claimed the right to intervene because Madurai was in their ecclesiastical jurisdiction, meant that the
dispute would have to be resolved in Goa. But by the time Palmeiro arrived
at the viceregal capital, the affair had already been forwarded to the Supreme
Council of the Inquisition in Lisbon and from there to the Papal Curia. In

1619, just months after he became visitor, Rome demanded another examination of the case at Goa. Palmeiro would therefore be one of the main players in the denouement of a dispute that had lasted for over a decade.

To understand Palmeiro's role in the final stage of this controversy, a brief sketch of its previous phases is necessary. The affair centered on the proselytizing strategy employed by Roberto Nobili, one of the early members of the Jesuit mission to Madurai. That enterprise had been inaugurated by Gonçalo Fernandes (1541–1621), a Jesuit who had worked for years among the Parava Christians of the Fishery Coast in southern India. When the ruler of Madurai invited Fernandes to reside in his capital in 1595, the Jesuit took up his offer, thinking that he could mint the coin of conversion from this show of political favor. Yet once he left the coast, where Portuguese traders and Indian Christians were established presences, Fernandes found himself in another world. Madurai was an important Hindu religious center with massive temples and frequent devotional displays. It was infertile soil for planting the seed of the gospel, as far as Fernandes was concerned. Few townspeople were interested in risking their social standing by adopting this new religion. Fernandes therefore concentrated his pastoral efforts on the Parava migrants, hoping to lure others through his pious example. But seeking conversions at this court city was largely a fruitless endeavor for a foreign missionary dressed in the simple black robes of the Society of Jesus, one who kept company with the downtrodden—those few who adopted his religious teachings.[15]

Nobili, who had been sent to join Fernandes in Madurai in 1606, opted for a change of strategy. With the approval of his superiors in Cochin, the following year he left Fernandes and adopted the lifestyle of a sannyasi, or ascetic. He opened a new residence in Madurai, across the city from that of Fernandes, and went about in the light-colored robes of an Indian holy man. Configuring himself as a "Christian Brahman," Nobili sought to attract his peers from that highest caste in India's social order. His plan was to make the Christianity he preached and practiced appealing to the social and political elite by distancing it from its associations with the Portuguese and low-caste indigenous Christians. As the scion of one of the most influential families in Italy, Nobili felt justified in distinguishing himself from the Portuguese and insisting that his form of Christianity was distinct from that of the Portuguese in Cochin or Goa.

The conversion of a handful of Brahmans at Madurai—the reward for Nobili's efforts to transform himself in order to create the political and

FIGURE 3.1. Depiction of a Jesuit in India, painted in the seventeenth century by an unidentified artist at the Mughal court. Note the simple black robe that the priest wears, along with sober interior gown and simple hat.

cultural conditions for proselytization—appeared to justify his actions. Following his policies to their logical conclusion, Nobili adopted for himself and permitted his neophytes to retain the outward symbols of their social rank: the three-threaded string worn over the shoulder, the sandal paste worn on the forehead, and a specially grown tuft of hair. He also encouraged a form of ablution before hearing the mass, adapting local concepts of purity to Christian rituals, and changed some of the religious terminology inherited from the indigenous Christians of Southern India (the so-called Thomas Christians) that were used by the Jesuits. And in order to avoid the defilement that came from mingling with the impure, Nobili severed his public links to his fellow Jesuits. These extreme forms of cultural adaptation proved too much for Fernandes, who sent a scathing critique of Nobili's practices to his superiors in Cochin. This denunciation was the first salvo in a protracted propaganda war whose battles would be fought in Madurai, Cochin, Goa, Lisbon, and Rome.[16]

Unfortunately for Fernandes, Nobili was a skilled controversialist. He would not be silenced in this dispute without a fight. Nobili vigorously defended his positions in writing and in person, insisting that the indigenous form of dress and the Brahman insignia were merely political symbols or markers of social status in Madurai—they were emphatically not religious signs declaring one's adherence to Hindu religious tenets. To support his claims, Nobili cited passages from Sanskrit texts that addressed the divide between the secular and the religious in Indian thought.[17] Crucially, his patrons included Alberto Laerzio (1557–1630), his provincial superior, and Francesc Ros (1557–1624), a former Jesuit who was archbishop of Cranganore, a see located to the immediate north of Cochin (this archdiocese was originally called Angamalé, and it is sometimes referred to in historical sources as the Archdiocese of Serra). Interventions by these two men, whose power within the Society of Jesus in southern India and in the secular church was unrivalled, meant that Nobili was able to avoid the final censure of his policies on several occasions in the 1610s.

Several issues converged in the dispute over Nobili's actions. First, there was the question of whether Nobili had crossed the line into condoning paganism with his adoption of Indian cultural practices. Fernandes held that the caste system could not be detached from the Hindu religious context, so the use of its symbols by Christians implied the approval of non-Christian beliefs. Second, there was the issue of how closely Christianity needed to be

FIGURE 3.2. Portrait of Roberto Nobili drawn by Baltasar da Costa (1610–1673). This portrait is found at the end of Costa's manuscript copy of Nobili's catechism and was likely drawn in the mid-1650s near the time of Nobili's death in 1656.

allied with the political and cultural practices of the Portuguese. As the Nobili affair was debated at increasingly greater distances from the mission field,
this aspect of the dispute would gain prominence. The specifically European
aspects of Christian practice would be judged in light of their theological
necessity, although no definitive solution was discovered during the early
modern period. To be sure, church doctrine covered matters relating to belief
as well as items of practice, including the loci of authority invested in men
such as archbishops, bishops, and the judges of the Inquisition—under whose
jurisdiction Nobili and his converts fell. To cast doubt upon their authority
or to reject it was tantamount to schism. Third, Nobili's attempt to distance
himself from his fellow Jesuits provoked a rupture within the Society of Jesus. Although his intentions were *ad maiorem Dei gloriam,* his actions represented an affront to the spirit of fraternal charity that he had sworn to observe. All of these issues would have to be resolved before the Madurai affair
could come to a close.

So the affair had dragged on for over a decade prior to Palmeiro's arrival.
One of the primary reasons was that authorities both inside and outside the
Society of Jesus had made conflicting pronouncements. Palmeiro's predecessor, Nicolau Pimenta, twice inspected the Madurai mission during his two
terms as visitor. Pimenta was not impressed, and he condemned the practices
employed by Nobili and his neophytes. But Archbishop Ros insisted that this
condemnation was based on inadequate knowledge of Indian texts, and so
Ros appealed to the order's Roman curia to permit further investigation. Superior General Aquaviva and his successor Vitelleschi agreed, indicating that
they were favorably disposed to Nobili's methods. Yet the involvement of the
archbishop of Cranganore removed the case from the Society's sole jurisdiction. Ros's rival, the archbishop of Goa, Cristóvão de Sá (whose predecessor,
Aleixo de Menezes, had favored Nobili), also demanded to be heard on the
issue, owing to his status as primate of the Orient. Sá insisted that Nobili be
judged and condemned by the Inquisition, viewing the matter through the
prism of the practices employed in the region around Goa, where entry into
the Catholic church often entailed as much a spiritual conversion as a cultural one. Nobili's powerful allies in Rome brought the dispute to the highest
authority and secured a papal brief issued by Paul V in 1616, which kept the
Jesuit sannyasi from being condemned by Archbishop Sá. But the pope's decision was that the matter required further investigation: Rome mandated
that the two archbishops hold a conference to analyze the questions that were

raised by Nobili's methods. The Supreme Council of the Inquisition in Lisbon and its branch in Goa deferred to Rome's decree, which arrived in India in December 1617. This papal pronouncement was seconded by another brief issued the following year, which reiterated the pope's desire for a conference of theologians to be held.[18]

As this summary of events suggests, the controversy was considered to be of great importance and contained several dramatic moments. Twentieth-century scholars and theologians made much of Nobili's visionary attitudes and of his revolutionary stance toward the adaptability of Christianity to non-European cultures.[19] By turn, they denounced Nobili's detractors as blinkered reactionaries incapable of grasping the subtle arguments in favor of cultural accommodation. But these issues were not foremost in the minds of the affair's participants, who had little sense of the ramifications their positions might have in theological debates that would take place centuries in the future. The doubts they raised about Nobili's methods reflected the situation of the Portuguese in India, the proven usefulness of the methods of Jesuit missionaries stretching back to the days of Francis Xavier, and their knowledge of Indian religious and philosophical texts.

Gonçalo Fernandes, in particular, is frequently painted in deprecatory hues.[20] Yet long experience in the mission field gave heft to Fernandes's arguments against Nobili.[21] From the senior missionary's perspective, there were practical matters of mission management at stake—the most important of which was the place of Christianity and its Jesuit proponents within the panorama of religious belief in southern India. Fernandes, who had reached his late seventies when these disputes came to a head, feared that potential converts would not be able to spot the uniqueness of Christianity if it was cloaked in outward signs borrowed from the multiple contemporary forms of Hinduism. He therefore argued for the eradication of ambiguity, regardless of the associations that potential converts might make between Christianity, low caste or outcaste converts, and the Portuguese. Moreover, Fernandes demonstrated on several occasions that indigenous sources and Brahman informants could be used, just as Nobili had used them, to defend his claim that there was no clear separation between the secular and the religious in southern India. But his recourse to experience, that is, to the repeated invocation of "what I have seen in this land", was no match for Nobili's exposition of the issues in terms of theological definitions and patristic antecedents.[22]

André Palmeiro was predisposed to favor Fernandes's arguments over those of Nobili. After all, the ecclesiastical authorities in Goa, supported by a series of church councils held in Portuguese India in preceding decades, and several members of the Society with experience in India had argued persuasively against Nobili. But the Visitor still wanted to hear him out. The occasion for their meeting was the conference mandated by the pope that was convened at Goa in early 1619. As one of Palmeiro's subordinates in the Province of Malabar, Nobili was obliged to obey the Visitor's summons to appear in Goa. According to one modern scholar of the conference, Palmeiro had sent a "thundering letter" to Nobili, demanding that he abandon his dubious methods. This letter has not been identified for the present study, but it seems likely that Palmeiro revealed his displeasure at how Nobili had argued in public against his detractors—especially those outside of the Society of Jesus in the church hierarchy. Not only were such actions contrary to Jesuit vows, they were damaging to the order's reputation. In his letter the Visitor had reportedly promised to force the missionary to kneel before the archbishop of Goa and beg his forgiveness for having contested the prelate's sentences.[23] In one of Nobili's letters Palmeiro is quoted as saying that in his theological disputations at Coimbra he had strongly disputed the retention of the Brahman thread by Christian converts. Invoking the name of one of the victims of Cicero's invective, Palmeiro averred that he had argued this issue "with more than a Vatinian hatred." That being so, the Visitor had insisted, he had made up his mind that his first action as inspector of the Province of Malabar would be to "completely destroy the Madurai mission, so that not a trace of it would remain."[24]

Nobili cited Palmeiro's words verbatim because he occasioned a change of heart in the Visitor. During their private encounters at Goa in the weeks before the conference, Palmeiro came to agree with Nobili's interpretations. To the dismay of the archbishop of Goa, the meeting he convoked with high dudgeon in early February 1619 turned out to be far from an auto-da-fé. Nobili was indeed called on the carpet, but he came with influential allies. Not only did Palmeiro—the man who, Nobili reminded his audience, had been considered as second to none by the *Doctor Eximius,* Francisco Suárez—show himself favorable to Nobili's explanations of the signification of the Brahman thread and the other practices employed in Madurai, but the junior of the two inquisitors, João Fernandes de Almeida, did as well.[25] According to Nobili's account of the conference, Palmeiro declared: "After I weighed Father

Roberto's reasons and arguments, I made an effort and, pressed by my conscience, changed my plans and my opinions." It was his duty "as a Christian and a religious," Palmeiro added, to examine the issues of missionary policy raised in this dispute; he did not do so simply because papal briefs demanded. Palmeiro judged Nobili's arguments about the secular nature of the Brahman insignia to be conclusive. He therefore urged the clerics at the conference to accept Nobili's positions as a worthy strategy for vanquishing paganism, emulating "the readiness and the benevolence of Our Mother the Church to offer easy access to eternal salvation for all people, and not force them into Hell."[26]

At the risk of condemning those indigenous converts who were genuine Christians while they retained their caste status as Brahmans and its external symbols—those people referred to in his invocation of the term *non ad Orcum compellere*—Palmeiro sided with Nobili. The other Jesuit theologians present at the conference, as well as Archbishop Ros, followed suit. Their votes on the matter were registered in the official acts of the conference, along with the counterarguments offered by the archbishop, the senior inquisitor, and the representatives of the other religious orders. This information was collected for immediate dispatch to Rome. The imminent departure of the Lisbon fleets meant that the final reports were produced in haste—so much so that those who sided with Nobili had little time to produce their own account of the proceedings. Letters to the inquisitor general in Lisbon and three brief statements (one of them by Palmeiro) declaring the secular nature of the Brahman insignia and rituals used by Nobili were nevertheless included in the bundle of documents sent to Europe.[27] But these documents were too few to outweigh the lengthy statements denouncing Nobili's policies, treatises that had been prepared far in advance of the conference. Fearing their position was poorly represented, both Nobili and Palmeiro sent their own accounts to the Jesuit curia, hoping to steel the superior general for his eventual hearings before the papal court.

"On the Madurai affair," Palmeiro declared to Nuno Mascarenhas, the Portuguese Assistant to Superior General Vitelleschi, "His Holiness has been informed in writing about what happened in the meeting that took place upon his orders in this city, whose archbishop can be heard with much passion." The Visitor felt that the official report failed to convey the excessive terms used by this prelate to defend his views and further lamented not having time to construct an appropriate response to the archbishop's points. Palmeiro decided that the best strategy was to send three sets of blank paper bearing his signature to Rome, "so that the priests who receive it there can draw it up as they see best."[28] This move was uncharacteristic of the Visitor, but the stakes were high: the archbishop reportedly asserted that the Brahman thread would only be permitted over his dead body. According to the archbishop of Cranganore, his counterpart in Goa was given to "screaming" and took the opportunity of his first Lenten sermon to accuse the Society of Jesus of "favoring idolatry and the ceremonies of the devil."[29]

Palmeiro experienced an intellectual conversion in the early weeks of 1619. As he would have done in a Coimbra classroom, he had heard the two sides of a disputation and concluded that Nobili's arguments were sound. Insofar as the theological foundations of the Madurai mission and Nobili's practices were concerned, Palmeiro wrote, "there is nothing to question." But he felt it necessary to insist with his superiors in Rome that this was not a matter that could be resolved by logic alone. The Visitor was well aware that there were practical considerations that he could not judge until he saw Nobili's church with his own eyes. Palmeiro thus closed the letter that he penned after the Goa Conference by urging the superior general to suspend final judgment until he had made an inspection of the mission station at Madurai.[30] But before he could do that, he had to travel to Cochin. Only after he confronted the situation at the headquarters of the Province of Malabar would he undertake the arduous voyage overland to see Nobili's mission station in person. Rome would therefore have to wait nearly two years to hear Palmeiro's final word on the Madurai affair.

Palmeiro's intellect and administrative competence made a favorable impression on the Portuguese viceroys and other members of the colonial administration during his time in Goa. As inspector he was obliged to travel about the Estado da Índia and beyond, and that made him a valuable adjunct of their imperial projects. So as Palmeiro readied himself to depart for southern India in late February 1619, the viceroy solicited his help. The Count of Redondo wrote to the crown that the new visitor was "a religious who gives a great example and has many talents, and who is considered as such in this city."[31] Palmeiro could therefore be entrusted with important tasks, such as inspecting the Portuguese fortresses in the region of Cochin. The viceroy lamented the miserable state of the empire's defenses to Madrid, reporting that he had ordered the repair of the walls of Onor (Honnavar), but that most of the sea fortifications of Quilon (Kollam) needed rebuilding, too. He commissioned Palmeiro to work in conjunction with the *vedor da fazenda* (royal treasury official) in Cochin to appoint Jesuits to survey the fortifications of Cranganore (Kodungallur). The Visitor was to report to the viceroy on "all the work that needs to be done, and what it will cost, and if there is someone who can handle the construction, and the price for each wall, so that the money can be allotted and the work commence immediately."[32] Palmeiro would have occasion to reap the reward of his participation in the viceroy's projects in the form of patronage when he returned to Goa.

The Visitor headed south to Cochin in the early spring of 1619. His journey by sea covered the nearly five hundred miles of coastline between Goa and that second most important city in the Estado da Índia. Santa Cruz de Cochin, the Portuguese settlement situated a short distance from the court of the rulers of Cochin, had been the center of the pepper trade during the sixteenth century. Almost a decade older than Goa, the Portuguese colony was home to a prosperous merchant community whose commercial links reached to Sri Lanka and the Malay archipelago. Estimates of the city's population in the late sixteenth and early seventeenth centuries indicate that it had between ten and fifteen thousand inhabitants, about of third of whom were Portuguese or Luso-Asian.[33] Descriptions from Palmeiro's time suggest that Cochin's heyday as a trading entrepôt was past since the spice trade had increasingly become centered on Goa, but it does not appear that the city was in terminal decline—especially since it was repeatedly targeted in the seventeenth century (and eventually captured in 1663) by the Dutch East India Company. Visitors to Portuguese Cochin remarked upon the city's solidly built houses and beautiful churches as well as on the ethnic and religious diversity of its population.[34] Indian and European Christians as well as Jews, Muslims, and Hindus could be found in the kingdom of Cochin, although in Santa Cruz the presence of Catholic institutions was pervasive. The Portuguese city was the seat of a bishop whose see stretched to Colombo and Malacca. Of its several religious communities, the Franciscans had the oldest and largest, with the Dominicans, Jesuits, and, lastly, the Augustinians filling in the panorama of the regular clergy.[35]

Palmeiro took up residence in the Colégio de Madre de Deus, where he joined a community of seventy-one priests and brothers.[36] Not counting the colleges and residences in the city of Goa and its environs, this was the largest concentration of Jesuits in Asia. The first of them to reach Cochin was Francis Xavier in 1544, and the first group to settle in the city arrived in 1549. The order's residence, which was transformed into a college in 1560, expanded over the following decades owing to grants from the crown and local Portuguese benefactors. According to one contemporary description, the college church was among the more sumptuous churches of Portuguese India: it had a massive gilt altar with an eight-paneled retable, shipped from Lisbon, that was "excellently painted."[37]

Like the Society's major houses in Europe, the College of Cochin was primarily an educational institution. In 1618 its staff included two professors of speculative theology, two professors of moral theology, one philosophy instructor who read the *Curso das Artes*, two masters of "humanities," and a

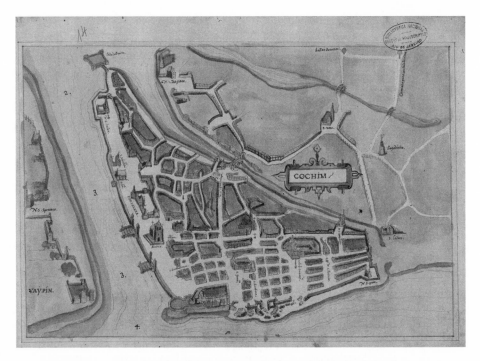

FIGURE 3.3. Map of Cochin drawn circa 1610 by Manuel Godinho de Erédia (1563–1623). This map, oriented with north on the left side, gives the best indication of the site and scale of the Jesuit college. That edifice, shown at the lower center right, was destroyed in the second half of the seventeenth century after the Dutch captured the city.

teacher of reading and writing. Annual letters from this period indicate that, just as in Portugal, the lower school's classes were taught by younger Jesuits (often brothers), and that an average of a dozen novices studied at the college.[38] It is not clear how many other students there were, but their numbers were significant enough to warrant the creation of a devotional confraternity. In addition to their pedagogical tasks, the Cochin Jesuits provided pastoral care to the local population. Sermons and organized devotions were a constant at their church, as were the activities of pious brotherhoods. One of these groups gathered the Portuguese residents under the invocation of the Blessed Virgin while the other was reserved for the *gente da terra,* that is, indigenous Christians. In the words of one report from 1620, these people scrupulously partook of the sacraments of confession and the Eucharist, gathered twice weekly for penitential discipline, and thus were "taken as an example by the whole city."[39]

The size of the Jesuit community at Cochin made that city the logical starting point for Palmeiro's inspection of the Province of Malabar. In 1619 its 24 priests, 14 scholastics, 13 temporal coadjutors, and 18 novices made up nearly half of the province's total of 156 Jesuits.[40] Palmeiro spent the first few months of his inspection taking stock of the college and its two dependent residences at Santo André (Arthunkel), thirty miles to the south, and at Tanur, seventy miles to the north. He also visited the College of Cranganore, located at a fortress town situated at a strategic juncture along the main inland waterway twenty miles north of Cochin. That residence was home to eight priests and a brother who lived alongside Archbishop Francesc Ros.[41] These Jesuits were responsible for visiting the dispersed parishes of the Syro-Malabar or "Thomas" Christians, and for staffing the archdiocesan seminary at Vaipikotta, a short distance south of Cranganore. Relations between the Jesuits and the Syro-Malabar Christians had a tumultuous history, but it does not appear that Palmeiro played much of a role in it.[42] He is known for having tried to raise academic standards at the seminary by limiting its enrollment to twenty-five students and for reassigning some fractious Jesuits at Cranganore, but little else.[43]

Palmeiro's initial survey of the problems faced by the Society in southern India revealed internal fissures within the order: The College of Cochin was a hotbed of discord. Indeed, the Malabar Jesuits had lived in a climate of disunion since their province's founding in 1602. The main fault line ran between its Portuguese members and their Italian brethren; there was particular division over the question of the nationality of the superiors appointed to govern the college and the missions, but the differences extended to a divide over issues of proselytizing method. Shortly after Palmeiro's arrival in Cochin, he identified the once and future provincial, Alberto Laerzio, as the primary agitator. Laerzio was also the leader of the Italian faction. Resolving the problems between this group and its Portuguese opposite would thus be the Visitor's first task.

The issue of nationality, or of national sentiment, was one of the most persistent problems faced by the Society in the early modern period. The order was founded by men from a range of nationalities and was intended to be supranational in its undertakings and its outlook. Yet, despite the will to cosmopolitanism displayed by Ignatius Loyola and his early followers, the forces of regionalism and nationalism in contemporary Europe were not easily overcome. Clashes rooted in national identity were especially frequent among the Jesuits, owing to the order's centralized administration. In contrast to other orders that were largely administered at the national level, the Society accorded supreme authority to its superiors general. As the order expanded in the mid-sixteenth century, the nationality of the generals themselves became a matter of great importance for the papacy and for European monarchs as well as for the Society as a whole. In order to loosen some of the tensions created by national sentiment, the order was organized in assistancies that largely paralleled national boundaries. While the superior general might be a Spaniard, a Fleming, or an Italian, his assistants were drawn from the senior Jesuits of the European provinces. The Society's Roman curia thus reflected the cosmopolitan makeup of the first band of men who joined Loyola at Paris in the 1530s.

Beyond Europe, the boundaries of the order's assistancies reflected the reach of European colonial empires. The Spanish and Portuguese Empires were the first to see the creation of overseas Jesuit provinces, whether in New Spain, Peru, Brazil, or the Estado da Índia. The problem of nationality arose from the fact that these overseas administrative units contained vast mission districts that the Society could not staff only with Spanish or Portuguese Jesuits. Jesuits in the other European assistancies eagerly sought assignments to the overseas missions, especially to those in Portuguese Asia, where the saintly Francis Xavier had worked. Cognizant of the need for laborers in the vineyard, the Society's superiors general approved the petitions of non-Portuguese candidates for positions in the Asian enterprises that would give them a chance at missionary glory or martyrdom. Italian Jesuits were especially keen to work there. Not only had there been Italian missionaries in Maritime Asia from the time of Xavier, their assistancy lacked mission territories of its own. But the presence of "foreigners" in provinces within the Portuguese Assistancy at times led to frictions between Jesuits.

Tension over nationality was particularly acute in the Asian provinces when the number of "foreigners" grew and they rose to positions of governance. According to contemporary logic, a majority of Jesuits (and a virtual monopoly of superiors) in each province should be of the nationality of the home province of the assistancy. For example, one would expect that the three provinces of the French Assistancy (including its Canadian missions) would have French superiors, and that the Italian provinces would have Tuscan, Sicilian, Venetian, or Lombard superiors. But the creation of the Province of Malabar gave rise to a situation in which the Portuguese or Indian-born Portuguese were not an absolute majority. Acting as mission procurator for the Province of India (before its division), Alberto Laerzio traveled through Portugal, Spain, and Italy in 1599, returning with a record number of sixty-two recruits. The fact that over half of these men were Italians planted the seeds of discord among the Jesuits in southern India. And the fact that Laerzio also brought with him notice of the separation of the Province of Malabar from that of Goa as well as the appointment of Italians to key positions within the newly created province only made matters worse.

Scholars of the Asian missions have traditionally viewed resistance to this strong Italian presence as a symptom of Portuguese close-mindedness, xenophobia, "intellectual mediocrity", and "conquistador" mentality.[44] But one can safely assume that the arrival of a large contingent of Portuguese and their assumption of governing roles in an Italian province would have produced a similar uproar. A true meritocratic spirit was yet to emerge anywhere in early modern Europe, even if its origins can be spotted in the *Constitutions* of the Society of Jesus. Moreover, the matter of "foreigners" in predominantly missionary provinces had been debated at the order's Seventh General Congregation, a meeting of representatives of the whole Society held at Rome in early 1616. That meeting's decrees state unequivocally that any men who leave their home provinces to join others are obliged to integrate themselves into the provinces that receive them, and that no independent groups formed on the basis of nationality would be permitted within assistancies run by different nationalities. Any such divisions were deemed to be "contrary to the mutual

union of hearts and minds" and "conducive to the great harm of the Society."
Rejecting requests for the creation of independent groups based on nationality, the congregation urged the newly elected superior general to address the
sources of tension.[45] Muzio Vitelleschi did precisely that, dispatching a circular letter, one of the few that he would send during his long tenure, on this
topic in 1619—the same year that Palmeiro arrived in Cochin.[46]

It is necessary to move beyond clichés about national character, especially
those that posit Italian flexibility against Portuguese rigidity, in order to understand how Palmeiro dealt with the situation that he encountered at Cochin. The Visitor did not merely face two national groups struggling for
primacy within the Province of Malabar. He also encountered a clutch of
oversized egos. Three men in particular gave him cause for concern. The fact
that they were Italians—regardless of the genius of their ideas or methods—
and the coincidence that the few who dared speak against them were Portuguese has suggested that this was a simple issue of one nationality versus
another. Yet matters were not so clear-cut. What emerges more clearly from a
reading of contemporary documents is a clash between personality types,
pitting charisma against pragmatism. To balance these two forces was the
principal challenge for the superiors of early modern religious orders, especially those of the Society of Jesus. On the one hand, there were men moved
by a spirit that impelled them to mimic the grand gestures of the Apostles or
of missionary saints. These individuals are often described as visionaries mis-
understood by their peers; they were figures whose irrepressible energy found
outlets in the heroic, the tragic, or the pathetic. And on the other hand, there
were the men like Palmeiro, who deliberated over rules and costs. These individuals considered the context and ramifications of individual actions, pausing before committing themselves to endeavors that might jeopardize current
projects or future possibilities. In sum, this contrast reflects the divergence
between the classical aphorism *ne plus ultra* and its early modern variant
found most memorably on the heraldry of Emperor Charles V, *plus ultra*.

The first of the larger-than-life Jesuits that Palmeiro found at Cochin was
Antonio Rubino (1578–1643), a native of Piedmont who had come to India in
1602 and had spent his first assignments at mission stations in the court of
Vijayanagara at Chandragiri and, later, Vellore. As in the case of Roberto Nobili, Rubino's proselytizing efforts took place far beyond the reach of colonial
control. Rubino saw himself carrying out his true vocation as a missionary
in the mold of Xavier, so it was only reluctantly that he accepted the post of

rector at São Tomé de Meliapor (Mylapore) for a term ending in 1617.[47] Palmeiro encountered Rubino in the spring of 1619, upon his arrival in Cochin, where Rubino had come after a civil war destroyed the Vijayanagara mission. The Visitor listened to his pleas for a new assignment in a mission field, either "the Moluccas or Bengal." In such a setting, Rubino argued, he might have another chance to serve heroically. But the province needed good men to administer its colleges, and Rubino had experience as a rector. Palmeiro therefore sent him to be the superior of the College of Colombo in Sri Lanka. Writing to the superior general in Rome, Rubino complained that "Father Visitor never wanted to accept my excuse from this task." He resigned himself to his new post, declaring with his customary pathos that he was thus obliged to "purge my sins in such calamitous times."[48] But Rubino's pious dreams were only put on hold—in 1642 he would embark on a foolhardy mission to Japan, where he died under torture as a martyr.

The second uncontrollable personality at Cochin belonged to Alberto Laerzio, the man who had pushed for the creation of the Province of Malabar and still looked upon it as his own nearly two decades later. A man with great ambitions, he recruited scores of Jesuits in Europe. His dream was to take the Indian missions to the forefront of Jesuit activity in South Asia, removing them from the shadow of Goa. After all, no other region of the subcontinent had produced such results as the Fishery Coast and the districts of the Thomas Christians. Laerzio sought to build upon this success, prodding his confreres along and encouraging men like Nobili and Rubino who made audacious gambles. But not all appreciated Laerzio's forceful style. He was constantly at odds with the Bishops of Cochin and was often to blame for inciting their ire. The initial disputes over Nobili's methods provided the opportunity for Laerzio to pique Frei André de Santa Maria (r. 1588–1615), who disapproved of the innovations at Madurai. This bishop also moved to seize the Jesuits' churches on the Fishery Coast in 1608 (discussed in detail later), in part—according to his confreres—because of Laerzio's provocations in Cochin.[49] Santa Maria's ill will toward the Jesuits only diminished slightly in 1611, when Laerzio was removed from his post as provincial superior.

Palmeiro was disturbed to learn that an unofficial provincial congregation had once again elected Laerzio as procurator to Europe in 1619. Laerzio's commission empowered him to negotiate in Rome and Madrid for the recuperation of the Fishery Coast churches as well as for the restoration of the Jesuits' revenue-producing villages in Sri Lanka. These properties had been seized by Santa Maria's successor as bishop of Cochin, the Augustinian friar Sebastião de São Pedro (1560–1629).[50] In the last weeks of 1619 Palmeiro wrote at least five letters to Rome to alert the Jesuit curia to the problems caused by Padre Alberto's journey. This flurry of letter writing was typical for the Visitor, who would go into seclusion with an amanuensis to produce his yearly reports in the days before the ships left for Europe. In these missives he explained the chain of events that led to Laerzio's election as procurator—a process over which Palmeiro had no control, given his interpretation of his duties. It is clear that Palmeiro was against the decision. In a moment of exasperation with his fractious subordinates he wrote: "God help us."[51]

The Visitor's frustration was kindled by procedural problems. When Antonio Rubino, the former rector of the College of Colombo, arrived in early November 1619 to explain how Frei Sebastião had seized the Jesuits' rental properties, the senior Jesuits at Cochin became convinced that a special procurator needed to be sent to Madrid and Rome "to curtail the calumnies of the bishop."[52] When asked for his assent to hold an election, Palmeiro demurred, saying that he disapproved but that the decision rested with the provincial superior. First the Visitor declared that the voyage was an unnecessary expense; the Jesuits' position could be explained in a letter to which the king and pope would respond in writing.[53] Palmeiro also reminded the college's consultors that the Society had rules about the election of procurators. The post of procurator to Rome could only be created by a vote during a provincial congregation, and that year's congregation had voted against such a proposal. To call for a new vote out of turn and without a full slate of voting delegates, Palmeiro argued, would go against the Society's rules. The crisis brought about by the bishop's actions notwithstanding, the Visitor declared, the Cochin Jesuits could not ignore their order's procedures. But time was short, and they felt pressed to argue their case in Europe. In the span of a month before that year's fleets sailed for Goa and on to Lisbon, the provincial consultors riposted, it would be impossible to gather all of the voting members to hold another congregation. The vastness of the Province of Malabar that Laerzio had pushed hard to create negated the possibility of swift collective decisions—some of its senior men were two thousand miles away in Malacca, and others were four thousand miles away in the Moluccas.

Putting aside Palmeiro's reservations, the senior Jesuits at Cochin decided to hold their "little congregation," as he termed it. "Many things happened at this meeting which upset me," the Visitor wrote to the Roman curia, starting with the flagrant disregard of the Society's rules.[54] Provincial Gaspar Fernandes (b. 1564) gathered a group of "fourteen or fifteen" men at Cochin to debate, and Laerzio put himself forward as the best candidate for procurator.[55] According to Palmeiro, most of the Italians present spoke up in favor of his election, invoking a dispensation once received from Rome to justify their actions. Two of those present, the Portuguese André Machado (d. 1626) and the Italian Giacomo Fenicio (1558–1632), contested the legitimacy of the vote. The Visitor joined their dissent. He insisted that this bending of the Society's rules would give rise to "great displeasures among those who remain here, and has already begun to do so."[56] Adherence to established procedures was indeed the bond that held the order together. Palmeiro closed his discussion of the meeting's problems with the following declaration: "I confess to Your Paternity that I took it badly and find it strange, this turning of all of our orders, decrees, and instructions into so many wax noses, which can be bent this way and that. And today the opinion of the province is that there will not be a congregation and a procurator will not be sent; but tomorrow because so-and-so or some men want it, the procurator travels because some decrees or dispensations permit."[57]

It was not only the ad hoc election of a procurator that annoyed Palmeiro; the choice of Laerzio was also a problem. "I do not believe they hit the mark with the person they chose," the Visitor wrote to Assistant Mascarenhas in Rome. Laerzio was clearly not indispensable for resolving the province's affairs. First of all, Palmeiro noted, he was sixty-three years old. Second, Padre Alberto had irritable bowels and was "very diminished." Third, he would necessarily have to pass through Goa, where his presence would serve to antagonize the city's prelate. According to Palmeiro, the archbishop was disaffected with Laerzio "for something that he said." After the Nobili affair, the primate of the Indies was against "all of the foreigners, as he calls them, in these lands." Neither man was Indian-born, and the irony in this aspersion was not lost on the Visitor.[58]

Palmeiro was also concerned about Laerzio's record of zeal for recruitment. The last time he had gone to Europe, Laerzio had brought back more recruits than the poorly funded province could absorb. Knowing that new Jesuits would necessarily have to be trained and employed, Palmeiro thought of the future costs to the College of Cochin. In his opinion, the college's revenues were only sufficient for a few more than half of the number of men it supported.[59] It was therefore likely that Laerzio would attempt to leave the recruits he would certainly bring back from Europe in Goa. Doing so would mean that the Province of Goa would pay for training and supporting the men of another province. To be sure, Jesuit procurators from the East Asian missions had done just this, leaving their men in Goa to finish their schooling rather than taking them onward to Macau. Niklaas Trigault (1577–1628) had returned from Europe in 1618 with twenty new Jesuits for China, entrusting them to the care of the Province of Goa, which already had twenty others slated for the East Asian missions. Palmeiro alerted Rome that it was imperative that Laerzio be prevented from returning with a new crowd of recruits. At most, the Visitor admitted, the province could handle six men (far fewer than the twenty-nine Laerzio brought back to India in 1624).[60] In sum, Palmeiro argued, there was no reason for procurators to be disappointed if they did not bring scores of new recruits to the missions.[61] He would repeat this message in later missives the Portuguese Assistant, knowing that Laerzio would push for more men: "If they are a mob, we will lose."[62]

The cloud of disunion hung over the Province of Malabar after Laerzio's election. In a letter sealed on December 15, 1619, Palmeiro intimated that he could see the tensions rising in the wake of the "little congregation." Provincial Fernandes had argued against Laerzio's election and accordingly was rumored to be the principal author of the renewed strife. There was no doubt that Laerzio was a polarizing figure, but the antagonism between the Italians and the Portuguese ran deeper. "One of the things I hear and feel that causes much discord in these parts is the conviction that the Italian priests write there to complain about the Portuguese for any displeasure," Palmeiro wrote to Rome. Yet he knew that the responses from the superior general about such matters were typically generic, urging the fractious members of the Society to union in vague terms which attributed no blame. In Malabar, however, they were taken to mean, as Palmeiro put it, that "if you want to get along calmly, venerate the Italians, et similia."[63] The gloating he sensed on the part of Laerzio's supporters after his election did not help matters. The Visitor feared that greater problems would arrive along with a new cargo of sympathizers for Padre Alberto in a few short years. Palmeiro was at wit's end with the affairs at Cochin: The Province had so many insoluble problems, and most of them seemed to have sprung directly from the unbridled energies of its founder.

In addition to the irrepressible duo of Antonio Rubino and Alberto Laerzio, the third outsized figure encountered by the Visitor in the Province of

Malabar was Roberto Nobili. This priest had returned to Madurai to resume his mission while he awaited approval of his missionary strategy from Lisbon and Rome.[64] Recall that Palmeiro had informed the Society's Roman curia that he intended to visit Nobili's residence to consider his strategy in situ, as he had already considered it in the abstract. The occasion for this inspection arose in 1619, when Palmeiro went on a tour of southern India and Sri Lanka. Although this journey will be discussed later, it is necessary to examine here his thoughts on Nobili's mission. Upon returning to Cochin, Palmeiro prepared reports for Rome that clearly reveal his impressions from Madurai and explain his decisions with regard to the controversial enterprise.

The part of the Madurai mission that had provoked so much scandal was the product of proselytizing zeal. Nobili earnestly sought to bring about conversions by aiming for the top of the social hierarchy, hoping that the authority of elite converts would inspire those of lower status to adopt Christianity. In order to do so, he mimicked the behaviors of the Brahmans. His image as a learned man and an ascetic was crucial, he needed to appear as the equal to those he sought to convert. Here, Nobili acted on the words of St. Paul: "And I became to the Jews, a Jew, that I might gain the Jews".[65] This was an audacious move, and not without serious consequences. What Nobili risked in his gamble was not winning the Brahmans in spite of becoming outwardly like them. Without results, he would be no more than a priest in disguise. Moreover, Nobili was not alone in the work of expanding the Church in Asia. He was not like Paul, who was recognized as a leader within the Primitive Church. Nobili was simply a Jesuit who was subject to the authority of his superiors, including Palmeiro, as he was also to the bishops who enjoyed ecclesiastical jurisdiction over India. He was not free to innovate as he saw fit, especially when his notions clashed so frontally with the decisions of his senior brethren and the church hierarchy. As the thunderous response provoked by Archbishop Cristóvão de Sá after the Goa Conference in February 1619 demonstrated, Nobili's policies were pursued at considerable cost to the public reputation of the Society of Jesus.

If there was to be any justification for Nobili's choice to repeatedly disregard the opinions of his betters, it would have to come in the form of results. This concern for outcomes was a practical criterion, one that has escaped the attentions of scholars content to track Nobili's struggles in the name of cultural accommodation rather than to chart his proselytizing gains. But unlike modern commentators, the Visitor insisted that a theologian's abstract logic did not suffice to evaluate a radical shift in missionary policy. Palmeiro had been convinced by what he heard in Goa, but he would also have to be convinced by what he saw in Madurai. After all, the Society of Jesus was not given to conducting experiments in proselytization for their own sake. The business of making Christians was not an idle pursuit but one that demanded men, money, and a convincing message. Nobili and his colleague at Madurai, Antonio Vico (1565–1640), were two men whose talents might be set to other, less costly tasks. But if their message proved convincing—that is, if their method produced converts—it would be worth the trouble.

The Visitor's inspection of the Madurai mission took place in the autumn of 1619, after he had trekked through western Sri Lanka and along the Coromandel Coast of southeastern India. In contrast to his descriptions of the other stops on his journey, his account of his stay in Madurai is succinct. In few words, he describes the city's stout walls, water tanks, and richly endowed temples, not neglecting to mention the massive gilt wood ceremonial carts used to carry devotional statues in procession about the city. Of course, the principal object of his visit was not to inspect the Hindu temples but to see the city's three Jesuits in their two residences. "In one of them lives only one, dressed in black in our ordinary clothes," Palmeiro wrote, "in the other, two dressed in whitish-yellow *cabayas* and a cloth on the head."[66] Leaving aside Vasco Domingos (b. 1565) and his more conventional mission, the Visitor commented more fully upon the latter pair. The two men dressed in "holy disguise" were of course none other than Nobili and Vico. "I also dressed in these clothes," affirmed Palmeiro, "so that I could spend two days in seclusion with these priests, edifying myself with the very poor and very saintly life that they lead there." Most impressive, he claimed, was their diet, which consisted of "only a bit of rice and some vegetables stewed in the local fashion, very insipid and bland, and the best treat they have is to drink a bit of cow's milk." About Nobili's intentions, Palmeiro averred, there could be no doubt: These bodily sacrifices were made in order to "win for God and gather into the heavenly flock those souls which stray so far from Him and His ways." Palmeiro also remarked briefly on the peculiar layout of Nobili and Vico's church. This building had been made to accommodate its unique community, with different spaces for the various castes of Christians, "with the section for the most noble caste situated closest to the crossing."[67]

Arriving back in Cochin, Palmeiro sent to Rome his thoughts on the Madurai mission. The first issue addressed in his letters from December 1619 was Nobili's change of attire. By abandoning the standard black robes used by the Jesuits and adopting the dress of Indian ascetics, Nobili and his companion, Vico, had made themselves appear different from their brethren. Palmeiro, too, had donned these robes when he was at Madurai. To the Visitor, the question of dress was unimportant, as was the missionaries' insistence on their noble birth in their effort to appeal to others of high social standing. Unlike Nobili's detractors, he did not see problems with these elements of missionary strategy: "There is no need to remark on the fact that they go about dressed like Brahmans, or on other things which others object to, because I understand that these things can help them to attract people and gain their affection," Palmeiro asserted in his letter to Rome. Nor would he condemn their calling themselves "Brahmans of the King of Spain and of the Lords of Europe, because in all of this they speak the truth, and it helps with their intent."[68]

In Palmeiro's opinion, the doubts raised by his trip to Madurai were of a different order. The first serious problem arose from Nobili's repudiation of the colonial church hierarchy. The Visitor admitted that it might be beneficial for Nobili and Vico to give ambiguous answers when asked about their links to the Portuguese at Goa. After all, Goa and Cochin were far from Madurai. What was unacceptable, Palmeiro asserted, was to deny publicly that they had any relationship to their coreligionists. "Such an opinion and dissimulation cannot be maintained or perpetuated," he argued, "and it seems to me that I am not only certain of this, but have moral evidence."[69] What Palmeiro meant was that even Nobili's Brahman converts had to be aware of their having joined a church which included the Portuguese and which, in India, was subject to Portuguese ecclesiastical authorities. To deny or disguise this basic fact was schismatic.

It was likewise intolerable, he argued, for Nobili to reject the company of his brethren in the Society of Jesus. While the creation of two residences in Madurai was perhaps useful for creating two Christian communities, the charade had been carried too far. In sum, Nobili had been coherent to a fault. He observed Brahman norms to the point where his understanding of the avoidance of occasions for defilement meant that he could not interact with his fellow Jesuits. Not only in Madurai but even when he was far from his mission station, Nobili avoided being in the company of low-caste individuals (including his European confreres). Palmeiro's "moral evidence" of the peril of such thoroughgoing dissimulation was the following scene from the

Goa Conference, related here by the city's archbishop to the Jesuit curia with clear indignation:

> It is intolerable that Father Roberto comes to this city and stays in the Professed House without ever eating with his brothers, and not permitting his food to be what they eat. He only eats what he brought and what his Brahmans make for him. Moreover, when he goes to the New College [of São Paulo in Goa], and even when his Brahmans are not present, he eats nothing but the food that his Brahmans bring for him. This causes a great scandal, and people believe that he not only pretends to be a Brahman but that he surely embraces their superstitions, because even when it was not necessary for him to observe them, he did.[70]

A further major problem with Nobili's *fingimento,* his masquerading as a Brahman, was the fact that little had been gained by his audacious methods. More than the abstract issues, this reality was what Palmeiro had found most shocking. After all, Nobili had argued for over a decade that his policy would pay off in conversions, and that he would create a large and thriving community of influential Indian Christians. But in the fifteen years since Nobili had restyled himself after the indigenous fashion, Palmeiro reported, "no fruit has been produced." Even if he discounted the period from 1615 until 1619 when the mission was suspended, there were no conversions to speak of, "nor is there any hope that there will be, with the way they are running it."[71]

In the opinion of all experienced missionaries in the Province of Malabar, Palmeiro continued, the Madurai effort was *infructuosissima.* Many of them found that Nobili's innovations were "only a burden to the Society and a scandal to many others," but the Visitor was not in complete accord. It was possible to bring Brahman converts into the Church without obliging them to lose their social status, he felt. He declared that dispensations should be granted to Brahmans and other higher caste converts—although their paltry numbers did not yet seem to justify such formal measures. Here Palmeiro was forced to concede a point to the Society's intractable foe, the bishop of Cochin, Frei Sebastião de São Pedro. Since it was part of his diocese, the bishop had visited Madurai with the intention of performing the sacrament of confirmation for the Jesuits' converts. Arriving there, however, he found that Nobili "had not baptized anyone or made Christians, nor was he occupied with the conversion of souls." It was Frei Sebastião's impression that Nobili "intended only to be considered a learned man among the Brahmans."[72]

Palmeiro did not go so far as to call Nobili's work vanity, as the bishop did. Instead the Visitor saw "dissimulation and pretense . . . which will bear no fruit, since it has not yet made any worth considering."[73]

In the Visitor's judgment, Nobili's policies had been a bold attempt to re-direct the course of the path of evangelization in India, but they had failed to produce results. To modern ears, the adjective "bold" suggests courage in the face of pessimism, but to early modern ears it was associated with temerity or foolhardiness. Palmeiro's most succinct statement on the topic contains an-other of these terms whose meaning has changed over time, *fantástica*. Early moderns would not have understood this word to mean something wonder-ful but rather something unreal, something that exists only in the imagina-tion. Summing up his thoughts on the matter in his letter to Nuno Mascar-enhas, Palmeiro declared:

> My dear Father Assistant, I can certify to you that in its present form this mission is something fantastic, without substance or abundance. If it con-tinues in this manner it will only serve to defend the opinion of those who started it. It will also show disrespect to what we owe to God and our or-der, as well as that which truth and sincerity oblige us to defend in such serious matters.[74]

Part of Palmeiro's charge as visitor was to come up with solutions to the crises facing the Province of Malabar. But the problem of disunity caused by fac-tion or missionary zeal was not easily resolved. As a manager of men, the Visitor had few options: he could impose penances on his subordinates, such as fasting or prayer, but this was not likely to change the tenor of community life in Cochin. After all, Jesuits were obliged to do such things on a regular basis by the rules of their order. As the superior general's personal representa-tive, he had the power to employ drastic measures. Yet Palmeiro was aware that his moves might bring about even more disunion than already existed among his men. So he trod lightly.

It took the Visitor almost a year to devise his own strategy of dealing with the factions that still disrupted life at the College of Cochin. Prior to leaving for his inspection tour of the province, he tended to see the Portuguese as unduly put upon by the Italians. But his mood changed during his trek; he became convinced that the fighting at Cochin was childish and, above all, unbecoming for professed religious. Had the disputes arisen from a competition to see who could observe the Society's rules most scrupulously, he might have felt that the competing factions were justified in their struggles. But this was not the case. Palmeiro therefore showed himself less inclined to suffer the complaints of his countrymen about the Italian faction. This is not to say that the troubles of the past had been resolved in his absence; rather, he concluded that both sides in the dispute were wrong. "I worked as much as I could to make brothers out of all," wrote the Visitor to Assistant Mascarenhas, but there were some among the Portuguese priests who resisted his peacemaking.[75]

Palmeiro's strategy was to ask Rome for reprimands written by the superior general. He was keen to have one such letter addressed to Francisco de Aragão (b. 1584), one of the college's theology professors. Palmeiro declared to the curia that although Aragão had good qualities, he also had "a restless and bellicose nature," and that Antonio Rubino had been justified in branding him a troublemaker.[76] The Visitor urged Mascarenhas to send a letter reminding Aragão about the need for unity, a notion dear to the heart of Muzio Vitelleschi. "It is important that he be sent a serious warning," Palmeiro concluded, deciding that this was the best way to deal with senior Jesuits.[77] It appears that the curia took the Visitor's suggestions seriously, since Rome sent a pointed rebuke to another individual whom Palmeiro had identified as a disturbance. Provincial Fernandes received a rebuke for his handling of the "little congregation" and for letting the factional fighting get out of hand. Worse still for Fernandes was Rome's stipulation that the letter be read aloud by the Visitor before the assembled Jesuits at the college.[78]

Of all the weapons in Palmeiro's disciplinary arsenal, reassignment was among the most potent. But he only used it in extreme circumstances, preferring first to solicit rebukes from Rome. Letters from the superior general reminding individual Jesuits of their vows of poverty, chastity, and obedience were usually effective means for cowing the recalcitrant, but not always. For instance, Cristóvão de Abreu (ca. 1572–1621), a professed Jesuit and former rector at Cranganore, had given Palmeiro trouble at Cochin, so Abreu received a notice from the curia warning him to shape up. But instead of accepting the Visitor's criticism, Abreu wrote back to Rome to complain about the Visitor's harshness.[79] Raising the stakes did not resolve the matter in Abreu's favor: Palmeiro sent him to Goa (where he died shortly afterward).[80] In another case, Giovanni Maria Campori (1574–1621) also had to be sent away from the Province of Malabar, where he had worked alongside the arch-bishop of Cranganore. Despite his skill as a minister in the Cranganore re-gion, Campori had been a leading figure in the Italian faction during the disputes at Cochin. Palmeiro brooked no resistance in his decision, even that of Archbishop Ros. Writing to Rome to complain about the Visitor's deci-sion, Ros claimed that the removal of Campori was no less than cutting "the feet and hands off the good governance of this Christian community."[81] Al-though he did not say it, this personnel change clearly seemed a small price to pay for unity among the Jesuits in the Province of Malabar.

The problems created by the zealous missionaries' experiments were harder to solve. The Madurai affair had been forwarded to Rome, and final judg-ment would have to come from there. Even if a blessing for Nobili's methods did come from the papal throne, his mission had already cost the Society dearly in terms of money, men, and reputation. What was Palmeiro to do? He could not simply shutter the enterprise; he knew that would bring on an uproar from its supporters (and unnecessary gloating from the Jesuits' adver-saries). Palmeiro at least had to wait until Nobili's démarches to the Lisbon Inquisition and the Holy See received a response.

The only means at the Visitor's disposal was to convince Nobili and Vico to abandon their passive methods of evangelization for a more aggressive strategy, even if in a native guise. If they were to gain converts, they would have to leave the monastic seclusion where their image of asceticism constituted their pros-elytizing lure. A more active strategy would have them not simply seek to be seen as learned men but to put their learning toward the goal of actively mak-ing new Christians. The measure of success was not to be the reputation for holiness but the numbers of neophytes, be they of the Brahman caste or of lower ones. In order to avoid singling out Nobili and Vico, however, Palmeiro made the drive for conversions the first rule he issued for the whole Province. This way there would be no ambiguity about which strategy worked best in the mission territories: "The priests will inform the rectors of their districts each month about any new catechumens that there are and of the adult bap-tisms they have performed. Even if no one has been converted, they will tell the rector, and the rector will give the same accounting when he writes to the Provincial so that he understands what is going on."[82]

Rome eventually decided in favor of Nobili. That is, the papacy granted approval to his interpretation of the Brahman insignia as secular symbols, not religious ones. In January 1623 the apostolic letter *Romanae Sedis Antistes* provisionally approved their use by Nobili and his elite converts. The time was ripe for Jesuit petitions to the Papal Curia, since Gregory XV, like his predecessor Paul V and his successor Urban VIII, favored the Society. The Holy Office of the Inquisition in Portugal also approved of Nobili's arguments (although its judges would have little leeway after the papal pronouncement). It was of considerable help to the Society in this matter that the inquisitor general was Fernão Martins Mascarenhas, five of whose younger brothers had joined the Society of Jesus. Mascarenhas had also been Palmeiro's colleague at the University of Coimbra, and two of his brothers held important positions within the Province of Portugal: Provincial António Mascarenhas (d. 1648) and Assistant Nuno Mascarenhas.[83] It was also a good thing for the Jesuits that the decision from Rome was a long time coming. Recall that the archbishop of Goa had used the strongest terms possible to condemn Nobili's methods, promising that he would never live to see the Brahman insignia permitted in his archdiocese. He did not. The news reached Goa two years after the corpse of Frei Cristóvão de Sá e Lisboa had been committed to the earth.

Rome's approval of Nobili's methods did not solve the problem raised by Palmeiro, that of missionary results. And the Visitor's request for rebukes from the superior general for his fractious subordinates would not necessarily bring peace to the College of Cochin. Time would be required to address those problems, so the Visitor turned about to face the other challenges found in the Province of Malabar. The distances he would have to cover to inspect the Society's far-flung missions were great, but they seemed far less of a burden than life in the midst of factional strife or under the critical glare of archbishops and inquisitors. The superior general had sent him to visit the province, so he set out with a sigh of relief to do just that.

4

In the Footsteps of the Apostles

In the early spring of 1620 André Palmeiro set out from Cochin on a 1,900-mile journey to inspect the Jesuit Province of Malabar. He went on this trek in order to gauge the work of his men, visiting their colleges and residences, and speaking to each of his subordinates individually. Palmeiro traversed the heart of his appointed district over an eight-month span: He sailed first to the Fishery Coast, a mission area that was in turmoil because of a dispute between the Jesuits and the bishop of Cochin. From this southernmost region of India, Palmeiro traveled by sea to Colombo and proceeded overland to northern Sri Lanka. From there he again crossed the Gulf of Mannar and sailed along the Coromandel Coast as far north as São Tomé de Meliapor. After visiting the pilgrimage sites associated with the Apostle Thomas, Palmeiro turned south once again toward the Fishery Coast before heading north on foot overland to Madurai. The final leg of his trip took him southward once again to Cape Comorin, the southern tip of India, and then northward back to Cochin along the coast of Travancore.

This ambitious inspection tour only included the Jesuit colleges and residences in the central region of the Province of Malabar. To visit the whole province would have been nearly impossible: this Jesuit administrative unit spanned nearly four thousand miles. Beyond the southern region of South Asia, it included a set of mission stations in Bengal, Burma, and the Moluccas as well as a college in Malacca. The Province of Malabar was the brainchild of Alberto Laerzio, a veteran from the College of Cochin who had served as procurator to Europe in 1598 and had insisted in Rome that the Jesuit superiors at Goa ignored the enterprises situated in Southern India and Sri Lanka. His wish for an independent province was granted in 1602 when Superior General Claudio Aquaviva carved a new administrative unit from the "Province of India." The resulting two units were called the Province of Goa and the Province of Malabar.

Despite the immense size of these two Jesuit provinces, they made sense in geographic terms: The annual monsoons and the logic of communications split Maritime Asia into two roughly coherent spaces. The Province of Goa corresponded to the western half of the Indian Ocean, encompassing the

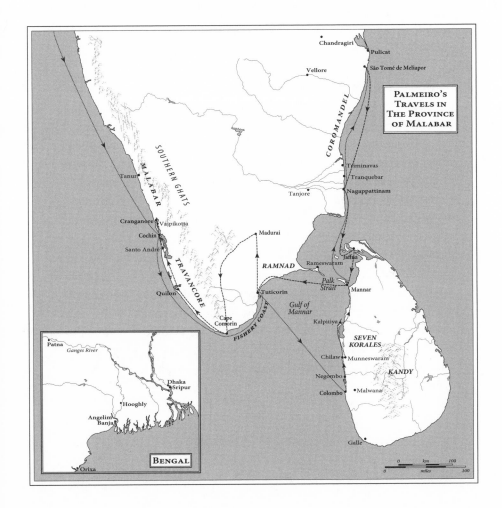

region that stretched from the Zambezi Valley in Mozambique northward along the coast of East Africa and around the Arabian Sea to Goa; and the Province of Malabar matched the ocean's eastern half, stretching from Malabar to Sri Lanka, from the Coromandel Coast to the Bay of Bengal, and finally along the Malay peninsula and the island chains that now constitute Indonesia all the way to the Moluccas. The regular monsoon winds that blew across the Arabian Sea made the Province of Goa comparatively easy to administer from the viceregal capital. Governing the Province of Malabar was another matter entirely. It was far too large to manage, even with favorable winds. While the Malabar, Fishery Coast, Coromandel, and Sri Lankan residences could be kept in regular contact with the provincial headquarters at Cochin, communications with Malacca, Ternate, and Bengal were time-consuming and difficult. Thankfully for Palmeiro, the majority of the province's Jesuits lived in the former area, so he could concentrate personally on mainland South Asia and Sri Lanka and complete his visitation by sending deputies to the more distant regions.

After Palmeiro returned to the College of Cochin at the end of his tour, he compiled a lengthy account for the superior general in Rome. His travelogue contains lively descriptions of the people that he encountered, the places that he visited, and the indigenous customs that he observed. It tells of a contested corner of early modern Maritime Asia, where Jesuits clashed with the bishop of Cochin, Portuguese armies fought against the indigenous rulers of Sri Lanka, and Portuguese traders competed against rivals from Northern Europe. After all, the Province of Malabar was the creation of Jesuit administrators who ignored the region's divisions. The account of the Visitor's travels therefore tells of colonial cities, lands with leaders allied to the Portuguese Estado da Índia, and regions under the control of native lords. His narrative describes a landscape that was at once exotic and familiar. It was a place where he saw flora and fauna unlike any he had ever seen and where he witnessed the manifestations of religious traditions vastly different from his own. But it was also a region where he found a strong Christian presence, since it was home to ancient Christian traditions as well as to communities that were the fruit of recent missionary endeavors.

Palmeiro sailed away from Cochin on March 16, 1620. The winds blew his vessel southward over four days toward *Pescaria*, the Fishery Coast. This area,

named for its pearl fisheries, stretched beyond Cape Comorin (Kanyaku-
mari) at the tip of the Indian subcontinent to Tuticorin (Thoothukudi), the
region's largest port. Since the 1540s it had been the center of the Jesuit missions to the Parava caste communities.[1] In the first decade of the seventeenth century, however, a major dispute between the bishops of Cochin and
the Society had seen the Jesuits expelled from the region against the will of the
indigenous Christians. The shadow of this dispute darkened much of the area
through which Palmeiro traveled. He would play an important role in the
conflict's resolution, and the affairs of the Fishery Coast would not be far
from his mind during the whole of his term as visitor of the Province of
Malabar.

Pescaria was home to one of the largest concentrations of indigenous Christians in India. It was not part of Portuguese domains, but its ruling clans
enjoyed close ties to the colonial state. Portuguese traders and Franciscan
missionaries had visited the area in the early sixteenth century, and the friars
had claimed numerous conversions among the members of the Parava caste.
The initial missionary élan in the area gradually tapered off, however, providing an opportunity for Francis Xavier to create a pastoral presence there in
the 1540s. His Jesuit successors made considerable advances in their proselytizing efforts and for sixty years ministered to the area's Christians in a capacity similar to that of parish priests.[2] During that period the Paravas enjoyed a
relative degree of freedom from the control of their lords, the nayakas of
Madurai. They were also free from the impositions of the bishops of Cochin,
who preferred to administer the area through vicars forane (in Portuguese,
vigários de vara). Since the Jesuits were already there, the bishop typically
granted the title of vicar forane to one of their number, thereby entrusting a
Jesuit with a limited degree of ecclesiastical authority over the Parava Christians. A major Portuguese expansion could not be expected in the region,
and, as the bishop knew, it was impractical to export European norms of
church administration from colonial cities to areas outside imperial control.
Better to let the Jesuits handle pastoral matters in the area—especially the
delicate task of negotiating with the rival clan heads who vied for positions of
prestige.

Like the region's pearls, the Christians of *Pescaria* were a valuable prize
coveted by Europeans. With age, and polished by skilled hands, they grew
in luster. The Jesuits were not shy of trumpeting their successes on the Fishery Coast, much to the chagrin of their rivals in Cochin. Not only did the

Franciscans resent the fact that the Jesuits had moved into areas where their friars had once worked, but the bishop saw a thriving Christian community within his dioceses that he did not administer directly. Tensions between the bishops and the Jesuits over the Fishery Coast came to a head at the turn of the seventeenth century, when the papacy created the Archdiocese of Angamalé in 1599 for administering the Syro-Malabar church (the so-called Thomas Christians). Rome did not define its frontiers precisely, a fact that meant that its archbishops would struggle for decades with the bishops of Cochin over the boundaries between their two jurisdictions. Moreover, Rome did not make the bishop of Cochin subordinate to the new archbishop. The papacy further complicated matters by appointing a Jesuit, Francesc Ros, to the new see, while members of the mendicant orders served as bishops of Cochin. The struggles for precedence among the religious orders were thus replicated within the church hierarchy.

The conflict grew worse within a few years of the creation of the new arch-diocese as Ros was successful in his petition to move the headquarters of his see. The Portuguese had long referred to the districts of the Thomas Chris-tians as the *Serra,* or mountains to the north and east of Cochin, so an arch-bishopric was created with its seat in that region. But Ros preferred as safer spot within the fortress of Cranganore, twenty miles north of Cochin, an area that had been within the diocese of Cochin. The pope and the king ap-proved, changing the name and seat of the archbishopric to Cranganore. In response to this perceived affront, the bishop of Cochin moved to take con-trol of the churches staffed by the Jesuits on the Fishery Coast in order to compensate for what had been taken from him.[3]

By definition, missionary endeavors are temporary affairs. From the perspective of Rome, Christian communities created by missionaries must sooner or later become parishes within dioceses. So it was to be expected that the Jesuits would at some point relinquish control over their churches and that members of the secular clergy would fill their role as parish priests. But when should this transition occur? In many corners of the early modern world, the Jesuits created mission churches that grew to considerable size. They rightly felt a sense of proprietorship over the communities of neophytes that they had formed, and the same was true for the missionary enterprises run by other religious orders. Neither the Jesuits nor the friars were keen to alienate their spiritual patrimony. But members of the regular clergy served at the pleasure of the bishops who enjoyed jurisdiction over their mission districts.

The Jesuits (or the friars) could be dismissed if their bishops could replace them with an alternative clergy. But the men of the Society held a trump card: They knew that the king of Portugal enjoyed the right of patronage over the church in the Estado da Índia and adjacent territories. Skillful diplomacy at Goa and Madrid by the Jesuits could therefore get the bishop's decision overruled.

The dispute between the Jesuits and the bishops of Cochin over the Fishery Coast produced a dramatic clash. Indigenous politics provided the occasion for the bishop's gambit: At the turn of the seventeenth century, the nayaka of Madurai sought greater control over the far southern reaches of his domains, areas that had long been neglected. In order to flee his impositions, in 1603 the Jesuits took several thousand Parava Christians to live on an island in Tuticorin harbor, the Ilha dos Reis (Hare Island). Sensing an opportunity to even the score against the archbishop of Cranganore, Bishop Frei André de Santa Maria in 1607 appointed a Franciscan as vicar forane to reside among the Jesuits' Christians on the island. This vicar was charged with convincing the Paravas to return to their homes on the mainland, over the protests of the Jesuits. The bishop also reached an accord with the nayaka that permitted him to evict the Jesuit colony on the island and to send members of his diocesan clergy to staff the parishes along the Fishery Coast. With a Portuguese fleet serving at his orders the following year, the bishop coordinated the invasion of the Ilha dos Reis and demanded that the Jesuits submit to his authority. The men of the Society immediately presented their grievances in Goa and Madrid, but the response was slow in coming and even slower in being implemented. In the meantime, the Jesuits could have bided their time, waiting for the old bishop to die and the storm to pass. But Provincial Alberto Laerzio was given to bold moves. In 1608 he chose the nuclear option: Laerzio renounced the Society's claims to the Fishery Coast churches, ceding their care to the bishop in perpetuity.

Laerzio's gesture was fully in character. In other words, it was full of bluster and potentially ruinous for the Jesuits. Thankfully for them, the crown was not interested in Laerzio's wounded pride. Madrid wanted the Jesuits on the Fishery Coast and so decided to override the bishop's decision. In 1614 King Philip II (of Portugal, Philip III of Spain) commanded Frei André de Santa Maria to return the churches, but the bishop died before the order reached India. The throne therefore had to repeat this command in 1619 to Frei Sebastião de São Pedro, the new bishop of Cochin. Word of this second order had not yet reached the Fishery Coast by the time Palmeiro arrived there in 1620. The Visitor surely knew what was coming from Madrid, so he tried to be as diplomatic as possible when he disembarked at Tuticorin. He took his role as peacemaker seriously and sought to calm the nerves that had frayed during the years of conflict. Palmeiro sought out the company of the Franciscans, accepting their offer of lodging during his brief stay in the city. In exchange for their hospitality, the friars requested that he preach for them. (Palmeiro's reputation in the pulpit had evidently preceded him to this far corner of South Asia.) The Visitor gave a sermon on March 25, the Feast of the Annunciation. But the good news that he announced was not the final pacification of the Fishery Coast Christians under the aegis of the Society of Jesus. That would have to wait until he came back to Tuticorin on a future trip.[4]

Palmeiro set sail again on the day after giving his sermon, this time across the Gulf of Mannar toward Sri Lanka. The intersection of winds and currents at the southernmost tip of India and the constant proximity of shoals make for treacherous navigation. Palmeiro sailed in a *champana* (in his words, "a most unstable kind of vessel") into a stiff wind that produced waves greater than any he had seen during his voyage from Europe to Asia.[5] Winds of this type are common in the Gulf of Mannar as winter turns into spring, and Portuguese sailors, taking their cue from the wisdom of the South Asian mariners, typically avoided the region at the time of the Southwest monsoon, that is, in the late spring, summer, and early autumn months.[6] According to Palmeiro, the crew of his boat wanted to cut across the gulf at its nearest point and then beat southward along the coast. "But since this way of navigating makes Colombo much farther," he wrote, "I turned myself into a pilot in seas that I did not know but about which I was informed, and with the help of a compass which I happened to bring along, I took us on a route that carried us to Colombo in four days." Obviously pleased with his audacity, the Visitor also noted that his ship reached the principal Portuguese colony on Sri Lanka ten days before another ship that had left Tuticorin on the same day but had chosen the safer route.[7]

The first stop on Palmeiro's inspection tour was the College of Colombo. This establishment was home to nine priests and a coadjutor, making it one of the larger communities of Jesuits in the province. The college's rector was Antonio Rubino, the reluctant administrator who yearned for missionary glory.[8] Although it was much smaller than its counterpart at Cochin, the College of Colombo also had both educational and pastoral functions. One of Palmeiro's main tasks at the college was to inspect its physical structures and establish plans for their expansion. His impression was that the college was far too small to accommodate its classes in reading, writing, and Latin grammar while maintaining its role as one of Colombo's main devotional centers. The annual letter for the year of Palmeiro's visit mentions frequent sermons given at the college church, including one by the Visitor himself. (He recorded that he preached in all the colleges he visited, "which the rectors obliged me to do."[9]) There were also weekly sessions of penitential discipline on Fridays, and during Lent (while the Visitor was in Colombo) the schoolchildren were led around the city's streets to its different churches by a teacher carrying luminaries and a cross while singing the litanies.[10]

Palmeiro's most pressing order of business in Colombo was to preside over the resolution of yet another conflict with the bishop of Cochin. Seeing that affairs in the Fishery Coast were not turning out in his favor, Frei Sebastião de São Pedro looked elsewhere to check the privileges of the religious orders in his diocese. The Jesuits and the Franciscans held titles to numerous villages in western Sri Lanka. Rents from these properties paid for the support of the College of Colombo as well as for Jesuits and friars who worked in the area. In the summer of 1619 the bishop seized the properties that belonged to the religious orders within his jurisdiction. There was nothing like a threat to their sources of income to force the Jesuits and the friars to stop their quarrelling and make common cause.

Rubino had been among the first to alert his superiors in Cochin to the bishop's move. He was the one who brought the news to the provincial headquarters, which led to the summoning of the "little congregation" against Palmeiro's wishes. Although the bishop's move spelled disaster for the Jesuits—it stripped them of most of their revenue in Sri Lanka—Rubino seemed to enjoy the excitement. In the calamity, his dream for virtuous suffering was realized. Writing to the superior general in the autumn of 1619, Rubino reiterated his frustrations about not being in a mission but asserted that the harassment of the bishop at Colombo was nearly equivalent to persecution by non-Christians. In the storm, Rubino found the college "a very good mission because presently we have no lack of poverty nor any small amount of suffering."[11] There was no doubting the ill will of the bishop of Cochin. But where the 1620 annual letter spoke diplomatically of the problems caused by "some people with little love for the Society," Rubino did not mince words: "This bishop bears a great hatred for us, and has said on occasion that he will destroy the *Companhia* and turn everything into dust and ashes."[12] But São Pedro's move was as unsuccessful as his predecessor's earlier strategy on the Fishery Coast. The difference between the two bishops' actions was that the response from Goa was much swifter in the Sri Lankan case: As soon as the news reached Fernão de Albuquerque (1540–1623, r. 1619–1622), the new governor of the Estado da Índia, he overturned São Pedro's decision.[13]

In order to make the restitution of the Jesuits' villages complete, the Visitor had to deliver the patents that he had received from Goa to the supreme Portuguese commander in Sri Lanka. This individual was none other than Constantino de Sá de Noronha (1586–1630), the *capitão geral*, a major protagonist in the wars that the Portuguese and their Sinhalese allies waged against the northern kingdom of Jaffna and the interior kingdom of Kandy. In 1620 he was in the third year of his long, two-phase captaincy (1618–1620, and 1623–1630) and had already acquired the legendary status that both Portuguese and Sri Lankan chroniclers would celebrate for decades.[14] The middle of the seventeenth century witnessed the climax of Portuguese power on the island, and much of it was due to Sá's acumen as a military commander. Upon learning of Palmeiro's arrival, Sá left his headquarters at Malwana, twelve miles to the east of Colombo, to receive him. The encounter between the two went as planned, the Visitor reported, "and God saw fit that the affair was concluded in less than three days with strange applause from the whole city." He was right to remark on the curious expression of joy, since the affair was a dispute between ecclesiastical rivals. "It seems to me that there was no citizen or Portuguese who did not come to congratulate us on the outcome," he wrote, "which we owe mainly to the general Constantino de Sá de Noronha."[15]

Gathering clouds of war cast shadows over the celebrations at Colombo. As a result, Dom Constantino could not linger with Palmeiro but had to turn his attentions toward a revolt in the kingdom of Jaffna.[16] For Palmeiro, the captain's battles were part of a virtuous struggle against idolatry. The Visitor was content to see his men assisting the Luso-Sinhalese armies, displaying their spiritual valor alongside men who demonstrated its martial counterpart. Palmeiro's travelogue contains excerpts from letters he received from António Soeiro (1576–1638), a priest who traveled with the troops sent to join the fight. Under the command of Luís Teixeira de Macedo this detachment was sent to relieve the beleaguered Filipe de Oliveira (d. 1627). According to Soeiro, Teixeira's troops proceeded north with such speed that they "more flew than walked," fighting their way into Jaffna and there "committing cruelties such as cutting children in half and the breasts off women." Palmeiro offers no comment about Soeiro's account of these episodes of brutality. Indeed, his passive tone suggests approval of the tactic, which successfully dissuaded others from taking the field until the reinforcements from Colombo joined up with Oliveira's army. The Visitor's own words barely conceal his glee at the news of a surprise attack on Jaffna, leading to the capture of King Sankili II (d. 1620) and his Brahman courtiers.[17]

Palmeiro also greeted the news of Portuguese military successes in northern Sri Lanka warmly, since the next stops on his inspection tour were in that region. After concluding his inspection of the College of Colombo, he set out for the Society's villages and residences along the island's west coast. In the district of the Seven Korales, there were six residences staffed by one priest each. Palmeiro set out on foot to cover the fifty miles to Chilaw, then proceeded a short distance inland to Munneswaram. This village was the site of an important Hindu temple that had been razed by Portuguese troops in the 1590s and its lands given to the Society. Palmeiro summoned the priests for a meeting there, since it seemed the most central point in the region, and interviewed them together and separately.[18] He also visited the local Christian communities, where he was received with celebrations. The Christians set out vases filled with flowers in the streets and even "laid down great bolts of cloth on the ground to be walked upon, which is what they do to receive the priests, and even their princes; although this special gesture was only done for me in the places where our villages are."[19]

It was during his overland journey along the coast of western Sri Lanka that Palmeiro first paused to appreciate his exotic surroundings. The press of affairs in Goa, Cochin, and Colombo weighed too heavily on the Visitor's mind for him to contemplate the vast differences between the flora and fauna of Portugal and South Asia. Indeed, apart from the brief mention of his quest to find a "porcupine stone" (porcupine bezoar) in Cochin for his superiors in Rome, Palmeiro made no mention of the Asian *naturalia* that so captivated his learned peers in Europe.[20] Far from the bickering of his subordinates or the anxieties brought on by disputes with bishops, Palmeiro found calm and opened his eyes to the nature around him. In the Sri Lankan wilderness, he discovered serendipity:

Over this whole route, most of which is thick forest and some parts very cool, with lemon trees and other local fruits, I saw very abundant packs of does and deer, in other places herds of wild buffaloes and some elephants. In Kalpitiya, which is an island of ours on which some amber washes up during storms, I found teeth from a dugong *(peixe-mulher),* which lives in a lake many leagues long that the sea forms there. This animal is called a "woman-fish" because it has breasts upon which it suckles its young that are very similar to those that women have. In this lake there are infinite fish, and very good ones. The local people bring us many bunches of them both in the morning and the afternoon out of the obligation, since we are their lords.[21]

After crossing the "lake" at Kalpitiya, later renamed Dutch Bay, the Visitor headed north for sixty miles toward the island of Mannar. He remarked on the flatness of the landscape and the scarcity of water, so dire "that our bearers drank mud in the puddles where the elephants drank and washed themselves." Mannar itself, he reported, had once been a rich city owing to the pearl fisheries nearby, but the oyster beds had disappeared. By 1620 it was reduced to misery. To be sure, some things were abundant at Mannar: according to Palmeiro, one pataca bought "one hundred and thirty-two partridges, with red feet and beaks like those in Portugal, although smaller, but in the taste and shape of the breast just like those in Portugal." Goats, calves, and fish could also be had at bargain prices, but that mattered little in light of the city's desolation. "All of the churches on this island, except for the one in the fortress," he wrote, "once belonged to the *Companhia,* and today they are as lost as the others in these parts."[22]

At this port city the Visitor learned more about the movements of the Portuguese troops on Sri Lanka. Knowing that the victorious army was heading southward again from Jaffna, he summoned António Soeiro to meet with him at Mannar. Palmeiro was moved when he learned that the priest had traveled barefoot over many miles for the encounter. "With my own hands, I helped to wash his feet," Palmeiro wrote, "which seemed to me very noble with their calluses and rough treatment by the roads." The Visitor's travelogue contains effusive praise for Soeiro and his military ministry. It appears that the Jesuit was a talisman for the army: Such was the soldiers' love for Soeiro, Palmeiro claimed, "that they are convinced that they are safe in his presence." Captain Teixeira averred that he would only permit Soeiro to leave his company as a corpse for burial.[23] As a result, Soeiro could not tarry

at Mannar—while the two men spoke, Teixeira was waiting with his whole
army six leagues away. The soldiers were on their way back to the Seven Korales to rejoin Dom Constantino's army and capture a pair of rebels. On two
occasions in his text Palmeiro invokes the bravery of the Sinhalese troops allied to the Portuguese. He also dilates approvingly on gory details, such as
the severed heads that littered the battlefields across southern and central Sri
Lanka.[24] The feats of arms clearly piqued his interest; he would have occasion
to get more battle reports later in his journey.

In late May 1620 Palmeiro sailed across the Gulf of Mannar and through the
Palk Strait to Nagapattinam. By sailing from Sri Lanka to the Coromandel
Coast, he headed into danger. Here the Visitor was no longer under the um-
brella of Portuguese power but rather in a region where Northern European
rivals openly contested the Iberians. In fact his passage northward along the
Coromandel Coast was delayed out of fear for the Dutch vessels in nearby
waters that had recently taken several Portuguese prizes.[25]

Palmeiro arrived at Nagapattinam in the first days of June and lodged at
the Society's college, home to three priests and two brothers. The small size of
this residence reflected the limited nature of Portuguese interests in the region. Their thin presence on the Coromandel Coast was why competing colonial interests in India had established their first bases there. Representatives of
the Dutch East India Company forged an alliance with indigenous lords that
permitted them to put down roots at Pulicat, almost two hundred miles to the
north, and Danish traders were negotiating for a similar arrangement at Tranquebar (Tharangambadi), only eighteen miles north of Nagapattinam.[26] Just a
month after Palmeiro headed onward, the Jesuit António Dias (1573–1625) had
to force the Danes out of the Society's church at Tranquebar through an appeal
to the local lord, Raghunatha (r. 1600–1634), nayaka of Tanjore (Thanjavur).[27]
On the Coromandel Coast, the presence of Protestant rivals occasioned atypical cooperation between the religious orders. The Visitor mentioned that his
arrival coincided with the octave of the Feast of the Visitation (May 31), during which Franciscan friars joined the Jesuits to put on "large fireworks displays every night in their and our houses." On the last day of the feast a procession was held and, of course, Palmeiro was asked to preach.[28]

The Visitor traveled onward only when a Portuguese fleet arrived on the
Coromandel Coast. The fleet was commanded by the captain of São Tomé de

Meliapor, 170 miles to the north of Nagapattinam. São Tomé was the site of a Portuguese colony that grew up around the pilgrimage sites linked to the Apostle Thomas. The discovery of relics by Portuguese explorers in the early sixteenth century had spurred the settlement's growth, but it never became the major center of trade on the Bay of Bengal that its promoters in the court and church had expected. Instead, São Tomé survived through the good graces of nearby indigenous lords, functioning as a retirement community for the Estado da Índia's soldiers.[29] Jesuits had been at São Tomé since the time of Francis Xavier, and in 1620 there were four priests and three brothers in the city.[30] Thankfully for Palmeiro, the climate between the secular clergy and the religious orders was less stormy than it was in Sri Lanka or in Cochin. In contrast to his peers in Goa and Cochin, the bishop of São Tomé was cordial toward the Jesuits. Luís de Brito e Menezes (ca. 1570–1629), an Augustinian who had been elevated to the city's bishopric in 1615, was an acquaintance of Palmeiro's from Coimbra. He received the Visitor cordially, granting Palmeiro permission to say mass as often as he pleased at the altar where St. Thomas's relics were kept.[31]

The Visitor's stay in São Tomé was the spiritual high point of his journey through the Province of Malabar. For a man who attached great importance to the presence of the holy and to the validity of relics, the city's shrines were loaded with significance. According to traditions (some of them disputed, but not by the Visitor), Thomas, the same man who had placed his fingers in Christ's side, had lived in this corner of India and performed many miracles there. Thomas had left family, friends, and country to travel to the end of the earth, where he suffered a grisly martyrdom—a fate that, Palmeiro confessed upon his deathbed, he had always desired for himself.[32] So it was with reverence that the Visitor described how the bishop gave him a privileged viewing of the relics: "the lance with which they martyred the saint, and some of his bones; and a vase filled with earth mixed with blood which he spilled."[33] Palmeiro also visited the two "mounts" six miles outside of São Tomé: the greater hilltop shrine, where an ancient cross that miraculously bled on the feast of Our Lady of the Expectation (December 18) was found; and the "Little Mount," where the apostle was known to have meditated. He wrote:

On the Little Mount, which belongs to our *Companhia* and where we have some well-appointed houses, there is a cave to which the Holy Apostle used to retire and pray. This cave is the most devout and secluded place

that I have seen until now, all covered over by a rock and far more impressive than that of Nossa Senhora da Lapa in the Kingdom of Portugal.[34] It
has an altar upon which mass is said, and I said it there, as well as on the
Great Mount. I greatly desired to be able to retire here for eight days and
do the Spiritual Exercises, but this place is all in an uproar and revolt because there is no king to rule over it, so we came out to these two mounts
and stayed for only two days, and we could not do them without armed
men to defend us.[35]

Palmeiro evidently found it hard to reconcile the regular routines of Jesuit
spirituality, most of them based on the communal life of the Society's colleges, with his obligation to continue his inspection tour. His personal devotions had been disturbed by his travels, and his pious desires were often
blocked by circumstances, leaving him to contemplate at several reprises the
virtue of obedience that had impelled him on his journey across Asia.

São Tomé de Meliapor was the farthest point that Palmeiro would reach
on his round trip from Cochin. But after more than four months of travel, he
had had enough of his visitation. He wrote that he preached on the feast of
Ignatius Loyola (July 31) at São Tomé and wanted to leave the city "with my
face already turned towards Cochin." The presence of Danish ships anchored
off the nearby coast and the contrary winds of the summer monsoon gave
him pause. He nevertheless forged ahead, writing to António Dias to plan a
rendezvous at Triminavas (Thirumullaivasal), a town fifteen miles from the
Danish menace. Palmeiro arrived at the appointed spot and inspected the
humble church that Dias had built. The Visitor was impressed by the two
hundred Christians who had joined his flock that year, a number Palmeiro
deemed to be "a lot in this land."[36] The pair traveled by sea to Tranquebar
and then by land to Nagapattinam, from where Palmeiro and a Parava crew
sailed to Tuticorin.

The voyage toward the Fishery Coast was the most perilous part of Palmeiro's 1620 journey. Contrary winds forced the Visitor's ship to sail close to
the coast until it reached Adam's Bridge near Rameswaram. The travelers
took precautions against the Marava people who lived in the coastal region
and who were known for raiding parties that preyed on the Portuguese and
the Paravas.[37] The Parava crew of Palmeiro's ship was terrified and preferred
to backtrack up the coast and sail across to Jaffna on Sri Lanka instead of
heading directly through the Palk Strait to Tuticorin. The Visitor claimed

that only the grace of God ensured their safe passage against the monsoon winds: Not only were there towering waves, but there was a "wind so strong that it ripped the sail, the boat straining hard and leaking through."[38] After a brief stopover in Jaffna, where he was received by the Portuguese commander Filipe de Oliveira at the newly built fort and taken on a tour of the battle-fields of the recent rebellion, the Visitor set sail toward Mannar with four small vessels. Despite contrary winds, crashing waves, and protests from the sailors, he insisted on making the fifty-mile trip, but the fleet was forced to seek a haven as the ships drew close to the shoals near their destination. Not wanting to wait out the storms and constrained by the crews of the other three ships to lead them through the channels (whose configuration Palmeiro surely did not know), the Visitor took charge:

> It was so risky that we gave ourselves up for lost. The skiff was more than half full of water, so we had to bail it out with pots and whatever was at hand. Even the sailors who knew that route started fainting, and those who knew how to swim got ready to do so. The other skiffs that followed us could see our danger, and the fury of the sea had forced them to shore, but to me it seemed that we would incur greater risk in landing than in sailing ahead. And so standing with a staff in my hand at the end of tar-paulins which covered the deck, in part encouraging them with my voice and in part threatening them with my staff, I rallied the sailors to ready the oars and turn the stem into the waves. These broke with such fury and invaded the skiff in such a way that I got soaked from head to toe, even though I was standing with a waxed blanket wrapped around me. In truth, had I known half of how bad it would be, I would not have got into such danger, because the skiff we traveled in was not longer than one of those little boats in Lisbon harbor and less tall. The waves in those shoals, along with the winds that blew, were a fury from Hell and so risky to cross that a great number of ships are lost every year. I am convinced that we were saved in that labor by Our Holy Virgin, whose litanies we had prayed be-fore embarking.[39]

Driven by Palmeiro, the crew navigated the shoals successfully and made it across to the southern coast of India, but they had not escaped all danger. The winds left them no option but to land in hostile territory north of Tuti-corin, where they were exposed to attack by Marava bandits. To make mat-ters worse, the Visitor's vessel had been separated from the other ships in his party. When he disembarked, he ordered the men to ready the rifles they had brought and to prepare some grenades in case of an encounter.[40] If there was to be any fighting on their overland trek to Tuticorin, Palmeiro wrote, "I and my companions would surely be the most important actors." But, in his words, "God seemed to have wished to blind our enemies and deliver us"— although it appears that the real reason for their surviving unscathed lay in the fact that, just two days before the group's arrival, Marava marauders had seized some larger ships.[41] There was no peace even when Palmeiro arrived at Tuticorin on October 1. There he found conflicts raging between the Paravas and the priests sent by the bishop of Cochin, so he planned a short stay in *Pescaria*. The Franciscans welcomed him once again, and invited him to preach in their church on the Feast of St. Francis, October 4.

Despite his fatigue after seven months of travel, Palmeiro felt obliged to inspect Roberto Nobili's mission. He therefore turned northward and traversed the eighty miles between Tuticorin and Madurai with an unnamed companion. "In many places on this journey I was amazed by the charity shown to travelers," Palmeiro wrote, "because we frequently found stalls where cool water was given to travelers for free, and in one place they added hot water for those who wanted to drink or wash themselves." At other stops along his route he was offered cooked rice, leading him to remark that "such hospitality is not seen among the Portuguese, although they know better how much such actions would earn them grace and glory from God." It appears that the Visitor was following along the main pilgrimage route linking Madurai, via Ramnad, to the major Hindu shrine at Rameswaram, an island that forms part of Adam's Bridge.[42] Palmeiro was shown the generosity with food and water intended for Hindu pilgrims, but he found other problems when it came to finding accommodation at night. The only places that offered a welcome were the area's temple complexes, which were accustomed to the passage of strangers. Palmeiro chafed at such Spartan accommodation, which he declared was borne of an unfounded prejudice:

> Along this route we always lodged in the porches of the temples. In no way would they let us retire into any house because we were taken to be of low caste, so low that with our mere presence in their house they would be brought down, or as they say, polluted. Those who hold this opinion are miserable little blacks who live in shacks made of clay and covered with palm leaves, worse than the local pigsties. Moreover, they are nearly dead

of hunger and go about naked, not only because of the heat of the land but because they have nothing to wear. Taking us for dirty and lowly, they thus despise us, and there are neither reasons nor arguments to drive this from their heads. This is one of the greatest impediments that these people have to receiving our holy law, since they think that in dealing with us and communicating with us, they lose their caste and are dishonored. God open their eyes, so blind do they go about, and arouse their natural reason, if ever so slightly, which would be enough to make them aware of the nonsense with which the Devil has ensnared them![43]

The temple complexes of Southern India provided Palmeiro with a fine vantage point for observing Hindu religious practices. Recall that his approval of Nobili's methods was based on a specific vision of indigenous society and religion that Palmeiro intended to verify from his own perspective. Crucial to any such evaluation would be the firsthand observation of not only the Madurai mission but also of common Hindu practices elsewhere in South India:

> Since we retired in these porches which are located next to the doors leading to the temple courtyards, we naturally became aware of some of the things that went on inside the temples. As night fell, we heard various trumpets and flutes that they played very well, although not in harmony. We also heard the dancers and singers. These are ordinarily girls and women of evil customs who typically go about dancing and singing with great nimbleness, according to the local people, and call out the most obscene things. The women also attend the meals of their god, which consists of a bit of rice that the Brahmans cook for them.[44] Afterwards, they leave the god to rest for about an hour. Then they return with the same instruments and music to arouse the god and invite it to come out into the streets and homes in search of occasions for lasciviousness. With this noise and celebration they take the god in a type of procession about the perimeter of the temple. In one of these parades I saw a hunchback dressed in women's clothes singing very handsomely, albeit in their style, with as much range of voice as the women that I saw in Portugal. . . . One cannot believe the sumptuousness and magnificence of some of the façades and frontispieces of the temples of these gods; I never saw any church or sanctuary of ours in Portugal which was their equal. A great hurt it caused in our breasts to see more honor given to the Devil and to the obscenity of his servants, than to the true Lord God of all.[45]

Naturally Palmeiro's reactions to Hindu rituals were negative. What is interesting here is his tone of frustration, a counterpoint to the usual missionary bravado. Reflecting on the temple dancers and the musicians, he wrote of the failed attempts made by his traveling companion to deploy rhetoric in the service of conversion, invoking the futile attempt by Saint Paul to convert King Agrippa: "A few times we tried to do it but they always replied in their manner, *in modico persuades christianos nos esse.*"[46]

The Visitor's travelogue contains only a few lines about his stay in Madurai. As noted earlier, he had much to say about Nobili's mission in his other letters to Rome. He therefore did not feel obliged to offer more than brief remarks about the massive temples at Madurai and the curious layout of Nobili's church. Palmeiro is similarly laconic about the other Jesuit church in the city. The tone of his comments on Madurai suggests that his travelogue was intended for circulation beyond the Society's Roman curia. So he avoided making comments that might reveal a personal judgment on the Madurai mission. After all, it had only been a year and a half since the Goa Conference, and the church authorities in Europe had not yet reached a final decision on the Nobili affair. Anything that could be construed as contrary to the eventual ruling from the Inquisition and the Papal Curia was best eschewed to prevent the Visitor's words from being used against the Society of Jesus.

Once he had seen Madurai, Palmeiro could return to Cochin satisfied that he had faithfully discharged his orders. He made a point of not going back to the Fishery Coast, trying to stay away from further involvement in the region's conflicts. The Visitor instead traveled south with his unidentified escort over the 150 miles toward Cape Comorin, a trek that involved "much expense and labor on my part, traveling along the base of some most high mountains for six days without stopping." During this voyage, Palmeiro passed by several towns which he described as "walled marvels", with mighty towers of finely hewn white stone.[47]

In this extreme southern corner of India, Palmeiro was impressed by the seemingly ubiquitous pockets of Christians, people who had migrated inland from the coast in the decades since the conversion of their clans and lived scattered about the region's villages. The Visitor recounted how their coreligionists discovered him and his companion as they prepared to spend yet another night on a temple porch. The pair was swiftly ushered to a Christian home, where they were given cots to sleep on. In another village the indigenous Christians rushed to greet him and his companion as soon as they heard the news of their arrival, "throwing themselves at our feet, and lying down completely on the ground, and going away most happy after being allowed to kiss our robes." Palmeiro responded to their affection by distributing alms and tried to persuade them to return to the coast, where they might receive the sacraments more regularly. "They answered me with tears in their eyes," the Visitor reported on the basis of his companion's translation, "that without the priests back on the coast, they would not go back."[48] Of course, the priests they meant were the Jesuits who had been expelled by order of the bishop of Cochin.

Despite the kindness of the local Christians, the rigors of the journey began to take their toll on the Visitor as he drew nearer to his destination. He complained about the continual impositions from the tax collectors, the *juncaneiros,* whom he encountered along his route to the southernmost tip of the Indian subcontinent.[49] "I was so tired from my trip and wearied by these men," Palmeiro wrote, "that when I came in sight of a cross at Cape Comorin, knowing that I had come to a Christian land, the pleasure and satisfaction of my soul were so great that I thought I had entered into glory."[50]

The final leg of his journey followed the coastline north through Travancore. Here the great numbers of local Christians enabled him to go from town to town with a larger escort, "the principal men of each place accompanying us until we arrived at the next." After covering the 90 miles from Cape Comorin to Quilon, he inspected the work of that city's three Jesuit priests and one brother "with the greatest possible hurry." Palmeiro completed the final 80 miles of his nearly 1,900-mile round trip to Cochin on the first of November 1620. In that autumn season Palmeiro made a gesture of thanksgiving to the Almighty as he closed the long account to the Jesuits' Roman curia recounting his travels:

> I have related . . . some aspects of my journey, and if I learn that God will have been served by it even slightly, I will give Him infinite praise, considering all the time that I took for these labors well spent. But only He knows this, and to Him I offer what I did, and I trust that in His infinite mercy He will give me the spirit and the mettle to suffer greatly for His love, employing the little that I can and that I am worth in His service.[51]

———————

The Visitor had just over a month between his arrival at Cochin and the departure of that year's fleet for Goa. By mid-December, he would need to have a report on his journey complete so it could be consigned to the Portugal-bound Indiamen. But his job as inspector was not finished when he closed the account of his travels; he also had to make decisions about how to correct the abuses he had detected at the colleges and missions in the province. These decisions were formalized in a series of rules that Palmeiro drew up and forwarded to Rome for approval. Despite the expansive powers that the superior general had accorded him, Palmeiro needed Rome's approval before his commands would be integrated into the province's official rules. Thankfully for him, Rome does not appear to have second-guessed any of the decisions he made during his years in Asia.

The Visitor sent formal reports to Rome to ensure that the Society's superior general would fully understand the reasons for his decisions. These documents appear to have been lost, but a letter to Nuno Mascarenhas, the Portuguese Assistant, has survived. Mascarenhas was the executive secretary for all of the Portuguese provinces; he had Vitelleschi's ear. It was also important that Mascarenhas and Palmeiro had been rector and consultor at Coimbra and were friends. The bond between the Visitor and the Assistant was crucially important in 1620. Alberto Laerzio was on his way to Rome and could be counted upon to present a different version of the affairs of the Province of Malabar to the superior general. After all, Laerzio had been an important figure in the province since its inception in 1602, and he seemed to enjoy respect at the Society's curia. But in Palmeiro's view, he was responsible, at least indirectly, for many of the problems detected during the inspection of the province. The Visitor's letter to Mascarenhas was therefore strictly confidential; it offered a candid assessment in a tone of fraternal exhortation.

The Visitor's diagnosis indicated that the worst problem was a lack of rigor among his subordinates, especially those men in positions of authority. Even in his day, it was a cliché that the heat of the tropics eroded European forms of discipline, and Palmeiro was quick to cite this reason for the *largueza* of his subordinates. In his view, they showed very little application to their tasks: "They are very given to resting and fleeing from any occasion for bother." Palmeiro liked to make an example of himself, even at his (relatively) advanced age, and his eight-and-a-half-month trek and heroic gestures around South India were calculated to spark imitators. Yet, he conceded, "owing to its ordinary heat, this land of India relaxes our nature and weakens it, making it less apt for work, whence we should not be surprised that there is less diligence."[52] Perhaps it was at the suggestion of his acclimated men that he had written to the superior general before going on his journey to request that "certain liberalities" not permitted in Europe should be permitted in India, but the sight of such license being taken without prior approval from Rome made him change his mind.[53]

The first victim of the torpor that he detected was discipline, which was corrupted throughout the province. If there was one man who had no patience for the slackening of rules, it was Palmeiro. He was keen to ensure that orders from Rome were observed to the letter and that the Society's rules were followed punctiliously, especially those pertaining to religious decorum. In keeping with the broad process of the reformation of Catholic life under way in contemporary Europe as well as with his notions of the dignity of the clerical estate, Palmeiro insisted on the firm separation between the religious and secular spheres. His rules for the Province of Malabar include several instances where he insisted upon a greater degree of seclusion for his men. For example, Palmeiro forbade Jesuits to take musicians to the gardens of the province's rural estates and likewise prohibited them from having trays of food brought by laymen for picnics. He also banned bathing in the water tanks at the colleges of Cochin and Colombo without special permission, to be granted only in exceptional circumstances. By no means, the Visitor commanded, were two Jesuits to wash in the same tank, and no one was to bring a servant to wash him.[54]

For Palmeiro, modesty was second only to obedience. His rules about bathing sought to ensure that the Jesuits washed by themselves or in the presence of a coadjutor who kept a lookout for prying eyes, and that they bathed only in places "where no women will pass along normal paths." More broadly, Palmeiro insisted on the firm separation of the spaces in Jesuit compounds into which layfolk were admitted. As far as the Visitor was concerned—calling attention to manifest abuses in Quilon and Cochin—the laity were to be permitted no farther than the naves of the Jesuits' churches. In keeping with this spirit, Palmeiro ordered that "married men should by no means be allowed to retire with their wives" into the cave of St. Thomas at the Little Mount in São Tomé de Meliapor. Another common practice he found objectionable on grounds of modesty was the giving of gifts, especially of Madras gingham cloth *(gingões)*, to visiting superiors at the College of São Tomé, which he prohibited except in rare circumstances. And the use of silk by any of the Society's servants was suppressed by Palmeiro, "because that type of clothing does not benefit people who serve religious who profess poverty."[55]

After compiling the rules that he had written for the province and preparing his reports for the curia, Palmeiro focused his attention on the parts of the Province of Malabar that he had not inspected in person. These were mission districts situated far beyond São Tomé, the most distant point that the Visitor had reached on his tour, namely, the Moluccas, Bengal, and Malacca. Only after he had learned about Jesuit life in those areas could he consider his inspection complete. Ideally, he would have sailed to these regions to visit his men, but his travels had left him with little appetite for such an endeavor. Palmeiro therefore appointed a set of deputies to inspect them in his stead.

The prospect of conducting an inspection of the farthest of these districts, the Moluccas, never crossed Palmeiro's mind. It was simply too far away: a round trip to this small group of residences would have taken him away from Cochin for almost a year. The closest Jesuit house in the Moluccas was at Makassar on the island of Sulawesi, 4,400 miles from Cochin along the standard sailing routes. The main residence on the island of Ternate was another thousand miles to the northeast by ship. The eight priests and two brothers in this "Moluccas Mission" stood at the front lines of the battles between the Dutch East India Company and the Spanish of the Philippines, under whose protection the Jesuits lived.

Jesuits had worked in insular Southeast Asia since the time of Francis Xavier in the 1540s. Portuguese traders seeking nutmeg, cloves, and mace had taken the early Jesuits to the area, but the Portuguese presence in these faraway waters had waned over the decades. By the early 1620s the distant outposts of the Portuguese Assistancy in the Moluccas were maintained primarily to defend the enterprise that their saintly ancestor had begun.[56] It was evident that there was little fruit to be garnered: Not only had the contemporary expansion of Islam in the area run parallel to (and faster than) the evangelization efforts of the Christian missionaries, but the feuds between rival European powers and their local allies did little to facilitate the Jesuits' goals. Moreover, most of the islands' peoples remained beyond the reach of would-be colonizers from Manila or Malacca. Without the constant presence of European Catholics, the Jesuits claimed, there was no hope for sustaining Christian communities in the area.[57]

In 1620 the Visitor appointed a professed Jesuit from the College of Cochin, Manuel de Azevedo (1581–1650), to inspect the Makassar and Ternate residences. The choice of this particular priest was not received well by Provincial Gaspar Fernandes, who wrote to the superior general that Azevedo was "somewhat stiff, and given to harsh words, and of less experience than is necessary in those parts."[58] Palmeiro cared not a whit for Fernandes's objections; the Visitor wanted discipline in the Province of Malabar, and Azevedo would not be shy about denouncing laxness.

Azevedo's report revealed that the residences in the Moluccas were in scandalous condition. Leaving aside the specter of illness and death that haunted the mission, he reported finding severe discipline problems in many of the missionaries. Azevedo dwelled at length on the behavior of Lorenzo Masonio (or Mazzoni, 1556–1631) and Andrea Simi (1580–1634). He accused this pair of excess—in particular, of being profligate with the mission's funds and enjoying too much intimacy with their servants. As Palmeiro's deputy, Azevedo came armed with a wide range of powers. He issued prohibitions against engaging in trade, a recourse that the Jesuits in the Moluccas had long relied upon to substitute other forms of income. Azevedo also banned displays of largesse to the mission's servants, specifically the purchase of expensive clothes and the paying of dowries. Moreover, he prohibited the frequent festivities held at the Jesuits' quarters, events that he had learned were nothing but drunken dancing parties.

Azevedo heard from the Spanish officials as well as from the Franciscan friars that the Society's reputation was in question. His measures were thus taken in order to defend "the credit and honor of the *Companhia*," he insisted. What else could he do besides expel the troublesome priests from the mission? In the end he decided to banish three of them from the Moluccas. Two of the priests, Lorenzo Masonio and Jorge da Fonseca (d. 1627), were, Azevedo claimed, too old to be of use to the mission and served "only to annoy and alienate people." The third, João Baptista (1557–ca. 1630), showed signs "not only of old age, but also of insanity." As for Andrea Simi, the proper punishment was to send him on a mission to Manado at the northeastern tip of Sulawesi without his beloved servants. Surveying this calamitous panorama from the mountain of debts incurred in Ternate, Azevedo closed his report to Palmeiro on a despondent note: "This is the sanctity and fruit produced in *Maluco*. It is a disgrace for the Society. I do not exaggerate, what I say is pure truth. They had no manner of religious life here, and others could not recognize us as members of the Society because of these affairs. It was as if our own men had forgotten their ministries."[59]

Palmeiro received this report upon his return to Cochin in November 1620. After his tour the Visitor had no patience for the type of laxness of which Azevedo spoke. It is therefore curious that Palmeiro reacted with ambivalence rather than commendation. The Visitor did not approve of all of his deputy's punishments, and even abrogated some of them. For example, he allowed Lorenzo Masonio to remain in Manila, where he had gone from Ternate, instead of obliging him to travel to Cochin. Palmeiro would even permit Masonio to return to the Moluccas as his deputy in 1624 (although Masonio did not actually go).[60] The Visitor also conceded that elderly João Baptista should spend his last years in Malacca, and received Jorge de Fonseca warmly upon his return to Cochin.

What accounted for Palmeiro's indulgence toward these dissolute priests? Their age, in all likelihood. The Visitor was not shy of punishing his younger subordinates or men who had spent their lives in the comfort of the Society's colleges. But the forty-one year-old Azevedo had moved vigorously against a trio of veterans: Masonio was sixty-three and Baptista was sixty-two; Fonseca's age was not recorded at the time of his death, but it was known that he had spent twenty-five years in the Moluccas. Men such as these, who had long worked in dangerous missions at the ends of the earth, deserved respect in their twilight years. Palmeiro, for one, found Fonseca to be a "a priest of much virtue and great example" and treated him well upon his return to India. The Visitor went so far as to send Fonseca to Goa, where he would be better cared for in his last years.[61]

Less is known about the inspections that Palmeiro commissioned in the other three distant corners of the Province of Malabar. No reports survive to testify to inspections conducted in Burma or at the College of Malacca. To be sure, the "Burmese mission" had been founded by two Jesuits who were taken as captives to the inland city of Ava in 1613. One of the pair, Manuel da Fonseca (d. 1652), was still living there in Palmeiro's day, but his opportunities to proselytize were limited.[62] It is likely that the Visitor sent an inspector to Malacca since the city's college was one of the more richly endowed Jesuit establishments in Asia and home to nine priests and brothers. No report of such a visit has been identified for this study, although it is possible that he asked Diogo Valente, Palmeiro's former Coimbra colleague who had been named bishop of Japan, to inspect the College of Malacca on his way to East Asia in 1619.[63]

It is certain that Palmeiro sent a deputy to Bengal in 1621, although no report of this inspection has survived. This individual was André Machado, one of the professed Jesuits at Cochin who had joined Palmeiro in opposition to the "little congregation." Machado traveled to Hooghly (Hugli), a small colony of Portuguese traders more than 1,500 miles from Cochin.[64] Annual letters from the period give an indication of what Machado's inspection would have involved. The "Bengal Mission" counted seven priests who circulated among five residences. Its headquarters was at Hooghly, where two priests competed with a group of Augustinians for the attentions of Portuguese traders, their Eurasian families, and indigenous converts. A hundred miles south, near the mouth of the Hooghly River at Angelim (Hijili), was the second residence, where a solitary Jesuit ministered to the local Christians as well as those at Banja. A third residence, referred to as Orixa (Orissa) and possibly situated at Pipili a further 200 miles south of Angelim along the coast, was home to another priest, while the fourth house was situated at Sripur, a town 140 miles east of Hooghly in the environs of Dhaka. The fifth residence was at Patna, 350 miles to the northwest by river from the chief residence of the Bengal Mission. In Patna the Jesuits frequented the court of Muqarrab Khan (ca.1556–1646), a Mughal official and former governor (subahdar) of Gujarat who had been baptized at Goa.[65]

The results of Machado's inspection are difficult to know, but it appears that Palmeiro made at least one decision with regard to the Bengal mission as a result of his trip. In 1622 the Visitor elevated the Hooghly residence to the status of a college. Competition with the Augustinians was one reason for this move, but there was also the fact that the Jesuits had built a capacious new church. Floodwaters from the Hooghly River had destroyed their first sanctuary, and the patronage of local Christians enabled them to construct a more dignified residence. The Society's newfound prestige would nevertheless be short lived. A decade later, in 1632, a Mughal army destroyed the city, and its missionaries were carried off as prisoners to the imperial court at Agra in north central India.[66]

———————

The curia of the Society of Jesus was evidently pleased with Palmeiro's work in the Province of Malabar. His handling of the factional strife at the College of Cochin seemed to have been effective and his participation in the Madurai affair judicious. A clear indication of the superior general's approval would be his renewal in the post of visitor.

Already in 1619, before he embarked on his tour, Palmeiro wrote to Rome that an inspector acting alone in one of the Asian provinces could not resolve all the problems facing the Jesuits in India. That is, the challenges needed to be addressed by a visitor with powers over both the Province of Goa and the Province of Malabar. The creation of the Province of Malabar had dismembered the old Province of India unequally, except in geographic terms. The Province of Goa enjoyed far more financial resources than the Province of Malabar, a fact that gave rise to resentment on the part of the Cochin Jesuits. In order to balance out this inequality, there needed to be a visitor responsible for both of them. André Machado, Palmeiro's deputy in Bengal, had written to the curia with precisely this suggestion in 1619, insisting that a joint visitor could apportion the Society's resources in a more equitable manner.[67] The Visitor himself intimated the same in a letter to Assistant Mascarenhas that year. He argued that a "general visitor" would be able to send alms to the cash-strapped Province of Malabar from the richly endowed Province of Goa.[68] To be sure, Palmeiro was not sending a job application to the superior general. In 1619 he was already dreaming of contemplative repose. Rome thought otherwise. Somewhere between India and Europe, the Jesuits' correspondence from Cochin and the superior general's letters from the curia crossed paths. In the patent that Muzio Vitelleschi signed on January 16, 1620, Palmeiro was named visitor of both Indian provinces.[69]

While he waited for a response from Europe, the Visitor turned his attention to the problems facing the College of Cochin. Personnel problems aside, the college was in dire straits. Because it was the headquarters of a sprawling province, its founders should have made sure that it had sufficient revenues to support a large community of priests and brothers devoted to pastoral and educational activities as well as its two dependent residences. Alas, they did not match its elevation in status with a corresponding rise in endowments. It did not take long for Palmeiro to identify the problems on the Jesuits' balance sheet at Cochin. Already in 1619, less than a year after his arrival, he wrote to Rome in exasperation: "This college is going down without help."[70]

What could Palmeiro do? His impulse was to reduce the college's classes, thereby dispensing with some of its staff. But the college had been founded partly by a royal donation, which obliged the Jesuits to offer a full complement of courses. Better still would be to reintegrate the Province of Malabar into the Province of Goa, but this was also impossible. Another option was to look for succor among the laity. Jesuit colleges in early modern Europe, like other religious institutions there and in Europe's overseas colonies, could expect to receive substantial donations or even complete endowments from noble benefactors or wealthy merchants. Donors offered liturgical ornaments or paid for burial space within the churches of religious orders as well as for perpetual masses to be said for the souls of the dead.[71] But in Cochin in the seventeenth century, the downturn in trade reduced the number of possible patrons willing to make such bequests.[72] According to the province's 1621 annual letter, even coming up with the funds to celebrate the beatification of Francis Xavier in May of that year had been a challenge: "This city is broke and its citizens are less well off than they were before, and this comes at a time when our need is greater than ever."[73] Provincial Fernandes was more candid when he wrote to Rome that year: "The city and its residents give nothing, since everything here is just about finished, and it is certain that if God Our Lord does not assist us with His special providence, I do not know where it will all end up."[74]

From the Visitor's perspective, there was no easy solution to the crisis. Between its large community, its numerous obligations, and the people who depended on the Jesuits for alms, the College of Cochin appeared to be doomed. Writing to Nuno Mascarenhas in 1621, he asserted that the reigning poverty was so great that no abundance of alms would be enough. It was not just the basic necessities that were lacking at Cochin, Palmeiro had no money to send to the missionaries in the far corners of the province. Among the requests received by the Visitor was a solicitation for some valuable object from his subordinates in Bengal, who intended to trade it for ready cash. His reference to these requests from within the Province of Malabar was intended to send an unsubtle hint to Rome: Palmeiro had nothing to spend on luxuries for his brethren in other provinces or at the curia. He offered details about the lackluster pearls and the cheap bezoar stones that he sent to the superior general as per Rome's request, and he did not fail to mention the wine he had been asked to send to the Jesuits in China and the Persian rug and taffeta that his former colleagues in Braga had solicited from him. In closing, he wrote: "I write to Your Reverence about these trifles, so that you will not wonder why I do not comply, as is my obligation, in as much as possible. In truth, Your Reverence would have compassion for me if you saw what goes on in this college, that is, how all of its staff come to me every day crying and asking me to give them what this house lacks, the annoyances that they give me, and the molestations I go through."[75]

In the midst of his worries about the financial viability of the Province of Malabar, Palmeiro was handed responsibility for the Christians of the Fishery Coast. He had known that the crown was in the process of seeing to the restoration of the Jesuits' churches there, and the moment finally came in January 1621.[76] If the men of the Society had to make due with little before this vindication, they would now have to make do with less: *Pescaria* was the site of over forty-five churches and roughly twenty thousand Christians.[77] But his concerns in this matter were not simply financial; the Society's prestige was on the line.

Palmeiro's first task was to negotiate the final restoration of the Jesuits' churches with the viceroy and the bishop of Cochin. He was under no illusions about his rival at the cathedral. In a letter he wrote to Rome on the eve of the restoration, the Visitor declared that the bishop "is our enemy, and always was." If that was so, then there was a degree of uncertainty to what otherwise looked like a straightforward affair. The Jesuits knew that they would get their churches back, but would they also get the status of vicars forane? This status would ensure their independence from the bishop's meddling on the Fishery Coast, something the Jesuits identified as the root cause of their previous troubles. If they had to work under the control of one of the bishop's appointees, the bitterness of the past would surely return. Palmeiro argued that a Jesuit needed to be named *vigário de vara* but that the bishop was "so shifting and inconstant, that if he gave us this jurisdiction today, he would take it away tomorrow."[78]

To insist that Frei Sebastião de São Pedro cede control over part of his diocese to a Jesuit was a delicate matter. After all, the restoration of the churches was nothing other than the king's rebuke of the bishop's moves, and it followed hot on the heels of another reprimand for his attempted seizure of the villages belonging to the religious orders in Sri Lanka. Palmeiro therefore summoned a meeting of ten senior priests at Cochin, where it was agreed that discretion was the better part of valor. The Jesuits were better off accepting the Fishery Coast churches whether or not a Jesuit was made vicar. If they refused the churches and another order sent men in their stead (which "they would do most willingly," Palmeiro noted), the Society's reputation would suffer. "Without a doubt," the Visitor declared, "people would think that because we wanted to settle a score, or merely for reasons of vanity, we abandoned an endeavor of such important service to God." Furthermore, Jesuits in Bengal, in the Moluccas, in Bassein (Vasai), and in the region of Goa worked under the authority of external vicars without incident. Indeed, the Society's men had done so for forty years in *Pescaria*.[79] The best policy, Palmeiro affirmed and his colleagues agreed, was to "go in with much zeal, example, and labor to overcome unedifying memories and past scandals."[80] In the end they were not given the title of vicar forane.

Meeting the challenge of the Fishery Coast was easier said than done. In 1621 the cash-strapped Jesuit province had few resources of money or of manpower to tackle a responsibility of this magnitude. Moreover, Palmeiro observed, the clerical changes and local unrest had taken their toll on the area's Christian communities: "This *Christandade* is almost completely lost, and it will be finished unless it receives help."[81] Obliged by conscience but also by corporate pride to seize the moment, he gathered the means necessary for the task. According to that year's annual letter, there was no lack of willing candidates at Cochin: "Everyone at this college offered himself to Father Visitor André Palmeiro for the undertaking, but only four attained this blessing."[82] In fact, there were simply not enough priests to spare for the Fishery Coast while still fulfilling the college's pastoral and educational obligations.

This was the moment when Palmeiro's status as joint visitor of the Provinces of Goa and Malabar became useful. His new powers enabled him to summon the men that he needed from Goa, and to requisition funds. To be sure, he had to tread softly to avoid creating new problems. Palmeiro remembered what had happened when he had made a request for men for the Fishery Coast from the Province of Goa in 1618. When he broached that subject with Provincial Jácome de Medeiros (1573–1625), this colleague "showed himself most difficult, and rebuked some priests who expressed the desire to be sent there."[83] But things were different in 1621. Palmeiro could command compliance from the provincial superior in Goa. Assuming that he would need to staff fourteen churches (a far cry from the total, but enough to secure the Society's claims to the region), he appealed to the new provincial in Goa, Luís Cardoso (1564–1628).[84]

The team Palmeiro put together in the early spring of 1621 consisted of fourteen men, including the provincial superior to act as their escort. Several of them were from Goa while others were veterans of the Fishery Coast or men with long experience in Southern India. Perhaps the most surprising selection in this group was Gonçalo Fernandes, the former adversary of Roberto Nobili. Despite his advanced age—he was over eighty years old—Fernandes begged Palmeiro to let him return to Tuticorin. The Visitor feared for the life of the veteran Jesuit, but Fernandes insisted that he wanted to be buried at the feet of his mentor, Henrique Henriques (1520–1600). Fernandes was therefore taken on a stretcher from his sickbed at the college to the ship, completing this final pilgrimage to the region where he had spent forty years as a missionary.[85]

The best description of the Jesuits' return to the Fishery Coast in March 1621 is found in that year's annual letter from the Province of Malabar:

> The reception that the Paravas gave to the priests was a testament to the *saudades* and desires that the Patagins and the rest of the people had to see them once again in their lands.[86] And so when they received the news that the priests were coming on the fleet, they traveled far out to sea to welcome them in vessels with pavilions and flags, firing off musketry salvos, and playing all the sorts of festive instruments that they typically play. When the priests disembarked, the Paravas carried them to the shore on their shoulders. So great was the multitude of people who gathered from nearby areas that the priests could not even be seen in the crowd when they were set down on the beach. The way along which the priests were to proceed on foot was decorated with branches from various trees, as far as Tuticorin and the church of the old college, which is still there. They also laid down very fine cloth and some of their *cabayas*, just as the people of Jerusalem had done for Jesus on Palm Sunday.
>
> The same was done for each of the priests when they took control of the churches to which they had been appointed by order of Father Provincial. These priests were taken from other places where some of them were superiors and others simply residents. Only their ability and their zeal were taken into consideration, not their age or how long they had been superiors. Such was the case of a priest who was about 76 years old, and had spent many of those years as rector in different colleges. He is now very pleased to be in a parish. Another priest came from Goa, where he had read theology for a few years. This priest asked most fervently that he be allowed to trade his place among the cool shade of the trees of Salcete for the sun and sands of *Pescaria*.[87]

The bond between the pastors and their flock was strong, as the Visitor had seen during his journey through the region. The memory of his trip to the Fishery Coast would remain with him for years; Palmeiro, for one, would not forget the indigenous Christians of this remote corner of India. His oversight of Jesuit affairs in *Pescaria* would not slacken during his term as joint visitor of the Province of Malabar and the Province of Goa, even when he traveled to the viceregal capital to enter the highest circles of imperial administration.

It was the Visitor who coordinated the appointments of priests to the Fishery Coast and channeled funds from Goa to the area for the maintenance of the clergy, the upkeep of their churches, and alms for poor Christians. His commitment to the preservation of the Jesuit presence in the region ensured that, by the end of 1623, there were ten Jesuits divided between Tuticorin and the other churches. Palmeiro saw to it that Antonio Rubino, the former rector of the College of Colombo, was named superior of the region's residences. In *Pescaria*, Rubino was certain to confront enough hardships to fulfill his pious desires. The Visitor also sent four more priests to restore the Jesuit presence at Mannar in western Sri Lanka, where the Society's churches had been abandoned over time. Palmeiro had seen with his own eyes that there were significant numbers of native Christians in the region. Many of these people were Paravas who had migrated to the southern coast of the Gulf of Mannar in search of new pearl fisheries or as part of a royal plan to secure the northern end of Sri Lanka by importing Christian allies to the area.[88] And the Visitor's cordial encounter with the Portuguese commander Filipe de Oliveira resulted in the creation of another new Jesuit community at Jaffna. Four priests were sent to open a residence inside the city's new fortress, from which they could minister to the Portuguese soldiers and proselytize the indigenous people.[89]

Such was the Visitor's commitment to the Christians of the Fishery Coast that he made another visit to the area nearly five years after his 1620 inspection tour. His special trip from Goa via Cochin to Tuticorin was prompted by an outbreak of violence among rival clans of Paravas. Letters from Rubino describe a struggle for precedence among men seeking the title of caste head (*pattankatti*). The selection of one individual by the Jesuits in 1621 had led to the rise of factions, with some Parava leaders threatening to petition the bishop of Cochin to send back his diocesan clergy. In Rubino's opinion, the Jesuits were partly to blame for the discord since they had made an infelicitous choice for caste head. He also suggested that some of the priests working in the area were ill suited for the task of ministering to the Paravas—an accusation that impugned the judgment of the provincial superior and, by extension, the Visitor. By 1623 the situation had soured to the point where it sparked a violent uprising. Reprisals between the main factions of Paravas had claimed several lives, including a fatal stabbing on the steps of the main church of Tuticorin, and the Jesuits found themselves once again expelled from the city.[90]

Palmeiro returned to the Fishery Coast in the final months of 1624 to play the role of peacemaker. Writing to Rome, he summed up the reason for his decision to go back to distant *Pescaria* by informing the superior general of the recent disturbances there, "caused in part by some bad Christians, and in part by the local heathens." Although a fragile peace seems to have been reached by 1624, Palmeiro felt compelled to visit the area again. In his view, provincial superior Gaspar de Andrade had not kept a close watch on affairs in Tuticorin. Andrade certainly had no plans to visit the Fishery Coast. According to Palmeiro, it was "owing to some personal distaste" that the provincial superior did not devote himself to "the calming of the Christians and the good governance of our men."[91] When the Visitor arrived on the Fishery Coast once again, his men made a great show of gratitude to their steadfast patron. Rubino was especially effusive in his praise for Palmeiro's intervention, writing in a letter to the provincial superior that "this Coast was resuscitated, and all of us with it" by the Visitor's appearance. The local Christians put on dancing displays and other festivities to celebrate his arrival, and waited eagerly for him to preside over the reconciliation of the different factions. Whether the new climate of détente was due to Palmeiro's skills at pacification or the mutual exhaustion of the warring clans is not clear, but peace had finally returned to the region. "The Coast was amazed to see such feasting," wrote Rubino about the celebrations upon the Visitor's return; but it was all worthwhile, honoring as it did "the one who does things, who favors the Coast, and who works for it."[92]

———————

Palmeiro spent his first years in Maritime Asia trekking around the fringe of the Portuguese Estado da Índia. From his base in Cochin he traveled along the contested southern shore of the subcontinent, on the edge of the battlefields of Sri Lanka, and to areas completely beyond colonial control, such as to Madurai, Coromandel, and Travancore. But in all of these journeys, there was no place that he visited more often than the Fishery Coast. This was the "Christian land" to which he came toward the end of his long walk in 1620; it was where, upon seeing the stone cross that the Portuguese had erected at Cape Comorin, he thought he had "entered into glory." Indeed, he would have his own glory in *Pescaria* after he helped bring the Jesuits back to the region in 1621. His mission in the region would be finished when he solemnized the peace among the Parava Christians three years later. This final gesture marked the end of Palmeiro's major interventions in the Province of Malabar, and his successes enabled him to focus his attentions elsewhere. Upon his appointment to the post of joint visitor of the provinces of Malabar and Goa, he had no shortage of matters to attend. Indeed, Palmeiro had half a world of concerns: The powers that he received from Rome gave him authority over all Jesuit affairs between the Cape of Good Hope and the Spice Islands. That space was equivalent to most of the Estado da Índia (excepting Southeast and East Asia), which meant that the reach of his power was nearly equivalent to that of the Portuguese viceroy. Clearly, he could no longer remain at provincial colleges or on distant shores. The time had come for the Visitor to move to the heart of the empire.

5

Among Archbishops, Emperors, and Viceroys

André Palmeiro returned to Goa in 1621 a changed man. When he lived at the capital of the Estado da Índia two years earlier, he was a visiting dignitary; upon his return, he was the superior general's personal representative. As visitor of the provinces of Malabar and Goa, he was the most powerful Jesuit in India, entrusted with maintaining the public image of the Society of Jesus at the heart of the Portuguese Empire in Asia. Considering the Jesuits' important standing within the colonial clergy and the close ties between the Portuguese church and the Portuguese state, Palmeiro was an indispensable man. While his primary task was to attend to the Jesuits' internal affairs, he was continually obliged to deal with outsiders because the order's concerns were so intertwined with imperial projects. In the other parts of the Estado da Índia where he had already been, the outsiders he had to deal with were bishops, captains, and regional lords; by contrast, in Goa he was a key interlocutor for archbishops, viceroys, and emperors. At the viceregal capital, the Visitor became a potentate in his own right.

Palmeiro's journey into the heart of Portuguese administration in Maritime Asia required him to articulate an imperial vision. Not only did the scale of his powers within the Society of Jesus demand it, but so did the geographic extent of his jurisdiction—stretching from southeastern Africa to the Spice Islands. No longer could he confine himself to domestic quarrels, such as those he had sought to defuse at Cochin among the fractious men of the Province of Malabar. And no longer could he concentrate so closely on questions of proselytizing method that arose in distant mission fields. At Goa, Palmeiro had to think big: the Visitor's charge was now akin to guiding the Society in Maritime Asia as if he was the admiral of a fleet of carracks crossing the Indian Ocean, not as if he was standing at the prow of a skiff in the Gulf of Mannar. Palmeiro would have to consider how to administer the Jesuits in the various colonial cities spread along the coast of western India. He would have to cast his eyes across the vast ocean that extended before him, thinking of Mozambique, Ethiopia, and Gujarat. And he would also have to consider the inland regions that stretched beyond the Western Ghats, considering how best to deploy Jesuits within the Mughal Empire. Of course, all of this would have to be accomplished without losing sight of the vast expanse of the Province of Malabar, where he still held the post of visitor.

Not only was Palmeiro required to have his own vision, he also had to create visions for others—visions of the glory, piety, and competence of the Society of Jesus, that is. As a major figure in an age that expected displays of status by high-ranking individuals and groups, the Visitor had to take part in events aimed at enhancing his order's standing. Despite his penchant for self-effacement, at Goa Palmeiro had to become a public figure. After all, he was housed under the same roof as the body of Francis Xavier when word of the canonization of the Apostle of the Orient arrived in India. Palmeiro was therefore a prominent figure in the celebrations organized by the Jesuits in 1623 to celebrate their new saint. He was also a key figure in diplomatic relations conducted by the Society at the courts of the Mughal emperors and the emperors of Ethiopia. It was crucial that Palmeiro select the right priests for those missions in order to preserve the image created by illustrious Jesuits from times past in the minds of such powerful rulers. And, of course, the powerful ruler who lived at the viceregal palace a short distance from his quarters was never far from the Visitor's thoughts. To the Portuguese viceroy, Palmeiro would have to represent a vision of piety and rectitude if he and his order were to continue to enjoy the fruits of royal patronage.

Goa was a court city, a capital like its counterparts in Lisbon, Madrid, and Rome. The influential inhabitants of those places shared much with their peers at the capital of the Estado da Índia. That is, their politics were as much global as they were local. Between the far horizons of empire and the immediate surroundings of the court city, focus was lost. This was true as much of

Palmeiro as it was of other imperial officials. As a loyal servant of the *Companhia,* he zealously guarded Jesuit honor in the public forum that his fellow courtiers most prized, the court city itself. And so the Visitor was drawn into the Goanese disputes that pitted his men against other religious orders, the church hierarchy, the city council, and the royal judges. The minutiae of these debates were of great concern to Palmeiro because they involved questions of politics and prestige as well as large sums of money. His faithful devotion to the Society's cause would put him to the test again and again during his stay in Goa, especially in the Jesuits' repeated conflicts with the friars who were their most tenacious competitors in Maritime Asia.

———————

The Visitor traveled to Goa after coordinating the Jesuits' return to the Fishery Coast in the spring of 1621. Exactly when he sailed north from Cochin is not clear: Nothing from his own pen has been discovered for this study for the two-year period from January 1621 until January 1623. Fortunately, it is possible to track Palmeiro's movements during this period in the writings of others. In February 1622 Fernão de Albuquerque, the outgoing royal governor of Portuguese Asia, listed the Visitor in the register of the clerical elite that he prepared each year. Albuquerque described him as "a very virtuous and prudent religious, who has all of the most important qualities that a prelate requires."[1] And in May 1622 a Jesuit who accompanied the ill-fated expedition to relieve the Anglo-Persian siege of Ormuz wrote that Palmeiro had given him a letter in Goa earlier that year.[2]

The Province of Goa, originally called the Province of India, was very different from the Province of Malabar. The main similarity between the two Jesuit administrative units lay in the broad swath of the globe encompassed by each: In the Province of Malabar, roughly four thousand miles separated Cochin from the farthest mission station at Ternate, while in the Province of Goa, the same distance stretched between the Jesuits at Lahore and their brethren in Mozambique. Beyond their comparable scale, there were few other similarities between the two provinces. To begin with, the Province of Goa counted 273 men in 1621, in contrast to the 152 priests and brothers in the Province of Malabar.[3] The men of the Province of Goa were divided among eight colleges with dependent residences and two "missions." In this regard it resembled more the Society's European provinces than its counterparts in Asia, which were principally composed of mission territories. The

Province of Goa had a professed house, colleges with large teaching faculties where the full complement of academic subjects was offered, and a network of residences spread throughout Portuguese colonial settlements.

The center of the province was the city of Goa itself, where more than 150 priests and brothers lived. These men were divided up among the professed house, the novitiate, and the colleges of São Paulo o Velho (the older) and São Paulo o Novo (the newer). The Jesuits at the Professed House contributed to the pastoral care of the city's residents alongside the other religious orders and the diocesan clergy, and were also charged with running the royal hospital. The Colégio de São Paulo o Novo was similar to a medium-sized Jesuit college in Europe; it offered classes in speculative and moral theology as well as philosophy, Latin grammar, and rhetoric. In 1621 twenty-nine of its eighty-two resident Jesuits were students of philosophy or theology. Here Palmeiro would have encountered a form of community life reminiscent of

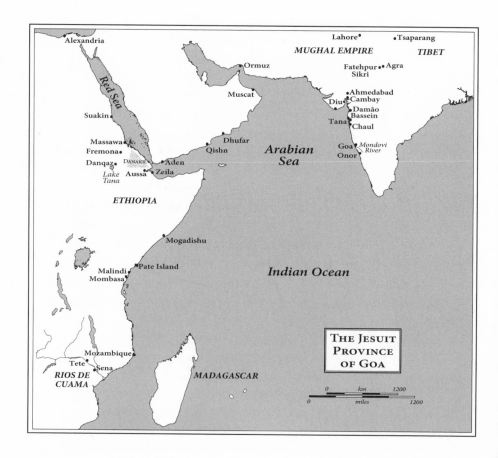

his time at the Colégio de Santo Antão in Lisbon or the Colégio de Jesus in Coimbra.

Outside the court city, the Province of Goa extended to the far side of the Indian Ocean. In Salcete, the region to the south of Goa, the Jesuits maintained another college in the town of Rachol and staffed nineteen parish churches (the Franciscans administered the parish churches to the immediate north of the city in the area called Bardes). Farther north of Goa, the Society had colleges in the string of Portuguese fortresses that dotted the western coast of the subcontinent: in Chaul, Tana (Thane), Bassein, Damão (Daman), and Diu. And far across the Indian Ocean, more than three thousand miles from the colonial capital (but a frequent stopping point for the *Carreira da Índia*), was the province's college at Mozambique. These colleges performed the same functions as the Society's smaller institutions back in Europe; that is, they held classes in reading, writing, and Latin grammar for young boys and lessons in moral theology for parish priests. The Province of Goa also included three "missions," groups of small Jesuit communities living beyond the boundaries of empire. These were the enterprises at the Mughal court cities of Lahore and Agra, in the highlands, in several towns and at the imperial court of Ethiopia, and in the Portuguese settlements of the lower Zambezi River valley.[4]

The Visitor arrived in the Province of Goa with administrative habits acquired in Malabar. His first impulse was not to remain in Goa but to strike out on an inspection tour of the colleges and residences that could be visited on a reasonable trip from the capital. He therefore concentrated his inspection on the colleges and residences situated to the north of the capital, the region called the *Província do Norte* by the Portuguese. In the early modern period this "Province of the North" stretched from Chaul, just south of the site of modern Mumbai, to Diu, situated on the northern coast of the Gulf of Cambay. Unfortunately, the letters that describe Palmeiro's journey there appear to have been lost. Other correspondence of his makes mention of his visit to the area, a trip that he completed by year's end in 1622.[5] He indicates that he traveled as far as Diu and back, a round trip of more than 800 miles. It stands to reason that his inspection tour of the Province of the North took him to Chaul, 235 miles northwest of Goa, and then onward up the coast to Tana, Bassein, and Damão. From this last port, he would have sailed across the Gulf of Cambay to Diu.

The Jesuit colleges in the *Província do Norte* were located in the centers of Portuguese colonial entrepôts. In many respects, the Jesuit presence in the

Province of the North was similar to the Society's establishment in western Sri Lanka. Like their counterparts in that corner of the Province of Malabar, Jesuits stationed at the northern area's colleges offered pastoral care and rudimentary education and at times served as parish priests for the Christian communities located beyond the walls of the Portuguese fortresses. The Province of Goa also drew considerable revenues from rent-producing lands near Tana, Damão, and Bassein in the same way that the Province of Malabar received revenues from villages in the Seven Korales region of Sri Lanka. But in the case of these northern holdings, revenues came from palm groves and other agricultural lands that reverted to both the Province of Goa and the Province of Japan (which encompassed the East and Southeast Asian missions).[6] Annual letters from Palmeiro's day describe construction at the College of Diu as well as the Jesuits' technical assistance to the engineers who built fortifications at Damão.[7] The Visitor would have been particularly concerned to make sure that these projects were executed carefully, and that the Society of Jesus received credit for putting its intellectual resources at the service of the Estado da Índia.

Palmeiro's visit to Diu and Damão brought him to the doorstep of the Mughal Empire. The Gulf of Cambay was the frontier between "India"— that is, what the Portuguese colonies on the coast were called—and *Mogor,* what the Portuguese called the domains of the Mughal emperors. It was an ideal vantage point for Palmeiro to assess the Jesuits' possibilities farther to the north without traveling the more than five hundred miles to the imperial court cities. The Mughal mission was created in 1578 when Emperor Akbar (b. 1542, r. 1556–1605) sent a request to the Jesuit provincial in Goa for men to attend his court in Fatehpur Sikri. The purpose of the priests' journey was for them to dispute religion against representatives of other traditions, with the emperor acting as judge. Although Akbar claimed he would adhere to the religion whose men made the most convincing case, the Jesuits at length understood that his purpose was to gather ideas for a new theology in which the emperor himself would be worshipped. Despite their frustrated hopes of generating a mass of conversions through a Mughal Constantine, the Jesuits decided to remain in the sovereign's shadow for political reasons. They knew it was wise to respond to imperial favor when it was so readily offered. Owing to the efforts of the skilled linguist Jerónimo Xavier, the grandnephew of the Apostle of the Orient, the Jesuits continued to be welcome at the Mughal court during the reign of Akbar's son, Jahangir (b. 1569, r. 1605–1627).[8]

FIGURE 5.1. Depiction of the durbar (court) of the Mughal Emperor Jahangir (r. 1605–1627). Painted circa 1625 and attributed either to Manohar Das or Abul Hasan, this image shows one of the court Jesuits, Jerónimo Xavier, at the lower left. Copyright © 2014 Museum of Fine Arts, Boston.

When Palmeiro arrived at the northern edge of "India," the Mughal mission counted six members. The role of these Jesuits was primarily diplomatic; their time was largely spent following the court around northern India, where they attempted to curry favor with influential figures and the emperor himself. The value of these efforts was reckoned to be great. Not only did they ensure a channel of communication between the viceroys at Goa and the Mughal emperors but imperial favor ensured protection for missionaries working elsewhere in northern India, where Jesuits often were impolitic in their deprecatory pronouncements about Islam and Hinduism. The priests ministered to small communities of Christians in the court cities of Agra and Lahore as well as to Christian Armenian merchants who lived throughout the Mughal domains. In all, their flock numbered near one thousand souls in Palmeiro's day. Despite this low number, the Jesuits maintained hopes that some important courtier or perhaps even the emperor himself (they insisted that he was Muslim in name only) might submit to baptism. In 1623 mission superior António de Andrade (1580–1634) conceded that the Jesuits' efforts at the Mughal court had not met with much success. Striking a defensive tone, he noted that although the results of his mission could not be compared with those produced by his confreres in Japan, China, or Ethiopia, those missions required "many, many years before they gave the fruit which they do today." The wait, however, was surely worthwhile: As Andrade wrote and many of his confreres believed, "it all comes down to making one of these kings Christian, because all will follow behind, since they are greatly dependent on him."[9]

The Visitor showed himself to be indulgent with Andrade and the Mughal mission despite their meager tally of conversions. This attitude stands in contrast to his decision vis-à-vis Roberto Nobili at Madurai, from whom Palmeiro demanded results. The Visitor seems unlikely to have believed that there might be a sudden reversal of fortune, but he was confident that political goodwill that had lasted since the 1580s was more valuable than experiments in dissimulation. Not only did the Jesuits appear to bask in Emperor Jahangir's favor (after a period of coolness a decade earlier on the occasion of hostilities between the Portuguese and the Mughals), they also enjoyed the patronage of Mirza Zul-Qarnian (1592–1656). This Armenian Christian was an important administrator and one of the most favored figures at the imperial court.[10] Jesuit reports from the early 1620s gush with praise for Zul-Qarnian, who repeatedly showed them great generosity. Francesco Corsi

(1573–1635), Jerónimo Xavier's former companion, informed Palmeiro about a princely donation that the Armenian courtier intended to make to the missionaries. The purpose of Zul-Qarnian's gift was to endow a college at Agra through the purchase of revenue-producing villages in the *Província do Norte,* near Damão. The matter had been sent to Madrid and Rome for approval, and both the crown and the Jesuit curia had urged Corsi to accept the donation.[11] Despite the fact that this news had arrived in the Province of Goa while Palmeiro was inspector there, he left the matter unresolved.[12]

Perhaps the Visitor preferred expanding the Jesuits' proselytizing activities in Mughal lands rather than outfitting a new college. During his 1622 trip to the Province of the North, he contemplated recommencing the defunct mission in Gujarat with an eye to ministering to the Armenians (and thereby pleasing Zul-Qarnian). In letters from the Mughal court, António de Andrade had insisted with Palmeiro that he consider sending men and money to open mission stations somewhere deeper inside the Gulf of Cambay or even inland. Rather than go himself, Palmeiro sent António Rodrigues (b. 1553), the former rector of the colleges of Diu and Damão, on a reconnaissance tour.[13] In Rodrigues's judgment, the logical sites for a mission station would be in Cambay (Khambat) or Ahmedabad, but he informed Palmeiro that there was little hope for success in either city. Forging ahead in spite of this negative evaluation, the Visitor decided to send Juan de Velasco (1581–1630), one of his most trusted companions in India, to Ahmedabad. Velasco nevertheless found little to detain him in the Gujarati city: "There were only two or three Armenians, who irredeemably live with concubines," he told the Visitor, "and because they are sellers of wine and very fond of it, they are often carried away by it, and they neither go to mass themselves nor send their servants who are Christians."[14]

The prospects for new missions in Gujarat were not good, and the Visitor learned from his trip to the north to turn a deaf ear to Andrade's pleas. In him, Palmeiro once again found himself confronted with a visionary who seemed detached from reality. He had dealt with men like this in the past, and the memory of Alberto Laerzio and Antonio Rubino was still fresh in his mind. The Portuguese Andrade had made his case for new missions in Gujarat in seemingly sensible terms: he argued that missionaries from another religious order might open a residence in the region and use it as a base for traveling to the imperial court. Once there, it was assumed, the friars would spoil the Jesuits' relationship with Jahangir in the same way they were believed to have ruined the Society's diplomatic efforts elsewhere in Asia, especially in Japan. Palmeiro was unconvinced of the efficacy of this strategy. A Jesuit or two in Ahmedabad or Cambay, the Visitor contended, would not dissuade zealous friars. Could such rivals not go to somewhere closer to the court "where our men have never set foot, or even to where we are?", he asked in a letter to Rome. (This is precisely what happened in 1623, when a pair of Franciscan friars arrived at court and Giuseppe de Castro (1577–1646) presented them to Jahangir and even acted as their interpreter. Such assistance to the Jesuits' rivals was something that the Visitor deemed "quite unnecessary".[15]) As for the pastoral needs of a handful of lackluster Armenian Christians in Cambay and Ahmedabad, Palmeiro contended that an itinerant priest would suffice. A new residence was out of the question: "If we had to detain our priests in cultivating so few people," he concluded, "they could be in any city in India, because there are more Christians in any of the cities which belong to the Moors or Heathens than in those two."[16]

Like Laerzio and Rubino, Andrade was a source of trouble for Palmeiro. As superior of the Mughal mission, Andrade held a position of considerable importance. Rome knew that he was talented, like Rubino, and had twice appointed him to the post of provincial. But his effusive character, given to excessive displays of emotion, jarred the Visitor. Palmeiro recognized Andrade's qualities, and in particular that he seemed to have a special gift for dealing with Jahangir. But this was not enough: After a later meeting, the Visitor noted that Andrade's appearance was shabby and lacking the dignity required by his station as mission superior and, above all, courtier. Worse than this, Palmeiro observed, was the "overabundance of generosity that he has with his friends." In other words, Andrade played the role of the pauper in public and the role of rich man in private. What he needed to do was project a sober dignity at all times. The Visitor reminded him that he could not expect his superiors in Goa to pay for his extravagances at the Mughal court (although Palmeiro mentions that former provincial Jácome de Medeiros had promised Andrade to give him "whatever he asked for").[17]

Despite these warnings, Palmeiro could only do so much to restrain a man who lived hundreds of miles away and who handled important diplomatic affairs. Andrade had not done anything to warrant censure beyond being himself. Palmeiro could not summon him to Goa or remove him from his post as superior of the Mughal mission without evidence of a transgression against his vows or against the Society. It was therefore with evident frustration that the Visitor related Andrade's crowning folly to the superior general—a journey that, for all its temerity, would preserve Andrade's name for posterity far more effectively than any of the Visitor's treks. On March 30, 1624, Andrade and a companion left Agra to head into the Himalayas. Their journey, the first visit to Tibet by European travelers in the modern age, led to the creation of a short-lived mission at the city of Tsaparang, in the Kingdom of Guge.[18] What bothered the Visitor is that he was not consulted about the Mughal mission superior's journey, only learning about his departure for parts unknown from the colleagues Andrade had left behind in the court city. Palmeiro's brief mention of this news to Rome provides yet another example of his exasperation with subordinates with visionary tendencies:

> The priests in *Mogor* are much favored by the king. The superior of that mission, Father António de Andrade, upon learning that there was a Christian community some long days' journey from the place where he was staying with the king, took off to discover those people. He took as his companion a brother who was with him. And already far along on his route, he wrote to the priests in Mogor a letter which reads as follows: "Eight days from here we will enter the lands of Tibet (that is how the people of this Christian community are called). We have an almost infallible certainty that they are Christians and good people. I will write immediately on what I find." It will be of much glory to God and honor to the Society if this new Christian community is discovered. Nevertheless, he should not have set out along such a distant route without an order from us. Father Francesco Corsi thinks that Father Andrade had some revelation from God about this journey.[19]

The Visitor's clashes with Andrade led him to the conclusion that the problem of leadership he had diagnosed in the Province of Malabar was common throughout the Indies. Returning to Goa after his trip to the *Província do Norte,* he was further confirmed in his judgment. For him, Jesuit superiors needed to be mature men and adept managers; they could not be visionaries or given to unrestrained impulses. The Society's resources were limited and needed to be shepherded by Jesuits whose feet were firmly planted on the ground. Although Palmeiro realized that zeal, even visionary zeal, was necessary for advancing the missions, he firmly believed that men who had such qualities needed to remain in subordinate positions. And since the superior general was the one who controlled promotions within the provincial hierarchy, the Visitor saw it as his job to alert Rome to the perils of promoting the unfit. This was no easy task: After all, reports that reached Europe about the Asian provinces put considerable stress on the heroic figures who embodied the missionary ideal. Seeking candidates for leadership positions in the documents sent to Rome from the overseas provinces, the curia's eyes would return over and over to the names of such men. Yet as Palmeiro would argue, the task of missionizing was not equal to the task of governing. Just like the rival trade companies that had begun to appear in Maritime Asia in the Visitor's day, the *Companhia* also needed competent, loyal servants.

The death of João Borges on February 27, 1623, prompted Palmeiro to urge the superior general to attend to the lack of good men in India.[20] Borges (b. 1572), the well-loved superior of the Professed House in Goa, was a *homem feito,* a fully-trained man. From the Visitor's perspective, he was someone who possessed the requisite spiritual depth, pastoral skill, and administrative wherewithal that was expected of mature Jesuits. In Palmeiro's experience, such men were relatively common among the Jesuits in Europe but altogether rare in Asia. He thus urged the superior general to send more competent individuals, "men of worth and spirit to carry forward and augment what so many of our holy priests founded and planted in this Orient."[21]

At the heart of the matter was a problem of supply in Europe, Palmeiro contended. Good men from the European provinces were dissuaded from heading to the missions, being considered too valuable or too competent to be sent away. Recall that Jesuits had to petition the superior general for assignments to the overseas provinces, and Rome's response to these petitions relied on information from their superiors. Men of talent might be steered away from their missionary desires if it was deemed that their skills were needed in Europe *ad maiorem Dei gloriam.* So the overseas provinces obtained most of their men disjointedly. The Jesuits in Asia were not handpicked by the superior general from the mass of European priests and brothers. Most of them were sent to Asia as young men, long before they had proven their competencies in any ministry besides the teaching of grammar. Their primary qualifications were an acceptable level of academic skill and a sufficient level of pathos, communicable in writing, about their desires for missionary glory or pious suffering. In a word, those sent to the missions were dispensable men.

The Society's system was not set up to send "made men" to the overseas provinces and, in Palmeiro's view, it showed. He had written to his former colleagues in Portugal to beg for talented Jesuits, and they had shrugged. He therefore wrote to Rome to decry "the little effort that the superiors there put into finding good men," and insisted that the Province of Portugal's indifference toward the missions had a chilling effect on the level of zeal in the Asian provinces. If the Society's superiors in Europe cared only to ensure that the best men remained at home, Palmeiro continued, "and it is publicly known that the most ordinary men are sent to these parts, each and all grow cold, as those who come here tell us, to our great displeasure." Here he put his finger on the problem: the mission provinces needed the zeal of great priests and the competence of great administrators, just like the European provinces did. And for this need to be met, vocations for the missions had to be encouraged in Europe among the most talented Jesuits. When he made this plea to Rome, Palmeiro might as well have been speaking for himself. Unlike the mood he sensed in the letters from Portugal, he did not consider the overseas provinces to be a death sentence: "It was not like this in times past and will not be in the future if it is understood that not everyone who is sent here is lost, and that these parts also need men of greater talents to work alongside those who do not have as many."[22]

The example of times past loomed large in Palmeiro's mind while he was in Goa. The city streets that he walked and the squares where he participated in demonstrations of piety were the scenes of heroic episodes from Jesuit history. Concentrating on his immediate surroundings rather than the vastness of the Estado da Índia was the way for him to understand the depth—not just the length and breadth—of the Jesuits' presence in Asia. The order had been there for three-quarters of a century, and the register of its illustrious members who had passed through Goa was long. It was therefore a great consolation for Palmeiro to take part in a celebration of the greatest Jesuit missionary of all, Francis Xavier. The news of Xavier's canonization at Rome in 1622 was greeted with great joy when it reached Goa in March of the following year.[23]

At the capital of the Estado da Índia, Xavier was a local saint. Not only was his incorrupt body kept at the Jesuits' Professed House, a sanctuary dedicated to Jesus, but the city had been the site of Xavier's first pastoral and missionary actions in Asia. His words and deeds were still in living memory—for the very old, of course; he had died on the China coast in 1552—across Portuguese Asia when the beatification process was begun in 1615. And Jesuit accounts from the years leading up to his official recognition by the papacy in 1619 reported a surge in miracles, inexplicable healings in particular, that occurred through Xavier's relics in Goa, Cochin, and on the Fishery Coast.[24] For instance, annual letters from the Province of Goa gave details of how Xavier's surplice, kept in a silver chest, was sent out across the city to perform cures at the bedsides of the infirm, and how splinters from the wooden casket in which his corpse had formerly been kept were distributed as relics.[25]

Xavier's canonization, proclaimed by Pope Gregory XV in March 1622 at the same time as that of Ignatius Loyola, Teresa of Avila, Isidore of Madrid, and Philip Neri, demanded an impressive display of pageantry from the Goa Jesuits. Since the news reached the city near the start of the summer rains in 1623, the festivities were delayed until the dry season. So ambitious was the Jesuits' plan that they put off the celebration from Xavier's feast day (December 3, the anniversary of his death) until January 1624, so that they could be sure of fine weather and, above all, so that the magnificent processional carts would be completed. The Visitor had an important role to play in these events. He is the only individual—with the exception of Loyola and Xavier—who is mentioned by name in contemporary accounts of the festivities. But both Palmeiro and Loyola himself are only mentioned in passing in these reports; the celebration was all about Xavier, from the high masses to the elaborate processions to the four-day-long reenactment of his life in the square in front of the Professed House. And the Jesuits spared no expense to honor their illustrious predecessor: "The favor of the Saint was felt in the happy success," wrote one observer; "there was such an abundance of gold, pearls, and jewels, and they were of such great value; yet no noteworthy accident or loss occurred."[26]

The celebrations began on January 21, 1624, with the rolling out of five mobile pyramids whose points "were equal to the highest ceilings of the buildings." These wooden structures, covered with painted scenes, emblems, and heraldry as well as gold and silver, were stationed at five important civic spaces: the squares in front of the viceregal palace, the cathedral, and the Bom Jesus church as well as before the entrances to the two Jesuit colleges, São Paulo o Novo on the city's west side and São Paulo o Velho on its east end. Bearers dressed in Indian clothing pulled the pyramids across the city from São Paulo o Novo. They were escorted by three cavalry squadrons representing Asia, Africa, and Europe and composed of the best students from the Society's college and seminary.[27] Pietro della Valle (1586–1652), an illustrious Roman traveler who journeyed about the Levant, Persia, and India in the 1610s and 1620s, provides an eyewitness account of the second phase of the festivities, which began on February 10.[28] Della Valle describes the solemn vespers held at the Bom Jesus that night, followed by a nighttime parade, or *encamisada,* with numerous young riders, gallantly dressed and carrying torches, escorting a flag bearing the likeness of the saints.[29]

FIGURE 5.2. Map of Goa drawn circa 1614. The three Jesuit institutions are located on the edge of the city center: At the left side, below the tip of the lake, the Colégio de São Paulo o Velho; at the center right, the Professed House of the Bom Jesus, Palmeiro's residence; and at the far right, the Colégio de São Paulo o Novo. Note the two Augustinian residences, Santo Agostinho and Santa Mónica, situated adjacent to São Paulo o Novo.

On February 11 the city's élite gathered at the Bom Jesus for a solemn mass. The Visitor presided and preached on the virtues of the Apostle of the Orient. Regardless of how erudite or moving Palmeiro's sermon was—no copy of it has survived—it was outdone by the play put on outside the church later that afternoon. The 1624 annual letter from the Province of Goa recorded that the drama lasted four days and drew a vast audience: "The Count Viceroy was present, with all of the nobility, citizens, magistrates, town council, and captains. All the windows were crowded with people. In the stands below them in the streets, no place remained unfilled. Even Heathens and Moors took pleasure in seeing something they had never seen before. The piece was serious, the audience greater on each successive day, and the scenes so distinguished and devout that they caused much joy, as well as calling forth tears of devotion."[30] Della Valle remarked that the spectacle was *una macchina non men stravagante che grandissima,* with more than three hundred actors, gallant dances, and many stage inventions including "carriages, ships, galleys, tournaments, heavens, hells, mountains and clouds." With the exception of one day when Viceroy Francisco da Gama (1565–1632) was ill, the play went on recounting Xavier's whole life and concluded only after discoursing on his death on Shangchuan Island in southern China and the transport of his body to his final resting place in Goa, a few paces from the stage.[31]

The high point of the festivities was the procession held on February 19, which started at São Paulo o Velho and covered a mile before it ended at the professed house. So splendid was this event that the Jesuits published a description of the processional carts and the allegorical figures they carried, which was not only distributed locally but sent to Europe. According to a different report, the procession was nearly as long as the distance of the route it followed, "the streets, alleys, bazaars, windows, squares and plazas being clogged with so many people." The Viceroy, the high nobility, and the cathedral clergy watched from the balcony of the Inquisitors' palace in the heart of the city, with da Gama commanding the procession to pause so he could appreciate the carriages fully; "only grudgingly did he let each move out of his sight."[32]

The procession had seven principal "triumphal carts," every one accompanied by riders and dancers, as well as a "ship of the church militant." This carrack must have been a sight to behold: Its three decks were lined with saints and martyrs, its four masts were decorated with emblems of the virtues, and its seven sails were painted with the gifts of the Holy Spirit, while

Gregory XV held the rudder and Ignatius Loyola and Francis Xavier held an astrolabe and compass for charting the course. The seven floats represented the victories of the two Jesuit saints, depicting their heroic actions against death, the devil, sin, and idolatry. This last triumph had special resonance in Goa, where church and state had moved forcefully to eradicate the presence of any vestige of non-Christian traditions. The richly dressed female figure of Idolatry processed alongside her companion, Blindness, who bore a shield painted with the picture of a mole. Idolatry dueled with Faith before being laid low, while her blinkered companion was made a prisoner of Truth. Atop the accompanying float was a massive tree, invoking both the tree from Nebuchadnezzar's second dream and the local banyan trees, many of which were sacred to Goa's Hindu population before the Jesuits petitioned the Inquisition to have them chopped down.[33]

The place of honor at the end of the procession was reserved for Xavier himself. The Jesuits processed according to rank before the golden standard bearing the saint's image that the city council had offered to the Society on proclaiming Xavier a patron of Goa. In order to ensure that there would be no fighting for precedence among the city councilmen or other local notables who sought to march, Palmeiro decided to carry this banner himself. He was followed by the silver casket that held the saint's corpse. According to one report, the silver of the casket by itself weighed 7 arrobas, or roughly 150 pounds, cost more than six thousand *pardaus* (a princely sum), and was covered with images depicting Xavier's miracles and episodes from his life.[34] To avoid discord among the Jesuits over who would have the honor of carrying Xavier's casket, the Visitor decided that a team of Franciscans would bear it aloft on their shoulders. The two Jesuit reports of the events pass over in silence the fact that these friars were the only members of a different order who participated in the procession. Della Valle, however, goes right to the point on the question of the rivalries between the religious orders that led to their absence: "None of the other religious orders in Goa appeared, because they said they would not go in the Jesuits' processions because the Jesuits did not go to those of the others."[35]

Della Valle's comment about the petty fighting between the different orders was on the mark. The canonization feasting held by the Society of Jesus was a Jesuit triumph alone; and when the music, the dancing, and the crowds went away, the resentments between the city's religious orders remained. Indeed, given the tenor of the rancor that emerges from contemporary documents, it is hard to believe that there were any friars present at the celebrations at all. The climate of spite was seen by della Valle as unbecoming of religious, but it would be wrong to assume that similar rivalries and unseemly exchanges were unknown elsewhere—they were as common in his native Rome as they were in Lisbon, Madrid, or elsewhere in Catholic Europe. The struggle for precedence and privilege was as common among early modern clerics as it was among the nobility (from whose ranks many religious came), and it was a primary reason why tracts and sermons about the virtue of humility retained their freshness over the decades. Della Valle nevertheless insisted that the infighting at Goa was worse than elsewhere: He claimed that the city had a surfeit of religious, an overabundance of processions each year, and an excess of ecclesiastical wealth. As an example of their childish behavior, he also recounted how the Jesuits got back at the Dominicans (just one of many rival groups) by refusing to ring their church bells on May 28 when all the other churches in Goa heralded the news of the beatification of Albertus Magnus and Ambrose of Siena.[36]

Feuding between the religious orders in the Estado da Índia was constant during the early modern period. Since honor and prestige were on the line, Palmeiro did not shy away from confrontation. His loyalty was above all to the Society of Jesus, and he was a man of his time: He fought against the friars when it was necessary for the good of the *Companhia*. And such was the climate in Goa that he had no lack of occasions for confronting his order's rivals. Beyond the tit-for-tat business of bell-ringing and processions, there were also more serious forms of conflict. But rather than dismiss these disputes in the manner that della Valle did, as the consequence of there being too many big fish in a small pond, it is important to examine the reasons why the bitterness between the religious orders persisted for so long. After all, the men who kept these feuds alive for decades were individuals who were expected to exemplify the virtue of charity.

The most intense battles that occurred during Palmeiro's term in Goa were the Jesuits' disputes with the Augustinians over real estate in the court city. These were delicate affairs for the Jesuits, since the friars were closely allied to the church hierarchy. To be sure, both groups had their own spiritual clienteles among elite and plebeian ranks of society who stood ready to back them up, but the presence of bishops and archbishops—to whom the Jesuits owed obedience—made their fights with the Augustinians more risky. Much to the Jesuits' displeasure, the death of Archbishop Frei Cristóvão de Sá e

Lisboa, their opponent in the Nobili affair, had led to Frei Sebastião de São Pedro's appointment as ecclesiastical governor until a new archbishop was named. Recall that São Pedro was the Society's old bugbear from Cochin, the bishop who had attempted to thwart the Jesuits on the Fishery Coast and in Sri Lanka. Despite the fact that the royal governor had written to Madrid to ensure that no friar be consecrated, especially not Frei Sebastião de São Pedro, king and pope would see fit to promote this Augustinian to the rank of archbishop in 1625.[37]

The affair that roiled the early 1620s was just as dramatic as the dispute over Roberto Nobili's missionary tactics. It was a fight over the expansion of the Jesuit college that stood adjacent to two Augustinian houses. From the friars' perspective, their Jesuit neighbors were intent on robbing them of both their view and their quiet. What happened was that the Society sought to expand the Colégio de São Paulo o Novo so that it could accommodate the hundreds of students who took classes at the old college on the other side of town. The Colégio de São Paulo o Velho was situated in a low-lying area blamed for repeated fever outbreaks. Far more attractive was a spot the Jesuits had acquired on the upper slope of Nossa Senhora do Rosário hill, which dominated the western edge of the city. The elevation at this site ensured exposure to healthy winds, and it was for this reason that the Society had maintained a small residence for its convalescing members at the spot since 1578. In the early seventeenth century, the Jesuits moved their novitiate there as well.

Since the Jesuits' original building was small, with nothing but a chapel, a small patio, and quarters for only a few men, it had caused no great stir among the area's other residents. But their 1617 plans for major expansion on the site in order to house their teaching facilities, seminary, and novitiate were deeply disturbing to the Augustinian friars at the nearby convent of Nossa Senhora da Graça, no less than to the Augustinian nuns at the convent of Santa Mónica, across the street. Given the slope of the hills on this side of Goa, the planned expansion of São Paulo o Novo would place the Jesuits' new bell towers in the line of sight from the friars' convent to the Mandovi River. Moreover, there was the problem of bringing the school children who received instruction at the old college over to the Society's new site. The nuns of Santa Mónica were displeased with the idea of so many children crowding near their door each day and with the possibility that wandering eyes (peering from the Jesuits' higher windows) might invade their privacy. In other words, "not in my backyard."

The Jesuits initially brushed aside the Augustinians' objections and commenced construction in 1615, but the level of tension between the two groups rose along with their rooflines. In order to secure the personal approval of Viceroy Jerónimo de Azevedo (r. 1612–1617) for their plans, the Jesuits had agreed not to build a public church where typical pastoral activities such as preaching and confessing (with their concomitant crowds) would take place. Construction could therefore proceed, but it began with the demolition of a set of rental houses that the Augustinians owned. Not only did this gesture irk the friars and the nuns, but it was clear that the Jesuits had acted in bad faith in their agreement with the viceroy. Their plans included building a major church and a large residence that would dramatically increase the Jesuits' presence in that part of the city. Seeing that the viceroy's permission had not been submitted to the chancery for approval, the Augustinians appealed to the city council and the *Relação,* the royal court in Goa, in the early summer of 1617. The friars' goal was to stop the construction work, which had moved at a rapid pace. They intended to force the Jesuits to move their students, novices, and seminarians back to São Paulo o Velho on the other side of the city, or at least abide by their vow to limit the scope of activities held at the new college.[38]

In this clash between the Jesuits and the Augustinians, appeals to outside authorities became necessary. The two most important political forces in Goa, the viceroy and the city council, backed opposing sides, so it was necessary to appeal to higher powers. The nuns, friars, and town councilors petitioned the king in Madrid, but the Jesuits knew how long it would take for word to travel to Europe and return. One Augustinian account describes how the Jesuits pushed their workers to complete the new buildings during the rainy season of 1617, before the fleets reached India. This way they could claim that the work had been finished before they knew the crown's decision.[39] King Philip had written to express his disapproval of the Jesuits' project that year, but he had ordered his viceroy to resolve the affair locally. Knowing that the viceroy was on their side, the Jesuits refused to desist, and their workmen "instead continued with greater energy, working on holidays." By the end of 1618 the viceroy and the judges of the *Relação* received orders from Madrid to force the Jesuits to take part of their students back to São Paulo o Velho. This move would send the young boys of the Latin grammar and rhetoric classes out of the Augustinians' vicinity, leaving only the more mature philosophy and theology students at the new site. Since the specter of

disease still haunted the old college, it is unclear if these orders were enforced. What is clear is that the Jesuits' provocations had brought the Augustinians to their wits' end. In early 1619 the royal governor wrote to the king to
tell about how the friars came out to block the workers from continuing at
the new college. This affair, he concluded, "could not but end with the heathens noticing and the Christians being scandalized."[40]

But the building of São Paulo o Novo had already caused scandal, and not
simply because the friars were unjustly robbed of their view and a handful of
houses. More important in the eyes of the *Câmara,* the friars, and the citizens
was the dishonor caused to the nuns of Santa Mónica. Because of the slope of
the terrain, the Jesuits' new classrooms overlooked the convent, and their windows afforded views into three of the nuns' four dormitory areas. Far from
being a place of pious enclosure, as the convent's founders and its inhabitants
desired, Santa Mónica was forever under the gaze of the college's boys. According to a formal complaint signed by seventeen nuns, the boys had taken
to tipping their hats when the prioress appeared at her window as well as making "other gestures, nods, and discourtesies." On a par with these insults was
the stench from the *secretas,* latrines, that wafted toward the convent from the
new, more crowded college, borne by the (formerly salubrious) winds. Fearing
contagion, the nuns asked ships' pilots to visit the site with compasses to confirm the direction of the winds and draw up a deposition with a scribe and a
judge. The nuns further complained that the student commotion at the college was a continual disturbance, and that the proximity of the public ministries of the Jesuits' church was "an assault on our thoughts."[41]

Such was the popular outcry over this violation of the nuns' honor (and their
role as guarantors of divine favor within the city) that the Jesuits relented—at
least in part. In 1621 they agreed to move their seminary back to the old college.[42] But the Jesuits resisted the friars' demands that they remove their
other classes and novitiate, despite royal commands that they only keep their
theology classes at the new site.[43] Although their position was untenable, the
Jesuits called on their allies in the viceregal palace at several reprises as the
dispute dragged on over the years. It was no secret to the Augustinians that
viceroys were on the Jesuits' side. Jerónimo de Azevedo "was sure to favor
them in everything," the friars' version of the events declared.[44] In assessing the
situation for the crown, his successor, Fernão de Albuquerque, dismissed
the Augustinians' arguments, telling the king simply, "They do not want to be
close to the men of the *Companhia,* and are ashamed to speak directly about

it." Albuquerque argued further on the Jesuits' behalf in 1621, declaring that the crown should look kindly on them because "they have more Christian communities and missions under their care than all of the other orders combined." Moreover, the Jesuits had assisted with various engineering projects in the Estado da Índia.[45]

The unease caused by this dispute in Goa, Madrid, and even Rome finally blew back against the Goa Jesuits when Palmeiro was in charge. With the arrival of the fleet from Lisbon in late 1623 the Visitor learned that the Society's curia was also against the plans for the new college. But if the Goa Jesuits were to back down in the face of such pressures, they needed a way to save face. They found their refuge in a close reading of the founding charter of the novitiate, an institution that the Jesuits had hoped to house in their new college. Palmeiro learned that the novitiate could only keep its endowment if it was "never united to a college." If the Jesuits contravened these terms, they would lose the endowment; its funds would revert to the *Misericórdia,* a charitable confraternity.[46]

Acceding to Rome's wishes, the Visitor called together the professed priests of the college to discuss the predicament in January 1624. These Jesuits debated vigorously over whether to create an enclosure for the novices at the new college, or to find a way to train them at São Paulo o Velho without endangering their health. Letters from four participants at this gathering reported that Palmeiro refrained from making a pronouncement and instructed all present to send their opinions to Rome.[47] The Visitor forwarded his thoughts to the superior general under separate cover, recounting the history of the conflict with the Augustinians and the positions taken at the meeting. Seeing that the Jesuits had few options, he argued for retreat: the novitiate should be moved to the old buildings. Past promises, royal decrees, and the terms of the novitiate's endowment were reasons enough, but Palmeiro also remarked that the incidence of disease near São Paulo o Velho had lessened.[48]

The Jesuits were mistaken in thinking that the resolution of this affair was in their hands; while they awaited Rome's opinion, Madrid forced the issue. Viceroy Francisco da Gama summoned Palmeiro in the late spring of 1624 to inform him that the crown had decided in favor of the Augustinians. The friars were "squeezing him" to ensure that the Jesuits did not delay moving their novitiate any longer, the viceroy claimed. As a result, da Gama intimated, he could not continue to "shut the mouths of the friars" if the Jesuits continued to stall. And owing to the decline in fevers, the Jesuits could no longer count on support from a majority of the judges of the *Relação* who were entrusted with promulgating royal decrees. The question that Palmeiro had to answer was how the Jesuits would retreat. So the Visitor called a gathering of more than twenty professed members of the Society, where he won support for his decision to move the novitiate back to the old college. "We resolved to do it, as it was done, in the month of July," he wrote to Rome, "to the great applause of the whole city, which celebrated this move as a reason for being certain that we would not completely abandon São Paulo o Velho."[49]

And so the Jesuits held another procession across the city of Goa in 1624, but this one served to signal a defeat for the Society. In addition to the legal excuses they had for abandoning part of their plans, they found another in their recognition of the will of the city's inhabitants. After all, the old college had been founded by Francis Xavier and had housed his wonder-working relics for years. As the site of pious memories, São Paulo o Velho could therefore not be left to ruin. The tone of Palmeiro's letter recounting this retreat to the curia nevertheless revealed that he felt the pain of the Society's wounded pride. He held out the possibility of disease as a trump card, half hoping it would vindicate the Jesuits' years of delays in obeying royal orders. Sickness was virtually guaranteed in Goa's climate, he recognized, whether at the new college or the old one. If, however, there was a significant increase of the rates of disease, Palmeiro asserted, "then we will be more justified and enabled to make some other move."[50]

Despite being checked in their plans by the Augustinians and their allies in Goa, the Jesuits still enjoyed the goodwill of the Portuguese viceroys. Like his predecessors, Francisco da Gama showed himself a friend of the Society— even when the Jesuits overplayed their hand, as they had in the case of the new college. In that affair, da Gama realized that Palmeiro, his primary interlocutor, was not responsible for the tensions that had built up. As a result, the viceroy bore the Visitor no ill will. Indeed, it appears that their frequent interactions in political matters turned them into friends.

This friendship was mutually beneficial, since da Gama had few friends in Goa. Despite the fact that he was the great-grandson of Vasco da Gama and held the hereditary title of Count of Vidigueira, he was hated in both popular and elite circles. To give but one example of the rancor da Gama faced in Goa, his enemies smashed the statue of his illustrious ancestor just as he embarked for Lisbon at the end of his first term as viceroy, 1597–1600.[51] According to one modern scholar, Francisco da Gama was "haughty, distant, very conscious of his dignity as viceroy . . . , rigorous in fulfilling obligations, whether his own or those of his subjects, be they noble or plebeian."[52] In other words, he was just like Palmeiro—with the exception that the Visitor was never described as haughty. The viceroy sought Palmeiro's advice on matters relating to imperial governance and tried to have him included in the administrative councils of the Estado da Índia. For instance, in 1623 he appointed the Visitor to the *Mesa da Conciência e Ordens,* the royal tribunal that dealt with ecclesiastical affairs, but Palmeiro excused himself and the post went to the viceroy's fourth choice, the Augustinian provincial.[53]

FIGURE 5.3. Portrait of D. Francisco da Gama, Count of Vidigueira, during his second term as viceroy of the Portuguese Estado da Índia from 1622 until 1628.

The Visitor was da Gama's preferential contact within the Society of Jesus. Unlike the priests of the Province of Goa—in particular, the senior Jesuits who lived in the capital and thrived on rivalries with the other orders—Palmeiro had a broad vision. He represented the Society itself and was scrupulous enough in the defense of the order's standing and image to put relations with the crown above local interests. When da Gama needed help supervising the repairs to the fortifications in Sri Lanka, he turned to the Visitor. When the viceroy learned of the murmuring in Cochin that Jesuit servants were secretly unloading cargoes away from the city's customs house, he alerted Palmeiro.[54] And when the king wanted to know who was responsible for the circulation of a virulently anti-Jesuit tract in Goa, da Gama made sure to alert the Visitor about the progress of his investigations.[55] In a further demonstration of the strength of the bond between the two men, the viceroy continued to correspond with the Visitor after Palmeiro headed to East Asia. In return for his friendship, and in view of the fact that the Lisbon Jesuits were seeing to the education of his young son, Vasco Luís da Gama (1612–1676), the viceroy declared his loyalty to the Society and swore to fight for its interests. "While I am alive," he wrote to Superior General Muzio Vitelleschi in January 1624, "it will always be present in my mind to serve Your Paternity and the *Companhia* in whatever affairs may arise."[56]

More than once, Palmeiro had occasion to test the viceroy's willingness to come to the Jesuits' aid. As has been shown, the crown did not always favor the Society in colonial affairs, and at times Madrid sent orders prejudicial to its missions. Palmeiro's friendship with da Gama helped to alleviate these royal impositions or block them altogether. One such case provides a useful illustration of the benefits of this alliance. It concerns the Jesuits' presence in Southeast Africa and a misunderstanding over the crown's orders. When Francisco da Gama sailed to Goa for his second term as viceroy in 1622, he was charged with inspecting the fortifications and the royal hospital on Mozambique Island. That small Portuguese outpost was of great strategic importance to the crown since its fortified harbor stood at an important juncture along the Cape Route. The Jesuits maintained a college there, in a building situated on a plot known as the *fortaleza velha,* the old fort. Thinking that the Jesuits' college compromised the colony's military defenses, the crown twice ordered the priests to decamp to another site. Palmeiro and the superiors of the Province of Goa protested that the "old fort" held no military value when it was purchased in 1614, and that the king was misinformed.[57] But convincing the crown of its error was no simple task; the Jesuits could not do it alone.

Viceroy da Gama had ample time to inspect the fortifications of Mozambique on his way to India. He had been shipwrecked in the area after an encounter with a Dutch fleet and had to bide his time before heading to Goa.[58] He surveyed the massive new fortress that had recently been completed and verified the state of the older defensive works on the island. The "old fort" that had stood at the middle of the island, although indicated on contemporary maps in the hands of royal advisors, had long since crumbled, and its carved stones had been taken away to be used for other constructions. In the viceroy's letters to the king, da Gama described how he had gone to hear mass at the Jesuits' modest church one morning and, despite searching, "did not find any vestige or sign of the old fort, but only the memory one had been there once." He therefore refused to evict the priests, though he made assurances of his readiness to comply with the royal will if need be.[59] When Palmeiro met with the viceroy in Goa in 1623, he learned of da Gama's gesture toward the Jesuits at Mozambique and duly relayed his gratitude to the Society's Roman curia. The Visitor noted that da Gama had insisted that the Jesuits remain at their church and informed the king "of the truth he had seen with his own eyes." Of course, it was one thing to tell the crown it was misinformed and another to receive a formal declaration rescinding a royal order. Further pressure from the viceroy on the Jesuits' behalf would almost certainly be necessary. In Palmeiro's view, there could be no retreat from the Jesuits' position in Mozambique, and da Gama would have to see the matter through to the end: "We will not abandon this site," he wrote, "because it is the best in the town for our ministries, being in its center, and for that reason our church is the most frequented by the residents, who greatly esteem the *Companhia*."[60]

Madrid at length came around to the Jesuits' position with regard to the College of Mozambique. After all, the men of the Society were very useful to the crown in East Africa. In addition to maintaining their own network of communications in the region that funneled valuable information to royal administrators, the Jesuits also assisted in diplomacy and care for the sick. Although there were only five priests and two brothers attached to the college on Mozambique Island, they accepted the task of administering the colony's royal hospital. Before the Jesuits took over this institution, an important facility in a land known for its epidemics, the building in which it was housed collapsed due to mismanagement.[61] In addition to goodwill from the crown, the Jesuits received salaries from the royal treasury in return for ministering to the sick.[62] The Society's men also contributed to maintaining a Portuguese presence in the Zambezi River valley (known as the *Rios de Cuama*), four hundred miles away from Mozambique, with residences at Sena in the lower river valley and Tete, 260 miles farther upstream.[63] One of the most experienced Jesuits in this region, Giulio Cesare Vertua (b. 1584) of the Sena mission, served as an invaluable assistant to the governor of the Portuguese colony when he led an embassy in 1623 to the new *monomotapa*, lord of the upper Zambezi highlands.

The Visitor knew that these services were more beneficial to the crown than to the Society of Jesus. But in return for royal and viceregal patronage, it was a fair trade. The Jesuits were indeed present in Mozambique, but their efforts had not produced much spiritual fruit. Palmeiro had deputized Francisco de Azevedo (1578–1660), the former rector of the College of Diu, to inspect the missions at Sena and Tete in 1623, and while Azevedo did not discover any problems among the Jesuits, he did not find a significant community of indigenous Christians. Giulio Cesare Vertua, a fifteen-year veteran of the missions in that area, wrote to Palmeiro to insist that the problem lay in the fact that the area was administered by the Jesuit rector in far-away Mozambique who "does not deal with the *cafres* but only takes care of his college."[64] The same lack of success was seen on Madagascar, where the Jesuits had gone in the late 1610s at the crown's suggestion to search for shipwrecked Portuguese sailors and their descendants. Luigi Mariana (1581–ca.1640) had spent nearly seven years in the island's southern regions and even claimed the conversion of a prince, who was baptized at Goa. But Mariana's departure put the enterprise on hold, leading Palmeiro to send two men back to the island with orders not to return to Goa without permission. In spite of his desires to correspond to the crown's wishes, the Madagascar mission was futile. By 1624 the Jesuits had been expelled from the island and Palmeiro desisted, declaring that "all understood that God did not want to open the eyes of the multitude who live on that island."[65]

The Jesuits' activities in Mozambique and Madagascar were merely a sideshow to the Society's interests elsewhere in East Africa. They placed far more importance on the success of the mission to Ethiopia, which reached its period of greatest flourishing during Palmeiro's time as visitor. That particular enterprise had begun in the middle of the sixteenth century and was erected on the diplomatic foundations that the Portuguese had established with rulers of the Ethiopian highlands (identified by them as the Prester John of medieval legend). The Ethiopians were a Christian people, so the Jesuits' mission in their lands was similar to their work among the Syro-Malabar Christians of Southern India or the Armenian Christians scattered about South Asia. The Society's aim was to reform an existing church. That is, they intended to make Roman Catholics out of the Ethiopian Christians. The Jesuits sought to enact changes similar to those occurring in contemporary Europe, where the standardization of liturgical practices and the insistence on papal supremacy were central aims of the Tridentine reformation. Several Jesuits had been named Latin Patriarchs of the Ethiopian church by different popes in the second half of the sixteenth century, but none of them had garnered much success in their attempts to introduce the Roman rite. Longstanding religious customs were not easily replaced, and the links between the Ethiopian church hierarchy and the Orthodox Patriarchs of Alexandria not easily severed.

It was clear that reform along Roman lines would only come about in Ethiopia if its rulers forced the indigenous church to adopt new ways. Hence, the handful of Jesuits who worked in that land during the late 1500s concentrated their efforts on the court. They claimed few converts to Roman Catholicism among the Ethiopian clergy. The laymen and women who adopted the Roman rite were primarily the descendants of Portuguese soldiers and traders who had come to the area as part of the ambassadorial retinues of the mid-sixteenth century. The Jesuits' pastoral work over the course of the decades had nevertheless led, by the early seventeenth century, to the establishment of a small network of churches, centered on Fremona in the Tigray region and extending around the shores of Lake Tana.[66]

The Jesuits' strategy in Ethiopia focused on the person of the emperor, but results were long in coming. During his many years in Ethiopia, Pedro Páez (1564–1622) won the favor of Emperor Susenyos (b. 1572, r. 1606–1632). In 1621, Susenyos (to whom Jesuit sources frequently refer by his formal title, Seltan Sagued) decided to adopt the Roman rite. The following year he began to impose changes on the practice of religion in his domains. Although several members of his court joined him in his embrace of Roman Catholicism, the move caused uproar among the indigenous clergy and galvanized resistance among Susenyos's political foes. It was only the news of triumph, however, not word of the complications, that reached the Jesuits at Goa in 1622: in Ethiopia the emperor had made a solemn promise to Catholicize his domains with the help of the Society of Jesus.

The call from East Africa spurred the Visitor into action. Palmeiro had to appoint new men for the Ethiopian mission and, most importantly, find a way of getting them there safely. Getting his men to the mission field was a considerable challenge because of the erosion of Portuguese naval power in the Red Sea and near the southern coast of the Arabian Peninsula. And it was not just at sea where the Jesuits had problems; after disembarking, they still had to travel through hostile territory up to the Ethiopian highlands where their mission was located. Palmeiro's challenge therefore required him to consider what was known of East African geography in order to select a safe path for his men.

Even at the capital of the Estado da Índia in the 1620s, there was little knowledge of the African interior. The Portuguese colonial state's interest in Ethiopia had waned since the mid-sixteenth century, and the political and economic reach of the Portuguese extended little beyond the coast, except in the Zambezi River valley. So scant was Portuguese knowledge of the interior that even the relative position of Ethiopia was not known with certainty—it was located somewhere north of Mozambique, somewhere west of the Horn of Africa, and somewhere south of the Red Sea. The nature of early modern maritime trade, which split into two East African contact zones with the Somali deserts in the middle, helps make this lack of information understandable. But Palmeiro still needed to know where to send his men, and there were a few things of which the Portuguese were sure: First, the steady rise of Ottoman power in the Red Sea made the old route to Ethiopia, via the port of Massawa (in today's Eritrea), dangerous. Second, there were rivers that went inland from most of the ports that were visited by Portuguese traders on the Swahili coast. If Ethiopia was located in the mountains, it was likely that these rivers had their origin in those highlands. Third, it was easy enough for teams of Jesuits to reach any of the East African ports from Goa. If the Estado da Índia did not have the necessary information, Palmeiro would have to send his men out as explorers. They would collect the knowledge that the colonial state lacked, surveying the different avenues from the coast to Ethiopia and reporting back to him. As he wrote to the superior general after the reports of the first Jesuit explorations were made, "if God is served to open for us some safe and easy route it would greatly help that mission, whose only difficulty is getting there."[67]

Palmeiro's reconnaissance of East Africa began in the south. The Jesuit curia had sent orders that he should contemplate a route inland from Mozambique—Rome's maps were even worse than Goa's—although the Visitor knew this was an improbable option. The notion that it might be an easy path up the Zambezi River was, after all, only slightly more farfetched than Rome's suggestion that he consider the trailheads in Angola on the other side of the continent, an idea that Palmeiro dismissed out of hand.[68] Neither Palmeiro nor the Portuguese royal officials knew that Ethiopia was 2,300 miles from Mozambique. They imagined that the lakes rumored to exist above the region of the *Rios de Cuama* (near Tete) would connect with the rivers of Ethiopia. And so Palmeiro asked Luigi Mariana, a veteran of the Mozambique mission, to inquire if it would be possible to proceed northward from the Zambezi Valley, past the lands of the Maravi peoples and the powerful chieftain Muzura, to the region of the lakes and onward from there to Ethiopia.[69] Mariana went to Sena and Tete, where he asked the Portuguese settlers and their indigenous relations in the area about the possibilities for such a trek, but his reply to the Visitor was negative. No one that Mariana found was willing to undertake such a journey since the lord Muzura was the sworn enemy of the Portuguese. Even if a way around Muzura's lands could be found, however, Mariana was not convinced it would be easy. "It suffices to mention the serious illnesses that those who enter these rivers customarily suffer from, and of which little needs to be said," he wrote to Palmeiro. Moreover, Mariana added, there were sure to be "long voyages that will have to be made along wearisome rivers and in such small and cramped boats" as well as unknown and possibly hostile peoples along the way. "But as for myself," he offered to the Visitor, "I am ready to do all that which holy Obedience ordains."[70]

The chances of finding a successful passage to Ethiopia increased, if only marginally, at points farther north along the East African coast. Thus, in early 1624 the Visitor sent two men to the region of Malindi in what is now Kenya. These Jesuits were Juan de Velasco, a valued assistant whom Palmeiro described as his "feet and hands," and a recent arrival to India, Jerónimo Lobo (1595–1678). This team was instructed to survey the nearly six hundred miles of coastline from Mogadishu to Mombasa and report to the Visitor if they found a viable route inland. The Visitor's reason for sending men to ex-

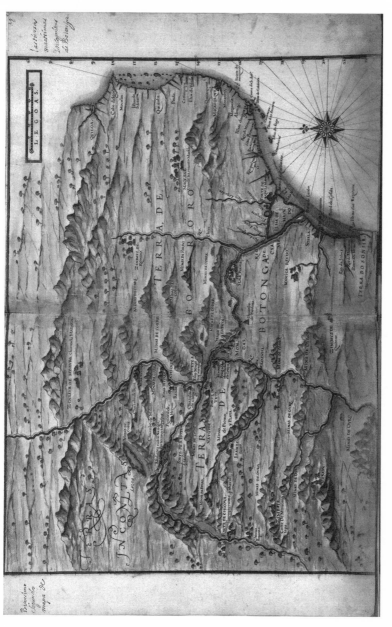

FIGURE 5.4. Map of Mozambique and the lower Zambezi River valley, known as the *Rios de Cuama* by the Portuguese. This map, from the "Tavoas Geraes de Toda a Navegação" drawn by João Teixeira Albernaz the elder (fl. 1602–1648) in 1630, shows the limits of Portuguese knowledge of the East African interior.

plore this region was the intelligence that the Galla (or Oromo) people who lived in that region were at peace with the Ethiopian emperor, whose lands were rumored to be nearby.[71] Good relations with the Muslim traders along most of this coastline meant that Portuguese ships were frequently present. To be sure, scholars have shown that there was only intermittent peace between the Ethiopian polity, the Oromo, and, further afield, the coastal kingdoms.[72]

Velasco reported to Palmeiro that the rumors of peace were exaggerated and an overland route would be difficult. The nations situated adjacent to the Ethiopian emperor's lands were "in continual war amongst themselves." On Pate Island (now part of Kenya), Velasco and Lobo learned more from "a Moor who had travelled through all of these lands and is the only one we find with perfect knowledge of them." Their informant told them that they could expect the constant threat of warfare, numerous obligatory gifts for the "little kings of the backcountry," and the burden of outfitting a train of pack animals. The result would be "a flood of expenses." Velasco and Lobo concluded that their only possibility was a route north from Mogadishu, but that city was in revolt and its lord (who had been friendly to the Portuguese) in exile. Realizing that they had reached a dead end, Velasco and Lobo found passage to Diu, where they waited for new orders from the Visitor.[73]

From his inquiries among the Portuguese traders and officials at Goa as well as from information that had arrived from Ethiopia, Palmeiro learned of one more route that he might investigate. This path lay through the kingdom of Zeila, starting at the port of the same name (now Saylac, Somalia) and on toward Ethiopia to the west. The ruler of Zeila was understood to be at peace with both the Ethiopian emperor and the ruler of Qishn (on the northern side of the Gulf of Aden, now part of Yemen), with whom the Portuguese enjoyed good relations. The mission superior in Ethiopia, António Fernandes (1568–1642), wrote to Palmeiro to express his doubts about the Zeila route, suspecting that the country's ruler was not friendly. Brushing aside this trepidation, Palmeiro and his consultors at Goa elected to send two men to Zeila. The Visitor assumed that if they could not get beyond the port, they could turn back in the same way Velasco and Lobo had done, "and if they go farther, we will uncover our intended goal."[74] The two priests, Francisco Machado (b. 1587) and Bernardo Pereira (b. 1588), were warmly received in Qishn and shown hospitality in the port of Zeila. Fernandes made plans to descend from Ethiopia toward a rendezvous with the pair, who had proceeded on a ten-day trek inland to the court of the kingdom of Zeila at Aussa.

Letters sent from the port of Zeila by Machado and Pereira reached Goa in the summer of 1624, heralding their safe passage thus far. Content with his gamble, Palmeiro forwarded the good news to Rome in November of that year.[75] But the Visitor later learned that he had sent the two missionaries into danger. When the news that they were coming from Zeila reached the imperial court in Ethiopia, the emperor "immediately gave them up for dead."[76] According to contemporary accounts, the emperor's advisors had made a costly error when they suggested possible routes to the Jesuits in Ethiopia (who had passed on their information to their confreres in Goa). Instead of writing that they could safely proceed through Danakil, the letters said Zeila. Certainly a trek across the harsh terrain of the Danakil Depression (otherwise known as the Afar Triangle) would not have been easy, but it would have been less dangerous than a reception at the court of Zeila. The rulers of that land had not forgotten how they had suffered at the hands of both the Ethiopians and the Portuguese in times past. Initially welcomed at Aussa in August 1624, the missionaries were imprisoned and killed upon the ruler's orders.[77]

The result of these failed prospections meant that the Visitor had to consider the route through *o Estreito*, that is, the Bab-el-Mandeb Strait at the mouth of the Red Sea. Despite the Portuguese fear of the Turks and Arabs, the 2,500-mile route from Diu to Massawa or Suakin (in modern Sudan) and then inland toward Fremona proved to be the safest one. This came as a surprise to Palmeiro in light of the fact that the four Jesuits led by Manuel de Almeida (1580–1646), whom he sent to the Ethiopian emperor in 1622, had great difficulty even getting to the Red Sea. Delayed by bad weather, pirates, and English and Dutch fleets, Almeida's group took over eight months to reach Suakin, including a delay at Dhufar (now Salalah, Oman) during which the Jesuits were forced to hide aboard their ships while they waited for the winter winds to change.[78] But another group of four priests sent by Palmeiro from Goa in early 1624 were able to reach Ethiopia swiftly via the Red Sea route. Apparently eager to maintain good relations with Susenyos, the Ottoman pasha at Massawa showed the Jesuits courtesy and facilitated their journey onward.

Manuel de Almeida arrived with his companions at Danqaz, site of the imperial court, in February 1624, bearing greetings for the Ethiopian emperor from the Society's superiors in Rome and Goa. Susenyos reportedly heard the Jesuit envoy read the letters from Assistant Nuno Mascarenhas and Palmeiro "with much happiness," and enjoyed the gifts he received: a reliquary, Chinese embroidery, devotional paintings, and a valuable crucifix. The Visitor sent a set of rosary beads made of amber from Goa, but it appears that the emperor best liked the set of musical instruments, including a harp and a harpsichord. They were, he claimed, "all things from heaven."[79] By the autumn of 1624 Palmeiro felt justified in proclaiming his jubilation about the events in Ethiopia to Rome. Despite the slow progress of some of the men he had sent, ten priests had made their way through dangerous territory to reach the mission field. "Infinite thanks will be given to God Almighty for such a great mercy," he wrote, "that this year we put more people in Ethiopia than we were able to do in any of the more than sixty years past."[80]

In the mid-1620s Ethiopia was a Jesuit success story. Elsewhere in the Provinces of Goa and Malabar, Palmeiro encountered leadership problems, but Ethiopia appeared to be on the right track. Its superiors were worthy men who enjoyed the favor of the emperor and members of the high nobility; they seemed capable of carrying forward the ambitious task before them. The final effort that Palmeiro would need to coordinate with regard to Ethiopia was the safe transit of the recently appointed Latin Patriarch, Afonso Mendes, to the imperial court. Being intent on reshaping the Ethiopian church along Roman lines, Susenyos requested a representative appointed by the papacy—not simply a member of a religious order like the other missionaries—to reform and ordain the indigenous clergy.[81] With the safe passage of Mendes, a priest who had been Palmeiro's fellow theology professor at Coimbra, and his two auxiliaries to the mission field, the Visitor could trust that Ethiopia would have firm ecclesiastical guidance, exercised by people loyal to the Society of Jesus. He could then turn his attention to the other matters that demanded his attention.

As the Society's senior representative in Goa, Palmeiro had an important role to play in helping his former colleague get to Ethiopia. After all, the "conversion" of the emperor and the creation of a Latin Church in that country was the result of Jesuit efforts, so the order's spiritual patrimony was at stake. The Visitor therefore delayed his return to resolve the affairs of the Fishery Coast in order to ensure that Mendes's passage through India went well. The problem that both he and the new Jesuit provincial, the elderly Francisco de Vergara (1550–1634), saw was that the currents of rumor around the Estado da Índia would be swifter than the winds and waves carrying the patriarch to his destination. If Muslim powers in the region learned that such a high-value prelate was heading through their lands, they might capture him and hold him for a princely ransom.

Vergara and Palmeiro sent word to Mozambique, where the fleet carrying Mendes in 1623 would be sure to stop, that the patriarch should disembark incognito at Goa. The plan was to have Mendes and his two auxiliary bishops proceed from the docks to the College of São Paulo o Novo in covered sedan chairs. From there they would head to one of the Jesuit houses in Salcete dressed in the Society's standard black robes. It was crucial, Vergara explained in a letter to Superior General Vitelleschi, that Mendes not be seen with his episcopal insignia before reaching Ethiopia. Vestments or other symbols of the high clergy would be a sure giveaway of his illustrious status. But Palmeiro forgot to exercise the necessary discretion when his old friend the patriarch arrived in late May 1624. Provincial Vergara was away from Goa during that period and could only lament how the Visitor had blown Mendes's cover. "Father Visitor bears some of the blame," Vergara wrote to the Jesuit curia in November of that year, specifying:

> I was visiting Salcete at the time, and so they disembarked publicly and with the same ceremony entered the college, and right away put on their pontifical insignia, and the most important people in the city came to visit them. They donned in public their vestments, the rochet and mozzetta, and together they were present at some feasts in our houses, and so they were shown to the whole city and to all the others in India, and already they know in Diu of Mendes's coming as patriarch and bishop of Ethiopia. This fame will soon race along aboard the ships that travel to the Strait of Mecca, and the pasha of Massawa and Suakin will know and seek them if they go to Ethiopia.[82]

The other share of blame belonged to the Latin Patriarch of Ethiopia. Mendes wrote to Rome how overjoyed he was upon his arrival to see Palmeiro, "with whom I shared great friendship in Portugal," and how they resumed their amicable dealings in Goa.[83] But even if the Visitor had urged his former colleague to lay low, the symbols of Mendes's rank proved an irresistible temptation. Francisco de Vergara noted that the patriarch caused the Goa Jesuits dismay by walking about the city with "all of his pontifical insignia with two or three Portuguese servants before him." Would that he had avoided this show and proceeded "apostolically and without pomp, as the other bishops had done when they first arrived"—taking Estévão de Brito (ca. 1570–1641), the former Jesuit who was recently consecrated archbishop of Cranganore, as an example.[84]

It was not just the patriarch but also his auxiliaries who caused problems during their stay at Goa. Mendes had sailed to India in the company of two other Jesuits, Diogo Seco (1574–1623) and João da Rocha (b. 1587), but Seco had died on the way. The choice of these three men had caused unease at the Jesuit curia in Rome because neither the king nor the papacy had consulted the superior general. Philip III had declared Mendes as his candidate for the patriarchate to Gregory XV after hearing the theologian give an oration at Évora in 1619. Responding to royal pressure, the papacy issued letters patent for the new Latin Patriarch, but the news only reached Muzio Vitelleschi once the patents had been sent to Portugal. The choice of Diogo Seco and João da Rocha, Mendes's two auxiliaries, appears to have been worked out between Mendes and the crown. It is unlikely that the Jesuit hierarchy in Portugal would have permitted Rocha to go, since he had not yet made his fourth-vow profession.

Wanting to be sure that Catholic bishops arrived in Ethiopia, the crown insisted that the papacy send letters announcing the appointment of these two men as auxiliary bishops, along with patents for their consecration. (The designation of three bishops was intended to ensure successors if any of them died prematurely, as indeed was to happen with Seco.) The papacy, however, ordered that the youthful Rocha not be consecrated until some later point and not before his departure from Lisbon. Vitelleschi was sufficiently annoyed at this display of royal and papal disregard for his prerogatives that he sent orders to India for Palmeiro to seize Rocha's episcopal patents and give him some other assignment in the Province of Goa. And when reports of Rocha's indiscreet behavior at the colonial capital arrived in Rome, they gave force to the superior general's decision to insist that the papacy revoke his patent outright.[85]

During his voyage to India, João da Rocha decided to step into the shoes of the deceased Diogo Seco, who had been consecrated in Lisbon. Rocha considered himself his colleague's successor, and so, upon disembarking at Goa, he put on Seco's vestments in public. "Wanting to show himself something of a bishop," as Provincial Vergara described the scene, he kept the Goa Jesuits embarrassed throughout the summer months of 1624.[86] But when the mails arrived from Rome in the autumn of that year, Palmeiro delivered what Mendes called the *bombarda*. The Visitor brandished his own letters from Rome to take away the ones that Rocha had received. From the patriarch's perspective, this punishment was "well deserved, owing to the juvenile ardor with which he snatched up the rochet, without paying due respect to those who most deserved it."[87] The Visitor reported that Rocha was "greatly saddened by this mortification" but nonetheless submitted to the superior general's orders. Needless to say, the demotion of a bishop-elect to the rank of a simple priest would be all the more embarrassing for the Goa Jesuits if Rocha were given a public ministry. So Palmeiro called his consultors to find another assignment, perhaps somewhere in Salcete, away from the rumor mills on the banks of the Mandovi. Upon hearing the news from the Visitor, Rocha "went down on his knees, saying that he would serve in a kitchen until his death." But such an extreme measure was unnecessary and, as Palmeiro was happy to inform Vitelleschi, Rocha adapted well to his new post.[88]

When he wrote to Rome to explain how he had handled the Rocha affair, the Visitor could not contain his bewilderment that the young priest he had known as a student at Coimbra was ever considered for the episcopacy: "If Your Paternity will give me the liberty to say this," Palmeiro wrote, "Father João da Rocha did not demonstrate such commendable behavior in Portugal that, at his age and without being professed, he should have been named for this dignity." The crux of the problem, in Palmeiro's judgment based on his (now considerable) experience of dealing with bishops in mission territories, was that Rome and Madrid often selected men who had no notion of the situations over which they would exercise jurisdiction. Clearly it was a good thing for the Society of Jesus that its men were consecrated bishops in Europe, where the public display of ecclesiastical dignity raised the order's prestige. (Loyola had expressed reservations about his men joining the secular church hierarchy but at length permitted them to accept offices and titles.) But the type of episcopal pomp that was just the thing for enhancing authority in Europe did not necessarily produce the same effect in Asia and often was counterproductive—as Mendes's display at Goa demonstrated. Invoking Archbishop Brito of Cranganore again, Palmeiro stated his view of how appointments to the church hierarchy should be made in the lands beyond Europe: "It could be that the Society will gain more and it will cost the king less if, when bishops are appointed for the missions and they have to be from the *Companhia,* they are chosen from among the priests who are already in these parts, because they already have experience and will assume the role with less clamor."[89]

But it was not in the Visitor's hands to see one of his men named patriarch; he had to get Afonso Mendes to Ethiopia safely. He accomplished this task by the autumn of 1624, plotting a route through the Red Sea. Palmeiro realized the problems caused by his earlier disregard for caution and urged the patriarch to dress simply as he sailed around the Arabian Sea. Mendes wrote to Rome before his departure for Diu that he intended to go in the customary robes of a Jesuit, and that he had been coached on the necessary responses to give if he was marked as the patriarch: "I can respond that I am a priest who can ordain others." It was decided that his route would take him to Massawa, and he went in confidence that the Ottoman pasha in that city would give him no trouble. Mendes carried a valuable present that he hoped to offer in the right circumstances in order to smooth his passage, if it stalled. Heading to Ethiopia without a designated successor nevertheless gave the patriarch pause "because everything today is hung on the strand of my life, which is very weak and little secure."[90]

Palmeiro was more concerned about the patriarch's being able to present himself with sufficient authority before Emperor Susenyos. This worry had been one of the primary reasons why the Visitor had decided to remain at Goa until he saw Mendes off. "I hope that the patriarch does not lack anything on this mission," he declared to Vitelleschi in Rome. Palmeiro spent the early autumn of 1624 gathering money for the patriarch. Viceroy Francisco da Gama was asked for alms for Mendes, and these were duly given. The Visitor identified vestments and ornaments that Mendes could carry with him to his new African church. For example, among the liturgical paraphernalia in the Society's churches, Palmeiro found a silver vessel that bore the indication "for the patriarch." Although there was no clue about which patriarch it might have been intended for, the Visitor decided it was best entrusted to Mendes. Monies obtained by the patriarch in Goa were used for buying the gifts he would have to give to the pasha as well as to the emperor.[91] By the end of 1624 Mendes would be on his way to Ethiopia, and Palmeiro would leave Goa for Cochin in the comfort that he had overseen another success.

The Visitor left Goa in November 1624 to return to the Province of Malabar. Palmeiro's departure from Goa reminded his subordinates at the colonial capital that he was not only their leader; he was still the administrator of the two provinces and responsible for them both. One of the pressing matters that prompted his return to the Province of Malabar was his desire to visit the Fishery Coast again. This trip by sea, which covered more than 680 miles each way from Goa, sought to resolve Jesuit personnel questions related to the revolt among the Parava Christians.

There were also other matters in the "South" that demanded Palmeiro's attention as he ended his term as visitor of both Indian provinces. News from Europe permitted him to settle, at least partially, some affairs in the Province of Malabar that had been left unresolved for half a decade. Problems of men and money had caused Palmeiro great anxiety during his stay in Cochin, but it appears that his time in Goa had given him a different attitude toward these issues. For example, the return of Alberto Laerzio to Goa on September 2, 1624, in the company of fifteen priests and fifteen novices did not disturb the Visitor, despite his earlier concerns about how a large crop of recruits could be supported by the impoverished Province of Malabar. Indeed, Palmeiro decided to escort these new arrivals personally to Cochin, taking in his company the newly consecrated archbishop of Cranganore, Estévão de Brito. In contrast to his attitude toward the ill-advised choice of João da Rocha, the Visitor was content with Rome's selection for Cranganore. Brito had long served among the Syro-Malabar Christians and knew the region of his future see well. The Visitor was present when Patriarch Mendes performed the investiture ceremony for Brito in late September, and had high hopes that the new archbishop would govern in tranquility.[92]

The other matter demanding the Visitor's presence in Cochin was the fallout of the papacy's decision on Roberto Nobili's contested missionary practices. In January 1623 Rome had ruled to approve his methods, issuing the apostolic letter *Romanae Sedis Antistes* that arrived in Goa later that year. The news rekindled the embers of conflict at the capital as well as in Cochin, where Palmeiro forwarded the information in January 1624.[93] The attitudes of some of Nobili's former supporters had changed since the Goa Conference of 1619. The two inquisitors in Goa considered that the Jesuits felt the pope's pronouncement to be scandalous; in particular, the permission granted for high-caste converts to retain the Brahman symbols of the tuft of hair and thread "was not well received, even among many of the most important members of the Society."[94] Palmeiro therefore balked when the superior general sent word that he was to take part of the excess revenues of the Goa colleges and apply them to Nobili's mission. "It will never be acceptable for the priests of either this or that province for me to send it to Madurai," he replied to Rome, "because the priests of these provinces generally do not approve of that mission." Fearing that the general's order would stoke the flames of past conflicts over Nobili's enterprise, Palmeiro continued: "I speak to Your Reverence in all sincerity. Many will say that it still stands only because it was created by Italian priests." In order to preserve the unity among different nationalities within the Society that was so dear to Vitelleschi, the Visitor chose instead to take the revenue in question to the Jesuits on the Fishery Coast. Had it gone to Madurai, he informed the general, the Goa Jesuits would certainly "take the opportunity to express disgust at your orders."[95]

By 1624 Palmeiro had served as inspector in India for six years. He was aware that his second triennial term was soon to end, but he did not dare slacken the reins of governance until he received permission from Rome to do so. In the mails that traveled to Europe early that year, he offered to resign his post, citing his advanced age. "I will not disappoint in what is desired of me, but I am more ready to rest than to bear other burdens," he wrote. This desire to retire was logical—he was fifty-five years old—but Rome was apparently pleased with his calm hand on the tiller of the Society's ship in Asia. Sensing that the superior general might ignore his invocations of fatigue as he had done in the past, Palmeiro made them anyway to be sure that none would accuse him of being hungry for power. "God and the good of our *Companhia* are what matters above all," he asserted in the same letter, "and so I will not shield my body from work, since my life will not be greatly shortened by the fulfillment of duty."[96]

The Goa Jesuits had mixed feelings about Palmeiro's reappointment as visitor. It was to be expected that a man who had clashed with some of the senior priests would have his detractors. While they might not have invoked the tired adage about the corruptive nature of absolute power, they began to intimate what Poor Richard would later make a proverb: Fish and visitors stink in three days. Jácome de Medeiros, the former provincial officer who had chafed at Palmeiro's orders early in the Visitor's term, put the matter gingerly to General Vitelleschi in early 1624. It would have been impolitic to speak poorly of his superior, and so Medeiros tried a different tack; he suggested that Palmeiro was too indulgent. Medeiros admitted that Palmeiro's example was beneficial and that his goal was "to console all and offend no one." But this lack of severity, he claimed, was taken by some as license, and what was seen as complacency resulted in some discredit to the Visitor. He further argued that Palmeiro should be given a respite from his charge. After all, Rome had acceded to a request from a provincial congregation that no provincial superior in Goa serve for more than three years, and the Visitor's term had far exceeded that limit. No inspector should be allowed to serve for a longer period than a provincial, Medeiros urged, "all the more so since he is more absolute in power; unless he is an angel come down from heaven."[97]

Others had noted Palmeiro's agreeable character but had not seen cause for concern in it. Provincial Francisco de Vergara was adamant that the Visitor continue in his post. He was nearly seventy-five years old and needed Palmeiro's geniality and vitality to help him govern the Province of Goa. Patriarch Afonso Mendes insisted that affability was the Visitor's best quality because it ensured the unity of his fractious subordinates. Writing to Assistant Mascarenhas, Mendes explained how he had made inquiries among the Goa Jesuits in the summer of 1624 about Palmeiro, most likely at the curia's request. "No one accused him of anything but gentleness; but his gentleness also knows how to hold the rod," Mendes wrote, affirming also that "the example of his person is most rare in these parts, and very necessary."[98] Mendes repeated this confidential evaluation to Vitelleschi, declaring that there was no undercurrent of complaints about Palmeiro except among some who wished he would employ more rigor, more swiftly. "But these times are not of iron," Mendes countered, "nor are better cures performed with iron than with a gentle touch."[99]

The Jesuit curia did not wait to get these evaluations from Goa. If the superior general thought it impolitic for Palmeiro to continue as visitor in India, his talents could be put to good use elsewhere. There were other parts of Asia where his administrative skills were in demand, and where he would be a fresh face at the top of the Society's hierarchy. On December 21, 1624, a new patent was issued at Rome making him visitor of the East Asian missions.[100]

It is worthwhile pausing to consider the curia's decision. By his own admission, Palmeiro had little desire to undertake such an ambitious task. But he was a seasoned leader whose administrative competence and scrupulous observance of the duties of his office had been proven on successive occasions. Moreover, he was trustworthy, had long experience, and was already in Asia. And if it was necessary for the curia to save face in Palmeiro's reassignment, the fact of his already long tenure in India and that of a climate of tumult among the Jesuits in Macau offered the occasion for issuing a new order that would not appear to be the fruit of sour grapes at Goa. From the perspective of Rome, Palmeiro was therefore an ideal candidate for the post of visitor for the Province of Japan and the recently created Vice-Province of China.

The curia's decision was not so well received by the Jesuits on the shores of the South China Sea. Although a congregation representing the Province of Japan in 1623 had made an explicit request for a new superior to be sent from the outside, the Macau Jesuits had reservations about those who arrived with experience in South Asia. After all, "India" was the Estado da Índia, or the territories under colonial influence, something vastly different from the mission fields where indigenous rulers held sway and where East Asian cultural norms prevailed. The Jesuits who had immersed themselves in the cultures of East Asia were the first to suggest that the experience of "India" was of little use in China and Japan and might even be detrimental to their missions.

There was no more candid spokesman for this view than João Rodrigues (ca. 1561–1633), the most accomplished linguist among the Japan Jesuits and an important figure among the missionary exiles from that country living in Macau.[101] Rodrigues felt that someone like Palmeiro, despite his obvious talents, would be tainted by the attitudes he was sure to have acquired during his time in India. Rodrigues wrote to Rome twice about his reservations, urging the curia not to assume that all "Indias" were equal. He cited the example of Francisco Vieira (1553–1619), who had come from India to serve as visitor of the Province of Japan in 1615. For Rodrigues, who had lived in East Asia since his teenage years, Vieira was indelibly marked by his time among the indigenous people of Goa, "had a variety of different ideas, and was unable to satisfy these nations, or at least did not grasp the ideas that were different from those of the *Canarins* in India."[102] After he met Palmeiro in Macau, Rodrigues wrote again to the superior general about the variety of Asian cultures and the need for superiors who would take the unique qualities of East Asia into account. That superiors sent from the outside would forever compare the policies used in China and Japan with those employed in India was his prime concern:

> Those men who have governed other new Christian communities have opinions that need to be changed. They are not easily satisfied with things at variance with their experience, and so they adjust only with great difficulty to how things work here. This is especially true with those who stay in Macau and do not live here among the Christian communities where they can see with their own eyes what goes on and thereby gain the necessary experience. Men who have seen things here do not change the rules made by other superiors after many years' experience, or without much

counsel and consideration, communicating everything to our Father General who approves their rules. Superiors who have governed other *christandades* but do not work in these raise questions at every step, saying that this or that is not done in this way where they came from, nor is it permitted there. They are right to do so, for there is one way for the *Canarins* of India and other Christian communities of barbarian blacks from those parts, many of whom are slaves of the Portuguese, and another way for the Japanese, Chinese, and Koreans, people who are so civilized and ingenious in the sciences, government, and everything else that they are in no way inferior to our ways in Europe.[103]

João Rodrigues had hoped that a visitor would arrive at Macau from Europe without a lengthy layover in India. He was quick to brand Palmeiro a "superior from India," despite the Visitor's three decades' worth of experience in Portugal. But if Rodrigues feared that the shadow of India would color the East Asian missions in Palmeiro's eyes, he was mistaken. The Visitor's track record in Goa or Cochin had not shown him as disposed to riding roughshod over the carefully constructed policies of experienced men, or of approaching the task of governance with lash in hand. It is ironic that the man who had been criticized in India for a lack of rigor was likened to a slave driver. Rodrigues was nevertheless forced to concede that he was only making assumptions about Palmeiro. "Since he is so capable," Rodrigues wrote to Vitelleschi, "he will adjust very well, but it will cost him."[104]

––––––––––

Palmeiro's letters to Rome concerning his impending voyage to Cochin at the end of 1624 were the last missives that have been preserved from his time in India. By the time his orders arrived in Goa, it was autumn of the following year. Where he was at that time, whether in Cochin or Goa, is not known. The Visitor had completed his task in South Asia and was bound for a new set of challenges. The affairs of Ethiopia, the Mughal lands, and the Portuguese colonies on Indian Ocean shores would no longer be his concern, and his later writings make no mention of the issues that had preoccupied him in the Provinces of Goa and Malabar. To be sure, he left the Indian provinces with the satisfaction that he had successfully discharged his obligations to the *Companhia*. The curia and, above all, the superior general, had smiled benevolently on his efforts and had sent him off to take up other weighty responsibilities.

Bidding farewell to his friends from Portugal and India, he embarked at some point in the spring of 1626 on the 4,200-mile route from the capital of the Estado da Índia to its easternmost outpost. Ships heading from western India would typically leave Goa in the spring, aiming to clear the southern tip of Sri Lanka before the beginning of the Southwestern monsoon in early June. With the push of these winds, the fleets would traverse the Bay of Bengal and the Andaman Sea before moving swiftly through the Straits of Malacca. Often Portuguese ships would put in at Malacca for restocking, then head past the future site of Singapore before swinging northward toward the coast of modern Vietnam and onward across the South China Sea. When he arrived at Macau, he was truly in another world.

PART TWO

At Empire's Edge

6

The View from Macau

In the middle of the summer of 1626 André Palmeiro arrived on the China coast. He would spend the last nine years of his life in East Asia, governing the Jesuits' enterprises in that region from Macau. This small Portuguese colony at the mouth of the Pearl River was the headquarters for the Society's Province of Japan and Vice-Province of China. In contrast to the Indian provinces, these administrative units stretched far beyond the reach of colonial control: Between Siam and Japan, only Macau was in Portuguese hands. But even in that port city, neither the Portuguese and Eurasian residents nor the royal officials sent from the metropole were sovereign. Thanks to the negotiations that had permitted the establishment of the "City of the Name of God in China", officials representing the Ming state kept watch on the colony from just beyond its walls. So while there were numerous Portuguese and Luso-Asians who circulated across the waters of East Asia, there the Estado da Índia was little more than a name. The indigenous powers of East and Southeast Asia ruled on land while the Portuguese at Macau tried to draw profits from the movement of trade over the sea.

The same ebb and flow of commerce in East Asia waters enabled the creation of the Jesuits' Province of Japan. Portuguese fleets, like the one that carried the Visitor from his assignment in Goa to his post in Macau, bore the Society's men from the order's headquarters to mission fields across the region. Jesuits had followed the path of commerce first to Japan, where their mission had begun in the mid-sixteenth century. Toward century's end they used the pretext of accompanying Portuguese traders to the biannual Canton fairs to lay the foundations of their enterprise within the Ming Empire. (Eventually the growth of a mission within that land would justify the creation of a semi-independent unit, the Vice-Province of China.) In the early seventeenth century priests and brothers from the Society accompanied the Christian exiles who left Japan along the commercial routes that linked that land to Southeast Asia, establishing missions in the kingdoms of Cochinchina, Tonkin, and Siam. By the time Palmeiro arrived at Macau, a reconfiguration of Portuguese trade in the region permitted the Jesuits to travel easily to ports from Hainan Island to Siam to the Philippines.

So the winds of trade had borne the Jesuits about the China Seas for over three-quarters of a century by 1626. But the weather had begun to turn. When Palmeiro reached Macau, the Japan mission was mired in crisis: All of the Catholic clergy had been exiled by shogunal decree in 1614; the priests who remained and the clandestine church to which they ministered were the targets of a tenacious persecution that had the eradication of Christianity from Japanese soil as its goal. Indigenous forces also acted against the Jesuits in China, where an attack on the missionaries and their nascent church had only abated in 1623. As a result of that upheaval, the Society's mission within the Ming Empire was not firmly established even after half a century of effort. Moreover, the proselytizing strategies that the Jesuits had employed in China provoked discord within their order. It was still too soon to judge whether the new missions in mainland Southeast Asia would produce fruit, but it seemed certain that much would depend on whether the Jesuits could secure the good will of the region's rulers—and that outcome was far from guaranteed.

Palmeiro's vantage point over the Jesuit enterprises in East Asia differed greatly from the one he had occupied in India. In Macau he stood at a distance from the Japan, China, and Southeast Asia missions, rather than at their center. Persecution made it impossible for him to travel to Japan, and the mission in that land was the Society's most important concern in the region. The Province of Japan had been named after the site where the Jesuits had found the greatest degree of missionary success in East Asia, but Palmeiro had to govern its men from afar. Even making contact with the Jesuits in Japan was difficult, and the Visitor had to attempt a variety of stratagems to get men and money past the Japanese authorities who enforced the official ban on Christianity. Things were different in the Ming Empire, where the Jesuits enjoyed fame in the circles of scholar-bureaucrats who were the country's ruling elite. But their presence was sanctioned only through the patronage of influential figures, some of whom had become Christians, rather than by the will of the Chinese emperor. According to imperial law, foreigners could only enter China in the context of tribute embassies or during the periods of the Canton trade fairs. These restrictions were barriers of more importance to Palmeiro than the Great Wall; they stood between him and his men. But as the Visitor would learn, the Ming realm was not as impermeable as its laws made it out to be. Whereas it would be suicidal to attempt an inspection of the Japan mission, a journey across China to visit the Jesuits who were scattered across that land was possible, albeit challenging.

───────────

Palmeiro disembarked at Macau in July 1626.[1] What did he find there? The Portuguese colony, founded in 1557 through a combination of economic logic and diplomatic savvy, was a city of roughly twelve thousand inhabitants.[2] While the theorists of empire in Lisbon or Madrid might refer to Macau as a *conquista,* the place was in reality a minute territorial concession made by the Ming emperors. The Chinese authorities tolerated the settlement so long as it made no pretense toward expansion. The relationship between the colony and the Ming state was tense; the early 1620s had seen moments of conflict between the city's inhabitants and the Chinese officials who kept a close eye over the city from their yamen just beyond the gate leading into China proper.[3]

Situated too far from Goa to rely on the Portuguese viceroys (and resistant to overtures from the Castilian lords at Manila), Macau's city council acceded to mandarin demands in order to maintain their place in the lucrative trading world of East Asia. The *Senado da Câmara,* composed of Portuguese or Eurasian merchants, was perhaps the most independent civic body in the Portuguese Empire, and among the most prosperous.[4] The Macau merchants' riches were derived from their position as intermediaries in the exchange of Japanese silver for Chinese silk, a role the Portuguese had assumed when official relations between the Ming Empire and the Japanese state were severed in the mid-sixteenth century. The principal activity of Macau's urban oligarchy was therefore to organize the purchase of Chinese textiles at the Canton fairs and to outfit fleets to ply the route to Nagasaki. While the political situation in Japan and the presence of Dutch and English rivals was beginning to destabilize this enterprise in the mid-1620s, it still produced fabulous wealth for its Portuguese participants and would do so until 1639. Espying instability and seeking new opportunities, the colony's merchants had also begun to build their trading activities in the ports of mainland and insular Southeast Asia.[5]

A small city with a wide network of trading links, Macau was the ideal site for the Jesuits' headquarters in East Asia. Portuguese merchants had transported the Society's first missionary, Francis Xavier, on some of his journeys in the region and they had maintained the ships upon which his successors traveled. The largesse of these traders helped to endow Jesuit missionary endeavors in Japan, and later China, as well as in Macau itself, where the Society's Colégio de Madre de Deus was opened in 1594. In return the Jesuits who were trained in the Japanese and Chinese languages served as diplomatic and economic mediators with the indigenous authorities and traders in Kyushu and Guangdong. Eventually, the Jesuits would also use Macau as a base for their efforts in Tonkin and Cochinchina, that is, the kingdoms on eastern coast of mainland Southeast Asia. From its humble beginnings as a way station for missionaries traveling onward to Japan in the late sixteenth century, the Jesuit college grew into one of the Society's largest establishments in Asia.[6] While the Japan mission had thrived—until the expulsion of the Jesuits (and all other Catholic clergy) by shogunal decree in 1614, that is—the college had been home to a community of approximately forty-five men, just over half of whom were priests.[7] But with that rude blow to the main mission in East Asia, it became home to a community of exiles more than twice as large as its buildings were constructed to house.[8] By the mid-1620s there were more than sixty-eight priests and brothers at Macau living in the college complex just below the recently built *Fortaleza do Monte*.[9] This considerable number made the Jesuit community in the city the largest Catholic religious group in East Asia and a major political and economic force in the colony.

The Society enjoyed close links to the city's merchants and resisted attempts by either crown or Church to alter Macau's patterns of autonomous rule. In the years preceding Palmeiro's arrival, the Jesuits had become involved in major scandals in Macau with the royal governor and with the city's other clergy. Tensions that had been building since the exile of the missionaries from Japan came to a head shortly after the city's meager armed forces, under Jesuit command, repulsed a Dutch attempt to capture Macau in June 1622. The appointment of the colony's first royal governor, or *capitão geral,* in the following year was perceived as a threat to the independence of the city council as well as to the Jesuits. Most importantly, the Society lost its recreation ground on the *Monte* next to their college as a consequence of the restructuring of the city's defenses and the stationing of a detachment of soldiers, whose watchtowers afforded views into the Jesuits' quarters. In contrast to the good relations that the Society's men enjoyed with Viceroy Francisco da Gama in Goa, they chafed under his deputy, Francisco Mascarenhas, in Macau during the years of his rule, from 1623 to 1626.[10]

Worse than their relations with the captain general were the Jesuits' interactions with the other clergy in the cramped colony. After the 1614 debacle in Japan, Macau saw their mutual recriminations intensify, with Jesuits, Franciscans, Dominicans, and Augustinians casting blame for the missionaries' expulsion from Japan. The climate got worse in the early 1620s in a dispute over the governorship of the local diocese. Despite the fact that only about six members of each of the three mendicant orders were regularly in the city, friars from these orders enjoyed episcopal dignity in the early seventeenth century.[11] Upon his departure for Portugal in 1615, Frei João Pinto de Piedade (1553–1628) left the governorship of the bishopric in the hands of his fellow Dominican, Frei António do Rosário (d. after 1639). But when rumors of the bishop's renunciation of his see reached Macau in 1623, the city's parish clergy chose to elect a different ecclesiastical governor. The tug-of-war between the Dominicans and the diocesan clergy reached a stalemate in the following months when Rosário refused to step down.

The Jesuits took the side of the lower clergy in this dispute, but they did not come out on top. Incited from the pulpit to take up arms by the former provincial of the Province of Japan and rector of the College of Macau, Valentim Carvalho (1560–1631), the rebellious parish priests started a riot. Shots were fired at the Dominican convent. In a gesture aimed at calming the situation, the city council and the parish priests held a new election where they chose as governor Diogo Valente, the (former Jesuit) bishop of Japan, who was in the city awaiting an opportunity to travel to his beleaguered diocese. Although the captain general crushed the popular revolt and its leaders were sent to Goa for trial by the Holy Office, the Jesuits' support for the uprising caused scandal. In 1625 Carvalho was recalled to Goa, where he would spend his last years. This was a move made under the pretense that he was to take up a leadership post in India, but there is no record of him acting as a superior in the Provinces of Malabar or Goa. Valente was also summoned to Goa by that city's archbishop and held under a ban of excommunication for usurping another's episcopal dignity. News of the affair reached Palmeiro in India by late 1624.[12] Part of his charge in East Asia was therefore to rein in the excesses caused by his confreres and attempt to reestablish the Society's bruised reputation.

In addition to the challenges that Palmeiro would have to confront in Macau itself, he was also entrusted with finding solutions for the problems facing the Province of Japan and the Vice-Province of China. As the names of these units indicate, Japan was the center of the Jesuits' efforts in East Asia, with the China mission and the incipient enterprises in Southeast Asia occupying secondary places. The main reason for this state of affairs was that Japan had seen the most spectacular growth in conversions, whether coerced or not, in the preceding half-century. Estimates of the size of the Japanese mission church at the beginning of the seventeenth century suggest that there were nearly three hundred thousand Christians, the majority of whom lived on the island of Kyushu. There were also pockets of Japanese Christians found on Honshu, with significant communities located in the region of Osaka and in the island's northern reaches.

The Jesuits' strategy of intermingling politics and economics with their religious aims led to their being viewed as adversaries by the military hegemons bent on the unification of Japan. At the time of their expulsion in 1614, many of the Jesuits embarked for Macau thinking their exile would be brief, that the political storm provoked by Tokugawa Ieyasu (1543–1616) would abate, and that they would soon be allowed to return. But the tempest did not pass under the rule of Ieyasu's son Hidetada (1579–1632), either for the missionaries in hiding or for their flock. Over the first decade of these final persecutions, the number of Japanese Christians and the number of Jesuits (not to mention friars) was greatly diminished through a rigorous campaign aimed at eradicating all traces of Christianity from Japan. Reports of gruesome martyrdoms of both clergy and laity made their way to Macau, where they fostered a climate of anxiety and despair before being forwarded to Goa, Lisbon, and the rest of Europe.

Hope springs eternal, however, and the Jesuits at Macau plotted for years how to regain their foothold in Japan. Concern for their abandoned Christians was foremost, but there was also a strong desire for martyrdom among certain members of the Society. The men who ardently desired to return to the mission field in the face of mortal peril orchestrated elaborate ruses in order to disembark clandestinely in Nagasaki. More were reluctant martyrs who moved in the shadows from one peasant's hut to another before the shogunal authorities tracked them down. Some of those whose desire to minister to the living was stronger than their will to gain a heavenly palm followed the migration of Japanese Christian exiles to Southeast Asia. Starting in the 1610s Jesuits living in the port cities of the kingdoms of Tonkin and Cochinchina (as well as Cambodia and Siam) began missionary enterprises that would later expand their focus to include indigenous populations.

The Society's mission to China had likewise begun as an offshoot of the Japan mission, but its pedigree stretched back further, to the early 1580s. Although the growth of the China enterprise was slow, especially in numbers of neophytes, its early superiors had forged successful alliances (and had made some conversions) among the high-ranking imperial servants. But the strategy of engaging mandarins had been met with ambivalent results, and had even played a role in an outbreak of persecution in 1616—just two years after the Jesuits' expulsion from Japan. This crisis had passed by 1623, a few years before Palmeiro arrived in Macau, but its legacy was a climate of contempt among the exiles from Japan and their confreres in China. The resentment came from Superior General Vitelleschi's decision in 1619 to create an independent Vice-Province of China from the withering Province of Japan, and the internecine tensions were further exacerbated by rumors of excess among the would-be Jesuit mandarins in Beijing that reached the exiles at Macau.[13]

Regardless of the new élan that seemed to be taking hold in China and the promising beginnings of the missions in Southeast Asia, Palmeiro's main concern after his arrival was the embattled Japan mission. The unfolding tragedy, he asserted, was "what is most substantial" in East Asia; all other enterprises were sideshows.[14] His first task was to find some way of helping his confreres across the sea, but that was nearly impossible in the late 1620s. Once again he was obliged to elaborate a strategy for shuttling men and money across oceans in the face of certain danger. But how? In contrast to his efforts at Goa to smuggle the Latin Patriarch of Ethiopia past the hostile

Muslim powers of the Arabian Sea, the subordinates that he needed to send to Japan could hope for no kind reception at their destination. Mortal peril was a fact of life for the Jesuits living underground in Kyushu and Honshu, as it would be for the temerarious few who attempted to join them. At least the exiled Jesuits at Macau could call on substantial reserves of knowledge about the geography of the mission territories and faithful contacts among the Portuguese and Japanese traders who traveled back and forth to Japan. Relying on their counsel for the elaboration of his plans, Palmeiro would not be shooting in the dark.

The Visitor had to base his decisions on the most current information available at Macau, and the news that arrived from Nagasaki in 1626 and 1627 was disheartening. The persecutors of the Japanese mission church had pursued their goal with tremendous zeal. Hundreds of Christians had been captured, tortured, and executed. More than just a handful of missionaries, too, had fallen victim, further reducing the meager numbers of priests in Japan. Most upsetting for the Jesuits on the China coast was the news of the imprisonment of their provincial, Francisco Pacheco (b. 1566), in December 1625, especially because he was betrayed by a former Christian. Another two Jesuits, Giovanni Battista Zola (b. 1575) and Gaspar Sadamatsu (b. 1565), were also captured that year and held in the fortress of Shimabara, while a third priest, Baltasar de Torres (b. 1563), was seized in a village near Nagasaki. These men would face their inevitable executions in 1626, whereas their lay assistants were dispatched at the moment of their capture.[15]

The discovery of this clutch of priests led the shogun's men to redouble their efforts to flush out the remainder and extinguish the embers of fervor among the Japanese Christians. By the end of the following year, news of men and women being drowned at sea, burned at the stake, or scalded to death in the boiling springs on Mount Unzen reached Macau.[16] João Rodrigues Girão (1558–ca. 1629) described how the persecution had grown in intensity in 1627, with the agents of the state, especially the daimyo Matsukura Bungo no Kami Shigemasa, who used "varied and strange torments never before used in Japan." Rodrigues Girão's enumeration included the following horrors reserved for people unwilling to apostatize:

> Stripping both men and women naked and exposing them to shame, either hanging them from on high or plunging them into the frozen waters of winter; mauling them; holding them over the fire so as to burn them, or

burning them with lighted faggots, and, in the case of a pair, roasting them alive like so many Saint Lawrences, and leaving them in such a state that they gave up the ghost a few days later; branding almost all of the men and some women with a burning iron so as to imprint the word 'Christian' on their foreheads and cheeks; cutting the fingers off the hands of even small children; and, finally, insulting them and shaming them, and doing things to them which are too vile to write.[17]

FIGURE 6.1. Depiction of the death of Francisco Pacheco at Nagasaki in 1626. This image is found in the catalogue of martyrdom reports published at Lisbon in 1650 by António Francisco Cardim, titled *Elogios, e Ramalhete de Flores borrifado com o Sangue dos Religiosos da Companhia de Iesu* (Eulogies, and Bouquet of Flowers sprayed with the Blood of the Religious of the Society of Jesus).

The rigors of persecution had a chilling effect in some areas. Self-preservation began to trump loyalty among the plebeian Christians, and the priests were forced to seek refuge in the countryside near the towns and cities where they had once preached. Reports made their way to Macau of secret hiding places built under Christian homes where priests could find refuge. One letter described how three friars from different orders were sequestered under a trapdoor, and how Baltasar de Torres had initially managed to escape detection in similar hideaways.[18] Another report described how Juan Bautista de Baeza (1557–1626) spent his last years; after an illness left him paralyzed, he lay in a wooden box from whence he would minister to his flock.[19]

The healthy missionaries needed to travel abroad by themselves, whether to carry out their pastoral duties or to simply avoid capture, and there were many spies who were ready to claim the bounties offered by the shogun and his agents. Yet in spite of all of the danger in the regions of Nagasaki and adjacent Shimabara, glimmers of hope appeared with regard to the other parts of Kyushu and the two more remote centers of Japanese Christianity, the region around Osaka and the areas of Aizu Wakamatsu and Sendai in the northern reaches of Honshu. Closer to the seat of shogunal power and therefore less suspected of subversion, these latter regions were spared—at least at first—from the harshest manifestations of persecutory wrath. Rodrigues Girão could therefore send word to Europe that, beyond Kyushu, the rest of the underground Jesuits were safe, and that the Christian communities were at peace, "if it can be called peace."[20] Crucially for the missionaries and their *christandades*, baptisms were reported to have continued apace, with two thousand claimed by the Jesuits alone in 1626.[21]

From 1,300 miles away in Macau, Palmeiro contemplated his options. His first impulse was to travel to Japan to conduct an inspection in person, since such an expedition would give him firsthand knowledge about the situation there and how best to support his men and their flock. (The Inquisitors in Goa had conceded him special powers to punish Christian backsliders among the Japanese when he made his planned arrival in the mission field, although this task does not seem to have been high on his list of priorities.[22]) This plan for a voyage to Japan was dismissed as fancy quickly enough. It was too dangerous for an inexperienced European such as Palmeiro to travel about the Japanese countryside while the agents of the Nagasaki commissioners, the shogun's representatives in that former Christian center, had placed bounties on the heads of all *padres*.

One of Palmeiro's predecessors in the office of visitor, Francisco Vieira, had attempted such a trip in 1618 to little effect. Raids had begun in Nagasaki shortly after his arrival in that city, and on the night of December 13, Carlo Spinola (1565–1622), the Jesuits' procurator, and others had been captured. Vieira and his companion, Cristóvão Ferreira, who were hiding in a house nearby, decided to flee the city by ship in order not compromise their hosts. Separating from Ferreira, whose language skills and long experience in Japan enabled him to reconnoiter the territory, Vieira chose to seek a safe haven. Vieira spent forty days traveling by sea, disembarking only in remote anchorages before rejoining his confreres in the area that the Jesuits called Shimo, the northwestern part of Kyushu. According to Vieira's account, he had experienced "so many aches, indispositions, and pains, that I thought my life was ending; but it consoled me to see that I was expiring while persecuted for the Faith, and abandoned without remedy in imitation of the Blessed Francis Xavier, who died alone in a shack on one of the Chinese islands."[23]

Palmeiro's deathbed protestations of a lifelong desire for pious suffering to the contrary, he did not have a martyr complex. The Visitor was clearly aware that he could do more for the Japan mission by channeling resources to it from Macau than by putting himself into harm's way. Once the tenor of anxiety over the dying Japan mission reached a fever pitch, it would be up to his successor, Antonio Rubino, to attempt such a foolhardy expedition in 1642.

From Palmeiro's perspective, the best policy was stealth. But he needed to find a way to get men and money to Japan in a way that would neither reveal the positions of his subordinates nor jeopardize the links between Macau and Nagasaki. This latter consideration was foremost because the cessation of trade between the Portuguese colony and the Japanese port would immediately sever the lines of communication between the Jesuits on the China coast and their confreres and Christians across the sea. The threat had been made by the Japanese authorities, and the Castilians at Manila had already paid the price of exclusion from Nagasaki for transporting friars and Christian paraphernalia.

Macau's city fathers urged Palmeiro and the other missionary clergy to restrict what was sent on Portuguese ships to the bare minimum, for fear they would suffer the same fate. In the year of the Visitor's arrival in Macau, traders from Japan brought back reports of a rigorous inspection of that year's cargoes in Nagasaki. "A thousand laws" were promulgated in 1625 and 1626 to keep anyone or anything from disembarking without permission, it was claimed, and the inspectors demanded to know if there was any contraband such as devotional images or mass wine on the ships.[24] As the members of the Macau *Senado* explained to João Rodrigues, the Society's procurator, the penalty if such things were found or if any priests were discovered would be that the Japanese would "burn the ships, kill the people, and break off trade forever."[25]

So the first challenge was simply to maintain contact with the men in the mission field. On the fleets that sailed for Nagasaki in fall of 1626, the Jesuits sent two letters: one from Palmeiro indicating the line of succession in the office of Provincial from Pacheco to Mateus de Couros (1568–1632), and another from Rodrigues accompanying the 1,500 cruzados destined for the priests.[26] The procurator explained to Muzio Vitelleschi how the letters were carefully sealed between lead sheets so that they could be tossed into the sea if danger threatened.[27] It appears that although the 1626 missives made it safely to their addressees, letters sent in the following months had to be consigned to the waves to avoid detection. According to a letter from Couros in Japan that year, his reports to Macau were sent in code, but this was no guarantee of an easy flow of information.[28] Palmeiro wrote to Rome in May 1628 to recount how two monsoons had passed without his being able to make contact with his subordinates in Japan. Palmeiro lamented that he could not even send a reprimand to Giovanni Battista Porro (1576–1639), who had shown himself less than charitable to his confreres during their underground travels. The Visitor admitted that he had great difficulty finding a courier for his correspondence, "if it is not a small package that fits into a shoe or other such hiding place." Few were those who dared even to carry these letters, making it impossible for him to send private messages to specific priests. It was out of the question, Palmeiro insisted to the superior general, to forward letters from Rome since Vitelleschi's name and the wax seals on his letters were hard to conceal.[29]

A second challenge was to get money from Macau to Nagasaki and into the hands of the missionaries. One of the harsh realities that Palmeiro encountered upon his arrival on the China coast was that the Province of Japan was far from being wealthy. Lacking the option of investing in revenue-producing lands (with the exception of rental properties in Macau), the Jesuits had secured a dispensation from Rome to invest in the Japan trade. In spite of the disgust that the image of men sworn to poverty doubling as merchants had provoked in Europe and elsewhere in Asia, this had been the most reliable means for supporting the mission. But the vagaries of the silk–silver exchange had trended downward in the 1620s as the political climate in Japan put strictures on trade and some years passed without fleets traveling to Nagasaki.

If there was one man who was able to make the best of the flagging trade in East Asia, it was João Rodrigues. He had longer experience in the Japan trade than nearly anyone else in contemporary East Asia, and it was a boon for the Jesuits that he was willing to serve as procurator. Rodrigues knew the markets on both sides of the China Sea: the silk buyers in Nagasaki and its sellers in Canton. (Indeed, it was thanks to his diplomacy at Canton that Macau's trading links with China had been stabilized after a period of tension in the early 1620s.) Rodrigues knew the value of the silk trade to the Jesuits and was not willing to see this financial lifeline to the Japan mission severed through mismanagement. But he also had a clear sense of the limited size of the Society's investments. He made a candid disclosure of the province's finances to Palmeiro, during which he dispelled the illusions harbored by the Visitor from his time in India: "He arrived with the idea that there was some hidden treasure in this province and was amazed when he found it with old and new debts." To compound the problem of meager resources, the province's funds were stretched increasingly thin. Committed to new missions across Southeast Asia and forced by Rome to send money to the Vice-Province of China, Rodrigues claimed that his superiors had been so many Jobs, suffering patiently in the face of continual demands and molestations.[30]

The simplest way for Palmeiro to get money to his men in Japan was through the silk trade. Rome permitted the Jesuits to purchase fifty piculs of silk each year for indirect sale through agents in Japan. The exchange for silver that occurred at Nagasaki could, if done carefully, remain there to pay the rising expenses of the priests in hiding. The continual movements of individual men and the danger of investing money in Japan, not to mention the poor Christians to whom they were obliged by conscience to offer alms, all contributed to the rising costs of the mission.[31] But the proceeds from the silk trade could only benefit the persecuted *padres* if the Society's curia did not insist that a percentage go to support the other missions. In 1627 Palmeiro rejected the superior general's suggestion about raising the percentage of the yearly silk cargo dedicated to the China mission since the Vice-Province of

China had other resources. In a letter to the curia the following year, he declared that the alms collected in Macau were sufficient to feed the Jesuits at the Portuguese colony. Little remained, however, for supporting the other missions, or even for the maintenance of the college buildings. All at Macau eyed the proceeds from the silk trade, expecting it to perform miracles, Palmeiro wrote. But "although God can make them happen, we have seen that it is unwise to pin the fate of regular governance on such hopes."[32]

Of all the Visitor's strategic concerns with regard to the Japan mission, getting men to the mission field was the greatest. According to one letter from November 1627, there were only sixteen priests and brothers left in Japan, and not many friars beyond that number.[33] Given the problems of transferring money or even correspondence, the challenge of transferring men seemed nearly insurmountable. Sending men directly from Macau was out of the question, but perhaps they could reach Japan from someplace else.

The most promising possibility that occurred to Palmeiro was Southeast Asia, since there were ships that traveled to Kyushu from the ports of Cochinchina. So, in addition to sending supplies to the missionaries in that kingdom, he arranged for five priests to travel back across the South China Sea to Japan. But the dire straits of the trading community at Macau meant that Palmeiro had difficulty finding a ship to carry his men westward so that they might eventually find a passage back to the east. The yearly Japan fleet from the Portuguese colony had been blockaded in port by the Dutch for several months in 1627, and the disappearance of these European rovers meant that the danger had moved elsewhere in the region.[34] Dutch fleets sailing along the Vietnamese coast would surely prey on Portuguese vessels in the area, just as they sat in wait in the Straits of Taiwan for ships heading for Japan. Sending men to Cochinchina for travel back across the South China Sea to Nagasaki would expose them to danger twice. The route through Vietnam to Japan was therefore not a reliable one for the yearly provisioning of the mission, so Palmeiro had to consider other options.

A way through China was more feasible. After all, Chinese traders were not uncommon visitors to Japan, despite the severing of relations between the two nations in the sixteenth century. In fact, Jesuits and friars living in Japan after the start of the persecutions had at times adopted Chinese dress since it offered some excuse for the priests' exotic countenances. Palmeiro had ordered two priests to live in seclusion on the Ilha Verde, a small island in

Macau's inner harbor where the Society maintained a residence, telling them to keep a low profile while waiting for their hair to grow out so they could "play the role of Chinese." In these final years of the Ming Dynasty, Chinese men prided themselves on their long hair, a fact that made the imposition of the queue under the Qing emperors all the more insulting.

Once their disguises were ready, the Visitor's intention was to send Gaspar do Amaral (1594–1646) and Paulo Saito (1577–1633) up along the coast toward *Chincheo,* as the Portuguese called Fujian Province, to find passage to Japan. The Fujianese ports of Quanzhou and Fuzhou had long been important trading centers, and their residents were linked by commerce and blood to the sojourning communities across Southeast Asia and the Philippines. Most importantly for the Jesuits was the fact that their junks also plied the routes to Kyushu and elsewhere in Japan, but Palmeiro reported to Rome that the China Jesuits were not confident that missionaries would be able to travel successfully onward from there. Their worries stemmed from an attempt made by the Dominicans in 1627 to go from Manila to Fujian and onward to Japan, which ended badly when the friars were betrayed to the Japanese authorities. But Palmeiro dismissed this concern, judging that the Dominicans had been careless in entrusting their money to their hastily chosen fellow travelers, something he would not do. The Jesuit pair were to travel on a large boat with trusted intermediaries, presumably drawn from the ranks of the Jesuits' mission church, "because greed will easily blind other, less interested parties, than the Chinese."[35] Alas, Palmeiro's plan was nevertheless not successful, and it would only be in 1632 that Saito alone would make it to Japan (albeit disguised among the passengers of a Chinese ship).

Beyond the immediate needs of the Japan mission, the Visitor needed to plan for its future. After all, he knew that many of his men were old and left debilitated by the continual trials that they had to endure. It was possible to set the province's men to growing their hair and to teach new recruits how to speak Japanese, but the dangers faced by Europeans in the mission territories obliged him to seek to revive an idea that had met with results earlier on: the recourse to indigenous clergy. Muzio Vitelleschi had written to Palmeiro to urge him to reestablish the seminary for Japanese boys, who would surely be able to infiltrate their homeland more easily than Portuguese, Italians, or Spaniards. To be sure, the Province of Japan had been one of the pioneers of integrating Japanese men into its ranks, first as brothers and later on as priests. Regardless of the presence of a number of turncoats at the outbreak of the persecutions (whose duplicity gave some of the European Jesuits pause[36]), most of the Society's Japanese members had shown loyalty to the order and the Church, all the way to the point of martyrdom.

The Jesuits at Macau hoped for a return to their former mission fields; they refused to believe that their exile would be permanent. So it was only a decade after their expulsion and in despair for the dwindling numbers of clergy who could serve in Japan that co–provincial superior Valentim Carvalho acquired a set of buildings where a number of the Jesuits' Japanese lay assistants were to commence training as seminarians. For reasons that are unclear, although ones likely linked to the upheaval fomented by Carvalho in the dispute over the city's bishopric and diocesan clergy, this incipient training facility was dissolved and its postulants sent away despite their vocations. When ordered by Rome to repair the damage done three years later, Palmeiro remarked: "God forgive Father Valentim Carvalho for what he destroyed, giving so many good men who today serve in Japan to other orders!" The Visitor nevertheless had found four candidates for a new seminary. Two of these were the sons of exiled Japanese noblemen who had recently arrived in Macau. Accordingly, Palmeiro could declare to Rome his intention of rebuilding the Japanese church with its native sons.[37]

The tide of anxiety felt by the exiled Jesuits and their confreres in Macau ebbed and flowed, as news and rumors washed up on the coast of southern China. In Palmeiro's missives to Rome, he invoked an epic register to contrast the constancy of many Christians with the weakness of others who inevitably bent under the relentless persecution. "We have heard tell of excessive rigor on the part of those who persecute, but also of excessive fervor on the part of those who suffer and triumph;" he wrote, "many have fallen, whether under the severity of torture, the power of the tyrant, or the unceasing labors which are great enough to dent even bronze breastplates, but many have remained constant and many have done so with excellent valor." But only divine intervention would be able to free the missionaries and their flock from their torments, Palmeiro asserted. Even those who followed the news of the persecutions in faraway Macau were affected because they found themselves "obliged to live with these fears; and it certainly seems better to die of the torments than to live always in fear."[38]

To compound his state of worry over the safety of his fellow Jesuits and their flock, the Visitor had learned that his priests were not at peace with the friars who suffered alongside them. In central Honshu in the area around Osaka (a region called "Kami" in contemporary European sources), the Jesuits had

seen their Franciscan peers offering the sacrament of confirmation to their
neophytes, a sacramental prerogative reserved for bishops. Scandalized by
this apparent novelty, one of the Jesuits, Francesco Boldrino (1575–1633), denounced the friars as "ignorant and idiots." But the Franciscans insisted
that they were only acting in accordance with a papal permission given to
their order by Adrian VI in 1522 when the missionary efforts in the New
World were just beginning. That bull specifically accorded mendicant friars (Franciscans, Dominicans, or Augustinians) the capacity to administer
the sacraments, except Holy Orders, in lands where there was no bishop present and at times when there was a grave necessity.[39] To be sure, this privilege
was conceded by the papacy two decades before the Society of Jesus was
founded and, despite the large number of special permissions granted to the
Jesuits after 1540, had not been extended to their missionaries. Yet since the
clergy were competitors even in such extreme circumstances, the Japan Jesuits begged Palmeiro to ask Rome to send a similar privilege. Recalling his
time as a professor of sacramental theology, he argued that confirmation was
"created precisely for such dangerous times, when it gives a special grace and
energy truly necessary in Japan."[40]

Although the anxiety ran high in Macau, Palmeiro tried his best to transmit words of encouragement back to the men in the mission field. In a letter
addressed to the head missionary, Mateus de Couros, but intended for all of
the priests and brothers in Japan, he described the beleaguered Jesuits as "the
vanguard of the *Companhia,* the luster of our order." Palmeiro cited passages
from Tertullian on the virtues of martyrs, underscoring the bonds of blood
forged between the early Christians who suffered under the Roman emperors
and these latter-day ones who suffered under the shoguns. Invoking his personal sentiments, he described the fruits produced by the sufferings of the
Jesuits in Japan, hiding in shadows and ditches before meeting their ends on
pyres, in the hearts of other members of the Society of Jesus:

> When you are all hiding in those pits before you are dead and buried for
> the love of Christ, you should not think that you are hidden and exiled.
> For I swear that you are like the seeds of fragrant herbs that are hidden in
> the soil awaiting their moment of birth, and which then spring forth in
> such beautiful, sweet-smelling flowers to please and console not only our
> Society, but also the whole world. And although it is considered sterile, fire
> brings forth such fruit in that land. The flames which engulfed our priests

and the ashes to which they were reduced are producing spirits so generous that, borne as they are in fire and breathing fire, they desire to perish in fire so that they may be born again. And you and all of the others priests over there would believe me if you saw, as I have seen and felt, the fervor and holy zeal that we have in this Province which has been heated by our proximity to the flames of the pyres upon which our holy priests expired. All of us in the Society, we who reside in India, we who live in Portugal, we who are in Europe, have felt the stirrings of the spirit and the kindling of such fires and desires to travel to that land and to suffer for Christ alongside you, seeking this chance with not only great emotion, but also with abundant pleas.[41]

Palmeiro felt it important to reassure his suffering companions that their fate was what so many other Jesuits desired, and that their toils in Japan produced zeal the world over. His words attempted to make the best out of a desperate situation, although it was clear that more priests and Japanese Christians would die as martyrs before the persecutions ended.

The Jesuits' suffering in Japan seemed to lessen by the end of 1628, or so claimed the reports from the mission field that reached Macau. During that year the Visitor had received several letters from the priests hidden in the hills beyond Nagasaki and could transmit the good news to Rome. The best information was that all of his men were in good health, with the exception of the Provincial Mateus de Couros, who reported suffering heart pangs that left him "without a pulse and without energy for some time." Some of the missionaries had nearly come into the grasp of pursuers, but they had escaped to at least temporary safety. Other good news was that the Dutch appeared to have worn out their welcome in Japan and risked being expelled. Reports of a Dutch outpost on the island of Taiwan as well as Dutch maltreatment of Japanese traders there had raised shogunal ire and led to an embargo, much to the pleasure of the Portuguese (who were also under trading strictures at the time).[42] "Those who know about Japan say that they are done for," Palmeiro wrote of the Dutch, "because the Japanese never go to such lengths unless their resolve is to cut off trade for good." But perhaps the best news that came from Japan was a rumor that the Tokugawa lords were on the verge of easing their prohibitions against the practice of Christianity. Giovanni Battista Porro had heard that the *xogum velho*, Hidetada, had reportedly shown mercy at Edo to a group of exiles from Nagasaki. The old shogun had apparently told the young one, Tokugawa Iemitsu (r. 1623–1651), that the Christians were not seditious and that their secret gatherings were only for the purpose of "discussing how to best live according to their law." If Iemitsu was convinced of this, Porro told Palmeiro, who duly informed Vitelleschi, it might mark a turning point.[43]

———

The brief glimpse of sunlight through the clouds that hung over the Japanese Christians allowed the Visitor to turn his attention elsewhere in East Asia. While Palmeiro would take a keen interest in the nascent efforts in Vietnam, it was the China enterprise that most forcefully clamored for his attention. His arrival in Macau was highly anticipated by the Jesuits in the Ming Empire, whose Vice-Province of China enjoyed partial autonomy from the Province of Japan.

The events that led to the separation of the China mission from its counterpart in Japan are worth recounting briefly here. In 1612, two years before the outbreak of the persecutions in Japan, China mission superior Niccolò Longobardo (1565–1654) had sent a procurator to Rome to plead for an administrative split between the Jesuits in the two Asian empires. Against the wishes of the Japan Jesuits, Superior General Vitelleschi acceded to the petitions carried by procurator Niklaas Trigault. The small size of the China mission (with only eighteen men in 1615), the news of an outbreak of persecution in Nanjing in 1616, and the subsequent expulsion of the missionaries from the two imperial courts of Nanjing and Beijing urged caution. In the end, a vice-province and not a full-fledged province was created. Word of this incomplete separation of the China mission from the Province of Japan reached East Asia with Trigault in 1619, exacerbating the tensions between the two groups of beleaguered Jesuits at Macau. The bitterness remained seven years later when Palmeiro reached the China coast, and was not mitigated by positive reports from across the sea in Honshu or Kyushu.

At the heart of the conflict between the Japan and China Jesuits was the ambiguous nature of this new unit. Unlike the Society's other provinces, the vice-province had no colleges of its own and no permanent novitiate; it was simply a collection of residences. Its independence from the Province of Japan lay in the autonomy enjoyed by its superior, the vice-provincial, who was to make decisions based on the advice of his consultors in China. This new superior, typically resident in Hangzhou, was thus able to distribute men and money throughout China without having to appeal to the provincial and his advisors who lived in Japan or, as the persecution in that country progressed, in Macau.

The vice-provincial's stock of missionaries and silver were derived from the resources of the Province of Japan. Since the Japan Jesuits maintained that the excision of the China mission from their province was tantamount to treason, they resisted concessions, financial or otherwise, to their confreres. Macau, for them, was part of Japan, regardless of its geographical placement; and the investments made in the silk trade, despite their reliance on the Canton fairs, belonged to the province, not the vice-province. Holding an office that placed him above both provincial and vice-provincial in the Society's East Asian hierarchy, Palmeiro had the task of mediating between the two groups. While his sympathies naturally tended toward the priests living in the shadows in Japan, his scrupulous attention to duty reminded him of his obligations to his subordinates in China. Although they had ceased to be the targets of persecution by indigenous rivals in 1623, they too needed and deserved his paternal presence.

In the autumn of 1628 a window of opportunity opened for Palmeiro to conduct an inspection tour of the vice-province. Although he was reluctant to be away from Macau while the specter of persecution hovered over Japan, the Visitor knew that the mails from that country would only arrive when the monsoon winds shifted in the middle of the following year. Instead of pining away for news on the China coast, he resolved to accompany an embassy sent from the city of Macau to Beijing. His goal was to visit as many mission stations as possible along the main route from Canton to the imperial court, straying off of it only to visit the Jesuits in the Jiangnan region around the Yangzi River delta. Over the course of the year that it took him to complete this ambitious roundtrip, he would cover more than three thousand miles. Even for a man who had traveled extensively throughout South Asia, this was a daunting prospect: the report that he penned about his journey begins with a reflection on his sixty years of age and the possibility that his trek into China would take him to his grave. Whereas he averred that he did not feel the pains of old age, his gray hair dispelled any illusions of youthful vigor that he might have harbored. Thankfully for Palmeiro, it was possible to travel throughout the Ming Empire by boat, in a sedan chair, or by horse or mule, giving him confidence that he would be able make the trip "without so many bodily labors."[44]

Palmeiro's descriptions of his travels, written after his return to Macau in the autumn of 1629, reveal that this journey was not simply for the purpose of encouraging his subordinates. There was, first of all, the fact that the China mission had never been inspected in the nearly four decades since its inception. With the glare of the triumph and tragedy in Japan detaining the attentions of all of his predecessors, the task of visiting the mission stations beyond the walls of Macau had been given to members of the mission itself. In other words, no superior from outside of the restricted circle of China Jesuits had ever examined the policies and behaviors used for political and proselytizing purposes within the vast space of the Ming Empire. And even those who had been sent into China as deputies of the visitors in Japan or at Macau had not been well received by their confreres in distant Hangzhou or Beijing: An inspection conducted by Manuel Dias the younger (1574–1659) in 1614–1615 was met with resistance by senior Jesuits who insisted that the time was not yet ripe for such a visitation—despite the fact that the mission had been founded in 1579 and firmly rooted since its founder, Matteo Ricci, had settled in Beijing in 1601. Because the account of his travels was destined to be read by a wide audience, Palmeiro cited the need for good administration as the rationale for his trek. "The particularities of governance and the specific points which fall to the visitors of these provinces," he asserted, "will never be finely tuned if they are always handled according to what others say and not in light of what the visitors have seen or have discovered for themselves."[45]

As he had done during his visit to Madurai in the Province of Malabar, Palmeiro played the Doubting Thomas. After living among the Japan Jesuits at Macau for over two years and hearing the opinions of veterans such as João Rodrigues, the Visitor had developed suspicions about the way things were being done in China. Once again the question of scandal loomed over Jesuit activities, and Palmeiro's job was to ensure that if rumors spread from East Asia back to Europe, they would be unfounded. In his private correspondence with the superior general, the justification for his journey was not simply the need for good governance but five specific questions that needed to be answered.

All five issues related to the missionary strategies employed by the Jesuits in China, and most of them challenged the "accommodation method" that had been articulated by Matteo Ricci. In order to impress his hosts and gain a foothold in the imperial capital, Ricci had cast himself in a Chinese guise, in his clothing, in his manners, and in his language.[46] Passing himself off as a *xiru,* or "Western (Confucian) scholar," he intended to transmit the Christian message to a literate Chinese audience. Ricci's goal was obtained during his lifetime: He became well known at court, and his fellow Jesuits who followed the same strategy were, in general, tolerated by imperial officials. Despite the seven-year period of instability referred to as the Nanjing Persecutions, which lasted from 1616 until 1623, Ricci's policies were largely imitated by his successors in the China mission, and the "accommodation method" continued until the Visitor's day. But although the Japan Jesuits had done their own accommodating to the cultural norms in their host country, they were convinced that their confreres had exaggerated in their desire to please the Chinese. Thus, in the Ming Empire, as in Madurai, Palmeiro was obliged to evaluate whether the missionaries' interpretation of the Pauline example of becoming "all things to all men"—a phrase also dear to Ignatius Loyola—had gone too far.

As was the case in India, the Visitor did not object to the use of indigenous garb, comportment, or language if they served the purpose of producing conversions. But the news from the Jesuits inside China that reached Macau never stressed the numbers of baptisms; indeed, it intoned a continual refrain about the difficulty of spreading Christianity and the need for caution. So it is perhaps unsurprising that the first reason that Palmeiro gave for his visit to China was to evaluate the impact of this proselytizing strategy. Why, he asked, were there so few Christians despite the presence of Jesuits within the Ming Empire for forty years "with so much labor and expense"?[47]

Directly related to this fundamental question was a second query about the missionaries' behavior among the Chinese scholar-bureaucrats, or mandarins, who stood atop of the social scale. Contrary to the dated commonplace that they belonged to a nation content with itself and disinterested in the outside world, Ming-era literati were consumed with curiosity. Ricci had sensed this and had appealed to their desire for knowledge by producing treatises in Chinese on Western thought and, most famously, maps of the world. But surely the Jesuits' role as exotic purveyors of curiosities was intended only as a means to an end, Palmeiro assumed, to be relegated to the background once they had secured the necessary political patronage. But the rumors that reached Macau told otherwise. Nearly two decades after Ricci's death in 1610, Palmeiro therefore asked, were the Jesuits still so dependent on their patrons that they continually needed to cater to Chinese intellectual appetites? In Macau it was believed that the missionaries wasted their time being overly solicitous to their mandarin interlocutors, behavior that resulted only in "conversation and not conversion."[48]

The third question that prompted Palmeiro's trek through the Ming Empire had to do with the way in which the Jesuits presented themselves to their Chinese audience. In order to mitigate the strangeness of their countenances, the first Jesuit in China, Michele Ruggieri (1543–1607), as well as his junior companion Ricci, had adopted a form of dress reminiscent of the ones used by the Buddhist clergy. But when Ricci reevaluated his strategies after Ruggieri's departure from China in 1588, he decided that this association was counterproductive in light of the low esteem in which many of the indigenous monks were held. In 1595 Ricci therefore clothed himself in the garb similar to those of the Chinese literati. But whereas the "Western Brahman" Roberto Nobili had stripped himself of the black cloak of his fellow Jesuits in favor of a loincloth and shawl, the "Western scholar" Matteo Ricci had adopted the silk robes of the scholar-officials. Although this was a controversial gesture in light of Ricci's vow of poverty, his superiors had permitted the extravagance in order for him to put the mission on a solid footing in China. After all, the Japan Jesuits had worn silk during the early years of their mission, and it was unclear if its use had not served to facilitate the missionaries' interactions with high-status individuals. Yet when reports of Jesuits in silk reached India in the late 1560s, a new superior was sent to Japan to ban the use of this fabric and replace it with humble cotton.[49] Later on, the Japan Jesuits still knew the power of such symbols of worldly pomp in East Asia and thus did not rush to criticize Ricci's strategy (which had been blessed, at least implicitly, by Visitor Alessandro Valignano).

New problems arose for the China Jesuits when reports of their use of silk began to circulate beyond the Society and past Macau. Instead of moving to conceal this controversial policy, the China Jesuits chose to celebrate it: Niklaas Trigault paraded about Europe in this sumptuous garb, posing for at least two portraits of himself and overseeing the publication of a famous engraving of Ricci bedecked in silken finery. In this silk, observers outside the Society (and several within) saw vanity or, worse still, the deadly sin of lust. But like his predecessors, and in keeping with his indifference over the outward signs that caused furor in India, the Visitor did not object in principle to the occasional use of silk. The news from within China that reached Macau nevertheless told of some Jesuits who wore their silk "courtesy robes" when it was unnecessary, that is, outside of the moments when they made calls on influential figures. Palmeiro was intent on discovering if this disregard for the Society's commonly held vows was true, and if there were indeed missionaries whose personal wardrobes contained "three or four robes of this kind."[50]

The fourth question that spurred the Visitor's inspection was the matter of the terms used to express Christian concepts in Chinese. Just as in his intervention in the disputes in India over Nobili's policies, Palmeiro was a late arrival to a raging debate. The "Terms Controversy," a prelude to the more well-known "Rites Controversy" of the late seventeenth and early eighteenth centuries, had begun shortly after the first wave of Jesuit exiles from Japan arrived in Macau in 1614.[51] Its prime mover was João Rodrigues, who had been expelled from Nagasaki in 1610 and whose deep interest in East Asian languages and responsibilities as mission procurator had taken him on a two-year tour of China from 1613 until 1615.[52]

As a result of his travels in the Ming Empire and his interviews with literati Christians, Rodrigues became convinced that Matteo Ricci had been too zealous by half in his policy of accommodation. In addition to changing his attire, Ricci had selected Chinese terms to express Christian concepts instead of using neologisms; that is, he found what he considered to be appropriate equivalents and used them as acceptable vehicles for his religious message. Whereas in Japan God was *Deusu* (from the Latin, *Deus*) and things Christian were *Kirishitan,* in China God was *Shangdi* or *Tianzhu,* heaven was *Tian* (which sometimes doubled for God), angels were *Tianshen,* and the soul was *Linghun.* The Chinese terms were selected by Ricci from the Confucian canon and therefore served the dual purpose of negating suspicions about Christianity's foreign origins and confirming the wisdom of the sages of Chinese antiquity (in the same manner that Greek and Roman thought provided a useful moral and philosophical framework for Christian theology).

Although Ricci's move has been considered a stroke of genius by modern commentators, his contemporaries were less convinced of its merits. After all, the Japan Jesuits had had good reasons for inventing words rather than selecting terms from the rich vocabulary of their hosts. Rodrigues and his confreres knew that the millennial philosophical traditions of East Asia were thoroughly imbued with religious significance, and that there were few characters without multiple meanings. More than any others, the canonical texts of the *Four Books* and *Five Classics* had been the object of metaphysical glosses for centuries, and the most important interpretive school of the late Ming period, the Neo-Confucians of the Song Dynasty, relied extensively on Buddhist and Daoist terminology. Ricci had assumed that he could invoke the humanist motto, *ad fontes,* and his Chinese readers would follow him much in the same way that European scholars of the Renaissance had sought to understand biblical sources by stripping them of the centuries' worth of interpretive accretions. Rodrigues argued that Ricci had put too much faith in his readers' capacities or volition; he had erred by using terms and phrases that his Chinese readers would associate with their religious traditions, thereby identifying Christian concepts with paganism. In short, for the veterans of Japan, there were no uncorrupted terms in the Confucian lexicon.

The problem lay in severing the link that Ricci had forged between Christianity and Confucianism, most importantly with regard to the term *Shangdi,* "Ruler on High," which figured prominently in his printed works. In the 1610s the Japan Jesuits showed themselves to be against Ricci's usage, nearly to a man, while their counterparts in China largely defended the terms, insisting that Confucius's original text—not the later glosses—were what mattered. But over the ensuing decade, divisions emerged among the China Jesuits as well, with the detractors recognizing the impossibility of disassociating the terms from the standard metaphysical and religious reading of the literati. The debate within China between the two sides raged when Palmeiro arrived at Macau in 1626, and the Visitor gave his permission to a conference to be held at Jiading, a town near Shanghai, in order to discuss the issue. Despite the repeated requests that he be present at the proceedings, he insisted that his lack of knowledge of Chinese (or Japanese) would make his attendance irrelevant: he was a theologian, not a linguist. Just as in the Nobili affair, Palmeiro knew his judgment was valid for matters of missionary intentions, not for parsing the significance of Asian writings. Instead, the Visitor requested that the rector of the College of Macau and former missionary in Japan, Pedro Morejón (1562–1639), compile the arguments from both sides of the question in 1627 that he might weigh its moral dimensions.[53] Such matters were fully within the scope of the Visitor's competence, but he did not rush to judgment.

The meeting of the China missionaries took place in January 1628, but it did not resolve the issue. At the insistence of some older missionaries, the priests at Jiading unanimously affirmed the need to abandon the more controversial terms, especially *Shangdi.*[54] Regardless of this accord, the terms' defenders did not strike them from their Christian vocabulary. Moreover, both sides continued to debate the terms in polemical treatises that contained no shortage of insults and attacks unbecoming of members of the Society of

Jesus. From the perspective of the terms' defenders, there was an urgent need to clarify and strengthen their position because it appeared that they were sacrificing Ricci's legacy, to which they owed so much. On the opposite side of the issue, the detractors insisted that the use of the terms was nothing short of teaching heresy and abetting idolatry, and such use ran the risk of bringing the wrath of Inquisition upon the Society.[55]

The Visitor took the measure of silencing both sides in order to bring peace to the China Jesuits. Two men were castigated for their excesses in arguing their positions: João Rodrigues, who had not only written a treatise denouncing the terms but who had also arranged for the printing of a doctrine primer with his preferred terms at Canton, and Rodrigo de Figueiredo (1594–1642), a younger missionary who responded to Rodrigues's challenge in a harsh tone.[56] Palmeiro also sent a request to the inquisitors in Goa to appoint him deputy of the Holy Office in Macau. He clearly intended to use the powers of that office to stifle any outside discussion of the Jesuits' Chinese controversies before he and the superior general were able to resolve the matter internally.[57] With the threat of scandal growing more serious by the day, Palmeiro's resolve was strengthened to find a solution within China to the intractable problems of Ricci's legacy.

The final question that the Visitor sought to answer inside the Ming Empire was how to provision the mission more efficiently. Here again the policy of accommodation to Chinese norms posed problems for the missionaries since it implied distancing themselves from the Portuguese at Macau. Matteo Ricci had downplayed his links to the colony as he made his way to Beijing, and his successors had followed suit for two reasons. First, there were longstanding prohibitions against foreigners residing in China outside of the context of tribute embassies or beyond the duration of the biannual Canton fairs. If the Jesuits were representatives of the Portuguese, they would have been expected to abide by the same rules and restrict their activities to brief, officially sanctioned sojourns at Beijing or Canton. But their goal was to remain in China in order to proselytize, a vocation not contemplated for foreigners by the terms of Ming law, so the Jesuits sought to keep their links to Macau as ambiguous as possible to their Chinese hosts.

The second reason was the problematic nature of the Portuguese colony in the eyes of the Ming authorities. Recognizing that their distant homeland, *Daxiyang guo,* or the Great Western Ocean, was 10,000 *li* away—as contemporary Chinese poets would have it—and that the cannons mounted on European ships were useful for combating the piracy endemic to the Pearl River delta, the Chinese had granted the Portuguese permission in 1557 to administer a spit of land with a capacious harbor. But within twenty years of that diplomatic victory, news reached Chinese ears that foreigners from the same distant lands with the same types of ships had conquered the nearby islands of the Philippines with the same types of artillery. And another group of violent seafarers, albeit with red hair instead of brown, also began to show up in East Asian waters in the first decades of the seventeenth century and even attacked Macau (unsuccessfully) with cannons in 1622.[58] Unaware of (or indifferent to) the distinctions between Portuguese, Spaniards, and Dutch, members of some mandarin factions began to voice fears that these foreigners might turn their evident military strength against the Ming Empire and use their outpost at Macau as a staging post.[59] It does not require a great leap of imagination to see how suspicious Chinese officials would have seen the Jesuits who resided in the principal cities of the empire as a network of spies plotting the inevitable invasion.

Despite the fact that the Jesuits did not want to broadcast their links to Macau, they still needed to draw sustenance from the Portuguese colony. The problem of getting men and money beyond Guangdong Province had dogged the Jesuits from the start, and while the first leg of any journey into China— from Macau to Canton—was relatively easy, moving deeper into the empire posed significant problems. These difficulties were compounded by the intensifying climate of mandarin suspicion toward the Portuguese at Macau in the last years of the Wanli reign (1572–1620). For reasons having little to do with the Europeans in the South China Sea and much to do with the rise of factionalism among the imperial bureaucrats, an unresponsive emperor, and the incursions of Manchu raiders from across the northern borders, a climate of anxiety, both political and spiritual, grew among the members of the late Ming elite.

Concerns about the Jesuits' designs and, above all, their ties to the Portuguese, found voice in memorials to the throne as well as in anti-Christian tracts that circulated during the Nanjing Persecutions. Even after the climate of persecution had passed in 1623, the problem of outfitting the mission remained: financial and manpower resources still needed to find their way to the Jesuits spread across the empire from Xi'an to Shanghai. Moving material from Macau into China was risky, Palmeiro asserted, even when it traveled in the hands of the Society's Chinese (though Macau-born and culturally

Portuguese) temporal coadjutors. His concern for provisioning the vice-province therefore accounts for the presence of so many references to the costs of food and transport in his travelogue.

Curiously, the vagaries of imperial politics in the waning years of the Ming Dynasty were responsible for Palmeiro's entry into China in 1628. While some official factions were fearful of the Portuguese and their weapons, others saw them as holding the keys to the empire's salvation. Dissimulating their knowledge of Macau as the source of spiritual succor, a handful of Christian mandarins argued that the city could offer material defense in the form of superior technology. Palmeiro saw an opportunity for infiltrating China—that is, for passing undetected from the Portuguese camp to that of the China Jesuits—when these officials' proposals were accepted by the Dragon Throne.

In the autumn of 1628 the city of Macau received a request from Beijing for a detachment of artillery experts to help with the defense of the northern frontier. Convinced that the European guns and mathematical skills would give the Chinese armies a decisive advantage against the invading Manchus, the Vice-Minister of War, Xu Guangqi (1562–1633, baptized Paulo in 1603), arranged for a military embassy. This was the second such visit; a first group of Portuguese gunners had gone to northern China in 1622, but an accidental misfire of one of their cannon had led to their being sent back to Macau. The renewal of raids from across the northern border prompted Xu to seek permission for another group, a move that resulted in the appointment of Gonçalo Teixeira Correia (d. 1632) as ambassador. His 1628 embassy was small, consisting of four gunners and ten pieces of artillery, three of bronze and seven of iron, to be transported to Beijing. At the insistence of the city fathers of Macau, João Rodrigues was appointed to the group to act as the interpreter, a role he had fulfilled for several years as Jesuit procurator at Macau and trade liaison at Canton.[60] The Portuguese group thus provided cover for Palmeiro and his Macanese companion, Brother Domingos Mendes (ca. 1579–1652), who masqueraded as part of the embassy until it had progressed beyond the Chinese border patrols.[61]

The relationship between the Visitor and the ambassadors provides a useful illustration of the rapport between the Jesuits and the Portuguese empire in East Asia. Clearly there was the same symbiosis in personal relationships as seen in the heart of the Estado da Índia at Goa and Cochin, where high-ranking Jesuits enjoyed the friendship and patronage of members of the colonial elite in exchange for pastoral, intellectual, and diplomatic services. Owing to their skills in Asian languages and their residence in various Asian courts, Jesuits were invaluable intermediaries between the Portuguese and rulers in Agra, Beijing, or Kyoto. The close relationships between the Jesuits and "the Portuguese" (whether laymen, churchmen, or colonial officials) were less clearly beneficial in East Asia than they were in South Asia. While the association between the Portuguese and Christianity had created problems for individuals such as Roberto Nobili, who sought to remove his religious message from the practices of the colonial population, this was one of the few instances of such stigma in India. In the case of Ethiopia, the Zambezi Valley, the Fishery Coast, and the Mughal lands of northern India, the Jesuits' links to the Portuguese were known to prospective converts, even if the bond was merely one of shared language and religion.

In East Asia, however, the Jesuits' links to Macau were the source of more problems. Within China, as noted earlier, it was not the ecclesiastical links between the Jesuits and the Portuguese—because there had been few jurisdictional conflicts between the secular and regular clergy over the missions until the later seventeenth century—that caused tension but their political and economic bonds. And in Japan an interest in preserving the lucrative silk–silver trade obliged the Portuguese to distance themselves from the Jesuits. Yet the distance between the two groups in either Asian context was projected for political expediency: clearly it served the interests of both the Portuguese and the Jesuits that the two groups be considered as separate in the minds of East Asian authorities.

This is not to say that the objectives of the Society and the Portuguese ran parallel to each other. Indeed, Jesuit voices were responsible for halting the march of empire in Asia, most directly when they dismissed incipient Castilian plans for conquering Southern China in the 1580s (which were, incidentally, most elaborately articulated by a Castilian Jesuit).[62] And, as mentioned earlier, Jesuits were behind the civil unrest aimed at the crown's representatives in the 1620s. Geography gives a good indication of the degree of overlap between the concerns of the Society of Jesus and the Portuguese Empire. Whereas in South Asia, the high concentration of coastal fortifications and other outposts meant that the Jesuits often worked within colonial contexts, or at least near to them, in East Asia the Society's men were found far beyond the limits of Portuguese control—which was only effective in Macau, Malacca, and on parts of the high seas. The vast majority of the Jesuits' endeavors in East Asia were therefore conducted in territories outside of Portuguese control, so it was logical that their diplomatic efforts primarily sought to ensure the survival of their Christian communities and the ability of their men to preach in relative security.

One can see how the Jesuits oscillated between their public allies in this region clearly in the figure of João Rodrigues. He earned the sobriquet *tsūzu,* or interpreter, during the years in which he acted as a courtier to the Japanese military hegemon Hideyoshi but ended his diplomatic career serving as the representative of the city of Macau before the Canton mandarins and the court of the Chongzhen Emperor. Palmeiro played a similarly ambiguous role: While he needed the Portuguese embassy in order to travel the first furlong into the Ming Empire, he would part company with his compatriots near the northern edge of Guangdong Province to conduct affairs among Christian scholar-officials in Beijing and Hangzhou for the benefit of the *Yesu hui,* the Society of Jesus, not the Portuguese. From the perspective of both the Jesuits and these Chinese Christians, it was most important to sustain the fledgling church in the face of repeated attacks against the missionaries (and their indigenous allies) by political or religious rivals. These were affairs in which the Portuguese had no say but that were nevertheless matters of life and death for Jesuits and neophytes alike.

———

The Portuguese embassy left Macau on its route up the Pearl River on December 11, 1628.[63] It would take a long time, the first four and a half months of a ten-month odyssey, for Palmeiro to arrive at the southernmost mission station of the vice-province. The delays and slow pace of travel would give the Visitor plenty of time to reflect on life in the Ming Empire, permitting him to jot down the observations he would compile after his return to Macau in the autumn of 1629. His account of his travels to northern China and back is the most substantial single text that he authored since he compiled his lecture notes on Aquinas at Braga over two decades before.

Palmeiro's *itinerario* takes the form of a letter to the superior general, but it is clear that the text was destined to be read by individuals inside and outside of the Society at several points between Macau and Rome. The desire for news from China was evident among readers in early seventeenth century, and the Jesuits followed the publication of Niklaas Trigault's version of Matteo Ricci's journal, titled *De Christiana Expeditione apud Sinas* (first ed.,

Augsburg, 1615), with annual reports from the mission field printed across Europe. But in contrast to Palmeiro's account, these relatively brief texts are more edifying than descriptive in character, peppered as they are with accounts of missionary triumphs and miraculous events.[64] Indeed, the next major Jesuit description of China would not appear off European presses until the early 1640s, when Álvaro Semedo (1585–1658) published his *Imperio de la China* (first ed., Madrid, 1642; rev., Rome, 1643). By that time the final rupture of the Macau-Nagasaki link and the death throes of the Ming Dynasty obliged the Jesuits to raise funds more aggressively in Europe.

Despite its merits as a mixture of ethnographic detail, philosophical reflection, and travel narrative, Palmeiro's account of his adventures in China never appeared in print. This fact is surprising, given the Jesuits' reputation as self-promoters of the first order. While the Visitor's text is clearly not as ambitious in scope as the books written by either Trigault or Semedo, it does contain reflections on Chinese culture, and especially the imperial bureaucracy, that make it similar to other contemporary accounts that were printed. But the fact that texts were not typeset does not mean that they were not widely read; manuscript culture persisted long after the advent of print in Europe, and dispatches from the Jesuit mission fields are prime examples of the types of handwritten texts that enjoyed wide circulation.

Why did Palmeiro's text not make it into print? The primary reason lay in the fact that its author did not write as a publicist or mission booster. His purpose was to inform the superior general about his travels and about the state of the China mission, mentioning both the good and the bad. Palmeiro was too scrupulous in his attention to duty to omit the unflattering aspects in his impressions, and he did not trumpet heroic aspects of missionary life where they did not exist. The Society of Jesus relied on patronage or its own financial resources to have some missionary texts printed in Europe, and it reserved those expenditures for writings that contributed to the goal of raising more funds for its overseas enterprises or for celebrating the triumphs (or heroic sufferings) that would enhance the order's prestige. And since the policies of the Jesuits in East Asia often raised suspicions in Europe, the defense of the Society's strategies in print was especially important; their famed appreciation of certain aspects of indigenous Asian thought and culture served to provide the justificatory context for their actions. As an outsider to the China mission, the Visitor had a unique perspective among the Jesuits in Asia: he enjoyed greater independence in the presentation of his impressions than his subordinates and was not afraid to level criticism of Asians and Europeans where he saw fit.

Let us follow Palmeiro on his journey through the Ming Empire. The first leg of his voyage was marked by concern that he might be discovered by the Chinese authorities and deported to Macau. Perhaps overestimating the skill and the zeal of the official patrols, he kept a low profile among the members of the embassy as his ship navigated toward Canton. The Visitor remarked on the "hundreds of embarkations, which they call warships" (but what he thought were clearly not) that filled the Pearl River. But invoking a refrain that he would intone at every mention of native soldiers—a prejudice that he inherited from the writings of Ricci and other European authors who had described the Ming Empire since the 1560s—Palmeiro dismissed this multitude as the only sign of Chinese strength. Few were capable of professing arms in the European manner, he maintained, but they nevertheless had enough eyes to spot intruders. Palmeiro made a distinction between military valor and astuteness, asserting early in his text that the Chinese had plenty of the latter. Indeed, one of the greatest dangers of the Portuguese military mission to the court was that it intended to train Chinese artillerymen in the manufacture and use of European-style cannon. "They do not lack the ingenuity to learn, if they have the spirit to do it, but they lack this and the king lacks confidence in them," the Visitor claimed to have heard from an important mandarin in Beijing, "because it is rightly feared that after they are well-trained in the art of artillery, they will flee to the Tartars for any trifle to teach them to use it against the Chinese."[65]

The danger of being seen by the Ming Argus struck fear in Palmeiro's heart, so he kept to the shadows even after the embassy had reached its first stop in Canton. The Portuguese group would have to wait there until it received permission to head onward, a span of several weeks. During that time, Correia, Rodrigues, and the gunners were lodged in a temple on an island, possibly the Haizhuangzi situated across the Pearl River from the city walls. Palmeiro described the site as a pleasant park where games and banquets were held continually. But he expressed fear at the continual swarm of people who came to see the embassy and, above all, that those who came to speak with his assistant, Domingos Mendes, and the other unnamed brother who escorted them to Canton would expose him.

The Visitor instead chose to hide aboard a boat moored nearby, in a room "no greater than seven palms wide and twelve long" where he had nothing but a cot and a handful of books. "I had enough time during the day, because it was all mine," he wrote, "to give hours to God in prayer and those that were left over to be employed in lessons." Each day at dawn Palmeiro would emerge to say mass in an improvised chapel found in the rented lodgings of his compatriots, returning to the cold damp of what he called his lair or den. But this was the middle of December, and the sixty year-old Jesuit felt the effects of the elements: the boat's covering was filled with holes, permitting him to see the stars at night and subjecting him to "a cold so great that my bones felt paralyzed by the pains that I suffered."[66]

Despite his desire to offer up his sufferings in the hopes of greater rewards later on his voyage, Palmeiro at length yielded to the requests from Rodrigues and Correia to join them in their apartments on land. Death from exposure seemed a distinct possibility in light of the continual delays to which the Portuguese party was subjected by dithering bureaucrats. But even with spacious accommodations, Palmeiro's spirit was not at ease living within a Buddhist temple in such close quarters to the *bonzes,* its clergy. He contrasted the clean altar of his daily sacrifice to the True God with the praises offered by monks to the Devil in the precincts beyond the walls of the Europeans' lodgings. More shocking than the mere presence of what he deemed idolatry was the lascivious atmosphere of the temple's halls and groves. "It seems to me that there is no day during the whole year when crowds of boys and other dissolute people do not come to this temple to hold great banquets, and to carry on drinking," he wrote. "And what is worse is the rest, which, if it cannot be written about, can be understood:. . . that the most common place for all kinds of men to engage in debauchery is in the temples and shrines of these *bonzes* and the houses of their idols, even though in Canton and many other cities of this kingdom there is a great quantity of boats which only serve for banqueting and other forms of decadence." Palmeiro made a point of informing his audience that this vision of sinful sloth and luxury was valid for the entirety of China, confirming the notion of a close bond between moral laxity and idolatry present in the minds of his readers.[67]

The embassy spent nearly three months, until the end of February 1629, stalled at Canton. Annoyed by the delay yet reassured that he blended in with the other Portuguese, Palmeiro at length felt confident to expand his knowledge of the massive city spread out along the Pearl River. He mentions two trips by boat around Canton (since foreigners were forbidden from passing through its gates) as well as the scaling of a hill on the grounds of a temple, most likely the Zhenhai Tower on Yuexiu Hill, which afforded a broad vista. From this vantage point he could see that Canton was larger than his native city of Lisbon in terms of its layout, its scale, and its number of inhabitants. In terms of the beauty of its architecture, the elegance of its people, or in the scale of its monuments, he declared the city was among the best in China, although it could hardly compare with those in the Portuguese capital or elsewhere in Europe.[68]

Palmeiro was nonetheless impressed with the sheer volume of trade that transpired at Canton, claiming that he estimated the number of boats in the city's waterways at more than fifteen thousand—twice as many as he had heard were in Venice—"and if someone told me there were more, I would not think they were lying." On a similar scale were the number of silk looms, which Palmeiro heard numbered over five thousand in Canton alone. Clearly dwelling on the widespread use of silk in China and especially among his fellow Jesuits, he reflected on the far greater number of hands occupied "in weaving and preparing one of life's gifts and luxuries, since decorating the body that wears it is the only purpose that silk serves, it offers no true health to man."[69] Palmeiro would recall the luxuries of Canton when it came time for him to hand down rules about how the Jesuits should live, even in the midst of such worldly temptations.

Spending time with João Rodrigues, the Society's longtime procurator in Japan and Macau, alerted Palmeiro to the contours of commerce in the China Seas. In light of the doubts raised among other Europeans about the Jesuits' engagement in the silk trade, it was important for the Visitor to evaluate the situation for himself. After all, the Society had invested heavily in rental properties in Macau, just as other orders had done, but the proceeds were too meager to support endeavors on the scale of the missions in China, Japan, and Southeast Asia. The profits that the Society reaped from the cargoes it dispatched to Nagasaki were substantial, but the worsening political situation there and the threat that Portuguese trade might be terminated prompted him to consider alternatives. Regardless of the vagaries of the political moods within China vis-à-vis the Portuguese, Palmeiro seemed certain that they would always have access to the emporium at Canton. He further praised the type of trade that they carried on there, remarking that the Europeans earned profits on the order of 60 percent or 70 percent when trading for gold (silver was more actively sought in China), and that there was an abundance of high-quality musk and tutenag (an alloy also known as "Chinese copper"). Attempting to plan for an uncertain future, he underscored the value of these items in India and Europe, suggesting them alternatives for the Macau-Nagasaki route.

Thankfully, in light of what Palmeiro saw, the logistical problems of Jesuit trade were greater than its moral ones. It is a commonplace that early modern theologians viewed commerce in moral terms, condemning it as a form of avarice. The Visitor was no exception—he was well aware of Aquinas's reservations about priests engaging in trade and the explicit mention of the perils of greed.[70] But the Visitor reassured his readers that there was "no cleaner and more honorable trade in the world" than that of the Portuguese at Canton since they only trafficked in "things of great value and cleanliness." He therefore deemed it licit for the Jesuits to participate in this trade in order to fund their apostolic endeavors and noted with satisfaction that other goods such as meat and grain could be acquired cheaply in China. This is not to say, however, that he put aside the moral lenses through which he viewed Canton; far from it. The weeks of delay, the presence of what he deemed false religion, the spiritual mood typical of the beginning of the Lenten season, and, above all, the fact that, as foreigners, no missionaries could live among the *Cantonistas* made the abundance of worldly goods arrayed before his eyes even more distasteful. His verdict on the inhabitants of Canton was severe:

> They are more closed to God than all of the rest of these kingdoms since they are closed to the Portuguese, of whom they are terrified and afraid, and so they shut the doors to those who could open heaven's gates. There is no way to get in to proclaim to them the truth of our Holy Faith, and so they have an excess of delights which dim their reason and they lack those who could enlighten them with rays of truth. What can thus be expected but that having spent their lives in such loose living, and so blind to reason, they spend eternity in the torments that their profligate and decadent lives have earned them?[71]

The tone that Palmeiro struck in his account of Canton is uncharacteristic. While he did not often shy from condemning non-Christian practices during his travels in India, he rendered an especially harsh judgment on southern China. He had wandered into the midst of more than a few Hindu and Buddhist communities and had encountered plenty of Muslims during his sojourns in Maritime Asia, but nowhere in his writings does one see such a condemnatory refrain. Surely his incapacity to protect his fellow Jesuits in Japan contributed to his somber mood, as did the incongruity of Macau, whose official name was "City of the Name of God in China," lying a stone's throw from the gates of Gomorrah, and the "impertinences of the mandarins" who blocked the route into China for him and his men. But the spreading shadows had become too opaque to have arisen from frustration or annoyance, even in an age known for witnessing the birth of melancholy.

It was instead another wave of bad news that had knocked the Visitor off his feet. While Palmeiro was in Canton, a Chinese Christian arrived with word from Vice-Provincial Manuel Dias the younger. In addition to the plans that Dias had for a rendezvous with Palmeiro at Nanchang in neighboring Jiangxi Province, the messenger spoke of the sudden death of Niklaas Trigault in Hangzhou the previous November. The loss of the former procurator and publicist, who was also the author of a useful guide for studying the Chinese language, was a great blow to the China Jesuits. "This news made a strong impression in my breast," the Visitor wrote, "both because of the great need that this mission has for laborers so well-trained and so skilled, and because it described his death as so swift that he succumbed almost as soon as he felt it coming on." According to this report—and in keeping with later accounts of the event for public consumption—Trigault had just finished confessing in order to say mass when he retired to his room where he was found dead moments later, his body still warm. This was the story that Palmeiro heard at Canton, but he would hear another one at least by the time he reached Hangzhou. When he compiled the notes he used for writing his travelogue, he decided to say little about Trigault's death; such events were "divine judgments, and although we cannot understand them, we should venerate them."[72]

The same individual who brought the Visitor this tragic news also helped him shake some of his funk and refocus his mind and spirit. The Christian begged Palmeiro to visit his home in the vicinity of Canton to baptize a young son, an invitation which the Jesuit decided to interpret as a positive omen. Not only did he get to administer the sacrament, but he also learned that his confreres had produced a greater number of baptisms throughout China than they had done at any point previously. The Visitor claimed that the annual tally had never surpassed one thousand until 1628, when it exceeded that goal by a wide margin. Indeed, the arc of conversions was trending upward at the time, finally giving Palmeiro hope that there would be a great harvest "in this field which we have sown for so long, with sweat from the brow, with expense, and with the loss of life."[73] What China lacked, he contended, was for God to turn His eyes upon it—although he feared that this might bring wrath instead of mercy, "for what they have not done, or for having gone too slowly in doing it."[74]

After weeks of waiting, the Portuguese embassy recommenced its route to the north, and Palmeiro with it. He watched as two mandarins attached to their group, "dressed in pontifical style, after their fashion," sacrificed pigs to the spirit of the river, and then distributed the meat to the travelers. The boat that the Cantonese authorities had outfitted for the passage to Nanxiong, the last port before the Mei Pass at the northern reaches of Guangdong Province, was more capacious than the one they had sailed in from Macau. Chinese boats would be an endless source of fascination for Palmeiro: descriptions of their multitude, their furnishings, and their inhabitants abound in the account of his journey. To be sure, he spent the better part of his ten-month stay in China floating on the rivers of the Ming Empire, and so had made plenty of observations about them. The boat to Nanxiong was well appointed; the cabin he shared with Rodrigues and Mendes was large enough for a table and chairs, and had three bedrooms with enough space for their supplies. Palmeiro's description of his quarters contains one of the more vivid reports of what life was like in the floating lodgings that he came to know so well:

> In truth, I was appointed the most dignified and honored cabin of the three, but it had a considerable downside: in the stern of all of these boats there is a secluded spot with private access where the owner of the boat lives with his whole family. There are also hens for laying eggs, ducks being raised, a dog for the watch, and a pig for the slaughter, meaning that at the crack of dawn and at many reprises during the day I heard children crying, the pig snorting, the roosters crowing, the dog barking, and the ducks squawking. In their boats (and there is none which does not have them), the Chinese put little statutes of their idols, and if the boatman is poor he has at least a painted image, in front of which they light candles and burn incense every day. There is no poverty so great which impedes this devotion. . . . And as I learned that the place where the idol was located was close by, I ordered that the foot of my bed be turned toward it. Since I could not tread upon it with my feet, at least in this way I could defile it through my intentions.[75]

During their passage up the Pearl and later Bei (North) Rivers, the Portuguese group beat against the current. For most of the time they were pulled along the rivers' towpaths, but the force of the waters made it appear to Palmeiro that the boats were being "carried on the shoulders of men" rather than cruising over water. He watched as he drifted by what he considered to be innumerable towns and villages, all of which seemed to occupy much ground but appeared very poor. Therein lay the paradox of the Chinese landscape: although the low-lying buildings suggested poverty, the sheer amount of boats crammed with goods proved the existence of riches. Palmeiro concluded that the industriousness of the local people was a sure sign of their prosperity, even though he asserted that they dealt in small goods that sold cheaply. In other words, they profited from selling in quantity, and not in quality. But not all who lived along the river route appeared to escape misery: the Visitor's account describes a rabble of soldiers—"if such poor and vile folk are worthy of the name"—who crowded the riverbanks to kowtow before the boats of traveling mandarins. These men were obliged to ask if the officials required their services, and most often were pressed into service towing the boats as far as the next garrison. At one point during Palmeiro's journey, a tardy response on the part of a local captain of one of these teams earned a brutal punishment by the mandarin attached to the embassy, including his being chained by the neck and lashed with a bamboo cane. "What feats can be expected of soldiers who are whipped?," the Jesuit asked, "Only what these do, which is steal."[76]

This trip up the Bei River was also a journey into the history of the Jesuit mission in China. Despite the fact that the Jesuits' enterprise had only commenced forty years before Palmeiro's visitation, they had already abandoned a set of missions. The tense political situation in Guangdong Province with regard to foreigners, who were only permitted to stay in a specific area near Canton twice yearly for the duration of the trade fairs, made it difficult for them to remain on a permanent basis. And although the first foothold that the Jesuits had gained in China had been due to the success of Michele Ruggieri and Matteo Ricci in winning the friendship of important provincial officials, the prevailing attitude among the mandarins in Canton was intolerant of their presence. From their initial quarters at Canton, they had decamped in 1582 to Zhaoqing, the province's administrative capital further up the Pearl River, and eventually to Shaozhou on the Bei River in 1589. Unlike elsewhere in the Ming Empire, where their welcome was less controversial, the Jesuits were unable to overcome elite and plebeian suspicions about their presence in Guangdong. The hostile atmosphere prompted them in 1613 to move to Nanxiong, a town at the province's northern border, but that residence was abandoned when the Jesuits regrouped after the flames of persecution that lasted until 1623 died down.

So Palmeiro's progress through Guangdong Province afforded him a view of the ruins of the China mission's early years. In his description of Shaozhou, he relates his sadness at the fact that the Jesuits had lost their residence and that there was no clear way of regaining it. "There are some Christians here, many of whom came to visit me," he wrote, mentioning two sons of a dead mandarin, one of whom was poised to ascend to official rank. "I spoke to them through an interpreter," Palmeiro continued, "because I did not know how things were in this community. I found them to be well-intentioned, but ignorant, . . . naturally, without anyone to cultivate them, they will grow wild." His invocation of this agricultural metaphor, one used frequently in Jesuit sources, suggests something of the nature of the relationship that the missionaries had with their Christians. In order for the neophytes in the missions to progress toward the standards that the Society envisioned for ideal lay Christians, their pastors needed to be present; they could not simply baptize and leave. The Visitor and João Rodrigues nevertheless responded to the pleas that they perform a few infant baptisms before continuing onward. With a despondent tone, Palmeiro remarked that he had offered the Shaozhou community "all of those ministries which could be done in such a short stopover, which amounted to making the necessary exhortations about their obligation to live as Christians."[77]

Things seemed better at Nanxiong, further upstream, where the Visitor found a group of approximately one hundred neophytes. He recounted how the children were sent to him for his blessing and to demonstrate how they could recite their prayers. Palmeiro was pleased at this display, remarking that "it was as if they practiced them every day at school, but it was their parents who taught them at home," and was satisfied to learn that the local adults had all said their confessions that year to a visiting missionary.[78] Although ideally a priest would reside among such a community, Palmeiro conceded that the Christians of northern Guangdong could be cultivated reasonably well by the same Jesuit who traveled to Macau each year to seek salaries and supplies for the vice-province.

The panorama that stretched from the edge of Palmeiro's boat as it reached the northern end of the Guangdong river system prompted him to reflect more deeply on material resources. Like previous visitors to the Ming Empire (and most later visitors), he was overawed by the sheer quantities of everything he saw. As he was progressively reassured that the China mission was not a futile effort and that the Jesuits' actions did elicit some spiritual benefit, his curiosity returned and fixed on the commerce that seemed to flourish around him. Outside of Nanxiong, he remarked on the presence of many large boats filled with tanks for raising prized fish for sale throughout China. Palmeiro was most interested in how these fish were fed, noting that their diet of plants produced the opposite effect in them than it did in other animals, where it increased the meat's flavor. The Chinese appeared to enjoy their fish insipid, valuing tenderness over taste. It was for this reason that the boatmen he saw fed their captive hatchlings raw egg yolks, and themselves lived on the boiled whites. Palmeiro describes his conversation with a Chinese man who "knew all of this very well because he had performed this job many times," and who insisted that this diet of yolks (mixed with rice for bigger fish) produced very tender flesh, despite the fact that forty eggs were necessary each day for each boat.[79]

The press of boats filled with merchandise moving up and down the Bei River, one of the major transportation arteries of the empire, also led the Visitor to question how much the state derived from taxation. European observers since the time of Marco Polo had heard of the immense wealth of the imperial court and the splendor of the emperor's palaces, but these riches seemed to contrast starkly with the poverty that Palmeiro saw on the riverbanks of Guangdong Province. His questions about the source of imperial revenues were not dispelled by his reckoning that the massive quantity of small-scale traders, each paying a paltry sum at the customhouses situated along principal routes, eventually added up to considerable amounts. Palmeiro recalled that the Portuguese who traded at Canton never paid more than 1.5 percent on the silk they purchased, and at other customhouses "even less is paid," and so the conundrum remained in his mind.[80]

While at Beijing a few months later, he put the question to Xu Guangqi, *Doutor Paulo,* "who is one of the most important men in China and who has few above him in the government of the kingdom and, who it is believed, will soon have none."[81] Xu was indeed on the verge of being appointed *Gelao,* or Imperial Grand Secretary, and had enjoyed a long career in Ming administration. He explained to Palmeiro that there was "not a palm of ground in the whole of this monarchy that does not pay rent to the king," and that given the vast size of China—by Palmeiro's calculation of his route to the north it spanned over twenty degrees of latitude—this tax would amount to a staggering sum.

Another source of revenue was explained by Licenciate Inácio, that is, Sun Yuanhua (1581–1632), a military mandarin and one of Xu's disciples.[82] In addition to the sum of seven million in gold (these are Palmeiro's terms) from the land, there were also other taxes on "houses, their purchase and sale, and even on fishing in the rivers," although such things were not unheard of in Europe. Most importantly, Sun contended, there was also a tax that each man paid to the throne upon reaching sixteen years of age and yearly thereafter, the *ting*, "and this obligation to pay this tribute is so strict and exacting that even the king himself pays it in order to give the example to his vassals." Again, the vast size of the Chinese population—estimated at about 150 million in 1600—spelled massive revenues for the throne.[83] But neither Palmeiro nor his bureaucratic interlocutors were under the illusion that these potential revenues actually made their way into imperial coffers. As the Visitor noted: "I was told by a very important person that, in truth, the collecting of this tribute is very weak, that the king permits this state of affairs, and the highest mandarins know it and dissimulate."[84] Even despite this fiscal ineptitude, Palmeiro concluded that the empire's size was the reason for the Dragon Throne's legendary wealth—although the incapacity of the Ming state to quell peasant revolts and block invasions from the north would give the lie to such impressions within a decade of Palmeiro's trip through China.

———————

In late March 1629 Palmeiro left the company of the Portuguese embassy at Nanxiong to strike out on his own toward the Society's Vice-Province of China. But even before his boat arrived at this last port in Guangdong, he had already severed his ties symbolically: he put aside the customary black robe of the Society of Jesus and donned indigenous dress. Once in his new disguise, the Visitor summoned João Rodrigues and Gonçalo Teixeira Correia to say good-bye: "Seeing me in those clothes so different from what they were used to moved them to no little degree, and I confess that I was overcome as well." In order to complete the ruse, Palmeiro and Domingos Mendes took to an inn for a few days before leaving on March 26 to head through the Mei Pass and to the other rivers that would carry him further northward.[85] He covered the twenty-two miles from Nanxiong to Nan'an (today's Dayu, named after the Dayu Ridge that separates Guangdong from Jiangxi Province) in a sedan chair, which afforded him yet another perspective. So many people with so much merchandise clogged this artery that the Visitor had a hard time making headway; he insisted that "the press is ordinarily so great, and far greater than what one would find on the most trafficked street in Lisbon during its busiest day." The Jesuit pair had to stop "at every step," owing to the pairs of porters pushing their way along with their loads of goods hung from a pole borne upon the shoulder. Palmeiro was clearly impressed by these laborers, whom he compared to the *mariolas* (now meaning "rascal," but then simply "porter") of Lisbon, but who seemed capable of bearing greater burdens.[86]

Had Palmeiro been of a poetic disposition, he might have evoked the scene around him at this important juncture on his voyage in more eloquent terms. After all, at the Mei, or "Plum," Pass he stood at the edge of a different world. Heading down into Jiangxi Province beyond Dayu Ridge, he entered the heart of the Ming Empire. In the mind of contemporary Chinese, there was a distinction between the distant southern province with its semitropical climate and the vast central regions of the Yangzi River and Yellow River watersheds. Dayu Ridge was the point of separation between the two, and for that reason it became a recurring theme for generations of poets, including Ou Daren (1516–1595), a minor Guangdong scholar-official considered one of the province's foremost sixteenth-century poets.[87] One of Ou's poems, titled "Coming through Plum Pass as the Evening Clears," vividly invokes the symbolic importance of the route over which Palmeiro traveled in late March 1629. At the edge of the realm, everything was peaceful and all nations, the Portuguese included, came to show their respect to the magnificence of the Great Ming, as the Chinese styled their empire:

Sunset clings to a thousand peaks
That recede into the distance as we clear Plum Pass.
As the sun settles, the monkeys fall silent
And people head home along skyline trail.
From central China it breaches the south mountain frontier,
From the South China Sea it channels the Europeans.
Here the kings of the world's nations converge;
Here in the autumn breeze the battle horses stand idle.[88]

On the last day of March Palmeiro and his companion embarked again upon China's rivers. Once he began to drift along in Jiangxi Province, Palmeiro was traveling along river systems that would carry him most of the way to Beijing. Along the eight-day leg to Nanchang, he was most impressed by the bridges made of boats that spanned the Gan River and its tributaries at Ganzhou. But the fact that he was traveling in secret meant that his tension rose as he approached the barriers. Most memorably, he recalled stopping at one such bridge that was composed of forty-two boats each lashed together, and that bore a small customhouse and watch post. By the time the two Jesuits reached this point, the passage had been closed for the evening, but Palmeiro's confrere decided to make immediately the necessary announcement to the mandarin responsible for supervising the bridge. The servant procured the stationery required for writing a *tiedan,* which the Visitor described following manner: "A courtesy paper which is very common among the Chinese, innumerable quantities of which are sold in stores; each has seven, eight or more folds of paper, neatly done, depending on what is being requested of the person to whom it is sent and, in addition, a pocket made of the same paper. . . . It is inexcusable to forget this courtesy." The note briefly mentions the name of the petitioner and requests that he be admitted to make due reverence, formalities that Palmeiro found hard to explain in writing and "even seeing them done slowly were hard to understand."[89]

If Palmeiro harbored reservations about his disguise, a servant of his made matters more complicated by presenting him as a member of the scholarly elite. Without the Visitor's knowledge, he invented a Chinese name and calmly asserted to the official at the bridge that his master was "a literatus who was a relative of a very well known Christian mandarin." When Palmeiro reprimanded the servant for these lies, the man countered that there was nothing dishonorable about what he had done or said because "since the mandarin whose relative he made me was indeed the spiritual son of the *padres* who converted him, and I was the father of all of them, I was thus also his relative." Despite these good intentions and the swift response produced by the invocation of this pious genealogy, Palmeiro still commented that "there is no error so great that men will not find a cloak with which to cover it, or for which they will not find an excuse to diminish it." Impressed by the caliber of the illustrious passenger, the official in charge of the bridge ensured that the Jesuits sped on their way. They were even exempted from paying the fee, a gesture Palmeiro accepted without qualms since he was certain that their boat carried no taxable merchandise.[90]

As the Visitor's boat floated downstream to his first rendezvous with the men of the vice-province, his spirits seemed to have rebounded from the frustrations and disappointments that had marked the first months of his journey through China. He recounted the pleasant vistas of the wheat fields at the rivers' edges, and his delight at hearing the daybreak songs of the nightingales "that I have heard in no other place since I have been in the East." Prompted by the melodies of nature, he once again set to contemplating the richness of creation, just as he had done in the wilds of Sri Lanka when he found himself at elephants' watering holes. Like many of his European contemporaries who wrote during this advent of modern science, he saw nature through a moral lens, and understood that the behavior of the creatures of the Earth contained lessons for men. This time his speculations concerned the cormorants he saw roosting along the riverbanks, the uses that man had found for these birds, and the moral conclusions to be drawn from their habits. Palmeiro's reflections offer a fitting pause in the narrative of his journey, providing a momentary distraction before his attentions were once again focused on the weighty tasks of his office:

> In many places here I saw those fishing crows that dive into the rivers to search for fish at the bottom and between the rocks, just like ferrets do inside rabbit burrows. People told me that the antipathy between these crows and fish is so great that when someone gets a fishbone stuck in their throat, if they crush some of the bones of these birds into powder and blow it through an incision onto the spot where the bone is stuck, the powder will immediately grind and destroy it in such a way that neither causes pain nor makes the bone emerge. What great hatred is demonstrated in this animosity, because not even death, which ends everything, can stop it.[91]

It took the Visitor almost half the time he would spend traveling through China to reach the first mission station that he would inspect. Weeks of delay and the snail's pace of progress through Guangdong Province had kept him from reaching even the southernmost Jesuit house until early April 1629. Nearly four months had passed since he had embarked at Macau, over the course of which the hectic pace of Palmeiro's schedule slowed to nearly a standstill: in his isolation on the bustling Chinese waterways, he could do nothing except sit, pray, sleep, or observe his surroundings. The five questions that had impelled him on this journey remained unresolved, and even the work of providing encouragement to his fellow Jesuits had yet to begin. If nothing else, his mood changed for the better after he passed through the Mei Pass and into Jiangxi Province, away from the frontier region where he feared the Ming border patrols. He would need a positive outlook if he was to complete the ambitious trek ahead of him—he had only traveled 575 miles, or just over a sixth of his total distance—and to deal with the thorny issues of accommodation that were burning in the minds of his subordinates.

7

To Beijing and Back Again

On April 7, 1629, André Palmeiro arrived at Nanchang, the capital city of Jiangxi Province, where he found Vice-Provincial Manuel Dias the younger and Brother Manuel Pereira (1575–1633). "The joy that I had upon meeting them can easily be understood," the Visitor recalled, "since they were the first of those whom I had entered this kingdom to seek, and having them with me gave me such contentment in my soul that I felt satisfied with my past labors and was encouraged to face the others that awaited me."[1] After months of travel, he had finally crossed the buffer zone that separated Macau from the vice-province and was ready to conduct his inspection of the Jesuits' China enterprise. The route traveled by Palmeiro would take him to many of the mission stations spread throughout the Ming Empire, along the main north–south artery that linked Canton to Beijing.[2] Concerned that his absence from Macau would be detrimental to the missionaries in Japan (although he knew his capacity for intervention there was extremely limited), he did not stray far from this path. He would make no visit to the Jesuits' houses in the Chinese west, at Xi'an (Shaanxi Province), Jiangzhou (Shanxi Province), or Kaifeng (Henan Province). Likewise, he omitted a detour to the southeastern coast, to Fuzhou in Fujian Province.

The Visitor's journey would take him into the central regions of Jesuit activity in China: Jiangxi Province, the imperial capital, and the Jiangnan region at the Yangzi River's lower reaches. This last area, from Nanjing to Shanghai, had the greatest concentration of Jesuit residences and was the final area on Palmeiro's tour. To be sure, to claim that there was any sort of concentration of residences is misleading because the Society only maintained eleven houses in all of the Ming Empire in 1629. The Jesuits' presence in China was minuscule and, above all, widely dispersed. Even in the Jiangnan region, where they had houses in a handful of cities and tended communities of Christians in many towns and villages, their presence was insignificant against the immensity of the indigenous backdrop. What would most impress Palmeiro was the daunting scale of the Ming Empire, its massive size, its staggering population, its continual bustle of commercial activity. That the Jesuits were not lost in its midst was itself a miracle.

The central paradox of their efforts in China was precisely this: a handful of foreigners from the far side of the world had managed to attract attention vastly disproportionate to their numbers. While it would be a gross overreach to brand the seventeenth century (or any other) as a "Christian century in China"—as Charles Boxer famously did in a provocative hyperbole for Japan during the period from 1549 until 1650—the cultural recognition that the Jesuits received and the religious conversions that they occasioned are undeniable. Even before he reached Nanchang, Palmeiro had seen results of the Jesuits' work in China among the orphaned Christian communities of Guangdong Province as well as in the widespread knowledge of the *xiru*—"Western (Confucian) scholars" as Matteo Ricci and his confreres had styled themselves—among the empire's literati elite. From Jiangxi Province to the north, the Visitor would see even more evidence of the missionaries' presence and assess the challenges that they faced in their attempt to leave an even more discernible mark on the vast Chinese canvas.

Sight was Palmeiro's principal means for evaluating the China mission. Hearing had proved an unreliable means for evaluating the Jesuits' policies and methods in that country since he had listened to many contradictory opinions voiced in Macau and from within the vice-province. Moreover, without knowledge of Asian languages and customs—he could never equal his missionary brethren in that—he was unable to evaluate his subordinates' testimony.

Palmeiro was confident that his eyes would not trick him. He had seen vast stretches of South Asia, and, most importantly, he had seen how the Jesuits conducted themselves in those mission fields. Crucially, he had evaluated

experiments in missionary policy in India and knew how to spot errors in the
way the men of the Society comported themselves. Within China, Palmeiro
would have to see proof of the success of the Jesuits' disputed strategies, or at
least gauge the scale of the difficulties that they faced, in order to make up
his mind about the vice-province. That is, he would have to see communities of devout Chinese Christians being run by skilled pastors, and he would
have to see the fruits of cooperation between imperial officials and missionaries that served the mission either by ensuring its political protection or by
expanding its size. But woe betide those Jesuits who exaggerated in their

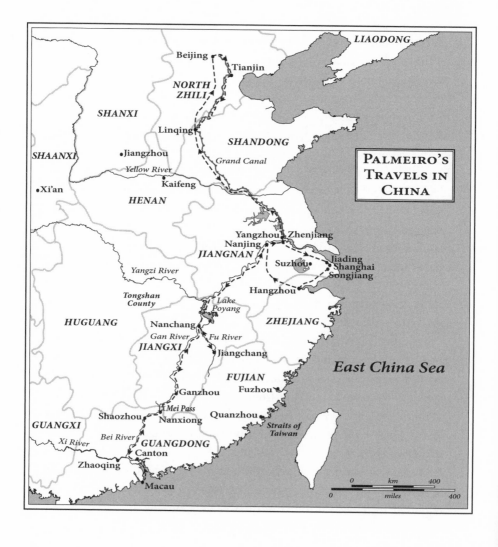

accommodation to Chinese cultural norms, those who wore silk robes when it was not necessary or those who carried themselves in a manner too reminiscent of that of mandarins. Palmeiro had a clear vision of what it meant to be a Jesuit, an identity that he might permit reshaping in a Chinese mold, just as he had permitted its reshaping in a Brahman one, but only if this change produced results that were clearly recognizable as Christian.

———

The first tableau of missionary life that the Visitor beheld in the vice-province was a study in contrasts. The initial pleasure of his meeting with Dias at Nanchang dissipated swiftly when the vice-provincial officer related the recent news from the mission: Pieter van Spiere (b. 1585) had been murdered in late December as he traveled to neighboring Huguang Province. Indeed, Palmeiro lamented upon hearing this news, "the displeasures of this world are not only weighty, but swift in coming." Given the loss of Niklaas Trigault in November, the death of yet another missionary came as a considerable blow: The vice-province was left with seventeen priests and four brothers, eight of them over fifty years old.[3] Doubly damaging was the fact that both men who died were from Douai in Flanders (one contemporary Jesuit insisted they were born on the same street), and in Palmeiro's opinion, "one Fleming can do the work of two men."[4]

The news of van Spiere's death served to remind the Visitor that despite the absence of persecution in China, the business of missionary work was still dangerous. Not only religious hatred or political motivations were responsible for the deaths of the Jesuits in East Asia but also criminal acts. Van Spiere had been sailing in the company of two servants to visit a mandarin Christian named Puon, baptized as Simão, who had requested a priest to spend Christmas with him and his family in Tongshan county (in the southern part of today's Hubei Province). The trio left Nanchang on December 16 and carried only limited luggage, but the weight of the Jesuit's altar stone and chalice gave the boatmen the impression that they were transporting a large quantity of silver. Van Spiere and his servants were seized by the crew while they slept, bound hand and foot, and, despite their offer to surrender their meager possessions in exchange for their lives and their silence, were tossed overboard. When Vice-Provincial Dias received word from Huguang that the priest had not arrived, he sent a party of trusted servants and local Christians to investigate, but not before the official Puon commenced legal proceedings against the boatmen. Van Spiere's body was never recovered from the Yangzi, and Palmeiro could only conclude that God, "who numbers the smallest hairs of those who suffer for Him, will always have an eye on it so as to make it appear in greater glory on the Day of Judgment."[5]

If on the one hand the news of this tragedy shook Palmeiro's confidence, the celerity of Chinese justice against the murderers on the other hand impressed him. This incident was one of several occasions that he had to contemplate how mandarins meted out punishments. As one who had spent years contemplating divine justice to prepare his lectures on moral theology and had witnessed its human counterpart in the secular and ecclesiastical realms in Portugal and during his travels, Palmeiro was a keen observer of justice in China. The orderliness of the Ming state and the effective enforcement of its laws had been a source of admiration for European observers since the first Portuguese travelers arrived in the early sixteenth century. The primary reason for their disquisitions lay in the fact that they had firsthand experience of detainment at the hands of Chinese officials for transgressing the regulations for foreign trade at Canton.[6] Jesuit authors, in particular Adriano de las Cortes (1580–1629), who was imprisoned after surviving a shipwreck on the empire's southern coast in 1625, but also others who did not have to suffer its rigors, dwelled at length on indigenous justice.[7] Of course, the missionaries in the Ming Empire were entirely at the mercy of imperial officials, so their knowledge of this topic sprang from the need for self-preservation.

The main concern that spurred Palmeiro's observations was whether Chinese officials obeyed any reliable norms. That is, he was keen to know if the Jesuits could count on their impartiality and their adherence to comprehensible patterns of judicial procedure, especially in light of the fact that there was no supreme court of appeal for foreigners. Given that the missionaries' fate was often in mandarin hands, but also that Chinese justice could act as a brake on persecution (especially if persecution emanated from popular milieux), it was crucial to understand how officials wielded their power. What Palmeiro saw was not completely reassuring. His initial impression was that the authority of Chinese officials was only vouchsafed by their excessive severity. During his trip with the Portuguese gunners, he had witnessed how the official who accompanied the embassy punished a petty thief, applying torture in the form of thumbscrews and chastisement with lashes of a bamboo cane. Ironically for a man who had served as a deputy and a commissioner of the Inquisition as well as a preacher at an auto-da-fé, he left no doubt of his revulsion at what he perceived to be a lack of clemency and the brutality of commonly used punishments.[8] What would happen if the wrath of Chinese officials came down upon the Jesuits and their Christians? Having already suffered brutal punishments during the Nanjing Persecutions in 1616 and 1617, they had good reason to fear capricious officials.

With regard to Pieter van Spiere's murder, Palmeiro was nevertheless pleased that justice was done where there was "such inhuman guilt." Here the Jesuits' links to scholar-officials were crucial: Simão Puon composed the accusations against the boatmen and had them delivered directly to the magistrate in the hometown of the murderers but without alerting the vice-provincial. The Visitor suggested that the Jesuits would not have been able to bring suit, and that the case had to be transferred to another official, but that in the end a fitting sentence was passed. Justice was served, he contended, by the deaths of the convicted: four of the accused were to die "cruelly, being cut up slice by slice while they were still alive," while a fifth "whom they did not find to be so guilty, was to die by beheading." Of course, capital punishment was commonplace in Europe for the crime of murder, and Palmeiro reserved his criticism for the practice of slow slicing.[9] He considered this practice cruel and unnecessary since it only served to transform a simple execution into mortal torture. There was no need to torment those who were bound for the scaffold since their wicked souls had already earned punishment for eternity. Palmeiro was likewise sure that the same fate was reserved for three other accomplices in van Spiere's murder who managed to flee before they could be detained. "Those who slipped through the hands of human justice, which does not grasp all," he concluded, "will nevertheless not evade the divine ones, from which nothing escapes."[10]

The picture was rosier when the Visitor turned to consider the fruit of the missions instead of the tragic loss of a missionary. If one of Palmeiro's tasks in China was to gauge the number of Christians that had been produced by forty years' worth of proselytizing, he was not disappointed with the results in Jiangxi Province. There he found solid communities that grew in spite of the persecutions that had obliged the Jesuits to seek refuge under the protection of mandarin allies. At Nanchang he found one hundred neophytes, "and there would have been more if the recent storm had not dispersed them and forced us to work discreetly." Although the Jesuits had not managed to win the friendship of more than a handful of officials (they received only hostility from others), their decision to follow the path of humility with regard to their adversaries appeared in Palmeiro's estimation to be a wise one. "The literati in this city have at times risen up against us," he remarked in reference to an episode in 1607, when the missionaries were accused of fomenting subversive doctrines: "By suffering in silence, even if we have not reduced them in everything, we have softened them in such a way that they will not only not bite, but not even bark."[11]

The results of the Jesuits' work were even clearer at Jianchang (today's Nancheng, in Fuzhou district), where Palmeiro arrived on Holy Saturday, April 14. Despite his disappointment at having to spend Holy Week on the Fu River, he was pleased to find Gaspar Ferreira (1571–1649) and Brother Francisco de Lagea (1585–1647) tending a community of over 1,200 Christians. This pair of Jesuits had performed 140 baptisms in the previous year and by Easter 1629 had already done 54 with another 30 adults waiting their turn while they were catechized. Palmeiro recalled being visited by "very honorable Christians" during his weeklong stay at Jianchang, and he expressed his confidence that the local *christandade,* that is, its community of baptized men and women, would grow considerably in future years.

After a brief stay in Jiangxi, Palmeiro embarked for points farther north in the company of Vice-Provincial Manuel Dias and Brother Domingos Mendes. While he drifted along, his thoughts once again returned to the different aspects of Chinese culture that he could study from his floating observation post. He was particularly interested in the manifestations of filial piety that he learned about from one boatman, who observed a fast to fulfill a vow he had sworn for the health of his mother. While the Visitor was not convinced of the practice of this fast—"it does not consist in only eating once, since they could eat a thousand times a day if they wanted to do so, but only in avoiding eating meat, fish, eggs, butter, and little else; rice, vegetables, beans, and other such things can be eaten as much as they want"—he admired its justification. (This was evidently not the Buddhist *zhai,* which would have displeased Palmeiro as much as it did his fellow Jesuits.) The boatman informed Palmeiro that he had vowed to fast for five years in recompense for the labors that his mother had suffered in giving birth and raising him. "It is hard to believe the zeal and great piety that one sees in China on the part of children and descendants towards their fathers and mothers during their lifetimes, and especially when they grow old," the Visitor insisted. Other Europeans who had come to an understanding of Chinese culture also remarked on the strict observance of filial piety, but the practice seems to have made a particularly strong impression on Palmeiro because he had been forced by his own vows to abandon his natural family, and even his adopted one—his spiritual family, the Society of Jesus in Portugal—when he was sent to Asia.[12]

Palmeiro's positive comments on this aspect of indigenous morality reinforced the notion, present in the writings of many of his contemporaries who visited China, that the Ming Empire only needed Christian revelation to crown its moral and political achievements. The high degree of civilization and the elaborate articulation of the Chinese state were clear proof of the validity of its moral foundations; to be sure, the Jesuits held that these were the result of a stricter observance of the precepts of natural law that God had imprinted on the minds of all men. In this regard the Chinese were similar to the Greeks, and especially to the Romans, who had propounded worthy moral principles, albeit without reference to Christianity, and whose texts could be found at the heart of the curriculum taught in Jesuit colleges. Unlike Matteo Ricci or the other China Jesuits, the Visitor could not identify the specific textual sources of the moral principles that exalted the responsibilities of family members and different social ranks toward each other, but he could see their benefits in practice. Most obvious to him was that their commitment to caring for family members accounted for the considerable longevity of the Chinese since "among them there is a great number of old men who, although they do not appear old because they have no beards, are nevertheless aged because they abound in years."[13]

The fact that the ideals of filial piety were commonly held in China had social benefits beyond the purely individual or familial. Palmeiro learned that the invocation of duty to one's parents could serve as a buffer against injustice among scholar-officials, in whose ranks were found the Society's most important patrons. In the context of a disquisition on the problems raised by the Ming censorial system, in which certain officials enjoyed the power to impeach other office-holders without recourse, the Visitor related how the excuse of caring for one's parents offered an expedient way of saving face while being forced to relinquish a civil post.[14] Since among the Chinese there was "no badge of honor greater than for a man to abandon all in order to attend to, or, as they say, to raise his father or mother," such assertions could be used for cover when censorial accusations were unjust—or simply when they threatened to ruin a promising career.

The responsibility for displaying filial piety extended after death as well, a fact that accounted for the Jesuits' being able to remain at Beijing to care for Ricci's grave. But Palmeiro was also aware that its scrupulous observance was a double-edged sword since it obliged civil officials to abandon their posts for a three-year mourning period when a parent died.[15] He makes specific reference to Wang Zheng (1571–1644, baptized Filipe in 1621), a scholar from Xi'an whose career was interrupted twice, the second time just as he completed one mourning period. Although it would have been perhaps more advantageous for the Jesuits to enjoy the protection of another high-ranking mandarin, they still seized the opportunity when "this disgrace, if it can be called that," occurred to open a new residence in Wang's hometown. Their convert's forced retirement nevertheless afforded him time to work with the missionaries in composing books on European machines, studies that circulated widely owing to the great prestige of his *jinshi*, metropolitan (or "doctor") degree, earned in 1622.[16]

While the camaraderie of Manuel Dias during the 350-mile journey from Nanchang to Nanjing enabled Palmeiro to deepen his knowledge of Chinese culture and how the Jesuits might best use it to their advantage, it did not wholly distract him from the scenery of China's waterways. The breadth of Lake Poyang, the largest body of fresh water in China, and the Yangzi River both captured his attention. He noted that the Yangzi's abundant waters produced "such waves and such storms that the Chinese call it the Son of the Sea, because it not only seems like the sea in its size but also in its wildness."

Travel was slow along the river despite the favorable currents, owing to the contrary winds, with the boats tacking constantly to make headway. Palmeiro remarked on the pleasant prospect of "more than five hundred sails running on the river, some heading east, some west," a sight that led him to contemplate the range of vessels he saw during his travels in China. He noted the presence of ships large and small, of massive boats with three or even four masts as well as of capacious pleasure barges moored near cities and outfitted for banquets and theater performances. But it was the sheer abundance of vessels that made the strongest impression on him, as it did on other contemporary European travelers. He could not help but resort to the same type of phrase that had made descriptions of China seem fabulous since Marco Polo's day: "The boats that sail on this river . . . are found in such a great multitude that they must be seen to be believed." Perhaps realizing that his superlatives about Chinese boats would strain the belief of his readers, he included some more precise data:

> The boats are so remarkable and in such a multitude, both on this great river and on other, smaller ones, that while I sailed along on one of the latter, my curiosity was aroused to count the number of those I encountered. I counted only the ones that came from the opposite direction, leaving aside those that were moored and those sailing along with us. With the use of a clock that timed an hour, I never saw less than a hundred coming towards us, and often saw above 130 or more. The result was that every day the number of vessels coming towards us was greater than a thousand.[17]

It took Palmeiro's party thirteen days to reach Nanjing, arriving at the former Ming capital city on May 4, 1629. He noted the city's status as a court, with the same offices and tribunals as in Beijing and even a "representation of the king's presence" to which officials showed obeisance. Once again, he returned to the idea of dissimulation, or pretending to be what one is not, which had so bothered him while he was at Madurai in Southern India, invoking the illusions and reality that he had encountered several times during his travels in Asia. In a brief comment he revealed himself *desenganado,* disillusioned with the world and its artifices, where by common consent "imagination makes truth equal to lies."[18]

But if on the one hand the court at Nanjing was "all faked," on the other hand the city's Christian community was quite real. Palmeiro described three men who learned of their arrival and hurried to the quayside to say their confessions to Manuel Dias. There had been no Jesuit residence in Nanjing since the 1616 persecution, an event that remained fresh in the memory of the city's Christians and local officials. But when the Visitor learned of a growing body of catechumens (at least twenty-five by the reckoning of the locals) who desired baptism there, he instructed Dias to send a priest to the city as soon as possible. Despite the potential for danger, Gaspar Ferreira had journeyed to Nanjing in 1628, and Rodrigo de Figueiredo, sent shortly after Palmeiro's later stopover in Hangzhou, spent enough time there to perform fifty baptisms and hear scores of confessions. The ease with which these two men visited the city, as well as the presence of an estimated five hundred Christians, prompted Palmeiro to urge Dias to reopen the Nanjing residence.

The vice-provincial's delay in resuming this mission was for the Visitor a sign of excessive caution. While there had indeed been persecutions and violence, the Jesuits could not huddle forever in the shadows. Timidity, Palmeiro felt, was no less of a problem than dissimulation, and the Jesuits had a moral and spiritual duty to preach the gospel in the face of peril. "There will be danger and risk in a priest residing in that city," he conceded, "but danger exists everywhere, and yet we still were able to pass through or live with it where we are, and moreover it is certain that without risking much, one cannot gain much."[19]

Speeding on their way down the Yangzi, Palmeiro and Dias continued together for another fifty miles until they reached Zhenjiang, where the river intersected with the Grand Canal. Sending Dias south to Hangzhou with a series of questions to discuss with his consultors, Palmeiro turned north and reembarked along the route for Yangzhou. At that city the Visitor's traveling companion, Domingos Mendes, sent word to a wealthy Christian family whose patriarch had died at the age of eighty-eight, only four days before their arrival.

At Yangzhou Palmeiro had another experience that served to allay some of the preconceptions he had brought with him into China about the vanity and fruitlessness of the Society's enterprise. The two Jesuits were invited to the family's home, where they were visited by the elderly widow, who insisted on speaking to Palmeiro. "With a holy plainness, she began to speak to me about God with such emotion and lucidity that I left very consoled," he recalled. Most moving for him was the story of her husband's final moments, when the dying man revealed to his wife that he had seen saints and angels amassing at the door to take him to heaven. Palmeiro departed unsure if this Christian was truly aware of his heavenly destination or if he was merely voicing the "imaginings of frenetic unconsciousness," but he concluded that in either case it was certain that those who so fervently believed could be sure of their place in heaven. And if the Jesuits could claim to have had some part in invoking such strong strains of piety—Francisco Furtado (1589–1653) had rushed from Hangzhou to administer extreme unction to this Christian—then their efforts were hardly in vain.[20]

Mendes and Palmeiro spent three days in Yangzhou preparing themselves for the final leg of their journey to Beijing. Although it might be expected that the two would travel north on the Grand Canal by boat, they proceeded overland for the remaining 550 miles. Ever conscious of his clandestine status, Palmeiro saw himself forced to rent a covered sedan chair for the journey. He explained that there were two types of chairs: one carried on the backs of porters "which are less expensive, but also less comfortable," and others that were enclosed and slung between mules, "which convey greater authority." Although his desire for humility urged him to take the simpler conveyance, discretion argued for the more expensive one, and the party set out for the north with a total of seven mules (including one each for the three servants who traveled with them). On May 13 they left on their route across the coastal lowlands and great northern plain, where Palmeiro remarked on the flatness of the wheat fields which stretched to the horizon: "All of this route is so flat and equal, and so lacking in mountains or hills that for great stretches of distance I could not spot any piece of land which stood out above another."[21] Yet if there was nothing that broke the monotony of the land, there was plenty of variety in the food available in the first regions he passed through on this route to attract his attention. He noted how inexpensive meat and poultry were, and appeared especially content to encounter types of wheat bread, either steamed or baked, some of which reminded his stomach of his distant homeland.

The conditions that the Jesuit party experienced on their way north became more severe as they left the well-watered coastal regions and entered the dry inland expanses of Shandong Province. Palmeiro was especially critical of the quality of the lodgings available along the way, something he found surprising given the fact that it was one of the most heavily traveled routes in China and that he passed by "many very noble cities, many walled towns, and many very large villages". It was not the quantity of inns, he related, but the fact that they were poor structures "without vistas to please you, without breezes to cool you, and without beds for you to sleep in." Although he admitted that all travelers carried their own cots and that there was always somewhere to set them up, he found the accommodations to be dirty and uncomfortable. Worse still, from Palmeiro's perspective, was the lack of good water on the route to Beijing. "In such a great distance overland," he averred, "I never once drank any that was not salty." His troubles were compounded as the climate became drier and the party entered regions stricken by drought. When he attempted to send the servants to purchase meat in one city, he learned that the local officials had banned the sale of pigs or other animals in order to impose a general fast that intended to coax heaven into sending rain. Unfortunately for Palmeiro, the same forced privations were imposed all throughout the northern plain as he headed across it, and were even declared in the imperial court a scant few days before his arrival.[22]

The rigors of this journey began to take their toll on the Visitor as he neared the imperial capital. He recalled the clouds of dust kicked up by the beasts of burden that traveled along the same road as his party, estimating that he had seen "a hundred thousand mounts for rent, many mules, many horses, and an infinite number of donkeys." Some passing rainstorms in the southern part of his route turned the road into a muddy mess, while at its northern reaches the sunbaked earth was ground into a fine dust by the legions of carts and animals who passed over it. Clouds of dust left their residue on everything, he recalled, even finding their way deep inside his luggage. "When this dust is combined with the heat of the intolerable stillness," Palmeiro wrote, "it weighed upon me so heavily that I was convinced that my life was ending and if I did not indeed meet death, I at least saw its shadow come over me." Brother Mendes urged him to rest, fearing that he would end his days on earth before he would end his journey through China. With the fortunate application of a medicine that Mendes prepared for him, Palmeiro returned to form and was able to continue onward. The memory of the sight of the Grim Reaper was enough to urge caution, however, and he ordered his sedan chair adapted so he could be carried lying down instead of sitting.[23]

Despite these hardships, the road to Beijing was not without its comic interludes. Of course, it was Palmeiro that was a source of amusement for the Chinese whom he encountered, owing to his exotic countenance:

It is hard to believe how fascinated they were with my beard and hair. When I got out of the sedan chair, walked into or out of the inns, or simply sat down, all of them gathered around to see me, whether it was because I was something new or something monstrous. All of them were curious to ask, albeit cautiously, how old I was. When they were told the truth, they claimed that the servants were lying to them and that they had shaved off a good number of years. One time while I was at an inn, there was a petty mandarin staying in an adjacent room who paused before leaving in the morning to get a good look at me. I made a gesture of respect when I passed by him, and he returned the courtesy, but he could not hide his curiosity and so asked the servant to reveal how old I was. The servant responded by adding twelve years (because since I was 62, he said I was 74), and the mandarin retorted that he had shrunk my age, since clearly I was much older.[24] In the end, the brother who traveled with me and the servants resolved to respond to anyone who asked that I had not yet reached 100 and with this answer they would be silenced.

Among the curious, however, there was a man who declared that he was certain that I was 99 years old. When I asked him why he did not say 100, but rather subtracted one, he told me that it was out of respect for the person of whom he spoke and also because it was some good fortune to take one away from a round number. There is no doubt that they believe this because they typically do the same for the numbers of other remarkable things: for instance, the number of boats that carry supplies to the court are typically 9,999, and others which they call "horse ships" are 999 in number, and so forth with the same superstitions for other things. The reason that these men think me so aged, although I am not as old as they believe, was because, they told me, I have a full grown beard which was going white at the ends. Since all of the Chinese carry in their imagination that there are men who possess the art of prolonging their lives or who owing to some special fate are destined to live so long, they judged that I had this good fortune. And so what they desired for themselves, they celebrated in me.[25]

The Visitor's party arrived at Beijing "with the special help of Heaven" on June 2, the eve of Pentecost. But before proceeding to the Society's residence within the city walls, they retired to the enclosed garden at Zhalan where the Jesuits had a cluster of buildings near Matteo Ricci's tomb. From this site, roughly three and a half miles from their primary residence at the court (the Nantang, "Southern Church"), Palmeiro sent word to Niccolò Longobardo to announce his arrival. The response informed the Visitor that he was eagerly awaited by a "most important mandarin," Sun Yuanhua, that is, "Licentiate Inácio", whose departure in the capacity of military official for Liaodong, the northeastern region beyond the Great Wall, was imminent.[26] Proceeding into the capital, Palmeiro met with him briefly after Sun heard mass and confessed before heading off to the embattled frontier. The Visitor was introduced to Dr. Paulo, that is, Xu Guangqi, the following day. The news of the Jesuit superior's arrival was greeted with joy among the local Christians, and he spent the early part of his stay receiving visits from Xu's relatives and "a goodly number of literati" whose courtesies he repaid scrupulously at the encouragement of Longobardo and the other court missionaries.

After the burgeoning churches of Jiangxi Province and other communities of Christians scattered along the route from Canton to Beijing, the size of the capital's community was a disappointment. Palmeiro estimated that it numbered about 250 men and women, a tally that was quite small for such a large city. Nevertheless, there seemed to be a clear explanation for the fact that nearly three decades of missionary activity at the court had produced such meager results. Above all, there was the difficulty of proselytizing in the open, since the Jesuits lacked formal permission even to reside in Beijing, not to speak of official tolerance for their preaching. "Only the divine arm will secure that liberty," Palmeiro confessed, being convinced that the pronouncements against the missionaries issued from the court at the time of the Nanjing Persecutions just over a decade previously still overshadowed them. Asserting that "even the slightest hint of desire to favor foreigners" was a grave crime among imperial officials, he was astonished that so many important mandarins frequented the Jesuits' residence daily. "It seems that the opinions on the sciences that we know and profess, and which they greatly prize, validate us in their eyes and embolden them," Palmeiro insisted, "or, as I am convinced, Divine Providence facilitates the intimate dealings they have with us at this house, so that the ordinary folks and the literati do not find our prolonged stay strange."[27]

Palmeiro therefore concluded that the Jesuits' permanence at court and their continual dealings with mandarins and literati were the key to the whole missionary endeavor. Their presence at Beijing might indeed lead to "conversation and not conversion," as he believed prior to his visitation, but even this seemingly idle activity was crucial for the success of the mission. To be sure, the China missionaries had insisted upon this since Ricci's day, but their opinion was only verified for the Jesuit hierarchy when Palmeiro, the first outside superior to inspect the mission, saw its effects with his own eyes. Although he does not mention it in his travelogue, Palmeiro was aware of Xu Guangqi's ambition to have the Jesuits involved in the reform of the Chinese calendar. The integration of the missionaries into this project would come later in 1629 and would have the immediate impact of dispelling the clouds of doubt about the legality of their stay in the capital.[28] But even before this important step was taken, the widely known links between the scholar-officials and the missionaries at court had facilitated the spread of the Jesuits throughout the imperial provinces. Thus, the fame of their ties to members of the late Ming elite ensured that local officials tolerated the Jesuits elsewhere for fear of offending their betters in Beijing. "In the other cities of the kingdom, they do not fear welcoming foreigners who are so well-known and so celebrated at court," Palmeiro concluded, "and in this way the door is opened for the Gospel."[29]

The Jesuits' missionary activities were an open secret at the Ming capital. The Visitor remarked that their church was "very pretty and gilded, but not public", that is, its façade did not declare it to be a church and its gatherings were held so as to not arouse suspicions. This means that the Jesuits did not offer sermons and catechism lessons on other days than those when they said mass, as was typically done in Europe and the European colonies, but performed these ministries on Sundays and holy days. Special meetings were held for women in the four houses that the missionaries maintained in different neighborhoods, where the priests would periodically appear to say mass, hear confessions, and teach doctrine. Palmeiro was impressed by the quality of the pastoral care that his subordinates offered to their flock and by the eager response of Beijing's Christians, as seen through their desire to receive the sacraments. But what most moved him during his stay at court was the sight of mandarins serving at the masses said in the missionaries' church. Such was the majesty of the Eucharist, Palmeiro asserted, that it obliged "men such as these, who are normally so haughty, to put on a surplice and wear it while standing before a public assembly." After what the Visitor had seen of the behavior of Chinese officials, the sight of them acting as altar boys beside the Jesuits was genuinely amazing.[30]

Another clear indication of acceptance of the missionaries in Beijing was that Palmeiro spent a good part of his two-week stay in the city touring its monuments. This was not unusual for Chinese visitors, especially the scholar-officials who participated in the highest levels of the civil service examinations or others who came for trade or administrative duties, and printed guides to the city's monuments were readily available.[31] But Palmeiro was perhaps the first European tourist to visit Beijing in the modern era and record his impressions for posterity. Unlike his Jesuit brethren, whose writings described aspects of life at the capital and their efforts to create a mission church within its walls, the Visitor was only visiting.

His wanderings in Beijing were not a strategic reconnaissance of the mission field, but they were not an innocent tour of the city's highlights either. Here we can see the hand of the China Jesuits in shaping Palmeiro's impressions of the imperial capital, since it was clearly they who constructed his itinerary. For the men of the vice-province, it was crucial that the Visitor leave with an appropriate level of awe at the magnificence of Chinese civilization. After all, many of the doubts that had sparked Palmeiro's journey (doubts incubated among Jesuits in Japan, India, and Europe) arose from the missionaries' difficulties of rendering their understanding of China into European terms. Palmeiro had already seen much to impress him on his journey from Macau, but a tour of the capital city was necessary for fixing the context for the China Jesuits' actions in his mind. He had to marvel at the size of the emperor's palaces and the ramparts of the city's fortifications, he had to wonder at the dimensions of its towers and statues within its temples, and he had to stand in awe before the multitudes from across Asia that assembled at court if he was to transmit to Rome an unambiguous message about the scale of the missionaries' apostolic challenge and the value of the results they had produced.

What did Palmeiro see in Beijing? The first stop on his tour was a trip to see a section of the walls. Then, as now, the city's fortifications were a sight to behold. Most likely owing to the private collaboration on astronomical matters between the Jesuits and Xu Guangqi, Palmeiro was taken to see the imperial observatory that was situated atop a bulwark near the city's eastern edge. There he learned that the wall's topmost level consisted of a platform wide enough for two coaches or four horses to proceed in parallel, but he judged that there was room for three coaches. His figures were admittedly impressionistic because, as he remarked, "as a foreigner I did not dare to measure the wall"—fearing that suspicious eyes might judge his gestures an act of espionage. Palmeiro nevertheless got a good sense of the scale of the city from this vantage point. He noted the evenly spaced guard pavilions along the wall, the ample distance found between the wall and the city's houses (something uncommon in European walled cities), and the massive number of bricks—1,200,000 of them—imported from Linqing in Shandong Province to construct it. He could also perceive the rectangular layout of the city, judging its walls to be four leagues or more in length (roughly fourteen miles) and noting that the perimeter of the old Yuan Dynasty walls had been extended considerably. Indeed, he asserted, the part enclosed by the newer walls would be enough for "a good-sized city in any part of the world."[32]

On top of the wall at the old imperial observatory Palmeiro also saw the astronomical instruments that had been placed there during the Yuan Dynasty. He remarked on an armillary sphere and "a curious quadrant" made of bronze that had sat exposed to the elements for three hundred years but, he claimed, were "as clean, and their decorations as sharp, as if they had been erected only a few days before." This spot would be the site of some of the most famous episodes of the Jesuits' mission to China, although in June 1629 they had yet to assume the mantle of court astronomers. By early September of that year the throne would accept Xu Guangqi's suggestion that the "Western scholars" be integrated into the calendar office of the Imperial Astronomical Bureau. So it was only a few months after Palmeiro's visit that a new array of Jesuit-built instruments would be set alongside the ones placed there during the reign of Kublai Khan in the thirteenth century. Within fifty years of Palmeiro's visit the famous missionary-astronomer Ferdinand Verbiest (1623–1688) would refurbish the observatory with the bronze instruments still visible today and remove the old pieces from the top of the wall to its base.[33]

Although the Forbidden City remained true to its name, the Visitor was taken on a tour of the palace's perimeter. This trip around its walls led him to claim that the imperial residence covered "not only the greater part of the city, but the best part of it". From the outside, he could see the stream that flowed through the palace grounds as well as the hill at its northern edge, which he deemed adequate for catching a cool breeze. He also saw the massive south-facing palace gate, in front of which he passed on two occasions, and remarked on how the officials entering the Forbidden City would dismount far from its doors in order to give the example of humility before the throne. Palmeiro related that the buildings inside the palace walls were constructed in the same one-story style as the city's other buildings, but that they seemed much taller than the rest when viewed from atop the observatory platform. Surely, he claimed, the palace's halls were well-appointed, comfortable, and commodious since "such a great monarch was born in them, lives in them, never leaves them, and dies in them." But this was not enough to convince him of their absolute worth, and Palmeiro retained the judgment about indigenous architecture that he had formulated when espying the city of Canton six months earlier: "With regard to the beauty and the architectural plans, all of the greatest buildings and the most sumptuous temples of Beijing are not only inferior to what we have in Europe, but fall so short that they are not even worth comparing."[34]

His visit to the exterior of the Forbidden City prompted a reflection on life inside the palace walls, which, of course, he did not witness. Palmeiro's point of comparison was to the monarchs of Europe, whose image contrasted sharply with that of the Ming emperors. Most disturbing to him was the fact that the inner court, that is, inside the palace walls, was staffed entirely by eunuchs and women. There was therefore no way for the Chinese emperor to attain Palmeiro's European ideal of royal virility since it could never emerge in this company. If the presence of female caresses was bad enough for a

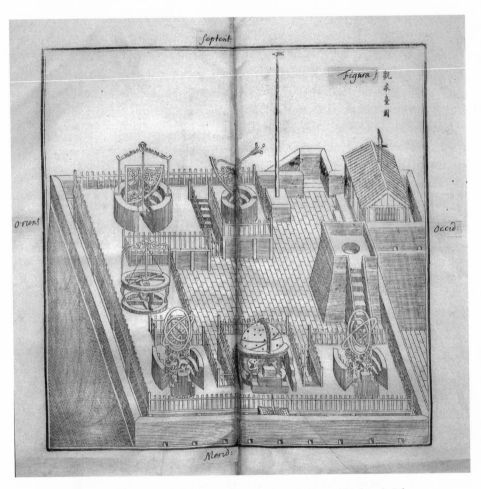

FIGURE 7.1. View of the Imperial Observatory from Ferdinand Verbiest's *Liber Organicus Astronomiae apus Sinas restitutae,* printed at Beijing in 1674. Although this image shows the observatory platform after Verbiest reorganized the astronomical instruments in 1670, it nevertheless gives a sense of the same spot that Palmeiro visited in the summer of 1629.

king, he argued, it was worse that the Chinese monarch lived *encantoado, ou ainda encantado,* that is, cornered and enchanted, "by the ghosts of men." There was nevertheless hope for the young Chongzhen Emperor (1611–1644), who had risen to the throne in 1627 and had reportedly spent his formative years outside of the palace. While he did live "buried alive" amid eunuchs and ladies, the prince did not appear to be dominated by them like his predecessors had been. But Palmeiro contended that these early signs were not enough to cement the emperor's potential. Clearly what was missing was the light of reason to penetrate the shadows of his magnificent palace-tomb and for him to submit to baptism, or at least to sanction the preaching of Christianity openly in his lands. "We all ask God, and especially those who live here in China," he asserted, "offering sacrifices and doing penitence (and some doing a great deal), to send a ray from heaven into the soul of this young man, so that he recognizes the truth that we preach and opens a wide gate for the spread of His holy law in this great kingdom."[35]

The Visitor's tour of the Ming capital also included stops at some of the city's temples. In his opinion, although there was a great abundance of religious buildings in Beijing, they were all more or less alike in style. Moreover, he insisted that the ones he saw were dirty, filled with "dust and spider webs which either shrouded the best parts of them or made them appear very ugly." His hosts insisted that Palmeiro enter into two of them in particular, praising the high quality of the devotional art he would see, and he duly obliged them. Of course, their recommendations were not without purpose. Their suggestions of temples to visit were not motivated only by aesthetic concerns, since the court Jesuits did not insist that he see the Temple of Heaven with its famous round tower. Their aim was to ensure that the Visitor beheld a vision of Chinese religion that would underscore the difficulty of the missionaries' endeavor: he needed to be shown a plethora of gods, and he needed to see massive idols. Regardless of its beauty, the Temple of Heaven had neither of these things. Further evidence of a "guided tour" comes from the fact that Palmeiro did not visit the Kong Miao, the Confucius Temple, despite its symbolic centrality to the intellectual life of scholar-officials, including the Jesuits' mandarin Christians. Although the Jesuits were certainly aware of its existence and knew that it was the site of rituals similar to those performed in other shrines (at least to the untrained eye), the Visitor's opinion that these were done for "pure reason of state" was best not to be challenged by too vivid a spectacle of incense and prostrations before statues.[36]

So Palmeiro was shown the two pernicious sects that the Jesuits identified as their primary rivals. First he was shown the "sect of the *Tausus*," that is, the Daoists, with its panoply of deities.[37] From his remarks about the presence of seventy-two "chapels" at the first one he visited, it appears that he went to the Dongyue Temple located a short distance outside the Chaoyang Gate.[38] The chapels he saw were arranged around a courtyard, with a large pavilion in the center. Like many other tourists in later generations, he experienced the frustration of not getting to see what was touted as the most impressive part of the temple "because it was closed and no *bonzes* could be found to open it."[39] He was nevertheless impressed by the contents of the smaller chapels, each of which held statues of "spirits, as the Chinese call them," bearing the symbols of their ethereal offices. Then as now, these terracotta statues represented the gods of the underworld who meted out punishments or issued rewards in the afterlife. Palmeiro was struck by the realism of these figures, reporting that the ones who were held to succor the poor or the afflicted "had faces whose expressions promised gentleness," and those whose duty was to chastise the wicked "had wrinkles on their foreheads, bulging eyes, and protruding teeth." But even though the devils were depicted performing gruesome punishments, he concluded that "they were no less graceful than those who rewarded virtue, and no less of a sight to see."[40]

The second temple that Palmeiro visited belonged to Buddhism, the other tradition considered by the Jesuits a principal adversary in their battles for souls.[41] While it would have been relatively easy to find a Buddhist temple in the capital, the court Jesuits needed to impress the Visitor not just with grandiose architecture but with an impressive devotional statue. Their choice of the Wofo Temple, the home of the Sleeping Buddha in Beijing's northwestern suburbs, reveals that they wanted to appeal to what they assumed to be Palmeiro's understanding of idolatry. The abundance of Daoist gods that he saw at the Dongyue Temple sufficed to demonstrate the complexity of pagan cosmology since it showed many ranks of deities with different functions, but the statues there were human-sized. It was important for the Visitor to see something big if he was to understand the solidity of Buddhism within China. Seeing a massive statue of the Buddha would also underscore the difficulty of uprooting this originally foreign tradition from Chinese culture.

At the Sleeping Buddha temple, Palmeiro noted that the eponymous figure was an accurate likeness: "stretched out on a bed with a pillow under his head, and a hand by his cheek just like someone who enjoys sleeping." He was also taken by its huge size, estimating it at "twenty palms," and by the other large statues placed along the shrine's walls.[42] What particularly stood out in Palmeiro's mind was the fact that each year, he claimed, the queen would send a blanket to cover the Buddha: a lighter one in summer and a heavier one in winter.[43] Of course, the Visitor's take was anything but complimentary about pious gestures made to any deity other than the Christian God. Referring to the royal blankets, he asserted that they were of no comfort to the Sleeping Buddha: "Both one and the other weigh him down in Hell where he is, because unmerited honors which serve to alleviate discomfort in this world are only burdens in the next."[44]

Palmeiro's visits to different monuments in the Ming capital also permitted him to see the bustle of everyday life. Like other seventeenth-century European visitors to Beijing, he marveled at the number of people who crowded its streets. Such was the press of merchants, officials, functionaries, and servants in the city's main thoroughfares that they were "impossible to cross, one being always jostled about." In contrast to those in the other Chinese cities that he had seen, he reported that the capital's streets were unpaved and therefore "totally insufferable". As was the case with the road that had brought him to the capital, the slightest rain made them so muddy that "you cannot even take one step," and the baking heat gave rise to clouds of dust that "not only blind your eyes but block your throat." Thankfully, there were plenty of horses, mules, and donkeys for hire: "There is no part of the city where you can not find thousands of them, if you ever needed thousands." Whoever rode about the city always wore a veil, he remarked, one loose enough to see through but fine enough to protect the honor of those who rode less than adequate mounts. A final aspect that drew his attention was the fact that all riders of rented mounts were accompanied by servants who walked on foot holding the reins, a practice that rendered skilled and fearful riders equal.[45]

In this spectacle of humanity on the streets of Beijing, Palmeiro found little to compare with what he remembered from his days in Lisbon or Coimbra, or even Goa. The Ming capital to him seemed somehow lacking in the type of magnificence that one expected at a court because all of the splendor was concentrated on the person of the emperor and was not spread about to a rich, competitive nobility: "In all of this multitude that one finds in the streets, there is nothing to draw the eyes; there are no talented horsemen, there are no coaches, there are no people in different costumes as there are in the more populous cities of Europe, and even in some of the smaller ones." While he did concede that occasionally one saw high-ranking officials proceeding through the streets, Palmeiro claimed they were accompanied by less impressive trains than what he had seen in other Chinese cities. Once again the centrality of the emperor reduced even the most important mandarins to secondary roles at court, accounting for their somewhat muted public presence in Beijing. By contrast, in the provincial cities where Palmeiro had been, he claimed that the officials who went about in sedan chairs were typically accompanied by "three or four times more pageantry."[46]

The fact that the court Jesuits had many high-status Christians among their acquaintances meant that Palmeiro had a privileged perspective on late Ming governance. As we have seen, he was particularly interested in the habits of the mandarins since in their ranks the missionaries found the keys to social acceptance and political protection. But like many other contemporary Europeans who wrote descriptions of China, he found the intricate working of the imperial bureaucracy to be fascinating.[47] For a man like Palmeiro, who had risen to a position of prominence without the privilege of birth and solely by dint of his intellect, there was much to recommend in the Ming system. The Chinese civil service was the nearest approximation to a meritocratic political framework that the premodern world would produce: entry into its ranks came through examinations, and promotions came through more of the same. Nobility counted little, and family ties were intentionally severed when provincial assignments were made. Although there were gentry clans whose members gained entry into the mandarinate generation after generation, and even if exemptions from the lowest-level examinations were available for purchase, these were exceptions to the general rule of social ascension through merit. While it was certainly not the case that Palmeiro saw no virtue in noble birth, he nevertheless admired this system of government predicated on proven wisdom.

But whereas other Jesuit authors dwelled on the examination system that permitted entry into the civil service, Palmeiro was more concerned with the system in practice and, in particular, the checks that it placed on the abuse of power. Justice was one of his most important preoccupations, and the Ming bureaucracy offered ample cause for reflection. During his description of Beijing, he revisits a discussion of the role of the imperial censors in curbing the excesses of provincial officials, and complements it with a disquisition on the relations between the highest mandarins and the throne. It was natural for these themes to have attracted the Visitor's attention because he, too, held a position at the summit of a bureaucratic administration; he was charged with inspecting the work of others and enjoyed the power to promote or demote them in a nearly absolute fashion (by invoking the vows that bound the Society of Jesus). Moreover, he served at the pleasure of the superior general in Rome and was expected to send his own type of memorials in which he not only described his activities but also struck the requisite tone of humility before his own superior. It should not be forgotten that although Palmeiro's powers were wide-ranging, the majority of his subordinates were professed Jesuits; that is, they were also senior members of the Society and could not simply be commanded about, except in exceptional circumstances. Along with great power, Palmeiro knew, came great responsibility, among the missionaries no less than among the mandarins. The Ming censorate and the other supreme levels of Chinese governance were therefore a distant mirror of the Visitor's own office and a worthy source of comparisons.

While he was at Beijing, Palmeiro learned about an inspection of the ranks of the mandarinate. This "examination" was coordinated by the most important of the six supreme tribunals, the Ministry of Personnel, the "Lipù," *Libu,* and administered by a set of "visitors, that they call Tu cha yuen, which is a great dignity." Although Palmeiro's description of these inspections does not precisely match the system of Ming administration presented by modern historians, these other visitors were clearly members of the Ming Censorate, that is, the Chief Surveillance Office or *Ducha yuan.*[48] These inspectors were charged with evaluating imperial bureaucrats as a result of periodic visitations (the civil servants, not the military mandarins, who had their own evaluation system, and as Palmeiro remarked, "truly in China, *cedant arma togae*"[49]). They carried out their task in two cycles for the lower grades of mandarins: once every three years for provincial officials, and once every six years for court officials.[50] Palmeiro was present in Beijing for the announcement of the results of the latter inspection cycle, which ended in 1629, and his confreres showed him the list of the names of the officials who were dismissed from their posts, most likely published in the capital gazette.[51] Clearly it was the Jesuits' relations with so many court mandarins that piqued the missionaries' interest in this evaluation since it promised not only to elevate their patrons but also to vanquish their enemies. But there was also the fact that the Society of Jesus also had a system of triennial evaluations that was used by the order's superior general for making appointments within each province, a system with which Palmeiro was intimately familiar.[52]

It was not only the number of court mandarins mentioned in the gazette—211 officials—that impressed Palmeiro but also the reasons cited for their dismissal. Excepting the 32 who were retired because of old age or ill health, the rest were demoted for reasons of inadequacy, temerity, inattention, greed, or cruelty.[53] The last two of these categories (although only accounting for nine mandarins) particularly drew his attention: he noted that the greedy and the cruel did not just lose their rank but were reduced to plebeian status. "A just sentence, and good punishment," he remarked, "that they become equal to commoners and lose the grade that they had, for those who out of greed sank to the level of base interest or those who through cruelty showed themselves to be like brutes." Palmeiro found the publication of these sentences, as well as those for the inspection of the provincial mandarins, to be especially praiseworthy since it served as both chastisement for the wicked and warning for the rest.[54]

For the highest levels of imperial officials, however, the inspection system was different. According to Palmeiro, mandarins from the second, third, and fourth grades were obliged to offer memorials to the throne in which they recognized their shortcomings and requested dismissal.[55] Typically the response simply brought orders to carry on but sometimes contained words of praise, such as in 1629 when the Chongzhen Emperor paid a compliment to Xu Guangqi. It was an especially propitious moment for Dr. Paulo, since the throne's laconic note seemed a foreshadowing of the greater rewards that Xu would share with the Jesuits at court: "You have always shown that you have an abundance of virtue and wisdom, and so I order that you continue in your office."[56]

While there was not a regular inspection of high-ranking officials like Xu, they were nevertheless subject to criticism by imperial censors, who were charged with sending memorials to the throne on aspects of good governance as well as about mandarin misbehavior. Jesuit authors in the early seventeenth century were especially keen to explain the function of this office, which they called "Tauli" or "Coli" (possibly derived from *ke-dao*, that is, functionaries of the Ming censorial apparatus).[57] Entrusted with defending the moral and political welfare of the empire, the censors submitted memorials to the throne in order to denounce malfeasance. Those who were impeached were obliged to relinquish their posts without recourse. If they resisted, "memorials rained down" upon them in public, forcing them to resign.[58] The Jesuits were interested in the actions of these inspectors since their power could be (and, at times, was) brought to bear on the missionaries' patrons or their adversaries within the imperial bureaucracy. Impeachments could cause problems if they were not motivated by the highest ideals of justice and virtue, as Palmeiro's informants suggested to him. Of course, critics were never lacking. Accordingly, the Visitor related, the ministry was obliged to rotate a minimum number of censorial officials out of office twice each year, so as to prevent them from abusing their power to degrade other officials without appeal. "It is a risky style of government, and exposed to great evils," Palmeiro asserted, "since it takes only the hatred of one ill-inclined individual to cast down a great number of innocent men."[59]

Recent history in China had demonstrated how the actions of a few could have deleterious effects on imperial governance. Competition among factions of scholar-officials in the mid-1620s, in particular rivalry involving the members of the Donglin Academy from the Jiangnan region, had ended in bloody purges in the years just before Palmeiro's visit to Beijing.[60] His interlocutors at the court were more than aware of the climate of intrigue and factionalism that plagued imperial politics. Notwithstanding, the Visitor claimed that "they say" the censors rarely caused the downfall of innocent men. That is, it was commonly held that only the guilty paid for their crimes since the memorials written by the censors passed through other hands before the throne endorsed them. Moreover, the censors were aware that if they acted unjustly, they too would be called to face justice; and "some argued" that the possibility of one unjust official was a small price to pay for a system in which powerful censors could prevent large-scale abuse.

For Palmeiro, it was clear that there were enough weights and counterweights in the Ming system to ensure that justice prevailed most often, and that the state was administered fairly. This was his goal for the Society of Jesus too, so his reflections on the mandarins served to stimulate his thoughts on how best to navigate the positions of his combative subordinates, especially with regard to the contested missionary policies that he had entered China to judge: "In the end, good governance, as well as any other good, resides in the middle path; that is, not to believe everything that you hear, so that you avoid being led into error, nor to concede to every counterclaim without rigorous examination, so that you are not tricked by others."[61]

After two weeks at the capital, the Visitor was ready to depart once again for the south. His final activities included consulting with the priests about how best to win more secure terms of residency in Beijing. According to the court Jesuits and their friends in the bureaucracy, the greatest chance for success would only come from a memorial to the throne. Any response, however vague (given the novelty of such pronouncement), could be brandished before opponents as a shield, but an unambiguous statement was the desired result. Palmeiro gave his approval to a draft text of the memorial that the Jesuits intended to submit and suggested that they might accompany it with the lavish gifts given by Maximilian of Bavaria (1573–1651) to Niklaas Trigault in 1617 and intended for the Chinese emperor. It is unclear which of the duke's gifts Palmeiro referred to here, calling it only "a present so lustrous," since Maximilian had sent a number of automatons made of silver, a desk of drawers filled with curiosities, and a set of books with gilt illustrations of biblical scenes.[62]

Although these gifts had been at the Jesuits' residence for almost a decade, the specter of persecution that had shadowed the missionaries until the early 1620s and the ensuing upheaval at court during the later Tianqi reign (1621–1627) had made it impossible to present the items to the throne. The Jesuits' good fortune on June 21, 1629—less than a week after the Visitor left the capital—was to be summoned to predict an eclipse, an event that led to their appointment to the calendar reform project of the Imperial Astronomical Bureau later that year. This coup wound up obviating the need to present gold and silver curios to the emperor in order to gain permission to remain in Beijing, and meant that the Jesuits would hold on to the duke's gifts for a while longer.[63]

The Visitor left the capital on June 17, heeding the advice of Xu Guangqi and other literati that he travel on the Grand Canal rather than overland. Palmeiro was nevertheless concerned that there would not be enough water in the canal to ensure a speedy passage since he had heard of backups along that route that resulted in long delays. His impatience is palpable: "It is something very onerous for any passenger, but for someone who is in as much of a rush as I was on this trip it is not only a displeasure or annoyance, but a perpetual torment that grows worse as the delays grow longer and the need to move onward is greater." But with the assurances of a Christian boatman who was to act as his guide, Palmeiro headed for the embarkation point at Tongzhou, twelve miles from Beijing, in the company of Niccolò Longobardo.

This senior court Jesuit and former mission superior likely benefited from the time alone with the Visitor to add one last opinion on the issue of the terms used by the missionaries. Longobardo was one of the most fervent opponents of *Shangdi*, Ruler on High, and even was against the more widely used term *Tianzhu*, Lord of Heaven, which was suggested as a less contentious alternative. Perhaps it was simply a courtesy that he paid to his guest from afar, but it seems certain that Longobardo wanted to coordinate with Palmeiro since he would not be present at Hangzhou when the Visitor revisited the topic with the vice-province's consultors. The Sicilian Jesuit even stayed for a night with Palmeiro aboard his boat at the northern terminus of the Grand Canal before heading back to Beijing the following day.

In four days the Visitor made it to Tianjin, where he found "many thousands of boats moored" in the garrison city's port. While he traveled south his fascination for water transportation returned in spite of the heat of the "intolerable stillness" that he suffered along the route. He was particularly taken by the press of traffic along the Grand Canal and the number of towns and cities that he saw as he sailed for two weeks. Palmeiro also learned once again the value of having good contacts at the capital when he reached Linqing, where the first customs station was located. When stopped by officials, the boatman presented a license given to them by Xu Guangqi, which ensured them and their vessel "not only ready clearance, but also hasty passage." But the pace of their progress slowed soon after this checkpoint as they moved further south. Palmeiro described the system of hydraulic engineering along the Grand Canal as it intersected with other waterways in Shandong Province. He noted the large boards that were placed on the sides of the canal to ensure that it maintained a high enough level for ships to pass, and he recalled that at Beijing he had been assured that abundant rainfall would have meant there would be no such water retention barriers along his route.[64] "But when we got to Linqing where the first one is, I found everything backwards," he recalled, "because I waited for three days, which seemed like three years to me, and none of these were opened, holding up an infinity of boats, and even passenger vessels, that could not advance because the water level was so low."[65]

Having turned his back on the farthest point of his round-trip, Palmeiro was in no mood to wait for the water to refill the Grand Canal—something not likely in early July. Indeed, the Visitor's description of the parched North China Plain matches Chinese accounts of drought that returned to this area in 1628 and lasted for most of the remainder of the Chongzhen reign.[66] Inferring from the delay at Linqing what he could expect at the other forty-odd spots where the canal intersected with other rivers, and feeling rushed by the need to regain Macau by the time the Japan fleets brought news to the Portuguese colony, Palmeiro decided to strike out overland. Knowing that he would jeopardize his health and incur greater expenses, he ordered his servants to outfit mules and an enclosed sedan chair (again adapted for his comfort and safety). Palmeiro justified his choice by averring that "risking health in the performance of one's duty is unavoidable, and I thus considered the sum of money to be well spent, for wanting to save it at such times gives a whiff of avarice." This deadly sin, he remarked, consisted not only in the excessive pursuit of gain, but also "failing to spend when it is necessary."[67]

So on July 4 he set out again, within a few days reaching the same road along which he had journeyed north. Palmeiro was surprised to see that the wheat that was being grown along the route during his trip to Beijing in late May had already been harvested and the fields replanted with crops already nearing maturation a little over a month later. In central Shandong Province he saw cultures of corn as well as beans and other legumes, and insisted that the two quick harvests accounted for the abundance found in most of China. The combination of fertile soil and human industry also explained the lack of poor people "who beg and who importune you" in the Ming Empire, he claimed, a conclusion that he had reached "because I found so few of them in the great many places I went." Most of the beggars that Palmeiro spotted were blind; they went about striking sticks together to call attention to themselves or played on three-stringed lutes, most likely the guitar-like *sanxian*. "I found it quite amusing that most of these poor blind men marry blind women," he recorded, "and they work together to earn alms, carrying and playing lutes." Beyond this distraction, the Visitor made no other remarks about the route except to note that his health held out and that he reached Yangzhou after thirty days.

––––––––––

Once he had crossed the Yangzi River at Zhenjiang, Palmeiro found himself in the Jiangnan region. This area, stretching from Suzhou in the north to Hangzhou in the south and including the peninsular region of Songjiang and Shanghai, was where he would discover the last four residences to be inspected before he headed back to Macau. Here Palmeiro entered the garden of the Ming Empire, and he knew it: "This part of the land, which is more or less 100 leagues large, is the best in all of China in terms of its temperateness and its riches; the rivers and their branches, the boats great and small, and the bridges of stone and wood are innumerable here." Jiangnan was full of mulberry trees that were pruned, according to Palmeiro, in the manner of grapevines in Europe so as to yield tender leaves for the area's millions of silk-worms. The region was also the center of cotton production, especially in the area around Shanghai, where Palmeiro was amazed to learn that there were over ten thousand looms for weaving its coarse cloth.[68] Not only was Jiang-nan immensely productive, it was also the heart of the Jesuit vice-province. The Visitor knew that he would find the glory of the mission there; he was sure that he was about to inspect "the greater and the oldest part of the Chris-tian community that we have in all of China." His visits to the communities at Jiading, Shanghai, and Hangzhou would not disappoint him on this score, and they would help him to decide if the vice-province's progress still de-pended on fine silk or if humble cotton might suffice.[69]

The first stop on Palmeiro's 250-mile loop around the Jiangnan region was at Jiading, a town situated five days' journey southeast of Zhenjiang. Here he found João Fróis (1591–1638) and three novices living in a house that had been ceded to them by Sun Yuanhua, known to the missionaries as Licentiate Iná-cio. Palmeiro had met Sun at Beijing and was welcomed warmly by the four Jesuits and the local Christians from Inácio's clan. Although the vice-province lacked a formal novitiate, one endowed with rent-producing properties and a proper teaching staff, the Visitor was nevertheless pleased with what Fróis was doing at Jiading. In Palmeiro's judgment, he instructed the three former stu-dents from Macau in the Society's rules "with as much specificity and as much rigor as if he was performing the task at the Monte Olivete novitiate house in Lisbon."[70]

Despite paying such attention to detail and, above all, to the rules of the Society of Jesus, Fróis also managed to keep an eye on the 250 Christians in the town and the surrounding villages. Palmeiro related that the local people seemed eager to convert but that the Jesuit proceeded slowly so as not to raise the suspicions of local officials—especially because their patron was far away on the northern frontier. Indeed, the annual letter reported that only four-teen baptisms had been performed in the previous year, a rather paltry sum for the potential that the Visitor sensed.[71] The reason for Fróis's caution came from the supposed fear that the Jesuits would foment sedition in plebeian circles, especially in rural areas, under the cloak of religion. "A weak argument this is," Palmeiro retorted, "considering how few we are and how little we have; but the weak are afraid of everything and so we are forced to accommodate ourselves to them, because we depend so much on them and, besides that, we thus seek to win them over."[72]

The Jesuits in Shanghai, only seventeen miles away, were considerably less constrained. There Palmeiro found Pedro Ribeiro (1570–1640) in charge of a community that he claimed comprised 1,750 Christians, many of them cotton farmers and rural laborers. This Jesuit was the very image of missionary brio that the Visitor had wanted to find at all of the mission stations: the tireless priest constantly circulating among growing groups of neophytes, baptizing scores of souls each year, and shepherding them through the catechism. With 184 new Christians baptized in 1628 alone, Shanghai was the fastest expanding mission district in China and would remain the heart of Chinese Catholicism for generations.[73] Of course, this feat was only possible because of the patronage of local son Xu Guangqi, whose prestige in the Ming Empire was fast reaching its apogee. And, as was to be expected, the Xu clan, including Dr. Paulo's son and grandchildren, were at the heart of the welcoming party that received Palmeiro. He remembered the "notable courtesies" that they paid him in Shanghai, adding that he responded to their affections "in the same manner and coin, so that I did not remain in their debt."[74]

Palmeiro also found another Jesuit at Shanghai, the oldest member of the vice-province and a former mission superior from the days of Matteo Ricci. This was Manuel Dias the elder (1559–1639), a priest ten years older than the Visitor and nearly completely deaf, who was spending what was thought to be his final years at the Society's "little house". Palmeiro asserted that such quarters and the lack of community and medical care were a poor reward for so many years of service to the mission (not to mention a burden on Ribeiro, who had his hands full with the local Christians) and ordered Dias to Macau. Ironically, this missionary would outlive the Visitor by almost five years.[75]

After completing his inspection of at Shanghai, Palmeiro left for his final stop on July 26, 1629. Floating along for four days in the midst of rice fields and mulberry groves, towns and villages, he covered the one hundred miles to Hangzhou. To Palmeiro, it was "the queen of all of the cities I had seen in China, equal to or even surpassing Beijing in grandeur." Not only did he learn that the city's walls were four leagues in length, but looking out over the city from an overlook he judged it to have more extensive suburbs than the imperial capital. His comparison was not without reason, for in Hangzhou he played the tourist once again, as he had done in Beijing.

The Visitor's description of the southern city is far shorter than his account of the capital, though, and he only remarked upon two aspects of Hangzhou beyond his comments about the local Christians. The first of these was, of course, the famous West Lake, around whose shores the city was built. Palmeiro was struck by the beauty of the site, asserting that the fact that the lake's waters were continually circulated and not stagnant contributed to its pleasantness. He was also taken with the numerous "most beautiful" pleasure barges that served as floating banquet halls, where "the amount of wine that is drunk is equal to the amount of water one can see." All of these boats had room for long tables where all sorts of different types of food were to be found, including "meat, fish, fruit, and seafood, all eating what they please," and drinking spirits from dainty glasses "so small that they do not even hold enough wine to fill half of an ordinary chicken egg."[76] Despite the mouthwatering details of these descriptions, while he was in Hangzhou Palmeiro declined the one invitation to a banquet that he received during his year in China, an offer extended to him by an illustrious local Christian.[77]

On land the Visitor found the other aspect of the city that was to his liking. The two Jesuit houses in Hangzhou were located close to the city's principal thoroughfare, and he noted that he had spent a considerable amount of time walking slowly around its spacious "well-paved" streets. In contrast to the dust bowl that was Beijing, Hangzhou offered the possibility of pleasant strolls (although one can imagine that Palmeiro's pace was anything but relaxed). He recalled walking down the whole of the main north–south avenue from one city gate to another and being impressed by the ninety-seven stone arches that lined this route. The profusion of *pailou* (or *paifang*), as these arched gates were called, resulted from the high number of important scholars and officials whose memory was preserved in inscriptions on their topmost central panels. While the cultural significance of the arches was lost on Palmeiro, he could easily appreciate their beauty. More than seventy of these structures had fine carvings of flowers and animals not merely etched on the surface of their columns and friezes but sculpted out of the stone at such depth so as to appear ornaments rather than part of the original columns. "Although these arches have no architecture about them, and indeed lack it completely since they are totally insecure, with poor foundations or none at all, being simply placed on the ground," Palmeiro observed, "nevertheless their decorations are so beautiful and done with such skill that they would be greatly esteemed in any part of Europe."[78]

The safety with which the Visitor was able to travel about the city came from the fact that the Hangzhou Jesuits enjoyed the protection of important patrons, two of the three pillars of Christianity in late Ming China. The Society's two residences were in the houses of Yang Tingyun, called Dr. Miguel (1557–1628), and Li Zhizao, called Dr. Leão (1565–1630), both of whom had earned the supreme *jinshi* degrees and had long served in the imperial bureaucracy.[79] Esteemed scholars and reliable benefactors of the Jesuits, this pair had acted as the patrons of the Hangzhou church and had even sheltered the missionaries from the attacks of rival officials during the Nanjing Persecutions. But 1629 was the twilight of the lives of the first illustrious Chinese Catholics: Yang had died in early December of the previous year, Li would die in 1630, and Xu Guangqi would only live until 1633.

Palmeiro had seen the importance of the "shadow of Dr. Paulo" at Beijing, and in Hangzhou he clearly perceived the benefit that the presence of Dr. Leão and Dr. Miguel had for the mission: the Society had more priests and students living there than in any other place in China.[80] In return for their patronage, the Jesuits sought to address the intellectual and spiritual concerns of Yang and Li. Instead of pursuing an ambitious proselytizing strategy among plebeians as Pedro Ribeiro did in the Shanghai area, the five priests at Hangzhou devoted much of their time to translating European devotional and philosophical texts into Chinese. Although all of the city's Jesuits were occupied at least part of their time with composing books, the most renowned endeavor at the time of Palmeiro's visit was the translation of some of Aristotle's writings (*De Caelo,* and a combined version of the *Categories* and Porphyry's *Isagoge*) as well as part of commentaries of the *Cursus Conimbricense* produced by Francisco Furtado with the help of Li Zhizao.

Despite the presence of so many missionaries, Hangzhou's Christian community was relatively small at roughly four hundred members. It was nevertheless a fervent one, and Palmeiro was more than satisfied by the intensity of devotion in the city. The local Jesuits described to him the death of Yang Tingyun—which occurred only a few days after the death of Niklaas Trigault—in such terms that the Visitor became convinced of his salvation.[81] The extended families of Yang and Li were the core of the Hangzhou church, and it was with them that Palmeiro spent most of his time in the city.[82] He recalled exchanging gifts with Li Zhizao and other local Christians and re-marked on the luxurious presents of silk that he received from them—only to return the items forthwith. In order to cease the back-and-forth of this ritual, he offered "some little things," most likely small devotional objects, in the hopes that modest tokens would reinforce the message that he was a man of poverty and humility. More appropriate, he intended to communicate, was that he be invited to assist at Catholic rituals. Apparently his request was re-ceived. He records that he was present at several baptisms and was even in-vited to celebrate the sacrament for a stepchild of one of Yang Tingyun's daughters. "I baptized the child myself, because they asked me to and also because I take a certain pleasure in these things," he wrote, "and I would like it even more to live only to do such things, or to die doing them."[83]

This last statement is one of the few introspective moments in Palmeiro's writings. Curiously, it comes in a text that he knew would have a wide circu-lation, rather than in one of his private letters to the superior general. Was his avowal of the desire to be a missionary, rather than an inspector, aimed to foster vocations among the audiences for his text? Or was it a true reflection of an upwelling of fervor that he felt upon seeing the fruits of missionary la-bors, that is, when he saw a church thriving among non-European Christians on the far side of the world? In either case, he clearly felt envious of his con-freres at Hangzhou. He mentions in particular Rodrigo de Figueiredo and Francisco Furtado, who had both come from similar Portuguese origins as the Visitor but who incarnated the missionary ideal of intellectual and devo-tional vigor in the service of the gospel. With a touch of sadness, Palmeiro recognized that he was too old to learn a foreign language well enough to be useful in the missions, however strongly he might have desired to study. Con-tinuing in this vein, he wrote: "If God esteems desires, as we know He does, I still have to hope that he will reward me, if not for what I have done to convert many people to the faith, at least for what I have desired to do to convert them. He also knows well that part of the credit for conversions of course goes to those who send workers into the field, even though they do not go there, and so men will say that I did what I could to serve Him, even though it could never amount to all that He merits."[84]

Palmeiro ended his visit to the China mission in early August 1629 by gather-ing the vice-provincial consultors for a meeting. One of them, Manuel Dias the elder, he had brought with him from Shanghai and the others included Vice-Provincial Manuel Dias the younger (ex-officio) and, most likely, Lazzaro Cattaneo (1560–1640), one of the most senior missionaries. At this meeting Palmeiro reviewed the rules that had been issued by various superiors over the course of the preceding decades, especially those that had been issued upon the vice-province's founding. The Visitor averred that the variety of contexts in which the Jesuits worked in China, ranging from rural villages to the imperial court, demanded a range of specific orders, so the meeting centered primarily on establishing a new framework of rules. "I reviewed them all," he wrote, "adding here, removing there, and leaving all of those that I thought necessary arranged in the manner that, in light of the consultors' opinions, I judged to be most convenient."[85] Copies of the new rules were produced for distribution to all of the residences, as well as a circular letter explaining the nature of the changes to Jesuit life in China that the Visitor mandated.

The set of rules issued on August 15, 1629, touches on many aspects of missionary life, and with a degree of detail that suggests deep reflection on the physical and spiritual dimensions of the China mission. Some of the rules related to matters of immediate importance; these were issued in direct response to news that the Visitor learned in Hangzhou. Recall that the corpse of Niklaas Trigault had been found in his room there the previous November, and that the news had come as a shock to Palmeiro and his colleagues. Earlier in his voyage, the Visitor had learned of Trigault's sudden death, but in Hangzhou he heard the story told in a different way: the Flemish Jesuit had committed suicide. Word of Trigault's grievous sin was kept very quiet, even among the China Jesuits, and was not shared with the courier who brought the report to Palmeiro in Canton.[86] Contemporary writings about Trigault speak of his death only in veiled terms, and the truth would have remained a secret forever if not for the translation written above the sequence of numbers that relayed the news in numeric code. At the end of a letter that he wrote after his return to Macau, Palmeiro's words about the affair were brief: "It seems that the weight of this news threw me so off balance that I did not remember it: *Father Trigault hanged himself.*"

The Visitor claimed that he had investigated the case by asking all of the missionaries in Hangzhou if they could explain "such a rare event," but none were forthcoming. The only clue he found came from Cattaneo, who told Palmeiro that "*Shangdi* had killed him." Trigault's choleric character had been noted by his superiors soon after his arrival in China, and it appears that his symptoms were those of manic depression. Rightly or wrongly, the Visitor saw blood on *Shangdi*'s hands. To put it another way, the incessant quarrel among the Jesuits over the Chinese translation of the Holy Name had killed Trigault. "There are reasons to believe this is true," Palmeiro wrote with regard to Cattaneo's tip, "because he was so taken with that opinion." Accordingly, this committed defender of *Shangdi* was most likely driven to suicidal despair by the Jiading agreement in January 1628, ten months before Trigault's death, in which the Jesuits agreed to abandon the term. "If this is so," remarked Palmeiro about the polemical Ruler on High, "he paid Trigault well for the work done on his behalf." Nevertheless, the Visitor conceded, "these are divine judgments, which we cannot understand, but only venerate."[87]

Something nevertheless had to be done to right the wrong of Trigault's shameful death, which was clearly rooted in too heavy a commitment to the "accommodation method" or at least too great concessions to Chinese opinions in matters Christian. For Palmeiro, the first step in creating a morally acceptable method for the Jesuits of the vice-province was to vanquish *Shangdi*. His circular letter took aim at this problematic term, prohibiting its use and invoking the vow of obedience in order to enforce his will. This drastic move would not end the Terms Controversy immediately, for the Visitor would have to deal with the fallout of his command after he returned to Macau, but he felt that it was sufficient to stanch the open wound in the missionary corps that *Shangdi* had caused. Palmeiro stopped short of banning all of the disputed terms, approving the use of *Tianzhu* to signify the Almighty—over the objections of several missionaries, including Niccolò Longobardo in Beijing and João Rodrigues at Macau. He even took the further step against this group by ordering that the missionaries continue to employ Chinese terms and to avoid "except on rare occasions" the use of *cobitas,* that is, transliterations of Christian terms from the Portuguese or Latin. And Palmeiro created a system of text revision in which the names of both authors and reviewers would appear printed on missionary books, in imitation of the procedures of censorship employed in Europe and destined to ensure the use of common terminology among all Jesuits in China.[88] With these rules the Visitor challenged his subordinates to find other terms for Christian concepts, ones that were not reminiscent of the Confucianism that they had considered their closest point of contact to the indigenous elite.

Palmeiro did not wait around in Hangzhou to feel the effects of this bombshell. He did not have the time nor the inclination to debate the merits of the disputed terms, especially not as the summer drew toward its close and the winds would soon bring news from Japan. So three days after he issued his rules, on August 18, he left Hangzhou en route to Nanjing. Palmeiro's account suggests that he left in a rush upon hearing that the Portuguese embassy had reached that city and that he might be able to rendezvous with them if he traveled quickly across the 150 miles to his destination. While it would have been shorter for him to head overland to Jiangxi Province, his health demanded that he travel by boat to Nanjing, so he headed northwest to rejoin the normal route to the south. And fearing that he might not arrive in time to meet up with the embassy, he sent his companion, Brother Domingos Mendes, ahead to stall them if possible.

Palmeiro's haste paid off, and he found Gonçalo Teixeira Correia and João Rodrigues waiting for him at Nanjing. They were, he wrote, "in perfect health, but excessively annoyed by the lengthy delays, and fearful that these long waits would be followed by other, greater ones." In fact the Visitor had traveled nearly three times as far as the ambassadors in the span of nine months since they had entered China together. Both men recounted a "long litany of reverses" that they had suffered along the way from Nanxiong, where they had parted company, but Palmeiro discounted their complaints since they had been received lavishly by imperial officials at every stop.[89] The reason for the Visitor's eagerness to see the Portuguese embassy was not merely because they were familiar faces in the midst of the Ming Empire. No, he knew that João Rodrigues would receive his verdict against *Shangdi* in the wrong way, and Palmeiro did not want Rodrigues to gloat or otherwise antagonize the other Jesuits. Given the harsh words that had been exchanged on the issue and the unbecoming acts committed by either side, the Visitor surely intended to impose silence on him before he caused further damage to the Society.

***

Once he had tied up this loose end, Palmeiro rushed back toward Macau in order to learn what he could about the Japan mission. He also had to digest all that he had experienced in China and transmit his thoughts on the vice-province to Rome. It was perhaps for this reason that his travelogue hastily summarizes the final leg of his journey back to Macau, noting little more than his departure from Nanjing on August 27, 1629, and his arrival at the Portuguese colony on October 18 of the same year. So preoccupied were his thoughts that he did not expand on the adventures of that autumn, recording only that he traveled in less security southward than northward. He mentioned succinctly how bandits attacked his ship and claimed that "if it was not for the dexterity with which our crew responded by unsheathing swords, we would have ended our lives before we ended this journey."[90] In his mind were doubts about the way the missionaries behaved in China, and about the merits of their accommodation to Chinese culture, issues he would resolve along the way from the Yangzi River valley to the Pearl River delta. By December of that year, he had composed a series of letters that presented his impressions of the China mission and justified his decisions with regard to the vice-province. When he reached the Portuguese colony on the far southern shore of the Ming Empire, the time for hearing and seeing had come to an end. It was time for Palmeiro to speak.

8

Challenging Accommodation

On December 3, 1629, André Palmeiro accompanied a procession through the streets of Macau. It was the feast of Francis Xavier, patron saint of the Portuguese colony, and the Jesuits were obliged to hold the liturgical and devotional events intended to bring divine favor upon the city. The mood in Macau was somber: There had been no trade with Japan for two years and local fortunes, including those of the Jesuits, had withered. In this time of lean kine, tensions between the city's inhabitants mounted because, as Palmeiro declared, "if Japan is over for Macau, than Macau is all done for, and done for all". Remembering the ancient promise made to peacemakers, the Visitor took this opportunity to extend an olive branch to the Jesuits' ecclesiastical rivals. When organizing the procession, he offered the most important relic, an arm bone of Francis Xavier, to Frei António do Rosário, the governor of the bishopric of Macau and the colony's acting governor. This was the same prelate whose assumption of office had led to the revolt of the parish clergy in 1624, part of the series of events that culminated in the excommunication of the bishop of Japan, Diogo Valente, by the archbishop of Goa. But by 1629 those affairs had been resolved and the bishop of Japan had returned to the China coast. Palmeiro invited Valente to carry one of the gilt reliquary busts containing the heads of the three beatified Jesuit martyrs of Japan while he and a veteran missionary, Gabriel de Matos (1572–1634), carried the other two. By bringing these feuding parties together on such a solemn occasion, Palmeiro hoped he would "eliminate the feelings of distaste and displeasure which are never so fully hidden that they will not burst forth in scandal and cause the loss of reputation for the religious, something that has been diminished greatly in this city by past events."[1]

Palmeiro sought to restore the good name of the Society of Jesus in Macau and elsewhere in East Asia by such gestures of deference to secular and ecclesiastical authorities coupled with firm control over his subordinates. After all, the Jesuits were as much to blame for the upheaval of the early 1620s as were other orders and the secular clergy, and the Visitor knew it. The Jesuits' exile from Japan in 1614 had led to excess in Macau; even some members of the Society noted the "great liberty and debauchery" at their college. Shocked observers wrote about its doors being always open "to laymen and heathens, who paraded through the corridors and even into the rooms without anyone's noticing it, let alone forbidding it."[2] Although Palmeiro had quickly brought order from the chaos, he knew that more needed to be done. If the Society's reputation had been harmed by vice, it would be remedied by virtue. Accordingly, he insisted on the scrupulous observance of the Society's rules and, in particular, of its vows of poverty, chastity, and obedience.

Shutting the college's doors and limiting the Jesuits' comings and goings helped to ensure the community's chastity, and the strict adherence to the vow of poverty came easily enough in light of the colony's dire straits. Palmeiro was ambivalent about the disappearance of Macau's former abundance since in his view it had only served to tempt his brethren. This was a man known for wearing his cloaks until they were threadbare and for sharing his garments with the college's brothers at the peak of winter. His confreres knew that his meals consisted only of bread, rice, and a bit of boiled beef at lunch, with a slice of bread and a glass of water for dinner, and that only in his last years did he begin to take a sip of wine with his evening meal—"but not enough to fill a nutshell." Not content with giving an example of austerity rooted in a close reading of the Society's *Constitutions,* Palmeiro saw to it that all Jesuits in Macau adhered to his understanding of the rules. For example, the Visitor's notion of *santa pobreza,* holy poverty, was simple: When he was prompted by a request for a devotional print to be used for one Jesuit's individual prayers, he not only denied the request but ordered the college procurator to gather all such images from the priests and brothers and send them off to neophytes in the mission fields. And it was rumored in Macau that the

FIGURE 8.1. View of Macau drawn in 1665 by the Dutch cartographer Johannes Vingboons (1617–1670). The Jesuit compound is seen at the center left of the image, adjacent to the fortress. Palmeiro's catechumen house and church were located farther to left, on the city's edge, and the Ilha Verde, from whence he wrote his letters each year, is shown in the extreme left foreground.

higher than average number of deaths at the Jesuit college was directly related to the strict regimen of frugality (both in diet and leisure) that the Visitor had imposed upon its residents.[3]

Had Palmeiro not been a man of intense personal piety, his demands for
austerity and obedience might have been a more difficult sell. But so convincing was the image he presented to his subordinates that his authority was
rarely challenged. Indeed, his fellow Jesuits remembered him above all for his
attention to the Society's rules as well as his constant reminders to his less
observant subordinates. "There was no other fault that he punished with
greater rigor", remarked Palmeiro's necrologist about his regard for the virtue
of obedience. Given that the Jesuits had all vowed to obey their superiors,
and that Palmeiro was the representative of the superior general, great weight
was attached to the Visitor's orders and those from Rome that he was instructed to enforce. According to the procurator of the College of Macau,
Giovanni Battista Bonelli (1585–1638), one of Palmeiro's most common excla-
mations was: "This is an order from Father General, may it never be out of
my mind!" Despite the severity of this phrase and the harsh temper suggested by this character sketch, Bonelli observed, with amazement, the Visitor
"could combine such suaveness with such rigor and zeal in religious observance." Few complained about Palmeiro's insistence on adherence to the Society's rules, Bonelli remarked, "except for one or two, who disliked that he did
what he should, or that which was appropriate."[4] The changes that Palmeiro
wrought on the lives of the Jesuits at Macau did not pass unnoticed by the
colony's residents, some of whom whispered that he had made the college
into a *Cartuxa,* that is, a Carthusian monastery, where monks vowed to humble
simplicity lived in silence.

Pious exaggeration (or backbiting) aside, it is certain that Palmeiro's presence brought a climate of discipline to the College of Macau. Yet even its near-
monastic atmosphere was too raucous for the task of collecting his thoughts on
what he had seen in China. So in mid-December 1629, after waiting in vain
for three months for news from Japan that he might include in his letters to
Rome, he embarked for Ilha Verde. This small island, today surrounded by
reclaimed land, was located a mile from the college in Macau's inner harbor.
It was the site of a residence where the Jesuits typically took recreation in the
summer months, although it does not appear that Palmeiro ever visited the
island for that purpose. "We do not know if during that time," Bonelli recalled about Palmeiro's eight and a half years in Macau, "he ever walked

around that little island more than four or five times, and only then for the pleasure of the bishop or other such persons." No, the Visitor's primary reason for going to Ilha Verde was to compose his letters to Rome. The island offered silence and, above all, a lack of prying eyes and over-attentive ears. Whenever he arrived there, Palmeiro would proceed straight to his cubicle and leave it only to go to the chapel and the refectory.[5] It was not the pure air or pleasant vista that brought Palmeiro peace of mind but rather the realization that he had fulfilled his obligation to the superior general and had acted responsibly toward the Society of Jesus.

The Visitor had weighty matters on his mind when he sailed to Ilha Verde that December. He had to explain to Muzio Vitelleschi what he had seen in China, and he had to justify the measures that he had taken with regard to the Jesuits of the vice-province. During his stay on the island Palmeiro wrote six substantial letters (one of which has been lost) on different matters relating to the China mission. Taken as a whole, these missives constitute a critique of the policies of missionization that had been devised by Matteo Ricci and maintained by his successors, commonly known as the "accommodation method." Recall that Palmeiro was the first external superior to inspect the mission; the previous inspectors had been deputized from among the Jesuit corps in the Ming Empire. As an outsider—yet one committed to the long-range goal of expanding the mission's reach—Palmeiro brought a certain equanimity to his job of measuring the policies of his subordinates against their costs and outcomes. Unlike many of the China missionaries who wrote about their enterprise, the Visitor's goal was not to defend the policies of his subordinates but rather to analyze them. As such, he did not spare criticism where it was due, and did not fail to extend praise when it was merited.

The letters from Ilha Verde present an overview of the Jesuits' policies in the Ming Empire at a key moment in the evolution of their mission, at the time when their enterprise entered its maturity. For that reason it is important to examine Palmeiro's evaluation of the missionary strategy in some detail. Before doing that, however, it is necessary to briefly trace the emergence of the accommodation method and the problems that it posed half a century after the inception of the China mission.

The accommodation method, frequently referred to in modern scholarship by the Italian phrase *il modo soave,* has been considered the great achievement of the Jesuits in East Asia. It was the fruit of their realization that the coercive imposition of Christianity by Europeans was impossible in that region, where the Western presence was primarily based on trade and diplomacy. The man most readily associated with *il modo soave* was Alessandro Valignano, the one who elaborated this method with specific rules for the first important East Asian mission field, Japan. Valignano had arrived in that country after his colleagues had been there for three decades and, witnessing his subordinates' relative lack of success, ordered them to adapt themselves more fully to local cultural norms. His decisions about missionary method in Japan were tactical ones, not based on principle; he did not object to the more aggressive modes of conversion employed in India and Africa, where Christianity advanced at the point of the sword. Indeed, Valignano approved of the use of righteous force in the cause of making Japan Christian, too, urging on the converted samurai who torched Buddhist temples and sacked Shinto shrines. But when the time-tested method of *compelle intrare,* in St. Luke's formulation, was not viable, a different, "gentle" means of penetrating East Asian hearts and minds was necessary.[6] The rapid expansion of the Japan mission church as a result of the *modo soave* in the 1580s and 1590s was taken as proof of the wisdom of this policy.

What had worked in Japan was applied to China. Not only had Valignano given the first impulse to create a mission within the Ming Empire in the late 1570s, he was also a crucial source of encouragement for Ricci. Valignano knew that for there to be a mission in China, the Jesuits needed to employ some form of cultural accommodation in order to make missionary work acceptable to the governing elite, and to make Christianity attractive to prospective converts. But with its strong centralized state and powerful bureaucrats, China was not Japan. The means of accommodating to the dominant cultural patterns in the two lands thus could not be the same. In the Ming Empire, the "gentle method" had to be truly genteel. In the 1590s, with Valignano's approval, Ricci chose to appeal to the sensibilities of the scholar-officials who governed China. His strategy was to present himself as their intellectual peer, as someone who had precious wisdom to offer—such as a new vision of earth and a new conception of heaven. Over the course of his three decades in the Ming Empire, rather than deploying a coherent package of policies, conceived as a whole, he made a series of decisions in which he adjusted his approach to the business of missionization as time passed. Crucially, Valignano never entered China to evaluate Ricci's choices; that visitor trusted that they were made in good faith, *ad maiorem Dei gloriam*. And so in the Ming Empire, Ricci's version of the accommodation method was his own creation.

Modern scholars have lavished praise on Ricci and his method, seeing him as a harbinger of modernity. According to the standard line—an interpretation much repeated in the 1980s (on the anniversary of his arrival in China) and, more recently, in 2010 (on the anniversary of his death)—Ricci had an open mind and a tolerant spirit. Unlike his contemporaries who were little more than conquistadores masquerading as missionaries, Ricci was urbane. His was an intellectual effort to present the "West" to the "East", to share the glories of European civilization respectfully with the Chinese, whose language he had mastered and whose culture he valued. Ricci chose "science" as the central plank of his missionary platform, insisting that mathematics and astronomy were among the best means for attracting the attention of the Chinese elite. Once their curiosity had been piqued by his maps and prisms, he pursued the possibilities for dialogue with his hosts but never forced them to hear his religious message. Those Chinese who were sufficiently interested in spiritual matters might learn something about the teachings of the Lord of Heaven in a way that was sure to avoid offending their moral or philosophical sensibilities. Many of the other missionaries in the late sixteenth and early seventeenth centuries were incapable of such largeness of spirit: they would have brought the faith to the Ming Empire at the point of the sword. But Ricci was smarter than they.[7] To be sure, this clichéd view of Ricci bears only partial resemblance to the man who founded the China mission, an individual who was far more in step with his times and therefore less "modern" than we are led to believe.

As a result of this understanding of Ricci, there is no small amount of confusion about the accommodation method. What was originally a term used by mid-twentieth century theologians to discuss the specific forms of cultural adaptation made by clergy in non-European mission fields, "accommodation" became more expansive (and vague) when repeated in later decades by scholars working in other disciplines. In recent scholarship it is often invoked as a state of mind marked by openness and the willingness to enter into dialogue with other cultures. There, when "accommodation" is linked to Ricci, it substitutes for his perceived attitude toward East Asian culture. His study of Confucian texts and his immersion in the Chinese language as well as his writings in that idiom and his eagerness to discuss "science" (instead of simply religion) are posited as evidence of his desire to "accommodate" to his hosts.[8] But the insistence on these elements of his method—which are, of course, appealing to modern ears—obscure the fact that Ricci was a Roman Catholic missionary. It also suggests that "accommodation" to late Ming culture was his goal, when in fact it was the means by which he intended to make converts to Christianity.

Linking Riccian accommodation with modern attitudes also has the effect of turning its detractors into caricatures. There are, after all, antonyms for all of the terms of praise used to describe the man and his method. If Ricci was "modern", then those who disagreed with him were "medieval"; if he was tolerant, then his critics were bigots. But these judgments become difficult to understand when it is remembered that the first critics of Ricci's policies of accommodation (indeed, some of his most tenacious detractors before the middle of the seventeenth century) were to be found in the ranks of the Society of Jesus, and even within the China mission. There is no doubt that his strategy was a bold initiative in an era known for its resistance to innovation, and that the decision to permit missionaries to adapt to non-European cultures raised more objections in some domains than it did in others. The choice to adopt Chinese dress, for example, was less problematic to most Jesuits than the option to identify what were deemed to be glimpses of God in ancient Chinese texts. To be sure, many of the ideas associated with Ricci's work had been employed in Japan by an older missionary corps from which would come some of his most vociferous opponents. But while these fellow Jesuits would object to some of his decisions, none of them questioned the necessity of learning Asian languages, studying indigenous writings, or becoming familiar with native philosophical traditions. These were matters of common consent even among those members of the Society who objected to other elements of Ricci's policies. In sum, if there was debate among the Jesuits on this issue, it centered on the degree of accommodation to be made to East Asian cultures, not on the necessity of accommodation itself.

The most persistent caricatures found in explanations of the accommodation method are those based on national character. Seeking to understand why Valignano and Ricci pursued a strategy that appeared to be so modern in some of its contours, scholars have underscored what the two men shared and what their detractors lacked. This crucial element was nothing other than their place of birth. Logically, if Ricci rejected the uncompromising attitudes of his peers, it was because he was not Spanish or Portuguese but "Italian". Needless to say, there was nothing *soave* about the Iberians; they marched to the orders of the Inquisition and were intrinsically incapable of appreciating any culture except their own. Witness, we have heard, how they ran rough-shod over Latin America, Africa, and the Philippines, and how they ruth-lessly crushed the blissful state of *convivencia,* that is, the "living together" of the three Abrahamic religious traditions, in medieval Spain. Unlike their Spanish and Portuguese counterparts, however, Ricci and Valignano were raised in the cradle of humanism and suckled at the bosom of the Renais-sance. As "Italians", they presumably shared more than geography with the great minds of their age, regardless of the well-known cultural and political diversity of the peninsula. And never mind that the same "Italy" had produced Savonarola and Machiavelli, or that both of those Italian Jesuits in Asia took their principal inspiration from two "Spaniards", Ignatius Loyola and Francis Xavier; as Italians, Ricci and Valignano were naturally inclined toward toler-ance. In short, *il modo soave* was the embodiment of the Italian Renaissance in East Asia.[9]

But as has been demonstrated in the case of the Madurai mission, clichés of national character are of little use when trying to understand the Jesuits in early modern Asia. The accident of Ricci's birth did not determine how he would approach the challenge of spreading the gospel in China, just as it did not forecast how Roberto Nobili would carry out his mission in southern In-dia. More importantly, the national origins of the Jesuits who worked along-side either one did not bind them to respond to Ricci's or Nobili's policies in a particular way. And it should not be forgotten that although the Madurai affair only involved a handful of men, since Nobili himself was the prime mover of his personal method and worked only with a few collaborators, Matteo Ricci's decisions had consequences for all of the China Jesuits be-cause his public success in China obliged them to replicate his style.

It is simply incorrect to assume that the nationality of a given missionary would have disposed him either positively or negatively toward accommoda-tion, or that those Jesuits who raised objections to aspects of that policy some-how had insufficient appreciation for Asian cultures. There were in fact several Portuguese priests, most importantly João Rodrigues, who labeled some of Ricci's policies misguided and even pernicious. But it is surely too much to decry this individual, who composed elaborate, expert, and in some regards still unexcelled handbooks of Japanese language and culture, as unwilling to engage with non-European cultures. The principal critic of Ricci within the China mission was one of his compatriots, but perhaps the Sicilian origins of

Niccolò Longobardo made him less "Italian" than his Marchese confrere. Conversely, among the most ardent defenders of Ricci's legacy were Rodrigo de Figueiredo and Álvaro Semedo, both Portuguese. André Palmeiro's mixed review of Ricci's policies—not in the airy realm of theory, but in the earthy one of practice—in which some were praised and others condemned further argues for dismissing the simplistic and anachronistic dichotomy between benighted Iberians and enlightened Italians.

Another, more subtle, way of explaining the arguments over the accommodation method sees a split between "insiders" and "outsiders." This interpretation, advanced primarily by China scholars, albeit with a pedigree stretching back to Jesuit writings from the mid-seventeenth century, sees Ricci and his successors as possessed of superior knowledge of late Ming realities owing to their long years of studying Chinese language and culture.[10] If Ricci had adopted a certain form of indigenous dress and had chosen to express Christian ideas in specific Chinese terms, this line maintains, it was because he had penetrated the marrow of native philosophy and had found the best way for transplanting his ideas into the body of Chinese culture. Ricci's fame in contemporary China has been taken as confirmation of the wisdom of his choices, and the problems that ensued when his policies were challenged (most famously during the Rites Controversy) were occasioned by men who did not know Chinese culture. Outsiders, in this view, trained their lenses on China but only saw reflections of non-Chinese realities; when they looked at the Ming realm, they only saw shadows of Japan or India. The first group of doubting outsiders were the Jesuits from Japan, followed by the Society's superiors sent from Goa, a group whose ranks included Palmeiro. But as has been shown, even the Japan Jesuits chafed when their visitors were sent from the Society's Indian Provinces at the orders of the superior general in Rome. Furthermore, this split between insiders and outsiders within China assumes that the insiders were uncritical of Ricci's methods and the outsiders saw them as aberrations—an understanding disproven by the same criteria which argue for discarding "national" categories. To give but a few examples, Palmeiro, the consummate outsider, found much to praise in Ricci's legacy while Niccolò Longobardo and Manuel Dias the younger, both veteran insiders, raised serious doubts about some of its aspects.

Evidently these men had some grounds for criticizing aspects of the accommodation method—reasons that were not the fruit of pernicious Eurocentrism or inadequate sensitivity to Chinese culture. Their objections were rooted in their identity as Jesuits and their goal of making conversions to Christianity. For them Ricci's decision to adapt his image to Chinese patterns obliged him to distance himself from the commonly held identity of the Society of Jesus: he made himself a freelancer in what was, by tradition and by vow, a uniform regiment. While Ricci had grounds for his policies in Christ's command to "go forth and teach all nations" as well as in the desire of Paul, repeated by Ignatius, to be "all things to all men", his decisions became problematic the further removed they were from the recognizable pattern "Jesuit." To some of his brethren, especially those from outside his mission, Ricci's image of a "China Jesuit" seemed at times more "Chinese" than "Jesuit". Those two concepts were not opposites, of course, nor did they exist at the ends of a spectrum. But it was nevertheless certain to his critics that Ricci had made some decisions that were not in keeping with their notions of what was appropriate for the Society's members. And, after his death in 1610, as the China Jesuits followed his lead farther in their line of accommodation, even some of them began to feel that they were on unsteady ground. Instead of abandoning the race, these men wanted to ensure that they were on the right track and that their religious message was understood by the Chinese without ambiguity.

How did Ricci's methods create problems for his peers? The primary challenge that the China Jesuits, and indeed all missionaries, faced was that of presenting concepts in a different idiom. At its heart the accommodation method was an attempt at translation: Ricci and his successors had taken Roman Catholicism and had translated parts of it into Chinese. The Jesuits had brought a rich symbolic vocabulary to East Asia and attempted to find appropriate matches for their concepts and rituals in the indigenous register. Some initial choices nevertheless needed to be reconsidered in light of their outcomes. For example, the use of Buddhist-style robes to signify "religious authority" (or at least "ritual practitioner") was abandoned after the 1580s in favor of other garments that carried the connotations of "intellectual authority" without religious overtones. By dressing as indigenous scholars, however, they elided the distinctions between clergy and laity in the eyes of their beholders. Lacking a perfect translation for the role that the Jesuits aimed to play in China, Ricci had chosen to present an image of himself that resembled "authority" more than it did "religion". This gamble paid off in renown (if not in conversions), and encouraged him to make other translations that he hoped would serve his goal of creating firm political foundations for the

Jesuits' proselytizing endeavors. Ricci also attracted converts to the translation of Catholicism that he presented in the Chinese language, and his successors followed suit with further renderings of "appropriate lay Catholic piety"
in the same mode. But translation is an art that combines precision and elegance when done properly. Ricci's translations were surely elegant, as evinced
by the fame that he garnered among the late Ming elite; the question was
whether they were precise enough to communicate who the Jesuits were and
what the nature of their religious message was.

In addition to being an exercise in translation, the accommodation method
was also an exercise in rhetoric. What was missionary work if not an attempt
at persuasion? Training in this art was central to Jesuit education; it was the
culmination of the study of classical languages and the necessary precursor to
the study of philosophy and theology. The terms and rules of Greek and Roman rhetoric, distilled from Aristotle, Cicero, and Quintilian by Cipriano
Suárez (1524–1593) in textbook form for use in the Society's schools, were never
far from the minds of Jesuit priests. In fact, most of them had not only studied rhetoric but had also taught it. So the shared techniques of classical oratory
constituted a central piece of intellectual baggage that all Jesuits carried overseas since rhetoric offered a range of tools for constructing a mission church.

In China Matteo Ricci had relied heavily on one such instrument, metaphor. With the expected verve of a charismatic figure, he made clear links in
his mind between what he saw in China and what he knew of himself and his
ambitions. Benefitting from poetic license, Ricci insisted that European realities had clear counterparts in China. He saw himself as an educated man
and thus referred to himself as a *xiru*, "Western scholar" or *xishi*, "Western
literatus". His black Jesuit robe conveyed authority in Europe, so he clothed
himself in robes which projected an equal amount of standing in China. And
he wanted to communicate his message about the Heavenly Lord, so he mined
the canonical literature of his hosts to find terms that spoke of supreme celestial majesty. To Ricci's defenders, these were shortcuts taken by a man convinced of his divine purpose, one possessed of a pious impatience that impelled
him forward. His use of metaphor justifiably asserted equivalences between
European and Chinese realities in order that his interlocutors might swiftly
understand who he was and what his message was.

As any reader of Cipriano Suárez knew, metaphor was not the most reliable tool in the rhetorician's kit. But Suárez's explanations give us some indication of why Ricci had relied upon it as much as he did. In *De Arte Rhetorica*

(first edition, 1562; revised 1565), Suárez remarks that metaphor "was produced of necessity from a scarcity and poverty of words, but afterwards its use became widespread because of its power to please and to divert."[11] Indeed, the lack of precise vocabulary had prompted Ricci to seek alternatives, and at first his choices proved felicitous. In Suárez's estimation, the attractiveness of a metaphor (which he gives in Greek) was the primary reason for its use:

> It is amazing why all are more charmed by *metaphora* than by unimaginative and merely logical association of words. For if an object has no proper term of its own . . . necessity demands that you supply from elsewhere what you do not have. Even where there is a large vocabulary of proper terms, however, men are much more charmed by transferred words, if the transfer does not violate sense. The reason for this is that a *metaphora* is a resemblance restricted to one word, and our minds are wondrously captivated by resemblances. There is this difference, nevertheless, that in a resemblance we compare some object to what we wish to explain; a *metaphora* is substituted for the object.[12]

Herein lay the challenge of the deployment of metaphors, whether in pulpits, at lecterns, or in the mission field. It had surely been Ricci's intention to avoid misunderstanding, and some of the metaphors he used with poetic elegance produced the desired results of securing political acceptance in China and stimulating some important conversions. But these facts did not negate the perils of the overreliance on metaphors or their misuse, dangers for which Suárez offered a clear word of caution: "We must be on guard not to believe that every privilege the poets enjoy is suitable for orators."[13]

In his cubicle on "Green Island" André Palmeiro questioned whether the maturing China mission still needed to rely so heavily on ambiguous translations and metaphors. It had been more than three decades since Ricci had changed into his literati robes and had begun crafting the image that his successors would copy. In the meantime, the Jesuits had become identifiable to many members of the Chinese elite as learned men, and to a smaller number of them as spiritual masters. In the mission's infancy, Ricci's policies had gained the missionaries fame, a truth that the Visitor clearly recognized. But Palmeiro was less convinced that all of his decisions retained their utility in 1629, nearly two decades after the mission founder's death. Moreover, Palmeiro was not sure if all of Ricci's translations were accurate and wondered whether they would not benefit from alteration. Accordingly, he posed fundamental questions about the vice-province: Why were there so few Christians despite so much intellectual energy spent on mission strategy? If the current approach was not working, then which social groups should be the targets of the Jesuits' energies? To what extent should the missionaries adopt the customs of the scholarly elite in order to ensure protection, secure patronage, and facilitate proselytization? How much should the Christian message and Catholic behavior be adapted to Chinese cultural and devotional norms, if at all? Finally, should the China Jesuits declare their links to Macau, or should they avoid making their relations to the Portuguese colony more widely known? In sum, to what extent should the Jesuits be identified for what they were: European priests belonging to the Society of Jesus who intended to win converts to Christianity among the Chinese?

The first major issue addressed by Palmeiro in his letters to Rome was the low tally of neophytes in China. Among the reasons that had prompted the Visitor to undertake his strenuous round trip to Beijing—a trip in which he suffered "greater labors and discomforts than those typically endured on the *Carreira da Índia*"—was the meager harvest of souls.[14] If the Jesuits were convinced of their purpose and certain of divine favor for their apostolic endeavors, why were they so ineffective at making converts in the Ming Empire? According to Palmeiro's numbers, based on the ledgers he found at the vice-province's residences, there were no more than six thousand Christians under the Jesuits' care.[15]

Such limited results were hard to justify after the Society's endorsement of the vision of the China mission described in the widely read and translated opus *De Christiana Expeditione apud Sinas*. There, Niklaas Trigault and Matteo Ricci gave the impression that the Jesuits had a clear understanding of how to present the gospel in the Ming Empire. Having surveyed the secular and religious panorama of that land, they claimed to know how best to target their message in order to create a thriving mission church. Their book was explicitly crafted as a tool for recruiting missionaries. Perhaps the China mission lacked men, but its method was sound, the book argued; it had already produced its first fruits. The problem was that the harvest had not matched the hype. The Jesuits' balance sheets left room for slow beginnings, and the

Society's superiors had not put pressure on them for four decades. But by 1629 it had begun to look like their vaunted strategy was not viable.

Was the problem the missionaries? Did they lack brio or had they lost their energy in the years of study needed to learn the language of the hosts? Palmeiro's response was an emphatic no: "I cannot attribute the slowness in the pace of conversion of this people to any lack of application among our men, nor in their fleeing from labor, because I do not understand it this way." The China Jesuits did not lack the will to proselytize, and indeed they seemed to have sufficient drive to not only convert "but to die converting." The Visitor was impressed by their energy, having seen them "study, tire themselves, labor, seek occasions for making many Christians," but to little avail.[16] If not the missionaries themselves, then what was to blame for the low number of converts? Palmeiro identified three related problems that he claimed were responsible for this predicament: widespread xenophobia, a lack of clear permission to reside in China, and an excess of timidity on the part of the missionaries. If the Jesuits could find a way past these hurdles, the Visitor concluded, the efforts would pay off on the scale that they merited.

A fundamental problem identified by Palmeiro was the fear of foreigners. But his invocation of Chinese xenophobia was not concerned with the rejection of the missionaries' religious or "scientific" ideas; it had to do with the fear, an anxiety that he had sensed and that other Jesuits had described to him, with regard to the presence of people who were not Han Chinese. In Palmeiro's words, "all over this kingdom, they are petrified and soon wilt before any foreigner," thereby making it nearly impossible for the missionaries to preach to anyone. The situation was especially bad, he claimed, in the southern province of Guangdong, where the mere sight of a Portuguese (or other European) led to shouts of "*Tamguei,* which means foreign devil". Accordingly, the Jesuits moved about with caution—much as Palmeiro had done in his enclosed conveyance on the road to Beijing—so as not to kindle the wildfire of fear at the first sight of a *fangui.* "Our men normally travel abroad in cities inside sedan chairs or in some other clandestine way," he asserted, "and if one of them is seen or if they are detected on the street, immediately the whole neighborhood and others who chance to see him look upon this new thing as if they were terrified."[17]

Not only were commoners afraid of the missionaries but even the members of the governing elite whom the Jesuits had to court for patronage and protection apparently feared associating with them in public. Palmeiro lamented that even "mandarins known to be good Christians" found it difficult to make their links to the Jesuits widely known. In light of the protection that Li Zhizao and Yang Tingyun had afforded the Jesuits during the Nanjing Persecutions, and the public patronage of Xu Guangqi and Sun Yuanhua at court and in Jiangnan, the Visitor was exaggerating when he claimed that "there is no one who dares to take them under his wing, who will not push them away and pretend that he does not know them if it is suspected, or even imagined, that he favors foreigners." Fear of the dreaded censor's memorial, Palmeiro suggested, was enough to drive away a large segment of the individuals that the accommodation method had been devised to attract. Even worse was his impression that things were not better at the place where preaching might produce a dramatic payoff. The Jesuits had tried to preach to the palace eunuchs, a group they were convinced would be easily converted and, most importantly, had daily access to the monarch, but xenophobia was said to block their way. "When some of them came to our house, they did it undercover, saying that they did not dare to do it in the open, since we were foreigners," Palmeiro reported. "And so they are scared, even in the city of Beijing, where we have lived for so many years and where we are known and esteemed."[18]

A further problem identified by the Visitor was the ambiguous legality of the Jesuits' presence in China. Ricci had been allowed to reside in the court city, and his successors were allowed to tend his grave outside Beijing's walls, but those were the only pronouncements that gave any missionaries the privilege to remain within the Ming Empire. After the two court Jesuits at the time of the Nanjing Persecutions, Sabatino de Ursis (1575–1620) and Diego de Pantoja (1571–1618), had been sent to Macau shackled inside wooden cages in 1617, even this limited permission had been revoked.[19] Thus, for most of the history of the mission the Jesuits resided in the Ming domains illegally. But the fact that some of the enforcers of Chinese laws were the missionaries' patrons made it possible for them to remain not only at court but also in some provincial cities.

Whereas the prestige of Li, Yang, and Xu in mandarin circles had served the missionaries as a buffer against attacks in the 1620s, what would happen when they died? Palmeiro was concerned that without the protection of these "doctors", the Jesuits might once again face persecutors, but this time without help. This was no way to secure the foundations for their project; if the collapse of the Japan mission served as a lesson, it was that without unambiguous permission from a supreme authority, the Jesuits were building their church on sand. Hampered by uncertainty and thereby forced to proceed with caution, Palmeiro concluded, the mission's slow pace of expansion in China would never increase. From his perspective the challenge was clear: "If while so withdrawn and almost completely prevented from performing our office of preaching the gospel, we do not find some way of opening a straighter path, even at the risk of danger, we will always have this impediment, not only doing little but being forced to do little, which is a double misery."[20]

What the Jesuits needed was a straightforward pronouncement from the Chongzhen emperor permitting them to reside anywhere in China in order to preach the "Law of Heaven". Even if the young sovereign might not be the next Constantine, he might at least make some pronouncement (one that would carry the force of law) in favor of the missionaries. With a declaration of approval from the throne, the Jesuits would become legal residents of the empire, and mandarin fears about associating with them would dissipate. And with the passage of time, it was assumed, plebeian resentment for the foreign preachers would likely subside. But it was no easy matter to petition the throne for a regime of exception that would apply to the Jesuits, one group among the many foreigners who came to China as traders or tribute-bearers. Although Li Zhizao and Xu Guangqi had mentioned the missionaries' capacities in military matters in memorials to the throne that led to the 1623 and 1628 Portuguese embassies from Macau, these appeals did not refer to religion.[21]

While he was in Beijing in June 1629, the Visitor had asked his subordinates and the Jesuits' mandarin allies if the missionaries should submit a memorial to the throne. Palmeiro's idea, long contemplated by the Jesuits, was to request explicit permission for the missionaries to reside in China in order to spread their religious message. Back in Macau six months later, Palmeiro informed Superior General Vitelleschi that the missionaries at court were waiting for the right moment for this move. The draft memorial intended to appeal to the Chongzhen Emperor's sense of filial piety, remarking that his grandfather, the Wanli Emperor, had shown kindness to Matteo Ricci. Further, it underscored the Jesuits' utility by declaring: "We are ready to serve him with the books that explain our knowledge, and to communicate to his vassals the wisdom found in them." Such a memorial was nevertheless a gamble since it threatened to bar the Jesuits from court—and the empire—if it was rejected. Palmeiro was justly reticent about wagering all on the goodwill of the palace officials: "It may happen that, once alerted through this memorial that the juridical status of our stay in Beijing is in doubt, they will fail to approve what was permitted before, and then who will stand up for us?"[22]

While popular fears and imperial pronouncements were beyond the Jesuits' control, there was something that Palmeiro felt the missionaries could do to expand the Chinese church. While he freely admitted that his subordinates were right to go slowly, he asserted that the numbers of Christians would not swell if "the priests do not dare to preach the sacred gospel more freely." In other words, he found his men to be timid: "I am persuaded that there is some excess in this, that we have an abundance of fear that is excessive." Palmeiro chided them for not proclaiming their message more forthrightly, casting the issue in moral terms: "It is very important to proceed with discretion and caution, but not with fear and cowardice. To be afraid when circumstances demand is the effect of virtue and it is what prudence teaches, but a fear measured by reason is what must prevail above all." This appeal to reason, tempered by a clear vision of Chinese political culture and the strength of the perceived xenophobia, was best summed up in an analogy that Palmeiro made about the missionaries and their goal: "It is certain that we are dealing here with glass and it would take just a touch to smash it all to pieces, but glass does not always break when you take it in your hands; although there is a risk, it can be used if you are careful with it."[23]

Acting on his diagnosis the Visitor took steps to force his subordinates out of their seclusion. In his understanding of the mission's history, none of the major persecutions faced by the Jesuits "had arisen from our being considered foreigners or for preaching our law". Rather, he placed the blame for earlier crises on specific missionaries or particular adversaries. That is, the Jesuits had not suffered blanket accusations but rather ad hominem attacks—even if they were couched in xenophobic commonplaces—and this was why they had been able to rebound. For instance, in the case of the Nanjing Persecutions, Palmeiro fingered Alfonso Vagnone (1568–1640) as the primary culprit, since this Jesuit was considered to have antagonized that city's officials.[24] Surely a medium existed between Vagnone's behavior and the excessive reserve that the persecutions had produced. Accordingly, in his letters the Visitor urged General Vitelleschi to send a circular back to China in which he would encourage the Jesuits to "be a bit bolder".[25] For his part, Palmeiro put an exhortation to courage as the first point on the topic of "Preaching the Gospel" in the rule book that he distributed from Hangzhou. Here he rejected "political" behavior (a topic on which he would have much more to say), which sacrificed virtue for expediency and constituted a way of masking one's true intentions so as to avoid giving offense: "Even though caution and discretion in preaching the sacred gospel in these kingdoms of China are very important and even necessary, excessive fear and a political means, whereby we aim to follow such a prudent method that we avoid making bold steps or proclaiming our message, must be completely avoided. Likewise, we should not display such timidity that we show fear when there is no reason for being afraid."[26]

An obvious question was involved: To whom should the Jesuits direct this new boldness? That is, in which groups would it make the numbers of converts grow? In the mission's first years, it seemed that the most promising group was the literati whose members were eager to hear about Ricci's *xixue,* "Western learning." But much effort had been expended on such men to little effect. Certainly the Jesuits had made a few important converts, but they were the exception, not the rule. By and large, the evangelic seed scattered among scholars had fallen amid thorns and failed to mature. By contrast, the missionaries spread through the provinces had demonstrated that tallies of baptisms were far higher in the lower social strata. Palmeiro had seen this in Jiangxi and Jiangnan, where most of the Jesuits' converts lived in rural hamlets. But while the Visitor recognized that there was much that could be done among such people, he knew it was risky: "Were it not for the danger that we might appear to be gathering these plain folk into our hands in order to incite riots, it would be very easy to make a large Christian community." Moreover, as he had been told by the Jesuits' mandarin allies "who know best the humors of their peers" in provincial government, it would be unwise for the missionaries to pursue a vigorous strategy in plebeian circles because "throughout the empire it has always been deemed dangerous for foreigners to freely gather simple people."[27]

Although Palmeiro did not issue prohibitions about preaching in rural areas—where the chaos of dynastical upheaval would permit conversions on a larger scale in the later 1630s, 1640s, and 1650s—he did urge caution. Whom else did he think the Jesuits should try to convert? The palace eunuchs in Beijing were a strategic group. These individuals, whom Palmeiro disparaged with broad strokes in his depiction of court life, nevertheless had to be taken into account because, among other things, they went "about with the king in their arms"; moreover, they were "easily led, because they do not profess letters."[28] Targeting the eunuchs would produce results, such as the conversion of

Pang Tianshou (d. 1647) and perhaps a dozen others by Niccolò Longobardo in the 1630s, but it would never lead to the scores of converts that the Jesuits expected.[29] Moreover, the change of dynasty, only a decade after Palmeiro wrote, brought to power rulers who would not be so dependent on eunuchs for conducting affairs of state.

The Visitor was under no illusions that Ricci had identified the best group for the Jesuits' message: scholars, especially those who entered the imperial bureaucracy. In general terms, they were literate and enjoyed social prestige. From a practical perspective, these qualities meant that the Jesuits could appeal to them via the printed word—something that the missionaries had done to undeniable effect among a few of them. But Palmeiro doubted that the virtues of a handful of men who had shown an interest in "Western learning" could be expected in the rest. Indeed, he considered it a paradox that the Jesuits were preaching a religious message to a group that was known for its atheism. While this is not the place to assess the accuracy of this well-known Jesuit interpretation of Confucian thought, it is appropriate to point out that Palmeiro and many of his peers were convinced that the literati "believe that everything ends with the body and this life." Lacking fear of divine retribution, such men were given to vice—"letting the reins of the flesh slacken", in the Visitor's words—and thus rejected religious teachings that would censure their habits.

To make matters worse, Palmeiro considered, the Chinese system of social promotion through studies and examinations led to an intolerable chauvinism: "Everything depends on letters and being eminent in them; all seek to study for the purpose of being able to write and producing a good essay. There is no person so lowly that he does not believe that he can become the greatest man in China." Seeing the keys to success in the knowledge of the canonical books of the Chinese tradition, they saw no need to look beyond them. Rather than finding the ranks of native scholars animated by intellectual curiosity and a universalizing spirit, as the exchanges described by Ricci had led others to believe, the Jesuits seemed to encounter far more literati who dismissed their teachings out of hand. "They are so puffed up with it that they do not want to admit to learning the law of others," Palmeiro concluded. "So they are blind men with little knowledge, and all the blinder because they do not want to learn."[30]

Lacking alternatives, the Visitor concurred that it was worthwhile to target the literati. The experience of a few important conversions and the Jesuits' fame in literate circles argued for continuing to address Chinese scholars. Some of them had already listened to the Jesuits' message, and there was reason to believe that more would do so if they would pay attention to it. "Haughtiness prevents them from believing the truth that we preach to them," asserted Palmeiro, "but if there was greater ease in dealing with them or living near them, they would clearly see by our demeanor that we do not call ourselves 'masters' in order to dominate them, but only to guide them towards salvation." The scholars and officials who had become Christians served as the Visitor's primary evidence, but he also pointed to "the heathens who speak with us more often". So would the other Chinese scholars come to believe, he added, "if they would come a bit further inside to converse with us."[31]

It would appear from this reading of Palmeiro's letters that he was in full accord with the accommodation method articulated by Ricci and his successors. At a superficial level, indeed he was, and later generations of China Jesuits remembered him as having confirmed Alessandro Valignano's policies.[32] Palmeiro as much as admitted his general approval when he paraphrased a famous Ignatian dictum as follows: "In order to make Christians, we make ourselves similar to the Chinese, since we cannot turn ourselves into Chinese; we attempt to appear what we are not, so that they will become what we intend".[33]

There were nevertheless aspects of the accommodation method that the Visitor criticized. His objections lay at the level of practice and intended to make the Jesuits' strategy more coherent and more effective. It should not be forgotten that the accommodation method was not a mission statement; it did not exist on paper with specific points and clauses. Rather, it consisted in mimicking the style that Ricci had employed, a task which became increasingly difficult as the years passed and his memory faded. By 1629 this "policy" was in fact a jumble of policies, of ad hoc behaviors and phrases that appeared useful in different Chinese contexts. Certain priests working in northern cities did things in one way while others in the south employed different means, with the men of each residence (or regional set of residences) responding to particular challenges as they saw fit. The Jesuits adapted their behavior and their image to the variety of regional norms for the literati elite, accommodating themselves when and as necessary.

This range of practices, with much left to the judgment of individual priests, caused grave problems for the Visitor. Like other religious orders, the

Society of Jesus was bound by its rules. Yet in contrast to the Rules of Benedict, Dominic, or Francis, the Jesuits' *Constitutions* include more precisions about the norms for individual and group behavior. Taken as a whole, they create a vision of the order's common identity in which the repeatedly invoked expression *nuestro modo de proceder* stands for an implicitly understood, specifically Jesuit, way of doing things. For Palmeiro the problem was that across China there were multiple "ways" instead of one "way," and the men of the vice-province lacked specific rules tailored to life in the Ming Empire. Without such precepts, individual Jesuits risked accommodating themselves too much to the habits of the Chinese. Faulty judgment on the part of one missionary could lead to scandals that could cause all of them to suffer opprobrium or exile. And although the success of the Jesuits' missions largely depended on the initiative of charismatic individuals, it was Palmeiro's conviction that such men needed a framework to guide their actions. When he was in India, the Visitor had dealt with individuals who were guided by their visionary natures to head off in different directions, but they were a minority among the scores of Jesuits in that part of Asia. Those who demonstrated an excess of individuality, to use an admittedly anachronistic term, could be summoned by their superiors to return to the colleges where discipline often reigned and communal routines were the norm. But there were no such centers in the China mission; the vice-province was largely a collection of isolated priests living alone or in pairs.

To address this diversity, the Visitor had issued his compendium of rules to all of the members of the vice-province before returning to Macau in the autumn of 1629. To be sure, his predecessors had sent rules to the China Jesuits touching on specific aspects of missionary life, such as the structure of their language-study program.[34] But Palmeiro's rules touched on a wider-ranging set of practical concerns, giving form to the Jesuits' strategy. They also sparked complaints since they insisted on imposing limits on individual behavior. Both Francesco Sambiasi (1582–1649) and Giulio Aleni (1582–1649), each of whom had been in the mission field for two decades, wrote to Palmeiro to voice their objections. The Visitor claimed that he was taken aback by the comments made by Sambiasi, who thought Palmeiro's specific rules unnecessary. To Sambiasi, it was enough to "abide by our rules in so much as the place and time permitted, and in everything else to accommodate ourselves to the Chinese."[35] But Ignatius Loyola and his early companions did not contemplate Asian realities when they wrote the *Constitutions,* leaving Palmeiro to retort about Sambiasi that "if our rules were enough, he would be correct, and in no small measure; since having many rules does not make our order, or any other, better governed." But in order to achieve the same union of hearts and minds that Loyola desired for the Society, and which its communal practices ensured elsewhere, the China Jesuits needed specific rules. Accommodation was a laudable goal for missionaries, the Visitor agreed, but it had to be done uniformly: "In so much as we accommodate in what is decent to the Chinese, we must have the same style, and this can only be achieved if we have certain terms and markers."[36]

Obviously there were points at which the individual initiative exceeded acceptable limits. But what aspects of missionary life needed restraining? Palmeiro was content with the way that the China Jesuits comported themselves with regard to their religious obligations as members of the Society of Jesus. He remarked that they lived with "great observance" of the order's common rules and did not "accommodate to the Chinese in anything that offends God or breaks any precepts."[37] The problems that he saw, therefore, had arisen from how the Jesuits comported themselves in those other moments when they were supposed to be claiming souls for the church.

Before entering China, Palmeiro had the impression that the missionaries were adapting themselves to the wrong aspects of indigenous culture; he feared that they were wasting their time with the rituals of courtesy that Ricci and others claimed to be the bedrock of literati mores. This prejudice was a problem of the Jesuits' own making since their writings had dedicated so much space to describing the indicators of civilization in the Ming Empire. In other words, those aspects of culture that educated Europeans considered a mirror of their own—Chinese books, scholars, laws, civil ceremonies— were the same ones that were considered by Palmeiro to be distractions from the Jesuits' apostolic endeavor. Instead of preaching the gospel, he thought, they engaged in an elaborate pantomime with indigenous scholars, "visiting and being visited; inviting and receiving invitations; in giving and receiving presents."[38] This type of behavior he labeled as "merely political"; that is, it consisted of vain gestures that served no discernible spiritual goal. From the perspective of an early modern commentator such as Palmeiro, "political" attitudes were pernicious since they often served to excuse immorality. Recall that the pejorative label *politique* applied to those individuals during the French Wars of Religion (1562–1598) who urged compromise on religious matters in the name of social stability.

The Visitor's inspection disabused him in the main of the idea that the Jesuits were spending too much time on ceremonial activities. Just as his visit to Madurai had enabled him to get past the external aspects of Nobili's strategy, so his journey through China had altered his views about several of the physical aspects of the accommodation method in that land. Just as he had found that Nobili's adventures in Indian costumes and behaviors were inoffensive (and unimportant in moral terms), so also he was not shocked by the general tableau of Jesuits in Chinese tints. "I examined this important point, and I found that in their dress, their food, their courtesies, and their manner, they all adhere to local customs," Palmeiro wrote, "and in this there is no flaw, nor anything worthy of note." Moreover, he asserted, these adaptations were indispensable "for the people of this kingdom, who are so disturbed by foreigners, to find us less strange."[39]

Adherence to indigenous ceremonies was de rigueur, but the Visitor did not find the Jesuits overly indulging themselves. Those courtesy visits, replete with tea and gifts, were necessary in Beijing but less so in other parts of China. For example, Giulio Aleni in Fujian Province was considered by Palmeiro to be "more political," spending much time in this type of activity but not extravagantly. Indeed, fear that the tone of the Visitor's rules might be overly severe, he reassured his subordinates explicitly. They were permitted to indulge in a cup of tea or a bite to eat during their visits "because it is a Chinese custom and they would find us very strange if we refused."[40] Things were different at court, where there was a continual stream of visitors who inquired about the Jesuits' mathematical, astronomical, and, to a lesser extent, spiritual teachings. "I do not call this excessive," Palmeiro remarked, "because we do not visit others, rather we suffer these visits by others".

The benefits that accrued to the men of the vice-province from these courtesies were clear: the good name of the Jesuits spread throughout China on the lips of scholars and officials. If there was a problem with the visitors at court, Palmeiro judged, it was because "most of the time is wasted in matters of pure curiosity, which contains much idleness." That is, the Beijing Jesuits were seen to spend hours talking about mechanics, optics, mathematics, and even ballistics in order to satisfy their interlocutors. Accordingly, the Visitor "gave serious advice" to Niccolò Longobardo and his companions that they should always steer conversations toward "God and the sacred mysteries". Natural philosophy or mathematics was merely a conversation starter; it should serve to draw Chinese minds to the Creator of the universe, not to creation.[41]

Two other customs that raised doubts for Palmeiro were banquets and the exchanging of gifts. But here again he saw some virtue in both if they were done with moderation. Accepting or offering invitations to banquets was entirely "political," the Visitor averred, but he did not feel that the Jesuits should be prohibited from this practice. Whereas the early accounts from China made it seem that the missionaries were obliged to spend their days in gluttonous revelry, Palmeiro knew it was not so. Attending banquets "neither bothers nor impedes, and even less conflicts with divine precepts or those of our order," he argued, adding that Francis Xavier and other saints attended heathen feasts to great profit. It was true, the Visitor noted, that certain inconveniences emerged when the Jesuits were invited during Lent or other fasting periods; worse, however, was the fact that Chinese banquets were often dinner theater. Early on in the mission's history, it appears, the missionaries' moral sensibilities were more frequently offended by the content of the plays they watched at the banquets they attended. Over time, however, it became known that the Jesuits disliked bawdy theater, an attitude that stemmed the tide of invitations that they received. Palmeiro claimed that the priests rarely, if ever, attended banquets or plays, noting that he had only been invited to one such feast during the ten months he was in China.

As for the ritual exchange of gifts, the same move from excess to moderation had occurred. "This is the custom of the land and it contains no evil," the Visitor declared, since even valuable presents could be returned without shame, and the Jesuits had no expensive gifts to offer (except to the emperor).[42] Even the gifts that the missionaries had, such as clocks and telescopes, were prized not for their value but rather for their novelty. So in order to preserve this crucial element of proselytizing bait, Palmeiro prohibited his subordinates from teaching the Chinese how to make such instruments themselves.[43]

There was, of course, one facet of the willing observance of Chinese customs that caused Palmeiro considerable consternation. If the missionaries were to carry out their visits in strict accordance to indigenous habits, they needed to wear the type of dress typically worn by literati during their ceremonial visits: silk robes. The Visitor devotes an entire letter to the question of silk, going into detail about the different types of ceremonial garments commonly used in China. His discussion centers on whether the Jesuits could dispense entirely with this luxurious fabric without sacrificing the social status that its use had helped them achieve.

Palmeiro's point of departure was the fact that the missionaries had no standard form of dress in the Ming Empire; there were no rules that stipulated the fabric or cut of their robes. Here again Palmeiro saw the perils of individual judgment. He nevertheless realized one thing in 1629: "There is no doubt that the time has not come, nor the appropriate conjunction arrived, for all of our men in China to wear a particular habit or an identifiable mark on their external attire by which we will all be known as a specific family or congregation." That is to say, unlike in Europe, where members of religious orders could be classified by the cut and color of their habits, the Jesuits in the Ming Empire wore a variety of vestments that made them appear as independent members of a learned society. Too much uniformity of dress would attract unwanted attention and potentially give rise to even greater suspicions about the missionaries' undisclosed intentions. "All must be one, but not known as one," Palmeiro continued, "nor should we declare this fact to the simple folks, but those who are more intelligent understand it perfectly without us having to explain it."[44]

Despite the variety of colors they used instead of the traditional black, Palmeiro claimed that there had always been doubts about the kind of fabric the missionaries should use. "Until my entry, all of them had silk *champaos*", he noted, referring to the outer robe as a *changpao,* "long gown"; but there were doubts about "the convenience or necessity of wearing them." To make matters clearer for the superior general, Palmeiro explained that there were different types of these floor-length robes. He began by describing the "courtesy *changpao*" by means of an analogy to Catholic liturgical vestments: "It is an exterior dress called a courtesy dress, because it only serves that purpose. . . . Your Paternity should imagine that it is like a dalmatic or a cope, which has its proper use in one place and for a particular ministry and is useless for others." Every one of the Jesuits in China had such a *changpao* to wear when calling on important figures, especially mandarins, or when receiving such men.

The missionaries had to have such robes, Palmeiro confessed; they were obligatory in social intercourse. But the substantial investment made in purchasing them was compensated by the fact that they were rarely used. A missionary would be obliged to wear a courtesy *changpao* when receiving or being received, but would quickly remove it after the moment of encounter, a fact that meant that these robes were used "few hours over the long years of one's life; in sum, they were only for being seen, not for being worn." Similar to the courtesy gown were other robes donned for funerals or public mourning, made of white silk. But according to the advice of the Christian mandarins and the senior Jesuits, Palmeiro could not dispense with these mourning robes or with the courtesy gowns.[45] The rules that he issued were explicit on this point, permitting the missionaries to have special silk robes for these specific occasions.[46]

FIGURE 8.2. Sketch of Johann Schreck (called Terrentius) in Chinese silk robes. This drawing was made by Peter Paul Rubens (1577–1640) in January 1618 at Brussels, while Terrentius traveled in the company of Niklaas Trigault on the latter's trip through Europe as mission procurator. The robe shown here is an example of the silk *changbao* that originated the controversy over silk among the China missionaries.

The focal point of the internal debate among the China Jesuits on the matter of silk was whether they should use it as their daily attire. For those who argued in favor of an everyday *changpao,* the robes conveyed an image of learned authority that the missionaries sought to project. Indeed, this is what Ricci had intended when he had adopted silk robes in the mid-1590s. According to Palmeiro, however, "the reasons that were given for wearing them at the beginning, when we first entered the kingdom, were still being defended in order to not give them up." Stated differently, the Jesuits had won the image battle and no longer needed rich fabric for projecting authority.

The Visitor claimed that the senior missionaries and their "mandarin friends" thought that there was no need for such robes, and he had seen with his own eyes that there were important literati at court and elsewhere who wore clothing made of more modest fabrics. "If it is good enough for them and, what is more, since we profess poverty," he wrote, "why should we have to wear a type of dress that proclaims riches?" Worse still, the use of silk robes seemed to have a corrosive effect on the missionaries' morals. Palmeiro asserted that those who defended their use based their arguments not on questions of authority but on "vanity and self comfort", since several of these men had "more than double" the typical number of gowns. In the most flagrant example of this unseemly attachment to luxury, the Visitor remarked that upon Niklaas Trigault's death "five robes of various different silks were found."[47]

The only way that Palmeiro saw to eliminate these problems was to ban the use of silk except on rare occasions. "Looking over the matter slowly," he wrote to Vitelleschi in a formulation reserved for only the most serious matters, "*in domino,* it appeared to me that I should order that the use of silk should not be allowed in ordinary *champaos.*" Not only would this move dismiss the temptation to luxury but prohibiting silk would also serve to "shut the mouths of the friars and other adversaries who get tripped up over it."[48] The rules that he issued while in Hangzhou left little room for debate: "Since today we are known as men who have no regard for external ostentation . . . such pomp and display can be dispensed with, and consequently the use of all types of silk, whether in shoes or robes, should be abandoned." The Visitor charged Vice-Provincial Manuel Dias the younger with gathering all such robes from the missionaries (and prohibited him from conceding special dispensations), permitting their use only on the infrequent occasions when missionaries were sent to new provinces.[49] Palmeiro further stipulated the types of cloth to be used for the Jesuits' robes, indicating heavier or lighter fabrics for the different seasons, as well as their black or blue color.[50] In closing his letter to the superior general on the subject, he lay to rest the lingering doubts that these prohibitions would somehow affect the Jesuits' standing in the Ming Empire. He pointed to the case of the Japan mission, where the use of silk was banned "and it was not for that reason that our men sacrificed their due respect and courtesy." For Palmeiro, the matter was simple: "Adequate dress, composure, modesty, and mature customs, add the respect that is due and summon as much authority as is not only useful, but indeed all that is necessary, for the conversion of the world."[51]

These physical manifestations of the accommodation method had served to make the image of the China Jesuits similar to that of the late Ming literati. We have seen that this approximation to Chinese standards posed no fundamental problems for Palmeiro; he mandated that his subordinates continue to use native dress and to observe the standards of elite conduct but in a way that did not compromise their vows of poverty and chastity. Far from being Eurocentric or insensitive to Chinese culture, his decisions urged the missionaries to employ modes of accommodation that were more befitting of their status as members of a religious order. They could do so because he also recognized that the work of establishing the mission had been largely accomplished by the first generation of China Jesuits. By 1629, the Visitor argued, the time had come to remove the exaggerated aspects of the missionaries' disguise so that their true identity could be more clearly discerned. Instead of persisting with the use of metaphors whereby the Jesuits were "Western literati"—that is, a European version of something Chinese—they needed to show, albeit cautiously, that they were different.

Nowhere was the shift from similarities to differences more urgently needed than in the formulation of the missionaries' religious message. The insistence, since Ricci's day, on the similarities between Chinese moral notions and Western ones had given rise to a host of ambiguities. Moreover, it had shown its limitations as a proselytizing strategy: few converts had been made from scholarly milieux. Palmeiro reserved his strongest words of criticism for his denunciation of this facet of the strategy used hitherto, asserting that it was a "great excess based on political and human accommodation, which I consider very damaging and prejudicial". In order to "facilitate the conversion of these Chinese," the Visitor wrote, "some of our men tell the literati that the law which we profess differs little from theirs." Furthermore, these Jesuits signified God by the term *Shangdi*, "which is the same that they use, if they recognize any god." Considering the fact that Palmeiro subscribed to the interpretation that the Chinese literati were atheists, "and those who are not adore the *pagodes*", this equivalence was scandalous.[52] Despite the fact that several of the missionaries judged these positions to be licit and useful for making conversions, Palmeiro asserted, "they are greatly mistaken."[53]

The Visitor saw three major problems with this strategy of approximation: a misunderstanding of the dynamics of conversion, the false equivalence between Christianity and indigenous teachings, and the limited use of shared moral principles. The first of these problems arose from the assumption that, when confronted with a choice between two largely equivalent doctrines, an educated Chinese would want to choose the Western one. If their teachings and the "Law of God" were so similar, Palmeiro observed, they would certainly not convert "so as not to seem capricious in trading the law that they had for one that was almost the same." Conversion was a serious business, and the choice to embrace beliefs (whether Christian or otherwise) was not made lightly.

Palmeiro here gave more credit to the prospective converts than his more "accommodationist" subordinates. Whereas those Jesuits operated under the assumption that their interlocutors would submit to baptism if they showed that Christian teachings differed little from indigenous precepts, the Visitor knew that conversions did not spring from facile equivalencies. It was at this point that the metaphors employed by Ricci and his successors reached their limits. Rhetoricians all, the China Jesuits should have recalled what Cipriano Suárez had made clear in his manual: "Just as the moderate and timely use of metaphors makes speech clear, so a repeated use both confuses and induces boredom."[54] In other words, overemphasis on rhetorical shortcuts or similarities, especially in proselytization, was counterproductive. In order for individuals to enter the church, they had to know that they would gain significantly from the rejection of their prior convictions or, in the case of atheists, from the adoption of religious precepts that complemented indigenous moral teachings. As far as Palmeiro was concerned, to assume that they would do so without firm assent (or that the Jesuits would want to build a church of literati followers who had not really converted), Palmeiro asserted, was "a political method, misguided in all respects."[55]

The second problem arose from the idea that Chinese scholars had some correct religious conceptions that might be useful in the Jesuits' proselytizing strategies. Ricci and his successors had divided Chinese religion into three main "sects": Buddhism, Daoism, and "the sect of the literati." Palmeiro used the more forceful term, "law," to describe the teachings of the literati, employing the same term that the Jesuits used for Christianity ("the Law of God"), Judaism ("the Law of Moses"), and Islam ("the Law of Mohammed"). By a convenient shorthand this third teaching has often been labeled "Confucianism" since its precepts were based on a reading of the *Four Books* and *Five Classics,* parts of which have been attributed to Master Kong. But there was no firm definition of "Confucianism" as a religious philosophy during the Ming Dynasty. What the Jesuits called "the sect of the literati" was precisely that, a group of people—the scholarly elite—defined by their ritual behaviors and moral teachings.[56]

This ambiguity made "the sect of the literati" problematic. Following Ricci's initial assessment, the Jesuits found much to praise in the moral lessons of the Confucian canon and considered some of its teachings to be as germane to Christianity as those of Aristotle or Cicero. But while the original Confucian texts eschewed terminology that was recognizably religious to Ricci, thereby leading him to conclude that the literati were atheists at heart, the standard glosses that accompanied most versions of those writings did not. Moreover, there was widespread mingling of concepts among the various "sects" in the Ming period, and the behaviors used to venerate Master Kong in specific Confucian sanctuaries were similar to those used in Buddhist or Daoist shrines. Contrary to what Ricci had argued, it was no easy task to untangle the literati strand from the knot of Ming religion.

Palmeiro, for one, did not see many obvious resemblances between the practices of the Chinese literati and those he associated with Christians (even Chinese ones). His objections began at the level of belief and proceeded to the level of behavior. From what the Visitor had seen and in light of what he had been told by his subordinates, he concluded that the literati were either atheists masquerading as idolaters or idolaters *tout court.* "The better part of these literati believe that there is no other life, and so spend this one as atheists," Palmeiro wrote, "and those that say there is life after death, who are fewer in number, adore the infamous *pagodes.*" Both groups nevertheless displayed the external signs of religious behaviors: "they have temples and in them idols, to whom they go to make sacrifices several times during the year". Such sacrifices were done "out of pure reason of state, since many of those who do it claim that there is no god or anything beyond what can be

seen." In either case, Palmeiro did not judge either group to display an obvious predisposition for becoming Christians based on their previous practice
of "the sect of the literati."

Turning his gaze to what he had been told were the doctrinal norms of
"Confucianism," the Visitor found little to praise. Moreover, he expressed
shock at hearing that some Jesuits proclaimed to the literati "that our law is
so pure and so different from that of the *pagodes,* but so congruent to theirs."
After all, even Ricci was not sparing with criticism for the fact that what he
considered to be manifest superstitions and immoral practices were widely
tolerated among the literati.[57] It was enough to put the "Law of God" and the
"law of the literati" side by side, Palmeiro argued, in order for clear contrasts
to emerge:

> If their law permits many wives and does not object to sodomy and other
> abominations, how can it be said that it differs little from that which we
> profess as Christians? If in their law there is either no God, or that divinity
> is not dealt with now, if there is no one essence and three persons, if there
> is no incarnation of one of those persons, if there are not any sacraments
> like our law has, and if these are all things that are of great importance,
> then how can it be said that both proceed in the same direction and that
> our law and theirs will reach the same ends? How can it be said that their
> precepts are so similar to the ones we have, when ours are so different from
> theirs in the purity of what they command and the means that they re-
> quire to be correctly observed?[58]

It seemed that the closest point of contact between "Confucianism" and
Christianity was in some of their basic moral teachings, but here Palmeiro
saw his third problem. To him the fact that the literati had some laudable
customs based on ancient writings and that these seemed to run parallel to
European norms was to be expected since God had imprinted impulses to
rectitude on the minds of all men. This was the effect of natural law, and Palmeiro had seen it during his travels in the Ming Empire. But he did not believe that this was a justification for eliding the differences between Christianity and "Confucianism" and insisting that the two laws were similar. "If
the priests believe that it suffices for this purpose to affirm that among the
books of the Chinese there are some moral documents that serve to instill
virtue," he argued, "I respond by asking what sect there has ever been or is
today that does not have some rules for correct living?" Taking an extreme

example, he continued: "What could be more contrary to the law of Christ than that of the enemy Mohammed? And nevertheless it professes only one God of the universe, and we know that among the Turks and Moors there are some documents and rules that are very conformant with reason. The same can be said of all of the heathens that live here in the East."[59] Coincidence was hardly a reliable ally in the battle for conversions.

These were grave criticisms of the proselytizing strategy of some of the China Jesuits, and were reported to Rome in condemnatory terms. Palmeiro summed up his points by insisting that the superior general should also be shocked that his men might traffic in such ambiguities or false similarities. "I understand that Your Paternity should find them strange, as things that are not simply wrong but very indecent," he exclaimed, adding: "This is putting Dagon with *Deus* on the same altar, this is in effect serving two different lords while only professing one as True."[60] Having made this reference to the Philistines' attempts to place the Ark of the Covenant on the same altar as the statue of their deity, he followed up by placing the blame for the low number of baptisms in China on those Jesuits who persisted with this line of argument with prospective converts.[61]

Despite his thunder, Palmeiro's attitudes toward his subordinates were measured. He did not spew prohibitions against the "political" missionaries because he knew such gestures would not only be counterproductive but unenforceable—that is to say, he knew that his only tools were the invocation of the Society's vows of obedience and was aware that even the sharpest instrument goes dull with overuse. Fortunately for him, there was the example of several missionaries whose presentation of Christianity, not displayed in a "Confucian" guise, could be commended to the others. While urging the superior general to make some statement on the matter, he addressed it with a specific reference in his rules. In keeping with his moderate approach to governance, Palmeiro balanced his rule so that it addressed both the overly zealous and the "political" in the Society's ranks:

> Although it is good and necessary in preaching our holy law not to refute the law of the *pagodes* and that of the literati with scandalous words, at which not only the sects but those who profess them take umbrage, it is nevertheless not good to dissimulate the errors in which they live and do not recognize in such a way that they think that our law and theirs are one, or more or less the same. Thus it is necessary to show them with modesty

and prudence the errors of their ways, so that by knowing them well, they will more swiftly give credit to the truth we teach.[62]

Another component of the accommodation method that caused the Visitor concern was the missionaries' choice of terminology. The "Terms Controversy" was, in its essence, a dispute over how the Christian message could be best rendered in the Chinese language. The crux of the disagreement was over the terms that had been used by Ricci and his successors to translate God and other theological terms, with the positive side defending their use and the negative side insisting on different translations or even transliterations from Latin. In Macau and in several cities within the Ming Empire, Jesuits had produced a mass of arguments on either side of the question. By one contemporary account, there were at least forty treatises dealing with the question dating back to Ricci's first writings on the subject in 1600, not to mention the discussions via correspondence or in person.[63]

Given that the high level of tension between the rival factions had already produced scandalous exchanges and acts (if Trigault's suicide is included), Palmeiro needed to resolve this question. His approach did not simply require him to adjudicate between contrasting translations and their theological implications, it also demanded that he find a solution that would please (as much as possible) the members of both the Province of Japan and its Vice-Province of China. Not only was Palmeiro responsible for both groups of Jesuits, he also knew that the issues involved were not restricted to the preaching of the gospel in China. As the Province of Japan gradually lost its core territories, it had acquired others in Southeast Asia that were fully in the Chinese cultural orbit. Missionary decisions taken within the Ming Empire, and especially ones linked to the spread of the Christian message through books that circulated throughout East and Southeast Asia, needed to be decided with both sets of Jesuits in mind. This is why the Visitor did not dismiss the concerns of João Rodrigues and the other Japan Jesuits out of hand when making his final decisions in the Terms Controversy.

It is unfortunate that the letter that Palmeiro wrote to Rome in 1629 dealing specifically with this question has been lost. There is nevertheless sufficient information in the other missives as well as in his rules to understand his argument. As mentioned earlier, he ordered the China Jesuits to cease using the term *Shangdi* to refer to God and invoked the virtue of obedience to enforce compliance. He also prohibited the use of the term *Tian*, heaven, but equally ruled against the use of *cobitas*, the Portuguese term for transliterations from European languages (although these had been used in Japan). In his rules Palmeiro aimed at ensuring that the Jesuits would use the same approved terms when they printed books in the Ming Empire. He gave the vice-provincial the power to appoint individuals to compose books, and insisted that this superior and a team of three inspectors censor texts before publication.[64] It was therefore unlikely that the problematic terms would continue to appear in Jesuit writings; to be sure, Palmeiro did not order the emendation of works by Ricci or other missionaries. Despite the rigor of his ruling, the final summation of his letters to Rome urged Superior General Vitelleschi to write back to the missionaries in China to reiterate that they should "not use that name *Shangdi* for now, since it is much safer to avoid it, and that they should exercise caution when using the name *Tianzhu*".[65] This statement suggests that Palmeiro knew that the superior general would have the final say in the matter, and that the solution proposed by the Visitor was intended to be a temporary one, albeit with no specified expiration date. Just as it had caused changes over the previous decades, so the future evolution of the mission might occasion further adaptations in strategy.

Given the passions aroused by the Terms Controversy, it was not surprising that Palmeiro's pronouncement was not the last word on the affair. Within months of the Visitor's departure from Hangzhou, where he had taken his decisions, letters with reactions from the China Jesuits began to arrive at Macau. Over the span of a year, both praise and blame was directed at Palmeiro. His response to these letters, summarized in his January 1631 letter to Rome, gives an overview of what he had written two years before and adds other insights about his rationale for banning some of the terms. The Visitor was unrepentant: "I judge on my conscience, and do so with such clarity, that in order to not offend God the most rigorous prohibition of the name *Shangdi* must be kept in force."[66]

Palmeiro was swayed by the arguments of the detractors of the terms, who insisted that they should not preach by using terms with multiple meanings, especially not when there were alternatives that presented no risk. Palmeiro cited the experience of the Beijing Christians whose pastor, Niccolò Longobardo, had long disputed the terms and asserted that even "those most impassioned for *Shangdi*" admitted there were viable alternatives. "On account of the present scandal and the danger of many falling into error because they use the name *Shangdi*," the Visitor concluded, "conscience obliges the use, without undue inconvenience, of other names." Far from being culturally insensitive, Palmeiro felt constrained by his office and his duty to the Society of Jesus to compel the Jesuits to return to the Chinese lexicon for a better translation. And instead of fearing censure by Rome, the Visitor knew that he enjoyed the superior general's complete trust. Muzio Vitelleschi had made it clear to Palmeiro that he did not intend to "tie his hands" in order for the Visitor to do what was necessary to resolve this affair.[67]

Observing the back-and-forth between the Visitor and those who objected to his rules is important for understanding the dynamics of the Terms Controversy since their exchanges highlight the fact that far more than an academic dispute was at stake. Personalities, questions of missionary strategy, and chains of authority played roles as important as the issues of translation. The most vociferous riposte against Palmeiro's orders came from Alfonso Vagnone, a Jesuit who had lived in China since 1605 and who was stationed in the western province of Shanxi. By December 1629, a few months after receiving the new rules, Vagnone had fired off two letters to his superiors in Macau and Rome. His letter to the superior general was blunt and his missive to the Visitor even blunter. To Rome Vagnone wrote that Palmeiro "passed like a lightning bolt" from Canton to Beijing and that with regard to the terms, "he did not want to hear anyone who held the affirmative opinion."[68] That is, the Visitor did not want to dwell in the vice-province to hear out those who defended *Shangdi* and *Tian*.

In Vagnone's opinion, there was only one way to handle this affair: Palmeiro should have gathered the missionaries together for an academic disputation, as was customary in Europe. Of course, the Visitor had insisted from the start that he did not understand Chinese and so was in no position to judge such a debate. But for Vagnone, it was necessary to "dispute and ascertain the truths of the matter, because this is the ancient method which has always been observed in the church." Perhaps speaking for himself, and apparently forgetting the Jiading meeting that had taken place only two years before, he asserted that without such an encounter "there will be no end to these controversies."[69] This was a prescient comment. The Terms Controversy turned out to be a prelude to the Rites Controversy, a conflict that remained unresolved until 1939.

In Vagnone's view, Palmeiro's ruling created more problems than it solved. By banning the use of *Shangdi* and *Tian,* the Visitor had blocked some of the primary channels for making conversions among the literati. No longer could the Jesuits point to the Confucian classics and say that those books contained glimpses of the Almighty (that is, if they were understood "correctly"). Curious scholars would arrive to speak with the missionaries and insist that their *Shangdi* was God, Vagnone argued, and when contradicted "either would laugh at us as if we do not understand their books, or spit in our faces, saying that we pretend to know their books better than they do, men who have spent their whole lives studying." He referred to episodes that had occurred in Xi'an, where Johann Adam Schall (1592–1666) was repeatedly badgered by a literatus on precisely this point, and at Kaifeng, where Francesco Sambiasi found himself "greatly embarrassed" and tongue-tied. Worse still, Vagnone added, the missionaries were forced to deny things found in the Jesuits' own writings: Both *Shangdi* and *Tian* appeared frequently in their most widely circulated books. Banishing them would encourage prospective converts to conclude that "we contradict ourselves or, at a minimum, that we do not understand their books as well as Father Matteo Ricci did". There were other consequences for those scholars who had become Christians, even if they understood the terms in the "correct" way. Vagnone asserted that the ban against *Shangdi* would "drive them away from us . . . as if we wanted to destroy the little light and testimony of God that they have in their ancient books." Moreover, he claimed that he had already been told by some Christian mandarins that they would not abandon the usage and would persist in the face of the priests' prohibitions "since they say that they understand their books better than we foreigners do."[70]

The letter sent by Vagnone to Palmeiro has been lost, but Palmeiro's summary and comments to the superior general give an indication of its tone. The sense of personal insult is palpable in the Visitor's account; nowhere else in his writings does he reveal such anger. Clearly Vagnone did not limit himself to raising questions about the practical implications of the new rules for Jesuit strategy. In the form of a rhetorical question, Palmeiro makes it clear that there was naked insubordination: "If it is to be that our subordinates affront us by calling us partial and claim that we give prejudicial orders, further threatening to denounce us to Your Paternity, when we as superiors do what we must in matters of such importance, who will have the courage to fulfill his obligations?"[71]

Unlike the episodes during his time in South Asia, when Palmeiro had been forced to act as the pragmatic brake on his subordinates' excessive zeal in light of personnel or economic constraints, in this case he was confronted with a direct challenge to his authority. In addition to sending him a harsh rebuke, Palmeiro considered summoning Vagnone to Macau for a dressing-down and even received letters from other senior missionaries and Vice-Provincial Manuel Dias urging the same. Recalling the specter of the 1616 persecutions, these voices feared that Vagnone "would cause some disturbance similar to what happened in Nanjing when we were exiled, for which they all blame him." The Visitor nevertheless demurred, citing the lack of trained priests and Vagnone's evident talents as a missionary and linguist. But the attacks had clearly touched a nerve, and Palmeiro expressed revulsion at being accused of unfairness: "I have lived many years in these Provinces of the Indies without being called partial, something I consider abominable, and only because I did not sway because my conscience obliged me not to, he brands me with this name with such effrontery."[72]

The Visitor's move had been an attempt to ensure a prudent uniformity in a mission field marked by differing degrees of accommodation to Chinese patterns. And according to him, he had not come from outside the Ming Empire with uninformed solutions—he had based his decisions on the explicit will of the China Jesuits. Palmeiro asserted that Vagnone had been the primary voice at the Jiading conference in January 1628 to insist that the assembled missionaries sign a resolution by which they agreed to renounce *Shangdi*. This document, along with many of the original treatises penned on the terms, has been lost, but Palmeiro's words are clear: "I left it as an order invoking the precept of obedience without adding anything."[73] If the Visitor had simply done what Vagnone had wanted, why was he so annoyed? Clearly Vagnone was setting up a smokescreen behind which to pursue his own strategy of using the term *Shangdi* while paying lip service to the misgivings of his brethren. Just as he hated seeing Jesuits dissimulating for "political" ends, Palmeiro detested seeing duplicity masquerading as virtue: "He accommodated himself to the resolution taken there in order to trick his brothers and the Society, freely using that term afterward to the scandal of his companions, and was upset that I obliged him with that invocation of obedience to keep his word."[74]

The Visitor's intervention in the Terms Controversy was further complicated by those who complained that he had not gone far enough with his prohibitions. In this group were the former superior, Niccolò Longobardo, as well as one of the mission's most experienced Macau-born Chinese coadjutors, Pascoal Mendes (1584–1640). The latter wrote to Rome from Beijing a year after Palmeiro's visit to alert the superior general to the danger of the term *Tianzhu,* which had been suggested as a less problematic alternative.[75] While the Visitor was aware of the potential problems of that term too—he had been duly informed about them by João Rodrigues, who rejected this option as forcefully as he did *Shangdi*—he saw even greater problems with its prohibition. Longobardo echoed Mendes's sentiments, experiencing an acute case of scruples about using the term *Tianzhu* (which he was convinced referred to a deity in the indigenous pantheon, and carried undue echoes of the banned *Tian*). In its stead, he opted for *Dazhu* (a rendering of *Deus* in Chinese characters meaning "Great Lord"), a term very similar to transliterations of the type that Palmeiro had prohibited.

To make matters worse, Longobardo drew up a memorial to the Chongzhen Emperor in 1631, intended to accompany the duke of Bavaria's gifts, that liberally used transliterations: "Not only for the name of God, but also for that of angel, devil, soul, hell, and a few others he used Portuguese names, which the priests of this mission found astonishing." Thankfully, the vice-provincial was in Beijing at the time and blocked this potentially embarrassing memorial from going out along with the duke's gifts. And perhaps since Longobardo did not launch his misgivings to the Visitor on a sea of threats and insults, Palmeiro's response to him was muted. He alerted the court Jesuit to his disobedience and asked the superior general to write to Beijing to tell Longobardo "not to be so anguished".[76]

Both Mendes and Longobardo also complained that Palmeiro refused to act on a related problem, the presence of the banned terms in the Jesuits' printed books. Mendes knew that their texts traveled much farther than the missionaries could and were certain to appear in Japan, Southeast Asia, and Manila—where there would certainly be friars waiting to censure the Jesuits or denounce them to the Inquisition.[77] While it was beyond the missionaries' capacities to hunt down the copies of their books that had been circulated since Ricci first started composing in Chinese, it was possible for them to emend those texts found in their residences or to correct future editions. But if men like Vagnone were convinced that the Jesuits would look bad if they contradicted themselves in speech, how would they look if they tampered with books that had already been widely praised? This issue had been mooted in the mid-1620s, before Palmeiro became Visitor, when General Vitelleschi had sent orders to China stating that no changes could be made to Ricci's books without express permission. In fact, Vagnone did not shy from reminding Palmeiro of this restriction when he wrote to complain about his partiality and insensitivity.[78] Rome was on the Visitor's side, however, and instead of imposing restraint upon Palmeiro, Vitelleschi in the early 1630s sent him permission to emend his subordinates' books.

Palmeiro's response to Rome upon receiving word of his expanded powers is a fitting testament to his capacity for governing his subordinates. It was also further proof that he did not act out of spite for East Asian culture and did not deny the capacity of the Jesuits' interlocutors to understand the Christian message in their own language. With careful guidance, his letters and his rules make clear, literate Chinese men (and women) could be made into Christians as virtuous as any whom he had seen during his travels about the Ming Empire. Even the risk of the Jesuits' books getting outside of China did not seem to trouble the Visitor since he assumed it would be a long while before any others reached the same level of linguistic competence as the men of the vice-province. Palmeiro described the power to emend as "very necessary" but countered that it was more important to proceed with caution, "waiting for the green humors that can been discerned in some to mature". Concerned that enacting such an order might touch off another round of disputes, he remarked that "it is to be feared that delirium and indecorous frenzies will spring up if they seek to cure their errors with hasty remedies." In order to prepare the ground for such changes, Palmeiro sent word to Vice-Provincial Manuel Dias for him to go about "softening the rebellious humors of two or three people"—at least Vagnone and Rodrigo de Figueiredo, but also in all likelihood Giacomo Rho (1592–1638). The Visitor further informed the superior general that he was keeping the news to himself since it would cause too much excitement in Longobardo and the opponents of the terms. If they found out in Beijing, the weary Palmeiro claimed, "I will have neither life nor rest until I order them to go ahead, but I believe above all that one must go slowly here and not create occasions for disputes in places that can only be reached by treks, and very long ones at that."[79]

———

There was one final aspect of the accommodation method that Palmeiro needed to review in his reports to Rome—the China Jesuits' hidden links to Macau. It was no secret in the Ming Empire that the missionaries were

foreigners from "the West," but the connection between that nebulous occi-
dental region and the Portuguese colony at the mouth of the Pearl River was
not explicit. In order to accommodate themselves to the perceived prejudices
of their hosts, the Jesuits had attempted to avoid being linked to Macau. But
this was yet another charade of the type that Palmeiro so disliked: The China
Jesuits were constrained to feign ignorance or even disavow their compatriots
(in the case of the Portuguese) or fellow Europeans. Even when the detachment of Portuguese artillerymen was summoned from Macau at the request
of the Tianqi Emperor in 1622 and again by the Chongzhen Emperor in 1628,
the missionaries felt compelled to shun them. With evident displeasure, the
Visitor noted that his men—Longobardo, the senior court Jesuit, and João
Rodrigues, the ambassador from the Portuguese colony—could not meet in
public in Beijing, "so that it would not be believed that we have any dealings
with Macau."[80] But the men of the vice-province were in fact dependent on the
colonial outpost. Their annual salary disbursements and new recruits both
passed through Macau, not to mention the wine they used for saying masses
and many of the devotional objects they distributed to their Christians.
While it may have been a good strategy to dissimulate their links to the Portuguese in the mission's early years, in 1629 Palmeiro pondered whether the
time had not come for the China Jesuits to remove their masks and reveal
their true identities as Europeans (and Portuguese, for nearly half of them).[81]

Prudence cautioned the China Jesuits against such a move and, here again,
the Visitor was guided by pragmatism. As with so many aspects of the accommodation method, this one dealt with perceptions. Convinced that Chinese eyes would see subversion if the Jesuits dressed alike, Palmeiro ordered
his subordinates to avoid using an identical cut and color for their clothes;
the same logic led him to concede that the missionaries had to avoid being
perceived as Portuguese. His subordinates had made it clear to him that the
label "barbarian" was commonly applied to the Portuguese (and other non-
Han peoples) and that there was an undercurrent of fear in mandarin circles
about the presence of potentially hostile peoples at the empire's borders. Removing the ambiguity about the links between the missionaries and the Macanese would have exacerbated these concerns, especially in light of the fact
that several of the Jesuits had lived in China for years and knew its terrain
and defenses well. Voices in imperial officialdom did not shy away from suggesting that the priests were a fifth column, spying on behalf of foreign powers and building a shadow army to assist in the coming invasion. The facts

that the Portuguese were trading partners with the Japanese, a nation with which the Ming Empire had fought a war in Korea just a few decades before, and that some Japanese resided in Macau only made the Europeans more suspicious. In light of these preconceptions, Palmeiro asked, what would the missionaries stand to gain by any public association with Macau?

The Visitor's rules on this matter urged the Jesuits to restraint. Communication with Macau was to be kept to a minimum. Palmeiro barred them from seeking pious donations from individuals in Macau or elsewhere in the Estado da Índia and likewise prohibited them from acting as intermediaries in overseas trade. Furthermore, he ordered them not to speak to the Chinese about their superiors in Macau or even those in Rome. Exceptions could be made, but only with "great caution, and with trustworthy people," such as Xu Guangqi or Li Zhizao. His discretion was extreme. In the rulebook that he wrote for circulation to all of the vice-province's residences, he avoided mention of Japan: "The same caution should be used inside China when speaking about our superiors and the things of the East and of the companions we have there." He also included a rule urging discretion in the liturgical prayers—even though these formulations were pronounced in Latin by celebrants whose backs were to their congregations—to avoid the chance that a translation might be made known. To prevent "scandal among the Chinese, if they believe that we recognize another outside of China as king and not the one they have," Palmeiro stipulated that the prayer of the collect (which in some masses mentioned European princes) was to be changed to mention only the name of the Chinese emperor.[82]

Regardless of these precautions, there was still the problem of the Jesuits' unavoidable movements between their Chinese missions and the Portuguese colony. In the minds of imperial officials, the link would be clear if the priests were spotted traveling to Macau. Lacking alternatives, Palmeiro insisted that the vice-province rely on its brothers, most of whom were "sons of Macau"— that is, those who were born in the Portuguese colony to East Asian parents but educated by the Jesuits at the city's college. With their unremarkable countenances, these coadjutors could move throughout the Ming Empire safely, securing the yearly salaries for the missionaries and escorting new recruits into China (as Domingos Mendes had accompanied Palmeiro). The Visitor took the further precaution of stipulating that the brothers who came to conduct these exchanges were not to travel all the way to the Portuguese colony but wait in Canton for their contacts. While his stated reason for this caution was the "great risk of their being discovered", it is clear that he remembered the incident in the early 1620s when a coadjutor had to be dismissed from the Society for unseemly behavior on one such journey.[83]

For such an arrangement to work, it was imperative that there were enough "sons of Macau" within the ranks of the Chinese Jesuits. On the eve of Palmeiro's 1628 trip, there were only four such men in the vice-province, and the youngest was already thirty-four years old.[84] While the idea of creating a novitiate either in Macau or somewhere within China was not a new one by that time, to muster sufficient willpower to act had proved difficult. Although there was a group of students from Macau living at Jiading under what he deemed to be the exemplary tutelage of João Fróis, Palmeiro was not impressed with this system for training coadjutors. While he could not envision the formation of Jesuits outside of the order's educational institutions (and the only college in East Asia was the one at Macau), he understood that it was necessary to have them trained in the Chinese language within the Ming Empire. If they completed their academic and novitiate training in Macau, it would take several additional years for them to master the spoken and written Chinese necessary for their tasks as catechists or couriers. Time was of the essence for the vice-province since the training of novices inevitably tied up manpower that could be dedicated to other ministries.

In the end Palmeiro agreed with the vice-province's consultors that a more ambitious training facility should be created somewhere inside the Ming Empire, outside Macau. His rules contain a significant number of stipulations about the training of novices destined to become brothers (not priests, given the lack of a seminary inside China), who were to be drawn primarily from the ranks of the Society's Asian or Eurasian students at the Colégio de Madre de Deus.[85] Yet the lack of men available for creating a formal training corps in the China mission kept these plans on paper during Palmeiro's lifetime.

While the Visitor was contemplating the issue of how best to support the mission from Macau, events were taking place within the empire that would create new opportunities for the China Jesuits. It was right at this moment that the missionaries were offered their first commissions as astronomers and mathematicians at the imperial court, positions that came with financial rewards that could make up for the lack of funds from the Japan trade. As Palmeiro was composing his letters at Ilha Verde in 1629, the Jesuits in Beijing were beginning their work of reforming the Chinese calendar. Before leaving Hangzhou in mid-August, he had learned that Xu Guangqi had proposed this project to the throne on the basis of the missionaries' accurate prediction of the eclipse on the previous June 21.

The events at court moved swiftly: by the autumn of 1629 Xu had assumed control of the "Calendrical Bureau" and installed it in a compound situated next to the Jesuits' Beijing residence. In order to assist in the project, Li Zhizao—Dr. Leão of Palmeiro's acquaintance—had been summoned from Hangzhou, but the true motor of this "scientific" enterprise was Johann Schreck (better known as Terrentius, 1576–1630), a German polymath who had briefly been a member of the Accademia dei Lincei before joining the Society of Jesus. If the Jesuits had any claim to have sent a true exemplar of the best of early modern natural philosophy to China, it was because of Terrentius. Unlike many of the other Jesuits, whose training in "science" was limited to the year (or half year) that they spent studying Aristotle's *De Caelo* or Euclid's *Elements,* he was the genuine article: a physician, botanist, mathematician, engineer, friend of Galileo and correspondent of Kepler.[86] Palmeiro had learned of Terrentius's appointment in early 1630, relaying the news to Rome that the calendar project had been entrusted to Dr. Paulo and Dr. Leão "and some Chinese mathematicians; but the *padre* will do everything, since the Chinese know little or nothing about these matters."[87]

Palmeiro knew that this involvement at court was another gamble. Not only was calculating the calendar a matter of state, one demanding a high level of mathematical expertise, but the imperial appointment meant that two of the most prominent Chinese Christians, Li and Xu, were working in the public eye. The fate of the mission—and potentially of the "Law of God" in China—hung in the balance since failure would inevitably bring scorn (or worse) upon the Jesuits and their followers. Accordingly, the Visitor had mixed emotions. On the one hand, he recognized what a boon success would bring: "This is the greatest thing that has happened in this mission. Upon it we can build the hopes to preach our law one day with some degree of freedom." But on the other hand, the experience of persecution in Japan, China, and elsewhere cautioned him against placing his hopes on events subject to the determination of non-Christians: "Since all of these Christian communities are in heathen lands, we can only have hopes that we will have success and not security." The elusive search for legal recognition in the Ming Empire might be resolved by imperial fiat, but Palmeiro would feel no calm until the emperor himself had become Christian. In China, as elsewhere in Asia, he continued, "if the principal leaders were Christians, we would be more firmly rooted, but because they are all heathens, displeasure with one Christian turns them against our law, and the failure to receive the profits that they hoped for easily annoys them, transforming them from feigned friends into open enemies."[88] Who was to say that Xu, Li, and Terrentius would not slip up or offend other powerful figures at court at great cost not only to the Jesuit mission but to the prospects for Christianity in China?

The events of the early 1630s at the imperial court were followed at Macau with great anxiety. From Palmeiro's vantage point at the extreme southern end of the Ming Empire, the events in faraway Beijing seemed to proceed at a dizzying pace while the fate of the mission hung by a thread. Not a year had passed since Terrentius had begun to work on the calendar when he died. To add insult to injury, the man upon whose shoulders the future of the vice-province depended had perished needlessly. On 11 May, 1630, Terrentius's genius got the better of him. "He killed himself," Palmeiro confessed, "because since he was so learned in medicine, he wanted to experiment on himself a cure for a light ailment with a type of sudorific which so weakened him that it finished him." This description is vague, but it appears that Terrentius had tried a Chinese herbal remedy to induce sweating, a cure for which his body was unprepared. At the suggestion of Xu and Li, two other missionaries, Giacomo Rho and Johann Adam Schall, were summoned to the court. But Palmeiro had his misgivings about this pair of forty-year-old priests: "I fear greatly that these two will not fill the void left by Father *Joam Terencio,* and that they do not have enough knowledge of that part of mathematics which is necessary for fixing the calendar; but helping one another, perhaps they will work more, and the redoubled industry of two men will exceed the knowledge of one, even if that one was better."[89] History would prove the wisdom of the choice, but in 1631 the skills of Schall and Rho were unproven.

In addition to the events within the walls of Beijing, action taking place elsewhere in northern China was also altering the Ming Empire in ways that would obviate the need for the Visitor's cautions with regard to links between the missionaries and Macau. The incursions made by the Manchu armies beyond the Great Wall became more frequent in the early 1630s, and the ineptitude of the Ming defenders served to compound anxieties at the capital and other northern cities. Palmeiro received word from inside China in early 1630 that prices had skyrocketed at Beijing, and that imperial officials were straining to maintain order. Rumors were circulated that the Manchu armies had been scattered or destroyed but, he averred, "those who know better, know that they are false and have only been forwarded by the mandarins to calm the common folk who seek to go fishing in these turbulent waters for what is not theirs." In distant Macau, the Visitor did know of one certain victory: The Portuguese artillerymen who had been taken north by Gonçalo Teixeira Correia and João Rodrigues had succeeded in putting one Manchu raiding party to flight with their guns in early 1630. After a triumphant reception at Beijing, the Portuguese were sent back to Macau with orders to return with an infantry detachment. Fortune would have it that Xu Guangqi was appointed as Vice-Minister of War, and it was his insistence that led to the surprising approval of this novel idea (over the strident voices of detractors within the imperial bureaucracy).[90] Dr. Paulo even wrote to Palmeiro at Macau to commend him on his good advice and to reiterate the request for Portuguese troops.[91]

Xu further singled out the Portuguese Jesuit who accompanied the gunners for special praise. He specifically noted that the Chongzhen Emperor was well pleased with João Rodrigues and that it was hoped he would accompany the infantry detachment back to Beijing. There is no small irony in the fact that the former interpreter to Toyotomi Hideyoshi, a man who had been expelled from Japan for participating in an excess of intrigues, was to play the part of the deus ex machina at the China Jesuits' masquerade. While the details of Rodrigues's fourth trip into the Ming Empire await the scholarly treatment to match their level of drama, it is enough to say that Correia and Rodrigues returned to Macau, where they assembled 150 Portuguese horsemen and an equal number of infantry and servants for the task. Evaluating the Manchu menace on the basis of one encounter, Gonçalo Teixeira Correia had ventured at the court of the Chongzhen Emperor that "300 Portuguese and a few loyal Chinese would be enough to scare off the Tartars, and even to punish them in their lands."[92] On the windy plain of north China, however, this gust of bravado was lost in a mutinous storm. The Portuguese detachment that had reached Shandong Province suffered at the hands of rebellious Chinese soldiers in early 1632, an event that cost Correia his life.[93]

Fearing the consequences that were certain if the Portuguese were associated with the mutineers, Rodrigues fled with the surviving troops to Beijing. The former Japan Jesuit headed straight to the imperial palace, where he submitted a memorial in his own name to the emperor. To his colleagues who had dithered over the wording of their own text for years, Rodrigues insisted that his goal was not to jeopardize the Vice-Province of China but rather to ensure the safety of Macau, "upon whose preservation depends the commerce of the two Indias which is so important to His Majesty and the missions." In his memorial, Rodrigues declared himself to be a member of the "*Jesu hui* (that is, the Society of Jesus, which is called thus in the Chinese language), a companion of Father Matteo Ricci of the same society." By associating himself with the founder of the China mission, he made a direct connection between Macau and the Jesuits in the Ming Empire. Pulling the mask farther off the Jesuits, Rodrigues declared that his vocation (like that of the other missionaries) was "to preach the Law of God to men for their salvation, and to do good by all and to seek the people's common good, without any desire for honors, dignities, offices or money. All of these things and worldly cares I had left behind in order to serve God Our Lord, our holy law, and religious profession." Regardless of the hand-wringing of the China Jesuits over the text of their memorial to the throne, of the potential fallout from the throne's reply, and of the ambiguous relationship between the men of the vice-province and Macau, Rodrigues addressed himself to the throne with characteristic frankness "because the priests who go about inside China never had the same opportunity as I did."[94]

Fortunately for all the Jesuits, João Rodrigues's final act of diplomacy before an Asian potentate ended well, and he left the capital with due remuneration and with the honor of the Portuguese intact in the eyes of the Chongzhen Emperor. The Ministry of War further issued a statement of praise of his work in Macau (taking him, much to Palmeiro's surprise, to be the Jesuits' superior), lauding him for helping to ensure peace and tranquility in the colony on the distant Chinese frontier.[95] In other words, Rodrigues did not bring down the Vice-Province of China with his reckless memorial or his temerarious behavior. Emboldened by the news that Palmeiro had sided with him (at least in part) on the question of the disputed terms, Rodrigues also did not shy from confronting his enemies.[96] He flatly ignored the Visitor's rules for the vice-province (which did not apply to him, since he was a member of the Province of Japan) by visiting temples with his interpreter for the sole purpose of challenging the Buddhist clergy to debates. According to Alfonso Vagnone—from whom Rodrigues would hear no kind words—he showed bad form in these debates, drawing ire and insults that led the Portuguese soldiers to remark that he "had once caused the downfall of the Japan

mission, and had now come to bring down the China mission."[97] Such head-
aches were most likely the reason why Palmeiro only gave a terse one-sentence
mention of Rodrigues's death at Macau in 1633 in a letter written the following year.[98]

For all that, the Visitor regretted the loss of Rodrigues. After all, he had
taught Palmeiro a valuable lesson: The "political" methods of the China Jesuits could safely be abandoned. That is, the aspects of the accommodation
method that Palmeiro found inappropriate for the members of the Society
were not crucial to the survival of the mission. Rodrigues never wore silk, he
never asserted that the teachings of the Chinese literati were roughly equivalent to those of Christianity, and he never denied that he was a Portuguese
priest—yet he still enjoyed the respect of the Ming officials with whom he
interacted. Putting aside the fear of offending the Chinese, he spoke candidly
of his mission in China. While Rodrigues might not have won any souls
among the members of the Buddhist or Daoist priesthood, at least those who
saw him debate or learned about his performance knew that he was an adversary of the indigenous clergy. If he could do all of these things in such a blunt
manner without reprisals, what could the men of the vice-province do with
their greater knowledge of China?

It was reassuring for Palmeiro to learn that the China mission did not
hang by a thread—to be sure, more pressing concerns over legions of Manchus pushed any mandarin worries over the handful of Europeans far into
the background—and that, in fact, the news from the men inside the Ming
Empire about the growth of the mission church had never been better.[99] Ordered by the Visitor to conform less to the culture of Ming literati, themselves on the verge of being cast from their pedestal by the invading Manchus, the Jesuits moved out with greater boldness into the mission field and
ushered in the longest period of growth in the history of their enterprise.[100]

9

Sunrise in the West

Ill winds blew through Macau in the late 1620s and early 1630s. The southwest monsoon brought word of struggles and setbacks in the new mission fields in Southeast Asia, while its northeast counterpart carried reports of the final destruction of the Japanese church as well as its flotsam. And to the north, the winds of war gathered in intensity as they prepared to blow across the Ming Empire, where episodes of famine, disease, and peasant revolts were becoming commonplace. The Portuguese colony that had prospered on the peaceful exchanges with various ports around the China Seas found itself battered by gusts from all sides, and its potential for survival repeatedly called into question. Yet if the merchants of Macau found themselves dangerously exposed to these storms, the Jesuits were in an even more perilous position. The Portuguese traders largely remained in coastal regions while the Society's men were deployed far inland, where they risked being cut off from their superiors and their sustenance. Palmeiro's final charge would therefore be to hold together the Jesuits' enterprises, protecting his men from the moral and physical hazards that arose in the tempest.

The Visitor faced a daunting logistical challenge. He had to provide for his men both in the colony and throughout the far-flung East and Southeast Asian missions with dwindling revenues. During the boom years of the silk-silver trade to Japan, the Jesuits could rely upon the largesse of pious benefactors for their temporal needs as well as on the Society's stake in that traffic. The Jesuits' prosperity was directly proportional to that of Macau itself since they were dependent on others for their welfare: their consignments of silk traveled on the colony's fleets, and their profits in silver were reinvested in the colony's commerce. Such an arrangement was felicitous for the clergy in Macau, since the port city had none of the standard resources such as fields, villages, or plantations with which orders were endowed elsewhere. But the sailings of the fleets to Nagasaki had become less frequent in the 1620s.[1] And there was no doubt about it: the end of the Japan trade would be calamitous for the future of the Society's missions in East Asia.

The Jesuits' procurators had been shrewd managers of their investments over the years, working under the assumption that the traffic between Macau and Nagasaki would continue to prosper even if persecution reduced their proselytizing activities in Japan to naught. They did not expect that the Portuguese traders would meet the same fate that had befallen the Catholic clergy, who were expelled from Japan in 1614 by shogunal fiat. A dozen years after that, however, it seemed that Macau's links to Nagasaki were becoming increasingly tenuous. Indeed, one of the shogunal commissioners who governed that Kyushu entrepôt was reported in 1626 to have remarked that the trade with Macau was "hanging by a hair."[2] Although another thirteen years would pass before the cessation of trade between the Portuguese colony and Japan, signs of trouble were evident. European rivals, primarily the Dutch in the Indonesian archipelago, increasingly disrupted Macau's commerce, and the shifting attitudes of Japanese rulers changed the terms of Portuguese trade yearly. As a result, the colony's merchants (and their Jesuit clients) were increasingly isolated from their sources of revenue. "Nearly four years I have been in Macau," wrote Palmeiro in late 1629 about the Portuguese fleets, "and in none of them has there been a voyage without incident. Only one fleet arrived from India in this whole time, and it brought only a paltry sum; and in these most recent years, there has not only been no money, but no ships have come at all."[3]

One question stood out above the others in the Visitor's mind: What would happen if the stream of silver that had flowed for nearly three-quarters of a century aboard Portuguese ships dried up completely before another fount was discovered? Recent events did not bode well, and Palmeiro's vision of the future without these resources was dim. Regardless of how good the Society's procurators had proved to be at making do with little, he worried that for

"such a great machine," *nem remendo, nem remedio há,* that is, there was neither repair nor remedy.[4] Worse still, the downturn in trade had created torpor
among the merchants of Macau. Lacking their annual renewal of capital, they
were discouraged from investing in new routes to replace the old ones. But
the Jesuits had already begun new missions in Southeast Asia, and they desperately needed the help of local merchants to send fleets to the West if they
were to keep in touch with their brethren. Abandoning the missions was just
as unthinkable as abandoning Macau itself; unlike the colony's other inhabitants, they could not depart to seek their fortunes elsewhere in the Portuguese empire. Vowed to stay put, the men of the Society were committed to
preserving their enterprises—to the last man, as in the case of Japan—so Palmeiro had to find new ways for keeping the missions afloat.

Two years after his first arrival in Macau, the Visitor decided to take matters
into his own hands. In order to safeguard the missions, he needed to break
away from the relationship of dependency with inconstant laymen. There
would be no more waiting around for the Portuguese merchants to offer the
Jesuits transportation to the mission fields or a means for getting their goods
to market. If the colony's traders were unwilling or unable to outfit ships capable of traveling to the regions where the Jesuits needed to go, then Palmeiro
would do it himself. So in 1628 he approved the purchase of a ship in the
Society's name that would sail between Macau and mainland Southeast Asia.
This craft would not only create a new communications link with his subordinates; the sale of its cargoes would also produce cash to sustain the missions. Despite the risky nature of this enterprise, Palmeiro was committed to
making it work. When the first ship that he obtained was wrecked near the
Philippines in 1628, he acquired another vessel; and so on as the years went
by, in order to sustain the missions. Based on indirect references in the Visitor's correspondence, it appears that the Jesuits eventually acquired three or
four ships before his death in 1635.[5] Contemporary sources refer to these vessels as *cho,* that is, a large junk-type vessel, typically used along the coasts of
mainland Southeast Asia.[6]

Palmeiro did not make this decision lightly, for it carried grave moral consequences. Professed religious were not supposed to engage in trade. As far as
they were concerned, speculation was reserved for theology. Moreover, the
Jesuits in East Asia had long been dogged by accusations that they had aban-

doned their vows of poverty for the pursuit of riches. Already during the time of Alessandro Valignano, the mere involvement of the Jesuits in the silk trade—that is, the consignment of cargoes on the yearly fleets sent from Macau and the brokering of silk in conjunction with Portuguese merchants

FIGURE 9.1. Sketch of various types of boats seen in the vicinity of Macau in 1637 by the English traveler Peter Mundy (ca. 1597–ca. 1667). The *cho,* or seagoing vessel, purchased by Palmeiro for the Society's traffic with Tonkin and Cochinchina would have been similar to the ship at the top right or center left. The large ship at the top is a naval vessel rather than a merchant ship.

at Nagasaki—had provoked scandal in Asia and Europe. But Valignano had brushed aside the naysayers' qualms *ad maiorem Dei gloriam* and had secured permission from Rome for the Society's procurators in Macau to obtain revenues from commerce for the expanding missions.[7] Palmeiro's conscience was thus not troubled by the continuance of that business, but the innovations that he permitted in 1628 were a different matter. While he insisted on bearing the responsibility for the Jesuits' trading activities (instead of placing that burden on the shoulders of the college's procurators), he was clearly disturbed.[8] It is therefore unsurprising that the Visitor's letters repeatedly invoke his reservations: "We were forced to outfit it," he wrote in reference to the first of the ships, "despite the inconveniences of our having our own vessel, because it carries cargo plainly for all to see and conducts trade in the public eye."[9] Palmeiro's decisions had placed the Jesuits' reputation on the line in a more risky manner than his predecessors' choices. He had, in short, created a commercial enterprise wholly owned and controlled by the Society of Jesus.

The Visitor may have been the last man ever to worry about gambling in Macau. And worry he did. Writing after the loss of the first ship, he lamented that he and his brethren were "forced to go about as merchants," and even so this dubious disguise did not provide them with enough to live on.[10] And in 1630 he voiced further concerns to Muzio Vitelleschi: "We can neither write to explain, nor can Your Paternity fully understand the labors that we must undertake to raise what is necessary for the missions in this city, or the inconveniences and indecency of the trade in which we engage, all of which are difficult to exaggerate." The fact that it was "the custom of the city" made their trade seem less strange, Palmeiro offered, "and knowing that we have reached this point out of respect for the service due to God is the only thing that can make it honorable."[11]

The unease nevertheless lingered. By 1633, five years after Palmeiro had purchased his first ship, he again raised the subject of the Jesuits' role in trade when corresponding with Rome. He was acutely aware of its cost to the Society's honor, especially when one of his ships sailed into Macau's harbor—"all cast their eyes upon it and declare that everything aboard belongs to the *Companhia.*" As if to mitigate the affront to clerical dignity for which he was responsible, he asserted that "everyone in this city does it, bishops, religious, parish priests, and confraternities, and others because there is no other way to raise what is necessary for living." It was hollow consolation, however, to point fingers at others in order to justify one's own actions, and there was one significant caveat that Palmeiro felt obliged to confess: Only the richest of the merchants of Macau owned vessels. Of course, he claimed that the *chos* outfitted by the Jesuits were "not among the largest ships, nor of the type that well-off merchants usually send." Even after half of a decade in the shipping business, Palmeiro had not conformed his conscience to necessity: the (now several) ships were "shocking, and can be dispensed with, even though the reasons that we have for sending them are so justified."[12] His confreres apparently agreed, and the Jesuit ships continued to sail long after Palmeiro's death in 1635.[13]

Beyond the moral problems raised by the Jesuits' involvement in trade, the Visitor was concerned with its many physical risks. The necessary evil that he had to accept involved borrowing money or selling assets from the procurator's resources at the College of Macau for investment in trade goods bought at Canton. Profits were uncertain, a fact that generated considerable anxiety during the months of waiting for vessels to make their round trips across the South China Sea. Among the greatest dangers was the presence of Dutch fleets in regional waters seeking to capture prizes. Palmeiro remarked that in 1627 and 1628, almost all of the Portuguese ships ran aground attempting to flee from these European rivals.[14] Even without the Dutch menace, other perils abounded. In 1630s the Visitor offered the following formulation of the challenges that he faced:

> We live with the fear of not having enough to live on. If it is time for the ship to sail, the storms at sea torment us on land because if they provoke its loss, they also cause the loss of our remedy. Beyond the risks of the winds, there are so many other dangers in these seas, such as pirates and shoals. And there are others upon the land among the Chinese, who, once they have our cash in hand in order to buy goods, either go bankrupt or pretend to be bankrupt. In sum, we always go about feeling the pain of present losses or fearing future ones.[15]

Despite the constant worry that involvement in trade provoked, Palmeiro's decisions and the talented stewardship of the provincial procurators kept the Society solvent. A mixture of loans and investments produced a stream of revenue, but little information about these deals has survived. The view of Jesuit trade in Palmeiro's day is likewise hazy. There are no detailed descriptions of the cargoes placed aboard the Visitor's ships or the investments made by Giovanni Battista Bonelli, who was procurator in the late 1620s, but the general outlines of their trade emerge from scattered references. Working through brokers at Canton, the Jesuits purchased goods and had them shipped to the storerooms attached to the College of Macau. Eighteenth-century descriptions report that the procurator's lodgings and warehouse were "after the church, the greatest thing at the college."[16] Originally built for coordinating the silk and silver cargoes of the Nagasaki run, the procuratorate was repurposed in Palmeiro's day for trade in a different direction. It was here that the procurator handled his dealings with local merchants and outfitted the Society's vessels bound for ports in mainland Southeast Asia.

Palmeiro mentions that the principal goods shipped from Macau on his ships were porcelain and silks, but specific information is scarce. António de Fontes (1589–after 1655), a missionary in Hanoi, described how one of the vessels got stuck on a sandbank as it traveled up the Red River to the court of Tonkin during a storm in the early summer of 1631. As the waves crashed, "much porcelain was lost, broken with the swaying and the great smacks against the ship, along with other trifles which were damaged and lost."[17] Drawing on their long experience in the silk trade with Japan, the Jesuits also sent cargoes of this precious fabric to Southeast Asian ports. In 1633 Palmeiro mentioned that his procurator negotiated silk, and that his ships were eagerly awaited by merchants and potentates alike in the region's courts. He also indicated that the ships returning from those regions brought back other types of silk or other fine textiles as well as benzoin, a fragrant resin.[18] It is likely that the Society's ships also carried silver, gold, cotton, and bronze coins called *caixas,* but Jesuit sources from the late 1620s and early 1630s do not mention these trade goods specifically.[19]

With this open participation in trade, the Visitor was obliged to work in concert with the procurator so as to defend this official from the scorn of onlookers in the colony or even his brethren at the college. To the surprise of some of his subordinates, among whom he was known for his desire for seclusion and contemplation, Palmeiro exerted himself in the early 1630s in building up relations with the local merchant community. He made yearly visits to the Society's various benefactors as well as to civic institutions such as the *Senado da Câmara,* the city council, and the charitable *Misericórdia* brotherhood at Christmas. And he was remembered after his death for his gift at reconciling two especially fractious groups, the crown officials and the representatives of the *Senado,* "which only he could resolve with his many talents and the authority that he had."[20] Palmeiro's engagement with these groups was not simply because of his desire to see other parties take over the responsibility for sending trading ships but also because as one group among other traders, the Jesuits necessarily created new rivalries. One Macau merchant originally from Braga, Francisco Carvalho Aranha, mentions how he enjoyed Palmeiro's friendship and that the Visitor readily shared the news that he received from Portugal in his personal correspondence.[21]

Such gestures made the Society's trading more palatable to others in the colony, but the same scruples that affected Palmeiro were more strongly felt by those who lived within the college. The Visitor described how, upon his return from inside the Ming Empire in late 1629, he heard a chorus of complaints about the debts that Procurator Bonelli had incurred in order to invest in trade. Here Palmeiro waxed almost poetic about the need for his brethren to overcome their reservations about the procurator's task, given that the survival of the Jesuits' missions was at stake: "During my absence, there were some who found it strange that the procurator had run up debts, but they are shocked at what they do not understand. In that line of work, nothing can be reaped if nothing is sown, or risked. It is true that the sowing is done on the waves of the sea, and that it is as risky as it is profitable. But what is to be done, since here we have no other fields to plow that will produce a harvest abundant enough for so many? It is a great evil, but a necessary one."[22]

———————

If such a zealous guardian of the Society's honor as Palmeiro was willing to risk opprobrium (and potentially the wages of sin) by engaging in trade, he was certainly driven by a powerful motivation. The Visitor pinned his hopes on the possibility for success in Southeast Asia. In that region's uncultivated mission fields, he thought his men might replicate the gains that had once been made in Japan and swiftly surpass those attained thus far in China. His decision to turn the Macau Jesuits toward the west was among the most important strategic moves that he made during his tenure in East Asia. Palmeiro's arrival at the Portuguese colony in 1626, twelve years after the order of expulsion of all Catholic priests from Japan, came at the moment when the hopes for recovering that country's church were fading and when the Province of Japan was in need of realignment. Instead of permitting his men to end their days pining away for their former mission fields, the Visitor devoted the available resources to creating new ones.

In Southeast Asia, the six kingdoms of Tonkin, Cochinchina, Champa, Cambodia, Laos, and Siam, as well as the Chinese backwater of Hainan Island, were little known to the Jesuits. Members of the mendicant orders had ventured from Manila to all of these regions except Laos and Hainan in the late sixteenth century, but the friars had not been able to create durable missions. Focused as they were on Japan and, to a much lesser extent, China for over half a century, the men of the Society had largely ignored the potential for spreading Christianity in mainland Southeast Asia. But prompted by the first waves of Japanese exiles to head for the region's coastal cities, in 1615 some former missionaries from Japan followed their dispersed flock to Cochinchina (Dang Trong, the southern central regions of Vietnam). And starting in the mid-1620s a handful of Jesuits from Macau would seek other communities of exiles in Cambodia, Siam, and Tonkin (Dang Ngoai, the northern regions of Vietnam). Biding their time in the foreign quarters of the region's port cities, some of the missionaries began to study the languages of the indigenous peoples and attempted to proselytize. Much to their surprise, the return on this investment was considerable. Reports of thousands of conversions, especially in Cochinchina and Tonkin in the late 1620s, encouraged the Visitor to shift some of his manpower resources toward these regions. The news also prodded him to consider areas that the Jesuits had not yet visited, such as Champa, Laos, and Hainan, and to elaborate plans for creating new missions in each.

Palmeiro's decision to allocate men and money to these missions was of the greatest significance for the spread of Christianity in Southeast Asia. Just as his predecessor Alessandro Valignano had acted as the godfather for the China mission, sending men and money to establish a diplomatic bridgehead in Canton in 1579, so Palmeiro fostered the growth of the enterprises to the west. Without his insistence on sending yearly missions and his demand that Jesuits engage with local potentates in order to secure approval for their activities, the missionaries' influence might have been limited to the dwindling numbers of Japanese exiles living among other merchant sojourners. Here again, as at the time when he had contemplated the coast of East Africa for routes to its interior, Palmeiro assumed the role of grand strategist. Using information collected from merchants and from the first missionaries to Cochinchina, as well as the basic notions of the region's cartography that circulated in Macau, he drew up a list of destinations for prospecting. First came a redoubled effort in Cochinchina, where a decade of sporadic Jesuit visits had stimulated hopes, then Siam and Tonkin, and so on, with the Jesuits' sallies from Macau expanding to other areas as the years progressed. By the end of Palmeiro's tenure as Visitor, the Society's Province of Japan would primarily consist of mission stations spread across Southeast Asia.

Crucially, as had been the case during his time in India, Palmeiro had a diplomatic corps at his disposal. This was especially true once some of the

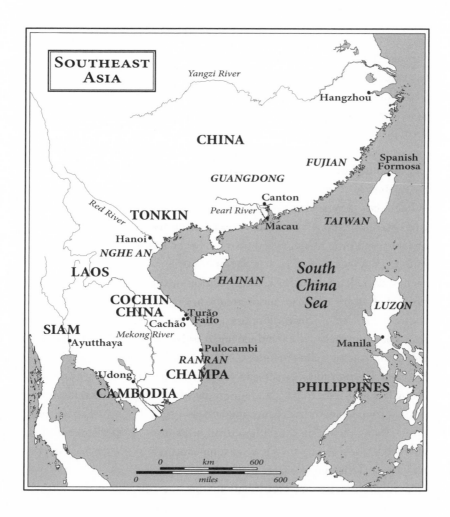

missionaries had learned the local languages or at least had identified inter-
preters whom they could trust. But in contrast to the Society's diplomatic
activities in South Asia, the Visitor's men in Southeast Asia primarily served
their order rather than the King or his viceroys. It was Palmeiro's goal to assess the area's different polities, gauging how likely it was for the Jesuits to
gain permission to reside in each, and how apt their inhabitants appeared for
accepting the Christian message. Upon receiving favorable responses to his
subordinates' prospecting journeys, he committed financial resources to acquiring luxury goods for the obligatory gift exchanges involved in diplomacy
and to endowing residences for the men selected for the new missions. The
Visitor's office at the College of Macau thus became a court in its own right, the
administrative center where trade and diplomacy were coordinated for nearly
a decade. It was also the destination to which correspondence and annual letters came from around the South China Sea, writings borne upon the same
Jesuit ships that carried the cargoes that were vital for supporting the missions. In sum, as head of his own trading company and leader of a diplomatic
corps that was received at a succession of courts across Southeast Asia, "Father
Visitor" became known as a minor potentate.

Undaunted by the frequent setbacks in these ventures, Palmeiro willed
the creation of a large new mission area that would flourish for over a century.
While this is not the place to detail the early evolution of the Jesuits' Southeast Asian missions—a story that still awaits a full scholarly treatment—a
brief survey of the region in Palmeiro's day and of the Visitor's methods is
in order.[23] As mentioned earlier, the first missionaries to the area followed
their scattered Japanese flock to the Vietnamese coast. There they found
two kingdoms in a state of intermittent war: The house of Trinh ruled over
the northern region from their court at Hanoi (called Ke Cho in Jesuit
sources), while their rivals from the house of Nguyen were sovereign in Cochinchina. The two clans vied for control of the lands nominally ruled over
by the Le Dynasty, but neither was able to win a decisive victory in the half-
century of hostilities that began in 1627. Cochinchina had several important
trading centers, including Faifo (modern Hoi An), Turão (Tourane; modern Da Nang), and Pulocambi (modern Qui Nhon), where merchants from
across Maritime Asia converged. Farther south along the coast, the remnants of the kingdom of Champa, which had flourished centuries previously,
enjoyed the independence of isolation from the concerns of its northern
neighbors.[24]

The Mekong River valley stretched inland toward the kingdom of Cambodia, a polity that had regained its autonomy from the Siamese rulers of Ayutthaya in the preceding decades. Upriver from Cambodia was the kingdom of Laos, a land separated from the Vietnamese coast by the long north–south mountain range that served as a porous cultural border between areas of Indian and Chinese influence. Still farther to the west was Siam, the dominant political force in the central part of mainland Southeast Asia during the seventeenth century despite its repeated struggles against the Cambodians and the Burmese.[25] All of these polities, with the exception of remote Laos, had been visited by Portuguese and Castilian traders during the late sixteenth and early seventeenth centuries—and most famously Fernão Mendes Pinto, whose tale of swashbuckling adventures was one of the most widely read books in early modern Europe. To be sure, the port cities of Southeast Asia had received foreign traders from around the region and beyond for generations, long before the Europeans arrived in the area.[26]

The long-standing patterns of trade in Southeast Asian emporia made Palmeiro's task easier, since the Jesuits could readily incorporate themselves among other outsiders. Securing sanction for proselytizing activities was a greater challenge, as was the engagement with indigenous rulers outside the formalized routines of trade or diplomacy. But the Visitor was confident. He trusted the abilities of his men, convinced that their linguistic gifts and persistence would permit them to get beyond the language barriers. Success, however, was not always certain.

The mission to Siam offers a good example of the challenges faced by the Jesuits. Six months prior to Palmeiro's arrival in the Portuguese colony, in early 1626, Pedro Morejón, António Francisco Cardim (ca. 1596–1659), and Romão Nishi (1567–1639) had sailed from Macau to Ayutthaya to negotiate for the release of a number of Spanish captives. While Morejón's diplomatic goals provided the primary reason for their journey, Jesuit sources make it clear that Nishi was sent to minister to the city's Japanese Christians while Cardim was to dedicate himself to learning the language in order to form a new *christandade*.[27] Although Nishi met with success, Cardim did not, despite the strides he made in the Thai language. To make matters worse, the confrere sent by Palmeiro to assist them, Giulio Cesare Margico (b. 1586), was poisoned in unknown circumstances in 1630. So meager was the Siamese harvest that Palmeiro approved its abandonment: In 1632 Nishi departed for Cambodia to minister to the Japanese Christians in that country.[28]

The Jesuits who traveled to Cochinchina and Tonkin met with slightly more success in spreading the Christian message, if not in guaranteeing permission for permanent residence or permission for their activities. The enterprise in Cochinchina began in 1615, but it grew very slowly despite the reports of significant numbers of conversions in Turão, Faifo, Cachão (Quang Nam garrison, close to Faifo), and Pulocambi. A handful of Jesuits had worked in these ports sporadically for a decade, but they were repeatedly expelled from their mission stations to other regions, such as the extreme southern area of Ranran (modern Phu Yen Province), or obliged to return to Macau.

When Palmeiro arrived at the Portuguese colony, their longest serving veteran was Francesco Buzomi (1575–1639), a priest who had been one of the first pair of Jesuits to visit the region. By the late 1620s the missionaries appeared to have won a degree of acceptance from the king, Nguyen Phuc Nguyen (r. 1613–1635), and his provincial officials, permitting them to staff all four of their residences with eight priests and two brothers. Despite this approval of their presence, official pronouncements against proselytizing indigenous people were issued that at times amounted to house arrest. The mission's center was Faifo, where in 1628 and 1629 there were four priests and a coadjutor. Since the missionaries lived among foreigners in this port, the Visitor took care to send the remaining Japanese priests and brothers from Macau to serve among their countrymen there, with the objective of reclaiming the exiles who had apostatized. The other Jesuits, who turned their attentions to the local populace, claimed scores of baptisms; in 1628 they recorded 404, and the following year 865.[29] But the missionaries experienced a reversal of fortune in 1630, when the royal mood soured over their failure to ensure that a shipment of prized medicinal herbs from China reached the Nguyen court. And when they proved incapable of paying bribes to hostile officials, the misdeeds of Portuguese pirates off the coast of Cochinchina offered the pretext for expelling the Jesuits.[30] In spite of this royal order, two of the missionaries, the Japanese priest Matias Machida (1581–1634) and mission superior Manuel Fernandes (1588–1634), remained in hiding at Faifo.[31]

News of similar qualified advances reached Palmeiro from Tonkin. The first Jesuit prospecting visit to that region took place in the year prior to his arrival in Macau, but the decision to allocate the resources necessary for starting a new mission was the Visitor's. In the springtime of 1627 Palmeiro appointed a veteran of the Japan mission, Pêro Marques (1576–1657), and a younger companion who had learned the Vietnamese language during visits to Cochinchina, Alexandre de Rhodes (1593–1660), to sail to the court at Hanoi with gifts for the king. Marques's first report told of their reception by Trinh Trang (r. 1623–1654), who was en route to campaign (unsuccessfully) against the Nguyen lords, and of the challenges encountered by the pair from the indigenous clergy and suspicious royal officials. The missionary nonetheless asserted that the Tonkinese "universally held foreigners in esteem, praising our things and disparaging their own."[32] Whether or not this was an important factor in the transmission of his religious message, Rhodes's preaching attracted not only attention at court but also a handful of high-status converts. Indeed, a member of the royal household was among the more than 1,200 baptisms reported by the Jesuits after their first year in the country. All did not proceed smoothly, however. When word reached the king's ears that zealous Christian neophytes had smashed devotional objects belonging to their former religion, the missionaries were confined to their quarters in Hanoi and, in the spring of 1629, expelled from the court toward exile in Cochinchina. But even when they were kept under house arrest and later banished from the court city, Rhodes and Marques kept up their work of proselytizing and recorded hundreds of conversions.[33]

The fact that the missionaries had arrived at the Tonkinese court in the company of Portuguese traders created an inseparable link between the two in the mind of the Trinh lord: The monarch was eager to conduct trade in order to sustain his struggle against the Nguyen. As such, the Jesuits would come to understand that their permission to reside in Tonkin was predicated on the regular arrival of the ship from Macau. When the vessel failed to arrive in 1628 or 1629—owing to a lack of Portuguese willing to outfit an expedition—the king decreed that the priests would have to return to the colony. Even the arrival of Palmeiro's ship with another pair of Jesuits at the end of 1629 was not enough to sway the sovereign to let them remain in his lands, and so the missionaries were forced to abandon the 5,602 converts they claimed to have made during their three-year stay, or, rather, to entrust them to their native catechists.[34] Yet by the time the priests returned on another trading ship in 1631, the number of converts had swelled by another 3,300, thanks to the efforts of these lay auxiliaries. Fortunately for the Jesuits, the royal mood had shifted, and Trinh Trang was pleased with the gifts of a pair of eyeglasses (plucked from a missionary's nose) and a mechanical clock sent by Palmeiro (repeatedly broken by the king's constant winding).[35] But it appeared that what had really occasioned this change of the king's heart was the hope that he might receive the same reward from Macau that he had heard awaited the Chongzhen Emperor at Beijing: a detachment of Portuguese soldiers equipped with artillery to rout his Nguyen adversaries. Upon learning that this was but a pipe dream, Trinh Trang "went completely cold," wrote António de Fontes, "and there was soon no lack of voices at court telling him that if we could not provide him this service, then he should not want us to be in his kingdom." Apparently, only the threat that the *Padre Grande*—that is, Father Visitor—might not send his ship back to Tonkin convinced the king to let a pair of Jesuits remain.[36]

The vagaries of the missionary presence in northern and central Vietnam prompted Palmeiro to consider sending men to still other parts of Southeast Asia. Despite the fact that the incipient missions in Cochinchina and Tonkin had reported tallies of conversions in just over a decade that the China enterprise had only claimed after half a century—a factor that convinced him to sustain the newer missions at great cost to the Society's honor—the Visitor had not exhausted the possibility of finding a spiritual El Dorado. On the ship that headed to Cochinchina from Macau in 1629, Palmeiro had sent orders for one of his men to visit the kingdom of Champa. The order of expulsion against the Jesuits in Turão, Cachão, and Faifo the following year offered an opportunity for such a venture, but the three missionaries who sailed to Champa wound up being treated as captives rather than diplomats. Only one of their number, Buzomi, managed to get away in the guise of an ambassador from that kingdom's sovereign to the king of Cambodia. The affair that at length brought Buzomi to Macau, about which more will be said later, convinced Palmeiro that proselytizing in Champa was fruitless. He would come to believe the same about Cambodia, where Matias Machida headed in 1631 after his clandestine pastoral work at Faifo was exposed. "It could be that his journey will be more effective than when our European men go," wrote the Visitor about this Japanese priest, "because those people give very little hope of producing fruit. Four Dominican friars were there for the past two years, and they made no progress, and in the end they left for Manila."[37]

The two final frontiers in the region for the Jesuits were Hainan Island and Laos. The shipping lanes from Macau to mainland Southeast Asia passed close to Hainan, but the impetus for sending missionaries to the island came from within the Ming Empire. In the wake of the disaster that ended the Portuguese military expedition to China in 1632, a military mandarin to whom contemporary sources refer as "Dr. Paulo", who was charged with escorting the remaining troops home and then heading to his post in Hainan, visited Palmeiro at the College of Macau. This Chinese Christian, the son of a convert who had been baptized by Matteo Ricci, begged the Visitor to appoint a priest to accompany him. Reluctant to let this opportunity slip by, Palmeiro selected Pêro Marques (although this Jesuit had no training in Chinese) along with a Chinese coadjutor to act as an interpreter.[38] The mission to Hainan would only begin to flourish, however, after Marques was replaced by a priest from within China with the requisite language skills.[39]

By contrast, Palmeiro had a long-standing desire to evaluate the most remote of all of the Southeast Asian lands, Laos, but he lacked an opportunity for sending one of his subordinates there. Already in 1631 he remarked to the superior general in Rome that the recent peace between the Cambodians and the Laotians might permit a Jesuit to travel far up the Mekong. "What is most important to know is if they are as boorish as those of Champa and Cambodia", the Visitor opined, because that would make them unworthy of further investments of men, money, and time, not to mention the fact that even more trading activity would be necessary if the Jesuits were to gather the necessary resources. With the priests in Cambodia focusing their efforts on the exiled Japanese community in that country, it seemed better to try another approach, so Palmeiro elected to send António Francisco Cardim to Tonkin to inquire about Laos from the traders who crossed the mountains to the southwest of Hanoi.[40] But Cardim's excessive melancholy and bad health (attributes he shared with his saintly brother, João Cardim, whom Palmeiro had known in Braga) obliged his colleagues to send him back to Macau, and it is unclear if Palmeiro received before his death the news gathered by the Tonkin Jesuits from a Vietnamese Christian who journeyed to the kingdom in 1634.[41] In the end, Palmeiro's project was only realized in 1642, when Giovanni Maria Leria (1597–1665) became the first European to visit Laos, if only for a brief stay.[42]

The Visitor had cast his net wide across Southeast Asia, but it appeared that the only promising regions were Tonkin and Cochinchina. His enthusiasm for these missions, however, did not mask the problems that arose along with the swift march of the faith. If anything, the quick pace of baptisms was the silver lining to the cloud of problems that hovered over these new enterprises; they were statistics that served to justify Palmeiro's decisions before the

Society's Roman curia. Yet the Visitor was nothing if not candid in the assessments that he sent to the superior general, and he did not obscure his frustrations. Beyond the logistical and diplomatic stumbling blocks that needed to be overcome in Southeast Asia, there were also challenges related to the development of the missions as religious enterprises. In contrast to the missions in Japan and China, Palmeiro assumed control over them just after the moment of their inception. He did not travel to Vietnam, however, to see how his subordinates were carrying out their proselytizing activities, nor how they were organizing their new Christian communities. His "visit" was done remotely from Macau, meaning that he had to rely on the initiative and judgment of the priests in the field for enacting sensible policies. But as we have seen elsewhere in this study, zeal was not always accompanied by rationality. From the mission field came disconcerting news, signs that the new enterprises were drifting off course.

One of the most important problems that Palmeiro detected in Vietnam concerned the trajectory of the developing mission church. Specifically, he was concerned that his subordinates had concentrated too much on making conversions and too little on administering the sacraments and explaining the obligations of the faith. While the tally of baptisms was of great importance to missionaries and their superiors alike, it was not sufficient. The moment of conversion for adults, or the baptism of infants and children, was properly meant as the beginning of what was intended to be a long process of spiritual and moral development. Over time, through the regular reception of the sacraments, the newly converted would progress along a path toward greater conformity with the behavioral norms of other (it is understood European) Catholic Christians. But what if the priests responsible for guiding them failed to offer those sacraments, or failed to insist on the necessity of frequenting church rituals? Palmeiro, for one, could envision the consequences of such omissions, so—suspecting that they had already occurred in Vietnam just over a decade after its missions had begun—he wrote to alert Rome and took steps to remedy the situation.

In the spring of 1628, before he outfitted the ship for Faifo, the Visitor held consultations in Macau with some of the more experienced men from the Cochinchina mission. His inquiries led him to the conclusion that the Jesuits had taken it upon themselves to alter the forms for administering the sacraments, at times dispensing with parts of the rituals altogether. By consequence, they were permitting their Vietnamese neophytes to practice a debased form of Catholicism, stripped down for the sake of expediency. "It is with great ease that our men leave aside the administration of the sacraments," Palmeiro confided to the superior general, "as well as some ceremonies which, although they are not essential, are nonetheless customary and expected by the church." Getting down to specifics, he reported that they made little use of holy oils at baptism ("and not just in villages far from our residences"), and that they infrequently, if at all, administered extreme unction. Palmeiro felt that these were inexcusable omissions, and he urged Rome to insist that the Jesuits should adhere as closely as possible to European ritual norms in the mission field.[43]

For trained theologians such as professed Jesuits, these were not trifling matters. The sacraments were, from the perspective of Palmeiro and his confreres, the necessary preconditions for salvation, that is, the human end of the eternal bargain made with Christ. And the salvation of souls was the whole reason for the Jesuits' presence overseas. While the priests in the mission fields no doubt felt justified in their choices to adapt rituals to their specific cultural contexts, concentrating first on what they deemed essential and introducing the complete forms of the sacraments by degrees, Palmeiro demurred. He had spent far too many years teaching Aquinas's interpretations of the sacraments at Coimbra to accept that their form and content could be so easily altered.

But it was not simply Palmeiro's anger that the priests who chose to alter the form of the sacraments needed to avoid. Other eyes were also focused on the Jesuits' missions. The Society's rivals would not hesitate to denounce them to the secular church authorities if they learned that the Jesuits strayed from established norms or permitted deviations among their Christians. The Jesuits' long history of disputes with the friars who administered the diocese of Macau (and controlled the archdiocese of Goa) was reason enough for Palmeiro to want to prevent new scandals. In 1628, with the matter of the bishop of Japan's excommunication by the archbishop of Goa over the contested administration of the see of Macau still unsettled, the Visitor's default position was to keep his men from attracting undue scrutiny. He therefore urged the superior general to command the Jesuits all across Asia to refrain from innovations in matters of church law. Palmeiro's suggested rule was that "in these *christandades,* and those in India, they should accommodate themselves as much as possible to the norms used among the Christians of Europe and those which are observed in the cities of the East where prelates reside."

Such an order from Rome would not simply be a good preventive policy, he contended, it was essential for the future of the Society's missions. In order to avoid giving their rivals valid reasons to accuse them, the Jesuits should toe the line instead of adapting at will as they had done. Putting his finger directly on the problem that would haunt the Jesuits in Asia for decades to come, he wrote: "It arises from these choices that when the members of other orders or even secular priests go at times to our Christian communities, they say that we want to be popes there and that we are creating a new church."[44]

Palmeiro's conscience was troubled by the accusations, yet he knew these were not simple issues. He admitted that his men were guilty as charged on some counts because he had proof that in the mission fields they "either remove or change the ordinary ceremonies." While he was certain that some of these changes in Cochinchina were the result of carelessness, he was equally sure that others were not. Most disconcertingly, Palmeiro confided to the superior general, some priests "very easily change or leave out points of positive law, as if it was within their power or discretion to accept or reject what they will."[45] This mention of *direito positivo* indicated that his concerns were not so much related to divine precepts mentioned in sacred scripture but to the norms of Christian behavior that had been established over the centuries by popes and theologians, and reaffirmed by church councils. Such things were not to be changed by whim, not even in the nascent mission fields.

There were, however, certain instances when the choice to bend church law was justifiable. It was evident to Palmeiro as well as to his subordinates that a degree of flexibility was needed if the Jesuits were to introduce Christianity within non-Western cultures successfully. Just how much flexibility to allow, however, was the problem. It was clear to Palmeiro that "some, or indeed many, of the accidental aspects of the administration of the sacraments and the explanation of the things of our Holy Faith" could not be immediately introduced in every mission field for reasons of cultural incompatibility. The progress of the church would at length permit their introduction, and the mission fields would converge with Europe. The Visitor further admitted that sacred history supported the Cochinchina Jesuits' position, since not all church customs were "used in the Ancient Church when the faith began to spread." Even so, he felt there needed to be a unity of practice, and that the "ordinary ceremonies" needed to be "ordinary" even among the newest neophytes in the Asian mission fields. "In everything that is possible, in both the essential and the accidental," Palmeiro wrote in evocation of Paul's Letter to the Ephesians, "it is important that there be one church and one baptism."[46]

One practical way for the Jesuits to dispel the suspicions that their enterprises were schismatic was to insist on the uniformity of Christian practice. This did not simply mean the use of standard forms of the sacraments and their regular administration; it also meant the application of church law, in so much as possible, in the mission field. Neophytes had to be made aware of the obligations of their new faith and had to be made to abide by its norms. The requirements that adults make confessions and receive the Eucharist yearly are but two examples. Others are the obligation to fast during Lent and the insolubility of the marriage bond. But it was unclear precisely when neophytes should be made aware of these requirements of Christian life.

The missionaries who changed aspects of the sacraments were acting in line with their understanding that it was not wise to reveal everything at once. To be sure, this was not a new question for the Jesuits, and it was not a quandary unique to the early modern period. Even St. Paul had worried about how soon to complement the Good News with the bad. The question of timing was therefore one of the most persistent problems for missionaries, and Palmeiro had no firm answer. But he was troubled by the fact that none of his subordinates seemed to have a plan for dealing with this issue. Questioned directly, none would have denied the place of positive law in Christian life, yet the Jesuits did not feel pressure to oblige their flocks to observe church practices. It was only when the contradictions became obvious, when they were caught permitting prohibited behaviors among their neophytes simply because it was deemed too soon to explain the accepted (European) Christian norms, that this situation would change.

One such case reached Palmeiro's ears from Cochinchina as early as 1628, when he learned that Francesco Buzomi had permitted some Christians in Cochinchina to repudiate their spouses, remarry, and afterward receive the Eucharist. Thankfully for Palmeiro, other Jesuits, not outsiders, brought him this news. Buzomi's confreres, and even some Japanese Christians living in Faifo, were shocked to see the missionary permitting something so contrary to church law. What was at stake was not whether indigenous marriages were valid in the eyes of the Church—a topic that had preoccupied the papacy as well as the missionary orders with regard to the neophytes of Latin America for nearly a century—but whether Buzomi was within his right to disregard positive law relating to marriage.[47]

Palmeiro's first reference to this topic is found in the same litany about Jesuit disregard for the administration of the sacraments, mentioned earlier. He noted his dismay that the neophytes in Southeast Asia had not been made aware that the Council of Trent had mandated the presence of parish priests at weddings. Although he admitted that it was too soon for all of the requirements imposed by the Church on European Christians to be made known in the missions (especially since the decrees of Trent were not universally promulgated in Europe itself in the 1620s, and because there was no secular clergy as of yet in Vietnam), Palmeiro judged that Buzomi had gone too far. It was one thing to defer to local marriage customs when converts chose to marry non-Christians, and a far different matter to permit baptized adults to repudiate their spouses. Neophytes who decided to marry, the Visitor insisted, needed to be aware of the nature of Christian matrimony and the Church's expectations for married couples. Palmeiro knew that his predecessors had worked with other theologians to reach a form of accommodation to Japanese marriage customs, and had assumed that a similar policy was followed in Southeast Asia.[48] Realizing the error of this assumption, he wrote to reprimand Buzomi and sent orders on the subject to Manuel Fernandes, mission superior in Cochinchina.[49]

The affair was not resolved quickly. In the mails that returned to Macau in the summer of 1628 Buzomi attempted to defend his position. He claimed he had done no wrong in dissolving the marriages since the men and women involved did not know that Christian matrimony was supposed to be indissoluble. Since the neophytes were only observing the local customs, which permitted divorce, and Buzomi had not yet introduced the points of positive law relating to matrimony, he had to treat them as blameless when they came to receive the Eucharist.

The main issue, the missionary contended, was whether it was better to err on the side of furthering the spread of the faith or to impose restrictions with the possible consequence of driving away neophytes and prospective converts. Arguing for flexibility over restriction, Buzomi pointed to scripture. He claimed that one need but look to the Acts of the Apostles, who did not reveal all of the limitations of Christian matrimony to their neophytes when they set off to preach across the world. There was also ample proof in the writings of the Church Fathers to defend his position. Their texts described the Primitive Church, one very similar to the mission churches of Asia, where the vestiges of pre-Christian life were not uprooted immediately but over

time. In that distant age as well as during Buzomi's day, Christian obligations were difficult to impose when the Church lacked the "helping arm" of
temporal power. It was therefore best to refrain from demanding too much of
neophytes. God agreed, Buzomi argued, and he pointed to the fact that He
permitted polygamy among the Hebrews in order to increase the numbers of
the faithful.[50] There was also the example of Francis Xavier, who specifically
discouraged the teaching of the complete rules of Christian marriage to neophytes. To these historical observations, Buzomi added one last argument
based on events of more recent vintage: His personal experience in Cochinchina suggested that insisting on the indissolubility of marriage would "infal-
libly make our law even more rejected and hated, and thought to be contrary
to good reason and the public good of the kingdom."[51]

Palmeiro was unimpressed by these arguments. He declared that Buzomi
had offered an ill-founded justification; his historical points were imprecise
and his citations of recent practice among neophytes in Asia were incorrect.
European customs had been introduced into the Japanese church, and the
China Jesuits had long prohibited the common practice of keeping concubines to their converts. Palmeiro therefore stood behind his rebuke as well as
his insistence that positive law be introduced, gradually, in Vietnam. From
the Visitor's perspective, it was reasonable to expect that the new Christians
in Cochinchina and Tonkin be held to the same standards as their coreligionists in the Ming Empire or in Japan. But Palmeiro did not want his
opinion to enforce what was, for him, a matter of universal importance. He
preferred to solicit a gesture of solidarity from Rome, since the declaration of
precepts of positive law in the missions had important ramifications for the
Society's missionary efforts around the globe. "Even though I have already
done what I can and I will order all of those who are in my district, because
this is how I understand my charge," wrote Palmeiro to Muzio Vitelleschi,
"nonetheless with the authority and respect that is due to Your Paternity all
should be encouraged to accommodate themselves."[52] Rome agreed, and there
is proof that the superior general wrote directly to Buzomi with specific rules
for how to observe positive law in the mission fields.[53]

In light of the fact that the China mission was nearing a half-century of
existence in 1629, it stood to reason that Palmeiro sought some consolation
from the veteran missionaries within the Ming Empire on the question of
church law in the missions. But his trip through China only served to add
further troubles to his conscience since in that land he found disregard for

Christian obligations on a scale far greater than in Cochinchina. While the Jesuits in China had been zealous in promoting what Portuguese sources call the *Ley de Deus,* the Law of God, they had not insisted on the law of the Church. Writing to Rome after his return to Macau, the Visitor made clear his "great discontentment" that the priests had agreed not to oblige their Chinese Christians to observe the precepts of positive law. While they did "exhort them to observe the feasts and fasts of the bishoprics of the East," he wrote, "they do not tell them that they are obligations." The consequences were calamitous:

> From this fact it arises that nowhere in this *christandade* does anyone fast, not during Lent, nor on the Ember Days, nor on vigils; at all of these times, and on Fridays and Saturdays, they eat meat. From this fact it arises that no one is obliged to confess, and I heard from priests who spoke to me about individual Christians, people with whom they dealt personally, that it had been years since they had said their confessions. And the same is true about taking communion, and even among people very worthy of receiving it. From this fact it arises that almost all of them marry very close relatives, but if they deem this acceptable they should at least have or request a dispensation. They hear mass when they want and when they can, since they are not obliged to do it, and the same can be said for any other obligation that arises or can arise from positive precepts.[54]

In sum, the Christianity preached by the Jesuits in China was closer to its Chinese name, *Tianzhu jiao,* that is, the "teaching of the Lord of Heaven," than it was to its Portuguese designation, *a Ley de Deus.* It encouraged correct piety but did not demand it. And this greatly concerned the Visitor:

> I do not approve of this doctrine. Indeed, I am greatly shocked by it, and I made my shock clear to the priests. I do not see that it is in the power of the preacher of the gospel and the minister of the Christian community to make known only those aspects of positive law which he deems fit. It may happen, and reason demands as much, that an *epikeia* may be used in this place or that, or at such time or another some law might not be enforced, because such judgments are based on the attention of a given legislator, or are based on what can be expected in particular circumstances. But I do not think it right, nor should it be possible, to absolutely reject and give up every point of positive law in one fell swoop.[55]

Recalling the arguments that Buzomi had employed to justify his actions, as well as those no doubt put forward by the Jesuits inside the Ming Empire, Palmeiro buttressed his position. He cited the long tradition of the elaboration of positive law and the evident fact that it was observed by the Primitive Church. So the use of citations from the Patristic Age about the behavior of Roman neophytes was disingenuous—"those who converted had also been heathens previously, and when they adopted our law, they adopted its obligations." Furthermore, there was sufficient evidence from the progress of the mission church in Japan that the introduction of positive law had not been counterproductive. Palmeiro insisted that most of church law was explained to the Christians of that country, and that dispensations existed for the cases in which there was a valid reason. This was particularly true in cases of marriages with too great a degree of consanguinity, but the newness of the church in Japan was considered to be "reason enough" for conceding dispensations. Palmeiro's general rule for the mission territories was therefore similar to the practice of the papacy (which maintained the Apostolic Dataria for handling such cases) with regard to European Christians: "I understand that it is necessary to declare many precepts as obligations, and to use dispensations for those things which circumstances demand and which we can give."[56] Consequently, he clarified his position for the China Jesuits by including a specific reference to the issue in the compendium of rules that he issued for the vice-province in 1629. In a phrase couched in as much diplomacy as he could muster in light of his frustrations, he declared: "Although in these early times not all of positive law which was used by the Primitive Church and which is used in well-governed *christandades* can be made known to the Christians, nevertheless it must be made known suavely in those cases where there are not grave inconveniences, so that in a few years all of it may be made known to them."[57]

This position brought the Visitor back to the question of marriages, and his concerns for the China mission were similar to those he had expressed in relation to Vietnam. Once again the Jesuits had elaborated a general policy of deference to local customs when they should have insisted on the obligations of marriage and its sacramental quality, acting at variance with church law only in particular circumstances. In China the missionaries had decided not to administer the sacrament of matrimony to any Christians "regardless of how well-versed in doctrine or how devout they were" without the special permission of the vice-provincial. During his inspection tour Palmeiro tried to understand why they had chosen this policy since none of the missionaries would give him a full explanation. Clearly they did not mean for the priests who were present at marriages not to say they were administering a sacrament. More likely, in the Visitor's view, the Jesuits preferred to let their Christians follow local custom. In either case, Palmeiro insisted that the Chinese Christians should be made aware that their marriages involved vows they were obliged to pronounce solemnly in a state of grace and observe for perpetuity. Perhaps, he wrote to the superior general, the China Jesuits had decided that if they could not observe the decrees of the Council of Trent with regard to the presence of priests at marriages scrupulously, it was best to avoid creating ambiguities. That is, if they could only be present at some marriages, then the other ones (those where they could not be present) would be invalid. It appears, however, that Palmeiro was giving his men a considerable amount of credit on this score in light of their general disregard for positive law. The Visitor, as well as the China Jesuits, knew that the decrees of the council had not been made known in China, and neither was it convenient to make them known in 1629. In Europe, he wrote, variation existed from place to place in how marriages were conducted, "and even the Roman Ritual commands that they be performed according to the standard customs of each land."[58]

After issuing his orders, Palmeiro continued to monitor the behavior of his subordinates to see how quickly they moved to introduce the precepts of positive law. Either they chose to ignore his commands or they felt it too difficult to insist on Christian obligations in light of their tenuous terms of residence, since he received no clear sign that changes had been made. In 1633 the superior of the Cochinchina mission sent the Visitor a letter that gave him further cause for concern. Palmeiro had instructed Gaspar Luís (1586–ca. 1647) to alert him if any priest deviated from his orders on the topic of matrimony and to send the offender directly to Macau. While none of the Jesuits stationed in Cochinchina had strayed from the rule, Luís reported that Francesco Buzomi had passed through Ranran Province on his way to Cambodia in 1632 and had committed yet another scandal. Not only did Buzomi admit some "poorly wed" Christians—a woman who had abandoned her husband for another—to the sacraments (something Luís had refused to do) but he also performed a marriage in the local church. The local community, which found this act shocking enough, was doubly distressed when Buzomi approved of the wishes of a Christian woman to leave her baptized husband for an unbaptized man.

Luís had received word about these affairs from catechists whom he had sent to the region, and had made further inquiries in the areas where Buzomi had previously worked. In the district of Cachão, Luís and his companion, Manuel Fernandes, reported "great difficulty in pacifying the married couples who are scandalized by some poorly wed people here, whose unions the *padre* had recognized because he instructed his catechists not to reveal everything on this point." None of the married Christians in the district seemed to have a clear understanding of matrimony or the reason for the sacrament, the missionaries confessed. And if it was not enough that Buzomi bucked the Visitor's orders in regard to matrimony, Luís further reported learning from a Japanese Christian that the same priest had dispensed with the obligation to refrain from eating meat on a holy day. In front of an audience of over one hundred neophytes gathered in a church in Pulocambi, Buzomi had declared licit something prohibited by "the customs of this *christandade* and the orders of the Bishop of Malacca, as well as those of the superiors that are observed in these missions." The Japanese Christian refused to indulge along with his Vietnamese coreligionists, reporting to Luís that he answered the invitation of the local people by saying, "You can eat meat because you have permission from the priest. I cannot because I am Japanese, and I must respect the customs of my native land."[59]

The information in Luís's letter suggests that while most of the Jesuits in the Vietnamese missions had begun to divulge some of the points of positive law to their flocks, others resisted. It was clear that the task of spreading this new component of the Christian message was going to be slow, and that it would be met with resistance from some quarters. Luís indicated the confusion among the Cochinchinese neophytes, whose missionary pastors had given them conflicting messages, but he also revealed that the insistence on the indissolubility of marriage did not produce the cataclysmic outcome that Buzomi had predicted. Indeed, the introduction of positive law did not, in general, account for any major disruption in the spread of Christianity in Asia. Once again, as had been the case with the rigor that he had introduced in the China mission on the polemical term *Shangdi*, Palmeiro's scruples prodded him to take actions that were strongly contested by his subordinates but had effects that, in the end, proved less damaging than predicted. The example of the Christian communities in the Ming Empire is particularly instructive on this score. Although it would take almost a decade for the results of the Visitor's directive to the China Jesuits to be seen clearly, the 1630s witnessed the increasing insistence on the obligatory reception of the sacraments. Already in the second half of that decade the missionaries began to organize their individual *christandades* according to a regular yearly schedule during which all of their neophytes were to receive pastoral care at least once per year. Simultaneously, the Jesuits' Chinese Christians became increasingly aware of the Church's demands of fasting and regular prayer routines, aspects of Catholic life organized according to the precepts of positive law.[60]

It would be convenient to interpret the clash between Palmeiro and Buzomi as another instance of the struggle between Portuguese and Italians. In fact, this is precisely how one of the most influential early historians of the Asian missions viewed their infighting, ardently defending the missionary against the Visitor.[61] But there is no evidence from archival sources to defend such a thesis, unlike in the case of disputes in the Province of Malabar discussed earlier in this study, where national factions were descried by contemporaries. That Buzomi and Palmeiro diverged because of the former's zeal and the latter's pragmatism is also untrue. As evinced by his willingness to risk his and the Society's honor by engaging in trade, the Visitor's zeal for the missions to Southeast Asia was by no means inferior to his subordinate's, and Buzomi's letters explaining his diplomatic maneuvers at the courts of Cochinchina, Champa, and Cambodia reveal that he employed no less pragmatism than his superior. So this was not yet another case of unrestrained charisma that needed to be brought into line by strict orders. At issue between the two men was a confrontation between two distinct missionary strategies: one that centered on the figure of the missionary and the other that focused on the corporate unity of the Society of Jesus. In the first of these, individual priests who developed long-term relationships with their converts and auxiliaries were the heart of the missionary enterprise. And in the second, missionaries were interchangeable (insofar as their linguistic skills permitted) so long as the Society maintained a presence among the communities of neophytes. In the case of the Southeast Asian missions, Buzomi and his local knowledge represented the first type, whereas Palmeiro, with his insistence on church laws and the order's rules, represented the second.

This contrast between the specific context of the mission fields and the universal precepts of the Society of Jesus and the Catholic Church has been seen in other episodes of this study. In its most extreme form, there was the case of Roberto Nobili, who insisted not just on a particular way to adapt to indigenous culture in South Asia but on his unique ability—thanks to the circumstances of his illustrious birth—to accomplish the task of converting members of the Brahman caste. Less pronounced was the case of the China Jesuits who argued in favor of preserving all of Matteo Ricci's policies and were led by their experience to insist that only those men who had lived long enough in the Ming Empire should rule on how best to conduct the China enterprise. In similar fashion, Buzomi would point to his many years in Cochinchina as grounds for defending his policies; he knew the terrain and so should be heeded in matters of cultural accommodation. His defense in permitting neophytes to repudiate their spouses sprang from his understanding of the social norms in his mission field among non-Christians, regardless of which citations from church tradition he might mention to his confreres.

The Visitor, with Rome's blessing, was sent to Asia to serve as a counterweight to this strong insistence on local knowledge. His task was to represent that broader vision—including the Society of Jesus, the Church, the Province of Japan, and even the wider Asian cultural context—and to ensure that the missionary enterprises would continue even if some of the most experienced men perished. Palmeiro's charge was to consider what was best for his order, removing undue emphasis on individuals and ensuring that all of his men represented the Society rather than simply themselves. This was the perspective of the Jesuit curia, too, which gave its inspectors the powers necessary for ensuring that the missionaries never forgot that they were bound by vows to their order and their Church. It was also Palmeiro's duty to attempt to harmonize the different Asian enterprises as much as possible, so that his men would uniformly enjoy the same social standing in the different mission fields. If he succeeded at that task, he would be able to move his men from one mission to another without relying (except in special circumstances) on the particular talents of any one Jesuit.

The contrast between these two approaches can be seen in a pair of episodes that occurred at Macau in the early 1630s. The first was a dispute that arose over the use of facial hair in the Southeast Asian missions, while the second was a short-lived attempt to synchronize all of the enterprises within the Province of Japan. In the first episode a clash of opinions arose between Palmeiro and Francesco Buzomi in which the Visitor's consideration of the larger Asian context differed from the local knowledge of some of the missionaries in Tonkin.

Buzomi arrived in Macau in 1630 after the King of Cochinchina ordered the expulsion of Jesuits from his lands, leaving his companions as captives of the King of Champa. Such was the impression that the Jesuit made upon the potentates in Southeast Asia that he found himself pressed into service as ambassador of the King of Champa to his counterpart in Cambodia, and then from the King of Cambodia to the *Senado* of Macau. When Buzomi arrived at the Portuguese colony, he found Palmeiro busy coordinating the return of the missionaries to Tonkin by ordering, among other things, that they grow out their beards. The Visitor's command reflected his knowledge of the Ming Empire and its tributary states: He had learned that the Tonkinese were firmly within the Chinese cultural orbit, and he had seen firsthand the impression that fully grown facial hair made among the Chinese. In order for the missionaries to be considered venerable and authoritative, he thus decreed, they had to present themselves as mature men with impressive beards. In this way, they would be received with respect and honor at the Trinh court, just as they had been in China. What had worked in the Ming Empire, where the Jesuits had become fixtures at court with their hirsute appearance, was intended to work in same manner with Tonkinese officials and the king himself.

Writing to the superior general from Macau, Buzomi remarked on how strange he found this insistence on facial hair. Buzomi's intention was to call the Visitor's judgment into question: Palmeiro might know something of China, he asserted, but he knew little of Southeast Asia. For instance, "in China we change our clothes, in Tonkin we do not", he remarked. In order to cut short any suggestion that Buzomi's experience in Faifo might not be valid for Hanoi, he offered the following: "After all, Cochinchina and Tonkin are the same kingdom, and have the same language and customs, and it has only been twenty years that they split, and it is most likely that when the present king, who is a septuagenarian, dies, Cochinchina will unite with Tonkin."[62] And so, on the issue at hand he could assert that "it has been sixteen years that I have been living in Cochinchina and I have never found that beards were useful for making conversions." Indeed, Buzomi continued, the people there found long beards to be off-putting and called those who wore them goats. But Palmeiro seemed to care little for such knowledge, the missionary asserted, "whereby we can see that he is partial to beards." Those who argued against Buzomi claimed that facial hair "made a man more serious and handsome" but failed to demonstrate how this would make them more effective missionaries. Resigned to being marginalized, albeit with his sense of humor intact, he searched his mind for the best image of venerable greybeards and exclaimed, "I say we all become Theatines!"[63]

The second episode occurred after Buzomi had sailed for Cambodia and his confreres had returned to Tonkin. In this case, language presented problems and, potentially, opportunities. At the heart of the matter lay the fact that Jesuit books from China were circulating in Vietnam, enhancing the image of the missionaries' message as something respected in the Ming Empire. In the annual letter from Tonkin for 1630, António de Fontes wrote of how a Buddhist cleric had brought him a copy of one of Matteo Ricci's catechisms "saying that his father had traveled to China as an ambassador and had returned from there with this book forty years beforehand." According to Fontes's informant, his father had learned that "those who followed that book went to heaven", and that his father had brought the text to Tonkin because he had seen "inside of our house the tomb of five or six Chinese who had already gone to heaven."[64] In his correspondence with the Visitor, Fontes gave further proof of the value of books produced by the priests of the vice-province. He noted the difference between Nom, that is, spoken Vietnamese written in adapted Chinese characters, and the literary language of classical Chinese with Vietnamese pronunciation. Fontes described how it was necessary for his mission to have prayer books printed in China "which are of great authority in this and other kingdoms". Here he cited a criticism of Christianity that his colleagues in the Ming Empire had also had to face: unlike the Buddhist clergy, the priests had no weighty tomes.[65] "There will be no lack of heathens who will mock the Christians for saying the prayers in Nom, which is the common language of the land," Fontes argued, "saying that the Law of the Lord of Heaven and Earth does not have books, since the Christians used prayers in ordinary letters which is a very lowly thing, and of no authority."[66]

These reports set the Society's administrative minds working. In Macau, Palmeiro saw as many opportunities as he did potential dangers with the circulation of Chinese books to Vietnam. He had spent a large part of his journey through the Ming Empire wrangling with the question of terminology and had issued rules intended to force the problematic terms from the Chinese Christian lexicon. There were, however, more heads to the linguistic hydra than the Visitor had imagined: Ricci's texts from the 1590s contained more than a few dubious terms since he had produced them only a few years after the start of the mission. Who was to say that there were not other copies of texts considered corrupt by Palmeiro circulating in Tonkin or Cochinchina? He could only hope that the new texts he had urged his subordinates in China to print would make it beyond Chinese borders before more of the old ones did.

Some damage had already been done. It is evident that Palmeiro had heard rumors about the presence of the disputed terms in Southeast Asia since his orders to Gaspar do Amaral instructed this deputy visitor of the Cochinchina mission to prohibit them. Having been informed that the term *Shangdi* was being used for God, Palmeiro wrote, "I have prohibited it *in virtute obedientiae* among the Christians of China, and so Your Reverence will in no ways permit a similar usage." Instead, the Visitor ordered, "call God the Lord of Heaven and Earth, that the Christians call *Tientichu,* or another appropriate name that is not *Xamty.*"[67] To be sure, it was not clear whether or not the Jesuits in Vietnam had used this imported term excessively. The news from Cochinchina aroused anxiety. Fortunately, things were not the same in Tonkin. Indeed, it appears that the Jesuits in that country had taken a cautious tack: Fontes informed Palmeiro that the Tonkinese catechists often used the baptismal formula in Latin that Alexandre de Rhodes had taught them. But the pronunciation of the ritual phrase was so bad that Fontes decided to render it into Nom. Unsatisfied with this solution, he hoped Palmeiro would permit appropriate Chinese formulas to be used because "all of the Christians normally know some letters (not leaving aside the women, who will also study and understand the texts easily) and will be able to learn and know them in Chinese characters."[68]

The Society's curia in Rome had still another idea for confronting this complex linguistic situation in the Province of Japan, which encompassed the missions fields from Nagasaki to Ayutthaya. In light of the problems caused by the use of different ritual terminologies, Muzio Vitelleschi instructed Palmeiro to consider using only one language for all of the East and Southeast Asian missions. Apparently this order was based on the notion that Chinese was the common language of the region, an idea reinforced by years of missionary writings that mentioned the presence of Chinese texts in Japan, Korea, Tonkin, and Cochinchina.

While it was a measure of the intelligence of the men on the superior general's staff in Rome, this astute delineation of a Chinese cultural zone that extended far beyond the borders of the Ming Empire did not offer any easy solutions to the Jesuits' problems. It therefore fell to Palmeiro to inform Vitelleschi that there was no common language in the Asian missions, that there was no easy way to synchronize Christian vocabulary from Japan with the problematic renderings in China in order to provide a workable set of ritual designations for Vietnam (or, for that matter, China). Rome's order followed the type of administrative logic that flourished far from the mission fields: From the general's point of view, regard for Chinese culture indicated a cultural unity and linguistic affinity. After all, the curia knew that in the late sixteenth century the Jesuits in Brazil had created a new "common language" out of the disparate tongues of that land's indigenous peoples. While that *língua geral* drew on several distinct languages, it permitted missionaries to converse with speakers of all of them.[69] And so the Visitor complied with Rome's order, consulting as instructed with men trained in the region's languages at Macau and sending his findings back to Europe. The result of this effort was a curious comparative declaration of the Lord's Prayer and basic vocabulary terms in which it was not only made clear that Japanese, Chinese, and Vietnamese were too distinct for any such uniformization project but that even the so-called dialects of spoken Chinese were as distinct as Italian and Spanish.[70]

The contrast between these two instances of debate over mission strategy revealed the delicate balancing act that Palmeiro performed in Macau. One the one hand, he had his superiors in Rome, who encouraged him to think of the broadest context for the Society's actions and to consider policies which had proven useful elsewhere. And on the other, the Visitor had his men, some of whom had been deeply immersed in the cultures of the countries where they worked and knew the subtleties of their audiences' sensibilities. But since Rome's orders trumped other Jesuit initiatives, Palmeiro was bound to listen to the suggestions of the superior general and act on as many of them as possible. It nonetheless made sense to listen to what the missionaries had to say about strategy. Insomuch as he did not detect any problems with the methods employed by his subordinates, the Visitor was content for them to guide the missions as they thought best. On occasion, he did not deem it beneficial to let his men act in accord with their training and experience, as has seen in the previous discussions of the missions in India, the Moluccas, and China. The weights on Palmeiro's balance consisted of trust: the less he trusted the missionaries in the field, the more he trusted Rome and his own judgment, and vice versa. While he inclined to confide in those who knew the cultures of their appointed lands—an inclination shared by the Society's curia—he was constantly on guard to be sure that his trust was not abused. That is, he remained alert to see if the Jesuits would uphold the Society's rules and to respect church law, once he reminded them that these were the most basic expectations for the order's missionaries.

The question of trust goes a long way to explaining why Palmeiro did not give too much credence to Francesco Buzomi's views on matters relating to the Vietnamese missions. Buzomi's linguistic skills and cultural knowledge were patent, but other aspects of his character undercut its positive qualities. Not only was there the tone of insubordination in Buzomi's letter on the question of Christian matrimony (although this was nothing compared to what Palmeiro got from Alfonso Vagnone in China about his verdict on the Terms), Buzomi was also profligate. This quality was put on display at Macau when Buzomi reached the colony in September 1630 in the capacity of the King of Cambodia's ambassador. While this diplomatic mission, which inconveniently sought reparations from the same Portuguese merchants who were the Jesuits' patrons, was disturbing enough, what shocked the Visitor was that Buzomi disembarked with an entourage of five servants. Knowing the lengths to which Palmeiro had gone to find support for the missions in Southeast Asia, it was unconscionable for Buzomi to spend the order's money on a personal retinue. Worse still, the missionary lavished attention on his *moços* (literally, "boys," even if actually servants), and on one of them in particular. This was not the first time that Palmeiro had discovered one of his subordinates with a corps of assistants; recall that he learned that one of the Jesuits in the Moluccas kept a group of silk-clad servants. But that story had transpired on a distant island, far from the Visitor's eyes, and out of the sight of the Society's other superiors. This was in Macau. "All reprimanded him greatly," Palmeiro communicated to Rome in January 1631, "for his manner of spoiling his *moços* and spending lots of money on them."[71]

Buzomi had a long history of surrounding himself with indigenous assistants, something his confreres had repeatedly denounced. Already in 1623 the Jesuits at Faifo described his work at Pulocambi in the following manner: "Father Buzomi has two or three *bonsos ong sai* who do all the work for him. . . . If there is something to be settled or important messages, he sends his interpreter, or then again one of the *ong sai*." The terms *bonso*, derived from the Japanese word for members of the Buddhist clergy, and *ong sai*, the Vietnamese for the same, reveal that Buzomi was master of a proselytizing team.[72] The same source indicates that the superior of the Cochinchina mission did not permit the use of such assistants at Faifo. So who were these native helpers? From this description, it would seem that they were servants, but it is also mentioned that they served as catechists. Buzomi would emphatically declare in a letter to Rome written during his 1630 stay in Macau that his *moços* were indeed catechists, but their personal service suggested to others that they were servants.[73] In either case, their presence in Macau disrupted the hierarchical relationships between the Society's priests and its temporal coadjutors. Jesuit brothers joined the order with the expectation that they would perform menial tasks and serve as catechism or grammar instructors. They were expected to serve all and not be partial to any one member of the order. Buzomi's assistants, however, only desired his company. According to Palmeiro, "there is no brother who wants to work with him for this reason, because they all complain that the lies of a servant are worth more to the *padre* than the truth of a brother."[74]

At the heart of this matter was a question of trust. From Palmeiro's perspective, it was unacceptable that the missionary had failed to consult his immediate superior in Cochinchina on the question of how many non-Jesuits were to accompany him to Macau. And the notion that Buzomi showed himself partial to his servants only made matters worse. But from Buzomi's point of view, he was only responding to the loyalty that his assistants had shown him over the years. Writing to defend himself against the Visitor's criticism, he insisted that these Vietnamese men were catechists or *dojicos* (from *dōjuku,* a Japanese term meaning "cohabitant" and used to designate lay auxiliaries who performed a variety of services). One of them had been at Buzomi's side for sixteen years, he claimed, while two others had served at his residence for twelve years. Had he left them alone in Cochinchina, he asserted, their parents would have forced them to marry. And so Buzomi felt that he had no choice but to bring them to Macau—while leaving two fellow Jesuits as captives in Champa and two others in a disease-ridden corner of Cochinchina. "It seemed inhuman to deny them the right to accompany me in the good times," he wrote to the superior general, "when they had faithfully accompanied me in the bad."[75]

The Visitor found this a weak justification. This type of behavior exhausted his ability to trust Buzomi, he averred, taking account of the missionary's insistence that he be sent to open a new enterprise in Laos after completing his Cambodian embassy. "I have already given him multiple warnings,"

Palmeiro confessed to Rome, "and I will not dare send him to open any other mission because I consider him to be incapable of taking a balanced approach, what with his excessive generosity towards the servants and his pampering of them."[76]

This discussion of Buzomi's assistants at Macau raises the important question of the place of native auxiliaries within the Society's East Asian enterprises. The missionaries' reliance on indigenous assistants was part of their overall strategy, akin to the forms of appearance and proselytizing language that they employed. Even more than the use of a specific style of dress or translations of Christian terminology, however, the acceptance of outsiders into the Society's missionary enterprises was a complex matter. In this domain, trust was essential. The Jesuits (and other religious orders) were naturally reluctant to confide in individuals who were not bound by vows to obey their superiors. The issue of obedience, however, was only one aspect of the Jesuits' relations with their auxiliaries. There were also questions of material support and catechetical training. For instance, should the Society be obliged to pay for the living expenses of the auxiliaries or permit them to live in the missionaries' residences? In other words, what constituted "excessive generosity" toward these assistants? What kind of training should they be provided? That is, how much instruction did the missionaries need to give their assistants before permitting them to spread Christianity in the Jesuits' stead? More importantly, could recently baptized individuals be entrusted with the important task of teaching the tenets of their new religion to others?

Leaving aside the lay leaders of neophyte communities and the occasional slave attached to a specific residence such as the College of Macau, it is possible to identify three types of indigenous assistants who worked with the Jesuits in Asia: servants, *dojicos,* and catechists. The distinctions lie on a spectrum of activity ranging from menial chores on one side to active proselytizing on the other. Local legal and cultural contexts often dictated the nature of the relationships between the missionaries and these types of individuals, making it difficult to describe the precise nature of the tasks of each. For example, the common activities and hierarchical status of the Jesuits' *dōjuku* in Japan were based on the types of functions that such individuals would perform within Buddhist monastic communities.[77] Hence, it was impossible for the Visitor to establish a uniform policy toward them that would be applicable throughout the Asian missions. In light of the expectation that these auxiliaries would exercise functions overlapping with those of the Society's coadjutors, it is worthwhile including the Asian-born Jesuit brothers in this enumeration of indigenous collaborators. The role of *filhos de Macau,* those Chinese or Eurasian men from the Portuguese colony who became coadjutors in the China mission, has already been mentioned, but it will be necessary to dwell on their position within the Society at greater length here. Not only was there evident friction between Buzomi's assistants and the college's brothers, but the presence of different types of Asian assistants prompted the Visitor to attempt to establish some clearer rules for their role within the Society's temporal and spiritual activities.

The lowest rank of indigenous auxiliary was that of servant. As suggested by Palmeiro's comments, *moços* were expected to perform menial tasks in recompense for a low wage and a few benefits such as meals, clothing, and shelter. By the late sixteenth century, it had become standard practice for the Jesuits in Japan to retain *komono,* servants, at their residences, and the practice had been extended to other mission fields. The terms of service varied, with servants in the Ming Empire being indentured for a certain number of years rather than paid a monthly salary. (The conditions of their employment seem very similar to the practice of domestic slavery, as described for those *moços cativos,* "captive boys," at the College of Macau.[78])

The Visitor's 1629 rules for the China mission give indications of why this arrangement was better than securing salaried help: "It is most convenient to abide by the custom of this whole kingdom and for us to purchase children for our service, since experience shows us that these are the only ones who can be tolerated at home in terms of cleanliness and fidelity." Serving boys were to be appropriately dressed, "so that they go about clean and happily." They were not to be seen "undressed from the waist up", something Palmeiro had spotted at times in the Jesuits' residences. The Visitor further instructed the local superiors to treat the *moços* with "great care and love", not permitting them to work on Sundays and feast days, and giving the older ones money to purchase their own clothing. Having been entrusted with raising these boys, the Jesuits were instructed to teach them doctrine "and the things of God, according to their capacity." Those servants who showed intellectual talent were to be taught to read and write, so as to help with translations (from local dialects into Mandarin) and messages. Discipline in the form of corporal punishment was approved for the Jesuits' domestics, "ordinarily with the bamboo cane that is used in China". Older servants were to receive the lashes "on top of their pants, when they deserve it."[79]

The limited numbers of priests and brothers in China made trustworthy servants indispensable. Palmeiro insisted that they be trained how to use weapons so that they could accompany traveling missionaries. He knew that Pieter van Spiere had been killed by bandits while sailing to Huguang Province, and that the conditions of travel seemed to be becoming more dangerous as peasant revolts and Manchu raids became more frequent. The obligation of the vice-provincial superior to visit all of the Society's far-flung residences during the course of the his triennial term was sufficient justification for Palmeiro to include this note about armed servants twice in his rules.[80] Despite the obvious bonds of solidarity that such orders implied, and the fact that many of the Jesuits' servants had grown up in their company, the Visitor nevertheless sensed that the links between masters and servants were often too close. He was especially concerned lest individual missionaries would grow accustomed to particular servants and insist on their constant presence. Indeed, it seems that the Jesuits who had worked in the Japan mission had their own dedicated servants, and the memory of such practices lingered.[81]

From Palmeiro's view, however, such an attitude flew in the face of the Society's vows of poverty, and he issued commands prohibiting the Jesuits in the mission fields from having their own personal *moços*. With the exception of those men who were too old or too sick to care for themselves, all of the "boys" were considered to be in the service of the residence as a whole. The Visitor went into some detail regarding their duties. Taking up the example of foot-washing, he insisted that servants could only bring hot water to the missionaries; they could not actually wash feet. He further repeated the prohibition, issued by the superior general, against permitting "little servants or students of a tender age" to sleep in the same rooms as the priests or brothers (presumably for swifter service).[82]

Buzomi's arrival at Macau in 1630 with his retinue of assistants prompted Palmeiro to rebuke him face to face. Since the other missionaries in Cochinchina did not seem to indulge their auxiliaries to any great degree and, moreover, they were living clandestinely at the time, he felt no need to issue new orders for that mission. He did, however, compose a list of commands for Tonkin. When that mission resumed in 1631 with the sailing of one of the Visitor's ships, a new superior was appointed and specific rules were written for preventing the type of abuses that Buzomi had committed. Here Palmeiro sought to address the problems of individual Jesuits having *moços* and of the excessively kind treatment of these assistants. "The superior should remember that he should not have a specific boy for his service, nor give him clothing or other treats," wrote the Visitor, "because if the superior does such things, they will very easily catch on among the other priests. At the very least, he will have a hard time making them observe this rule if he does not keep it himself."[83]

It would appear that the temptation to acquire servants was strong, and that the Jesuits in the mission field sought the same type of domestic help to which they had grown accustomed in the Society's colleges. On this score, Palmeiro was well informed: he had his own *moço cativo* at the College of Macau "so as to not occupy a brother".[84] But the college was not the mission field. So under no circumstances would Palmeiro permit his men to travel to Macau with an entourage of servants. He stipulated that at most ("something that will rarely occur"), one servant could accompany a missionary who had to return to the Portuguese colony, a *moço* who could perform any of the ordinary servant duties.[85] The principal reason for this rule can be deduced from a passage that Buzomi included in a letter to Rome from early 1631, written against the hail of criticism that Palmeiro and others directed at him. There Buzomi insisted that his servants had not cost the college anything during their stay, and that they had even taken on the valuable task of teaching Vietnamese to two Jesuits and an Augustinian friar.[86]

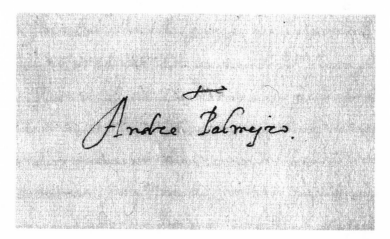

FIGURE 9.2. André Palmeiro's signature, from an original document at the Roman Archive of the Society of Jesus.

Palmeiro's rules for the China mission's servants attempted to strike a paternal balance between friendship and severity. He was inclined toward being generous to them—an attitude clearly tempered by the austerity that he demanded of himself—and knew the benefits of keeping his subordinates content. He had nevertheless detected instances of undue indulgence toward the hired (or indentured) help, attitudes that he considered incompatible with the order's financial position or the proper conduct of professed religious. Navigating between these hazards proved difficult: The Visitor had enough trouble managing the relations between Jesuits to worry excessively about how they treated their servants.

The tone of his orders for China suggests that he had to insist on a middle way, and certain remarks in his correspondence about the Vietnam mission indicate much the same thing. One of the potential dangers of too much severity toward servants was that they might leave the Jesuits' service embittered toward the missionaries and even Christianity. This seems to be the primary reason for his insistence that servants in China be treated with "care and love" and his appeal to good sense when instructing the vice-provincial to provide food and clothing for the servants. In Cochinchina, he trusted the superiors to enact similar policies, but apparently this was not always the case. For example, Buzomi's remarks on a clash that he had with Manuel Fernandes at Faifo over the treatment of servants reveal something of the undue severity at times imposed on the Jesuits' domestic help. The previous superior, Buzomi recounted, held that the servants should be given the same amount to eat as all others at the missionary residence. But Fernandes ruled that "it was enough to give them the leftovers from the table and, later on, that they should not have all of the leftovers, but only a plateful for all of them." Resuming governance in Faifo, Buzomi reinstated the older policy but had to confront accusations that he was excessive in his generosity. "Poor *dojicos!*" he exclaimed, thinking of how meager his generosity was when it only consisted of a full plate of food.[87]

Buzomi's use of a derivative of the Japanese term *dōjuku* to refer to the individuals who served at his house reveals the shades of ambiguity surrounding the ranks of the Society's auxiliaries. In the heyday of the Japan mission, *dōjuku* had been recruited in significant numbers (260 men of this status were recorded in 1604), a scale that would complicate their relations with the Jesuit brothers.[88] Studies of the early Japan mission insist that *dōjuku* were catechists, but it seems that by the 1620s, the Jesuits understood the position to require more menial rather than proselytizing functions. Buzomi's correspondence suggests that he saw a distinction between *dojicos* and catechists (he eschews the term *moços*), with the former being servants with occasional catechetical duties and the latter being dedicated proselytizers who lived independent of the Society's residences. Where Palmeiro saw servants and demanded that they be treated as such, Buzomi saw *dojicos,* that is, paramissionaries who were integral to the Jesuits' enterprises. Writing to Rome, Buzomi complained that the Visitor had "not yet understood how necessary it is for the missions to have *dojicos* and native catechists, and how little we can do without them."[89] At the heart of the matter was the fact that the hierarchical relationship between master and servant became blurred as soon as the Jesuits' domestic help became accessories to proselytizing. Buzomi was unapologetic about the way he treated his assistants: Whereas they might have begun their service as domestics, their willingness to help propagate Christianity among their compatriots elevated them in his eyes. Already in 1623 it was mentioned that his *ong sai* would be present when Buzomi gave catechism lessons, so that they could clear up any points that were not understood by his audience.[90]

So the range of duties expected of *dojicos* included catechetical work, something that had been the case since the late sixteenth century, but this was not their primary task in the new missions in Vietnam. Individuals specifically called *catequistas* focused exclusively on teaching doctrine and preaching to neophytes in the priests' stead in both Tonkin and Cochinchina. The fruit of their efforts—and the fact that the Jesuits were often confined to their residences—meant that these individuals did much of the actual missionary work. According to Buzomi, one of the catechists that he had brought with him to Macau in 1630 was "very skilled at preaching, and with his works and his personal example he not only enjoys great esteem from the Christians, but from the mandarins, too."[91] Other catechists were entrusted with visiting the dispersed communities of Christians, such as those in the far southern parts of Cochinchina, while the Jesuits tried to keep a low profile in the area of Faifo.[92]

In Tonkin, António de Fontes reported that he wrote sermons in Nom for his catechists to preach on feast days and the more important Sundays.[93] Missions to the countryside around Hanoi or to the other provinces of Tonkin were largely reserved for catechists, such as one named André who ventured south to Nghe An Province in 1631.[94] In the following year, while

Fontes accompanied the Trinh lord on a provincial tour and the other Jesuits studied language, two catechists named Chico and Tadeo handled most of the administrative duties of the Christian community, its churches, and its infirmaries (small-scale institutions created by their initiative). Chico, in particular, was entrusted to oversee "the expedition of burials, the expenses of the sick people, the support of the infirmaries, the printing of books, and the ordinary catechism lessons for all who wish to hear about our holy faith, besides sermons and doctrine lessons that he gives on Sundays and feast days for the Christians at the church when our men cannot be there."[95]

These types of activities required far more responsibility and initiative than those expected of *dōjuku* in the old Japan mission. And there was no mistaking the fruit that the Jesuits in Vietnam gathered through their efforts. Writing from Hanoi about the year's labors in 1632, Gaspar do Amaral mentioned the presence of seven catechists who assisted in ministering to the Christian community and performing 5,727 baptisms.[96] In the following year the number of catechists would double and the tally of baptisms exceed seven thousand.[97] The Visitor nevertheless had cause for concern. After all, how would the Jesuits control their catechists if, at times, they were unable to leave their residences?

Not wanting to prohibit his men's reliance on such invaluable helpers, he still urged them to keep a close watch on how the catechists were advancing the faith. Palmeiro was particularly concerned that unsupervised assistants would antagonize the Buddhist clergy or offend the religious sensibilities of non-Christians with acts of iconoclasm. This was precisely the charge leveled at the Jesuits by the rulers of both Cochinchina and Tonkin in the late 1620s, when the missionaries were expelled from both kingdoms. The assurance that such abuses would cease was one of the main conditions for their return a few years later. Hence, Palmeiro reminded Amaral not to permit catechists (or converts) to "knock down temples or rip up images of their gods in public, because it happens at times that the zeal of a few Christians thus impedes the conversion of many Christians."[98]

It appears that Palmeiro had encouraged the Jesuits in Tonkin to create an oversight mechanism for their catechists, but a few years would pass before the missionaries decided on the best way to meet this challenge. Amaral wrote to the Visitor in 1634 to describe how, as a result of an outbreak of persecution, all of the Christian communities were tended by catechists. These carefully chosen individuals were marked by special signs; they "cut their hair and swore four oaths". The four declarations were to never marry, to have no possessions, to dedicate themselves only to preaching, and to obey whomever the Jesuits appointed as their superior. This last point was particularly important since part of the oath specified that they would "at no time in the future appoint themselves leader, setting themselves apart from the others." In return for these sworn vows of poverty, chastity, and obedience, these elite catechists were given the designation *thay,* teacher or, in Amaral's words, "master of the law, which they hold as a great honor".[99]

From this same letter Palmeiro learned that the catechist corps in Tonkin did not live with the Jesuits in their mission stations but rather in separate residences in the three provinces with the greatest concentrations of Christians. This policy aimed to sever any relation of temporal dependency on the Society as well as to ensure that the Christian communities would survive if the priests were exiled. Amaral noted that this arrangement was preferable to having them in the mission stations, where there would be inevitable clashes with the servants. "Since this nation is naturally greedy," he wrote, "they ask for everything and want to be treated better than the other *moços* in their food, dress, and dealings." It was best to have no catechists in the Jesuits' residences, Amaral contended, because "having some and not others, there will be competition and then those who live with us will become haughty and the others will think that we despise them."[100] This new system reportedly produced its desired outcome: By the end of 1634 eighteen catechists had assisted three priests in producing a tally of 9,864 baptisms.[101]

In light of the perceived need for discipline among the catechists and the vows that they were obliged to make in order to receive the prized title *thay,* it seems strange that the missionaries did not insist on their becoming temporal coadjutors in the Society of Jesus. The strained finances of the Province of Japan are perhaps the best explanation since more men in the order's ranks would have obliged it to greater expenses at a time when ensuring sufficient revenues for a handful of priests involved uncertain commercial ventures.[102] It is also possible that the Jesuits did not want to risk political danger by bringing indigenous men into their ranks when the conditions of their residence in Tonkin and Cochinchina remained unsettled. And it may have been the case that the missionaries did not feel confident enough about their neophytes' faith to want them to join the Society.

While some scholars have posited a deep-seated Eurocentrism among the Jesuits as the primary reason why there were so few Asian members of the

Society, whether as brothers or priests, such a sentiment is not made explicit in the documents that have survived from Palmeiro's day.[103] That is, there are no claims in the sources from that period to suggest that the Jesuits in Macau or beyond thought that Asian men were unfit for entering their order purely because of their ethnicity. Other factors, most importantly the lack of worthy educational and novice training facilities, accounted for this dearth of local recruits accepted into the Society of Jesus. As convenient as it would be to assert that the Jesuits' racist attitudes constituted the insurmountable barrier that kept Vietnamese catechists from becoming brothers (or even priests) in the order, there is no contemporary evidence that would support this claim.

The issue of temporal coadjutors, whether of European or Asian extraction, within the Society gave the Visitor cause for concern during his time in Macau. Jesuit brothers had played vital roles in the Province of Japan since its inception, but the limits of the position of temporal coadjutor had never seemed adequate for the realities of the mission field. There was simply no avoiding the fact that the rank of brother was a subordinate one within the order, that it did not promise advancement to the priesthood. In Europe, and wherever there were colleges with significant communities of Jesuits, temporal coadjutors played key roles as managers of the Society's material resources. They served as sacristans, cooks, gatekeepers, clothing-makers, nurses, and procurators as well as acting as catechists and teachers of reading and writing to young children. Theirs was the path of humble service, one with an ancient pedigree in Christian religious communities. As Jesuits they gained the spiritual benefits that accrued from belonging to a religious order but without the weighty moral obligations of the cure of souls.

One should not assume that men who chose to live out their adult lives as temporal coadjutors simply saw that their ambitions for promotion to higher ranks had been thwarted by capricious superiors and resigned themselves to their lowly status. Indeed, those who joined the Jesuits in Europe during their youth knew that their future promotions beyond the initial rank of brother were not certain but were predicated on academic and spiritual merit. Most of the men who would eventually become priests in the Society of Jesus spent their early years in the order as brothers, before the decision was made whether or not to put them on a track toward the priesthood. For those who were slated to become temporal coadjutors or who joined with this intention, the conscious choice to remain brothers enjoyed reverence in early modern eyes not only for its indication of a commitment to service but also for its obligation to humility. (And even those who progressed toward the higher studies that would permit ordination were not necessarily destined to rise to the highest rank among the fourth-vow professed; many remained as third-vow spiritual coadjutors).

Palmeiro had known many brothers during his time in Portugal as well as over the course of his years in Asia. He had lived alongside them at Coimbra, where he and the other Jesuit professors and preachers depended on brothers to keep the college running while concentrating on matters academic themselves. At Braga, he had been in charge of a college staff that included several temporal coadjutors. While he was in India, Palmeiro counted on brothers to escort him to the far-flung spots that he would visit, from Diu to Colombo and Goa to São Tomé. He had lived at Cochin in the company of Pedro de Basto (1570–1645), the brother who was in charge of that college's clothing supply and who would, after Palmeiro's departure, enjoy renown for his gift of prophecy. The Visitor had also worked closely with many of the brothers at the College of Macau. Among his most familiar associates was Manuel de Figueiredo (1590–1663), who held the posts of procurator and pharmacist in the early 1630s. Palmeiro was effusive in his praise for this brother, mentioning his mercantile skills to the superior general in at least two letters.[104] And Figueiredo would be Palmeiro's constant companion during the Visitor's final illness, keeping watch at his bedside and making sure that he took the prescribed remedies. Palmeiro also sent brothers to the missions in the knowledge that they would serve as valuable auxiliaries to the priests. For instance, he sent António de Torres (1592–1680) and Belchior Ribeiro (1585–1671) to Faifo to assist with the Cochinchina mission. The common bond that united these men was the fact that they were all born in Europe and had either joined the order there as coadjutors or entered the Society after careers of soldiering or trade in Portuguese Asia.

The integration of Asian men into the ranks of the Society of Jesus proved a greater challenge. The Jesuit presence in the region was of recent vintage, and given the fact that there were few colleges (or other religious houses) that potential recruits could have seen, the European patterns of religious life were largely unknown. With the exception of those men who had visited a handful of colonial cities such as Goa, Cochin, or Manila, prospective Asian Jesuits would not have a clear idea of the different ranks and duties of brothers, spiritual coadjutors, or professed Jesuits. Even in Macau, where the Jesuit college was the largest of all of the city's religious houses, its population was atypical: compared with European colleges, it had a disproportionate number of fourth-vow professed. So it would only have been in exceptional circumstances that potential East Asian recruits would have known what European Jesuits expected of temporal coadjutors and what the possibilities for advancement were for brothers. To be sure, the majority of men who would have entertained vocations in early modern Asia had never visited any colonial city but simply endeavored to emulate their missionary pastors.

The result of this general lack of Jesuit models in the mission fields created a confusion of expectations. It should not be surprising that Chinese, Japanese, or Vietnamese Christian men would have entertained the goal of become priests. After all, it was not uncommon for their young peers to join (at times temporarily) the ranks of the Buddhist clergy and aspire to positions of prestige. It was precisely this dynamic that led to the acceptance of Japanese brothers into the Society of Jesus, many of whom were drawn from the ranks of the *dōjuku*. Some of these *iruman* ("brothers," from the Portuguese *irmão*) eventually, at the turn of the seventeenth century during the time of the first bishop to reside in Japan, were ordained, not all of them as Jesuits. To give one example, Justo Kazariya (or Yamada, b. 1559) died in 1629 after spending over forty years associated with the Jesuits, first as a *dōjuku*, then as a brother, and finally as a priest in Cochinchina and Cambodia.[105] By the time Palmeiro arrived in Macau, however, there was a dwindling number of Japanese brothers left, thanks to the persecutions. At the Portuguese colony, the only candidates considered for entry into the Society of Jesus were *filhos de Macau*, local men who were ethnically Chinese or Japanese and those of Luso-Asian parentage.[106] Without a seminary or a full complement of courses at the college, they were trained as brothers for service at Macau or within the Ming Empire. Palmeiro had known some of these brothers well and was certain of their capacities; recall that Domingos Mendes escorted him through China, and that he listened when Pascoal Mendes argued against the use of the term *Shangdi* and even *Tianzhu*. But it does not appear that Palmeiro sought to see these men ordained as priests; he was primarily interested in having a corps of temporal coadjutors to carry out the missions' difficult logistical tasks, such as serving as reliable couriers to Macau.[107]

The Visitor was averse to having the Society's various ranks collapsed into one. The order had always had brothers, and it needed them to support its ministries. While it was clear that those trained in Macau would be cognizant of their humble status, it was not certain that those men who joined in the mission fields would accept it. While it was too late to worry about this in

Japan—although there were some men who petitioned to be received into the order in Japanese prisons, those inescapable antechambers of martyrdom— and it was too soon to contemplate it for Tonkin and Cochinchina, the case of China caused Palmeiro anxiety. Ever since the inception of the Vice-Province of China in 1619, the question of training native auxiliaries for entry into the order had been debated both inside and outside the Ming Empire. The recruitment pool was primarily to be the young males of the mission church within China (instead of Macau), but no firm solution had been reached about the important question of where to train these Chinese men. Both the option to train them in the Portuguese colony and the choice to train them in China (possibly in the central southern region of Jiangnan) had their drawbacks, and it was only with hesitation that a plan had been made to create a "novitiate" at Jiading, near Shanghai. Palmeiro visited this site and voiced high praise for João Fróis, the Portuguese "novice master," in the account he wrote of his travels. But those words were written for public consumption. In his correspondence to Rome, he voiced a very different opinion, one that went right to the heart of the issues discussed here.

"I was not satisfied with the clothing and the education of the brother coadjutors," the Visitor wrote after his return to Macau in late 1629. Both of these points were related to the status of these men within the order, and he contended that the lack of a visible demarcation between the apparel and training of the priests and brothers in China would blur the distinction between them in the eyes of their intended audiences. First, Palmeiro asserted that there was no difference between how the coadjutors and padres dressed and that it was necessary for the brothers to use a more modest yet still respectable style of clothing. He argued that the ambiguity created by this vision of similarly attired priests and brothers—one reminiscent of the confused visual metaphor created by the priests' use of literati robes—had pernicious consequences: "Since they are all sons of Chinese families and they learn letters and polite speech from a tender age, they want to succeed at everything and want to be equal in all to the priests." The illusion that they were in training to attain the same rank as the priests was confirmed by their use of the same clothing, Palmeiro claimed, and he did not think it would be easy to correct the situation. "These outfits were given to them hastily, and now it is too late for a remedy", he lamented. That did not stop the Visitor from issuing orders for the clothing to be used by these men, but he did not specify the precise fabrics or style to be used (so long as they were not made of silk).[108]

The other point that drew Palmeiro's attention was the brothers' unfamiliarity with the Society's behavioral norms. He declared that they had "little or no training" within the order since they completed their novitiate within China, where there were no substantial Jesuit communities. That is, these recruits did not know how brothers were expected to behave toward priests or what they were supposed to learn during their formation. The fact that they were trained in small groups (even the Jiading house only had three students in the late 1620s) meant that they never learned the communal patterns of life that were the hallmarks of Jesuit life outside of the mission fields.[109]

The Visitor's rulebook thus laid out clear parameters for the comportment of temporal coadjutors, especially the Chinese students who intended to become brothers. He specified how they were to address priests using terms of respect, and how they were to be addressed by servants; he stipulated routine participation in the Spiritual Exercises as well as regular reception of the sacraments; and he indicated that the rules for brothers should be issued to all coadjutors in writing, or at least posted so that all could easily see them. The Visitor also established the daily routine of lessons and set down specific rules against unsupervised interactions or correspondence with outsiders. Read as a description of the behaviors that he witnessed among the China mission's actual and prospective brothers, Palmeiro's longest rule on the subject stands as a grave indictment: "In order for them to proceed with the due decorum that is expected of those who would be religious, they will not have things to eat in their cubicles, nor will they call each other or the servants bad names, nor will they speak at table, nor will they waste days in unnecessary chatting; and when they speak to each other, it will be with a low voice, showing modesty and calm in all of their actions, and they will be ready to do all of the penances that their superior orders them to do."[110]

It appears that the China Jesuits believed that their principal task with regard to these Chinese recruits was to provide them with the academic skills to assist with proselytizing. But in Palmeiro's view the missionaries had forgotten the crucial element of religious life, discipline. It is possible that, as foreigners, the Jesuits knew they did not have the authority to impose obedience on Chinese men within the Ming Empire. In any event, it was not clear just how much education was due to temporal coadjutors in order to make them into effective auxiliaries. Palmeiro approved a plan of language and philosophy studies similar to that intended for use by the Europeans who were assigned to the vice-province, in which brothers would learn to read and write Mandarin and Portuguese.

The Visitor did not agree that the education of coadjutors should extend to all of the realms of knowledge for which the Jesuits were known in China. Specifically, he countered a claim that the superior general had granted permission for the missionaries to teach the brothers mathematics. If discipline was already a problem among the vice-province's coadjutors, he maintained, training them in technical disciplines would further undermine any sense of subordination that they had to the missionaries. "It does not appear to me that Your Reverence would give such an order, were you were correctly informed," Palmeiro wrote to Vitelleschi, "since the learning of this science might serve to increase their haughtiness, because it is prized among the Chinese above all others." Worse still, he continued, "it could also serve as temptation to leave the *Companhia*." Without mentioning the name of Luís de Faria (b. 1594), he recounted the story of a brother who, "with only the knowledge of how to make some sundials and some spyglasses, caused infamous disorders, saying that with this art he already had the skills to earn his daily bread."[111] Palmeiro's rule about not teaching "seculars" how to make clocks and telescopes therefore applied even to the Society's indigenous students and coadjutors.[112] If nothing else could make the priests in China distinct from their auxiliaries, the Visitor appeared to argue, at least their knowledge of science would.

———

These hesitations about the education and discipline of Chinese brothers most likely are to blame for their diminishing numbers in the decades that followed Palmeiro's visit. And there was no new program to train Vietnamese brothers. In any case, the growth in the size of the Christian communities in both regions during the middle decades of the seventeenth century obliged the Jesuits to work through native auxiliaries. Unlike what had been the case in Japan, these individuals would not be brothers of the Society but either catechists (in Tonkin and Cochinchina) or leaders of lay brotherhoods (in China). With few priests in the mission field, the Jesuits tried to harness the strong upwelling of fervor on the part of some indigenous Christians by ceding their role as leaders over neophyte communities. And such were the responsibilities and social standing of the catechists in the Vietnamese missions that when the French bishops appointed by the Congregation of the Propaganda Fide arrived in that region after mid-century, they were promptly ordained as priests (much to the shock of the Jesuits). But that episode was far off in the future during Palmeiro's day, and his primary concern was to ensure that his men—from mission superiors down to coadjutors—were guided by the spirit of the Society's *Constitutions,* especially with regard to their vows of poverty, chastity, and obedience.

It was this spirit and the notion that all things should be done *ad maiorem Dei gloriam* that had made Palmeiro a gambler in Macau. He had wagered his order's reputation on the expansion of Christianity in Southeast Asia and had won the bet. The stakes were high: he had to make the Jesuits into ship-owners and merchants, avocations that were at odds with church tradition and the Society's vows. To be sure, it had not been Palmeiro's idea to begin the first missions in Southeast Asia, but he had vigorously pressed his luck once he assumed control over the Province of Japan. Turning some of his men away from the relentless tragedy unfolding in Japan, which was beyond human assistance, he sent mission after mission to Cochinchina and Tonkin with orders not to return to Macau unless their lives were threatened.[113] Even when circumstances obliged his men to sail away from their new mission fields or go into hiding, the Visitor's resolve was undaunted. The reward for his confidence in the risky diplomatic and commercial bets that he had made was evident in the growth of the Vietnamese Christian community. And so it was with evident pride that he wrote to Rome in April 1633 with news to be "greatly celebrated," since they told of the "most fervent progress of the new *christandade*" in Tonkin. Only the "infernal enemy" stood in the way, Palmeiro cautioned, since the devil had a long tradition of manipulating the hearts of pagan princes like the one upon whose favor the missionaries' hopes rested.[114] Yet it would appear that the devil's attentions were focused elsewhere, because the Visitor would only hear positive reports from Vietnam before his death in 1635. Satan was, of course, playing a different game where the stakes were far greater, winning on every spin of the wheel of fortune against the last Jesuits in Japan.

10

Sunset in the East

The ships that arrived in Macau in May 1632 brought the Visitor bad news from Nagasaki. Cristóvão Ferreira, one of the last European priests of the underground Japan mission, sent tales of torture, apostasy, and martyrdom from across the island empire. The reports told of persecutions of a rigor and intensity not experienced by Christians since Roman times.

Those persecutions provided the dramatic setting for acts of pious heroism. Writing in March of that year, Ferreira gave an account of how the Japanese Jesuit priest António Ishida (1570–1632) showed invincible constancy in the face of torment. Imprisoned alongside four European friars, Ishida was singled out for special punishment by the Tokugawa shogunate's chief agent for dealing with foreigners, the Nagasaki *bugyō* (commissioner) Takenaka Uneme no Kami Shigeyoshi.[1] Uneme's diabolical intention, claimed Ferreira, was to make them deny their religion "and in this way discredit our Holy Law and its ministers, breaking the spirit of the Christians so that, following their example, the Christians would more easily give up the faith." The persecutor also intended to "win credit and honor for himself before the shogun", but he had met his match in Ishida—or so at least thought Ferreira. After sending a scholar to win over the Jesuit by reason, and even suggesting that the priest merely make outward acquiescence to the demand for apostasy, Uneme ordered Ishida and six others, including two Luso-Japanese women, to be tortured.[2]

In the early days of December 1631, according to Ferreira, the prisoners were sent in chains to the far side of Tachibana Bay to the Takaku region and marched up the slopes of Mount Unzen, a volcano notorious for its sulfurous hot springs. Ishida and his companions, kept in seclusion from each other, were taken one by one to the edge of the "most furious tank and shown the great gushes that the boiling water made as a way to persuade them to leave the Law of Christ before they tasted so rigorous a torment." Unimpressed by the sight, Ishida and each of the others in turn were bound with ropes held by four men while the boiling water was poured onto their flesh. Over the course of the thirty-three days that they spent on Mount Unzen, Ishida, along with an Augustinian friar, and Beatriz da Costa, were submitted to this scalding on six occasions; the others received fewer dousings.[3] Ishida was treated with exceptional rigor since he had so willingly subverted the shogun's laws, but the punishments failed to move him. "The infidels were astonished," wrote Ferreira, when they found their victims "ever more constant, happy and desirous for suffering, and neither in Nagasaki or in Takaku was anything else spoken of but the invincible spirit and valor with which they suffered." Seeking to break them rather than kill them, Uneme appointed a doctor to treat their wounds after each scalding. But the *bugyō* at length was convinced by his retainers that the Christians would "exhaust all of the wells and tanks at Unzen", so he relented and summoned Ishida and his companions back to Nagasaki. By the time Ferreira closed his letter in late March 1632, the tenacious Japanese priest was languishing in prison while his tormentor headed for Edo to account for his governance before the shogun.[4]

Back on the China coast, the news of Ishida's trials weighed on the Visitor's conscience. It seemed that there was no stopping the bloody march toward the end of the Society's mission and Christianity's presence in Japan. Each report that arrived at the Portuguese colony told of torture, imprisonment, and execution, not only of the Jesuits but also of any friars who tried to disembark as well as any Japanese found to be harboring the priests or brothers. The number of men left on the other side of the East China Sea was inversely proportional to the intensity of the Jesuits' anxiety in Macau. As the names of the priests and brothers were gradually stricken from the roll of survivors, they implored the Almighty for some shift in the shogunal humor and for some measure of relief for the embattled church. Instead of resigning themselves to what appeared to be their fate, the Jesuits invested each glimmer of what they perceived to be divine favor with outsized significance. The consequent swings in their moods were great, although the cooler heads at Macau sought a rational perspective on the ineluctable outcome. As Palmeiro declared in a letter to Rome as he relayed more tragic news, "many times those of us who live in these parts are forced to hope, even without reason for hope."[5]

What could the Visitor do to alleviate the suffering of his remaining men in Japan and their beleaguered flock? He could send funds as well as encouragement aboard the Portuguese ships that sailed from Macau or Manila. He could also attempt to deliver men, but ever since the Japanese authorities had begun to offer bounties to those who denounced priests or brothers, that was

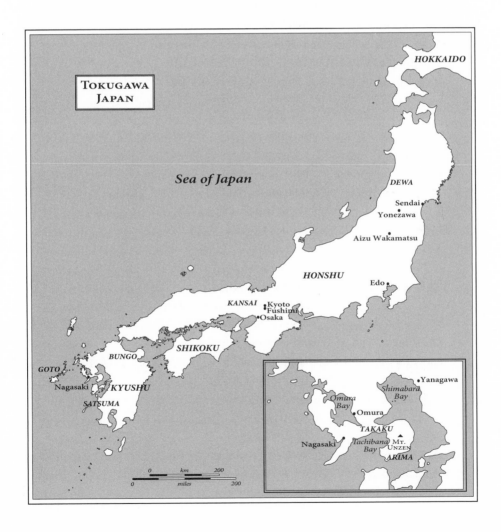

an increasingly dangerous gamble. Moreover, putting missionaries on merchant ships, even in disguise, would lead to reprisals against the Portuguese
traders that might sever the vital communication link between Macau and
Japan. While none of these paths was ideal, to leave the Jesuits and their
Christians completely without succor was unacceptable. Questions hung
over Palmeiro's head: Should he send the Japan hands remaining at Macau—
regardless of their advanced age—back to their old mission territories? After
all, they knew the language and the lay of the land; they would stand a better
chance of evading spies, turncoats, and the shogunal authorities than new-
comers would. Was there anything that might bring about a change in the
persecutory regime, such as the yearned-for death of the Tokugawa shogun?
Most importantly, why was God so reluctant to come to the aid of the Jesuits
and their Christians when they had heroically suffered for the faith? These
were the concerns that haunted the Visitor in the final years of his life, feeding the anxieties that would hasten his death in 1635.

The brutal persecutions that brought Japan's "Christian Century" to an end
are well known to scholars, novelists, and filmmakers. There was no shortage
of epic scenes for the Jesuits, the friars, and their followers: the hunt for the
remaining European priests in urban hideouts or in the mountain wilderness; the emotional coercion of the ceremonies during which Japanese lay
folk were obliged to tread upon Christian images called *fumie*; and the cruel
tortures and executions of Japanese and Europeans who confessed Christianity. From the moment that Palmeiro stepped ashore at Macau, he was a privileged witness to the events unfolding in Japan. As already seen, his first letters to Rome from the Portuguese colony described how he attempted to
smuggle messages and money to the mission field. This correspondence reported the many instances of fortitude in the face of persecution but did not
ignore the fact that its rigors had swelled the numbers not only of martyrs
but also of *caídos,* the fallen. The situation in Japan had grown more dire for
the Jesuits as the years passed; the mission that Palmeiro heard and read about
in 1626 was very different from the one he encountered in reports half a decade later. The shogunate's anti-Christian policies had worked with great ef-
ficiency, especially in the areas of Kyushu where the Christian presence had
been most deeply felt. At times in groups, but often one by one, the priests
and brothers fell into their persecutors' hands, weakening the bonds that held

the Japanese Christians to the bosom of the Church. When the last blows fell against the once-flourishing mission, Palmeiro would be among the first to hear.

Although the drumbeat of persecution had been maintained in Japan since the expulsion of the Catholic clergy in 1614, noises from other missions have drowned it out in this narrative. Palmeiro's realization that he had limited options, as well as a lull of news between 1627 and 1628, permitted him to turn his gaze elsewhere. But with the yearly shifts in the winds and the arrival of the silver fleets, the Visitor's mind was cyclically brought back to the fate of his men and the Christians in Japan. By the end of 1629, after Palmeiro had returned from inside the Ming Empire, he once again began to sense the pulse of the persecutions across the sea. Much like the waves created by the rising tides visible from the windows of the Colégio de Madre de Deus, the strains of suffering rose in a crescendo that increasingly took hold of Palmeiro's attentions. Instead of echoing the refrains of the previous decade, during which accounts of martyrdoms seemed balanced by tallies of baptisms in the hundreds or even thousands, the reports now were relentlessly grim. "I had hoped to send Your Reverence some more certain or better news from Japan," wrote the Visitor to the superior general after news reached Macau in late 1629, "but the desired outcome did not match my thoughts or feelings."[6]

These dispatches about the state of the Japanese Christian community came in *escuras metaforas,* dark metaphors. Palmeiro related how his men were so frightened of seeing their messages intercepted (and translated by turncoats) that they wrote in a nearly impenetrable register of veiled references. It was nevertheless certain, Palmeiro averred, that four more priests had been captured, "and by the terms used in the writing, it is understood that among them is one of ours." It was also certain that the mission church of Nagasaki, the former heart of Christianity in Japan, was "completely finished because with some of the new hardships that were imposed, what was still standing was laid low." Worse still, the rigors of the persecutions carried out by the Nagasaki commissioners had louder echoes elsewhere in Japan beyond Kyushu. The Visitor passed on word that in the northern regions, "where the *christandade* enjoyed some peace, there was a great number of martyrs." Indeed, Giovanni Battista Porro had written to Palmeiro in the summer of 1629 to describe the trials of his flock in domains of Date Masamune (1567–1636), the most important of the northern Honshu lords. First in the region of

Yonezawa in Dewa Province, and in the following year spreading eastward to the area of Aizu Wakamatsu and Sendai, the wrath of the shogunal authorities reduced these distant enclaves of Japanese Christians.[7] In Porro's words, this end of Honshu had before that moment "seemed to be another Mount Olympus, where neither the winds nor the rains of the lower regions could reach."[8] But as the military hegemon Toyotomi Hideyoshi had declared in 1587, Japan was the land of the gods, and the time had come for the gods to come back to this northern perch just as they had returned to Kyushu.

These reports of the spread of the persecutions convinced Palmeiro and his colleagues that the end had come for "the hopes of seeing so flourishing a Christian community restored to its former state."[9] As best he could, the Visitor thus had to engage in damage control. In this, both the living and the dead demanded his attentions: On the one hand he had to provide solace to his remaining subordinates, while on the other he had to ensure that the details of the martyrdoms were recorded for transmission to Rome. In other words, the Visitor had to remind the living that the sufferings of this world were fleeting and the glory of martyrs eternal. And for the sake of those who had sacrificed their lives, he had to undertake the grim accounting that would ensure that the memory of their martyrdoms would not be lost by the Universal Church.

Dealing with the dead proved to be the easier of these two tasks, but only slightly so. Issues of memory, precedence, and prestige had to be negotiated in Macau and in Europe, and they were far from consensual topics. Recall that the Jesuits were not the only order to claim martyrs in Japan; Franciscans, Dominicans, Augustinians, and at least one Trinitarian—not to mention hundreds of laymen and women—also won their palms during the decades of persecution. While their brethren believed that the souls of those who died confessing the faith were received immediately in heaven, the institutional church took longer to sort matters out on earth. In order to ensure that the martyrs of Japan received their due—from the simple cataloging of their names and the circumstances of their deaths by competent authorities, to their integration on the official lists of the blessed in Rome, and finally to the approved invocation of their memory (and intercessory power) in prayers and memorial masses—a vast bureaucratic effort had to be coordinated. Given the number of individuals who had died during the Tokugawa persecutions, it is not surprising that this process was a long one. Even if the papacy's customary slowness is taken to account, the beatification process (the obligatory first step toward recognition) was a laborious affair that took decades—much to the frustration of the martyrs' pastors and others in Macau, Manila, or elsewhere. To give but one example, the beatification of the twenty-six individuals crucified at Nagasaki in 1597 was only promulgated in 1627, thirty years after the events.[10] Yet the increased intensity of the persecutions in the 1620s eventually prodded Rome to make a swifter reckoning of the scores of martyrs who had died in that decade. The process of recognizing all the others killed on Japanese soil would continue long after the rigors of the persecution had passed and Christianity had been all but extinguished in Japan.[11]

In the late sixteenth century the papacy forcefully asserted its control over the official recognition of the blessed and the saints. With the creation of the Sacred Congregation for Rites and Ceremonies in 1588 and the articulation of standard procedures for beatification and canonization in the following years, Rome intended to put order in the chaos of popular devotions. The papacy's intention was to clear the thicket of localized cults and divergent liturgies established in centuries past for particular saints, and to introduce a rigorous investigation process by which all cults of sainthood would be either approved or rejected. Foremost in the minds of the popes was to ensure that Catholic devotions bore a Roman stamp. By bringing the beatification and canonization process fully under papal control, Rome would serve as the arbiter of the forms of piety permitted within Catholicism. Gone were the days when small-scale devotions, if approved by local church authorities, were considered acceptable. As should have been expected, the consequence of this centralizing move was an increase of lobbying efforts aimed at the Congregation of Rites, especially by religious orders. But priests, friars, and nuns were not the only ones interested in seeing their confreres recognized. Diocesan authorities also competed to have their local or regional devotions approved. Such was the onslaught of pious propaganda in favor of different candidates that Urban VIII moved to stem outside interference in Rome's deliberations. In 1625 he issued a brief (its main points would be reiterated by decree in 1634) that prohibited the public celebration of holy men or women, whether in sermons, publications, processions, or other devotions, until the papacy had recognized them.[12] These changes in the official procedures for making saints occurred just when the Japan mission church produced large numbers of martyrs, a fact that inevitably delayed the attribution of elevated status.

Although the representatives of the secular church and the religious orders had been keeping their own records of the martyrdoms at Macau, they had to wait for Rome's approval to open the beatification process. Once those instructions reached East Asia, the initial phases would be handled by special tribunals organized by the competent bishops; the bishop of China (a *sede vacante* controlled by an ecclesiastical governor since 1615), the bishop of Japan (once again resident in Macau after 1631), and the archbishop of Manila.[13] These authorities were charged with collecting testimony about the martyrs, authenticating it, and forwarding it to Rome. To be sure, the ongoing persecution in Japan made investigations in situ impossible. Matters were further complicated by the fact that the eyewitnesses were concentrated in Kyushu or Honshu. While it was not necessary when dealing with martyrs to show records of miracles or evidence of popular sentiment in order to complete the beatification process, constancy in confessing the faith at the time of death being considered sufficient grounds, Rome still needed proof. The recollections of missionary exiles and European traders in Macau and Manila were therefore the primary sources of the beatification cases for the martyrs of Japan.

The martyrdom investigations were a grave threat to the fragile peace that had been established between the religious orders in Macau. The reopening of files related to Japan was likely to renew the heated exchanges from the late 1610s between the orders over which group bore the responsibility for the expulsion of the priests from that country. And memories of the violent disputes between the friars and the Jesuits in 1624 over Macau's bishopric were still fresh, despite Palmeiro's attempts to make peace. It was no coincidence that he had chosen the reliquary heads of three Japanese martyrs, carried by the three most important clergymen in the colony on the feast of Francis Xavier in 1629, to bring closure to past feuds. But the simmering resentments would burst forth again just a few months later, in the first weeks of 1630, when the trials commenced at Macau. It only took the public airing of each order's pious memories to fan the embers of jealousy into flames.

There existed a climate of mutual recrimination between the religious orders over missteps in Japan, and while each order was keen to record the heroic memory of its martyrs, they did not necessarily see the actions of their rivals in the same light. For their part, the Jesuits would not cease to blame the friars for jeopardizing their efforts through repeated bungling. The friars would by turn accuse the Jesuits of trying to monopolize the memory of Japan, which had produced a sizeable crop of mendicant martyrs. Rome's 1625 gag order on public declarations of sanctity meant that the religious at Macau had spent half a decade celebrating their martyrs in private, and this, they

felt, was an unjust and unbecoming fate for their heroic brethren and followers. The beatification trials therefore represented the first opportunity for
them to loosen their tongues and insist on their martyrs' rightful places
among the blessed. But the vagaries of the mails between Europe and the
China coast meant that the requests from Rome reached Macau in haphazard
fashion and in letters that only mentioned some martyrs by name. Wounded
pride thus added to the habitual jockeying for prestige among the orders, adding another stratum to the seemingly inexhaustible mine of resentment between priests and friars.

As the Society's most important representative in East Asia, Palmeiro had
to coordinate his order's participation in the beatification process. His efforts
began even before the official trials began since it was inevitable that Rome
would, at some point, recognize the Jesuit martyrs. The Visitor's first step was
to identify among his subordinates those men who were sufficiently familiar
with Japan to describe the conditions of the persecution. Memory of the mission was fading fast in Macau in the late 1620s, a fact that would make it
harder to get the Jesuits' story straight. If they were to offer testimony about
events that had occurred in previous decades, it was necessary to get at least a
first draft of their mission's history down on paper. For this reason Palmeiro
requested two of his most experienced men, João Rodrigues and Pedro Morejón, to complete the history of the Japanese Church, which Rodrigues had left
unfinished years earlier. After all, there was no Jesuit as well versed in Japanese
affairs as Rodrigues, but he had been expelled from Japan in 1610; Morejón had
stayed on for a longer span, but he had gone into exile with most of the other
priests in 1614.

By the time Palmeiro set this pair to the task in 1627, the profusion of accounts that had been written by missionaries in hiding made it difficult to
identify a clear narrative thread. "They are proceeding very slowly," wrote the
Visitor the following year, "and the old *padres* are dying off, and with them
the necessary information."[14] Rodrigues himself had admitted as much in a
letter to the superior general where he contrasted his advanced age—although
he still had the energy for two more trips to Beijing—with the demands of
history writing that he reluctantly undertook. He knew what was at stake if
he did not finish his task: "The candle is going out, and everything will come to
an end," Rodrigues lamented. "New men will appear to fill books about these
parts and Japan, as others do with fables of the kind they write in Europe,
in such an abundance that if an angel came to wipe away the falsehoods

from those books, we would have an ample supply of blank paper for years to come."[15]

For Palmeiro, a narrow focus on more recent events in Japan was just as hard to obtain as a broad view of the mission's history. But owing to the need for accurate testimony for the beatification process, he also had to identify men whose knowledge was deep enough to ensure that the reports sent to Rome reflected what the Jesuits knew of the circumstances of their martyrs' sufferings. He also needed to choose a man with a combination of diplomatic skills and tenacity because whoever handled this affair would necessarily have to deal with representatives of the secular clergy as well as the other religious orders. Palmeiro's choice, once new requests from Rome were made public in 1630, was Pedro Morejón.[16] This Jesuit had twice served as a diplomat, in Siam as well as in Manila, and was considered deft at dealing with his Castilian compatriots. Such skills were crucial in the competition for Rome's attention from the other side of the world: It was a clear signal that the Jesuits would have to pursue their cases aggressively if the numbers of their martyrs were to get proportional recognition from the Papal Curia. There was no doubt that the Jesuits had contributed the largest number of priests and brothers to the tally of martyrs, but the mendicant orders were just as eager as they were to see their brethren beatified. And it was with evident pleasure that Frei António do Rosário, the governor of the bishopric of China, opened an inquiry in the spring of 1630 seeking details about the 1617 decapitation of his fellow Dominican Fray Alfonso de Navarrete.[17] While there were indeed four religious mentioned by Rome in this inquiry, one from each order including the Society of Jesus, it offended the Jesuits that their other martyrs did not enjoy pride of place. It was therefore a fortunate turn of events when Morejón learned at Manila in 1630 that the papacy had sent several other orders for inquiries to Asia by different routes.[18]

The inquiries held in Macau lasted for most of the first half of the 1630s. The testimony from the Navarrete trial consists of pages of questions and answers relating to the death of the four priests, including sworn statements confirming how their corpses were placed into two wooden boxes and cast into Ōmura Bay and relating that one of the boxes reemerged from the depths months later with the incorrupt bodies of an Augustinian and a Franciscan.[19] The governor of the bishopric of Macau also had orders to conduct another inquiry, this one "universal" instead of "particular" (that is, specifically about the four martyrs from 1617), but it appears that Morejón spent more time working with the bishop of Japan, who received instructions to conduct three different inquiries. This prelate was Diogo Valente, Palmeiro's friend from his days at Coimbra, who had returned to Macau in the autumn of 1631 after his ban of excommunication was lifted by both royal command and papal fiat. Although it was impossible for Valente to carry out his investigations in Japan, he could rely on his former confreres to provide information. Palmeiro was keen to facilitate this process and made sure that Valente had appropriate lodgings for carrying out his task (given that he could not reside in his diocese). The Visitor arranged for a set of buildings that belonged to the Jesuits in Macau to be put at the bishop's disposal and offered the assistance of the provincial procurator to help Valente coordinate his activities.[20] Much to the satisfaction of Palmeiro and the other Jesuits, Valente made a priority of his investigation of Carlo Spinola, the most famous figure in the Great Martyrdom of Nagasaki in September 1622.[21]

The bishop of Japan's other two inquiries were of a more general nature. He requested from the representatives of each order lists of the names of the religious and lay folk who had been martyred. Here, having a ready knowledge of the history of Japan was crucial, so Morejón was an ideal representative for the Society. He and his peers among the mendicants duly enumerated the dead but were compelled by the supervising judges to give names for every individual (rather than simply submit tallies consisting of references to "a friar," "a brother," or "a layman"). Ever vigilant of his order's honor, Morejón was keen to alert the Jesuits' Roman curia that this was not simply a disinterested accounting of those who had died. He insisted that the friars were on the one hand inflating their numbers of martyrs while on the other omitting—perhaps intentionally, he suggested—names of some of the Jesuits' Japanese coadjutors from the final tallies. When the documentation from Macau was complete in 1633, the Jesuits and the Franciscans cooperated in preparing eight full copies, sending half of them via Manila and Mexico and the other half via Goa.[22] The loss of those papers sent on the Portuguese *Carreira da Índia,* however, obliged Morejón to produce yet another set in 1635, complete with information about the latest martyrdoms.[23]

More difficult than wrangling over the memory of the dead was dealing with those who so ardently desired to die. It was one thing to manage men who faced frustration, imprisonment, or exile, as was the case in China or Southeast

Asia; it was a wholly different matter to direct men who knew they courted torture and martyrdom. Palmeiro's task was unenviable: He knew that in Japan the remaining Jesuits risked their lives with every move, but he could not command them to return to Macau. The men in hiding knew what they had to expect from both the agents of the Tokugawa regime as well as local authorities; they were conscious of the presence of spies and apostates who would benefit from the bounties placed on the missionaries' heads. And the Jesuits harbored no illusions about the tortures that awaited them if they were captured. Their lot was to minister to their persecuted flock while seeking to evade the man hunters and to show constancy in the face of oppression, all the while hoping for divine succor for the mission church. But what was the Visitor to do with those hardy souls who wanted to travel to Japan despite the evident dangers? What could Palmeiro say to men who willingly put themselves in harm's way—and who, by doing so, jeopardized the Macau–Nagasaki route? What advice or consolation could he give them, short of urging them to delay their perilous plans until the storm, God willing, had passed?

The situation of the last Jesuits in Japan greatly taxed his prudence and pragmatism. We know that Palmeiro did not dismiss the heroism of those who suffered in Japan, and we know that he believed the martyrs were the ornament of the Society of Jesus. His letters to the men in the mission field declared his admiration for those who experienced the cruel and unusual tortures invented by the Nagasaki commissioners and by zealously anti-Christian daimyo in the late 1620s. Writing to Mateus de Couros, who would die of exhaustion at Hasami in the hills behind Ōmura, Palmeiro declared that the dangers confronted by the priests in Japan "and the pits in which they are buried in order to animate their Christians, amount to more than the books written, the sermons preached, and the university chairs held anywhere in the world."[24] According to Giovanni Battista Bonelli, one of the Visitor's closest associates in the last years of his life, Palmeiro had an "insatiable thirst" for martyrdom. During Palmeiro's final illness, Bonelli questioned the Visitor if he regretted not being able to die for the faith in the same gruesome ways as his brethren in Japan. The response came: "Not just a pit or a pyre, I say, but pits, pyres, lions, and all of the machines of martyrdom, and if I had a thousand lives to give, a thousand lives I would give for the love of God."[25]

A similar sentiment comes through in the letters that the Visitor sent to Ishida, Couros, and others, but one wonders if these yearnings were not more the fruits of Palmeiro's commitment to showing solidarity with his men. It is certain that his sense of responsibility to the superior general and to the order prevented him from risking his life by going to Japan, at least until he was relieved of his post. Because he died in office, he never had the opportunity to turn his words into actions. His letters nevertheless speak to his convictions about the glory that awaited martyrs. He reminded Ishida in 1632 that to be a prisoner for the love of Christ was "the most noble title known to St. Paul", and that God prepared to hand Ishida, as a saintly confessor, "the golden key to His royal court". As far as the Visitor and many of his contemporaries were concerned, there could only be one outcome for the suffering of the priests and brothers in Japan, the palm of martyrdom. Human weakness did not enter into Palmeiro's equation. Ishida was sure to endure unto death, the Visitor was convinced, as he looked forward to the transfiguration that awaited the Japanese Jesuit when his torments reached their end:

Continue, my dear *Padre* António, on this path down which you have started. See to the end this enterprise that was begun, has continued, and is almost completed, producing so much divine glory and luster for our holy faith. Crowns of victory are already being prepared in the royal palaces of glory! Our saint is there with his arms open wide, waiting for his triumphant son to enter.[26] What lustrous enamels will beautify that body of yours, wounded all over by the boiling waters of Unzen? What sparkling necklaces will decorate that neck, where such great chains of iron were placed for the love of Jesus? What beautiful bracelets will shine on those arms, which were so damaged by binding shackles? What enviable luster will be given to those fortunate feet but new kinds of elegant *tabis* and shoes, in order to make up for the harm caused by heavy fetters?[27] Finally, what a fortunate exchange Your Reverence will make when you enter as a victor from this tiresome exile into that eternal homeland? How good will the torments of the past seem to you, once you are enjoying firsthand such distinguished rewards?[28]

Beyond reiterating a list of heavenly rewards drawn from Christian tradition, there was little that the Visitor could do for Ishida. The *padre* was in prison; whether he would live long enough to read Palmeiro's words could not be foretold. The Visitor signed his letter on July 12, just in time for it to be carried on the fleet that left Macau on July 15 and reached Nagasaki in August 1632.[29] Did Palmeiro's words inspire Ishida to face his final sentence with fortitude? Whether or not they motivated him, he found the strength to

resist until September 3, when he was burned alive over a slow fire at Nagasaki alongside three Augustinians and two Franciscans.[30]

The Visitor had slightly more room to maneuver in his management of the
men who were still at large. Two in particular are mentioned in his writings,
men whose actions caused him particular anxiety. This pair was Cristóvão
Ferreira and Sebastião Vieira (1574–1634), the last European priests who had
worked in Japan before the persecutions began in 1614. Both had joined the
Society at Coimbra during the 1590s, where Palmeiro was an instructor. And
both had successfully petitioned for assignments in the overseas missions
soon after entering the order. Ferreira sailed for India in 1600, traveling onward to Macau to complete his studies before reaching Japan in 1609. Vieira
completed his studies at Évora before sailing on the *Carreira da Índia* in 1602
and disembarking at Nagasaki in 1604. It is likely that the two got to know
each other at Macau, where Ferreira studied theology while Vieira served as
master of novices. Beyond that time spent together, their paths do not appear
to have crossed often in the mission field.

Before the edict of expulsion was issued, Cristóvão Ferreira studied Japanese in Arima and worked in the Jesuit residence at Kyoto. He stayed on in
the capital region after 1614, traveling incognito among the local Christians
and writing reports about persecutions. By 1617 Ferreira had returned to the
Nagasaki region to serve as secretary to the provincial officer, being charged
with composing many of the early martyrdom reports that were sent to Europe. With changes in provincial leadership, Ferreira would return to his old
mission districts in central Japan, spending the early 1620s in the Kansai region. As the Tokugawa authorities captured and killed more Jesuits, though,
Ferreira would be recalled to western Kyushu, where he once again served as
assistant to the provincial, moving in the shadows between huts on that island's remote mountains. Due to the limited number of professed priests as
well as to his presence near Nagasaki, Ferreira was one of the primary candidates to succeed Mateus de Couros when the beleaguered provincial officer
died. Unaware of how many men were in the mission field at liberty at a
given moment, Palmeiro issued an order in 1628 stating that the senior priest
at large assume the rank of vice-provincial (the rank of provincial being reserved for professed Jesuits appointed to that office by the superior general).
After many years of serving as the mission superior's right-hand man, Ferreira would assume the senior office himself in the summer of 1632, although
his tenure would only last for roughly a year.

Owing to his position near the top of the Society's hierarchy in Japan, Ferreira had privileged access to reports about the sufferings of his colleagues across the archipelago. He was the Visitor's eyes and ears in the mission field, the crucial coordinator of the news who kept the Japan enterprise linked to the rest of the Society through Macau. Messages sent to the remaining men would most likely travel through Ferreira's hands and then onward by trusted couriers. By the early 1630s, there was no one who knew more than he did about the gruesome tortures and painful deaths awaiting those Jesuits who were captured by the shogunal and domanial authorities. The priests' network of underground Christians, as well as the covert connections between the remaining clergy, ensured that Ferreira had access to the news of the persecutions as far away as Aizu Wakamatsu in northern Honshu. These connections also enabled him to get firsthand reports about the torture of Ishida and his companions on Mount Unzen within weeks of that future martyr's return to a Nagasaki prison cell. And among the dispatches that Ferreira sent to Palmeiro was a report in March 1632 about the cruel plan to send Christian beggars and lepers from the cities of central Japan to Manila as a sadistic test of Christian charity. He claimed that there were more than ninety of these unfortunates detained in Nagasaki, awaiting more to join them from the Edo region before embarking for the Philippines.[31]

While Cristóvão Ferreira had spent most of his missionary career moving between central and western Japan, Sebastião Vieira had spent his shuttling between Japan, the China coast, and Europe. Early on Vieira was assigned to the position of procurator in Macau, and later in Nagasaki. At the time of the expulsion of the priests, he embarked for Manila, from whence he found passage back to Japan in 1615. Back in Macau in 1619 he served as procurator for the Province of Japan for another three years before being elected from among his brethren to travel to Rome in 1623. Vieira's trip to Europe was a recruiting expedition, but it also aimed to communicate the heroic labors of the Japan Jesuits and their Christians to the Papal Curia and to complain to the Society's curia about the split between the Province of Japan and its recently created appendage, the Vice-Province of China. It took six years for Vieira to complete his round trip from Macau to Goa to Lisbon to Rome, but it is unclear whether he accomplished much. His primary intent was to obtain men and, above all, money for the Province of Japan (that is, funds that would not have to be shared with the China mission) and to bring about the creation of a dedicated post of procurator in Lisbon. Vieira also sought to lobby the papacy to issue a ban on friars traveling to Japan from Manila; such ventures only served to inflame the wrath of the persecutors, the Japan Jesuits were convinced. He did succeed in securing a large party of forty recruits for the East Asian missions, but only one of these would actually reach Japan.[32]

If nothing else, Vieira's voyage to the Eternal City had set his mind to accomplishing his own journey to eternity. He returned to Macau in late 1629 determined to find a way back to Japan, even if it meant death. Realizing that the Portuguese merchants did not want to risk seeing their trade with Nagasaki cut off in order to satisfy his temerarious desires, Vieira planned a route through Manila. But before heading to the Philippines, he caused Palmeiro's blood to boil. Frustrated by what he saw as the misallocation of the funds that properly belonged to the Japan mission, Vieira agitated among the old Japan hands at Macau to block any move by Palmeiro to transfer resources to the Vice-Province of China or to the missions in mainland Southeast Asia (which belonged to the Province of Japan). From Palmeiro's perspective, the burgeoning mission in the Ming Empire and the new enterprises in Cochinchina and Tonkin merited their share of the Society's resources, especially since there were so few Jesuits left in Japan and it was so difficult to get cash into their hands. Although Palmeiro himself was bitterly disappointed with the fate of the mission, he was not convinced that money would solve its problems. Vieira thought otherwise and confronted Palmeiro before embarking on his final journey to martyrdom.

The affair came to a head in early 1632, when Palmeiro claimed the 500 taels of silver that for years had been taken from the proceeds of the Japan procurator's trade for the China mission. This payment had been stipulated by General Vitelleschi at the time of the creation of the Vice-Province of China and had given the mission in the Ming Empire a crucial boost in its first decade. But with the news of successes at Beijing—that is, with the appointment of Jesuits to the Chinese calendar reform project and its concomitant financial rewards—Vieira was able to alter the mood in Macau. According to Palmeiro, he fomented a "great disturbance" at the college among his peers against the yearly payment. Vieira had complained loudly about the redistribution of funds from the Province of Japan's resources, convincing his brethren that the China mission "wanted to adorn itself with the jewels of others."[33] Although the Visitor was able to resolve the problem of the cash shortfall by having rental properties built in Macau and sending more silk to be sold in Japan, Vieira's maneuvers had crossed a line: Vieira had argued for a consultation to be held to debate the merits of the original order from the superior general, an order against which he had unsuccessfully lobbied in person at Rome. There was nothing that Palmeiro held in higher esteem than orders from the superior general, so he responded to Vieira's insubordination by issuing a stern rebuke. Writing to Vitelleschi, the Visitor told of how he had reminded Vieira that with regard to Rome's orders, "it was not his to consult, but only to execute." The encounter thus ended on a sour note and, as Palmeiro confessed to his superior, "for me, there were hurtful things in this affair, but the important thing is that we suffer them patiently." Indeed, the suffering was soon to be shared by all parties.[34]

The two men parted company when Vieira sailed to Manila in the late spring of 1632. The Visitor blocked his attempt to take a companion with him, a desire also refused him by the provincial officer in the Philippines: The Society's *Constitutions* were not a suicide pact. Vieira disembarked at Manila in the clothing of a Portuguese nobleman and quickly sought passage aboard a Chinese ship heading for Japan. He was fully aware of the danger of traveling on this route to Nagasaki and cognizant of the fatal gambles taken by his predecessors in similar circumstances, yet he wrote to a fellow Jesuit in Rome about how his mission was clear: "Not even Francis Xavier delivered himself over to the Chinese with greater enthusiasm to have them leave him at the markets of Canton," Vieira declared, "than I do now, delivering myself to the same people so that they will toss me on the beaches of Japan, although he did it with greater spirit, greater zeal, and greater perfection."[35]

And so he set sail in the summer of 1632, now wearing Chinese garb, aboard a ship whose crew comprised Japanese apostates and unbaptized Chinese. After spending several days hiding in a storage compartment, Vieira realized that the ship—despite the large bribe he had made to its captain in order to travel alone—also carried three friars. Not content to blow their own cover, Vieira lamented, they also blew his and jeopardized his mission: "The religious were not in the same confinement as I was, and they did not take the necessary caution," he recalled, "and because they were Spaniards, they necessarily drank their chocolate and had their meals prepared on the common stove."[36] The crew soon figured out who they were and, after deliberations about sailing instead to either China or Taiwan, opted out of fear to leave the four missionaries in a remote inlet of the Gotō Islands, off the coast of Kyushu. From this spot Vieira struck out on his own, convincing four Christian fishermen to accompany him on the final leg of his trip.

Word of Vieira's arrival in Japan spread quickly. He recorded that during the short span in which he was in the Gotō Islands in mid-August 1632, he received a letter from António Ishida, locked in prison, welcoming him back to the mission.[37] The Nagasaki commissioner heard of Vieira too, but apparently only learned that a priest who had gone to Rome had returned to Japan. *Romano,* as Vieira claims to have been called, was pursued first on the islands and later along the coast of Satsuma, where he had intended to travel until the winds pushed him northward. Vieira sailed instead toward Arima, entering Shimabara Bay and following its coast to its deepest reaches, living in a small boat and going ashore only in the company of trusted Christians. Among these, he ministered as he could, saying masses in improvised chapels, hearing confessions, and moving only under the cover of darkness. By the time he signed his account of his journey, "from this vessel and in between the islands of Japan", he had traveled all the way to the Yanagawa area of Chikugo Province.[38]

Already in 1626 João Rodrigues had declared that the Japan mission was in its *undecima hora,* its penultimate hour.[39] Over the next half dozen years, the persecutory rigor of the Tokugawa regime would run down the clock to its final minutes. By 1633 it seemed that the mission had reached its final seconds. It was in that year that one disheartening report followed another, with no break in the unrelenting wrath of the Nagasaki commissioners and their peers elsewhere in Japan. In the interval between the execution of António Ishida in early September 1632 and the fatal torturing of other Jesuits in October 1633, the mission was reduced almost to naught. Leaving aside a few Japanese brothers and, of course, the laymen and women who held fast to their religion, the Christian presence in Japan was fast disappearing. All that the Visitor could do at this point was to tally the numbers of the dead and forward his grisly statistics to Rome. Knowing that the mission was on the brink raised his level of anxiety, and each new report from the mission field recorded the steps leading to the final end of the missionary enterprise that had begun in 1549.

By the late summer of 1633 the already gruesome tableau had grown a few shades darker. That year's trading fleet returned to Macau with news of a new form of torture invented to extract information from the unwilling. If those who had resisted during the torment of the boiling springs of Unzen had been sincere in their challenge to the Nagasaki commissioners to invent a more brutal torture, their wish had been fulfilled. Outside the city on Nishizaka Hill at the end of July of that year, Brother Nicolau Fukunaga (b. 1569) was the first Jesuit to be subjected to the "new invention", being hung upside down and lowered halfway into a pit. After his legs and arms were bound, and incisions made in his temples to ensure enough blood was drained so that he remained alive, wooden boards were positioned to block the entry of light. Denied food or drink, Fukunaga lasted from Thursday, July 28, at three in the afternoon until the following Sunday morning at eleven. Two weeks later, Manuel Borges (b. 1584) experienced the same fate, along with two former *dōjuku;* and by the end of August, Giacomo Antonio Giannone (b. 1579) and his former catechist, João Kidera, had expired after three days in the *tormento das covas,* the torture of the pits, at Shimabara. Others, including three Dominicans, three Augustinians, and a handful of laymen, were also suspended in Nagasaki before the month of August ended.[40]

Worse than the reports that these captured priests, brothers, and lay Christians had died was the news that most of the remaining priests had been detained. At some point in August or September, Sebastião Vieira managed to pass a letter into the hands of the Portuguese traders at Nagasaki. He sounded the mission's death knell. He was one of the few priests who remained at large, perhaps still aboard his small boat in Shimabara Bay. Not wanting to tip off the authorities in case his letter slipped into their hands, Vieira wrote in metaphor on a scrap of paper. He described the perilous state of "the persecuted little flock, now very, very little", noting the deaths of three *senhores*— that is, priests—who had evaded captivity but been exhausted by their travails underground: Mateus de Couros, Francesco Boldrino, and Miguel Matsuda (b. 1578). To compound these losses, four more priests had been captured: Manuel Borges, António de Sousa (b. 1589), Sisto Iyo (b. 1570), and the acting superior, Cristóvão Ferreira.[41]

"If no help arrives, all will soon end," Vieira wrote, "and it is crucial for the good of many that all diligence is exerted to bring new, good aid." With this suggestion, he inferred that Palmeiro's intransigence against sending men to Japan was a fatal mistake. But he did not blame his superior directly. Instead, he invoked the old notion of the church as the Ship of St. Peter, and lamented the fate of its skeleton crew of missionaries:

With these events, the little boat has been left without a rudder and without a pilot to guide it through the on-going storm. No light is left to illuminate it, because all that remained was confiscated, writings as well as resources. The sailors on the ship recalled a resolution, an old order that they had which named the oldest boatman as pilot. By misfortune, it fell to this poor sinner, who naturally and greatly detests the poison that these events have made and make him swallow, since they embitter and damage his stomach so much. And so it is left defenseless, while those elsewhere do not assist as they can and as they must, as they have been advised to help. But if the storm continues as it has and if the master of the boat does not help out as he should, in a short while all of us boatmen will be done for, and the boat, left in the midst of such furious waves and tempestuous seas, will not last long.[42]

Would the storm abate in time for some survivors to escape its ravages? Vieira pinned his hopes on a change of regime in Edo, a remote chance that captured the imagination of those outside of Japan as well. "The author of this torment is but one," he claimed about the shogun Tokugawa Iemitsu, "without descendants, without close relatives, and, as the third generation of the house that began this torment, it seems that it will end with him."[43] The words of the psalms inspired Vieira in this line of thinking: *viri sanguinum et doli non dimidiabunt dies suos*—"bloody and deceitful men shall not live out half of their days".[44] He therefore concluded that "when another house and family takes power, there are truly valid hopes that some repose will follow after so many waves of blood, so much fire, and so many dead."[45]

While Vieira continued his ministry from the small boat that served him as "house, church, and pulpit", hearing confessions from over six hundred Christians by his count, many of his brethren languished in prison. Cristóvão Ferreira had been captured on August 3 and brought to the same Nagasaki jail that held several of his brethren and other religious, both European and Japanese.[46] In early September, however, Ferreira managed to smuggle a letter out of captivity, addressed to Palmeiro, written with a "a quill made of a sliver of bamboo". Echoing the sentiments that the Visitor had communicated to those awaiting martyrdom in previous years, he wrote of his desire to receive sufficient grace from God so to permit him to give his life "for His Law and Faith, and for His greater glory." Ferreira also mentioned how his list of the remaining priests had fallen into the hands of the authorities, recognizing that since "the informants are many, and the investigations that are made are great, few if any of them will escape." Already in the span of two months, he wrote, eleven priests had been captured: eight Jesuits including himself and three friars. Combined with those who had been martyred over the preceding year, he recorded that twenty-three priests were gone from the mission field. To make matters worse, Ferreira asserted that it was impossible (despite Vieira's wish) for new priests to get into Japan, and rather than being helpful, "their coming is the reason for the greater rigor we have felt." He nevertheless asserted that the eleven priests in the Nagasaki prison and the five more in an Ōmura jail were not daunted by the prospect of torture and death before them. "By the grace of God, all have much spirit and desire," Ferreira claimed, "awaiting that fortunate hour."[47]

By the time the Portuguese fleet sailed back to Macau in mid-October, there were more names to add to the long list of martyrs. Two Jesuits, Paulo Saito and Bento Fernandes (b. 1579), were suspended side by side over pits in Nagasaki on September 26, with the former refusing to expire before his trusted companion. According to one report, Fernandes was taken down to receive medical care before another round of torture, but Saito refused to give up the ghost. "Wondering at his constancy, the guards asked why he would not die," this report declared. "He responded that he would not die while padre Bento Fernandes was still alive, and so it was that they both died saintly at the same time, one in the pit, the other in the house, and their bodies were burned together like those of the other martyrs."[48] On October 5 João da Costa (b. 1574), who had returned to Japan disguised as a ship's pilot and who had ministered in the Bungo region on the far side of Kyushu for twelve years, was brought to the execution ground at Nagasaki. He expired after nearly four days of suspension over the pit, alongside Sisto Iyo, who lasted for five.[49]

Two weeks later, on October 18, the Nagasaki commissioners planned an even greater spectacle: eight pits were prepared for four Jesuit priests and two brothers, two Dominicans, and two of the Jesuits' lay auxiliaries. Among their number was Julião Nakaura (b. 1567), who had been sent as a young man to Europe in the company of three other boys in the 1580s as part of the famed Japanese "embassy" and had joined the Society upon his return to his homeland. According to contemporary testimony, Nakaura was given particularly brutal treatment by his tormentors before being sent to the pit. As a Japanese, he was subjected to "long and prolix beatings" to see if he would abjure, but these ended when "the tyrants were certain of his constancy and felt that they were wasting their time." Nakaura was joined over the *cova* by

António de Sousa, who had been exiled and returned twice since 1614 but had evaded capture until 1633 in the Osaka region. Sousa was marched, "with shackles on his feet and cuffs on his hands," from the site of his arrest to Nagasaki, roughly four hundred miles, and hung on the day of his arrival. This pair were accompanied by two Dominicans who had been captured with Sousa, as well as by another Jesuit, Giovanni Matteo Adami (b. 1576), who had been detained in Dewa, in northern Honshu, and brought to Kyushu for torture and execution.[50]

But the Nagasaki commissioners' greatest prize was the ringleader of the Jesuit mission, Cristóvão Ferreira. Not only was he in charge of the Jesuits, Ferreira was also the acting governor of the Bishopric of Japan (in the diocese itself), and so he was not only in possession of lists of the Jesuits who were still in the mission field, he most likely had records of where the surviving communities of Christians were located. With the proper pressure, he might reveal the hideouts of every last missionary in the realm. And so, alongside the others, he was hung over the pit, where he remained for five hours until he was taken down. At precisely this time the trading fleet from Macau was preparing to weigh anchor in Nagasaki harbor. The Portuguese traders were apprised of what was going on in the suburban plot where the martyrs had been taken, and had seen the fruit of the tormentors' work during their brief stay in the Japanese port. Yet they did not remain long enough to see the end of this last episode of pious heroism. The ship's crew had seen Ferreira taken down from the scaffold "to discover the rest of the padres, since he was the superior", and, from their vantage point on the ship's deck, "at the unfurling of the sails, already some of them claimed that they had returned him to the torment."[51]

This was the last update from Japan that Palmeiro would receive in 1633. The fleet reached Macau a few weeks later with the word of that autumn's martyrdoms, and that was the news that the Visitor forwarded to Rome. Fearing that the fleets headed to India might not make it safely to their destination, he sent the news on the Manila–Acapulco route as well in March of the following year. As was to be expected, Palmeiro informed the superior general of the grim news: "Although it is luster and honor for our order to have such glorious martyrs as there have recently been in Japan, and even the Catholic Church is much more greatly honored by such martyrdoms, nevertheless if that *christandade* is not completely destroyed, it is at least at risk of soon being so." But after enduring so many years of persecution, during which the

Jesuits had evaded their pursuers with the help of their Christians, it was clear that something had changed. For Palmeiro, the *annus horribilis* had two clear causes: The first was the increase in the rewards paid to those who denounced clandestine religious. The Nagasaki commissioners offered substantial bounties—four hundred taels of silver, it was claimed[52]—and "easily achieved the ends that they desired through this means, and so became aware that money can buy anything". The reward for denouncing Jesuits was made even greater than that offered for friars or laymen, "and with this infernal design in short order they seized ten priests and a brother from our *Companhia*."[53]

The other reason for the heightened intensity of the persecution was the arrival of the friars. Palmeiro was unequivocal about what he saw as the selfish and destructive aims of the mendicants from Manila, who produced no fruit for the mission church. Indeed, he declared, since "many religious wanted to enter Japan without knowing its language or customs, and they were immediately captured, the fury of the tyrant and his ministers was roused." Such foolish bids at heroism—or, stated otherwise, suicide—seemed unstoppable without some action by church authorities in Manila, Madrid, or Rome. Palmeiro knew that even a man with as much experience of Japan as Sebastião Vieira was putting others at risk by returning to the mission field, at least he might use his language skills and knowledge of the terrain to remain out of sight. But there was only one Vieira. By contrast, there had been almost yearly shipments of friars from Manila eager for martyrdom. Recall that on the ship that smuggled Vieira to Japan in July 1632 there were three friars, two Franciscans and a Dominican; on each of two other vessels that left the Philippines for Kyushu that same year were two Augustinians. While the friars who accompanied Vieira managed to avoid capture for a year, the others would remain at large for no more than a few months.[54] For Palmeiro, the lesson was clear, and he presented it bluntly to the superior general: "We do not know how or where to help the church in Japan, and we are most uncertain about what we must do. The best remedy would be to send more men, but if those who go are detected, it will be the greatest poison for that *christandade*."[55]

Palmeiro also recited the roll of martyrs in his missive. He told of the priests and brothers who suffered in Edo, Osaka, and elsewhere; and he asserted that the *tormento das covas* produced heroic resistance on a scale that "rightly amazed even the heathens." And he reported the deeds of the Japanese seminarians who had served the fellow members of their flock by delivering letters

from the priests and "reminding them of the obligations which were theirs as
Christians." Most of these had met their fate as martyrs, along with those
who had died of exhaustion; Vice-Provincial Ferreira, Palmeiro claimed, was
"already a glorious martyr." His sources informed him that there were only six
of the Society's priests left. Four of them were Japanese: Diogo Yūki (1574–
1636), Pedro Kasui (1587–1639), Martinho Shikimi (1577–1641), and Mâncio
Konishi (1600–1644). Two were Europeans: Giovanni Battista Porro and Sebastião Vieira.[56] Palmeiro had little knowledge of the four Japanese priests,
who were presumed to be hidden in central Japan. Porro, he knew, was lying
low in the northern region of Aizu Wakamatsu, and Vieira was somewhere
near the coast of Kyushu. The Visitor had heard of Vieira's travails, noting
that the authorities had sought him "with such industry, or even voracity,
that only if God hides him will they fail to catch him." Palmeiro informed
Vitelleschi that Vieira had had a close brush with disaster when an informant
grabbed the reins of his horse as he traveled one night. A fortunate intervention by his companions enabled Vieira to escape—"if it was not part of a divine plan that is preserving him for other things." What heavenly design this
might be was not yet clear to Palmeiro, and he closed his letter by lamenting
the "extreme desolation" of the Japanese church.[57] Unlike the reenactment of
another divine drama that took place in far-away Bavaria for the first time in
1634, there would be no resurrection in this passion play.

———————

The cascade of calamities in Japan affected not only the priests in the field
and their persecuted flock. Palmeiro, too, felt the suffering of the mission
church in his bones. At the advanced age of sixty-five, a long life for many
early modern people although shorter than the prodigious spans of many of
his Jesuit peers, he was cognizant of his mortality. He had lived for much of
his life with various bodily indispositions, from the stomach pains that he
suffered during his time at Coimbra to the fainting spell that he experienced
on the road to Beijing. He knew that his final hour might be close at hand and
that any sudden change in his fragile health could be fatal. Palmeiro mentioned this fact in his correspondence already in the mid-1620s, but he seemed
more certain by 1630. In that year's report to Rome, he intimated that it
would be his last: "The number of my years is not small, and the weakness
that I am feeling is great, so without any change there is no promise of long
life."[58] Four years later, death had not yet come, but neither had his health

improved. In 1634 he wrote to the superior general of pains that obliged him to be bled, "but which nonetheless passed quickly". Perhaps because of the gravity of the matters in the missions with which he had to deal, he tried to sound upbeat about his ailments. "Pain which does not last, even if it is great," he offered, "does not hurt so."[59]

The pains of his flesh paled in comparison with those of his spirit. The feeling of helplessness that Palmeiro mentioned repeatedly in his letters affected his health, and his response—typical for religious of his day—was greater rigor in prayer, abstinence, and penitence. Dishearteningly, Palmeiro's close associates and friends began to perish around him in Macau. In the late summer of 1633 the interpreter and diplomat João Rodrigues died after failing to treat a fracture.[60] Although the two men had occasion to argue at more than a few reprises, the Visitor confessed that his death "left us with a deep longing for the many things that he could do and for which he labored." And when an outbreak of fever spread throughout the colony in the early autumn of that year, it claimed the life of Palmeiro's close friend, Diogo Valente, the bishop of Japan. The two men had joined the Society within a week of one another at Coimbra in 1584 and had spent their formative years together. Like Palmeiro, Valente had received an unexpected appointment to work in Asia in 1617 and traveled to Goa only a year after him. After the tumult of the 1620s, which witnessed Valente's excommunication and later vindication, the pair was reunited in Macau in 1631. Palmeiro considered Valente a trusted confidant and sought his opinion on theological matters, such as the Terms Controversy among the missionaries in China.[61] Although the two men enjoyed each other's company for less than two years in the early 1630s, it is clear that they developed a bond whose rupture left Palmeiro even more sorrowful.

In contrast to his terse mention of Rodrigues's passing, the Visitor gave many details about the final sickness, death, and burial of his friend Diogo Valente. The bishop, Palmeiro wrote, "finished his days on October 28 from a malignant fever, but he died as he had always lived, giving a very singular example to all of his extraordinary devotion." The Visitor had stayed by the bedside of his companion for hours as the effects of the disease took their toll, listening to Valente's pious invocations to the Blessed Sacrament that had been placed in his room. Within earshot of the cathedral chapter and the city's illustrious laymen, Valente offered words "with such prudence, gentleness and interior feeling that all were brought to tears."[62] On the evening of his death Palmeiro remained in the bishop's room with a handful of other Jesuits to sing litanies but retired before Valente's passing, which happened just before two o'clock in the morning. Giovanni Battista Bonelli, whom the Visitor had deputized to spend the night at the bishop's door, was the first to alert Palmeiro, who rushed back to celebrate the first mass for Valente's soul at the altar in his chamber.

Within days of Valente's death, a massive bier had been constructed in the Jesuit church—not, as one might expect, in the city's cathedral out of deference to a bishop—to bear the prelate's coffin: a wooden structure "28 palms tall", that is, roughly six meters in height, in pyramid shape, and decorated with pyramids painted black and yellow with silver flourishes. In addition, the bier was festooned with candles, perfume jars, and incense sticks as well as blue and yellow taffeta bunting. The sermon offered by Mateus Gago (b. 1589) dwelled on Valente's indomitable patience, a quality tested on several occasions and proven by the fact that "never a word of complaint came out of his mouth against anyone."[63] In Palmeiro's opinion, the funeral proceedings were "as solemn as possible for this city", especially the burial in the main chapel of the Jesuits' church. These ceremonies were a just recompense on earth, but the Visitor was sure a greater one awaited Valente in heaven: "God shall have given him a great reward for all that he suffered, because the labors he endured while wholly innocent were also great."[64]

Palmeiro's participation in this funeral seems to have spurred him to thoughts of his own impending death. After all, as visitor, he was aware that the site of his own burial would not be too far from that of his friend and his predecessors: The *capela mor* of the Jesuits' church at Macau was also the final resting place for Melchior Carneiro (1516–1583), one of the first Jesuit bishops and a towering figure of the early missions in Asia; Luís Cerqueira (1552–1614), bishop of Japan during the heyday of the mission to that country; and Alessandro Valignano, Palmeiro's most illustrious predecessor in the office of visitor.[65] Looking over these tombs, Palmeiro knew it would not be long before he joined their company. He therefore took steps to prepare for a smooth transition to whoever would succeed him. It did not seem likely that Rome would appoint a new visitor from India to replace him in Macau but rather one of the senior men from the Province of Japan. According to the Society's administrative logic in the seventeenth century, there would be a list of successors in situ that had been sent from the superior general in years past (in fact, the letter that was opened after Palmeiro's death had been written on December 7, 1632). These *vias de successão* would indicate a replacement for

Palmeiro, an individual who would in turn by replaced by someone from outside of East Asia if Rome saw fit.

Palmeiro knew that the pool of potential choices for the post of visitor was limited. The most senior Jesuits in Macau included Pedro Morejón, Giovanni Battista Bonelli, Manuel Dias the elder, António Francisco Cardim, and Vicente Ribeiro (1577–1650). Of these, Morejón, the tireless diplomat to Manila and procurator for the Japan martyrs, was nearly blind, and Dias, a veteran of the China mission, was nearly deaf. The other three were younger and more energetic but did not have the same experience of governance as Dias and Morejón. Sensing that the general had indicated Dias as his successor, Palmeiro worked to ensure that this old China hand would take the job if it was indeed offered to him. Cardim, the rector of the College of Macau and provincial consultor, was summoned by the Visitor to receive instructions on how he was to open the succession letters and was given arguments to win over Dias. Recall that Dias, who was almost a decade older than Palmeiro, had spent most of his life as a missionary within the Ming Empire (although as a member of the Province of Japan on loan) and had only returned to Macau after the Visitor had found his incapacity hampering the work of his colleagues at Shanghai. But this did not mean that Dias was unfit for the job, Palmeiro argued, since his "judgment was intact; he was a most exemplary and dependable man, and would keep a firm hand on rules and religious observance." Moreover, Dias's deafness was not a problem since, the Visitor asserted, he could shout orders at will because he would have "a large room where he could deal with affairs in secret".[66]

The decision to win over Dias reveals that Palmeiro knew that the expanding China mission, rather than its collapsing counterpart, was the future of the Society's work in East Asia. Perhaps because he had covered the hundreds of miles to Beijing and had seen the growth of the Chinese church firsthand, the Visitor harbored special feelings for that enterprise. Had he made the trek to Japan to behold the mission church in that country before its destruction, he might have fought harder—if such was possible—to revive it. There is no doubt that Palmeiro was in a minority at Macau in his sentiments for the Vice-Province of China, since the dwindling numbers of those who did remember the glory of the Japanese church fought against him for every man and every ounce of silver that he diverted from their cause. We have seen how Sebastião Vieira complained that some of the revenue of the Japan trade was siphoned off for the China mission; he would riposte even more vigorously when Palmeiro reassigned some of the men he had escorted to Macau for the mission inside the Ming Empire.[67]

It was for this same reason that the men of the Province of Japan were filled with dread at the prospect of someone such as Manuel Dias, who had worked longer for the China endeavor than for the Japanese one, being named visitor or provincial. To be sure, Dias had been rector of the College of Macau for two three-year terms. But despite his seventy-five years in 1634, he represented the thin end of the wedge. From the perspective of Vieira and his peers, the appointment of men from the vice-province to positions of authority such as that of visitor for the Province of Japan would be a disaster. As António Francisco Cardim put it, China-trained superiors would turn their backs on the martyred mission: "It seems to them that all will be China and nothing Japan; that they will only help China, totally abandoning Japan, which has brought so much honor to the *Companhia*." Moreover, visitors or superiors from the China mission would likely try to detach the College of Macau from the Province of Japan and attach it to the Vice-Province of China. The coincidence of geography that had placed the headquarters of the Japan mission at the mouth of the Pearl River would be used as grounds for such a move, Cardim argued to the superior general in Rome, but it had to be prevented.[68] The fact that Palmeiro had refused to allow a procurator's journey to Europe to argue against the dismemberment of the college from the province was, in Cardim's view, a signal that even the Visitor's loyalty to the Japan mission was suspect.

Nothing could be farther from the truth, of course. As visitor of both province and vice-province, Palmeiro had to manage both. In his estimation, Dias was the best man to fill his shoes—since he had a breadth of vision that would enable him to care for China, Japan, and Southeast Asia. According to Cardim, Palmeiro was aware of the problems of having a Jesuit bred solely within the China mission take over his office. The Visitor was only too familiar with the bitter disputes between his men in the Ming Empire, as well as with their partiality toward Chinese culture and customs, to want to entrust any of their number with such power. But he also did not want to see the China mission neglected as it gained momentum, so he hoped that Dias's name would be found in the succession letters. Moreover, he saw his own brand of cautious confidence in Dias. Dias had the same type of vision that led Palmeiro to create parallel financing structures for the China and Japan missions, as well as the commercial ventures to support the Southeast Asian enterprises, and he had the same sensitivity that led him to insist on separate spiritual communities to tend to the needs of the Japanese exiles (and their pastors) at Macau as well as the colony's Chinese converts.[69] It was precisely in 1634, during the last months of his life, that the Visitor solicited funds from the Portuguese merchants in the city to endow a church for indigenous catechumens. The new church and meeting hall were dedicated to *Nossa Senhora do Amparo,* Our Lady of Protection, and were situated behind the college buildings so Jesuits trained in Cantonese or Mandarin could minister to Chinese Christians.[70]

The final scenes of the Jesuit drama unfolding in Japan occurred in the last weeks of 1633 and the first months of 1634. But no news from Kyushu reached Macau until later that year. A suspension of trade with Manila meant that there was no late spring news, and the annual fleet to Nagasaki only left Macau on August 1. Although a ship from the Spanish outpost on Formosa did call at the Portuguese colony on its way to the Philippines in the early spring, it brought no news from Japan. And it was by a stroke of good fortune that one of the ships in the yearly fleet from Macau to Nagasaki escaped the storm that forced the other three vessels back to the China coast that year. At least that vessel would make it to its destination on the late summer winds. Yet while this ship would bring an exceptionally valuable cargo of silver back to its home port, it would also come laden with disastrous reports and rumors.[71]

But before the autumn of 1634 some of this news did make its way from Japan to points west. In April of that year a ship from Nagasaki manned by Japanese Christians and steered by a Portuguese pilot reached Cambodia, where its crew encountered Manuel Coelho. This Jesuit had come from India with the ambition of traveling to Japan and was biding his time disguised as a "trader of shark skins and hides" while he waited for passage. "With tears in their eyes," the arrivals from Nagasaki recounted the martyrdoms of the previous year in vivid detail.[72] The sojourners also brought letters from the Portuguese who remained in Japan. These filled in details about the priests who had been subjected to the *tormento das covas* on October 18, 1633. Those who had weighed anchor that day for Macau had seen that Cristóvão Ferreira had been taken down from over the pit after five hours, but they did not know that the Dominican Fray Lucas del Espíritu Santo (b. 1594) had also been untied after twenty-four hours. The letters told that both men had been taken to the house of a justice official, and that rumor soon spread that both men apostatized. But a day later Fray Lucas was seen once again over the pit, where he expired. What had happened to Ferreira was not certain since he was not spotted again at the site of the martyrdoms.[73]

The letters from Japan also told Coelho about what had happened to Sebastião Vieira. On December 20, 1633, the priest had been captured along with four Japanese helpers and brought to a prison cell in Nagasaki.[74] Vieira's imprisonment coincided with the departure of the two Nagasaki *bugyō* for Edo, where they intended to relate their triumphs against the priests to the shogun. Lacking the time to properly torture the Jesuit, the commissioners brought him along part of the way and left him in the company of a Franciscan, Fray Luis Gómez Palomino (b. 1563), at a prison at Ōmura. According to the letters, the pair was kept in suspense for over thirty days, "waiting by the hour for word from the court so that by its command they would receive martyrdom." But the order that arrived on January 23 instead summoned them to Edo where the Tokugawa lord wished "to see them and to hear from their mouths some things that he wanted to know about them." And so Vieira and Goméz were sent across Japan in chains toward an uncertain encounter with the country's supreme ruler.[75]

Manuel Coelho was left to speculate about the fate of the three priests mentioned in these letters. In this exercise he was joined by the two authors of the letters as well as by the crew of the Japanese ship. A list of martyrs that Coelho was shown by the Portuguese pilot included a note suggesting that both Vieira and Ferreira had been taken to Edo (with no mention of the Franciscan).[76] Not much credence was given to the rumor that Ferreira had apostatized, so Coelho offered no comment about it. After all, it was unthinkable that a man who had suffered the effects of persecution for so many years and lived in the shadows for so long in order to sustain the faith in Japan could buckle under torture. As for Vieira, one of the Portuguese informants suggested that God had greater things in mind for him at Edo, and "even the heathens took it as a good sign" that the priests had been summoned to court.[77]

Was this final showdown to be the stage for a miracle? In the other letter, António de Oliveira Aranha, one of the two principal emissaries from the city of Macau to the shogunal court, declared that the three priests were doomed. "I trust in God that they will all give their lives for Him," Aranha affirmed, "unless something happens like that which the Japanese tell about some cases that occurred during the king's illness, about which they say many things which have to be seen to be believed."[78] This "king" was Tokugawa Iemitsu, and it was public knowledge throughout Japan that he had suffered from a disease that left him disfigured. While the disease was actually smallpox, contemporary European sources called it leprosy.[79] The shogun's humors had shifted with his suffering, making him unpredictable, or so the missionaries claimed. It therefore seemed possible that the Almighty might have wanted to vindicate the Japanese Christians and their pastors at this final hour by illuminating their chief persecutor. Coelho heard a clear echo of a pivotal moment in the history of the Primitive Church. He reported that one of the principal *bonzes* in Edo had suggested that the cause of Iemitsu's disease was the fact that he had ordered the killing of innocents, and in particular, the *padres* at Nagasaki. In desperation that neither his "chief sorcerer" nor his physicians could heal him, the Lord of the Realm (*Tenka-dono*) decided to summon the last "Southern Barbarian *bonzes*," to make a gesture of amends. "May it please the Divine Goodness that this be for the good and peace of that afflicted *christandade,* irrigated with so much blood of martyrs," wrote Coelho, "and that God may show the mercy to make this leprous tyrant *Tencandono* another Constantine who will be healed in body and soul, not with the blood of children to be poured out, but with the blood of the holy men that has already been spilled."[80]

The pilot and crew of the Japanese vessel in Cambodia had no more information to give Coelho. Only slightly better apprised of the situation were the members of embassy sent from Macau to negotiate trading conditions with the Tokugawa regime. This group, led by the colony's sometime governor, Gonçalo da Silveira, had been delayed at Nagasaki from the summer of 1630 until early 1634, when it was finally granted an audience at Edo. It appears that Silveira's embassy reached the shogunal capital just after Vieira and Fray Luis Gómez, in early March 1634.[81] A messenger from the Portuguese party found his way to Vieira's cell where the Jesuit passed on a brief description of his conditions in jail and that of his seven companions, six of whom were Japanese Christians. Once again he employed veiled references: "I write these rules almost in the dark, because upon arriving at this jail they took even our glasses, without which I am as good as blind, and breviary, and even a hand towel; these are omens that they will soon take our lives, which is what we most desire for the greater glory of God."

Knowing that there was no more need for subterfuge (and perhaps no option for such), he had worn the black robe and cape of a Jesuit through the streets of Edo. "These people can no longer feign ignorance of the Law of God," he wrote, "because we have preached it to them in the open and with much clarity." Vieira only had a "toothpick sharpened by fingernails," so he could not write long letters from his Edo jail, but he promised more news to his nearby correspondents.[82]

Gonçalo da Silveira received two more letters from Vieira in early April, during the embassy's stay at Edo. In these the Jesuit recounted his audience before the shogunal authorities (although not Iemitsu himself) and the heroic statements he had made in defense of the faith. Once again in his black robe, "but with the thumbs of my hands tied with cords to the ropes that bound me," Vieira had been brought before a pair of *bugyō* who interrogated him about his illegal return to Japan and denounced Christianity. "This is the blindness of the Jews," he wrote of his interlocutors' attitudes, "who more greatly esteemed the murderous thief Barrabas than the goodness and innocence of the good Jesus." In the days following this first audience, Vieira was interrogated again, this time in the Edo jail, alongside Fray Luis, whose weakened condition prevented him from speaking. During this meeting, the Jesuit was given paper and ink to write his answers and even permitted to produce a summary of Christian doctrine for the shogun, which he claimed to have accomplished "in less than fourteen hours". Reflecting on his encounters with the authorities, the sixty-three-year-old Vieira exclaimed: "It is no small praise and triumph for the Holy Faith, for the Shogun of Japan with all his power, to admit that he is scared of two old, weak, and captive religious."[83]

On April 7, 1634, Vieira wrote his last surviving letter to the members of the Portuguese embassy. In it he lamented not being able to write at greater length to the "Lord of the Green Island"—that is, his provincial officer back on the Ilha Verde in Macau. Vieira also begged that his correspondents would remember him to "the other friends of that country and in Nagasaki," and especially to the Silveiras, Gonçalo and his brother Jerónimo, who had received him so many times at their homes. He sent further greetings to *Senhor* Palmeiro, with a request that the Visitor reimburse the letter's bearer for the silver that had been given to Vieira on two occasions. In closing, he regretted only having one life to give for the love of God: "Even if I had a hundred, a hundred would not be enough; I would want to have a thousand bodies in which to be able to suffer much, much, much for his divine love."[84] But he had only one, and by early June it was suspended upside down over a pit, alongside those of his Japanese companions (five of whom Vieira accepted into the Society of Jesus in jail) and Fray Luis. Reports that reached the Silveira embassy on its way back to Nagasaki and onward to Macau told of the Jesuit's fortitude during the *tormento das covas* and how, after three days, on June 6, his head was set on fire. The flames which ravaged his body served to

FIGURE 10.1. Depiction of the death of Sebastião Vieira at Edo in 1634 from Cardim's *Elogios* (Lisbon, 1650). Vieira is shown suspended over the pit in a fashion similar to other depictions of that form of torture. But he is also shown engulfed in flames, in fulfillment of his prophecy that he would die by fire.

fulfill Vieira's prophecy that he would be consumed by fire, instead of simply expiring over the pit. Like the Japan mission itself, he had finally been reduced to ashes.[85]

———————

Facts and rumors reached Macau in the last weeks of 1634. What was to be believed? About Vieira, there were no doubts. His letters passed through Palmeiro's hands and eventually made their way to Rome. The martyr's friends in the colony were certain of his fate, and celebrated it in triumph as the new year began. Palmeiro's letter to Muzio Vitelleschi—the Visitor's last report to his superior—contains a lively description of the feasting, in which he was a reluctant secondary participant. Manuel da Câmara de Noronha, the city's *capitão geral,* who was "very friendly with the *Companhia,* but extremely so with Sebastião Vieira," had insisted that there be not just worthy but splendid celebrations.[86] Unlike the other martyrs who had suffered in Japan after years of clandestine service, Palmeiro noted, Vieira "had only just left the city for Japan, and had there a nephew, a very wealthy man, and many other relatives who loved him greatly." The citizens of Macau therefore spared no expense celebrating their friend's memory: "Many fires, both luminaries and fireworks; many days' worth of displays of horsemanship, always varied and pleasing; bullfights; strutting about, both by the soldiers from the garrison and by the Portuguese born here in the city; and much splendor in the clothing and very costly gowns." The most impressive display, Palmeiro claimed, was an *encamisada,* a torchlight procession on horseback, with riders in sumptuous livery. "Those people who have seen such feasts in Europe in cities, where patrons usually spent more," he added, "judged these celebrations to be just as grand."[87]

There is a tone of distress in the Visitor's last letter. Perhaps it came from an affliction, "a pain in my foot", that obliged him to take to bed. There was also the lingering memory of Palmeiro's dispute with Vieira before the martyr left to meet his fate. And it seems that the Visitor saw the celebrations as excessive, especially when there were unresolved questions about the fate of the other Jesuits in Japan. The captain-general had insisted on taking part in all of the festivities, especially in the processions and promenades, wearing a jewel-covered turban that was said to be worth "over twenty thousand cruzados". Following Noronha's lead, the Visitor remarked, "many others went about crazily dressed and, above all, to take pleasure in seeing how the men joined in and what they spent on it." Palmeiro's sentiments were best relayed in a play on a passage that he chose from the Book of Esther: *sic honorabitur quam Deus voluerit honorare*, "thus he shall be honored whom God has a mind to honor".[88]

At the Visitor's command, the Macau Jesuits refrained from organizing any public celebrations at the college. Noronha had begged Palmeiro to celebrate a high mass and offer a sermon about Vieira's heroic virtues, but Palmeiro refused. He cited the need for the "approval and consent of the Supreme Pontiff", that is, a dispensation from Urban VIII's prohibition on public celebrations of sanctity for the as yet unbeatified, especially in light of the recent beatification inquiries. He nevertheless felt that some official recognition was due to his fallen colleague, so he permitted luminaries to be placed before the college and church "with much display." He justified such demonstrations by noting that they were customary at times when military victories were announced or when news of the king's health was divulged. Palmeiro further sensed that there was a legitimacy granted to the public clamor, as if he could hear the voice of God speaking through the people of Macau. While the pope mandated that he refrain from proclaiming Vieira's surely blessed state in public, within the privacy of his order he felt compelled to declare to his superior that the celebrations of the martyr's *beau geste* contained a reflection of heavenly approval. In closing his letter, the Visitor averred that there had been "divine consent which smiled upon and strengthened these good human intentions, since they so greatly sought to honor him, as well as his valorous death, and his illustrious confession of faith, valorous in speech and in writing, which merited these favors." None other, Palmeiro recognized, had offered such a direct confession of faith to the rulers of Japan as Vieira. "Let him thus be greatly praised," the Visitor concluded, "and a door be opened for us, so that we can enter to follow the holy footsteps of such glorious martyrs."[89]

The din of the festivities in Macau, and even the preceding reflection on Vieira's valor, did little to calm Palmeiro's soul. The rumors from Japan were shocking, and the Visitor did not want to believe them. It is a great loss for our story that the *primeira via*, the first yearly report that he wrote in late December or early January 1635, has not survived. Perhaps the gravity of its suggestions led to the superior general placing it in a secret place. Vitelleschi must have hidden it well, if indeed the letter did reach Europe, since it cannot be located in the files at the Society's Roman archives that touch on scandals and other sensitive matters.[90] The word from Japan was that Cristóvão Ferreira had indeed apostatized, but there was no trustworthy testimony to confirm it. Lowered into the pit on October 18, 1633, he had surely been taken out, as many eyewitnesses had seen. It was plausible that this gesture corresponded to the desire of the magistrates to extract more information from Ferreira, not to his abandonment of the faith. But the rumors said no. Ignored at first as expressions of ill will circulated by the Jesuits' enemies, the word on the street eventually gained credence: The same *vox populi* that hailed Vieira affirmed that Ferreira had reneged over the pit.[91] For Palmeiro, the only way to ensure that this was no echo of the *vox Dei* was to implore God to dispel the horrifying specter of apostasy. To this end, he began a far more intensive regime of prayer and penitential discipline, fasting and flagellating himself in order to atone for any of his sins that might have contributed to the evident divine displeasure. We do not know if Palmeiro's rigorous penances resulted in a sign from the Almighty. But coupled with the abstinence that he customarily observed during Lent, they served to weaken his body to the point where he would succumb to an illness during Holy Week of 1635. Whether the Visitor's faith was shaken by the rumors about Ferreira or, on the contrary, his trust in providence was strengthened by his pious exercises is unknown. After speaking his mind so frankly for so many years, André Palmeiro fell into silence.

Conclusion

A Baroque Death

The illness that André Palmeiro mentioned in his last letter to Rome was among the first signs of his impending death. During the preceding months he had experienced dizzy spells as he walked about the college, episodes that occasionally obliged him to brace himself against his companions or the corridor walls. In January 1635 swelling in his foot, perhaps a form of gout, obliged him to take to bed. When this initial malady passed, others came in its wake. Over the next three months, the Visitor grew progressively weaker. His customary penances during the Lenten season, intensified by concern over the news from Japan, did not help his body to respond to its afflictions. And his diet, which before had been austere by the standards of early modern religious life, became even more limited. Although the rector of the College of Macau did not judge Palmeiro's illness to be life-threatening at the outset, at length he recognized that the symptoms were extreme. Doctors were therefore summoned and a rigorous cure prescribed, but the swelling that had been in his feet reappeared, in larger form, in his abdomen. Palmeiro's distended belly dramatically reduced his desire to eat, and such was his nausea that he could neither chew nor retain anything that he swallowed. The appearance of fever was the last sign that his days were numbered, and even his doctors admitted defeat. By the last week of March, just before the beginning of Holy Week, the Visitor had resigned himself to the fact that he would never leave his bed.

The events of Palmeiro's final illness and death were recorded by procurator Giovanni Battista Bonelli, his longtime associate. While notice of the Visitor's last days was also sent to Rome in the private correspondence of the provincial administrators and of his successor, the most elaborate account came from Bonelli's pen. This document was a "relation of the death and life" of the deceased, prepared shortly after burial. Such necrologies were commonly produced in the early modern period within the Society of Jesus, as they were in other religious communities. Some were printed, at times serving as evidence for beatification cases for individuals considered especially pious or heroic, but most of them circulated internally in manuscript. This was the case with Palmeiro's necrology, a document whose longest version stretched to twenty-eight folio pages.[1]

Not all Jesuits received posthumous recognition of this sort. For a majority of the rank and file, a brief mention in an annual letter sufficed to give notice of their passing. In this way the Society could keep a running tally of the prayers that individual members were obliged to say for the souls of their brethren. Some, however, were deemed worthy of more personalized remembrance. Professed Jesuits often earned longer discussions in the same yearly reports, where specific mention was made of the circumstances of their death as well as of their particular virtues and devotions. And the men who held important posts within the order were given far greater attention, as were those who enjoyed a reputation for sanctity. Their final hours and pious lives were recorded in the type of "death and life" account that Palmeiro received. Such accounts belong to a particular literary genre; that is, they were written according to certain rules of style and content. These necrologies typically consisted of lengthy accounts of the terminal illness; descriptions of the prayers, masses, and promises made for the health of the moribund; retellings of the drama of the moment of death and any pious ejaculations uttered; and reports of public and private mourning and funeral masses. Anecdotes about the lives of the deceased and discussions of how they demonstrated the principal virtues of religious life were also obligatory.

Palmeiro's necrology is an account of his dying moments, supplemented with vignettes about his life. It is the longest text written about him by an early modern author, and it contains the fullest collection of descriptions of his habits and personality. Given the number of important positions he held within the order, the reader may be surprised to learn that his peers dwelt on his final hours. Surely a recounting of his travels and his governance would have been a more appropriate testament to Palmeiro's life. Yet early modern religious did not see death as the end; rather, it was the beginning of eternal life, the shedding of the chains of human suffering, and the gradual ascension to the divine presence. Moreover, the cult of the *bona mors,* the happy death, enjoyed considerable regard among early moderns. The Visitor's contemporaries believed that the way one died gave indications about one's destination in the afterlife: a painful passing or one in which the body seemed tormented signaled a wrathful divine judgment, whereas a peaceful death, marked by calm acceptance and adequate time for the reception of the sacraments, indicated the promise of salvation. The proof of Palmeiro's virtue therefore lay in his behavior during his final moments.

According to Manuel Dias the elder, the man who would succeed him as visitor, Palmeiro "died in the same way he lived, as one who truly desired the other life, and in a manner which is called the death of the just."[2] This event was therefore worthy of recounting in detail, if only so that the superior general in Rome might know how his appointed servant had spent his last days in office. But the account of Palmeiro's death would also serve as justification for his decisions as inspector, and as an example of piety for other Jesuits. So Bonelli watched his confrere closely as his illness took its toll, taking notes about the Visitor's last words, his choice of devotions, and his tranquil passing. The procurator claimed to have spent many hours either standing at Palmeiro's bedside or sitting "in a spot where he could not see me" in order to copy down his last conversations with others. And Bonelli was not the only one who wished to occupy this hidden perch; several priests and brothers kept nightly vigils, only to be shooed away to bed by the college's rector deep into the night.[3]

Palmeiro's necrology was intended to be the first draft of a small chapter in the larger history of the Society of Jesus, and it provides insight into an important aspect of his life.[4] The account was the last collection of the Visitor's thoughts, and offers the best vantage on his spiritual life. Few descriptions of Palmeiro's interior life were discovered in the course of this study, a frustrating dearth of evidence in a biography of a priest, a theologian, and a Jesuit. The documents say little about his inner life, making it difficult to speculate about the Visitor's spirituality. What is lacking is material substantiating something that was evidently central to his life. The vagaries of time may be at fault principally, but Palmeiro himself was also to blame for the scarcity of sources. He made few records of his devotions and kept no spiritual diary, or at least none has survived. Nothing of the texts of his sermons has survived, either, although it is clear from other sources that he preached often. Indeed, one vignette from his last years in Macau tells of how a brother found him in his cubicle jotting notes for a sermon on the back of an envelope. When asked why the Visitor did not write on full sheets of paper, he replied that the scraps were good enough "for something of such little worth as his sermons."[5]

Palmeiro's correspondence and the other texts analyzed in this study are similarly laconic on this theme. It is evident from the many sets of rules that he issued to his subordinates that he prized his order's common routines of piety. He was insistent that the Society's devotions, such as the singing of litanies and the reading of lessons at mealtimes, be maintained, even by pairs of missionaries in remote residences. He likewise reminded his subordinates of the need to make time for reflection and individual prayer. But references to his own participation in these types of activity are scant. For example, he never mentions taking (or giving) the Spiritual Exercises and rarely offers any indication of his saying masses or intoning specific prayers. Such practices were the hallmarks of the Society's brand of spirituality and the reference point for all Jesuits, but about them the Visitor kept mum. His correspondence gives little indication of his personal devotions, with the exception of the occasional invocation of his trust in the Almighty for perpetuating the missions or justifying their martyrs. And so Bonelli's account of his deathbed discussions, insomuch as it offers testimony of Palmeiro's thoughts, gives a rare view into the heart of a man whose pen would not reveal its secrets.

That a priest from the height of the Catholic Reformation, one entrusted with weighty matters, should have written so little about his interior life confounds the historian. Surely the gaps in the record are no reflection of Palmeiro's spiritual state. For all of his activities, he was still a contemplative. The testimony of people who knew him avers that he was a deeply spiritual man who engaged in demanding devotional routines and never ceased to offer pastoral counsel to others. Yet it seems that the public nature of his office encouraged him to hide his expressions of piety from the gaze of others. According to Bonelli, Palmeiro "was given to hiding his penances and devotions," especially his frequent practice of corporal discipline. On only one occasion did the Visitor let a coadjutor know how frequently he flagellated himself, and this brother confessed to Bonelli being "shocked that a man who was so busy could do it so much." It was nevertheless with a certain satisfaction that the necrologist recorded that "there was one thing" that the Visitor could not hide: his daily trips to kneel for half an hour before the consecrated host.[6]

The best explanation for Palmeiro's silence on matters that were so important to him is that he viewed his devotions as private concerns to be shared only with God and his confessor (whose identity he does not reveal). In other words, his spiritual state was not an appropriate topic for business correspondence with the Society's Roman curia. Had he forged a more direct bond with Muzio Vitelleschi during his time in Europe, the Visitor's letters might bear more of a personal stamp and offer more elucidation of his spiritual state. But the two men never met, so their kinship remained professional and their correspondence concentrated on matters pertaining to the governance of the Society of Jesus.

––––––––

Bonelli's record of the dying Visitor's words and deeds asserts that he found solace in the promise of his eternal reward. To be sure, the events recounted in the "Relation of the Death and Life of Padre André Palmeiro" are like so many scenes in the paintings produced during the baroque era. Attention to reproducing exact details was not the artist's concern. Rather, Bonelli sought to create tableaux of the principal episodes of his death based on standard models of piety, relying on a palette of common tints and adjusting his compositions to appeal to his seventeenth-century sensibilities. Like the imposing scenes painted by Zurbarán or the Carducci brothers, Bonelli's text related and enhanced the dramatic moments of the Visitor's passing.[7] Based on the observations recorded by the procurator and his colleagues, the necrology paints an idealized portrait of Palmeiro's inner grandeur. In keeping with the expectations of its readers, the text presents a figure who would be recognizable to those who knew him personally as well as those who had simply heard of him or had received his letters in Europe.

A brief excursus into some of the conventions of baroque depictions of the *bona mors* based on specific examples is useful at this point. Vincenzo Carducci's *Death of the Venerable Odo of Novara,* painted by commission in 1632 for the Carthusian monastery of Santa Maria de el Paular in Castile, reveals many of the commonplaces of the genre. The artist depicted the dying monk lying on a low wooden platform, holding a crucifix, and in the company of six of his brethren. Historical accuracy was of little concern to Carducci; Odo of Novara died more than four hundred years before the pious scene was painted. Moreover, the figures are dominated by a vision of Christ in glory standing amid luminous clouds and beams of light. That said, the composition was based on the textual portraits of Odo of Novara found in Carthusian histories and intended for the private viewing of monks who were aware of their order's traditions. The artist's interest was therefore to represent the verisimilitude of an event rather than to reproduce a fact.

To the seventeenth-century observer, Carducci's painting sent a clear message about the venerable Carthusian's life: Odo of Novara was a paragon of humility and piety, he was revered by his fellow monks for his many virtues, and he was destined for the eternal life that his piety merited. The monk's commitment to poverty is demonstrated by the bare wood of his pallet, by the branches that protrude from below his blanket, by his simple sustenance of bread, soup, and water, and, above all, by his gaunt features. His piety is shown by the tight grasp in which he holds the crucifix at this decisive moment as well as by the devotional statue of Mary installed above his resting place and the pilgrim's staff that lies beside him. Further proof of the substance of Odo's sanctity comes in the mystical vision of the Savior that he beholds, the product of the exhortations of the monk who stands closest to him. Indeed, the vigorous bearded face of this middle-aged monk appears as a mirror image of the face of Jesus, who floats just behind his companion. At the foot of the dying one's bed, a group of Carthusians watches the scene: A trio of bearded monks (their graying facial hair serving as an indicator of their maturity and wisdom) kneels while two younger monks stand behind them, one of them reading from a book, most likely a devotional text. The monks' black robes and the gray floor and walls that color the edges of the painting in dark hues contrast with the bright burst of light coming from the mystical vision at its center. The difference between this world and the next could not be more striking, and Odo's vision of Christ at the hour of his death is a clear sign of his imminent departure for paradise.

Another instructive example of the "good death" can be found in the representation of the death of Ignatius Loyola painted by Domingos da Cunha (ca. 1598–1644), a Jesuit brother who was known as *o Cabrinha* ("the mulatto" or, literally, "the little goat"). In the early 1630s Cunha painted a cycle of large canvases for the nave of the church of São Roque at the Jesuits' Professed

House in Lisbon. His compositions were based on engravings found in an illustrated life of Ignatius that was published on the occasion of Loyola's beatification in 1609, a collection of images that served as the basis for the saint's iconography in Jesuit communities across the early modern world.

FIGURE E.I. Vincenzo Carducci, also known as Vicente Carducho, *Death of the Venerable Odo of Novara,* painted in 1632 for the Carthusian Monastery of Santa Maria del Paular. Although the main event of this scene is shown as it was in the artist's imagination, the three kneeling figures on the left side are portraits of the painter himself (1568–1638), the playwright and poet Lope de Vega (1562–1635), and the prior of the monastery, Juan de Baeza (d. 1641).

Cunha's painting follows the general lines of the original, showing Loyola in his deathbed surrounded by fellow Jesuits.[8] As expected, the scene is dark. The only lighter areas are Ignatius's bed and body, the faces of his companions, and the clouds above, which open to permit his soul to ascend to heaven in the company of an angelic orchestra. Shadows encroach from the painting's edges, and the somber mood is reinforced by the black robes worn by the men who crowd around the saint.

Cunha's painting shows the main themes of the story of Loyola's death with little concern for precision. The standard account of the event, found in the biography written by Pedro de Ribadeneyra (1527–1611) in 1572 and widely

FIGURE E.2. Domingos da Cunha (called *o Cabrinha*), *Death of St. Ignatius of Loyola*, painted circa 1630 for the church of São Roque at the Jesuit Professed House in Lisbon.

reprinted and translated in the following decades, claims that he died swiftly on July 31, 1556. According to that text, Loyola took to his bed one hour after sunrise, moments after reassuring his companions that his hour was near but that it had not yet arrived. Suddenly, however, he raised his eyes to heaven, lifted his hands in prayer, and expired with a "calm countenance." Loyola's brethren arrived in haste after hearing of his death, some acclaiming him a saint and others weeping copiously at his bedside.[9] Despite the established sequence of these events, Cunha collapses them into one moment. He places weeping mourners and late arrivals (the figure on the painting's right side carries his hat in hand, as if he had burst into the room), alongside a priest who bears a crucifix, as if this figure was in the midst of a final exhortation to one still alive. The painter also adds and enhances details so that the story fits into an expected mold: The dying saint's room has an aspergillum at the ready for sprinkling holy water as well as a (presumably devotional) book and lit candles arranged on his beside. Most strikingly, the bright light of the morning hours has been changed into the gloomy shadows of night. Cunha's composition thus achieves its purpose—to communicate the holiness of the saint's death—dispensing with incongruous verity in favor of expressive cliché.

Bonelli's account of the death of Palmeiro is constructed along similar lines. Conscience prodded him in the direction of verisimilitude, but Bonelli was free to include, alter, or omit moments at will. After all, the message that he communicated of Palmeiro's virtue was most important. Few of the Jesuits who would read the necrology in India or Europe had ever met the Visitor, and even fewer knew anything of Macau, the place where the events transpired. Precision was therefore unimportant, but the proper evocation of the Visitor's virtue was. Like Carducci and Cabrinha, Bonelli was a painter, not a photographer; his account was a depiction, not a snapshot. He lays on the pathos from his palette thickly, and enhances certain aspects to produce the desired effect. It is therefore not the specific details of the events in Bonelli's "Relation of the Death and Life" that are most important here but rather the tone that they communicate. Let us watch the baroque drama of Palmeiro's final days, moving through the sequence of pious episodes that Bonelli provides for our contemplation.

The narration of Palmeiro's death begins on March 24, the Saturday before Palm Sunday of 1635. When his nurse, Brother Manuel de Figueiredo, checked the Visitor's pulse and general condition this day, he came to the conclusion that "it was the will of God Our Lord to carry him off to Him."

Consequently, there was no further need to continue the prescribed remedies, and no hope that the masses and prayers that had been said, or the penances that had been performed for his health, might produce their desired
effect. This decision came as a blow to Palmeiro's friends, both inside and
outside the Society, who believed that he would recover. After all, the Visitor
was not very old, and the Macau Jesuits had made extraordinary devotions
on his behalf. The college's rector, António Francisco Cardim, ordered masses
and prayers, and installed the relic of Francis Xavier's arm bone in a magnificent display in a chapel near the infirmary, where the liturgy was said and all
the college's brothers were required to take communion. According to
Bonelli, Cardim also made a vow to Xavier (whose given name he had added
to his own out of devotion to the Jesuit pioneer), and "there were many in the
college who offered their lives to God in exchange for that of Father Visitor."
Outside the Jesuit compound, members of the other religious orders in the
colony also joined with their prayers. Bonelli recalled especially that Frei
Francisco de Sena, the governor of the city's bishopric, prayed the litanies
three times daily for Palmeiro's health, even though he too was sick in bed.[10]

As the moment of death drew near, Figueiredo prompted the Visitor to
receive the sacraments. After his nurse's suggestion, Palmeiro replied:

> My dearest brother, I have become convinced over the past days that I am
> dying, and it has been twenty days since I made a general confession. In
> order to show my appreciation for your great charity and that of the other
> priests and brothers, as well as not to upset them, I have not said goodbye
> to them all. . . . But I accept this news as if it was sent from heaven. A
> sweet news, a happy news, *quam dilecta tabernacula tua, Domine virtu-
> tum.*[11] Why should it be tomorrow? Why not today, Lord? Many times I
> have had happy news in my life, but this bests them all. . . . Do you think,
> my dearest brother, that this news disturbs my spirit? Not at all, this news
> is so joyful for me; it is like I am going to a great celebration. And if Our
> Lord takes me to a place where I will see Him, I will remember you, my
> dear brother, in thanksgiving for having been the one who gave me the
> news.[12]

Bonelli relates that Palmeiro would alternate between speaking to those present and praying aloud to God and the saints. On one such occasion he raised
his hands and lamented his misfortune at having to die in bed rather than in

the company of his heroic brethren. "Lord, I desired greatly to die on a pyre for love of You," Palmeiro declared, "but since I have never merited this from You, despite the many times that I asked it of You, and since You are pleased that I die in this bed, let Your will be done."[13]

The following day, when Palmeiro let his brethren bring him the Eucharist *per modum viatici,* the college's priests and brothers came together at his bedside bearing lit tapers. With this group assembled and the Blessed Sacrament held before him in Rector Cardim's hands, the Visitor made a declaration of faith. The rumors of Cristóvão Ferreira's apostasy were not far from the minds of the assembly, so he may have wanted to make a strong statement of his convictions. Having invoked the Holy Trinity, the Immaculate Virgin, and the events of Christ's life, the Visitor stated: "This I believe, Lord, because it is true, and because this is what the Holy Roman Catholic Church says." Continuing on, he asked for pardon for the failures in his service to God. Exclaiming "forgive me, Good Jesus, forgive me! Come Lord, enter into this soul!", he received communion and afterward requested extreme unction from the senior priests.

When these rites were finished, Cardim knelt at the bedside and, with tears in his eyes, asked Palmeiro's blessing and pardon for his many faults and for those of the other priests and brothers. They had taken the Visitor's customary severity as a continual, silent rebuke of their behavior, and they expected forgiveness in his final hour. With the whole Jesuit community before him on their knees awaiting his gesture, the Visitor replied by turning the request around: "It is I who should ask for pardon from all of you for the poor example that I have given. Poor, I say, I do not say good, because my example speaks very badly of me, as a superior who is obliged to give a good example." Turning his gaze back to Cardim, he said: "And it is I who ask for Your Reverence's blessing, because as a sinner, I have no blessing to give." Palmeiro continued his response to the assembled priests by praising the religious community where he spent the last years of his life. Despite the arguments and bitterness that had marked many months of his time in Macau, he declared his love for his brethren and his desire that the concord he had worked hard to achieve might outlive him:

> You ask me for pardon, but I have not been upset. Rather, I have been greatly consoled by the virtue of the priests and brothers of this college. I

love you all, and if you could see the place at which I hold you in my soul, you would see how high a spot you occupy. I commend these brothers to you, Father Rector, and I ask the superiors who will succeed me that you treat them with great tenderness. I have seen through long experience that this is all that is necessary for the good governance of our order. At its heart, this community is holy, and I say this because of what I have heard from all of you together and from each one individually. Believe me, Father Rector, when I say that this college is holy and I have always found in it an edifying lesson.

According to Bonelli, the assembled Jesuits tried hard to hold back their tears but, of course, there was no containing their emotion when the Visitor urged the senior priests to calm governance. At that moment, the "younger ones among the brothers raised such a great wailing, and the rest burst forth with moans and sobs," with even Palmeiro shedding tears. Before the crowd retired, though, Cardim reiterated his request and Palmeiro conferred his blessing. To those who remained, the Visitor remarked that he had never felt so much love from the men at the college.[14]

During the days that followed this farewell, Palmeiro's pious utterances grew more frequent. Bonelli recalled how he requested to hear his brethren read the "hymn of glory," an evocation of paradise popularly attributed to St. Augustine, and how he asked for a painting of heavenly glory to be put before him.[15] Had the Visitor not been so diligent in collecting devotional objects for sending off to the missions, this second request might have been easier to fill. But Rector Cardim remembered that in a coadjutor's cubicle there was a small painting of the Madonna and Child seated on a cloud surrounded by angels and accompanied by the five Jesuit saints, and "that in some way represented glory."[16] As soon as Palmeiro had donned his glasses, he began to recite the words of the hymn *Urbs beata Jerusalem,* Bonelli related. Fixing his gaze upon the figure of the Madonna, he said: "What a beautiful thing this is! Virgin lady, if they paint you so beautifully here on earth, how will you be there in heaven?" And then, focusing on the figure of Ignatius, Palmeiro continued: "I will find you there as well, my holy father! I am certain that you will be there waiting." Finally, thinking of his corporal mortifications over the years and of his strict obedience to his vows, he cast his eyes on the angels depicted among the clouds and declared: "Ah, what a beautiful thing it will be to behold the glory that I will see there! I do not doubt that I will go there, because I am certain that those five thousand lashes were not in vain. No, I am certain."[17]

On cue, the Grim Reaper cast his shadow over the main character as this play reached its climax. Alas, Bonelli's skill as a dramaturge fell short of the standard set by Palmeiro's contemporary, Lope de Vega. In the necrology, the Visitor began to grow impatient about his departure for heaven a week before his death. At one point, Palmeiro was overheard speaking aloud to himself when he thought himself alone: "What are you doing, Death? Who is holding you up? Why don't you come and free me from this miserable prison?"[18] And when a doctor came to him a few days later and pronounced that he seemed to be recovering his health, Palmeiro responded with disgust "that he neither wanted nor desired" such an outcome. And so it was with relief that he greeted the new downturn in his condition that occurred just before Palm Sunday. Thinking himself on the verge of taking his last breath, he asked to hold a crucifix and began to address the figure of Christ. As he was speaking, Cardim arrived and Palmeiro declared: "Father rector, is this what death is? Jesus! Jesus! I never thought it would be like this; without any displeasure, neither inwards or outwards. The saintly father Francisco Suárez was right when he said there was nothing so sweet as death, and I say it, too.[19] I never imagined death would be so sweet, and so agreeable. If I was not so certain that this was the reward of glory that I expected, I would distrust this peace I feel." Continuing on the same theme, he urged Cardim: "Tell those men out there that Death is not gloomy and sullen, but very light and comely. Tell them not to be afraid of her, since we are the ones who make her out to be ugly."[20]

Palmeiro's condition did not worsen precipitously, and he lingered long enough for thoughts of his unworthiness to return. At one moment, he called out for holy water to be sprinkled on his bed. The coadjutor who was at his bedside asked why the Visitor wanted such a thing done, and Palmeiro replied that it was a proven method against the Evil One. "The Devil wants nothing from you," the brother answered, to which Palmeiro responded that he "was a great sinner, although he didn't care a lick for the *demónio* since the mercy of God was upon him."[21] On the Friday before Palm Sunday, Cardim brought a group of priests and brothers to the Visitor's bedside to sing the litanies and to pray the office for the sick in agony.[22] Upon hearing his brethren intone the initial verse, *Proficiscere, anima christiana, de hoc mundo,* that is, "depart, O Christian soul, out of this world", Palmeiro spoke up: "Let us go then! Let us do it! Why do we not go?" When Cardim asked the Visitor for patience and handed him the college's precious relic of the True Cross and one of the Holy Thorns, he changed his tone. After kissing these remnants of the Passion, Palmeiro began to describe himself as an "abominable sinner with an infernal fury." Taken aback by his words, his brethren reaffirmed themselves that the Visitor had always been "a mirror of virtue, not only after he joined the *Companhia,* but also before." Nevertheless, Palmeiro asked those gathered by him for pardon and even insisted that they take his request to those who were not present. "And as Father Visitor said these words," Bonelli wrote, "the priests and brothers were around his bedside with their eyes overflowing with tears, and in such great pain and woe, that I cannot even explain it."[23]

Over the course of his last few days, the fevers grew more intense. Palmeiro lacked the strength even to turn in his bed, but on occasion he raised his arms and his voice to implore God to come for his soul. "When will it be, Lord? When will it be? Come! Come!," the brother at his bedside recalled him saying. One night in his final week, his attendants were awakened by the cry: "Delay no more, Lord! I yearn to be close to you more intensely than the wounded deer yearns for the watery spring."[24] According to Bonelli, Palmeiro repeatedly mentioned the bother that he caused his attendants, and all the priests and brothers whose sleep he disturbed by lingering on. During their normal waking hours, the Visitor spoke about spiritual themes to his numerous guests. Bonelli mentioned how he would ask Palmeiro to interpret various passages from scripture, "knowing that I gave him particular pleasure by this." Despite his fevers, Palmeiro responded to these queries as if he were still in full possession of his mental capacities. And so his brethren remained by his bedside during the first days of Holy Week, conversing with him until late into the night. But when Brother Figueiredo and Rector Cardim went to check on Palmeiro at four in the morning on Wednesday, April 4, they detected no pulse. Since he still seemed alive, however, Cardim ordered the signal bell to be rung and instructed the priests who gathered to pray once again the prayers for the dying. In Bonelli's account, only a half an hour after they had rushed to his bedside Palmeiro breathed his last.[25]

"As soon as I closed his eyes," the procurator wrote, "I went straight away to say a mass for him in the church, and other priests went off to do the same, not only in the church, but also in the college's smaller chapels." These would be the first of many masses said for Palmeiro's soul, and the first signs of the outpouring of grief that accompanied his passing. Bonelli noted that shortly after the pealing of the college's bells, "the most important people of the city came, with men filling the halls and women the church, all of them showing by the tears they spilled the pain and feelings inside them." Owing to the fact that the Tenebrae mass was set for that afternoon, there was no public liturgy for the Visitor until Maundy Thursday. When the Jesuits opened the church to mourners that next day, "all came, including the Captain General and most of the citizens." As if to match the prevailing emotional gloom, dark clouds passed over the city right in the middle of the mass. Despite the church's large windows, it became so dark that the Jesuits were obliged to light candles in order to be able to finish their memorial ceremony. "And after that, there came such a heavy rain which was accompanied by much thunder and lightning," Bonelli continued, "that it seemed to be true what people said, which was that heaven itself was showing signs of mourning and sadness."[26]

In keeping with tradition as well as to honor the city inhabitants' desire to reverence Palmeiro's body, the Jesuits erected a bier in the church and placed his corpse upon it. Men and women came in crowds, Bonelli claimed, to see him one last time and to kiss his hand. Such were the emotions caused by his lifeless body that many, both Jesuits and others, felt obliged to retreat into the shadows of the church's lateral chapels so as not to weep in public. Although it is not clear precisely when the burial was held, it seems likely that it happened soon after this final viewing. The approaching ceremonies of Holy Week demanded the use of the church, and Palmeiro's tomb was to be located in the main chapel.

Bonelli's text says little about the last paces of the Visitor's lifetime of journeys. He simply states that the Visitor was laid to rest next to Alessandro Valignano, "his predecessor in the office and now his companion in glory."[27] Turning to a list of the tombs in the Society's church at Macau produced in the mid-eighteenth century, one gets a better sense of Palmeiro's final resting place. The *capela mor* was the site for the burials of the most important Jesuits in East Asia—superiors within the order and Jesuits who had accepted ecclesiastical dignities. Starting at the high altar, the first rank of tombs with stone covers held the bodies of three bishops of Japan: Melchior Carneiro (who also held the title of Latin Patriarch of Ethiopia), Luís Cerqueira, and Diogo Valente. Filling out the elevated portion of the main chapel, just above the steps that led to the church's crossing and nave, lay a trio of early visitors, with Valignano on the right-hand side and Francesco Pasio (1554–1612) on the left. Somewhat squeezed by the small space yet right in the center of the chapel, "at the feet of the Patriarch," André Palmeiro was buried.[28]

The rush of events during Holy Week in 1635 left little time for communal reflection on the Visitor's virtues. The outpouring of emotions that his death occasioned mixed with the tears and laments typical of Good Friday and Holy Saturday, delaying the moment when the Macau Jesuits would pause to consider his life. And so the figure of Palmeiro was not so quickly forgotten. In the week after Easter, Rector Cardim addressed the Macau Jesuits to eulogize the Visitor in the form of the funeral sermon that had not been given at the time of his burial. As was characteristic, he took a verse from the Bible and constructed his thoughts around it. Cardim's choice was from the first Book of Kings: *Cognovit universus Israhel a Dan usque Bersabee quod fidelis Samuhel propheta esset Domini.*[29] He used this passage, Bonelli records, to evoke the great expanses where Palmeiro's virtues were known and revered. Just as Samuel was known throughout all Israel, so all of Portugal, Cardim asserted, knew of the Visitor's skill at letters and his heroic traits: "The noble lords, the prelates, and, in the universities where he lectured, both the great and the small all knew what a great servant of God he was." Continuing on, Cardim delved into Palmeiro's formidable qualities: "how he mortified himself, and how he so controlled his passions that he did not seem to have any; how experienced he was in the solid and true virtues; how distinguished was his doctrine; how his governing was so tender, so agreeable, so prudent, and so effective."[30]

It was not just Portugal that knew of Palmeiro's qualities, Cardim asserted; the ends of the earth had felt the Visitor's presence. His virtues were known "in all of India, at the court of the emperor of Ethiopia, in the lands of *Mogor* and *Narsinga*,[31] and in Tibet, Tonkin, China, and Japan." And so, the rector concluded, it appeared that Jacob's prophecy for his son Nephtali was fulfilled in the Visitor: *Nephtalim cervus emissus et dans eloquia pulchritudinis.*[32] With the swiftness of a deer, the *cervus emissus* of the biblical text, "out of obedience he ran about to visit the four provinces of the Orient: Goa, Malabar, Macau and China." Indeed, Palmeiro was the first higher official to enter inside the Chinese mainland. (Had he recovered from his illness, he would have covered even more ground—an order for him to return to inspect the Indian provinces was on its way to Macau when he died).[33]

The mention of the Visitor's obedience was important. Recall that Palmeiro had spent most of his life at Coimbra, rarely traveling beyond that city's limits; it was in that university town that he gained the intellectual renown which qualified him for his later work in Asia. When obedience obliged, he traveled, traversing vast expanses and taking his erudition with him. Palmeiro's words, Cardim claimed, were truly beautiful, being "those of a master and a doctor." His responses to any questions or doubts were "so firm and true, so much in accord with human and divine law, with the doctrine of the church fathers and the sacred councils, as well as with scholastic, mystical, and moral theology." And his sermons were "learned, serious, zealous, and magisterial." In sum, the college rector concluded, Palmeiro was "in all most learned and most eminent," an assertion to which "all of the priests responded that there were no virtues in which he did not greatly shine."[34]

The Visitor's travels have been the defining theme of this study and the primary reason for examining his life. As Cardim reminded his confreres in the eulogy, the Visitor's fame was spread nearly as far as transportation across the early modern world permitted. His obligation to govern the Society of Jesus had taken him across the breadth of the Portuguese Empire, save for an assignment in Brazil. It had carried him far beyond the limits of European power, deep into the inland regions of southern India, and all the way to the capital of the Ming Empire. Had circumstances not conspired against the Jesuits in Japan, he almost certainly would have attempted to visit that country as well.

His words also traveled. Indeed, they traveled much farther than he did, to the most distant mission stations in Asia. His voice was therefore the envy of colonial officials, from the Portuguese viceroy down to the captains of the empire's fortresses: Given safe transit, his orders would be obeyed immediately wherever they were received. From his writing desk at Cochin, Goa, or Macau, he issued decisions that had repercussions throughout the Portuguese Empire and beyond its borders. Missionaries in the Spice Islands, at the Mughal court, in the villages of Vietnam, in the highlands of Ethiopia, and the hinterlands of Mozambique maintained their ties to the Visitor through the exchange of correspondence. Taking into account the massive distance separating the farthest points in Palmeiro's travels as well as the intensity of his exchanges between Europe and Asia, one could argue that he had a global impact.

It is the mention of distance that conjures up the adjective "global." This word has recently attained a fetishistic quality as historians and other scholars seek premodern parallels to present trends in cultural and economic interconnectedness. But how useful is the term "global" for understanding André Palmeiro and the early modern Jesuit missionaries? There is no doubt that the Visitor saw much more of the world than the vast majority of his contemporaries. Acting on the orders of a distant superior, he left his academic life in Portugal for a global adventure. He willingly obeyed the command to travel to the ends of the earth; and everywhere he went, from Portugal all the way to the farthest shore of the Eurasian landmass, he found other members of the Society of Jesus. Beyond the stops on his global tour, there were more Jesuits working in missionary outposts. So "global" can be taken as a shorthand for "great distance." But there seems to be more. The will to travel about the world and the capacity to do so was a mark of the early modern Jesuits, a sign of the scale of the Society's ambitions. The order maintained a global system of communications for the purposes of governance and corporate unity. We have seen how the Visitor's correspondence not only kept him in touch with the superior general in Rome but also established channels of communication with his subordinates in their distant mission stations. And therefore "global" can be taken to describe the world-spanning network willed into existence by the Jesuits. It also suggests a far broader consciousness than that of earlier ages since even the members of the Society who never traveled beyond Europe were constantly reminded of their brethren in distant places. Surely this means that Palmeiro and his confreres were the harbingers of globalization, the process implied by such invocations of "global."[35]

But just as one swallow does not make a spring, so the vast ambitions of the Jesuits did not signal an enduring shift in world history. Simply to invoke the distances traveled by the men of the Society, or the coincidence of their presence in Portuguese or Spanish (or French) imperial outposts and beyond, does little to increase understanding of the separate spheres of action that the Jesuits inhabited in the early modern world. The word "global" used in this context is a subterfuge. It enables scholars of premodernity to claim more than their share, to maintain superficial or misleading similarities between the past and the present. None of this artifice serves the purposes of historical inquiry and therefore should be scrupulously avoided. "Global" raises a smoke screen that masks the limited capacity for action enjoyed by early moderns, regardless of the miles they traversed or the fact that they belonged to a centrally administered organization. To use this adjective is to take the story of Palmeiro and his confreres to a level of superficiality where all detail disappears and all actors are reduced to caricatures. It has therefore been the primary goal of this study to make the figures three-dimensional, to give depth and texture to the flat silhouettes that mar recent accounts of the "global."

We must nevertheless still reckon with the scale of the Jesuit presence in the early modern world and of the Society's ambitions. Did their activities and their consciousness not indicate a decisive turn toward a modern understanding of the world? Alas, no. It was not the world that became more interconnected because of Jesuits; rather, it was the Society that, owing to the limitations of communication in early modernity, became more thinly stretched as it spread out across the world. No one knew this better than Palmeiro, whose travels attempted to bring those far-flung Jesuits back into line with European norms. That their will impelled them to move ever farther to more distant mission stations did not make the Visitor's task easier. In fact, it exposed the fragility of Jesuit endeavor; it revealed the weakness that would be proven by the swiftness with which the Society's endeavors crumbled before the nineteenth century. So if the Jesuits' world—that is, their early modern network and their mission churches—offers a glimpse of the trailhead of globalization, it was one that led to a series of dead ends.

Not long after Palmeiro's passing, the vast web of Jesuit activity began to shrink. The visionary will of individuals in the middle of the sixteenth century, starting with Francis Xavier, had set into motion an expansion that attained its maximum extent in the early years of the following century. This first phase in the history of Jesuit expansion was complete by the time Palmeiro arrived in India, and the Society's reach in Asia had already begun to recede before the Visitor died. In some areas, fatal blows would fall upon important missions; others would show signs of decay or demonstrate a limited capacity for growth. Within a few decades of 1635 many of the Jesuit missions that he had sought to preserve and propagate during his fifteen years as visitor would be reduced to naught.

These Jesuit endeavors—the enterprises in Ethiopia, in parts of India and Southeast Asia, and above all in Japan—were so many dinosaurs condemned to extinction by the changes in the political climate of Maritime Asia. They were the glorious missions of the Society's early years, the fruit produced by the heroic piety of the order's founders and venerable elders. These missions had come about in the heady early years of Portuguese expansion, when the Iberians were relatively new presences on the political and economic spectrum of Maritime Asia. By the early seventeenth century, however, others had arrived from Europe to challenge Portuguese supremacy on the seas, and forces within the various mission fields beyond colonial control were mustered against the perceived destabilizing missionary presence. After the fall of the first major Jesuit enterprises in Maritime Asia, their memory inspired awe for what the priests of old had accomplished as well as regret for what had been lost. Crucially for the Society of Jesus, the fossils of these extinct missions offered valuable lessons on how to survive in unpredictable circumstances and at great distance from colonial protection. The smaller enterprises that had been in their infancy during Palmeiro's day would therefore emerge from the cataclysms of the end of this first cycle of Jesuit mission history in Asia better equipped for survival, at least until their adaptations were once again challenged by other, more powerful forces.

Let us survey the panorama of dead ends from West to East, following the same arc traversed by Palmeiro. In the early 1630s, just when a great Jesuit triumph appeared imminent, the situation soured in East Africa. Portuguese efforts to establish communion between the Ethiopian Christians and their Latin brethren began in the mid-sixteenth century and had reached their high-water mark during Palmeiro's tenure. The decision by Emperor Susenyos to align the indigenous church with Rome was considered a victory by the Jesuits, but it was a fleeting one. Despite the Visitor's efforts to chart new ways for his men and Patriarch Afonso Mendes to reach the Ethiopian highlands, their ambitious project of Latinization was scuttled upon the ascension of the next emperor, Fasiladas (r. 1632–1667). In 1634, even before Palmeiro's death, the Jesuits were expelled from that land, and the ancient Ethiopian rites and the native clergy restored to their former prominence. Palmeiro's friend Mendes and the corps of Jesuit veterans spent time in Ottoman captivity on their way back to India, where they passed the next decades strategizing about how to regain their lost mission. With the exile of their pastors, the Latin Christian communities created by the Jesuits in Ethiopia gradually disappeared. Whether the Visitor knew of these events is unclear since he does not mention them in his correspondence.

The fate of the Jesuits in South Asia beyond the bounds of the Portuguese Empire was not much rosier. Despite the continued presence of missionaries at the Mughal court, they made little progress in producing high-ranking converts or nourishing a significant community of native Christians in the cities of Northern India. And the expeditions that had left Agra for more distant lands to the north discovered only missionary deserts. In the mid-1620s António de Andrade's two journeys to the southern edge of Tibet had planted the seeds of a new church that some of his confreres attempted to cultivate in the succeeding decade, but to little avail. The conquest of the Kingdom of Guge by neighboring rivals and the great expense of providing gifts to the new sovereign, not to mention the meager harvest of converts, led the Society's superiors in Goa to order the end of this mission in 1635.[36]

On the southern fringe of the subcontinent, the outlook was similarly bleak, but for other reasons. Here, the aggressive attempts of the Dutch to capture the spice trade from Portuguese hands would carry them from one military victory to another over their Catholic rivals. And since the Portuguese arms that had protected the Jesuits' endeavors were vanquished, the Society's presence largely disappeared from Sri Lanka as well as from the Coromandel, Fishery, and Malabar Coasts. With the rise of the V.O.C.'s power, a new Christian fault line was introduced in Maritime Asia and the structures of the Catholic Church declined, even if the number of indigenous Catholics—the fruit of the efforts of Jesuits and others—would not diminish dramatically. The Society of Jesus, formerly at the center of the Catholic presence in southern India, would be displaced when the Dutch seized the Portuguese ports of Galle in 1640, Negombo in 1646, Colombo in 1656, Nagapattinam and Tuticorin in 1657, Jaffna in 1658, and Cranganore and Quilon in 1661. Although the capture of these ports made it difficult for the Jesuits to minister to their Christian communities in the towns of coastal southern India, the Paravas at length would win concessions from the V.O.C. to permit the Society's men in Madurai to visit them.[37]

Elsewhere, the Dutch were not so tolerant of the Jesuit presence. For instance, the churches at Cranganore, where Palmeiro had helped to create a seminary for indigenous clergy, would be abandoned after the surrender of that Portuguese fortress. Likewise, the College of Cochin, where Palmeiro had spent his years as visitor of the Province of Malabar, would fall into Dutch hands with the capitulation of the city in 1663. The Jesuit edifice, situated on the fringe of the former Portuguese city, would be destroyed during the Dutch refortification of Cochin in the years following the capture of the colony. According to one late-seventeenth-century description of the former colonial city, the main chapel of the Society's church, with its tombs of vener-ated missionaries, was located under a bulwark of a new Dutch fortification.[38]

Political rivalries, war, and upheaval also spoiled the Jesuits' plans farther to the east. The capture of Hooghly by Mughal forces in 1632 scattered the missionaries and their church, which was only reassembled years later else-where in Bengal. And the Society's "mission" in Burma only continued until the early 1650s because the lone Jesuit in that country, Manuel da Fonseca, was held in captivity at the royal court for thirty-eight years.[39] More devas-tating for the Jesuit presence in this region was the fall of Malacca to the Dutch. After resisting the attacks of the nearby Achinese over the course of several decades and lifting blockades by the V.O.C. in the 1620s, the Portu-guese surrendered the colony in 1641. The Jesuit church, sitting at the crest of the hillock at the center of the city, was turned over to Calvinist use by the new religious authorities. And although there were Dutch Catholic governors and even periodic visits by Jesuits traveling incognito, the Society would not regain its former place in Malacca.[40]

The loss of this strategic port caused grave problems for the Jesuit enter-prises in East Asia and threatened to rend the Portuguese Empire in two. Not only did the Province of Japan and the Vice-Province of China rely on the (sporadic) payment of a portion of the city's customs duties for their upkeep, they also used Malacca as a relay point for supplies and correspondence. But with Dutch ships blocking the well-traveled Portuguese routes from Goa to Macau, it would be very difficult for the Society to get men and money from one end of the Estado da Índia to the other. As a result, Jesuits in the later seventeenth century would attempt several different routes to reach East Asia, whether by proceeding across the subcontinent on foot, trekking from Europe across Central Asia, or sailing by way of Batavia on Dutch ships.

———————

Japan lies at the eastern terminus on this panorama of Jesuit dead ends. Al-though the Society suffered numerous disasters in the final years of Pal-meiro's life and soon after his death, none surpassed the definitive loss of that mission. The Visitor went to his grave with the knowledge that the once-glorious Japanese church was in its death throes. Although he knew of the widespread persecution of Japanese Christians, he did not live to hear of its bloodiest episode, the Shimabara Rebellion of 1637–1638. This episode was spurred by a tax revolt among the peasants in the former Arima domains near Nagasaki, the heart of the heavily Christianized area of western Kyushu. The Tokugawa shogunate's massive repression of this peasant uprising meant at the same time the eradication of the traces of Christianity in this territory. By the time the shogunal forces—aided by the shelling of a seaside stronghold by a Dutch ship—had crushed their adversaries in April 1638, the casualties among the populace were reported to have numbered over 37,000.[41]

During the decade he had spent in Macau, Palmeiro had heard that the Tokugawa rulers' tolerance for the Portuguese was waning, but he did not witness its end. In 1639 the shogunate suspended all contact between Macau and Nagasaki or any other Japanese port, issuing orders for the Portuguese to stay away. That the regime was deadly serious in making this decision was proven the following year by the execution of a large group of representatives of the city of Macau who ventured to Nagasaki to petition for the resumption of their lucrative trade.[42] A further embassy was attempted in the mid-1640s to reestablish relations between newly independent Portugal and Japan but met with a similar, if less violent, rejection.[43] None of these events led to the absolute destruction of the Christian presence in Japan. But they did represent the death of Palmeiro's and his confreres' hope that the faith and its preachers might again attain the measure of success they had enjoyed in that land before 1614.

The Visitor was in his grave when the Jesuits at Macau received the dreaded confirmation of what they justifiably came to consider the greatest indignity inflicted on the beleaguered mission. Cristóvão Ferreira's apostasy was verified by trustworthy reports from Nagasaki that arrived in June 1635. No longer could the Jesuits feign that the rumors were little more than the gossip of ill-informed or ill-intentioned plebeians. Truly for Ferreira the gap between beatification and repudiation was a syllable wide. As glorious as it was for the Society to have a legion of martyrs associated with its name, so shameful was it to have just one apostate. It is therefore instructive to consider in some detail how the Jesuits dealt with the fallout of Ferreira's act, even if it takes this narrative into the years after the Visitor's death. While it is impossible to say if Palmeiro would have handled matters in the same way as his successor, it is likely that before his death he traced the path that would be followed by his brethren. Recall that the Visitor's principal concern had been for the order, and specifically for the Society's honor. The Jesuits at Macau showed similar concern in their actions, of necessity repudiating a man to whom they had previously ascribed heroic qualities.

What had happened to Ferreira in Nagasaki after that fateful day in October 1633? The fleet that returned to Macau in the summer after Palmeiro's death brought conflicting reports, but one thing was clear: he apostatized during his torture over the pit and became the prized ward—and, indeed, collaborator—of the Nagasaki commissioners. Few except his captors had seen Ferreira, although some European traders and Japanese Christians claimed to have spotted him during the following year and a half. Enough sightings had been made by 1635, and the news traveled quickly away from Nagasaki. According to one contemporary, the scandal would not cause too much damage if "it did not go beyond Japan and China, but it is already speeding over the seas under full sail, greatly wounding the honor of the Society; it has already passed through the Strait of Singapore and soon will leave that of Gibraltar in its wake."[44] As ships carried the Jesuits' shame around the world, disbelief turned to revulsion and rejection. By begging for mercy at the hands of the heathen, Ferreira had forfeited the compassionate grace of the Almighty. Or so thought his confreres, who were left with no option but to wash their hands of him as swiftly as possible, and with as much bravado as they could muster—in order to prove that his self-serving weakness was not a suggestion of their own lack of strength.

It was Manuel Dias the elder, Palmeiro's successor, who dealt with the fallout. The new visitor gathered the evidence necessary for expelling Ferreira from the Society, first by writing to the apostate himself for confirmation and then by taking depositions from those who had seen him in Nagasaki. In a letter to the apostate in late June 1635, Dias sent news of Palmeiro's death and implored Ferreira to respond with some sign that the scurrilous rumors, such as that he was living with a woman, were not true.[45] But no answer came from Ferreira. It was only with the return of the fleets in November of that year that Dias received irrefutable testimony from Gonçalo da Silveira, the Portuguese ambassador to Edo. Silveira averred that not only was Ferreira alive but he was cooperating with his captors, serving as an interpreter for officialdom in Nagasaki.[46] Only two merchants from Macau, Manuel Mendes and Pedro Cordeiro, had spoken to Ferreira. To them, the apostate did not deny his actions. Instead, through a veil of tears, he insisted with Mendes that "whoever loses God because of his weakness can still do good." Mendes was as unconvinced as the Jesuits who read his report. What good could Ferreira possibly do, now that he had indelibly tarnished the Society's honor? Could it at least be hoped that Ferreira's fall had not yet turned him from

Paul to Saul? Dias asked his informants if the former Jesuit had become a persecutor of the Christians, and, in hollow consolation, Mendes declared: "I found that he was not."[47]

The scandal of Ferreira's apostasy did not cease with this news but grew as more details of his new life emerged. Dias was particularly interested in learning the extent to which the apostate had forsaken his vows since this evidence would be used as grounds for his dismissal. Although this information came shrouded in a haze of suppositions and rumors, it all pointed in one direction: Ferreira was more attached to the flesh than to the spirit. Testimony from Japanese exiles in Macau questioned by Dias confirmed that the apostate cohabitated with the Japanese widow of a Chinese merchant, although it was not clear if he did more than share the same residence.[48] More confusing were the assertions that Ferreira had sired children with other women elsewhere in Japan: One witness said he had a son, another that he had two, but none agreed on the ages of these boys, whether five years old, or seventeen, or fourteen, or nine. Any of these ages indicated that Ferreira had begun his path to mortal sin long before he reached the pit at Nagasaki, but there was no firm proof of a child; some witnesses declared that there was none at all. This lack of evidence nevertheless did not stop Dias from recording rumors that could only serve to confirm the suspicion of Ferreira's abandonment of his vow of chastity. In the testimony that he forwarded to Rome, Dias noted that his informants claimed to have heard of Ferreira declaring before Japanese officials at Nagasaki that, before his capture, he "had sinned with eight hundred women."[49]

Not only the prodigious scale of his rumored sins of the flesh disqualified Ferreira from the Society. His public declarations of apostasy and his assistance to the persecutors were also damning. Dias was keen to know if the fallen Jesuit had formally renounced his faith before the Japanese authorities, thereby voiding his other vows to his order. Indeed, the testimony reported, Ferreira had made a signed public declaration of his apostasy to city officials, a text that Dias duly had translated in his correspondence.[50] Other questions inquired if the apostate had made any specific personal declarations beyond this bureaucratic boilerplate, to which the reply came that "he reneged on the Most Holy Trinity, and that he said there was no other life," and what is more, he composed a treatise in which he denounced the Ten Commandments.[51] The witnesses further added that Ferreira had been seen taking part in a procession to a Buddhist temple, and that he willingly stepped on a sacred image in order to prove his disregard for Christian symbols. This gesture would become the principal ritual of the anti-Christian inquisition that the Tokugawa officials would carry out in subsequent decades. According to one Portuguese merchant who spoke with Dias's witnesses, a former Japanese Christian in Nagasaki claimed that "not even Martin Luther would do the things that the *padre* did."[52]

With a surfeit of evidence against Ferreira, Manuel Dias took the final step to banish him from the Society of Jesus. Had Ferreira been of a lesser rank, such as a brother or a spiritual (third vow) coadjutor, Dias could have dismissed him summarily. But the apostate was a professed Jesuit, and his expulsion required his indictment in Rome. After writing once again to Ferreira in July 1636 and receiving no response with the return of the fleets from Nagasaki that year, Dias forged ahead with a consultation at Macau for the purpose of dismissing the apostate.[53] Ferreira's continued presence in Japan and his apparently willing cooperation with the persecutors was a goad for the Jesuits. To be sure, Dias greatly feared that he might be expelled from Nagasaki to Macau, because in that case he would surely be tried before the tribunals of the Holy Office in India. A trial involving a professed Jesuit accused of apostasy would make matters far worse, giving the Society's rivals a chance to revive old disputes and to settle old scores. Recall that the Inquisition was staffed by theologians drawn from the religious orders as well as officials seeking to make names for themselves within its far-reaching bureaucracy. The whiff of unorthodoxy already detected by the Jesuits' detractors in Asia would turn into a permanent stench, were Ferreira to be put on trial. Breathing a sigh of relief at the fact that António Cardim was the local commissioner in Macau and that Álvaro Tavares (1575–1637), a senior Jesuit, was a deputy in India, Dias remarked to the superior general: "This case shows us how important it is for one of our men to always be part of the Inquisition in Goa."[54]

Some Jesuits, not content with defensive tactics against the threat of further scandal, decided to take the fight to Japan. Dias was not the only one at Macau to send missives challenging Ferreira. Giovanni Battista Bonelli addressed a long letter to the apostate, denouncing the harm he had done to the faith, the order, and the mission's heroic history. There the procurator described how the seventy-six-year-old Dias called a meeting where he declared his determination to "go in person to Japan to attend to the honor of the Society and present himself to the Tyrant in the stead of Your Reverence."[55] Indeed, the visitor reported to Rome that as soon as the confirmation of the apostasy reached Macau, three brothers, one of whom was Palmeiro's traveling companion, Domingos Mendes, offered to sacrifice themselves on a similar voyage.[56] But these men would not travel to Japan; that was the fate reserved for other Jesuits. The reckless missions of the late 1630s and early 1640s only served to compound the tragedy suffered by the Jesuits and the Japanese Christians. In 1637, in gratitude for a miraculous cure worked by Francis Xavier on his sickbed in Naples, Marcello Mastrilli (b. 1603) sailed for Kyushu (via Manila; Dias in Macau would not have permitted such a folly) where he intended to restore the faith and confront Ferreira.[57] Within a month of his arrival, on October 14 of that year, this Jesuit visionary died over the pit.[58] Five years later, Visitor Antonio Rubino, Palmeiro's former colleague from Colombo and the Fishery Coast, would be moved by the spirit to challenge Ferreira in person. Rubino's mission in 1642, and the one that followed the next year, led by the sixty-six-year-old Pêro Marques, would serve no purpose other than to produce more martyrs and a handful of other apostates.[59]

In the end, André Palmeiro was buried alongside the missionary dreams of the Society's first decades. Others, born later, remained alive, although it was only through twists of fate that they survived the reconfiguration of the Portuguese Empire in Asia in the later seventeenth century. This second generation of Jesuit missions, several of which Palmeiro had a hand in creating, would not produce the large scale drama of their earlier counterparts. None of these projects would achieve the renown and the tallies of conversions of the earlier missions; to be sure, their smaller size would permit an intensity of pastoral activity that perhaps ensured their survival. Among these enterprises were the missions in the Zambezi valley of Mozambique, where the Jesuits ran mission stations and large farms until the mid-eighteenth century, and the colleges and residences found in many of the Portuguese outposts on the western coast of India.[60] In the inland districts of southern India, away from the predations of the Dutch East India Company, the Madurai mission likewise survived long after Palmeiro's death. Here Roberto Nobili played the primary role until his death in 1656, after which Portuguese confreres such as João de Brito (1647–1693) continued his efforts.

The Jesuit missions in South Asia would attract a continuous stream of recruits long into the eighteenth century, despite the gradual waning of Portuguese power and the rise of French and English influence. As a result, Jesuit mission stations in Agra and Bengal would endure for decades and even serve as the launching point for new expeditions into the Himalayas. While the efforts of men like Ippolito Desideri (1684–1733), who traveled to Lhasa in the 1710s, seemed intent on surpassing the feats of Jesuits a century earlier, they met no greater degree of success. The ephemeral missions to different quarters of South and Central Asia produced nothing of lasting consequence beyond a greater knowledge of geography and ethnography among Enlightenment-era Europeans; no major mission church grew from their efforts.[61]

These dead ends far afield notwithstanding, the Society's presence within Portuguese India itself remained strong in the century after Palmeiro's passing. The Jesuit presence in Goa's *Velhas Conquistas,* more specifically in the district of Salcete, lost little of the intensity of its missionary impulse, leaving the foundations of a church that would continue down to the present, albeit one that would long be administered by others. Indeed, a new missionary effort begun in 1649 in Mysore, a region located to the southeast of Goa, would be a comparative success for the Jesuits in the second half of the seventeenth century. A further Jesuit enterprise, founded independently of the Portuguese Assistancy in the hinterland of the French colony at Pondicherry on the Coromandel Coast, also began in the 1700s. Known as the Carnatic mission, this small-scale endeavor flourished for a few decades, its men contributing to the creation of Indological studies in Europe.[62] But all was not well for the Indian Jesuits, even in the heart of the Estado da Índia. The remnants of the theological disputes of Palmeiro's day would be rekindled in the early eighteenth century, and would spread from India to Rome. In Europe, the Jesuits would be far less able than their predecessors to defend the positions of their missionary brethren in the disputes over the "Malabar Rites." This was an important factor that contributed to shifting the political tide against the Society of Jesus in the mid-eighteenth century.

Despite the disappearance of the Jesuits from Japan, their Province of Japan and Vice-Province of China would also survive the dramatic events of the 1640s and 1650s. As we have seen, it was largely through Palmeiro's efforts that the efforts in mainland Southeast Asia made it through their troubled early years. By the middle of the seventeenth century, the name "Province of Japan" was the epitaph for the martyrs of that land, but it was also something more—a challenge for the Jesuits who served in Tonkin and Cochinchina. From their headquarters at Macau, the Society's men who guarded the memory of Japan turned their gaze fully toward the nearby shores of the South China Sea. The missions to Vietnam would thrive during the late seventeenth and early eighteenth century, laying the foundations for the substantial church of the modern era in that country (a large Catholic community that was, of course, fostered by the French colonial presence in the 1800s). Realizing that there would be no resurrection to the East, the Macau Jesuits developed their links to Southern China and by 1658 were assigned by their superior general the southern three provinces, including Hainan Island, as their mission territory.

Palmeiro's dying exhortation to Manuel Dias to care for the China mission bore fruit. The Jesuits of the vice-province emerged from the cataclysm of the Manchu invasions of the mid-seventeenth century with few casualties. And when the dust settled in China, the rulers of the Qing dynasty recognized the missionaries as part of the religious landscape of their newly conquered territories. The expansion of the China mission during the late seventeenth century would nevertheless cause problems for both Europeans and Chinese as the Jesuits' missionary rivals took up again the theological disputes that Palmeiro had sought to lay to rest. To further complicate matters, Louis XIV chose to patronize French Jesuit endeavors to Siam and China that were mounted under the pretense of scientific inquiry and diplomatic exchange. These independent French missions, outside the control of Palmeiro's successors in the Province of Japan and the Vice-Province of China, would cause further strain within the Society of Jesus itself and leave the order exposed to threats from outside its ranks. At length, this wrangling helped bring about the scuttling of the China mission and served to incite the ire of European powers against the Society of Jesus.

The survival of some of the missionary enterprises that Palmeiro had administered was due as much to fortuitous political and economic circumstances and insulation from missionary rivalries and ecclesiastical politics as it was to the will of the Jesuits. None of these elements was guaranteed, and prayers would not necessarily prompt the Almighty to ensure the success of the Jesuits' desires. No one knew this better than the Visitor. Fifteen years of his life had been dedicated to managing the resources of his order and resolving the difficulties that emerged in the path of the missions. But before the centennial anniversary of Palmeiro's death had arrived, the Society of Jesus in Maritime Asia would be confronted by forces that Jesuit willpower could not overcome.

In the final decades of the seventeenth century, missionary rivals would appear in Asia to challenge the ways in which the men of the Society spread the gospel, obliging them to fight more battles of the sort that had been waged in Japan in the late sixteenth century. The difference with episodes that the Jesuits faced later on in Vietnam, China, and India was that they could no longer count on the power of the Portuguese Church, the Inquisition, or the Portuguese Empire. The papacy shifted its allegiances away from the Society toward other forces more directly under its control, and sent bishops and more tractable religious orders to sidestep or replace the Jesuits. Political and economic changes, both in Europe and Asia, also reduced the Jesuits' capacity to finance continued work in many of their mission fields, regardless of the value of their much-coveted landholdings in Portugal, India, and Africa. The final blow to their enterprises came when the Portuguese crown, which had supported Jesuit activities for over two centuries, revoked its patronage in 1759.

It was then that the first incarnation of the Society of Jesus, much like André Palmeiro himself, died a baroque death. The attack on the Jesuits in Portugal and the Portuguese Empire led by the Marquis of Pombal was the first act in the fourteen-year drama that culminated in the suppression of the "Old Company." In Portugal and its territories, Jesuits were imprisoned and many exiled to Italy or elsewhere. But there was no true safe haven for the men of the Society as different monarchs one by one also chose to expel the Jesuits from their lands. When the final blow came, with the decree of extinction issued by papal fiat in 1773, the Jesuit presence was already a distant memory in many of the lands where Palmeiro had worked. As in the Visitor's case, the Old Company's final moments in the late eighteenth century revealed truths long hidden, contained episodes of pious pathos, and exposed corruptions caused by age. While it is true that the order would be resurrected in 1814, and that it would flourish in some of its former mission territories again, the "New Company" was the creation of a different age and different men with different ambitions.

After 1759, with the Society discredited and disbanded in Portugal and its empire, others rushed in to take possession of the missions founded by the Jesuits and claim their schools and churches. It is for this reason that parts of the Colégio de Santo Antão, where Palmeiro received his earliest education, can still be seen today in a Lisbon hospital, and the Colégio de Jesus, where the Visitor spent his days as a student and a professor in Coimbra, can be visited when the doors of the New Cathedral and the university buildings are open. Likewise, one can see the cloister and church of the Colégio de São

Paulo in Braga, where Palmeiro served as rector, for the price of a bit of conversation at the reception desk of that city's seminary. And in Goa one can still pace the same halls where the Visitor walked at the Professed House because the tomb and the cult of Francis Xavier have been maintained in the adjacent Basilica of the Bom Jesus.

If this handful of buildings has survived as testimony of the Jesuits' presence across the early modern world, far more have disappeared. Setting aside the mission stations inspected by the Visitor which vanished without their resident pastors, most of the colleges in which Palmeiro stayed in Maritime Asia have long since crumbled. For example, the Colégio Novo de São Paulo, whose construction was overseen in part by the Visitor, was abandoned to ruin in the late eighteenth century along with most of the urban structures of Velha Goa. In similar fashion, only a ruined doorway remains to indicate the former site of Old St. Paul's, on the opposite side of the former capital of the Estado da Índia.[63] And because they were in Dutch hands already in the seventeenth century and English ones after that, the Jesuit colleges of the Malabar and Coromandel Coasts, as well as those in Sri Lanka, have been lost to memory. It goes without saying that the churches of Japan were destroyed with the same rigor that was applied to their pastors and their Christians. Inside China, the only remaining space of Jesuit activity that Palmeiro would have seen is the Old Imperial Observatory, heavily restored, in central Beijing. There one can still see the platform from where he looked out over the Ming capital before its collapse, at the farthest point on his journey across Asia.

In Macau, where Palmeiro ended his days, a fitting monument still stands to mark the passage of the early modern Jesuits. This is the façade of the former Jesuit church, known locally as the Ruins of St. Paul's. Standing atop a long flight of steps, it served as the city's most famous symbol before its imposing presence was dwarfed by casino towers. The ruins have been described as a sermon in stone, but they are better described as a tombstone for the Society's Asian missions. They are all that is left of the once-imposing structure that Palmeiro knew in the 1620s. The college and procurator's warehouse—buildings deemed most remarkable by early modern observers—have disappeared. The magnificent church that once stood behind the façade is gone. Abandoned after the suppression of the Society of Jesus, the church stood until the early 1830s, when it was destroyed by the combination of typhoon winds and fire. After that the graves of the Jesuits who had been buried in the church's nave and in front of its high altar were exposed to the elements. The forces of nature that brought down the roof of the Igreja da Madre de Deus also served to push up the stone slabs that covered the tombs in its floor. All of these markers of the Jesuits' former sanctuary are gone, and a piazza spreads out behind the old façade since the restoration of the area in the 1990s. Rectangular outlines that decorate the pavement remind visitors of the site of the tombs that used to exist below their feet. There is no other trace of the Jesuits or of André Palmeiro on this empty spot below Macau's hazy sky. No matter; those who visit the site after following the Visitor's footsteps will know where to seek him.

Abbreviations

Notes

Illustration Credits

Acknowledgments

Index

Abbreviations

1629 Orders	AP, Orders issued to the Vice-Province of China, Hangzhou, August 15, 1629 [and Macau, January 15, 1631], ARSI *JS* 100: 20r–39v
AHSI	*Archivum Historicum Societatis Iesu*
AHU	Arquivo Histórico Ultramarino, Lisbon
AL	Annual Letter (for the Jesuit Province or Vice-Province of . . .)
AN/TT	Arquivo Nacional/Torre do Tombo, Lisbon
AP	André Palmeiro (1569–1635)
ARSI	Archivum Romanum Societatis Iesu, Rome
AUC	Arquivo da Universidade, Coimbra
BAJA	Biblioteca da Ajuda, Lisbon, *Jesuítas na Ásia* Collection Codex
BC	Brief (Annual) Personnel Catalogue (of the Jesuit Province of . . .)
Beccari	Camillo Beccari, SJ, ed., *Rerum Aethiopicarum Scriptores Occidentales Inediti a Saeculo xvi ad xix,* 15 vols. (Rome, 1903–1917)
BNL	Biblioteca Nacional de Portugal, Lisbon
Bonelli 2	Giovanni Battista Bonelli, "Relação da Morte e Vida do P.ᶜ Andre Palmeiro Vizitador da Prov.ᵃ de Japão, e China", Macau, 1635, BAJA 49-VI-8: 91v–102v

Bonelli Relação	Giovanni Battista Bonelli, "Relação da Morte do Padre Andre Palmeyro", Macau, May 1635, BAJA 49-V-11: 265r–278v
BPADE	Biblioteca Pública e Arquivo Distrital, Évora
CA	Claudio Aquaviva (1543–1615), Superior General of the Society of Jesus
CF	Cristóvão Ferreira (ca. 1580–1650)
Chinese Itinerary	AP, Itinerary of Journey through China, 1628–1629, [Macau, January 8, 1630], ARSI *JS* 161-II: 118r–133r
FG	*Fondo Gesuitico* Collection at ARSI
Franco	António Franco, *Imagem da Virtude em o Noviciado da Companhia de Jesus no Real Collegio de Jesus de Coimbra,* 2 vols. (Coimbra, 1719)
Goa	*Goana-Malabarica* Collection at ARSI
Hist. Soc.	*Historiae Societatis Iesu* Collection at ARSI
Indian Itinerary	Account of Palmeiro's journey through Southern India and Sri Lanka, in AP to NM, Cochin, December 20, 1620, ARSI *Goa* 18: 25r–28v
JR	João Rodrigues (ca. 1561–1633)
JS	*Japonica-Sinica* Collection at ARSI
Leite	António Leite, "Fundação do Real Collegio de Coimbra da Companhia de JHS", [Coimbra, c.1640], BNL *Reservados* 4506
Liv.	*Livro* (Book)
LM	Raymundo Bulhão Pato and António da Silva Rego, eds., *Documentos remetidos da Índia ou Livros das Monções,* 10 vols. (Lisbon, 1880–1982)
Lus	*Lusitania* Collection at ARSI
MD	Manuel Dias the elder (1559–1639)
Mss. Liv.	*Manuscritos da Livraria* Collection, AN/TT
MV	Muzio Vitelleschi (1563–1645), Superior General of the Society of Jesus
NM	Nuno Mascarenhas (1552–1637), assistant (executive secretary) for the Portuguese Assistancy of the Society of Jesus
TC	Triennial Personnel Catalogue (for the Jesuit Province or Vice-Province of . . .)
TSO	*Tribunal do Santo Ofício* (Inquisition) Collection, AN/TT
Xu Volume	Peter Englefriet, Gregory Blue and Catherine Jami, eds., *Statecraft and Renewal in Late Ming China: The Cross-Cultural Synthesis of Xu Guangqi (1562–1633)* (Leiden, 2001)

Notes

Prelude

1. A list of those tortured and martyred between August and October 1633 is in Juan Ruiz-de-Medina, *El Martirologio del Japón, 1558–1873* (Rome, 1999), 697–721.

2. MD to MV, Macau, September 1, 1635, ARSI *JS* 18-I:234v.

3. Manuel Mendes de Moura was the nephew of Afonso Mendes, a Portuguese Jesuit who served as Latin Patriarch of Ethiopia.

4. Testimony by Manuel Mendes de Moura, in MD to MV, Macau, January 26, 1636, ARSI *JS* 18-I: 238v-239r.

Introduction

1. Statistics in William Bangert, *A History of the Society of Jesus* (St. Louis, 1986), 45, 96, and 98.

2. On Nadal, see John O'Malley, *The First Jesuits* (Cambridge, 1993), 11–14, and 63–65.

3. The evolution of the rules for visitors are analyzed in Guy Philippart, SJ, "Visiteurs, commissaires et inspecteurs dans la Compagnie de Jésus de 1540 à 1615: I," *AHSI*, 37 (1968): 3–128; Part II, covering 1573–1615: *AHSI*, 38 (1969): 170–277.

4. Further about Mercurian's challenges is in Mario Fois, SJ, "Everard Mercurian," in *The Mercurian Project: Forming Jesuit Culture, 1573–1580,* ed. Thomas Mc-Coog, SJ (St. Louis, 2004), 1–34, esp. 26–29.

5. Philippart, "Visiteurs, commissaires," Part II, 182–92, and 208–10. See also Dauril Alden, *The Making of an Enterprise: The Society of Jesus in Portugal, Its Empire, and Beyond, 1540–1750* (Stanford, 1996), 247–53.

6. No full biography of Valignano yet exists in English. See instead Josef Franz Schütte, SJ, *Valignano's Mission Principles for Japan*, trans. J. J. Coyne, 2 vols. (St. Louis, 1980–1985); George Elison, *Deus Destroyed: The Image of Christianity in Early Modern Japan* (Cambridge, Mass., 1991), 54–84; or J. F. Moran, *The Japanese and the Jesuits: Alessandro Valignano in Sixteenth-Century Japan* (London, 1992).

7. John 6:9.

I. Entering the Order

1. Mário da Costa Roque, "A 'Peste Grande' de 1569 em Lisboa," *Anais,* 28 (1982): 73–90.

2. Teresa Ferreira Rodrigues, "As Estruturas Populacionais," in *História de Portugal,* ed. José Mattoso, 8 vols. (Lisbon, 1993), 3:212–13.

3. M. Lopes de Almeida, ed., *Memorial de Pero Roiz Soares* (Coimbra, 1953), 19–20.

4. Franco, 2:575. Palmeiro's exact birth date is unknown. Jesuit personnel catalogues from the 1580s and 1590s suggest he was born shortly after January 1, 1569. See TC Portugal 1587, ARSI *Lus* 44-I:12v; and TC Portugal 1590, ARSI *Lus* 44-I:37r.

5. Bonelli 2, 96r.

6. Bonelli Relação, 270r.

7. Baltasar Teles, *Chronica da Companhia de IESV da Provincia de Portugal,* 2 vols. (Lisbon, 1645–1646), 2:17.

8. AL Portugal 1577, [Coimbra?], January 1, 1578, AN/TT Mss. Liv. 690:17v–18r; and AL Portugal 1578, Coimbra, January 1, 1579, AN/TT Mss. Liv. 690:38v.

9. Dominique Julia, "L'Elaboration de la *Ratio Studiorum,* 1548–1599," in *Ratio Studiorum: Plan raisonné et institution des études dans la Compagnie de Jesus,* ed. Adrien Demoustier and Dominique Julia (Paris, 1997), 29–69, at 33.

10. Anon. Jesuit author, "Alguas Cousas que se tem experiencia aproveitarem pera reger qualquer Classe," Évora, after 1562, AN/TT Mss. Liv. 1838:1–14.

11. AL Portugal 1579, Coimbra, January 1, 1580, AN/TT Mss. Liv. 690:63v.

12. Bonelli Relação, 270r.

13. Fernão Guerreiro, AL Portugal 1580, [Coimbra?], February 5, 1581, AN/TT Mss. Liv. 690:84v–85r.

14. AL Portugal 1578, Coimbra, January 1, 1579, AN/TT Mss. Liv. 690:38v.

15. On the first Jesuits in Portugal, see Dauril Alden, *The Making of an Enterprise: The Society of Jesus in Portugal, Its Empire, and Beyond, 1540–1750* (Stanford, 1996), 24–38; and Francisco Rodrigues, SJ, *História da Companhia de Jesus na Assistência de Portugal,* 6 bks. in 3 vols. (Porto, 1931–1950), vol. 1, bk. 1, 217–327.

16. AL Portugal 1584, [Coimbra?, January 1585?], AN/TT Mss. Liv. 690:128r.

17. "Livro dos Votos dos Irmãos Noviços," Évora, late sixteenth century, BNL *Reservados* 4468:3r. This version varies slightly from the modern form of the vows. See Ignatius Loyola, *The Constitutions of the Society of Jesus,* ed. and trans. George Ganss (St. Louis, 1970), 241–42.

18. BC Portugal 1585, ARSI *Lus* 39:7v.

19. Leite, 20.

20. António de Oliveira, *A Vida Económica e Social de Coimbra de 1537 a 1640,* 2 vols. (Coimbra, 1971), 1:179–87.

21. António Carvalho da Costa, *Corografia Portugueza,* 3 vols. (Lisbon, 1706–1712), 2:6.

22. Pedro de Mariz, *Dialogos de Varia Historia* (Coimbra, 1598), 2r.

23. For more, see Luís de Oliveira Ramos, "A Universidade de Coimbra," in *História da Universidade em Portugal,* 2 vols. (Lisbon, 1997), 2:361–93.

24. On the conflicts over the Colégio das Artes, see Mário Brandão, *O Colégio das Artes,* 2 vols. (Coimbra, 1924–1933), esp. vol. 2.

25. Teles, *Cronica da Companhia,* 1:101.

26. AL Portugal 1588, [Coimbra?, 1589?], AN/TT Mss. Liv. 690:153r.

27. TC Portugal 1590, ARSI *Lus* 44-I:37r.

28. Franco, 1:9. The *Desseoso,* written by Frei Miguel de Comalada in Catalan, was widely translated in the sixteenth century.

29. Franco, 1:11–12.

30. Ibid., 1:575–76.

31. Ibid., 1:582 and 577.

32. Ibid., 1:586.

33. Ibid., 1:577.

34. Bonelli 2, 98v.

35. Leite, 1.

36. BC Portugal 1585, ARSI *Lus* 39:7v.

37. AP, "Magnae Matris carmen genethliacon," in "Thesaurus rerum scholasticarum, quae à Patribus, ac Fratribus Collegij Conimbricensis scriptae sunt, ab Anno Domini. 1631," AN/TT Mss. Liv. 1963:107v–108v. On this collection of poetry and oratory, see Sebastião Tavares de Pinho, "Um Códice Latino da literatura Jesuítica quase desconhecido: o Cod. 1963 da Livraria dos Manuscritos dos ANTT," *Humanitas,* 57 (2005): 351–83. The author is especially grateful to Noël Golvers for his help with this transcription and translation.

38. Luis Fróis, "Tratado dos Embaixadores Iapões que forão de Iapão à Roma no anno de 1582," in *La première ambassade du Japon en Europe, 1582–1592,* ed. J. A. Abranches Pinto, Yoshitomo Okamoto, and Henri Bernard, SJ (Tokyo, 1942), 258.

39. Derek Massarella, ed., and J. F. Moran, trans., *Japanese Travellers in Sixteenth-Century Europe: A Dialogue Concerning the Mission of the Japanese Ambassadors to the Roman Curia (1590)* (London, 2012), 395.

40. On the Jesuits' teaching of Aristotle, see Charles Lohr, "Les jésuites et l'aristotélisme du XVIème siècle" in *Les Jésuites à la Renaissance: Système educatif et production du savoir,* ed. Luce Giard (Paris, 1995), 79–91. On the Coimbra Commentaries, see J. Pinharanda Gomes, *Os Conimbricenses* (Lisbon, 1992); and Jill Kraye, "Coimbra Commentators" in *Cambridge Translations of Renaissance Philosophical Texts* (Cambridge, 1997), 80–87.

41. TC Portugal 1590, ARSI *Lus* 44-I:37r.

42. Franco, 2:575.

43. Manuel Sequeira to CA, Coimbra, September 21, 1593, ARSI *Lus* 72:126v.

44. Sebastião Barradas to CA, Coimbra, January 10, 1595, ARSI *Lus* 73:1r.

45. Francisco de Gouvea to CA, Coimbra, November 18, 1595, ARSI *Lus* 73:67r–68v.

46. TC Portugal 1597, ARSI *Lus.* 44-I:140v; and João Correa, TC Portugal 1603, ARSI *Lus* 44-I:174v.

47. It is possible that Palmeiro studied theology at the same time that he taught either Latin or philosophy. The 1603 catalogue says he taught Latin for six years and seven months and studied theology for three years before teaching the four-year philosophy sequence beginning in 1599. See ibid.

48. TC Portugal 1597, ARSI *Lus* 44-I:137v; and João Correa, TC Portugal 1603, ARSI *Lus* 44-I:177r.

49. One biographical dictionary claims he was ordained in 1599, but this date does not appear in sources examined for this study. See Josef Wicki, SJ, "André Palmeiro" in *Diccionario Histórico de la Compañia de Jesús,* ed. Charles O'Neill, SJ, and Joaquín Maria Domínguez, SJ, 4 vols. (Madrid, 2001), 3:2961.

50. Leite, 62–64.

2. The Visitor in Training

1. On Martins, see Liam Brockey, "Jesuit Pastoral Theater on an Urban Stage: Lisbon, 1588–1593," *Journal of Early Modern History,* 9, no. 1–2 (2005): 3–50, esp. 28–36.

2. Martins began to teach doctrine in the streets of Lisbon in 1581, when Palmeiro was a grammar student. See Franco, 1:406.

3. Anon., Account of the death of Inácio Martins, Coimbra, March 1598, ARSI *Lus* 58:150r/v.

4. Ibid., 151r.

5. Ibid., 152r–153v.

6. Martim de Mello, Inquiry about the death of António Antunes, Coimbra, January 29, 1599, ARSI *Lus* 74:1r/v.

7. Ibid., 2r.

8. Anon., Account of the death of Inácio Martins, Coimbra, March 1598, ARSI *Lus* 58:151r.

9. "Livro das Sepulturas" from the Jesuit College Church, Coimbra, mid-sixteenth until mid-eighteenth centuries, BNL *Reservados* 4505:24v.

10. Manuel Sequeira to CA, Coimbra, August 20, 1593, ARSI *Lus* 72:122r.

11. *Actos e Graus,* 1597–1601, AUC, Dep IV-1a.D-1-1-19: bk. 2:24v (March 4, 1600).

12. João Manuel de Carvalho, *Diário da Peste de Coimbra (1599)* (Lisbon, 1994), 58 and 76.

13. Leite, 123.

14. Franco, 2:493–94.

15. Ibid., 493–506, and 515–16.

16. Leite, 123–24.

17. Franco, 1:233.

18. TC Portugal 1599, October 1599, ARSI *Lus* 39:20r.

19. Carvalho, *Diário da Peste,* 177.

20. *Actos e Graus,* 1597–1601, AUC, Dep IV-1a.D-1-1-19: bk. 3, 23v (July 31, 1601); and *Actos e Graus,* 1601–1604, AUC, Dep IV-1a.D-1-1-20: bk.1, 29r (July 31, 1602).

21. BC Portugal 1601, [January 1601], ARSI *Lus* 39:25r; João Correa, BC Portugal 1601, November 1601, ARSI *Lus* 39:36v; and BC Portugal 1602, January 1602, ARSI *Lus* 39:42v.

22. António Simões, *Assertiones Philosophicae ex libris de Physica ausculatione depromptae* (Coimbra, 1603); and João Pereira Gomes, SJ, *Os Professores de Filosofia da Universidade de Évora* (Évora, 1960), 238–39.

23. J. Pinharanda Gomes, *Os Conimbricenses* (Lisbon, 1992), 46–49.

24. AP, "Commentaria in universam Aristot: Dialtecticam," Coimbra, February 5, 1601, BNL *Reservados* 2441:17–105, on Porphyry's *Isagoge*; 106–401 on Aristotle's *Categories.*

25. This mathematics course is mentioned in the lists of classes at the Colégio de Jesus. See, for example, BC Portugal 1587, January 1, 1587, ARSI *Lus* 39:13v; and Third Catalogue Portugal 1606, April 1606, ARSI *Lus* 39:60r.

26. Gomes, *Professores de Filosofia,* 24–27.

27. João Correia, TC Portugal 1603, ARSI *Lus* 44-I:175r.

28. Francisco Rodrigues, "O 'Doutor Exímio' na Universidade de Coimbra," *Brotéria* 24 (1937): 5–19, esp. 16; Raúl de Scorraille, *François Suarez de la Compagnie de Jésus,* 2 vols. (Paris, 1912–1913), 2:7–49.

29. João Correa, TC Portugal 1603, April 1603, ARSI *Lus* 44-I:168r–196r, esp. 175r–176v.

30. Provincial Congregation Acts, Province of Portugal, Lisbon, April 1603, BNL *Reservados* 753:45r.

31. Ibid., 44v–45r.

32. Bonelli Relação, 275r.

33. Even in Lisbon there were few Jesuit doctors of theology. The two men who held the degree, Paulo Ferrer and Francisco Pereira, were both consultors for the

Inquisition, a position that required the highest academic degree. See João Correa, TC Portugal 1603, ARSI *Lus* 44-I:168v–169r.

34. "Auto do Processo sobre a execução da remissoria e compulsoria q se fizerão e processarão na cidade de Coimbra na causa da Canonização da Beata dona Isabel," Coimbra, February 1612, BNL *Reservados* 8446:159.

35. On the fourth vow, see John O'Malley, "The Fourth Vow in Its Ignatian Context: A Historical Study," *Studies in the Spirituality of Jesuits* 15, no. 1 (January 1983): 1–59.

36. The specific phrase is: "I further promise a special obedience to the sovereign pontiff in regard to the missions . . ." See Ignatius Loyola, SJ, *The Constitutions of the Society of Jesus,* ed. George Ganss, SJ (St. Louis, 1970), 238.

37. John O'Malley, *The First Jesuits* (Cambridge, 1993), 296–301; and John Padberg, SJ, "Ignatius, the Popes, and Realistic Reverence," *Studies in the Spirituality of Jesuits* 25 (May 1993): 1–38.

38. BC Portugal 1604, November 1603, ARSI *Lus* 39:50v.

39. Jean Delumeau, *L'Aveu et le pardon: Les difficultés de la confession, XIIIe–XVIIIe siècle,* (Paris, 1990), 92–93.

40. BC Portugal 1605, ARSI *Lus* 39:55r.

41. Fernando Taveira da Fonseca, "A Teologia na Universidade de Coimbra," in *História da Universidade em Portugal,* 2 vols. (Lisbon, 1997), 2:781–816.

42. António Mascarenhas, TC Portugal 1606, Lisbon, March 1606, ARSI *Lus* 44-I:221v (here: "now reading the third theology"); and BC Portugal 1608, ARSI *Lus* 39:63r (here: "vespers reader").

43. BC Portugal 1610, ARSI *Lus* 44-I:248v; BC Portugal 1612, ARSI *Lus* 39:70r; and TC Portugal 1614, ARSI *Lus* 44-II:310v.

44. AP, "Commentarii et disputationis in 3am parte Divi Thomae," Coimbra, 1611, BNL *Reservados* 2829; AP, Three Treatises on the Third Part of St. Thomas, [Braga, 1616?], BNL *Reservados* 5631.

45. AP, "Treatise on the Sacraments," in Three Treatises on the Third Part of St. Thomas, 3–82; AP, "Treatise on Baptism," in ibid., 83–149; and AP, "Treatise on Holy Matrimony," in ibid., 154–321.

46. Carvalho, *Diário da Peste,* 167.

47. Leite, 64.

48. António Mascarenhas, TC Portugal 1606, Lisbon, March 1606, ARSI *Lus* 44-I:221v; and BC Portugal 1610, ARSI *Lus* 44-I:248v.

49. Luke 12:48.

50. AP, "De Sancte Spiritus adventu: Carmen," [Coimbra, ca. 1610], in Anon., Humanities Miscellanea, BPADE CXIV/1–39: 119r–123v. I am especially grateful to Noël Golvers for his help with this transcription and translation.

51. *Conclusiones ex tertia theologiae parte. . . . Praerit Pater Andreas Palmeiro, Tuebitur Ioannes da Rocha in Collegio Societatis IESV* (Coimbra, 1614).

52. João Álvares, "Visita da Provincia de Portugal," [Coimbra?], 1613, AN/TT *Armário Jesuítico,* 5:42, 57, and 68.

53. Ibid., 124, 130, and 131.

54. Joaquim Veríssimo Serrão, *Viagens em Portugal de Manuel Severim de Faria, 1604–1609–1625* (Lisbon, 1974), 102.

55. On this dispute, see Mário Brandão and M. Lopes d'Almeida, *A Universidade de Coimbra: Esboço da sua História* (Coimbra, 1937), part 2:3–36, esp. 18–19.

56. Anon. Jesuit author, Report and Response on the Disputed Tithes, Coimbra, February 1609, AUC, Dep. IV-1.aE-21-2-5:17r.

57. Francisco Suárez, "Informacion por el Collegio de la Companhia de Iesus de Coymbra en la pretension de las Classes," in Mário Brandão, *O Colégio das Artes,* 2 vols. (Coimbra, 1924–1933), 2:ccix, ccxxix, and ccxxx.

58. Francisco Rodrigues, *História da Companhia de Jesus na Assistência de Portugal,* 6 bks. in 3 vols. (Porto, 1931–1950), 2:2, 247–249.

59. Simon Ditchfield, "Tridentine Worship and the Cult of the Saints," in R. Po-Chia Hsia, ed., *Cambridge History of Christianity, Vol. 6: Reform and Expansion, 1500–1650* (Cambridge: 2008), 201–24, esp. 207–16.

60. António Ribeiro de Vasconcellos, *Evolução do Culto de Dona Isabel de Aragão,* 2 vols. (Coimbra, 1894), 1:287, and 301–18.

61. "Auto do Processo sobre a execução da remissoria e compulsoria q se fizerão e processarão na cidade de Coimbra na causa da Canonização da Beata dona Isabel," BNL *Reservados* 8446:159–62.

62. The books Palmeiro cited included Diogo do Rosário, *Historia das Vidas & Feitos Heroicos & Obras Insignes dos Santos,* 2 vols. (Coimbra, 1577); and Pedro de Mariz, *Dialogos de Varia Historia* (Coimbra, 1594).

63. Vasconcellos, *Evolução do Culto,* 1:366–380.

64. Ibid., 395.

65. Gaspar Borges de Azevedo, Declaration concerning the Tomb of St. Isabel, in Vasconcellos, *Evolução do Culto,* 2:126.

66. Baltasar d'Azeredo, "Declaration" and António Sebastião, "Analogous Declaration," in Vasconcellos, *Evolução do Culto,* 121–22.

67. Tomé Nunes, Declaration concerning the Tomb of St. Isabel, Coimbra, March 26, 1612, ibid., 113–18.

68. Borges de Azevedo, Declaration, ibid., 125–26.

69. "Livro das Sepulturas" from the Jesuit College Church of Coimbra, mid-sixteenth until mid-eighteenth centuries, BNL *Reservados* 4505:1r.

70. Afonso Mendes to NM, Coimbra, June 14, 1614, BPADE CIX/2-13, doc. 49:1r.

71. Manuel Fagundes to Luís Pinheiro, Porto, May 17, 1614, ARSI *Lus* 74:122r.

72. An account of the Jesuits' response in Porto is in ibid., 122; on the Lisbon procession, see Anon. Jesuit to António Mascarenhas, [Lisbon, June 1614?], ARSI *Lus*

74:123r–124r; and the Évora sermon is in *Segunda Parte dos Sermoens do Padre Francisco de Mendoça* (Lisbon, 1649), 23–31.

73. Afonso Mendes to NM, Coimbra, June 14, 1614, BPADE CIX/2-13, doc. 49:1r.

74. Lamentations 4:20, *Spiritus oris nostri, Christus Dominus, captus est in peccatis nostris, cui diximus: In umbra tua vivemus in gentibus.*

75. Afonso Mendes to NM, Coimbra, June 14, 1614, BPADE CIX/2-13, doc. 49:1v–2r.

76. Miscellanea from the Jesuit College of Coimbra, BNL *Reservados* 1646:12r.

77. A. F. Neiva Soares, *A Arquidiocese de Braga no Século XVII: Sociedade e Mentalidades pelas Visitações Pastorais (1550–1700)* (Braga, 1997), 38–44.

78. José Sebastião da Silva Dias, "Braga e a Cultura Portuguesa do Renascimento," *Philosophica Conimbricensia* 1 (1972): 3–98, esp. 36–37.

79. It is possible that the two men met in Lisbon since Menezes was there as viceroy during Palmeiro's visits in 1614 and 1615. See Carlos Alonso, OSA, "Alejo de Meneses, O.S.A. (1559–1617) Arzobispo de Braga; III. Parte: Virrey de Portugal (1614–1615)," *Archivo Agustiniano* 68, no. 186 (January–December 1984): 151–81.

80. Anon. Jesuit author, Report and Response on the Disputed Tithes, Coimbra, February 1609, AUC, Dep. IV-1.aE-21-2-5:18v.

81. TC Portugal 1614, January 1614, ARSI *Lus* 44-II:334v.

82. BC Portugal 1615, ARSI *Lus* 39:89r.

83. Sebastião de Abreu, *Vida e Virtudes do Admiravel Padre Joam Cardim* (Évora, 1659), 144, 148, 149, 137, 165, and 172.

84. Ibid., 177–78, 181–82, and 197. Palmeiro's letter, reprinted in Abreu's text, was closed at Macau on November 15, 1631.

85. António de Abreu, Portuguese Provincial Congregation Acts for 1614, BNL *Reservados* 753:71r–75r, esp. 74v.

86. Jerónimo Álvares, Portuguese Provincial Congregation Acts for 1615, BNL *Reservados* 753:76r–81v.

87. Bonelli 2, 97r/v.

88. List of Superiors for the Provinces of Malabar and Goa, ARSI *Hist. Soc.* 62: 41.

89. Francisco de Morim, AL Portugal 1617, Coimbra, May 1, 1618, ARSI *Lus* 53:116r.

90. Bonelli 2, 95v–96r.

91. Ibid., 97r.

3. Manager of Men

1. On the *Carreira da Índia,* see C. R. Boxer, ed. and trans., *The Tragic History of the Sea (1589–1622)* (London, 1959), 1–30.

2. AP to MV, Cochin, December 20, 1620, ARSI *Goa* 18:25r.

3. Maria Hermínia Maldonado, ed., *Relação das Náos e Armadas da India* (Coimbra, 1985), 129.

4. Manuel Xavier, *Compedio Universal de todos os viso-reys, governadores, capitães geraes, capitães mores, capitães de naos, galleões, urcas, e caravellas que partirão de Lisboa para a India Oriental,* ed. J.A. Ismael Gracias (Nova Goa, 1917), 47.

5. Manuel Tinoco, AL Goa 1617, Goa, January 20, 1618, ARSI *Goa* 33-I:549r.

6. Compare to the arrival of Visitor Nicolau Pimenta: António da Veiga to the Fathers and Brothers of the Province of Portugal, Goa, December 18, 1596, in Josef Wicki, SJ, and John Gomes, SJ, eds., *Documenta Indica,* 18 vols. (Rome, 1948–1988), 18:743–67, esp. 765–66.

7. *Patentes superiorum et itinerariae 1599–1640* under "Provincia Malavarica", ARSI *Hist. Soc.* 62:58.

8. A. Disney, *A History of Portugal and the Portuguese Empire,* 2 vols. (Cambridge, 2009), 2:149.

9. On the administrative structures at Goa, see Catarina Madeira Santos, *'Goa é a Chave de Toda a Índia': Perfil Político do Capital do Estado da Índia, 1505–1570* (Lisbon, 1999); and M.N. Pearson, *The Portuguese in India* (Cambridge, 1987), 5–60.

10. On early modern Goa, see Teotónio de Souza, *Medieval Goa* (New Delhi, 1979), 109–51.

11. Bonelli Relação, 265r.

12. TC Goa 1618, Goa, ARSI *Goa* 27:35r.

13. Francisco Borges de Sousa and João Fernandes de Almeida to Fernão Martins Mascarenhas, Goa, February 22, 1619, in António Baião, ed., *A Inquisição de Goa: Correspondencia dos Inquisidores da Índia (1569–1630),* 2 vols. (Coimbra, 1930), 2:555.

14. Francisco Borges de Sousa and João Fernandes de Almeida to Fernão Martins Mascarenhas, Goa, January 30, 1618, in ibid., 554.

15. José Wicki, SJ, ed., *Tratado do Pe. Gonçalo Fernandes Trancoso sobre o Hinduísmo (Maduré 1616)* (Lisbon, 1973), xvi–xvii.

16. Studies of Nobili include Ines Zupanov, *Disputed Mission: Jesuit Experiments and Brahmanical Knowledge in Seventeenth-Century India* (New Delhi, 1999); Joan-Pau Rubiés, *Travel and Ethnology in the Renaissance* (Cambridge, 2000), 308–43; and Peter Bachmann, *Roberto Nobili, 1577–1656* (Rome, 1972).

17. Modern editions of this polemical literature include Wicki, *Tratado;* Roberto de Nobili, SJ, *Preaching Wisdom to the Wise,* ed. and trans. Anand Amaladass, SJ, and Francis Clooney, SJ (St. Louis, 2000); Robert de Nobili, *Adaptation,* ed. and trans. S. Rajamanickam, SJ (Palayamkottai, 1971); and S. Rajamanickam, SJ, *The First Oriental Scholar* (Tirunelveli, 1972).

18. Rajamanickam, *First Oriental Scholar,* 41.

19. Older views of Nobili include Augustin Saulière, *His Star in the East,* ed. S. Rajamanickam (Madras, 1995); Vincent Cronin, *A Pearl to India: The Life of Robert de Nobili* (New York, 1959); and D. Ferroli, *The Jesuits in Malabar,* 2 vols. (Bangalore, 1951), esp. 2:377–417.

20. Zupanov, *Disputed Mission,* 4; and Rajamanickam, *First Oriental Scholar,* 18–19, 223.

21. A subtle defense of Fernandes is in Wicki, *Tratado,* xi–xxvii.

22. See, for example, ibid., 312 and 317.

23. Ferroli, *Jesuits in Malabar,* 2:396. Ferroli repeats the assertion made in J. Bertrand, SJ, *La Mission du Maduré d'après des Documents Inédits,* 2 vols. (Paris, 1847–1848), 2:150. Neither author gives an archival reference.

24. Roberto Nobili to MV, Goa, February 15, 1619, ARSI *Goa* 51:288r.

25. Francesc Ros to [Fernando Martins Mascarenhas], Goa, February 9, 1619, AN/TT TSO *Consultas do Conselho Geral,* Liv. 207:64v.

26. Roberto Nobili to MV, Goa, February 15, 1619, ARSI *Goa* 51:288r.

27. Goa Conference Documents, Goa, January 31 to February 22, 1619, AN/TT TSO *Consultas do Conselho Geral,* Liv. 207:46r–208v; declaration by António Albertino, Goa, February 1619, ibid., 71r–72v; declaration by AP, co-signed by Balthasar Garces and Jerónimo Cota, Goa, February 13, 1619, ibid., 73r; and declaration by Roberto Nobili, Goa, February 13, 1619, ibid., 73v.

28. AP to NM, Goa, February 19, 1619, ARSI *Goa* 51:291r.

29. Francesc Ros to NM, Goa, February 6, 1619, ARSI *Goa* 17:249r/v.

30. AP to NM, Goa, February 19, 1619, ARSI *Goa* 51:291v.

31. João Coutinho to Philip III, Goa, February 15, 1619, in LM 5:169.

32. João Coutinho to Philip III, Goa, February 7, 1619, in LM 4:286.

33. Pius Malekandathil, *Portuguese Cochin and the Maritime Trade of India, 1500–1663* (New Delhi, 2001), 72–109, esp. 78.

34. A. Disney, *Twilight of the Pepper Empire: Portuguese Trade in Southwest India in the Early Seventeenth Century* (Cambridge, Mass., 1978), 10–12; and François Pyrard, *Voyage de Pyrard de Laval aux Indes orientales (1601–1611),* ed. Xavier de Castro, 2 vols. (Paris, 1998), 1:399–404, esp. 401.

35. José Alberto Tavim, "A Cidade Portuguesa de Santa Cruz de Cochim ou Cochim de Baixo: Algumas Perspectivas", in *Aquém e Além de Taprobana,* ed. L. F. Thomaz, 135–89 (Lisbon, 2002), 139–40.

36. Manuel Barradas, AL Malabar 1619, Cochin, December 1, 1619, ARSI *Goa* 56:369r. Some sources call this college "Colégio de São Paulo", but the official name was "Colégio de Madre de Deus".

37. Sebastião Gonçalves, *Primeira Parte da Historia dos Religiosos da Companhia de Jesus,* ed. José Wicki, SJ, 3 vols. (Coimbra, 1957–1962), 2:210–12.

38. Manuel Barradas, AL Malabar 1619, Cochin, December 1, 1619, ARSI *Goa* 56:369r.

39. Valentim Pinheiro, AL Malabar 1620, Cochin, December 20, 1620, ARSI *Goa* 56:379r.

40. Gaspar Fernandes, BC Malabar 1620, December 1619, ARSI *Goa* 29:23r–24r.

41. Gaspar Fernandes to NM, Cochin, November 30, 1619, ARSI *Goa* 17:279r.

42. The historiography of the Thomas Christians is vast. See, for example, Robert Eric Frykenberg, *Christianity in India: From Beginnings to the Present* (Oxford, 2008),

91–141; and Leslie Brown, *The Indian Christians of St. Thomas: An Account of the Ancient Syrian Church of Malabar* (Cambridge, 1956).

43. António de Araújo, AL Malabar, Cochin, January 1, 1622, ARSI *Goa* 33-I:697v.

44. See, for example, Rubiés, *Travel and Ethnology,* 321; Andrew Ross, *A Vision Betrayed: The Jesuits in Japan and China, 1542–1742* (Edinburgh, 1994), 205–6; and Nicolas Standaert, "Jesuit Corporate Culture as Shaped by the Chinese", in *The Jesuits: Cultures, Sciences and the Arts, 1542–1773,* ed. John O'Malley, SJ; T. Frank Kennedy, SJ; Gauvin Bailey; and Steven Harris (Toronto, 1999), 352–63.

45. John Padberg, SJ, Martin O'Keefe, SJ, and John McCarthy, SJ, *For Matters of Greater Moment: The First Thirty Jesuit General Congregations* (St. Louis, 1994), 256–57.

46. MV to Superiors of the Society of Jesus, Rome, March 7, 1619, in *Epistolae Praepositorum Generalium S.J.* (Antwerp, 1635), 435–48.

47. Joan-Pau Rubiés, "The Jesuit Discovery of Hinduism: Antonio Rubino's Account of the History and Religion of Vijayanagara (1608)", *Archiv für Religionsgeschichte,* 3 (2001): 210–56, esp. 213–18 and 236.

48. Antonio Rubino to MV, Colombo, October 22, 1619, ARSI *Goa* 17:265r.

49. AP to [NM], Cochin, December 1, 1619, AN/TT *Armário Jesuítico,* Liv. 3:304r.

50. On São Pedro, see Téofilo Aparício López, OSA, *La Orden de San Agustín en la Índia (1572–1622)* (Lisbon, 1978), 278–89.

51. AP to NM, Cochin, December 15, 1619, ARSI *Goa* 17:283.

52. AP to [NM?], Cochin, December 1, 1619, AN/TT *Armário Jesuítico,* Liv. 3:303r.

53. Ibid., 304r.

54. AP to NM, Cochin, December 1, 1619, ARSI *Goa* 18:80r.

55. AP to [NM?], Cochin, December 1, 1619, AN/TT *Armário Jesuítico,* Liv. 3:304r.

56. AP to NM, Cochin, November 30, 1619, ARSI *Goa* 18:117r.

57. AP to [NM?], Cochin, December 1, 1619, AN/TT *Armário Jesuítico,* Liv. 3:304r.

58. Ibid.

59. AP to NM, Cochin, December 15, 1619, ARSI *Goa* 17:283.

60. Josef Wicki, SJ, "Liste der Jesuiten-Indienfahrer, 1541–1758", *Aufsätze zur Portugiesischen Kulturgeschichte* 7 (1967): 252–450, esp. 291.

61. AP to NM, Cochin, November 30, 1619, ARSI *Goa* 18:117r.

62. AP to NM, Cochin, December 20, 1620, ARSI *Goa* 18:29v.

63. AP to NM, Cochin, December 15, 1619, ARSI *Goa* 17:283r. This letter is very difficult to read and has been cited incorrectly elsewhere. Cf. Ferroli, *Jesuits in Malabar,* 1:378–380; and Dauril Alden, *The Making of an Enterprise: The Society of Jesus in Portugal, Its Empire, and Beyond, 1540–1750* (Stanford, 1996), 270.

64. Valentim Pinheiro, AL Malabar 1620, Cochin, December 20, 1620, ARSI *Goa* 56:379r.

65. I Corinthians 9:20, *Et factus sum Judaeis tamquam Judaeus, ut Judaeos lucrarer.*

66. A *cabaya,* or *kebaya,* is a loose tunic worn in India and parts of Southeast Asia.

67. AP to NM, Cochin, December 20, 1620, ARSI *Goa* 18:28r.

68. Ibid, 29r.

69. Ibid.

70. Cristóvão de Sá to NM, Goa, February 15, 1620, ARSI *Goa* 18:7v.

71. AP to NM, Cochin, December 20, 1620, ARSI *Goa* 18:29r.

72. Frei Sebastião de São Pedro to Fernando Martins Mascarenhas, Goa, February 26, 1619, AN/TT TSO, *Consultas do Conselho Geral,* Liv. 207:79v.

73. AP to NM, Cochin, December 20, 1620, ARSI *Goa* 18:29r.

74. Ibid., 29v.

75. Ibid.

76. Aragão was labeled "coleric" in the Triennial Catalogue for 1613. See Pero Francisco, TPC Malabar, Cochin, November 1613, ARSI *Goa* 29:17v.

77. AP to NM, Cochin, December 20, 1620, ARSI *Goa* 18:29v.

78. AP to NM, Cochin, January 22, 1621, ARSI *Goa* 21:10v.

79. AP to NM, Cochin, December 1, 1619, ARSI *Goa* 18:81r; and Cristóvão de Abreu to NM, Cochin, December 24, 1620, ARSI *Goa* 18:34r/v.

80. António Rodrigues, AL Goa 1621, Goa, November 27, 1621, ARSI *Goa* 33-I:65lv.

81. Francesc Ros to NM, Diamper, December 9, 1620, ARSI *Goa* 18:20r/v.

82. AP, Rules for the Province of Malabar, [Cochin, December 1620], ARSI *Goa* 18:3r.

83. António Franco, *Imagem da Virtude em o Noviciado da Companhia de Jesus do Real Collegio do Espírito Santo de Évora* (Lisboa, 1714), 139; and Ana Isabel López-Salazar Codes, *Inquisición y Política: El Gobierno del Santo Oficio en el Portugal de los Austrias (1578–1653)* (Lisbon, 2011), 373.

4. In the Footsteps of the Apostles

1. On the Portuguese in *Pescaria,* see S. Jeyaseela Stephen, *Expanding Portuguese Empire and the Tamil Economy (Sixteenth–Eighteenth Centuries)* (New Delhi, 2009), 73–107.

2. Parava–Jesuit relations are discussed in S. B. Kaufmann, "A Christian Caste in Hindu Society: Religious Leadership and Social Conflict among the Paravas of Southern Tamilnadu", *Modern Asian Studies* 15, no. 2 (1981): 203–34; and Markus Vink, "Between the Devil and the Deep Blue Sea: The Christian Paravas, a 'Client Community' in Seventeenth-Century Southeast India", *Itinerario* 26 (2002): 64–98, esp. 70–75.

3. On the origins of this struggle, see Maria de Deus Manso, *A Companhia de Jesus na Índia (1542–1622): Actividades religiosas, poderes e contactos culturais* (Évora,

2009), 102–16; Léon Besse, SJ, *La Mission du Maduré: Historique de ses pangous* (Trichinopoly, 1914), 367–479, esp. 410–41; and Fernão de Queyroz, *Vida do Veneravel Irmão Pedro de Basto* (Lisbon, 1689), 58–82.

4. Indian Itinerary, 25r.

5. The *champana* is a small skiff, the equivalent of the East Asian sampan.

6. Jorge Flores, *Os Portugueses e o Mar de Ceilão: Trato, diplomacia e guerra (1498–1543)* (Lisbon, 1998), 33–42.

7. Indian Itinerary, 25r. On the Portuguese presence in Sri Lanka in the 1620s, see Chandra de Silva, *The Portuguese in Ceylon, 1618–1638* (Colombo, 1972).

8. Antonio Rubino to MV, Colombo, October 20, 1619, ARSI *Goa* 17:263r. On the College of Colombo, see Simon Gregory Perera, SJ, *The Jesuits in Ceylon in the XVI and XVII Centuries* (Madura, 1941; repr. New Delhi, 2004), 33–37.

9. Indian Itinerary, 25v.

10. Valentim Pinheiro, AL Malabar 1620, Cochin, December 20, 1620, ARSI *Goa* 56:389r.

11. Antonio Rubino to MV, Colombo, October 20, 1619, ARSI *Goa* 17:263r.

12. Antonio Rubino to MV, Colombo, October 22, 1619, ARSI *Goa* 17:265r.

13. Fernão de Albuquerque to Philip III, Goa, February 6, 1620, LM 6:147–48.

14. Rohini Paranavitana, "Sinhalese War Poems and the Portuguese", in *Re-exploring the Links: History and Constructed Histories between Portugal and Sri Lanka,* ed. Jorge Flores, (Wiesbaden, 2007), 49–62.

15. Indian Itinerary, 25r.

16. On this revolt, see Chandra de Silva, ed. and trans., *Portuguese Encounters with Sri Lanka and the Maldives* (Aldershot, 2009), 109–11, and 136–39.

17. Indian Itinerary, 25v. The date of the end of Sankili II's reign (and sometimes death) is given as 1619, but Palmeiro reports that he was called "prince" in Jaffna, and that he was sent to Colombo and onward to Goa in April 1620. See Silva, *Portuguese Encounters with Sri Lanka and the Maldives,* 128.

18. On Munneswaram, see Perera, *Jesuits in Ceylon,* 76.

19. Indian Itinerary, 25v.

20. AP to NM, Cochin, December 1, 1619, ARSI *Goa* 18:80v.

21. Indian Itinerary, 25v.

22. Ibid.

23. Ibid., 26r.

24. These battles are discussed in de Silva, *Portuguese in Ceylon,* 21–62.

25. Indian Itinerary, 26r.

26. Sanjay Subrahmanyam, "The Pulicat Enterprise: Luso-Dutch Conflict in South-Eastern India, 1610–1640", in his *Improvising Empire: Portuguese Trade and Settlement in the Bay of Bengal, 1500–1700* (Oxford, 1990), 188–215; and Ove Feldbaek, "No Ship for Tranquebar for Twenty-Nine Years; or, The Art of Survival of a Mid-Seventeenth Century European Settlement in India", in *Emporia, Commodities*

and Entrepreneurs in Asian Maritime Trade, c. 1400–1750, ed. Dietmar Rothermund and Roderick Ptak (Stuttgart, 1991), 29–36.

27. Valentim Pinheiro, AL Malabar 1620, Cochin, December 20, 1620, ARSI *Goa* 56:381r/v.

28. Indian Itinerary, 26r.

29. On São Tomé, see Sanjay Subramanyam, "Profit at the Apostle's Feet: The Portuguese Settlement of Mylapur in the Sixteenth Century", in his *Improvising Empire,* 47–67; and Ines Zupanov, "A Reliquary Town—São Tomé de Meliapor: The Political and the Sacred in Portuguese India", in her *Missionary Tropics: The Catholic Frontier in India (16th and 17th centuries)* (Ann Arbor, 2005), 87–110.

30. Gaspar Fernandes, BC Malabar 1620, December 1619, ARSI *Goa* 29:23v.

31. Indian Itinerary, 26r.

32. Bonelli 2, 99r.

33. Indian Itinerary, 26r.

34. "Our Lady of the Cave" is a mountaintop shrine near Sernancelhe in central Portugal where an image of the Virgin was discovered under a massive boulder in the late fifteenth century. The administration of the sanctuary was ceded to the Coimbra Jesuits in the 1600s.

35. Indian Itinerary, 26v.

36. Ibid.

37. On the Maravas, see S. Kadhirvel, *A History of the Maravas, 1700–1802* (Madurai, 1977), 6–32; and David Mosse, *The Saint in the Banyan Tree: Christianity and Caste Society in India* (Berkeley, 2012), 35–40.

38. Indian Itinerary, 27r.

39. Ibid.

40. *Panelas de polvora,* typically used in naval warfare, were clay pots filled with gunpowder, in other words, an early type of grenade.

41. Indian Itinerary, 27r/v.

42. Jennifer Howes, *The Courts of Pre-Colonial South India: Material Culture and Kingship* (New York, 2003), 82–83.

43. Indian Itinerary, 27v.

44. The *devadasi,* or "female servant of a god," was among the most important ritual personages at the Hindu temples of southern and western India. See Leslie Orr, *Donors, Devotees, and Daughters of God: Temple Women in Medieval Tamilnadu* (Oxford, 2000), 3–21.

45. Indian Itinerary, 27v.

46. Ibid. Palmeiro alludes to Acts 26:28, "In a little thou persuadest me to become a Christian."

47. Indian Itinerary, 28r.

48. Ibid.

49. *Juncaneiros:* from Malayalam *chunkam,* meaning duty or toll.

50. Indian Itinerary, 28r.

51. Ibid., 28v.

52. Ibid., 30r.

53. AP to NM, Cochin, December 1, 1619, ARSI *Goa* 18:81r.

54. AP, Rules for the Province of Malabar [Cochin, December 1620], ARSI *Goa* 18:4r.

55. Ibid., 4r/v.

56. On the Moluccas, see Leonard Andaya, *The World of Maluku: Eastern Indonesia in the Early Modern Period* (Honolulu, 1993); and on the Jesuit missions there, see Hubert Jacobs, SJ, ed., *Documenta Malucensia,* 3 vols. (Rome, 1974–1984), 3:2*–38*.

57. See, for example, João Baptista to MV, Ternate, March 2, 1619, in Jacobs, *Documenta Malucensia,* 3:392; and Valentim Pinheiro, AL Malabar 1620, Cochin, December 20, 1620, 3:411.

58. Gaspar Fernandes to MV, Cochin, December 6, 1620, ibid., 3:409.

59. Manuel de Azevedo to AP, Ternate, [second half of 1620], ibid., 3:414–429, esp. 417–419 and 428.

60. AP to MV, Goa, January 25, 1624, ibid., 3:457.

61. Ibid., 3:456.

62. Valentim Pinheiro, AL Malabar 1620, Cochin, December 20, 1620, ARSI *Goa* 56:390r/v. On the Jesuits in Burma, see Michael Charney, "Jesuit Letters on Pegu in the Early Seventeenth Century", *SOAS Bulletin of Burma Research,* 2, no. 2 (2004): 180–87.

63. Valente sailed from Goa to Macau in May 1619 and during the trip was nearly shipwrecked. His voyage was punctuated by a week spent in Malacca. See José Montanha, Catalogue of the Bishops of Macau, [Macau, June 6, 1746] AHU *Conselho Ultramarino,* Codex 1659 (n.p.); and Valentim Pinheiro, AL Malabar 1620, Cochin, December 20, 1620, ARSI *Goa* 56:382r.

64. On the Portuguese in Bengal, see Armando Cortesão, "Os Portugueses em Bengala", in *Esparsos,* 3 vols., ed. Armando Cortesão (Coimbra, 1974–1975), 3:386–404; and J. J. A. Campos, *History of the Portuguese in Bengal* (Calcutta, 1919; repr. Patna, 1979), 44–99.

65. Jacinto Pereira, AL Malabar 1621, December 27, 1621, ARSI *Goa* 33-I:667r–669r. More about Muqarrab Khan is in Syed Ali Nadeem Rezavi, "An Aristocratic Surgeon of Mughal India: Muqarrab Khan", *Medieval India* 1 (1992):154–67.

66. On the destruction of Hooghly, see Jorge Flores, "Relic or Springboard: A Note on the 'Rebirth' of Portuguese Hughli, ca. 1632–1820", *Indian Economic & Social History Review* 39, no. 3 (2002): 381–95, esp. 384–87.

67. André Machado to NM, Cochin, December 16, 1619, ARSI *Goa* 17:284r.

68. AP to NM, Cochin, December 1, 1619, ARSI *Goa* 18:80v.

69. *Patentes superiorum et itinerariae 1599–1640* under "India Orientalis" and "Provincia Malavarica", ARSI *Hist. Soc.* 62:57 and 58.

70. AP to NM, Cochin, December 15, 1619, ARSI *Goa* 17:283.

71. For a list of such donations in Cochin, see Gaspar Fernandes to MV, Cochin, December 6, 1620, ARSI *Goa* 18:18v.

72. A history of trade at Cochin in the early seventeenth century, albeit one at odds with the Jesuits' impressions, is in Sanjay Subrahmanyam, "Cochin in Decline, 1600–1650: Myth and Manipulation in the *Estado da Índia*", in *Portuguese Asia: Aspects in History and Economic History,* ed. Roderich Ptak (Stuttgart, 1987), 59–85.

73. Jacinto Pereira, AL Malabar 1621, December 27, 1621, ARSI *Goa* 33-I:659v.

74. Gaspar Fernandes to MV, Cochin, December 4, 1620, ARSI *Goa* 18:16v.

75. AP to NM, Cochin, January 22, 1621, ARSI *Goa* 21:10v.

76. Fernão de Albuquerque to Philip III, Goa, February 18, 1621, LM 7:132–34.

77. Queyroz, *Pedro de Basto,* 73.

78. AP to NM, Cochin, December 20, 1620, ARSI *Goa* 18:30r.

79. AP to NM, Cochin, January 23, 1621, ARSI *Goa* 21:13r.

80. AP to NM, Cochin, December 20, 1620, ARSI *Goa* 18:30r.

81. Ibid.

82. Jacinto Pereira, AL Malabar 1621, Cochin, December 27, 1621, in José Wicki, SJ, ed., *O Tratado do Pe. Gonçalo Fernandes Trancoso sobre o Hinduísmo (Maduré 1616),* (Lisbon, 1973), 319–20.

83. AP to NM, Cochin, December 1, 1619, ARSI *Goa* 18:81r.

84. AP to NM, Cochin, January 23, 1621, ARSI *Goa* 21:13v.

85. Fernandes died in early April, a month after his return to the Fishery Coast. See Wicki, *Tratado,* xvii, and 319–21.

86. The Portuguese term *saudade* means longing. *Patangins* were Parava village headmen.

87. Jacinto Pereira, AL Malabar 1621, Cochin, December 27, 1621, ARSI *Goa* 33-I:663v–664r.

88. Mention of this plan is found in Philip III to Francisco da Gama, Madrid, February 23, 1622, AN/TT Colecção São Vicente, Liv. 19, no. 39; and Constantino de Sá de Noronha to Philip IV, Malwana, December 1, 1623, AN/TT Colecção São Vicente, Liv. no. 276.

89. BC Malabar 1623, Cochin, November 1623, ARSI *Goa* 29:25v.

90. Antonio Rubino to MV, Punnaikayal, November 20, 1623, ARSI *Jap-Sin* 38:204r–205r. See also Besse, *Mission du Maduré,* 431–40.

91. AP to MV, Goa, November 1, 1624, ARSI *Goa* 9-I:109r/v.

92. Antonio Rubino to Francisco de Oliveira, Punnaikayal, January 2, 1625, ARSI *Jap-Sin* 38:206r.

5. Among Archbishops, Emperors, and Viceroys

1. Fernão de Albuquerque to Philip IV, Goa, February 18, 1622, LM 7:366–370.

2. Fernão Lopes to NM, Muscat, May 19, 1622, ARSI *Goa* 33-I:694r.

3. António Rodrigues, AL Goa 1621, Goa, November 27, 1621, ARSI *Goa* 33-I:647r; and Jacinto Pereira, AL Malabar 1621, December 27, 1621, ARSI *Goa* 33-I:659r.

4. António Rodrigues, AL Goa 1621, Goa, November 27, 1621, ARSI *Goa* 33-I:647r.

5. AP to MV, Goa, January 8, 1623, ARSI *Goa* 9-I:43r. On the Province of the North, see Glenn Ames, "The Province of the North: Continuity and Change in an Age of Decline and Rebirth, ca. 1571–1680", in *Portuguese Colonial Cities in the Early Modern World,* ed. Liam Matthew Brockey (Aldershot, UK, 2008), 129–48.

6. Charles Borges, *The Economics of the Goa Jesuits, 1542–1759* (New Delhi, 1994), 42–43, 91–93, and 185–88.

7. António Rodrigues, AL Goa 1621, Goa, November 27, 1621, ARSI *Goa* 33-I:652v–655v.

8. On Xavier at Jahangir's court, see Sanjay Subrahmanyam and Muzzafar Alam, "Frank Discussions: Catholics and Muslims at the Court of Jahangir, 1608–1611", *Indian Economic and Social History Review* 46, no. 4 (2009): 457–511. A somewhat dated introduction is in Edward Maclagan, *The Jesuits and the Great Mogul* (London, 1932).

9. António de Andrade, "Annua do Mogor," Agra, August 14, 1623, in *Documentação Ultramarina Portuguesa,* 5 vols., ed. António da Silva Rego (Lisbon, 1960–1967), 3:168 and 164.

10. On Zul-Qarnian, see Mesrovb Jacob Seth, *The Armenians in India: From the Earliest Times to the Present* (Calcutta, 1937; repr. Delhi, 1992), 1–87.

11. António Colaço to Philip IV, [Madrid, 1623?], AN/TT Colecção São Vicente, Liv. 19: no. 106. The favorable response, to which this document is appended, is signed Madrid, February 8, 1623.

12. The terms of Zul-Qarnian's donation are in Seth, *Armenians in India,* 38–47.

13. Rodrigues's first name is unclear. Palmeiro and Pietro della Valle refer to him as "Diogo Rodrigues" while Jesuit personnel catalogues mention only an António Rodrigues who meets Palmeiro's description. See Edward Grey, ed. and trans., *The Travels of Pietro della Valle in India,* 2 vols. (London, 1892), 1:138.

14. AP to MV, Goa, January 8, 1623, ARSI *Goa* 9-I:43r.

15. AP to MV, Goa, January 25, 1624, ARSI *Goa* 9-I:72r/v. On the friars, see Arnulf Camps, OFM, "Franciscan Missions to the Mughal Court", in his *Studies in Asian Mission History, 1956–1998* (Leiden, 2000), 60–71, esp. 61–67.

16. Here he means Muslim or Hindu cities. AP to MV, Goa, January 8, 1623, ARSI *Goa* 9-I:43v.

17. AP to MV, Goa, January 25, 1624, ARSI *Goa* 9-I:72r/v

18. On Andrade in Tibet, see Hugues Didier, ed., *Os Portugueses no Tibete: Os Primeiros Relatos dos Jesuítas (1624–1635),* trans. Lourdes Júdice (Lisbon, 2000), 11–68.

19. AP to MV, Goa, November 1, 1624. ARSI *Goa* 9-I:109r/v. Andrade's first report from Tibet would be addressed to Palmeiro, but it is unclear if the Visitor read it. See *Novo Descobrimento do Gram Cathayo, ou Reino de Tibet, pello Padre Antonio de Andrade da Companhia de IESV, Portuguez, no Anno de 1624* (Lisbon, 1626).

20. The necrology for Borges, a former missionary to Gujarat, is in João da Silva, AL Goa 1623, Goa, [December 1623], ARSI *Goa* 33-I:715v–716r.

21. AP to MV, Goa, March 21, 1623, ARSI *Goa* 9-I:45r.

22. Ibid.

23. Pietro della Valle states that the news arrived with a Portuguese *fidalgo* who came overland to India, reaching Goa on May 11, 1623. See Grey, *Travels of Pietro della Valle,* 1:170.

24. Georg Schurhammer, SJ, "Uma Relação Inédita do Pe. Manuel Barradas SI sobre São Francisco Xavier", in his *Varia* (Rome and Lisbon, 1965), 431–65.

25. João da Silva, AL Goa 1623, Goa, [December 1623], ARSI *Goa* 33-I:714v and 719r/v; and António Rodrigues, AL Goa 1621, Goa, November 27, 1621, ARSI *Goa* 33-I:650v.

26. Sebastião Barreto, Selection of AL Goa 1624, Goa, December 15, 1624, in Georg Schurhammer, SJ, ed., "Festas em Goa no Ano 1624", in his *Varia,* 493–96 plus facsimilie, at 495.

27. Ibid., 494.

28. Della Valle spent the first month of his stay in Goa, in April 1623, as Palmeiro's guest at the Professed House.

29. Grey, *Travels of Pietro della Valle,* 2:410.

30. Barreto, Selection from AL Goa 1624, in Schurhammer, *Varia,* 495.

31. Pietro della Valle, *Viaggi,* 2 vols. (Brighton, 1843), 2:764.

32. Barradas, Selection from AL Goa 1624, in Schurhammer, *Varia,* 495.

33. Anon. Jesuit, *Traça da Pompa Triunfal com que os Padres da Companhia de IESV celebrão em Goa a Canonização de Sancto Ignacio de Loyola seu fundador, e Patriarcha, e de S. Francisco Xavier Apostolo deste Oriente, no anno de 624,* in Schurhammer, *Varia,* facsimilie on unnumbered folios after 496. Nebuchadnezzar's second dream is recounted in Daniel 4:7–14.

34. Apparently the first scenes were recast in 1637, when Marcello Mastrilli brought an illustrated life of Xavier to Goa. See Georg Schurhammer, SJ, "Der Silberschrein des Hl. Franz Xaver in Goa. Ein Meisterwerk Christlich-Indischer Kunst" in his *Varia,* 561–67 plus facsimilie.

35. Della Valle, *Viaggi,* 2:765.

36. Grey, *Travels of Pietro della Valle,* 2:432.

37. Fernão de Albuquerque to Philip IV, Goa, March 31, 1622, AN/TT Colecção São Vicente, Liv. 19: no. 100.

38. Anon. Augustinian, "Memorias da Congregação de Santo Agostinho no Oriente", AN/TT Mss. Liv. 674:95r.

39. Ibid., 95v.

40. Fernão de Albuquerque to Philip III, Goa, February 7, 1620, LM 5:314–15.

41. Prioress Anna Madre de Deus and 16 other nuns, Report on the damage caused to the Convent of Santa Mónica by the Jesuits seminary and classes, Goa, February 13, 1618, AN/TT Mss. Liv. 674:133r–134v.

42. Fernão de Albuquerque to Philip III, Goa, January 19, 1621, LM 7:124.

43. Frei Diogo de Santa Ana, "Acta da Reunião", Goa, February 16, 1621, LM 7:271–73.

44. Anon. Augustinian, "Memorias da Congregação de Santo Agostinho no Oriente", AN/TT Mss. Liv. 674:95r.

45. Fernão de Albuquerque to Philip III, Goa, February 16, 1621, LM 7:99–102, esp. 101.

46. Manuel Gaspar to MV, Goa, January 8, 1624, ARSI *Goa* 9-I:62r.

47. Ibid.; Francisco Cerqueira and Juan de Velasco to MV, January 18, 1624, ARSI *Goa* 9-I:64r–66v; and Francisco Vergara to MV, Goa, December 30, 1624, ARSI *Goa* 9-I:116r/v.

48. AP to MV, Goa, January 26, 1624, ARSI *Goa* 9-I:77r/v.

49. AP to MV (Letter 2), Goa, November 2, 1624, ARSI *Goa* 9-I:105r/v.

50. Ibid.

51. Sanjay Subrahmanyam, *The Career and Legend of Vasco da Gama* (Cambridge, 1997), 18.

52. António da Silva Rego, "O Início do segundo governo do vice-rei da Índia D. Francisco da Gama. 1622–1623", *Memórias da Academia das Ciências de Lisboa, Classe de Letras* 19 (1978): 323–45.

53. Francisco da Gama to Philip IV, Goa, March 12, 1623, LM 9:39.

54. Francisco da Gama to Philip IV, Goa, March 12, 1623, LM 9:49; and Francisco da Gama to Philip IV, Goa, March 16, 1623, LM 9:59.

55. Philip IV to Francisco da Gama, Lisbon, February 1, 1623, ibid., 369.

56. Francisco da Gama to [MV], Goa, January 30, 1624. ARSI *Goa* 9-I:82r/v.

57. Philip IV to Francisco da Gama, Lisbon, February 9, 1622, in LM 8:70–71.

58. This battle is discussed in Donald Lockhart, trans. and ed., *The Itinerário of Jerónimo Lobo* (London, 1984), 27–40.

59. Francisco da Gama to Philip IV, Goa, March 15, 1623, LM 9:42–43.

60. AP to MV, Goa, January 21, 1624, ARSI *Goa* 9-I:67r.

61. Francisco da Gama to Philip IV, Goa, March 15, 1623, LM 9:17.

62. AP to MV, Goa, January 21, 1624, ARSI *Goa* 9-I:67r.

63. Further on this region is in António de Conceição, *Treatise on the Rivers of Cuama,* ed. and trans., Malyn Newitt (Oxford, 2009); and W. F. Rea, *The Economics of the Zambezi Missions* (Rome, 1976), 44–80.

64. Giulio Cesare Vertua to MV, Mozambique, October 3, 1623, ARSI *Goa* 9-I:56r–57v. Vertua's term *cafre* is the Portuguese rendering of the Arabic term *kafir,* meaning "unbeliever". The term *kaffir* has since acquired a pejorative, racist connotation.

65. AP to MV, Goa, January 21, 1624, ARSI *Goa* 9-I:67r. On Mariana's first expedition, see Aiden Southall, "White Strangers and Their Religion in East Africa and Madagascar", in *Strangers in African Societies,* ed. William Shack and Elliott Skinner (Berkeley, 1979), 211–26, esp. 214–17.

66. On the Jesuits in Ethiopia, see Leonardo Cohen, *The Missionary Strategies of the Jesuits in Ethiopia (1555–1632)* (Wiesbaden, 2009); and Hervé Pennec, *Des Jésuites au Royaume du Prêtre Jean (Éthiopie): Stratégies, rencontres et tentatives d'implantation, 1495–1633* (Paris, 2003).

67. AP to MV, Goa, January 25, 1624, Beccari 12:35.

68. AP to MV, Goa, November 1, 1624, Beccari 12:86.

69. On the Maravi, see Malyn Newitt, "The Early History of the Maravi", *Journal of African History* 23, no. 2 (1982):145–62; and Matthew Schoffeleers, "Father Mariana's 1624 Description of Lake Malawi and the Identity of the Maravi Emperor Muzura", *Society of Malawi Journal* 45, no. 1 (1992): 1–13.

70. Luigi Mariana to AP, [Mozambique], 1624, Beccari 12:112–14.

71. AP to MV, Goa, January 25, 1624, Beccari 12:36.

72. Harold Marcus, *A History of Ethiopia* (Berkeley, 1994), 34–40.

73. Juan de Velasco to AP, Diu, July 25, 1624, Beccari 12:75–81.

74. AP to MV, Goa, January 25, 1624, Beccari 12:36.

75. AP to MV (Letter 1), Goa, November 2, 1624, Beccari 12:89.

76. Lockhart, *Itinerário,* 50.

77. Manuel de Almeida, *Historia de Ethiopia a Alta ou Abassia,* Beccari 6:402.

78. Ibid., 366; and AP to MV, Goa, January 25, 1624, Beccari, 12:34.

79. Almeida, *Historia de Ethiopia,* Beccari 6:384.

80. AP to MV (Letter 1), Goa, November 2, 1624, Beccari 12:89.

81. Luís de Azevedo to AP, ["from the court of Ethiopia"], March 6, 1622, Beccari 11:520.

82. Francisco de Vergara to MV, Goa, November 17, 1624, Beccari 12:100.

83. Afonso Mendes to MV, Goa, November 9, 1624, Beccari 12:83.

84. Francisco de Vergara to MV, Goa, November 17, 1624, Beccari, 12:100.

85. Scholarship on this topic gives no satisfactory answer as to why Rocha's patents were revoked, but it seems clear that the superior general resented the fact that he had not been consulted. See Angel Santos Hernández, SJ, *Jesuitas y Obispos: Los Jesuitas Obispos Misioneros y los Obispos Jesuitas de la extinción,* 2 vols. (Madrid, 2001), 2:59–67.

86. Francisco de Vergara to MV, Goa, November 17, 1624, Beccari 12:101.

87. Afonso Mendes to NM, Goa, November 8, 1624, Beccari, 12:98.

88. AP to MV (Letter 1), Goa, November 2, 1624, Beccari 12:90.

89. Ibid., 91.

90. Afonso Mendes to MV, Goa, November 9, 1624, Beccari 12:84.

91. AP to MV (Letter 1), Goa, November 2, 1624, Beccari, 12:90.

92. AP to MV, Goa, November 1, 1624, ARSI *Goa* 9-I:109r/v.

93. AP to MV, Goa, January 25, 1624, ARSI *Goa* 9-I:68r.

94. Francisco Borges de Sousa and João Delgado Figueira to Fernão Martins Mascarenhas, Goa, February 17, 1625, in António Baião, ed., *A Inquisição de Goa: Correspondencia dos Inquisidores da Índia (1569–1630)*, 2 vols. (Coimbra, 1930), 2:621.

95. AP to MV (Letter 2), Goa, November 2, 1624, ARSI *Goa* 9-I:105v.

96. AP to MV, Goa, January 25, 1624, ARSI *Goa* 9-I:68v.

97. Jácome de Medeiros to MV, Goa, January 26, 1624, ARSI *Goa* 9-I:76r.

98. Afonso Mendes to NM, Goa, November 8, 1624, Beccari 12:98–99.

99. Afonso Mendes to MV, Goa November 7, 1624, Beccari 12:92.

100. *Patentes superiorum et itinerariae 1599–1640* under "Provincia Japonia", ARSI *Hist. Soc.* 62:59.

101. On Rodrigues in Macau, see Michael Cooper, SJ, *Rodrigues the Interpreter: An Early Jesuit in Japan and China* (Tokyo, 1974), 313–33.

102. JR to MV, Macau, November 21, 1626, ARSI *JS* 18-I:69r. Rodrigues here refers to the inhabitants of the region of Goa, speakers of Konkani.

103. JR to MV, Macau, November 30, 1627, ARSI *JS* 18-I:87v.

104. JR to MV, Macau, November 21, 1626, ARSI *JS* 18-I:69r.

6. The View from Macau

1. [João Álvares], Account of the Founding of the Tonkin Mission, [Macau, 1745], BAJA 49-V-31:9r.

2. On Macau's population, see G. B. Souza, *The Survival of Empire: Portuguese Trade and Society in China and the South China Sea, 1630–1754* (Cambridge, 1986), 12–45, esp. 32.

3. For example, see Jorge dos Santos Alves, "A 'Contenda da Ilha Verde', Primeira Discussão sobre a Legitimidade da Presença Portuguesa em Macau (1621)" in *Um Porto entre Dois Impérios: Estudos sobre Macau e as Relações Luso-Chinesas* (Macau, 1999), 127–62.

4. On Macau's *Câmara*, see C. R. Boxer, *Portuguese Society in the Tropics: The Municipal Councils of Goa, Macao, Bahia, and Luanda, 1510–1800* (Madison, 1965), 42–71.

5. See C. R. Boxer, *The Great Ship from Amacon: Annals of Macao and the Old Japan Trade, 1555–1640* (Lisbon, 1963); and Souza, *Survival of Empire*, 46–86, and 111–20.

6. On the College of Macau, see Liam Brockey, "A *Garganta*: The China Jesuits and the College of Macau, 1579–1623", *Revista de Cultura* (Macau) 5 (January 2003): 44–55.

7. JR, AL College of Macau 1611, Macau, November 1, 1612, in João Paulo Oliveira e Costa and Ana Fernandes Pinto, eds., *Cartas Ânuas do Colégio de Macau (1594–1627)* (Macau, 1999), 127.

8. MD, AL College of Macau 1614, Macau, January 2, 1615, ibid., 142.

9. Jerónimo Rodrigues, AL College of Macau 1627, Macau, November 14, 1627, ibid., 262.

10. See C. R. Boxer, *Fidalgos in the Far East, 1550–1770: Fact and Fancy in the History of Macao* (The Hague, 1948), 93–108.

11. Miguel Pinheiro Ravasco to Philip III, Report on the religious houses in Macau, Macau, October 16, 1621, AHU, Macau, *Caixa* 1: doc. 8.

12. AP to MV, Goa, November 1, 1624, ARSI *Goa* 9-I:109r/v.

13. On the China mission's early phase, see Liam Matthew Brockey, *Journey to the East: The Jesuit Mission to China, 1579–1724* (Cambridge, Mass., 2007), 25–77.

14. AP to MV (Letter 3), Macau, May 14, 1628, ARSI *JS* 161-II:99r.

15. João Rodrigues Girão to NM, Macau, February 18, 1626, ARSI *JS* 18-I:57v.

16. On the destruction of the Japanese church in Nagasaki, see J. S. A. Elisonas, "Nagasaki: The Early Years of an Early Modern Japanese City", in *Portuguese Colonial Cities in the Early Modern World,* ed. Liam Matthew Brockey (Aldershot, U.K., 2008), 63–102, esp. 80–102.

17. João Rodrigues Girão to NM, Macau, October 24, 1627, ARSI *JS* 18-I:78r.

18. João Rodrigues Girão to NM, Macau, April 26, 1626, ARSI *JS* 18-I:64r.

19. AP to MV, November 17, 1626, ARSI *Lus* 58:267v.

20. João Rodrigues Girão to NM, Macau, April 26, 1626, ARSI *JS* 18-I:65v.

21. João Rodrigues Girão to NM, Macau, October 24, 1627, ARSI *JS* 18-I:79v.

22. João Delgado Figueira and António Borges de Sousa, Inquisition Commission for AP, Goa, February 28, 1626, BAJA 49-V-6:248v.

23. Francisco Vieira to MV, Northwestern Kyushu, February 15, 1619, ARSI *JS* 17:239r.

24. João Rodrigues Girão to NM, Macau, February 18, 1626, ARSI *JS* 18-I:57r.

25. JR to MV, Macau, November 21, 1626, ARSI *JS* 18-I:66r.

26. Couros most likely died in Hasami village in Omura in 1632. See Hubert Cieslik, "The Case of Christovão Ferreira", *Monumenta Nipponica* 29, no. 1 (Spring 1974): 1–54, at 11.

27. JR to MV, Macau, November 21, 1626, ARSI *JS* 18-I:66v.

28. Mateus de Couros to MV, [Kyushu], October 5, 1626, in J. F. Schütte, SJ, *Introductio ad Historiam Societatis Jesu in Japonia, 1549–1650* (Rome, 1968), 250.

29. AP to MV, Macau, May 14, 1628, ARSI *JS* 161-II:103v–104r.

30. JR to MV, Macau, November 21, 1626, ARSI *JS* 18-I:69r/v.

31. AP to MV (Letter 1), Macau, May 14, 1628, ARSI *JS* 161-II:103v.

32. AP to MV (Letter 3), Macau, May 14, 1628, ARSI *JS* 161-II:99v.

33. JR to MV, Macau, November 30, 1627, ARSI *Jap-Sin* 18-I:86r. On the personnel information for the period from 1625 until 1639, see Schütte, *Introductio,* 248–66.

34. Some ships did reach Nagasaki that year from Macau, but they were neither the usual fleet nor bore the typical cargoes. See AP to MV (Letter 1), Macau, May 14, 1628, ARSI *JS* 161-II:103r; and Boxer, *Great Ship,* 114–15.

35. AP to MV, Macau, December 1, 1628, ARSI *JS* 161-II:105r.

36. For the Jesuits, the most shocking case concerned Fabian Fucan, a coadjutor who became a vociferous critic of the Society and Christianity. See George Elison, *Deus Destroyed: The Image of Christianity in Early Modern Japan* (Cambridge, Mass., 1973), 142–84.

37. AP to MV (Letter 1), Macau, May 14, 1628, ARSI *JS* 161-II:104r.

38. Ibid., 103r and 104r.

39. Frei Paulo da Trindade, a Franciscan theologian at Goa in the 1620s and 1630s, gave a generous reading to Adrian VI's vague bull. Trindade remarks that the sacramental power of the friars in such circumstances necessarily excludes Holy Orders, but makes no mention of confirmation. See his "Breve Recopilação do poder e autoridade que tem os comfessores mendicantes," Goa, February 20, 1619, BNL *Reservados* 6655: second treatise, unnumbered.

40. AP to MV (Letter 1), Macau, May 14, 1628, ARSI *JS* 161-II:103v.

41. AP to Mateus de Couros, Macau, July 27, 1627, BAJA 49-VI-8:100r–101r.

42. Boxer, *Great Ship*, 116.

43. AP to MV, Macau, December 1, 1628, ARSI *JS* 161-II:105r/v.

44. Chinese Itinerary, 118r.

45. Ibid.

46. The difference between "accommodation" and "inculturation," both theological terms relating to the transmission of Christianity to non-Western cultures, resides in the locus of action. Whereas with accommodation, those who present Christianity adapt themselves and their message to the dominant cultural idiom, with inculturation, the receivers of the outside religion transform its practices according to their patterns.

47. AP to MV, Macau, December 20, 1629, ARSI *JS* 161-II:109r.

48. Ibid.

49. Francisco Cabral to Francisco de Borja, Nagasaki, September 5, 1571, in J. F. Schütte, SJ, *Valignanos Missionsgrundsätze für Japan*, 2 vols. (Rome, 1958), 2:461–68, esp. 465–66; and Elison, *Deus Destroyed*, 55, and 414–15.

50. AP to MV, Macau, December 20, 1629, ARSI *JS* 161-II:109r.

51. An overview of the Terms Controversy, albeit without consideration of AP, is in Sangkeun Kim, *Strange Names of God: The Missionary Translation of the Divine Name and the Chinese Responses to Matteo Ricci's* Shangti *in Late Ming China, 1583–1644* (New York, 2004), esp. 119–96. See also Brockey, *Journey to the East*, 85–89.

52. On Rodrigues's first trip into China, see Michael Cooper, SJ, *Rodrigues the Interpreter: A Early Jesuit in Japan and China* (Tokyo, 1974), 278–89.

53. See Jean-Dominique Gabiani to Giovanni Paolo Oliva, Xi'an, September 22, 1680, appendix to Henri Bernard-Maître, SJ, "Un Dossier Bibliographique de la Fin du XVIIe Siècle: Sur la Question des Termes Chinois", *Recherches des Sciences Religieuses* 36 (1949): 25–79, at 71.

54. Palmeiro unambiguously states that Alfonso Vagnone insisted that the missionaries at Jiading all sign a pledge to abandon the polemical terms. See AP to MV, Macau, January 16, 1631, ARSI *FG* 730-I:13r.

55. Alfonso Vagnone to MV, Jiangzhou, December 18, 1629, ARSI *Jap-Sin* 161-II:108v.

56. Palmeiro's punishment for Rodrigues included a "public reprehension" and two days of fasting as well as the reciting of the penitential psalms with their litanies, twice. The Visitor wrote to the vice-provincial to impose a similar castigation on Figueiredo. See AP to MV, Macau, May 18, 1628, ARSI *FG* 730-I:3r.

57. João Delgado Figueira to [Francisco de Castro], Goa, February 1, 1630, in António Baião, ed., *A Inquisição de Goa: Correspondencia dos Inquisidores da Índia (1569–1630)*, 2 vols. (Coimbra, 1930), 2:653.

58. The Dutch attempt to seize Macau is best described in Boxer, *Fidalgos in the Far East,* 72–92.

59. On the Chinese debates about Macau, see Wu Zhilang, "The Establishment of Macao as a Special Port and the Ensuing Debates", in *Macau during the Ming Dynasty,* ed. Luís Filipe Barreto (Lisbon, 2009), 285–301.

60. The classic study of these military embassies is C. R. Boxer, "Portuguese Military Expeditions in Aid of the Mings against the Manchus, 1621–1647", *T'ien-Hsia Monthly* 7, no. 1 (August 1938): 24–36. Chinese debates over Portuguese military aid are discussed in Timothy Brook, "The Early Jesuits and the Late Ming Border: The Chinese Search for Accommodation", in *Encounters and Dialogues: Changing Perspectives on Chinese-Western Exchanges from the Sixteenth to the Eighteenth Centuries,* ed. Xiaoxin Wu (Sankt Augustin, 2005), 19–38.

61. On Mendes, see Isabel Pina, *Jesuítas Chineses e Mestiços da Missão da China (1589–1689),* (Lisbon, 2011), 310–15.

62. The machinations of Alonso Sanchéz (1547–1593) are discussed in Manel Ollé, *La Invención de China: Percepiones y Estrategias Filipinas respecto a China durante el Siglo XVI* (Wiesbaden, 2000), 51–64, and 115–50.

63. See Cooper, *Rodrigues the Interpreter,* 338.

64. A list is in Nicolas Standaert, *Yang Ting-yun, Confucian and Christian in Late Ming China: His Life and Thought* (Leiden, 1988), 227.

65. Chinese Itinerary, 118v.

66. Ibid., 119r. His expression is *tolhendo das cadeiras,* which generally refers to the pelvic bones.

67. Ibid., 118v–119r.

68. Ricci voiced the same negative opinion about Chinese architecture in his journals. See Pasquale d'Elia, SJ, ed., *Fonti Ricciane,* 3 vols. (Rome, 1942–1949), 1:29.

69. Chinese Itinerary, 120r.

70. Question 187 of the Second Part of the Second Part of the *Summa Theologica* deals with this issue.

71. Chinese Itinerary, 120r/v.

72. Ibid., 119v.

73. An analysis of the size of the Chinese Christian community is in Nicolas Standaert, "Chinese Christians", in his *Handbook of Christianity in China: 635–1800* (Leiden, 2001), 380–98.

74. Chinese Itinerary, 119v.

75. Ibid., 119v–120r.

76. Ibid., 120v.

77. Ibid., 121r.

78. Ibid, 121v.

79. Ibid.

80. On Ming taxation, see Timothy Brook, *The Troubled Empire: China in the Yuan and Ming Dynasties* (Cambridge, Mass., 2010), 47–49, and 117–21.

81. On Xu's career, conversion, and contributions to East–West dialogue, see Xu Volume.

82. On Sun's career, see Huang Yilong, "Sun Yuanhua (1581–1632): A Christian Convert who Put Xu Guangqi's Military Reform Policy into Practice", in Xu Volume, 225–59.

83. On the Ming population, see Brook, *Troubled Empire*, 42–45.

84. Chinese Itinerary, 121v–122r. Further on Ming taxation is in Ray Huang, *Taxation and Government Finance in Sixteenth-Century Ming China* (Cambridge, 1974), 82–188.

85. Chinese Itinerary, 121v.

86. Ibid., 122r.

87. Ou Daren met Michele Ruggieri in the 1580s and mentioned him in his poems. On this poet, see Zhang Xianqing, "Just a Poem: The Story of 'Xian Hua Si' in Cultural Encounter", *Chinese Cross-Currents* 7, no. 2 (April 2010): 112–31.

88. The author is grateful to Chen Huihung and Han Cheng-hua for identifying this poem, and to Timothy Brook for providing this eloquent translation.

89. The author would like to thank Timothy Brook and Dai Lianbun for help in identifying this element of Ming material culture.

90. Chinese Itinerary, 122r/v.

91. Ibid., 122v.

7. To Beijing and Back Again

1. Chinese Itinerary, 122v.

2. On travel in Ming China, see Timothy Brook, "Communications and Commerce", in *The Cambridge History of China*, 15 vols., ed. D. Twitchett and F. Mote (Cambridge, 1979–), 8:579–707, esp. 603–35.

3. Manuel Dias the younger, TC China 1628, [Hangzhou?, 1628], ARSI *JS* 134:307r–308r.

4. Rodrigo de Figueiredo, AL China, Hangzhou, August 22, 1629, ARSI *JS* 115-I:166v; and Chinese Itinerary, 131v.

5. Ibid., 123r.

6. C. R. Boxer, *South China in the Sixteenth Century* (London, 1953), 17–25 (on Galeote Pereira), and 168–85 (on Gaspar da Cruz).

7. Pascale Girard, ed. and trans., *Le Voyage en Chine d'Adriano de las Cortes, SJ (1625)* (Paris, 2001).

8. Chinese Itinerary, 121r.

9. On this punishment, see Timothy Brook, Jérôme Bourgon, and Gregory Blue, *Death by a Thousand Cuts* (Cambridge, Mass., 2008), 97–121.

10. Chinese Itinerary, 123r.

11. Ibid.; and, on the 1608 affair at Nanchang, see Pasquale d'Elia, SJ, ed., *Fonti Ricciane,* 3 vols. (Rome: 1942–1949), 2:448–61.

12. Ibid., 1:83 and 120.

13. Chinese Itinerary, 124r.

14. On the system, see Charles Hucker, *The Censorial System of Ming China* (Stanford, 1966), 30–66.

15. The situation for military officials was different. According to Palmeiro, "those who hold that it is necessary to mourn the loss of other lives for a long time can scarcely be expected to boldly risk their own, and also it would be more than a little contradictory for a soldier or warrior, whose profession is to fight and kill, to have to spend a great span crying over only one dead person." See Chinese Itinerary, 132v.

16. Ibid. On Wang, see Erik Zürcher, "Christian Social Action in Late Ming Times: Wang Zheng and his 'Humanitarian Society'", in *Linked Faiths: Essays on Chinese Religions and Traditional Culture in Honour of Kristofer Schipper,* ed. Jan de Meyer and Peter Engelfriet (Leiden, 1999), 269–86.

17. Chinese Itinerary, 124r.

18. Ibid., 124v.

19. Ibid.

20. Ibid., 125r.

21. Ibid.

22. Ibid., 125r/v.

23. Ibid., 126r.

24. Palmeiro was only sixty-one when these events transpired; the text reflects his age when it was written, in the months after his return to Macau.

25. Chinese Itinerary, 125v–126r.

26. Sun Yuanhua held the office of director of the Bureau of Operations at the Ministry of War and was responsible for provisioning the Liaodong army for its battles against the Manchu forces. See Huang Yi-Long, "Sun Yuanhua (1581–1632): A Christian Convert who Put Xu Guangqi's Military Reform Policy into Practice", in Xu Volume, 225–59, esp. 237.

27. Chinese Itinerary, 126v.

28. On Xu's successful attempt to incorporate the Jesuits into the calendar reform project, see Keizo Hashimoto, *Hsü Kuang-ch'i and Astronomical Reform: The Process of the Chinese Acceptance of Western Astronomy, 1629–1635* (Osaka, 1988), 28–52.

29. Chinese Itinerary, 126v.

30. Ibid.

31. Susan Naquin, *Peking: Temples and City Life, 1400–1900* (Berkeley, 2000), 252–58.

32. Chinese Itinerary, 127r.

33. Ibid.; Sun Xiaochun, "On the Star Catalogue and the Atlas of the *Chongzhen lishu*," in Xu Volume, 311–21, at 312; and Noël Golvers, *The Astronomia Europaea of Ferdinand Verbiest, S.J. (Dillingen, 1687)* (Nettetal, 1993), 46.

34. Chinese Itinerary, 127r/v.

35. Ibid., 127v.

36. AP to MV (Letter 2), Macau, December 20, 1629, ARSI *JS* 161-II:113r.

37. On the Jesuits' attitudes toward Daoism, see Liam Matthew Brockey, *Journey to the East: The Jesuit Mission to China, 1579–1724* (Cambridge, Mass., 2007), 296–302.

38. His report says that this temple was "inside the walls", but this seems to have been a slip. See Chinese Itinerary, 127v. The author thanks Susan Naquin for helping to identify this temple.

39. The Dongyue temple was not home to a large community of *bonzes,* the Jesuits' term for Buddhist or Daoist clergy, but was rather controlled by pilgrimage associations composed of laymen. See Vincent Goossaert, "Dongyue Miao/Shrine of the Eastern Peak (Beijing)", in *The Encyclopedia of Taoism,* 2 vols., ed. Fabrizio Pregadio (New York, 2008), 1:380–81.

40. Chinese Itinerary, 127v–128r.

41. On Jesuit attitudes toward Buddhism, see Urs App, *The Cult of Emptiness: The Western Discovery of Buddhist Thought and the Invention of Oriental Philosophy* (Kyoto, 2012), 11–144.

42. The recumbent statue is 5.2 meters long.

43. This "queen" was most likely Empress Dowager Li (1546–1614), renowned for her patronage of the capital's Buddhist temples during the Wanli reign. See Chou Tai-chi, "Li-shih", in *Dictionary of Ming Biography,* 2 vols., ed. L. Carrington Goodrich (New York, 1976), 1:856–59.

44. Chinese Itinerary, 128r.

45. Ibid.

46. Ibid.

47. Donald Lach and Edwin VanKley, *Asia in the Making of Europe,* 3 vols. in 8 bks. (Chicago, 1965–1993), 3:4:1579–93.

48. On the censorial apparatus, see Hucker, *Censorial System of Ming China,* 30–65.

49. Chinese Itinerary, 129r. The citation "let arms yield to togas" is from Cicero's *De Officiis.*

50. Palmeiro mistakenly states that the evaluation of court officials took place every five years, but one did coincide with his visit in 1629. See John Dardess, *Blood and History in China: The Donglin Faction and its Repression, 1620–1627* (Honolulu, 2002), 162. On the evaluation system, see Charles Hucker, "Governmental Organization of the Ming Dynasty", *Harvard Journal of Asiatic Studies* 21 (December 1958): 1–66, at 16.

51. The author thanks John Dardess for this precision.

52. On Jesuit personnel catalogues generally, see Adrien Demoustier, SJ, "Les Catalogues du Personnel de la Province de Lyon en 1587, 1606, et 1636", *AHSI* 43 (1974): 3–84.

53. Palmeiro's terms are accurate; the Chinese equivalents are in Hucker, "Governmental Organization", 15–16.

54. Chinese Itinerary, 128v.

55. High officials were expected to "confess their own faults" to the throne. See Hucker, "Governmental Organization", 16.

56. Chinese Itinerary, 128v.

57. Inspectors for the Ministry for the Personnel belonged to the Offices of Scrutiny and the Censorate, referred to collectively as *ke-dao,* and the generic term for functionary was *li,* so it is plausible that the "tau-li" and "co-li" were derivative terms. See Hucker, "Governmental Organization", 18 and 49–53; and John Dardess, *Ming China, 1368–1644* (Lanham, Md., 2011), 69–70.

58. Chinese Itinerary, 129r. On Ming-era memorial writing, see Silas Wu, "Transmission of Ming Memorials and the Evolution of the Transmission Network, 1368–1627", *T'oung-Pao* 54, no. 4–5 (1968): 275–87.

59. Chinese Itinerary, 128v–129r.

60. On the Donglin purge, see Dardess, *Blood and History,* 72–149.

61. Chinese Itinerary, 129r.

62. The gifts Trigault brought to China are listed in Edmond Lamalle, SJ, "La Propagande du P. Nicolas Trigault en faveur des Missions de Chine (1616)", *AHSI* 9 (1940): 49–120, esp. 75–76 and 104.

63. Benjamin Elman, *On Their Own Terms: Science in China, 1550–1900* (Cambridge, Mass., 2005), 93–94.

64. On the Grand Canal, see Joseph Needham, *Science and Civilisation in China,* 7 vols. in 27 parts (Cambridge, 1954–2004), 4:3:306–20; and Brook, "Communications and Commerce", 8:597–603.

65. Chinese Itinerary, 129v.

66. Timothy Brook, *The Troubled Empire: China in the Yuan and Ming Dynasties* (Cambridge, Mass., 2010), 249.

67. Chinese Itinerary, 130r.

68. Ibid., 130v.

69. Ibid.

70. Ibid. The Society's Lisbon novitiate was created in 1597, moving to improvised accomodations at the Monte Olivete site in 1603. Although the novice chapel
was consecrated in 1619, the novice lodgings were not completed until 1619. See
António Franco, *Imagem da Virtude em o Noviciado da Companhia de Jesu na Corte
de Lisboa* (Coimbra, 1717), 7–16.

71. Rodrigo de Figueiredo, AL China, Hangzhou, August 22, 1629, ARSI *JS*
115-I:161v.

72. Chinese Itinerary, 130v.

73. Rodrigo de Figueiredo, AL China, Hangzhou, August 22, 1629, ARSI *JS*
115-I:160v.

74. Chinese Itinerary, 130v.

75. Ibid., 130v.

76. Ibid., 131v.

77. AP to MV, Macau, December 20, 1629, ARSI *JS* 161-II:112v.

78. Chinese Itinerary, 131r.

79. On Yang and Li, see Nicolas Standaert, *Yang Tingyun, Confucian and Christian in Late Ming China: His Life and Thought* (Leiden, 1988), esp. 5–50; and Willard
Peterson, "Learning from Heaven: The Introduction of Christianity and Other
Western Ideas into Late Ming China", in *Cambridge History of China,* ed. Twitchett
and Mote, 8:810–18.

80. It is not clear how many Jesuit students were in Hangzhou in 1629. Palmeiro
says there were five at Yang's compound but then says that part of this number was in
Jiading. See Chinese Itinerary, 131v.

81. Chinese Itinerary, 131r.

82. On the Hangzhou church, see D. E. Mungello, *The Forgotten Christians of
Hangzhou* (Honolulu, 1994), 12–19.

83. Chinese Itinerary, 132r.

84. Ibid.

85. Ibid.

86. Liam Matthew Brockey, "The Death and Disappearance of Nicolas Trigault,
S.J.", *Journal of the Metropolitan Museum of Art* 38 (2003): 161–67.

87. AP to MV, Macau, [December 20] 1629, ARSI *JS* 161-II:117r.

88. 1629 Orders, 38v.

89. Chinese Itinerary, 133r.

90. AP, Variant copy of Chinese Itinerary, Macau, January 8, 1630, BAJA
49-V-6:553v.

8. Challenging Accommodation

1. AP to MV, Macau, [December] 1629, ARSI *JS* 161-II:116v.

2. Alfonso Vagnone to MV, Macau, November 1, 1622, ARSI *JS* 161-II:65v.

3. Bonelli Relação, 273r, 272v, 275v, and 274r; and AP, Order concerning the possessions of those who died at College of Macau, Macau, December 4, 1628, BAJA 49-IV-66:29v.

4. Bonelli Relação, 272v and 274r.

5. Ibid., 274r.

6. Luke 14:23: "And the Lord said to the servant: Go out into the highways and hedges, and compel them to come in, that my house may be filled."

7. See, for example, George Dunne, SJ, *Generation of Giants: The Story of the Jesuits in China in the Last Decades of the Ming Dynasty* (Notre Dame, 1962), 15–52; Andrew Ross, *A Vision Betrayed: The Jesuits in Japan and China, 1542–1742* (Edinburgh, 1994), 118–54, and 178–84; Jonathan Spence, *The Memory Palace of Matteo Ricci* (New York, 1984), 113–17; and Mary Laven, *Mission to China: Matteo Ricci and the Jesuit Encounter with the East* (London, 2011), esp. 26–27. The pioneering study that laid the foundations for later claims is Johannes Bettray, SVD, *Die Akkommodationsmethode des P. Matteo Ricci S.I. in China* (Rome, 1995). There Ricci's genius is clearly asserted. See, for example, ibid., xl.

8. See, for example, D. E. Mungello, *Curious Land: Jesuit Accommodation and the Origins of Sinology* (Honolulu, 1985), 13–20, and 44–73; Ross, *A Vision Betrayed,* 32–46; Laven, *Mission to China,* 20–22; Claudia von Collani, "Actors: Missionaries", in *Handbook of Christianity in China: 635–1800,* ed. Nicolas Standaert (Leiden, 2001), 309–21; and D. E. Mungello, *The Great Encounter of China and the West, 1500–1800* (Lanham, Md., 2011), 15–18.

9. D. E. Mungello, "A Confucian Echo of Western Humanist Culture in Seventeenth-Century China", in *Western Humanistic Culture Presented to China by Jesuit Missionaries (XVII–XVIII centuries),* ed. Federico Masini (Rome, 1996), 279–92, at 282; Howard Goodman and Anthony Grafton, "Ricci, the Chinese, and the Toolkits of Textualists", *Asia Major,* Third Series, 2, no. 2 (1990): 95–148; and Gauvin Bailey, *Art on the Jesuit Missions in Asia and Latin America, 1542–1773* (Toronto, 1999), 7–8.

10. This position is clearly annunciated in the voluminous history of the Jesuits' China mission by Daniello Bartoli (1608–1685), a text where Palmeiro's judgments were labeled hasty and ill-informed. See Bartoli, *Dell'Historia della Compagnia di Giesv, La Cina* (Rome, 1663), esp. 115–22, and 897–98. A modern version is in Paul Rule, *K'ungtzu or Confucius: The Jesuit Interpretation of Confucianism* (Sydney, 1986), 87–88.

11. Lawrence Flynn, SJ, "The *De Arte Rhetorica* (1568) by Cyprian Soarez, S.J.: A Translation with Introduction and Notes" (Ph.D. diss., University of Florida, 1955), 276.

12. Ibid., 278.

13. Ibid., 282.

14. Bonelli Relação, 265r.

15. AP to MV (Letter 1), Macau, December 20, 1629, ARSI *JS* 161-II:109r.

16. Ibid., 109v.

17. Ibid., 109v–110r.

18. Ibid., 109v.

19. Liam Matthew Brockey, *Journey to the East: The Jesuit Mission to China, 1579–1724* (Cambridge, Mass., 2007), 68–69.

20. AP to MV (Letter 1), Macau, December 20, 1629, ARSI *JS* 161-II:110v.

21. Huang Yi-Long, "Sun Yuanhua (1581–1632): A Christian Convert who Put Xu Guangqi's Military Reform Policy into Practice", in Xu Volume, 225–59, 227.

22. AP to MV (Letter 1), Macau, December 20, 1629, ARSI *JS* 161-II:110v.

23. Ibid., 109v–110r.

24. AP to MV, Macau, January 16, 1631, ARSI *FG* 730-I:13r.

25. AP to MV (Letter 1), Macau, December 20, 1629, ARSI *JS* 161-II:110r.

26. 1629 Orders, 23r.

27. AP to MV (Letter 1), Macau, December 20, 1629, ARSI *JS* 161-II:110v.

28. Ibid., 109v.

29. Nicolas Standaert, "Court-Converts", in *Handbook of Christianity in China: 635–1800,* ed. Nicolas Standaert (Leiden, 2001), 438–43.

30. AP to MV (Letter 1), Macau, December 20, 1629, ARSI *JS* 161-II:110v–111r.

31. Ibid., 110v.

32. Jean-Dominique Gabiani to Giovanni Paolo Oliva, Xi'an, September 22, 1680, in Henri Bernard-Maître, SJ, "Un Dossier Bibliographique de la Fin du XVIIe Siècle: Sur la Question des Termes Chinois", *Recherches des Sciences Religieuses* 36 (1949): 25–79, esp. 72–73.

33. AP to MV (Letter 2), Macau, December 20, 1629, ARSI *JS* 161-II:112r. On the Ignatian phrase, see John O'Malley, *The First Jesuits* (Cambridge, Mass., 1993), 112.

34. On these rules, see Brockey, *Journey to the East,* 243–86.

35. AP to MV (Letter 2), Macau, December 20, 1629, ARSI *JS* 161-II:112r.

36. Ibid., 112v.

37. Ibid., 112r.

38. Ibid.

39. Ibid.

40. 1629 Orders, 22v.

41. AP to MV (Letter 2), Macau, December 20, 1629, ARSI *JS* 161-II:112v.

42. Ibid., 112v–113r.

43. 1629 Orders, 29v. The rule is explicit: "Do not teach laymen to make spyglasses or clocks because it is not very fitting for our profession, and also because these things will be less esteemed if there are many of them."

44. AP to MV (Letter 3), Macau, December 20, 1629, ARSI *JS* 161-II:114r.

45. Ibid., 114r/v.

46. 1629 Orders, 22r.

47. AP to MV (Letter 3), Macau, December 20, 1629, ARSI *JS* 161-II:114v.

48. Ibid.

49. He begrudgingly granted permission for the use of a *changpao* "as light as wind" during the summer heat, remarking nevertheless that the use of such robes

"would open the door for some to use on many more occasions what is only permitted on one." Ibid., 115r.

50. 1629 Orders, 21v–22r. Palmeiro uses romanized Chinese terms and Portuguese terms of Asian origin that are hard to identify with precision. He divides the year into three seasons and insists that different fabrics be used in each season: cotton for winter, serge for spring and fall, and hemp for summer. The author thanks John Vollmer for his precisions on late Ming dress.

51. AP to MV (Letter 3), Macau, December 20, 1629, ARSI *JS* 161-II:115r.

52. *Pagode* is a generic term for non-Christian deities in Asia, used most frequently in Portuguese writings with reference to Hindu or Buddhist gods.

53. AP to MV (Letter 2), Macau, December 20, 1629, ARSI *JS* 161-II:113r.

54. Flynn, "The *De Arte Rhetorica*", 281.

55. AP to MV (Letter 2), Macau, December 20, 1629, ARSI *JS* 161-II:113r.

56. Lionel Jensen, *Manufacturing Confucianism: Chinese Traditions and Universal Civilization* (Durham, 1997), 32–75; and Mungello, *Curious Land*, 55–68.

57. Pasquale d'Elia, SJ, *Fonti Ricciane*, 3 vols. (Rome, 1942–1949), 1:94–107.

58. AP to MV (Letter 2), Macau, December 20, 1629, ARSI *JS* 161-II:113r.

59. Ibid., 113r/v.

60. Ibid., 113v.

61. 1 Samuel 5: 1–5.

62. 1629 Orders, 24r.

63. Bernard-Maître, "Un Dossier Bibliographique", 64–72.

64. 1629 Orders, 37v–39v.

65. AP to MV (Letter 6), Macau, December 20, 1629, ARSI *FG* 730-I:7v.

66. AP to MV, Macau, January 16, 1631, ARSI *FG* 730-I:12v–13r.

67. Ibid.

68. Alfonso Vagnone to [MV], Jiangzhou, December 18, 1629, ARSI *JS* 161-II:107r.

69. Ibid., 107r and 108r.

70. Ibid., 107v–108r.

71. AP to MV, Macau, January 16, 1631, ARSI *FG* 730-I:13r.

72. Ibid.

73. No trustworthy copy of the decisions made at Jiading has survived. The text purporting to be the conference acts in Domingo Fernández Navarrete's (1618–1688) writings is a forgery. See J. S. Cummins, *The Travels and Controversies of Friar Domingo Navarrete, 1618–1688*, 2 vols. (London, 1962), 2:427–28.

74. AP to MV, Macau, January 16, 1631, ARSI *FG* 730-I:13r.

75. Pascoal Mendes to MV, Beijing, June 1, 1630, ARSI *FG* 730-I:8v–9r.

76. AP to MV, Macau, May 8, 1632, ARSI *FG* 730-I:16r/v.

77. Pascoal Mendes to MV, Beijing, June 1, 1630, ARSI *FG* 730-I:9r.

78. Alfonso Vagnone to [MV], Jiangzhou, December 18, 1629, ARSI *JS* 161-II:108r.

79. AP to MV, Macau, May 8, 1632, ARSI *FG* 730-I:16r.

80. AP to MV (Letter 1), Macau, December 20, 1629, ARSI *JS* 161-II:109v.

81. [Manuel Dias the younger], TC China 1628, [Hangzhou, January 1628], ARSI *JS* 134:307r–308v.

82. 1629 Orders, 28v, 28r, and 25v.

83. On João Fernandes (b. 1581), who was dismissed in 1621, see Isabel Pina, *Jesuítas Chineses e Mestiços da Missão da China (1589–1689)* (Lisbon, 2011), 319–26.

84. [Manuel Dias the younger], TC China 1628, [Hangzhou, January 1628], ARSI *JS* 134:308r.

85. 1629 Orders, 34r–35v, and 37r/v.

86. On Terrentius, see Isaia Iannaccone, *Johann Schreck Terrentius: Le Scienze rinascimentali e lo spirito dell'accademia dei lincei nella cina dei Ming* (Naples, 1998); and Noël Golvers, *Johann Schreck-Terrentius: A Late-Humanist Jesuit Polymath and his Savant Network in Europe (1600–1618)* (Turnhout, forthcoming).

87. AP to MV, Macau, [January?] 1630, ARSI *JS* 161-II:143v.

88. Ibid.

89. AP to MV, Macau, January 16, 1631, ARSI *FG* 730-I:12r.

90. Timothy Brook, "The Early Jesuits and the Late Ming Border: The Chinese Search for Accommodation", in *Encounters and Dialogues: Changing Perspectives on Chinese-Western Exchanges from the Sixteenth to the Eighteenth Centuries,* ed. Xiaoxin Wu (Sankt Augustin, 2005), 19–38, esp. 31–35.

91. Xu Guangqi to AP, Beijing, [June 4, 1630], BAJA 49-V-8:743v–744v.

92. AP to MV, Macau, January 16, 1631, ARSI *FG* 730-I:12v.

93. Huang, "Sun Yuanhua", 251–56.

94. JR to MV, Macau, February 5, 1633, ARSI *JS* 18-I:121r.

95. Brook, "Late Ming Border", 33.

96. JR to MV, Macau, February 5, 1633, ARSI *JS* 18-I:122r.

97. Alfonso Vagnone to MV, Jiangzhou, June 1, 1632, ARSI *FG* 730-I:14v.

98. AP to MV, Macau, March 20, 1634, ARSI *JS* 161-II:150r.

99. AP to MV, Macau, January 16, 1631, ARSI *FG* 730-I:12r.

100. On the period from 1630 to 1663, see Brockey, *Journey to the East,* 92–124.

9. Sunrise in the West

1. By 1618 the "Great Ship" had been replaced by fleets of smaller vessels called galliots. See C. R. Boxer, *The Great Ship from Amacon: Annals of Macao and the Old Japan Trade, 1555–1640* (Lisbon, 1959), 90–91.

2. João Rodrigues Girão to NM, Macau, February 18, 1626, ARSI *JS* 18-I:57v.

3. AP to MV, Macau, [December 20] 1629, ARSI *JS* 161-II:116r.

4. Ibid.

5. AP to MV, Macau, April 28, 1633, ARSI *JS* 161-II:146r.

6. G. B. Souza, *The Survival of Empire: Portuguese Trade and Society in China and the South China Sea, 1630–1754* (Cambridge, 1986), 113.

7. J. F. Moran, *The Japanese and the Jesuits: Alessandro Valignano in Sixteenth-Century Japan* (London, 1993), 115–28.

8. AP, Notes for Japan Province Procurators, Macau, [December 1628], BAJA 49-IV-66:30r.

9. AP to MV, Macau, May 14, 1628, ARSI *JS* 161-II:101r.

10. AP to MV, Macau, [December 20] 1629, ARSI *JS* 161-II:116r.

11. AP to MV, Macau, [January?] 1630, ARSI *JS* 161-II:143r.

12. AP to MV, Macau, April 28, 1633, ARSI *JS* 161-II:146r.

13. Souza, *Survival of Empire,* 113.

14. AP to MV, Macau, December 20, 1629, ARSI *FG* 730-I:7r.

15. AP to MV, Macau, [January?] 1630, ARSI *JS* 161-II:143v. Palmeiro's complaint is echoed in other European writings. See Boxer, *Great Ship,* 125–26.

16. João Álvares, Description of the College of Macau, Macau, June 6, 1746, AHU *Conselho Ultramarino, Macau,* Cod. 1659, n.p.

17. António de Fontes to AP, Tonkin, June 25, 1631, BAJA 49-V-31:119v.

18. AP to MV, Macau, April 28, 1633, ARSI *JS* 161-II:146v.

19. Souza, *Survival of Empire,* 113; and Pierre-Yves Manguin, *Les Portugais sur les Côtes du Viêt-Nam et du Champa* (Paris, 1972), 230–31.

20. Bonelli Relação, 275r and 265v.

21. A. A. de Pina, SJ, "Macau no século XVII, Cartas de Francisco Carvalho Aranha, navegador e comerciante no Oriente", *Portugal em Africa,* 14 (1957): 343–60, at 350.

22. AP to MV, Macau, [December 20] 1629, ARSI *JS* 161-II:116r/v.

23. The most detailed history of the early phase of the Jesuit missions in Southeast Asia remains António Francisco Cardim, *Batalhas da Companhia de Jesus na sua Gloriosa Provincia de Japão,* ed. Luciano Cordeiro (Lisbon, 1894). See also Roland Jacques, *De Castro Marim à Faïfo: Naissance et développement du padroado portugais d'Orient des origines à 1659* (Lisbon, 1999), 142–58; and Tara Alberts, *Conflict and Conversion: Catholicism in Southeast Asia, 1500–1700* (Oxford, 2013), 17–87.

24. On this region, see George Dutton, Jayne Werner, and John Whitmore, eds., *Sources of Vietnamese Tradition* (New York, 2012), 147–248; Nguyen Tan Hu'ng, *Le Viêt Nam du XVIIe siècle: Un Tableau Socioculturel* (Paris, 2011), 25–103; and Li Tana, *Nguyên Cochinchina: Southern Vietnam in the Seventeenth and Eighteenth Centuries* (Ithaca, N.Y., 1998), 18–46.

25. From Palmeiro's perspective, which, like that of his Portuguese peers, was sea-based and not land-based, Burma was part of the Western Indian political and economic sphere.

26. On the trading world of Southeast Asia, see Anthony Reid, *Southeast Asia in the Age of Commerce, 1450–1680,* 2 vols. (New Haven, Conn., 1988–1993), esp. 2:62–131.

27. João Rodrigues Girão to NM, Macau, February 18, 1626, ARSI *JS* 18-I:58r.

28. Cardim, *Batalhas,* 286–90.

29. Gaspar Luís, AL Cochinchina Mission 1628, [Turão?], January 1629, BAJA 49-V-9:409r; and Gaspar Luís, AL Cochinchina Mission 1629, Turão, 1629, BAJA 49-V-9:422v.

30. Francesco Buzomi to MV, Macau, January 24, 1631, ARSI *JS* 68:21r–23r; and Gaspar Luís, AL Cochinchina Mission 1629, Turão, January 1630, ARSI *JS* 72:143r–159v.

31. AP to MV, Macau, January 16, 1631, ARSI *JS* 68:19r.

32. Pêro Marques to AP, Tonkin, July 25, 1627, ARSI *JS* 88:18r.

33. Alexandre de Rhodes to NM, Macau, January 16, 1631, ARSI *JS* 80:15v–16v.

34. Ibid., 16r.

35. António de Fontes to AP, Tonkin, June 25, 1631, BAJA 49-V-31:119v–120v.

36. António de Fontes, Partial AL Tonkin Mission June–December 1631, [Hanoi], December 31, 1631, BAJA 49-V-31:90r. The figure of the *Padre Grande* was also known in Cochinchina and lived on long after Palmeiro's death, until at least 1651. See Manguin, *Portuguais sur les Côtes,* 310–11.

37. AP to MV, Macau, January 16, 1631, ARSI *JS* 68:20r.

38. Pêro Marques, AL Hainan Mission, Hainan, July 29, 1633, ARSI *JS* 88:162v.

39. Bento de Matos, who had served with Giulio Aleni in Fuzhou, went to Hainan in 1635. See MD to MV, Macau, September 20, 1635 and October 16, 1635, ARSI *JS* 18–1:157r.

40. AP, Instructions given to mission superior Gaspar do Amaral, Macau, February 16, 1631, BAJA 49-V-31:42r.

41. Gaspar do Amaral, AL Tonkin Mission 1634, Hanoi, December 30, 1634, ARSI *JS* 88:189v–190v.

42. Cardim, *Batalhas,* 253–83.

43. AP to MV, Macau, May 14, 1628, ARSI *JS* 161-II:101r/v.

44. Ibid., 101v.

45. Ibid.

46. Ibid. Ephesians 4:5, "One Lord, one faith, one baptism."

47. On this issue, see *Administrer les Sacrements en Europe et au Nouveau Monde: La Curie Romaine et les* Dubia circa Sacramenta, ed. Charlotte Castelnaud-l'Estoile, Paolo Broggio, and Giovanni Pizzorusso, *Mélanges de l'Ecole française de Rome, Italie et Méditerranée* 121:1 (2009).

48. Jesús López Gay, *El Matrimonio de los Japoneses: Problema y soluciones según un Ms. Inédito de Gil de la Mata, SJ (1547–1599)* (Rome, 1964), esp. 45–78.

49. AP to MV, Macau, May 14, 1628, ARSI *JS* 161-II:101v.

50. Buzomi was on dangerous ground when he cited precedents from the Old Testament (such as Exodus 21:10 or Deuteronomy 21:15–17) that gave rules for equity in polygamous marriages. The topic he was addressing was divorce, and there was a clear example of a legal change on this topic in Matthew 19:7–8, where Jesus declares that Moses's permission of divorce is superseded by the new law.

51. Francisco Buzomi to AP, Faifo, July 3, 1628, BAJA 49-V-8:455r–456r.

52. AP to MV, Macau, May 14, 1628, ARSI *JS* 161-II: 101v.

53. Francesco Buzomi to MV, Macau, January 24, 1631, ARSI *JS* 68:21r.

54. AP to MV, Macau, December 20, 1629, ARSI *FG* 730-I:6r.

55. Ibid. The term *epikeia,* Palmeiro's *epicheia,* is from the Greek for "reasonableness." In the context of canon law, it implies a flexibility permitted in specific circumstances.

56. AP to MV, Macau, December 20, 1629, ARSI *FG* 730-I:6r.

57. 1629 Orders, 23v.

58. AP to MV, Macau, December 20, 1629, ARSI *FG* 730-I:6v. The first edition of the Roman Ritual was published in 1614.

59. Gaspar Luís to AP, [Cachão, 1633], ARSI *JS* 68:27r.

60. Liam Brockey, *Journey to the East: The Jesuit Mission to China, 1579–1724* (Cambridge, Mass., 2007), 94 and 331–39.

61. Daniello Bartoli, *Dell'Historia della Compagnia di Giesv, La Cina* (Rome, 1663), 613–20; 706–11; 765–71; 831–40; 914–35; 998–1003; and 1069–78.

62. Buzomi's understanding of the split between the Trinh and Nguyen lords is slightly off: he most likely refers to the death of Nguyen Hoang in 1613 and the succession of his son in Cochinchina. See Keith Taylor, "Nguyen Hoang and the Beginning of Vietnam's Southward Expansion", in *Southeast Asia in the Early Modern Era: Trade, Power, and Belief,* ed. Antony Reid (Ithaca, N.Y., 1993), 42–65, esp. 55–65.

63. Francesco Buzomi to MV, Macau, January 24, 1631, ARSI *JS* 68:23v. The Theatines were the Congregation of Clerics Regular, whose saints Gaetano Thiene (1480–1547), Andrea Avellino (1521–1608), and Paul IV (Gian Pietro Carafa, 1476–1559) were often depicted with bushy gray beards.

64. [António de Fontes], AL Tonkin Mission 1630, [Hanoi, early 1631], BAJA 49-V-31:58r.

65. Brockey, *Journey to the East,* 298–99.

66. António de Fontes to AP, Tonkin, June 25, 1631, BAJA 49-V-31:121r. Christian texts in Nom would indeed become a standard feature of Vietnamese Christian literature. See Brian Ostrowski, "The Rise of Christian Nôm Literature in Seventeenth-Century Vietnam: Fusing European Content and Local Expression", in *Vietnam and the West: New Approaches,* ed. Wynn Wilcox (Ithaca, N.Y., 2010), 19–39.

67. AP, Instructions for Gaspar do Amaral, Macau, February 16, 1631, BAJA 49-V-31:43v.

68. António de Fontes to AP, Tonkin, June 25, 1631, BAJA 49-V-31:120v–121r.

69. On the *língua geral,* see Charlotte de Castelnaud-L'Estoile, *Les Ouvriers d'une Vigne Stérile: Les Jésuites et la Conversion des Indiens au Brésil, 1580–1620* (Paris, 2000), 141–69.

70. AP to MV, Macau, May 8, 1632, with appended declaration on Chinese, Japanese, and Vietnamese, ARSI *JS* 94:6r–11v.

71. AP to MV, Macau, January 16, 1631, ARSI *JS* 68:19v.

72. Francisco de Pina to Jerónimo Rodrigues, Faifo, 1623, in Roland Jacques, *Portuguese Pioneers of Vietnamese Linguistics Prior to 1650* (Bangkok, 2002), 143; the terms are discussed on 83.

73. Francesco Buzomi to MV, Macau, January 24, 1631, ARSI *JS* 68:24v.

74. AP to MV, Macau, January 16, 1631, ARSI *JS* 68:19v.

75. Francesco Buzomi to MV, Macau, January 24, 1631, ARSI *JS* 68:24r/v.

76. AP to MV, Macau, January 16, 1631, ARSI *JS* 68:19v. Palmeiro nevertheless made Buzomi superior of the Cochinchina mission in early 1635, one of his last decisions. See AP to Francesco Buzomi, Macau, March 11, 1635, Real Academia de la Historia, Madrid, *Jesuitas, legajo* 22, fasc. 8, 457r/v.

77. On *dōjuku* in the Japan mission, see Boxer, *Christian Century,* 211–16, and 222–26; and Ikuo Higashibaba, *Christianity in Early Modern Japan: Kirishitan Belief and Practice* (Leiden, 2001), 20–28.

78. Palmeiro was reluctant to condone this practice, insisting that the term of service for *moços* be stipulated at purchase. "Even with the very little ones, it will not exceed fifteen or twenty years", he commanded. See 1629 Orders, 30v–31r.

79. Ibid., 36r/v.

80. Ibid., 30r and 33v.

81. Boxer, *Christian Century,* 217; and Higashibaba, *Christianity in Early Modern Japan,* 22.

82. 1629 Orders, 20v and 36r/v.

83. AP, Instructions given to mission superior Gaspar do Amaral, Macau, February 16, 1631, BAJA 49-V-31: 42r.

84. Bonelli Relação, 274v. Palmeiro requested that this slave be freed after his death since he had served at the college for twenty years.

85. AP, Instructions given to mission superior Gaspar do Amaral, Macau, February 16, 1631, BAJA 49-V-31:42r/v.

86. Francesco Buzomi to MV, Macau, January 24, 1631, ARSI *JS* 68:24v.

87. Ibid.

88. Boxer, *Christian Century,* 223.

89. Francesco Buzomi to MV, Macau, January 24, 1631, ARSI *JS* 68:24v.

90. Letter by Francisco de Pina, Faifo, 1623, transcribed in Jacques, *Portuguese Pioneers,* 45.

91. Francesco Buzomi to MV, Macau, January 24, 1631, ARSI *JS* 68:24r.

92. Gaspar Luís to AP, [Cachão, 1633], ARSI *JS* 68:27r.

93. António de Fontes to AP, Tonkin, June 25, 1631, BAJA 49-V-31:121r.

94. António de Fontes, Partial AL Tonkin Mission June to December 1631, [Hanoi?], December 31, 1631, BAJA 49-V-31:109v.

95. Gaspar do Amaral, AL Tonkin Mission 1632, Hanoi, December 31, 1632, BAJA 49-V-21:219v.

96. Ibid., 215r.

97. Gaspar do Amaral, AL Tonkin Mission 1633, Hanoi, December 30, 1633, BAJA 49-V-31:265r.

98. AP, Instructions for Gaspar do Amaral, Macau, February 16, 1631, BAJA 49-V-31:41v.

99. Gaspar do Amaral to AP, Hanoi, April 21, 1634, BAJA 49-V-31:303v.

100. Ibid., 304r.

101. Gaspar do Amaral, AL Tonkin Mission 1634, Hanoi, December 30, 1634, ARSI *JS* 88:171r.

102. AP to MV, Macau, [December 1629], ARSI *JS* 161-II:116r; and AP to MV, Macau, [January?] 1630, ARSI *JS* 161-II:143r.

103. Dauril Alden, *The Making of an Enterprise: The Society of Jesus in Portugal, Its Empire, and Beyond, 1540–1750* (Stanford, Calif., 1996), 255–266; and C. R. Boxer, *The Church Militant and Iberian Expansion, 1440–1770* (Baltimore, 1978), 2–30.

104. AP to MV, Macau, May 8, 1632, ARSI *FG* 730-I:16v; and AP to MV, Macau, September 17, 1633 ARSI *FG* 730-I:20r/v.

105. Gaspar Luís, AL Cochinchina Mission 1629, Turão, January 1630, ARSI *JS* 72:143r.

106. Only one Vietnamese brother, Inácio Xavier from Cochinchina, was accepted before 1650. See J. F. Schütte, SJ, *Textus Catalogorum Japoniae* (Rome, 1975), 1063.

107. See Isabel Pina, *Jesuítas Chineses e Mestiços da Missão da China (1589–1689)* (Lisbon, 2011), 241–93.

108. 1629 Orders, 22r.

109. The numbers dwindled rapidly: from eleven in 1626 to nine in 1627 and "some" in 1628. See AL China 1626, [1627?, n.p.] BAJA 49-V-6:308r, 322r/v, and 323v; MD, AL China 1627, Shanghai, May 9, 1628, BAJA 49-V-6:465r; and Rodrigo de Figueiredo, AL China 1628, Hangzhou, August 22, 1629, BAJA 49-V-6:584v.

110. 1629 Orders, 35r.

111. AP to MV, Macau, December 20, 1629, ARSI *FG* 730-I:6v.

112. 1629 Orders, 29v.

113. AP, Instructions given to mission superior Gaspar do Amaral, Macau, February 16, 1631, BAJA 49-V-31:41r.

114. AP to MV, Macau, April 28, 1633, ARSI *JS* 161-II:146r.

10. Sunset in the East

1. Takenaka Uneme held the office of Nagasaki *bugyō* from 1629 to 1633.

2. CF to AP, [near Nagasaki?], March 22, 1632, in Léon Pagès, *Histoire de la Religion Chrétienne au Japon depuis 1598 jusqu'a 1651,* 2 vols. (Paris, 1869–1870), 2:369–74.

3. On these tortures, see Juan Ruiz-de-Medina, *El Martirologio del Japón, 1558–1873* (Rome, 1999), 689–93.

4. CF to AP, [near Nagasaki?], March 22, 1632, in Pagès, *Histoire,* 2:373.

5. AP to MV, Macau, [January?] 1630, ARSI *JS* 161-II:143r.

6. Ibid.

7. Giovanni Battista Porro to AP, Aizu Wakamatsu, July 2, 1629, ARSI *JS* 61:286r–318v, in *Relatione della Persecutioni mosse contro la fede di Christo, in varii regni del Giappone ne gl'Anni MDCXXVIII. MDCXXIX. e MDCXXX* (Rome, 1635).

8. Giovanni Battista Porro to AP, Aizu Wakamatsu, August 5, 1630, ARSI *JS* 62:254v.

9. AP to MV, Macau, [January?] 1630, ARSI *JS* 161-II:143r.

10. Ruiz-de-Medina, *Martirologio*, 287–97. A mass for the three Jesuits, Paulo Miki, João de Goto, and Diogo Kisai, was permitted for the date of their martyrdom, February 5, in 1629.

11. Many of the Japan martyrs were beatified in the late nineteenth century, and some only in 2008.

12. On the canonization process, see Simon Ditchfield, "Tridentine Worship and the Cult of the Saints", in R. Po-Chia Hsia, ed., *Cambridge History of Christianity, Vol. 6: Reform and Expansion, 1500–1650* (Cambridge: 2008), 201–24; Simon Ditchfield, *Liturgy, Sanctity and History in Tridentine Italy: Pietro Maria Campi and the Preservation of the Particular* (Cambridge, 1995), 212–32; and Peter Burke, "How to Be a Counter-Reformation Saint", in Kaspar von Greyerz, ed., *Religion and Society in Early Modern Europe, 1500–1800* (London, 1984), 45–55.

13. The cathedral chapter of Manila conducted the beatification inquiries in 1630 and 1631, and requested relics of the three blessed Jesuits from Palmeiro. See Manila Cathedral Cabildo to AP, Manila, October 4, 1630, BAJA 49-V-9:76v–77r.

14. AP to MV, Macau, May 18, 1628, ARSI *FG* 730-I:3r.

15. JR to MV, Macau, November 30, 1627, ARSI *JS* 18-I:89r.

16. AP, Commission to Pedro Morejón, Macau, February 6, 1630, BAJA 49-V-8:744v–745r.

17. "Auto de Apprezentaçam de Letras Apostolicas que de Roma vierão sobre a Informaçám dos Martyres do Japam", Macau, April 27, 1630, BAJA 49-V-9:77v–83r.

18. Pedro Morejón to NM, Macau, October 17, 1635, ARSI *JS* 29:132r.

19. "Treslado das Perguntas do Interrogatorio e Artigos contheudos nas Letras Apostolicas da Sac. Congregação de Ritos", Rome, 1627 (translated Macau, 1630), BAJA 49-V-9:100r–110v.

20. Diogo Valente to MV, Macau, September 12, 1633, ARSI *JS* 21:341r; and Giovanni Battista Bonelli to MV, Macau, January 1634, ARSI *JS* 18-I:143r.

21. For the list of witnesses deposed in June 1632, see Pagès, *Histoire*, 2:380–82.

22. [Pedro Morejón], List of Jesuit Martyrs from 1617 until 1627, [Macau, 1633], BAJA 49-V-9:111r–115v.

23. Pedro Morejón to NM, Macau, October 17, 1635, ARSI *JS* 29:132v–133v.

24. AP to Mateus de Couros, Macau, July 27, 1627, BAJA 49-V-11:276v.

25. Bonelli Relação, 275v and 269v.

26. *Nosso Santo,* "our saint", was, of course, Ignatius Loyola.

27. *Tabis,* Palmeiro's *tābis,* are the traditional split-toed Japanese socks.

28. Bonelli Relação, 276r/v.

29. C. R. Boxer, *The Great Ship from Amacon: Annals of Macao and the Old Japan Trade, 1555–1640* (Lisbon, 1959), 127.

30. Ruiz-de-Medina, *Martirologio,* 689–93.

31. CF to AP, [near Nagasaki?], March 22, 1632, in Pagès, *Histoire,* 2:374. Lepers and beggars did indeed reach Manila from Nagasaki in 1631 and 1632. See M. T. Paske-Smith, "Japanese Trade and Residences in the Philippines, before and during the Spanish Occupation", *Transactions of the Asiatic Society of Japan* 42, no. 2 (1914): 683–710, at 707–8.

32. Josef Wicki, "Liste der Jesuiten-Indienfahrer, 1541–1758", *Aufsätze zur Portugiesischen Kulturgeschichte* 7 (1967): 252–450, at 292–93.

33. AP to MV, Macau, September 17, 1633 ARSI *FG* 730-I:20r.

34. AP to MV, Macau, May 8, 1632, ARSI *FG* 730-I:16v.

35. Sebastião Vieira to Vasco Martins, Manila, June 21, 1632, ARSI *JS* 38:305r.

36. Letter from Sebastião Vieira, "from this *fune* [vessel] between the Islands of Japan", February 18, 1633, in Franco, 1:159.

37. Ibid., 168.

38. Ibid., 187.

39. JR to MV, Macau, November 21, 1626, ARSI *JS* 18-I:69v.

40. Ruiz-de-Medina, *Martirologio,* 697–708; and Anon., List of Jesuit Martyrs from 1632 and 1633, [Macau?, late 1633], ARSI *Lus* 58:286r–287v.

41. Letter by Sebastião Vieira, [Kyushu, August–September 1633], ARSI *JS* 38:307r.

42. Ibid., 307v.

43. Iemitsu, who was in his late twenties in 1633, would produce an heir, Tokugawa Ietsuna, in 1641. The claim that Iemitsu had no close relatives is false, although his brother Tadanaga did commit suicide in January 1633 after the death of their father and a public disgrace.

44. Psalm 54:24.

45. Letter by Sebastião Vieira, [Kyushu, August–September 1633], ARSI *JS* 38:307v–308r.

46. Anon., "List of Jesuit Martyrs from 1632 and 1633, [Macau?, late 1633], ARSI *Lus* 58:287r.

47. CF to AP, Nagasaki, September 6, 1633, BNL *Reservados* 7640:41r.

48. Anon., List of Jesuit Martyrs from 1632 and 1633, [Macau?, late 1633], ARSI *Lus* 58:286r/v.

49. Ruiz-de-Medina, *Martirologio,* 715–16.

50. Anon., List of Jesuit Martyrs from 1632 and 1633, [Macau?, late 1633], ARSI *Lus* 58:286v.

51. Ibid., 287r. On the date of departure, see Boxer, *Great Ship,* 132.

52. Manuel Coelho, Report of the news that arrived in Cambodia from Japan on 20 April 1634, [Udong], May 20, 1634, ARSI *JS* 18-I:147r.

53. AP to MV, Macau, March 20, 1634, ARSI *JS* 161-II:150r/v.

54. The friars, Franciscans Ginés de Quesada and Juan Torrella and Dominican Giacinto Ansalone, are discussed in Ruiz-de-Medina, *Martirologio,* 690–91, 694–95, 726, and 728.

55. AP to MV, Macau, March 20, 1634, ARSI *JS* 161-II:150v.

56. Palmeiro also reported that there were two Dominicans and two Franciscans still at liberty.

57. Ibid.

58. AP to MV, Macau, [January?] 1630, ARSI *JS* 161-II:144v.

59. AP to MV, Macau, March 20, 1634, ARSI *JS* 161-II:150r.

60. Ibid.; see also Michael Cooper, SJ, *Rodrigues the Interpreter: A Early Jesuit in Japan and China* (Tokyo, 1974), 354.

61. AP to MV, Macau, September 17, 1633, ARSI *FG* 730-I:20r.

62. AP to MV, Macau, March 20, 1634, ARSI *JS* 161-II:150r.

63. Giovanni Battista Bonelli to MV, Macau, January 1634, ARSI *JS* 18-I:143v–144r.

64. AP to MV, Macau, March 20, 1634, ARSI *JS* 161-II:150r.

65. Benjamin Videira Pires, ed., "Um Campo Santo, de Macau", in Manuel Teixeira, *Macau e a Sua Diocese,* 15 vols. (Macau, 1940–1977), 8:202–43.

66. António Francisco Cardim to MV, Macau, [December? 1635], ARSI *JS* 161-I:159r/v.

67. AP to MV, Macau, September 17, 1633, ARSI *FG* 730-I: 20r/v.

68. António Francisco Cardim to MV, Macau, [December? 1635], ARSI *JS* 161-I:160r/v.

69. AP to MV, Macau, September 17, 1633, ARSI *FG* 730-I:20r/v.

70. António Francisco Cardim, *Batalhas da Companhia de Jesus na sua Gloriosa Provincia de Japão,* ed. Luciano Cordeiro (Lisbon, 1894), 22.

71. Boxer, *Great Ship,* 136–41.

72. Manuel Coelho, Report of the news that arrived in Cambodia from Japan on April 20, 1634, [Udong], May 20, 1634, ARSI *JS* 18-I:147r.

73. António de Oliveira Aranha to "Vicar of the Society of Jesus in Cambodia", [En route to Edo], March 1, 1634, part of Coelho's report, ibid., 150v.

74. Jorge Bastião to "Vicar of the Society of Jesus in Cambodia", [Nagasaki], February 28, 1634, part of Coelho's report, ibid., 150r.

75. Ibid.

76. Manuel Coelho, List of the Religious captured since May 1633, ibid., 149v.

77. Jorge Bastião to "Vicar of the Society of Jesus in Cambodia," [Nagasaki], February 28, 1634, ibid., 150r.

78. António de Oliveira Aranha to "Vicar of the Society of Jesus in Cambodia," [En route to Edo], March 1, 1634, ibid., 151r.

79. According to contemporary medical records, Iemitsu fell ill in March 1629 but eventually recovered. See Shinoda Tatsuaki, *Tokugawa shōgun-ke jūgodai no karute* (Tokyo, 2005), 61–62. I thank J. S. A. Elisonas for this information.

80. Manuel Coelho, Report of the news that arrived in Cambodia from Japan on 20 April 1634, [Udong], May 20, 1634, ARSI *JS* 18-I:151v. According to legend, Constantine was afflicted by leprosy before his baptism by Pope Sylvester. As a cure, he was prescribed a bath in the blood of three thousand infants. See Jacobus de Voragine, *The Golden Legend: Readings on the Saints,* ed. and trans. W. G. Ryan, 2 vols. (Princeton, 1993), 1:64.

81. Boxer, *Great Ship,* 138. On this embassy, see ibid., 120–26.

82. Sebastião Vieira to Gonçalo da Silveira, Edo, March 7, 1634, ARSI *JS* 38:309r.

83. Sebastião Vieira to Gonçalo da Silveira, Edo, April 2, 1634, ARSI *JS* 38:311r.

84. Sebastião Vieira to [Silveira embassy], Edo, April 7, 1634, ARSI *JS* 38:315r.

85. António Francisco Cardim, *Elogios, e Ramalhete de Flores Borrifado com o Sangue dos Religiosos da Companhia de Iesu* (Lisbon, 1650), 221.

86. Noronha was captain general from 1631 to 1635. See Boxer, *Great Ship,* 124–41.

87. AP to MV, Macau, January 21, 1635, ARSI *JS* 161-II:157r.

88. Esther 6:9.

89. AP to MV, Macau, January 21, 1635, ARSI *JS* 161-II:157r.

90. Such items would likely have been preserved in the *Fondo Gesuitico* collection at ARSI (although the central Jesuit archive was dispersed and reconstitued in the past, not always completely).

91. In late June 1635, Manuel Dias the elder wrote that the rumors of Ferreira's apostasy began to circulate "more than a year and a half ago"—that is, at the end of 1633—gaining credence in late 1634. But, Dias declared, the Jesuits only believed the reports which reached Macau via Cochinchina on June 12, 1635. See MD to CF, Macau, June 22, 1635, ARSI *JS* 18:230r.

Conclusion

1. Two versions of the text are in Lisbon, with a third at the Real Academia de la Historia in Madrid. While none of the texts are signed, it is clear from references within the text that Bonelli was the author. See Bonelli Relação; Bonelli 2; and "Relação da Morte e Vida do Pe. Andre Palmeiro Vizitador da Prov.a de Japão, e China", Madrid, Real Academia de la Historia, *Jesuitas, legajo* 22, fasc. 8:443–52.

2. MD to CF, Macau, June 22, 1635, ARSI *JS* 18:230r.

3. Bonelli Relação, 269r and 268r.

4. Parts of Bonelli's text are in Franco, 2:575–79.

5. Bonelli Relação, 272v.

6. Ibid., 275v.

7. See, for example, Bartolomeo Carducci's *Death of Saint Francis of Assisi* (painted 1593), Vincenzo Carducci's *Death of St. Bruno* (dated between 1626 and 1628), or Zurbarán's *Viewing of the Body of Saint Bonaventure* (painted 1629).

8. *Vita beati P. Ignatii Loiolae Societatis Iesu fundatoris* (Rome, 1609), 77.

9. Pedro de Ribadeneyra, *Vida del P. Ignatio de Loyola, fundador de la Compañia de Jesus* (Madrid, 1583), 223v.

10. Bonelli Relação, 268r.

11. Psalms 83:2, "How lovely are thy tabernacles, O Lord of hosts!"

12. Bonelli Relação, 266r.

13. Ibid., 266r/v.

14. Ibid., 267r.

15. This "hymn of glory" is from the pseudo-Augustinian compendium published in numerous early modern editions. The text, from verses drawn from Augustine's writings and found most frequently in chapter 26 of the "Meditations", is *Hymnus de gloria Paradisi Petri Damiani, Cardinalis Ostiensis, ex dictis B. Augustini*.

16. Bonelli says *santos*, but by 1635 there were only two canonized Jesuits, Loyola and Xavier. Six others were blessed: Stanislaus Kostka (beatified in 1605), Francis Borgia (1624), and Luigi Gonzaga (1605), and the three beatified Jesuit martyrs of Japan.

17. Bonelli Relação, 267v.

18. Ibid., 268r.

19. Accounts of Suárez's death at Lisbon on September 25, 1617, give one of his last phrases as: *Non putabam tam suave esse, tam dulce mori*. Palmeiro had surely read a manuscript report since an official version was only printed in the 1670s. See Antoni Ignasi Descamps, *Vida del Venerable Padre Francisco Suarez* (Perpignan, 1671), 317.

20. Bonelli Relação, 269r.

21. Ibid., 268v.

22. These prayers are also known as "Recommendation of a Soul Departing", *Ordo Commendationis Animae*.

23. Bonelli Relação, 269v–270r.

24. Ibid., 270v–271r.

25. Ibid., 271v.

26. Ibid., 271v–272r.

27. Ibid., 272r.

28. Between Palmeiro's grave and Carneiro's was only a thin stone. See Benjamin Videira Pires, ed., "Um Campo Santo, de Macau," in Manuel Teixeira, *Macau e a Sua Diocese,* 15 vols. (Macau, 1940–1977), 8:202–43, at 216.

29. 1 Samuel 3:20, "And all Israel, from Dan to Bersabee, knew that Samuel was a faithful prophet of the Lord."

30. Bonelli Relação, 272r.

31. Cardim calls two of the most important Indian states by Portuguese names, *Mogor* (the Mughal lands) and *Narsinga* (Vijayanagara, otherwise called *Bisnaga*).

32. Genesis 49:21, "Nephtali, a hart let loose, and giving words of beauty."

33. A patent for another assignment as visitor for the two Indian provinces was issued in Rome on January 9, 1634. Palmeiro's confreres in Goa lamented his passing since they had been "anxiously awaiting" his arrival. See *Patentes superiorum et itinerariae 1599–1640* under "India Orientalis", ARSI *Hist. Soc.* 62:57 and 58; and Álvaro Tavares to Manuel Severim de Faria, Goa, February 20, 1636, BNL *Reservados* 7640:115v.

34. Bonelli Relação, 272r.

35. Claims of this order are common coin in current literature on early modern "world history." See Luke Clossey, *Salvation and Globalization in the Early Jesuit Missions* (Cambridge, 2008); Geoffrey Gunn, *First Globalization: The Eurasian Exchange, 1500–1800* (Lanham, Md., 2003); Cátia Antunes, *Globalisation in the Early Modern Period: The Economic Relationship between Amsterdam and Lisbon, 1640–1705* (Amsterdam, 2004); and Miles Ogborn, *Global Lives: Britain and the World, 1550–1800* (Cambridge, 2008).

36. Hugues Didier, ed., *Os Portuguese no Tibete. Os Primeiros Relatos dos Jesuítas (1624–1635)*, trans. Lourdes Júdice (Lisbon, 2000), 53.

37. Markus Vink, "Between the Devil and the Deep Blue Sea. The Christian Paravas: A 'Client Community' in Seventeenth-Century Southeast India", *Itinerario* 26, no. 2 (2002): 64–98.

38. Fernão de Queyroz, *Vida do Veneravel Irmão Pedro de Basto* (Lisbon, 1689), 540.

39. H. Hosten, SJ, ed., and L. Besse, SJ, trans., "Father Manoel da Fonseca, S.J., in Ava (Burma) (1613–1652)", *Journal of the Proceedings of the Asiatic Society of Bengal* 21 (1925): 27–48, at 38.

40. Liam Matthew Brockey, "Introduction: Nodes of Empire", in my *Portuguese Colonial Cities in the Early Modern World* (Aldershot, 2008), 1–14, esp. 1–8.

41. George Elison, *Deus Destroyed: The Image of Christianity in Early Modern Japan* (Cambridge, Mass., 1991), 217–21.

42. C. R. Boxer, *Embaixada de Macau ao Japão em 1640* (Lisbon, 1933).

43. C. R. Boxer, "The Embassy of Captain Gonçalo de Siqueira de Souza to Japan in 1644–1647", *Monumenta Nipponica* 2, no. 1 (1939): 40–74, at 52–53.

44. Giovanni Battista Bonelli to CF, Macau, [July?] 1635, ARSI *JS* 18-I:302r.

45. MD to CF, Macau, June 22, 1635, ARSI *JS* 18:230r–232v.

46. Gonçalo da Silveira to MD, Macau, November 19, 1635, cited in MD to MV, Macau, January 26, 1636, *JS* 29:238r.

47. Testimony by Manuel Mendes, transcribed in MD to MV, Macau, January 26, 1636, *JS* 29: 238v–239r.

48. MD to MV, Macau, January 26, 1636, *JS* 29:238r–239r.

49. Testimony given by Japan exiles to MD and João Monteiro, Macau, 1636, ARSI *JS* 18-I:286r. See also Hubert Cieslik, "The Case of Christovão Ferreira", *Monumenta Nipponica* 29, no. 1 (Spring 1974): 1–54, at 26–27.

50. Deposition by a "thirty-six-year-old uncle" of Brothers Francisco and Pedro Marques, Macau, 1636, ARSI *JS* 18-I:296r/v.

51. The anti-Christian tract composed by Ferreira titled "Deceit Disclosed" is translated in Elison, *Deus Destroyed,* 293–318.

52. Testimony given by Japan exiles to MD and João Monteiro, Macau, 1636, ARSI *JS* 18-I:286v.

53. MD to CF, Macau, July 8, 1636, ARSI *JS* 18-I:250r–251r.

54. MD to MV, Macau, December 16, 1636, ARSI *JS* 18-I:264v.

55. Giovanni Battista Bonelli to CF, Macau, [July?] 1635, ARSI *JS* 18-I:302r.

56. MD to MV, Macau, January 26, 1636, ARSI *JS* 18-I:239v.

57. MD to Marcello Mastrilli, Macau, April 16, 1637, ARSI *JS* 29:153r–154v.

58. European sources claim Mastrilli was decapitated after being tormented, but Japanese sources indicate that he died over the pit. See Elison, *Deus Destroyed,* 197–99 and 204.

59. In addition to the members of these expeditions, the few remaining at-large Jesuits such as Giovanni Battista Porro and Martinho Shikimi would also apostatize under torture. See ibid., 197–203.

60. The classic study is W. F. Rea, *The Economics of the Zambezi Missions, 1580–1759* (Rome, 1976).

61. On Desideri, see Trent Pomplun, *Jesuit on the Roof of the World: Ippolito Desideri's Mission to Tibet* (Oxford, 2010).

62. Stephen Neill, *A History of Christianity in India: 1707–1858* (Cambridge, 1985), 90–93.

63. On the dismantling of Old Goa, see Paulo Varela Gomes, *Whitewash, Red Stone: A History of Church Architecture in Goa* (New Delhi, 2011).

Illustration Credits

Acknowledgments

The inspiration for this book came nearly two decades ago, when as a graduating senior I went looking for reading suggestions. The question that I put to my former professors was simple: What books should an educated person read? The responses were a varied lot, some recommending works in a specific field, others suggesting a range of literary selections. The first suggestion that caught my eye came on the typed list given to me by a professor of medieval history, Bill Dohar. Among titles such as *Kristin Lavransdatter* and *Augustine of Hippo,* he recommended Shusaku Endo's *Silence.* Only some of the items on the list contained brief comments, but the one that accompanied this suggestion jumped off the page the moment I read it and has stuck in my mind ever since then: "Woeful Jesuits in Japan."

This book is the fruit of the seed that germinated in the mid-1990s after I finished reading Endo's tale of torture, apostasy, and doubt. I returned to the story of *Silence* at several reprises during the years that I studied the Jesuits in China, its historical details prodding me to make a deeper investigation of the dramatic events in Japan. Through conversations and, above all, correspondence with Jurgis Elisonas, my interest in the history of the "Christian century" grew. It is to him that I owe a considerable debt of gratitude, not only for inspiring me to examine the early modern Jesuits but, above all, for his tireless reading, editing, and critiquing my work—not to mention his continual urging me to precision and clarity. I am grateful to have such a loyal friend and such a constant source of encouragement; this book would not have been possible without him.

The research necessary to produce this study was conducted over several years, and in many different libraries and archives. I am thankful for the professional dedication of numerous archivists, librarians, and curators for their prompt replies to my queries, and for their help in locating and providing access to the materials that I sought to use. My primary debt is to the director and staff of Archivum Romanum Societatis Iesu, the Jesuits' central archive in Rome. Fr. Brian Mac Cuarta and Dr. Mauro Brunello provided access, even via the Internet, to key documents for this study, and were always generous helping to facilitate my study. Of equal importance for my work was the staff of the Jesuit Province of Portugal at the *Brotéria* Library in Lisbon. Fr. António Júlio Trigueiros, Dra. Ana Rodrigues, and Dra. Ana Maria Pereira da Silva provided me with access to documents digitalized in the Jesuits' Roman collections as well as to rare publications found in their rich library of Jesuitica.

I am also grateful to the archivists and librarians at several other institutions overseas and at home. Dra. Cristina Pinto Basto provided invaluable support for my research at the Biblioteca da Ajuda in Lisbon and continued to make sources available to me when I returned to the United States. I owe special thanks to the archivist at Ajuda, Dra. Maria da Conceição Geada, who spent many hours teaching me how to read seventeenth- and eighteenth-century script and who never balked at any of my requests for obscure texts. At the Biblioteca Nacional, Dra. Lígia de Azevedo Martins offered kind assistance to me in the *Reservados* room where I sought to consult rare printed and manuscript materials. Likewise, Dra. Ana Maria Leitão Bandeira at the archive of the University of Coimbra kindly assisted me in my attempts to locate the protagonist of my study in the registers of that venerable institution. I am also grateful to the staffs of the Torre do Tombo (National Archive) in Lisbon and the District Archive of Évora who helped me to conduct my work speedily during my visits to Portugal. And here at home, I am thankful for the expert staff at Michigan State University Library, especially to Dr. Peter Berg and Dr. Xian Wu for their assistance with my project.

The search for traces of a man known for his modesty who lived four hundred years ago on the far side of the world is similar to the hunt for the proverbial needle. Many were the ideas about where to search that led only to dead ends, or which turned up more suggestions than facts. Yet without pursuing all leads, many discoveries in the archives would not have been made. I would therefore like to thank the librarians at the Biblioteca Nazionale Centrale in Rome, especially Dott. Valentina Longo, for helping to guide me during my search through their catalogues. In a similar manner, the staff of the Arquivo Histórico Ultramarino in Lisbon helped examine the indices and catalogues of the *caixas* in their archive although our search was in vain. I would also like to thank the anonymous teams of librarians and technicians who have devoted hours to digitalizing rare books, and for building the convenient search tools and organizational schemes that made this project possible to execute in a relatively short span. I am particularly grateful for the early modern Portuguese texts reproduced in the digital collections of the Biblioteca Nacional de Portugal, the Biblioteca Nacional de España, the Fundação Biblioteca Nacional in Brazil, and the Library of Congress.

This book was written after a major transition in my career, and I am thankful to the friends and colleagues at Michigan State who received me so warmly in 2009. It was an offhand compliment made by John Waller that convinced me to expand a preliminary article I had written about André Palmeiro into this study. For their helpful advice and encouragement during these past years, I would like to thank David Bailey, Peter Beattie, Denise Demetriou, Lisa Fine, Sean Forner, Karrin Hanshew, Walter Hawthorne, Charles Keith, Leslie Moch, Matt Pauly, Ethan Segal, Lewis Siegelbaum, Mindy Smith, Mickey Stamm, Ronen Steinberg, Gordon Stewart, Helen Veit, Erica Windler, and David Wheat.

Friends and colleagues beyond East Lansing also made valuable contributions to this project. My primary debt is to Noël Golvers of the Katholieke Universiteit Leuven, whose skill with neo-Latin texts is unparalleled and whose depth of knowledge of early modern Jesuit intellectual culture is unmatched. I am also grateful to Jim Amelang, Paolo Aranha, Francisco Bethencourt, Tim Brook, Peter Brown, Jorge Cañizares-Esguerra, Hui-hung Chen, Diogo Ramada Curto, John Dardess, Mark DeStephano, Simon Ditchfield, Freddy Dominguez, Ad Dudink, George Dutton, Carlos Eire, Ben Elman, Felipe Fernández-Armesto, Jean-Marie le Gall, Tony Grafton, Brad Gregory, Katie Harris, Martin Heijdra, Ronnie Hsia, Peter Lake, Howard Louthan, Tom McCoog, Eugenio Menegon, Nelson Minnich, Maria Filomena Mónica, Susan Naquin, Cristina Osswald, José Pedro Paiva, Federico Palomo del Barrio, Isabel Pina, Ana Fernandes Pinto, Joan-Pau Rubiés, António Vasconcelos de Saldanha, Kirsten Schultz, Ben Smith, Jake Soll, Nicolas Standaert, Sanjay Subrahmanyam, Ana Valdez, Kate van Liere, Filipa Vicente, John Vollmer, Molly Warsh, and Ines Zupanov. The production of a book is a laborious process in which many hands are involved, and this one was no exception. I am therefore especially grateful to Kathleen McDermott and the editorial staff of Harvard University Press for their professionalism and commitment to this project over the past year.

Part of the inspiration for this book came from the "company men" in my family. During the time that I took to write this book in Lisbon and East Lansing, I became the last male holdout from Kelly and Hayes Electrical Supply. My brothers, Michael and Christian, and my brother-in-law Rob, have taught me what it means to be loyal and have impressed me with their dedication, as has my father, who remains the heart and soul of their collective enterprise. If the *Companhia* that is described in these pages appears vivid and human, it is because I have spent many years observing these special individuals, together and separately. I am also grateful for the love and support that I have received over the years from them, as well as from my mother; my sister, Megan; my sisters-in-law, Kelly, Mandy, Ana, and Ana Margarida; and my brothers-in-law, João Pedro and Gonçalo. Time spent with them as well as my aunts and uncles, nieces, nephews, and cousins, both in America and Portugal, is what I enjoy most when my thoughts are not upon the distant past.

This book is dedicated to my wife, Mónica. Like its main character, she left a rewarding teaching career in Portugal for a trip to the far ends of the earth. For love of me, she said good-bye to friends and family in Lisbon for uncertain fortune in America. Our children, Beatriz and Leonor, have made this journey one filled with joy. If my academic career has flourished over the past decade, it is due to her strength and support as well as to her brilliant mind. I have no greater friend, no better editor, no greater inspiration, and no more comforting consolation than her. This book has passed under her rigorous scrutiny several times over and has benefited from her insightful comments. Indeed, several of the principal arguments presented here originated with her; in truth, the ideas in this book are as much hers as they are mine. This dedication is only a small token of my gratitude, but it is offered in the hope that it can repay some of abundant love and wisdom that she has given to me.

Index